Java Concise Reference Series

Swing and AWT

Java Concise Reference Series: Swing and AWT

Production Editor: Jeanine Downey

Java™, all Java-based trademarks and logos, and JavaScript™ are trademarks or registered trademarks of Sun Microsystems, Inc., in the United States and other countries. Newport House Books is independent of Sun Microsystems.

ISBN-10: 0-9818402-5-6
ISBN-13: 978-0-9818402-5-3

Published by Newport House Books
www.newporthousebooks.com

This book is dedicated to those who have served and sacrificed for our liberty.

Table of Contents

Preface

Classes and Interfaces

Index

Preface

This book, and others in the Java™ Concise Reference Series, is a complete, quick-reference guide for the standard Java library packages through version 7. Many books serve the purpose of a tutorial for the novice software engineer. Their content is useful when learning a new technology, but a complete and stripped down reference is essential when practicing software development once that technology is understood; this series fulfills that need. Tutorial and explanatory information has been eliminated so that the nature of the APIs is more understandable. This reference collection covers the core set of packages that every Java developer needs to create and maintain professional level software.

The Java software development kit has evolved into a highly complex, multi-layer system of classes; these reside in packages that are not always obviously structured. Most references on Java strive for clarity by mimicking this organization. In practice, software engineers commonly remember the name of the class they are looking to use, rather than its package name. For this reason, this book is organized alphabetically by class name. Within the *Classes and Interfaces* section, dictionary style headers allow for rapidly finding specific class definitions. The index provides facilities for finding classes within specific packages and by known class method names. We hope this and the other books in the series finds themselves on your desk at all times, providing fast and accurate API guidance.

Classes and Interfaces

javax.swing.**AbstractAction**

public abstract class **AbstractAction** implements Serializable, Cloneable, Action
{
    protected SwingPropertyChangeSupport **changeSupport** ;
    protected boolean **enabled** ;
    // Constructors
    public **AbstractAction**(Icon icon, String name) ;
    public **AbstractAction**(String name) ;
    public **AbstractAction**() ;
    // Static methods
    // Instance methods
    public synchronized void **addPropertyChangeListener**(PropertyChangeListener listener) ;
    protected Object **clone**() throws CloneNotSupportedException ;
    protected void **firePropertyChange**(Object newValue, Object oldValue, String propertyName) ;
    public Object **getKeys**() ; // Since 1.3
    public synchronized PropertyChangeListener **getPropertyChangeListeners**() ; // Since 1.4
    public Object **getValue**(String key) ;
    public boolean **isEnabled**() ;
    public void **putValue**(Object newValue, String key) ;
    public synchronized void **removePropertyChangeListener**(PropertyChangeListener listener) ;
    public void **setEnabled**(boolean newValue) ;
}

javax.swing.border.**AbstractBorder**

public abstract class **AbstractBorder** implements Serializable, Border
{
    // Constructors
    public **AbstractBorder**() ;
    // Static methods
    public static Rectangle **getInteriorRectangle**(int height, int width, int y, int x, Border b, Component
        c) ;
    // Instance methods
    public int **getBaseline**(int height, int width, Component c) ; // Since 1.6
    public Component.BaselineResizeBehavior **getBaselineResizeBehavior**(Component c) ; // Since 1.6
    public Insets **getBorderInsets**(Insets insets, Component c) ;
    public Insets **getBorderInsets**(Component c) ;
    public Rectangle **getInteriorRectangle**(int height, int width, int y, int x, Component c) ;
    public boolean **isBorderOpaque**() ;
    public void **paintBorder**(int height, int width, int y, int x, Graphics g, Component c) ;

}

---

javax.swing.**AbstractButton**

---

public abstract class **AbstractButton** extends JComponent implements SwingConstants, ItemSelectable
{
    public static final String **BORDER_PAINTED_CHANGED_PROPERTY** ;
    public static final String **CONTENT_AREA_FILLED_CHANGED_PROPERTY** ;
    public static final String **DISABLED_ICON_CHANGED_PROPERTY** ;
    public static final String **DISABLED_SELECTED_ICON_CHANGED_PROPERTY** ;
    public static final String **FOCUS_PAINTED_CHANGED_PROPERTY** ;
    public static final String **HORIZONTAL_ALIGNMENT_CHANGED_PROPERTY** ;
    public static final String **HORIZONTAL_TEXT_POSITION_CHANGED_PROPERTY** ;
    public static final String **ICON_CHANGED_PROPERTY** ;
    public static final String **MARGIN_CHANGED_PROPERTY** ;
    public static final String **MNEMONIC_CHANGED_PROPERTY** ;
    public static final String **MODEL_CHANGED_PROPERTY** ;
    public static final String **PRESSED_ICON_CHANGED_PROPERTY** ;
    public static final String **ROLLOVER_ENABLED_CHANGED_PROPERTY** ;
    public static final String **ROLLOVER_ICON_CHANGED_PROPERTY** ;
    public static final String **ROLLOVER_SELECTED_ICON_CHANGED_PROPERTY** ;
    public static final String **SELECTED_ICON_CHANGED_PROPERTY** ;
    public static final String **TEXT_CHANGED_PROPERTY** ;
    public static final String **VERTICAL_ALIGNMENT_CHANGED_PROPERTY** ;
    public static final String **VERTICAL_TEXT_POSITION_CHANGED_PROPERTY** ;
    protected ActionListener **actionListener** ;
    protected transient ChangeEvent **changeEvent** ;
    protected ChangeListener **changeListener** ;
    protected ItemListener **itemListener** ;
    protected ButtonModel **model** ;
    // Constructors
    public **AbstractButton**() ;
    // Instance methods
    protected void **actionPropertyChanged**(String propertyName, Action action) ; // Since 1.6
    public void **addActionListener**(ActionListener l) ;
    public void **addChangeListener**(ChangeListener l) ;
    protected void **addImpl**(int index, Object constraints, Component comp) ; // Since 1.5
    public void **addItemListener**(ItemListener l) ;
    protected int **checkHorizontalKey**(String exception, int key) ;
    protected int **checkVerticalKey**(String exception, int key) ;
    protected void **configurePropertiesFromAction**(Action a) ; // Since 1.3
    protected ActionListener **createActionListener**() ;
    protected PropertyChangeListener **createActionPropertyChangeListener**(Action a) ; // Since 1.3
    protected ChangeListener **createChangeListener**() ;

---

protected ItemListener **createItemListener**() ;
public void **doClick**(int pressTime) ;
public void **doClick**() ;
protected void **fireActionPerformed**(ActionEvent event) ;
protected void **fireItemStateChanged**(ItemEvent event) ;
protected void **fireStateChanged**() ;
public Action **getAction**() ; // Since 1.3
public String **getActionCommand**() ;
public ActionListener **getActionListeners**() ; // Since 1.4
public ChangeListener **getChangeListeners**() ; // Since 1.4
public Icon **getDisabledIcon**() ;
public Icon **getDisabledSelectedIcon**() ;
public int **getDisplayedMnemonicIndex**() ; // Since 1.4
public boolean **getHideActionText**() ; // Since 1.6
public int **getHorizontalAlignment**() ;
public int **getHorizontalTextPosition**() ;
public Icon **getIcon**() ;
public int **getIconTextGap**() ; // Since 1.4
public ItemListener **getItemListeners**() ; // Since 1.4
public String **getLabel**() ;
public Insets **getMargin**() ;
public int **getMnemonic**() ;
public ButtonModel **getModel**() ;
public long **getMultiClickThreshhold**() ; // Since 1.4
public Icon **getPressedIcon**() ;
public Icon **getRolloverIcon**() ;
public Icon **getRolloverSelectedIcon**() ;
public Icon **getSelectedIcon**() ;
public Object **getSelectedObjects**() ;
public String **getText**() ;
public ButtonUI **getUI**() ;
public int **getVerticalAlignment**() ;
public int **getVerticalTextPosition**() ;
public boolean **imageUpdate**(int h, int w, int y, int x, int infoflags, Image img) ;
protected void **init**(Icon icon, String text) ;
public boolean **isBorderPainted**() ;
public boolean **isContentAreaFilled**() ;
public boolean **isFocusPainted**() ;
public boolean **isRolloverEnabled**() ;
public boolean **isSelected**() ;
protected void **paintBorder**(Graphics g) ;
protected String **paramString**() ;
public void **removeActionListener**(ActionListener l) ;
public void **removeChangeListener**(ChangeListener l) ;
public void **removeItemListener**(ItemListener l) ;
public void **removeNotify**() ; // Since 1.6

```
public void setAction(Action a) ; // Since 1.3
public void setActionCommand(String actionCommand) ;
public void setBorderPainted(boolean b) ;
public void setContentAreaFilled(boolean b) ;
public void setDisabledIcon(Icon disabledIcon) ;
public void setDisabledSelectedIcon(Icon disabledSelectedIcon) ;
public void setDisplayedMnemonicIndex(int index) throws IllegalArgumentException ; // Since 1.4
public void setEnabled(boolean b) ;
public void setFocusPainted(boolean b) ;
public void setHideActionText(boolean hideActionText) ; // Since 1.6
public void setHorizontalAlignment(int alignment) ;
public void setHorizontalTextPosition(int textPosition) ;
public void setIcon(Icon defaultIcon) ;
public void setIconTextGap(int iconTextGap) ; // Since 1.4
public void setLabel(String label) ;
public void setLayout(LayoutManager mgr) ; // Since 1.5
public void setMargin(Insets m) ;
public void setMnemonic(char mnemonic) ;
public void setMnemonic(int mnemonic) ;
public void setModel(ButtonModel newModel) ;
public void setMultiClickThreshhold(long threshhold) ; // Since 1.4
public void setPressedIcon(Icon pressedIcon) ;
public void setRolloverEnabled(boolean b) ;
public void setRolloverIcon(Icon rolloverIcon) ;
public void setRolloverSelectedIcon(Icon rolloverSelectedIcon) ;
public void setSelected(boolean b) ;
public void setSelectedIcon(Icon selectedIcon) ;
public void setText(String text) ;
public void setUI(ButtonUI ui) ;
public void setVerticalAlignment(int alignment) ;
public void setVerticalTextPosition(int textPosition) ;
public void updateUI() ;
}
```

javax.swing.**AbstractCellEditor** [since 1.3]

```
public abstract class AbstractCellEditor  implements Serializable, CellEditor
{
    protected transient ChangeEvent changeEvent ;
    protected EventListenerList listenerList ;
    // Constructors
    public AbstractCellEditor() ;
    // Instance methods
    public void addCellEditorListener(CellEditorListener l) ;
```

```
        public void cancelCellEditing() ;
        protected void fireEditingCanceled() ;
        protected void fireEditingStopped() ;
        public CellEditorListener getCellEditorListeners() ; // Since 1.4
        public boolean isCellEditable(EventObject e) ;
        public void removeCellEditorListener(CellEditorListener l) ;
        public boolean shouldSelectCell(EventObject anEvent) ;
        public boolean stopCellEditing() ;
}
```

javax.swing.colorchooser.**AbstractColorChooserPanel**

```
public abstract class AbstractColorChooserPanel extends JPanel
{
        // Constructors
        public AbstractColorChooserPanel() ;
        // Instance methods
        protected abstract void buildChooser() ;
        protected Color getColorFromModel() ;
        public ColorSelectionModel getColorSelectionModel() ;
        public int getDisplayedMnemonicIndex() ; // Since 1.4
        public abstract String getDisplayName() ;
        public abstract Icon getLargeDisplayIcon() ;
        public int getMnemonic() ; // Since 1.4
        public abstract Icon getSmallDisplayIcon() ;
        public void installChooserPanel(JColorChooser enclosingChooser) ;
        public void paint(Graphics g) ;
        public void uninstallChooserPanel(JColorChooser enclosingChooser) ;
        public abstract void updateChooser() ;
}
```

javax.swing.text.**AbstractDocument**

```
public abstract class AbstractDocument  implements Serializable, Document
{
        protected static final String BAD_LOCATION ;
        public static final String BidiElementName ;
        public static final String ContentElementName ;
        public static final String ElementNameAttribute ;
        public static final String ParagraphElementName ;
        public static final String SectionElementName ;
```

protected EventListenerList **listenerList** ;
// Constructors
protected **AbstractDocument**(AbstractDocument.AttributeContext context,
    AbstractDocument.Content data) ;
protected **AbstractDocument**(AbstractDocument.Content data) ;
// Instance methods
public void **addDocumentListener**(DocumentListener listener) ;
public void **addUndoableEditListener**(UndoableEditListener listener) ;
protected Element **createBranchElement**(AttributeSet a, Element parent) ;
protected Element **createLeafElement**(int p1, int p0, AttributeSet a, Element parent) ;
public synchronized Position **createPosition**(int offs) throws BadLocationException ;
public void **dump**(PrintStream out) ;
protected void **fireChangedUpdate**(DocumentEvent e) ;
protected void **fireInsertUpdate**(DocumentEvent e) ;
protected void **fireRemoveUpdate**(DocumentEvent e) ;
protected void **fireUndoableEditUpdate**(UndoableEditEvent e) ;
public int **getAsynchronousLoadPriority**() ;
protected final AbstractDocument.AttributeContext **getAttributeContext**() ;
public Element **getBidiRootElement**() ;
protected final AbstractDocument.Content **getContent**() ;
protected final synchronized Thread **getCurrentWriter**() ;
public abstract Element **getDefaultRootElement**() ;
public DocumentFilter **getDocumentFilter**() ; // Since 1.4
public DocumentListener **getDocumentListeners**() ; // Since 1.4
public Dictionary<Object, Object> **getDocumentProperties**() ;
public final Position **getEndPosition**() ;
public int **getLength**() ;
public T **getListeners**(Class<T> listenerType) ; // Since 1.3
public abstract Element **getParagraphElement**(int pos) ;
public final Object **getProperty**(Object key) ;
public Element **getRootElements**() ;
public final Position **getStartPosition**() ;
public void **getText**(Segment txt, int length, int offset) throws BadLocationException ;
public String **getText**(int length, int offset) throws BadLocationException ;
public UndoableEditListener **getUndoableEditListeners**() ; // Since 1.4
public void **insertString**(AttributeSet a, String str, int offs) throws BadLocationException ;
protected void **insertUpdate**(AttributeSet attr, AbstractDocument.DefaultDocumentEvent chng) ;
protected void **postRemoveUpdate**(AbstractDocument.DefaultDocumentEvent chng) ;
public final void **putProperty**(Object value, Object key) ;
public final synchronized void **readLock**() ;
public final synchronized void **readUnlock**() ;
public void **remove**(int len, int offs) throws BadLocationException ;
public void **removeDocumentListener**(DocumentListener listener) ;
public void **removeUndoableEditListener**(UndoableEditListener listener) ;
protected void **removeUpdate**(AbstractDocument.DefaultDocumentEvent chng) ;
public void **render**(Runnable r) ;

```
      public void replace(AttributeSet attrs, String text, int length, int offset) throws BadLocationException
          ; // Since 1.4
      public void setAsynchronousLoadPriority(int p) ;
      public void setDocumentFilter(DocumentFilter filter) ; // Since 1.4
      public void setDocumentProperties(Dictionary<Object, Object> x) ;
      protected final synchronized void writeLock() ;
      protected final synchronized void writeUnlock() ;
}
```

---

javax.swing.text.**AbstractDocument.AttributeContext**

```
public static interface AbstractDocument.AttributeContext
{
      // Instance methods
      public AttributeSet addAttribute(Object value, Object name, AttributeSet old) ;
      public AttributeSet addAttributes(AttributeSet attr, AttributeSet old) ;
      public AttributeSet getEmptySet() ;
      public void reclaim(AttributeSet a) ;
      public AttributeSet removeAttribute(Object name, AttributeSet old) ;
      public AttributeSet removeAttributes(AttributeSet attrs, AttributeSet old) ;
      public AttributeSet removeAttributes(Enumeration<?> names, AttributeSet old) ;
}
```

---

javax.swing.text.**AbstractDocument.Content**

```
public static interface AbstractDocument.Content
{
      // Instance methods
      public Position createPosition(int offset) throws BadLocationException ;
      public void getChars(Segment txt, int len, int where) throws BadLocationException ;
      public String getString(int len, int where) throws BadLocationException ;
      public UndoableEdit insertString(String str, int where) throws BadLocationException ;
      public int length() ;
      public UndoableEdit remove(int nitems, int where) throws BadLocationException ;
}
```

javax.swing.text.**AbstractDocument.ElementEdit**

public static class **AbstractDocument.ElementEdit** extends AbstractUndoableEdit implements
DocumentEvent.ElementChange
{
    // Constructors
    public **AbstractDocument.ElementEdit**(javax.swing.text.Element[] added,
        javax.swing.text.Element[] removed, int index, Element e) ;
    // Instance methods
    public Element **getChildrenAdded**() ;
    public Element **getChildrenRemoved**() ;
    public Element **getElement**() ;
    public int **getIndex**() ;
    public void **redo**() throws CannotRedoException ;
    public void **undo**() throws CannotUndoException ;
}

javax.swing.tree.**AbstractLayoutCache**

public abstract class **AbstractLayoutCache** implements RowMapper
{
    protected AbstractLayoutCache.NodeDimensions **nodeDimensions** ;
    protected boolean **rootVisible** ;
    protected int **rowHeight** ;
    protected TreeModel **treeModel** ;
    protected TreeSelectionModel **treeSelectionModel** ;
    // Constructors
    public **AbstractLayoutCache**() ;
    // Instance methods
    public abstract Rectangle **getBounds**(Rectangle placeIn, TreePath path) ;
    public abstract boolean **getExpandedState**(TreePath path) ;
    public TreeModel **getModel**() ;
    protected Rectangle **getNodeDimensions**(Rectangle placeIn, boolean expanded, int depth, int row,
        Object value) ;
    public AbstractLayoutCache.NodeDimensions **getNodeDimensions**() ;
    public abstract TreePath **getPathClosestTo**(int y, int x) ;
    public abstract TreePath **getPathForRow**(int row) ;
    public int **getPreferredHeight**() ;
    public int **getPreferredWidth**(Rectangle bounds) ;
    public abstract int **getRowCount**() ;

public abstract int **getRowForPath**(TreePath path) ;
public int **getRowHeight**() ;
public int **getRowsForPaths**(javax.swing.tree.TreePath[] paths) ;
public TreeSelectionModel **getSelectionModel**() ;
public abstract int **getVisibleChildCount**(TreePath path) ;
public abstract Enumeration<TreePath> **getVisiblePathsFrom**(TreePath path) ;
public abstract void **invalidatePathBounds**(TreePath path) ;
public abstract void **invalidateSizes**() ;
public abstract boolean **isExpanded**(TreePath path) ;
protected boolean **isFixedRowHeight**() ;
public boolean **isRootVisible**() ;
public abstract void **setExpandedState**(boolean isExpanded, TreePath path) ;
public void **setModel**(TreeModel newModel) ;
public void **setNodeDimensions**(AbstractLayoutCache.NodeDimensions nd) ;
public void **setRootVisible**(boolean rootVisible) ;
public void **setRowHeight**(int rowHeight) ;
public void **setSelectionModel**(TreeSelectionModel newLSM) ;
public abstract void **treeNodesChanged**(TreeModelEvent e) ;
public abstract void **treeNodesInserted**(TreeModelEvent e) ;
public abstract void **treeNodesRemoved**(TreeModelEvent e) ;
public abstract void **treeStructureChanged**(TreeModelEvent e) ;
}

---

javax.swing.tree.**AbstractLayoutCache.NodeDimensions**

---

public abstract static class **AbstractLayoutCache.NodeDimensions**
{
    // Constructors
    public **AbstractLayoutCache.NodeDimensions**() ;
    // Instance methods
    public abstract Rectangle **getNodeDimensions**(Rectangle bounds, boolean expanded, int depth, int
        row, Object value) ;
}

---

javax.swing.**AbstractListModel**

---

public abstract class **AbstractListModel** implements Serializable, ListModel
{
    protected EventListenerList **listenerList** ;
    // Constructors
    public **AbstractListModel**() ;

```
        // Instance methods
        public void addListDataListener(ListDataListener l) ;
        protected void fireContentsChanged(int index1, int index0, Object source) ;
        protected void fireIntervalAdded(int index1, int index0, Object source) ;
        protected void fireIntervalRemoved(int index1, int index0, Object source) ;
        public ListDataListener getListDataListeners() ; // Since 1.4
        public T getListeners(Class<T> listenerType) ; // Since 1.3
        public void removeListDataListener(ListDataListener l) ;
}
```

---

javax.swing.**AbstractSpinnerModel** [since 1.4]

```
public abstract class AbstractSpinnerModel  implements Serializable, SpinnerModel
{
        protected EventListenerList listenerList ;
        // Constructors
        public AbstractSpinnerModel() ;
        // Instance methods
        public void addChangeListener(ChangeListener l) ;
        protected void fireStateChanged() ;
        public ChangeListener getChangeListeners() ; // Since 1.4
        public T getListeners(Class<T> listenerType) ;
        public void removeChangeListener(ChangeListener l) ;
}
```

---

javax.swing.table.**AbstractTableModel**

```
public abstract class AbstractTableModel  implements Serializable, TableModel
{
        protected EventListenerList listenerList ;
        // Constructors
        public AbstractTableModel() ;
        // Instance methods
        public void addTableModelListener(TableModelListener l) ;
        public int findColumn(String columnName) ;
        public void fireTableCellUpdated(int column, int row) ;
        public void fireTableChanged(TableModelEvent e) ;
        public void fireTableDataChanged() ;
        public void fireTableRowsDeleted(int lastRow, int firstRow) ;
        public void fireTableRowsInserted(int lastRow, int firstRow) ;
        public void fireTableRowsUpdated(int lastRow, int firstRow) ;
```

```
    public void fireTableStructureChanged() ;
    public Class<?> getColumnClass(int columnIndex) ;
    public String getColumnName(int column) ;
    public T getListeners(Class<T> listenerType) ; // Since 1.3
    public TableModelListener getTableModelListeners() ; // Since 1.4
    public boolean isCellEditable(int columnIndex, int rowIndex) ;
    public void removeTableModelListener(TableModelListener l) ;
    public void setValueAt(int columnIndex, int rowIndex, Object aValue) ;
}
```

javax.swing.undo.**AbstractUndoableEdit**

```
public class AbstractUndoableEdit  implements Serializable, UndoableEdit
{
    protected static final String RedoName ;
    protected static final String UndoName ;
    // Constructors
    public AbstractUndoableEdit() ;
    // Instance methods
    public boolean addEdit(UndoableEdit anEdit) ;
    public boolean canRedo() ;
    public boolean canUndo() ;
    public void die() ;
    public String getPresentationName() ;
    public String getRedoPresentationName() ;
    public String getUndoPresentationName() ;
    public boolean isSignificant() ;
    public void redo() throws CannotRedoException ;
    public boolean replaceEdit(UndoableEdit anEdit) ;
    public String toString() ;
    public void undo() throws CannotUndoException ;
}
```

javax.swing.text.**AbstractWriter**

```
public abstract class AbstractWriter
{
    protected static final char NEWLINE ;
    // Constructors
    protected AbstractWriter(int len, int pos, Element root, Writer w) ;
    protected AbstractWriter(Element root, Writer w) ;
```

```
    protected AbstractWriter(int len, int pos, Document doc, Writer w) ;
    protected AbstractWriter(Document doc, Writer w) ;
    // Instance methods
    protected void decrIndent() ;
    protected boolean getCanWrapLines() ; // Since 1.3
    protected int getCurrentLineLength() ; // Since 1.3
    protected Document getDocument() ;
    protected ElementIterator getElementIterator() ;
    public int getEndOffset() ; // Since 1.3
    protected int getIndentLevel() ; // Since 1.3
    protected int getIndentSpace() ; // Since 1.3
    protected int getLineLength() ; // Since 1.3
    public String getLineSeparator() ; // Since 1.3
    public int getStartOffset() ; // Since 1.3
    protected String getText(Element elem) throws BadLocationException ;
    protected Writer getWriter() ; // Since 1.3
    protected void incrIndent() ;
    protected void indent() throws IOException ;
    protected boolean inRange(Element next) ;
    protected boolean isLineEmpty() ; // Since 1.3
    protected void output(int length, int start, char[] content) throws IOException ; // Since 1.3
    protected void setCanWrapLines(boolean newValue) ; // Since 1.3
    protected void setCurrentLineLength(int length) ; // Since 1.3
    protected void setIndentSpace(int space) ;
    protected void setLineLength(int l) ;
    public void setLineSeparator(String value) ; // Since 1.3
    protected void text(Element elem) throws BadLocationException, IOException ;
    protected void write(char ch) throws IOException ;
    protected abstract void write() throws IOException, BadLocationException ;
    protected void write(int length, int startIndex, char[] chars) throws IOException ; // Since 1.3
    protected void write(String content) throws IOException ;
    protected void writeAttributes(AttributeSet attr) throws IOException ;
    protected void writeLineSeparator() throws IOException ; // Since 1.3
}
```

---

javax.swing.**Action**

```
public interface Action  implements ActionListener
{
    public static final String ACCELERATOR_KEY ;
    public static final String ACTION_COMMAND_KEY ;
    public static final String DEFAULT ;
    public static final String DISPLAYED_MNEMONIC_INDEX_KEY ;
    public static final String LARGE_ICON_KEY ;
```

```
    public static final String LONG_DESCRIPTION ;
    public static final String MNEMONIC_KEY ;
    public static final String NAME ;
    public static final String SELECTED_KEY ;
    public static final String SHORT_DESCRIPTION ;
    public static final String SMALL_ICON ;
    // Instance methods
    public void addPropertyChangeListener(PropertyChangeListener listener) ;
    public Object getValue(String key) ;
    public boolean isEnabled() ;
    public void putValue(Object value, String key) ;
    public void removePropertyChangeListener(PropertyChangeListener listener) ;
    public void setEnabled(boolean b) ;
}
```

java.awt.event.**ActionEvent** [since 1.1]

```
public class ActionEvent extends AWTEvent
{
    public static final int ACTION_FIRST ;
    public static final int ACTION_LAST ;
    public static final int ACTION_PERFORMED ;
    public static final int ALT_MASK ;
    public static final int CTRL_MASK ;
    public static final int META_MASK ;
    public static final int SHIFT_MASK ;
    // Constructors
    public ActionEvent(int modifiers, long when, String command, int id, Object source) ;
    public ActionEvent(int modifiers, String command, int id, Object source) ;
    public ActionEvent(String command, int id, Object source) ;
    // Instance methods
    public String getActionCommand() ;
    public int getModifiers() ;
    public long getWhen() ; // Since 1.4
    public String paramString() ;
}
```

java.awt.event.**ActionListener** [since 1.1]

```
public interface ActionListener implements EventListener
{
```

```
        // Instance methods
        public void actionPerformed(ActionEvent e) ;
}
```

javax.swing.**ActionMap** [since 1.3]

```
public class ActionMap  implements Serializable
{
        // Constructors
        public ActionMap() ;
        // Instance methods
        public Object allKeys() ;
        public void clear() ;
        public Action get(Object key) ;
        public ActionMap getParent() ;
        public Object keys() ;
        public void put(Action action, Object key) ;
        public void remove(Object key) ;
        public void setParent(ActionMap map) ;
        public int size() ;
}
```

javax.swing.plaf.**ActionMapUIResource** [since 1.3]

```
public class ActionMapUIResource extends ActionMap implements UIResource
{
        // Constructors
        public ActionMapUIResource() ;
}
```

java.awt.**ActiveEvent** [since 1.2]

```
public interface ActiveEvent
{
        // Instance methods
        public void dispatch() ;
}
```

java.awt.**Adjustable**

public interface **Adjustable**
{
    public static final int **HORIZONTAL** ;
    public static final int **NO_ORIENTATION** ;
    public static final int **VERTICAL** ;
    // Instance methods
    public void **addAdjustmentListener**(AdjustmentListener l) ;
    public int **getBlockIncrement**() ;
    public int **getMaximum**() ;
    public int **getMinimum**() ;
    public int **getOrientation**() ;
    public int **getUnitIncrement**() ;
    public int **getValue**() ;
    public int **getVisibleAmount**() ;
    public void **removeAdjustmentListener**(AdjustmentListener l) ;
    public void **setBlockIncrement**(int b) ;
    public void **setMaximum**(int max) ;
    public void **setMinimum**(int min) ;
    public void **setUnitIncrement**(int u) ;
    public void **setValue**(int v) ;
    public void **setVisibleAmount**(int v) ;
}

java.awt.event.**AdjustmentEvent** [since 1.1]

public class **AdjustmentEvent** extends AWTEvent
{
    public static final int **ADJUSTMENT_FIRST** ;
    public static final int **ADJUSTMENT_LAST** ;
    public static final int **ADJUSTMENT_VALUE_CHANGED** ;
    public static final int **BLOCK_DECREMENT** ;
    public static final int **BLOCK_INCREMENT** ;
    public static final int **TRACK** ;
    public static final int **UNIT_DECREMENT** ;
    public static final int **UNIT_INCREMENT** ;
    // Constructors
    public **AdjustmentEvent**(boolean isAdjusting, int value, int type, int id, Adjustable source) ;
    public **AdjustmentEvent**(int value, int type, int id, Adjustable source) ;
    // Instance methods

```
    public Adjustable getAdjustable() ;
    public int getAdjustmentType() ;
    public int getValue() ;
    public boolean getValueIsAdjusting() ; // Since 1.4
    public String paramString() ;
}
```

java.awt.event.**AdjustmentListener** [since 1.1]

```
public interface AdjustmentListener  implements EventListener
{
    // Instance methods
    public void adjustmentValueChanged(AdjustmentEvent e) ;
}
```

java.awt.geom.**AffineTransform** [since 1.2]

```
public class AffineTransform  implements Serializable, Cloneable
{
    public static final int TYPE_FLIP ;
    public static final int TYPE_GENERAL_ROTATION ;
    public static final int TYPE_GENERAL_SCALE ;
    public static final int TYPE_GENERAL_TRANSFORM ;
    public static final int TYPE_IDENTITY ;
    public static final int TYPE_MASK_ROTATION ;
    public static final int TYPE_MASK_SCALE ;
    public static final int TYPE_QUADRANT_ROTATION ;
    public static final int TYPE_TRANSLATION ;
    public static final int TYPE_UNIFORM_SCALE ;
    // Constructors
    public AffineTransform(double[] flatmatrix) ;
    public AffineTransform(double m12, double m02, double m11, double m01, double m10, double
        m00) ;
    public AffineTransform(float[] flatmatrix) ;
    public AffineTransform(float m12, float m02, float m11, float m01, float m10, float m00) ;
    public AffineTransform(AffineTransform Tx) ;
    public AffineTransform() ;
    private AffineTransform(int state, double m12, double m02, double m11, double m01, double m10,
        double m00) ;
    // Static methods
    public static AffineTransform getQuadrantRotateInstance(int numquadrants) ; // Since 1.6
```

public static AffineTransform **getQuadrantRotateInstance**(double anchory, double anchorx, int numquadrants) ; // Since 1.6

public static AffineTransform **getRotateInstance**(double anchory, double anchorx, double theta) ; // Since 1.2

public static AffineTransform **getRotateInstance**(double theta) ; // Since 1.2

public static AffineTransform **getRotateInstance**(double vecy, double vecx) ; // Since 1.6

public static AffineTransform **getRotateInstance**(double anchory, double anchorx, double vecy, double vecx) ; // Since 1.6

public static AffineTransform **getScaleInstance**(double sy, double sx) ; // Since 1.2

public static AffineTransform **getShearInstance**(double shy, double shx) ; // Since 1.2

public static AffineTransform **getTranslateInstance**(double ty, double tx) ; // Since 1.2

// Instance methods

public Object **clone**() ; // Since 1.2

public void **concatenate**(AffineTransform Tx) ; // Since 1.2

public AffineTransform **createInverse**() throws NoninvertibleTransformException ; // Since 1.2

public Shape **createTransformedShape**(Shape pSrc) ; // Since 1.2

public Point2D **deltaTransform**(Point2D ptDst, Point2D ptSrc) ; // Since 1.2

public void **deltaTransform**(int numPts, int dstOff, double[] dstPts, int srcOff, double[] srcPts) ; // Since 1.2

public boolean **equals**(Object obj) ; // Since 1.2

public double **getDeterminant**() ; // Since 1.2

public void **getMatrix**(double[] flatmatrix) ; // Since 1.2

public double **getScaleX**() ; // Since 1.2

public double **getScaleY**() ; // Since 1.2

public double **getShearX**() ; // Since 1.2

public double **getShearY**() ; // Since 1.2

public double **getTranslateX**() ; // Since 1.2

public double **getTranslateY**() ; // Since 1.2

public int **getType**() ; // Since 1.2

public int **hashCode**() ; // Since 1.2

public Point2D **inverseTransform**(Point2D ptDst, Point2D ptSrc) throws NoninvertibleTransformException ; // Since 1.2

public void **inverseTransform**(int numPts, int dstOff, double[] dstPts, int srcOff, double[] srcPts) throws NoninvertibleTransformException ; // Since 1.2

public void **invert**() throws NoninvertibleTransformException ; // Since 1.6

public boolean **isIdentity**() ; // Since 1.2

public void **preConcatenate**(AffineTransform Tx) ; // Since 1.2

public void **quadrantRotate**(int numquadrants) ; // Since 1.6

public void **quadrantRotate**(double anchory, double anchorx, int numquadrants) ; // Since 1.6

public void **rotate**(double vecy, double vecx) ; // Since 1.6

public void **rotate**(double anchory, double anchorx, double theta) ; // Since 1.2

public void **rotate**(double theta) ; // Since 1.2

public void **rotate**(double anchory, double anchorx, double vecy, double vecx) ; // Since 1.6

public void **scale**(double sy, double sx) ; // Since 1.2

public void **setToIdentity**() ; // Since 1.2

public void **setToQuadrantRotation**(int numquadrants) ; // Since 1.6

public void **setToQuadrantRotation**(double anchory, double anchorx, int numquadrants) ; // Since 1.6
public void **setToRotation**(double anchory, double anchorx, double theta) ; // Since 1.2
public void **setToRotation**(double vecy, double vecx) ; // Since 1.6
public void **setToRotation**(double anchory, double anchorx, double vecy, double vecx) ; // Since 1.6
public void **setToRotation**(double theta) ; // Since 1.2
public void **setToScale**(double sy, double sx) ; // Since 1.2
public void **setToShear**(double shy, double shx) ; // Since 1.2
public void **setToTranslation**(double ty, double tx) ; // Since 1.2
public void **setTransform**(double m12, double m02, double m11, double m01, double m10, double m00) ; // Since 1.2
public void **setTransform**(AffineTransform Tx) ; // Since 1.2
public void **shear**(double shy, double shx) ; // Since 1.2
public String **toString**() ; // Since 1.2
public void **transform**(int numPts, int dstOff, float[] dstPts, int srcOff, float[] srcPts) ; // Since 1.2
public void **transform**(int numPts, int dstOff, double[] dstPts, int srcOff, float[] srcPts) ; // Since 1.2
public void **transform**(int numPts, int dstOff, double[] dstPts, int srcOff, double[] srcPts) ; // Since 1.2
public void **transform**(int numPts, int dstOff, java.awt.geom.Point2D[] ptDst, int srcOff, java.awt.geom.Point2D[] ptSrc) ; // Since 1.2
public Point2D **transform**(Point2D ptDst, Point2D ptSrc) ; // Since 1.2
public void **transform**(int numPts, int dstOff, float[] dstPts, int srcOff, double[] srcPts) ; // Since 1.2
public void **translate**(double ty, double tx) ; // Since 1.2
}

---

java.awt.image.**AffineTransformOp**

---

public class **AffineTransformOp** implements RasterOp, BufferedImageOp
{
    public static final int **TYPE_BICUBIC** ;
    public static final int **TYPE_BILINEAR** ;
    public static final int **TYPE_NEAREST_NEIGHBOR** ;
    // Constructors
    public **AffineTransformOp**(int interpolationType, AffineTransform xform) ;
    public **AffineTransformOp**(RenderingHints hints, AffineTransform xform) ;
    // Instance methods
    public BufferedImage **createCompatibleDestImage**(ColorModel destCM, BufferedImage src) ;
    public WritableRaster **createCompatibleDestRaster**(Raster src) ;
    public final BufferedImage **filter**(BufferedImage dst, BufferedImage src) ;
    public final WritableRaster **filter**(WritableRaster dst, Raster src) ;
    public final Rectangle2D **getBounds2D**(BufferedImage src) ;
    public final Rectangle2D **getBounds2D**(Raster src) ;
    public final int **getInterpolationType**() ;
    public final Point2D **getPoint2D**(Point2D dstPt, Point2D srcPt) ;

```
    public final RenderingHints getRenderingHints() ;
    public final AffineTransform getTransform() ;
}
```

---

java.awt.**AlphaComposite**

```
public final class AlphaComposite  implements Composite
{
    public static final int CLEAR ;
    public static final AlphaComposite Clear ;
    public static final AlphaComposite Dst ;
    public static final int DST ;
    public static final AlphaComposite DstAtop ;
    public static final AlphaComposite DstIn ;
    public static final AlphaComposite DstOut ;
    public static final AlphaComposite DstOver ;
    public static final int DST_ATOP ;
    public static final int DST_IN ;
    public static final int DST_OUT ;
    public static final int DST_OVER ;
    public static final int SRC ;
    public static final AlphaComposite Src ;
    public static final AlphaComposite SrcAtop ;
    public static final AlphaComposite SrcIn ;
    public static final AlphaComposite SrcOut ;
    public static final AlphaComposite SrcOver ;
    public static final int SRC_ATOP ;
    public static final int SRC_IN ;
    public static final int SRC_OUT ;
    public static final int SRC_OVER ;
    public static final AlphaComposite Xor ;
    public static final int XOR ;
    // Constructors
    private AlphaComposite(float alpha, int rule) ;
    private AlphaComposite(int rule) ;
    // Static methods
    public static AlphaComposite getInstance(float alpha, int rule) ;
    public static AlphaComposite getInstance(int rule) ;
    // Instance methods
    public CompositeContext createContext(RenderingHints hints, ColorModel dstColorModel,
        ColorModel srcColorModel) ;
    public AlphaComposite derive(float alpha) ; // Since 1.6
    public AlphaComposite derive(int rule) ; // Since 1.6
    public boolean equals(Object obj) ;
```

```
    public float getAlpha() ;
    public int getRule() ;
    public int hashCode() ;
}
```

---

javax.swing.event.**AncestorEvent**

```
public class AncestorEvent extends AWTEvent
{
    public static final int ANCESTOR_ADDED ;
    public static final int ANCESTOR_MOVED ;
    public static final int ANCESTOR_REMOVED ;
    // Constructors
    public AncestorEvent(Container ancestorParent, Container ancestor, int id, JComponent source) ;
    // Instance methods
    public Container getAncestor() ;
    public Container getAncestorParent() ;
    public JComponent getComponent() ;
}
```

---

javax.swing.event.**AncestorListener**

```
public interface AncestorListener  implements EventListener
{
    // Instance methods
    public void ancestorAdded(AncestorEvent event) ;
    public void ancestorMoved(AncestorEvent event) ;
    public void ancestorRemoved(AncestorEvent event) ;
}
```

---

java.applet.**Applet** [since 1.0]

```
public class Applet extends Panel
{
    // Constructors
    public Applet() ;
    // Static methods
    public static final AudioClip newAudioClip(URL url) ; // Since 1.2
```

```
    // Instance methods
    public void destroy() ;
    public AccessibleContext getAccessibleContext() ; // Since 1.3
    public AppletContext getAppletContext() ;
    public String getAppletInfo() ;
    public AudioClip getAudioClip(URL url) ;
    public AudioClip getAudioClip(String name, URL url) ;
    public URL getCodeBase() ;
    public URL getDocumentBase() ;
    public Image getImage(String name, URL url) ;
    public Image getImage(URL url) ;
    public Locale getLocale() ; // Since 1.1
    public String getParameter(String name) ;
    public String getParameterInfo() ;
    public void init() ;
    public boolean isActive() ;
    public void play(String name, URL url) ;
    public void play(URL url) ;
    public void resize(int height, int width) ;
    public void resize(Dimension d) ;
    public final void setStub(AppletStub stub) ;
    public void showStatus(String msg) ;
    public void start() ;
    public void stop() ;
}
```

java.applet.**AppletContext** [since 1.0]

```
public interface AppletContext
{
    // Instance methods
    public Applet getApplet(String name) ;
    public Enumeration<Applet> getApplets() ;
    public AudioClip getAudioClip(URL url) ;
    public Image getImage(URL url) ;
    public InputStream getStream(String key) ; // Since 1.4
    public Iterator<String> getStreamKeys() ; // Since 1.4
    public void setStream(InputStream stream, String key) throws IOException ; // Since 1.4
    public void showDocument(String target, URL url) ;
    public void showDocument(URL url) ;
    public void showStatus(String status) ;
}
```

java.applet.**AppletStub** [since 1.0]

public interface **AppletStub**
{
    // Instance methods
    public void **appletResize**(int height, int width) ;
    public AppletContext **getAppletContext**() ;
    public URL **getCodeBase**() ;
    public URL **getDocumentBase**() ;
    public String **getParameter**(String name) ;
    public boolean **isActive**() ;
}

java.awt.geom.**Arc2D** [since 1.2]

public abstract class **Arc2D** extends RectangularShape
{
    public static final int **CHORD** ;
    public static final int **OPEN** ;
    public static final int **PIE** ;
    // Constructors
    protected **Arc2D**(int type) ;
    private **Arc2D**() ;
    // Static methods
    // Instance methods
    public boolean **contains**(Rectangle2D r) ; // Since 1.2
    public boolean **contains**(double h, double w, double y, double x) ; // Since 1.2
    public boolean **contains**(double y, double x) ; // Since 1.2
    public boolean **containsAngle**(double angle) ; // Since 1.2
    public boolean **equals**(Object obj) ; // Since 1.6
    public abstract double **getAngleExtent**() ; // Since 1.2
    public abstract double **getAngleStart**() ; // Since 1.2
    public int **getArcType**() ; // Since 1.2
    public Rectangle2D **getBounds2D**() ; // Since 1.2
    public Point2D **getEndPoint**() ; // Since 1.2
    public PathIterator **getPathIterator**(AffineTransform at) ; // Since 1.2
    public Point2D **getStartPoint**() ; // Since 1.2
    public int **hashCode**() ; // Since 1.6
    public boolean **intersects**(double h, double w, double y, double x) ; // Since 1.2
    protected abstract Rectangle2D **makeBounds**(double h, double w, double y, double x) ; // Since 1.2
    public abstract void **setAngleExtent**(double angExt) ; // Since 1.2

public void **setAngles**(double y2, double x2, double y1, double x1) ; // Since 1.2
public void **setAngles**(Point2D p2, Point2D p1) ; // Since 1.2
public abstract void **setAngleStart**(double angSt) ; // Since 1.2
public void **setAngleStart**(Point2D p) ; // Since 1.2
public abstract void **setArc**(int closure, double angExt, double angSt, double h, double w, double y,
    double x) ; // Since 1.2
public void **setArc**(int closure, double angExt, double angSt, Dimension2D size, Point2D loc) ; //
    Since 1.2
public void **setArc**(int closure, double angExt, double angSt, Rectangle2D rect) ; // Since 1.2
public void **setArc**(Arc2D a) ; // Since 1.2
public void **setArcByCenter**(int closure, double angExt, double angSt, double radius, double y,
    double x) ; // Since 1.2
public void **setArcByTangent**(double radius, Point2D p3, Point2D p2, Point2D p1) ; // Since 1.2
public void **setArcType**(int type) ; // Since 1.2
public void **setFrame**(double h, double w, double y, double x) ; // Since 1.2
}

---

java.awt.geom.**Arc2D.Double** [since 1.2]

---

public static class **Arc2D.Double** extends Arc2D implements Serializable
{
    public double **extent** ;
    public double **height** ;
    public double **start** ;
    public double **width** ;
    public double **x** ;
    public double **y** ;
    // Constructors
    public **Arc2D.Double**(int type, double extent, double start, Rectangle2D ellipseBounds) ;
    public **Arc2D.Double**(int type, double extent, double start, double h, double w, double y, double x) ;
    public **Arc2D.Double**(int type) ;
    public **Arc2D.Double**() ;
    // Instance methods
    public double **getAngleExtent**() ; // Since 1.2
    public double **getAngleStart**() ; // Since 1.2
    public double **getHeight**() ; // Since 1.2
    public double **getWidth**() ; // Since 1.2
    public double **getX**() ; // Since 1.2
    public double **getY**() ; // Since 1.2
    public boolean **isEmpty**() ; // Since 1.2
    protected Rectangle2D **makeBounds**(double h, double w, double y, double x) ; // Since 1.2
    public void **setAngleExtent**(double angExt) ; // Since 1.2
    public void **setAngleStart**(double angSt) ; // Since 1.2

public void **setArc**(int closure, double angExt, double angSt, double h, double w, double y, double x)
    ; // Since 1.2
}

java.awt.geom.**Arc2D.Float** [since 1.2]

public static class **Arc2D.Float** extends Arc2D implements Serializable
{
    public float **extent** ;
    public float **height** ;
    public float **start** ;
    public float **width** ;
    public float **x** ;
    public float **y** ;
    // Constructors
    public **Arc2D.Float**(int type, float extent, float start, Rectangle2D ellipseBounds) ;
    public **Arc2D.Float**(int type, float extent, float start, float h, float w, float y, float x) ;
    public **Arc2D.Float**(int type) ;
    public **Arc2D.Float**() ;
    // Instance methods
    public double **getAngleExtent**() ; // Since 1.2
    public double **getAngleStart**() ; // Since 1.2
    public double **getHeight**() ; // Since 1.2
    public double **getWidth**() ; // Since 1.2
    public double **getX**() ; // Since 1.2
    public double **getY**() ; // Since 1.2
    public boolean **isEmpty**() ; // Since 1.2
    protected Rectangle2D **makeBounds**(double h, double w, double y, double x) ; // Since 1.2
    public void **setAngleExtent**(double angExt) ; // Since 1.2
    public void **setAngleStart**(double angSt) ; // Since 1.2
    public void **setArc**(int closure, double angExt, double angSt, double h, double w, double y, double x)
        ; // Since 1.2
}

java.awt.geom.**Area** [since 1.2]

public class **Area** implements Cloneable, Shape
{
    // Constructors
    public **Area**(Shape s) ;
    public **Area**() ;

```
    // Static methods
    // Instance methods
    public void add(Area rhs) ; // Since 1.2
    public Object clone() ; // Since 1.2
    public boolean contains(Point2D p) ; // Since 1.2
    public boolean contains(Rectangle2D r) ; // Since 1.2
    public boolean contains(double h, double w, double y, double x) ; // Since 1.2
    public boolean contains(double y, double x) ; // Since 1.2
    public Area createTransformedArea(AffineTransform t) ; // Since 1.2
    public boolean equals(Area other) ; // Since 1.2
    public void exclusiveOr(Area rhs) ; // Since 1.2
    public Rectangle getBounds() ; // Since 1.2
    public Rectangle2D getBounds2D() ; // Since 1.2
    public PathIterator getPathIterator(double flatness, AffineTransform at) ; // Since 1.2
    public PathIterator getPathIterator(AffineTransform at) ; // Since 1.2
    public void intersect(Area rhs) ; // Since 1.2
    public boolean intersects(double h, double w, double y, double x) ; // Since 1.2
    public boolean intersects(Rectangle2D r) ; // Since 1.2
    public boolean isEmpty() ; // Since 1.2
    public boolean isPolygonal() ; // Since 1.2
    public boolean isRectangular() ; // Since 1.2
    public boolean isSingular() ; // Since 1.2
    public void reset() ; // Since 1.2
    public void subtract(Area rhs) ; // Since 1.2
    public void transform(AffineTransform t) ; // Since 1.2
}
```

java.awt.image.**AreaAveragingScaleFilter**

```
public class AreaAveragingScaleFilter extends ReplicateScaleFilter
{
    // Constructors
    public AreaAveragingScaleFilter(int height, int width) ;
    // Instance methods
    public void setHints(int hints) ;
    public void setPixels(int scansize, int off, int[] pixels, ColorModel model, int h, int w, int y, int x) ;
    public void setPixels(int scansize, int off, byte[] pixels, ColorModel model, int h, int w, int y, int x) ;
}
```

javax.swing.text.**AsyncBoxView** [since 1.3]

public class **AsyncBoxView** extends View
{
    protected AsyncBoxView.ChildLocator **locator** ;
    // Constructors
    public **AsyncBoxView**(int axis, Element elem) ;
    // Instance methods
    protected AsyncBoxView.ChildState **createChildState**(View v) ;
    protected void **flushRequirementChanges**() ;
    public float **getBottomInset**() ;
    public Shape **getChildAllocation**(Shape a, int index) ;
    protected AsyncBoxView.ChildState **getChildState**(int index) ;
    protected boolean **getEstimatedMajorSpan**() ; // Since 1.4
    protected float **getInsetSpan**(int axis) ; // Since 1.4
    protected LayoutQueue **getLayoutQueue**() ;
    public float **getLeftInset**() ;
    public int **getMajorAxis**() ;
    public float **getMaximumSpan**(int axis) ;
    public float **getMinimumSpan**(int axis) ;
    public int **getMinorAxis**() ;
    public int **getNextVisualPositionFrom**(javax.swing.text.Position.Bias[] biasRet, int direction, Shape
        a, Position.Bias b, int pos) throws BadLocationException ;
    public float **getPreferredSpan**(int axis) ;
    public float **getRightInset**() ;
    public float **getTopInset**() ;
    public View **getView**(int n) ;
    public int **getViewCount**() ;
    public int **getViewIndex**(Position.Bias b, int pos) ; // Since 1.3
    protected synchronized int **getViewIndexAtPosition**(Position.Bias b, int pos) ;
    protected void **loadChildren**(ViewFactory f) ;
    protected synchronized void **majorRequirementChange**(float delta, AsyncBoxView.ChildState cs) ;
    protected synchronized void **minorRequirementChange**(AsyncBoxView.ChildState cs) ;
    public Shape **modelToView**(Position.Bias b, Shape a, int pos) throws BadLocationException ;
    public void **paint**(Shape alloc, Graphics g) ;
    public synchronized void **preferenceChanged**(boolean height, boolean width, View child) ;
    public void **replace**(javax.swing.text.View[] views, int length, int offset) ;
    public void **setBottomInset**(float i) ;
    protected void **setEstimatedMajorSpan**(boolean isEstimated) ; // Since 1.4
    public void **setLeftInset**(float i) ;
    public void **setParent**(View parent) ;
    public void **setRightInset**(float i) ;
    public void **setSize**(float height, float width) ;

```
        public void setTopInset(float i) ;
        protected void updateLayout(Shape a, DocumentEvent e, DocumentEvent.ElementChange ec) ;
        public int viewToModel(javax.swing.text.Position.Bias[] biasReturn, Shape a, float y, float x) ;
}
```

---

javax.swing.text.html.parser.**AttributeList**

```
public final class AttributeList  implements Serializable, DTDConstants
{
        public int modifier ;
        public String name ;
        public AttributeList next ;
        public int type ;
        public String value ;
        public Vector<?> values ;
        // Constructors
        public AttributeList(AttributeList next, Vector<?> values, String value, int modifier, int type, String
            name) ;
        public AttributeList(String name) ;
        private AttributeList() ;
        // Static methods
        public static int name2type(String nm) ;
        public static String type2name(int tp) ;
        // Instance methods
        public int getModifier() ;
        public String getName() ;
        public AttributeList getNext() ;
        public int getType() ;
        public String getValue() ;
        public Enumeration<?> getValues() ;
        public String toString() ;
}
```

---

javax.swing.text.**AttributeSet**

```
public interface AttributeSet
{
        public static final Object NameAttribute ;
        public static final Object ResolveAttribute ;
        // Instance methods
        public boolean containsAttribute(Object value, Object name) ;
```

```
    public boolean containsAttributes(AttributeSet attributes) ;
    public AttributeSet copyAttributes() ;
    public Object getAttribute(Object key) ;
    public int getAttributeCount() ;
    public Enumeration<?> getAttributeNames() ;
    public AttributeSet getResolveParent() ;
    public boolean isDefined(Object attrName) ;
    public boolean isEqual(AttributeSet attr) ;
}
```

java.applet.**AudioClip** [since 1.0]

```
public interface AudioClip
{
    // Instance methods
    public void loop() ;
    public void play() ;
    public void stop() ;
}
```

java.awt.dnd.**Autoscroll** [since 1.2]

```
public interface Autoscroll
{
    // Instance methods
    public void autoscroll(Point cursorLocn) ;
    public Insets getAutoscrollInsets() ;
}
```

java.awt.**AWTError**

```
public class AWTError extends Error
{
    // Constructors
    public AWTError(String msg) ;
}
```

java.awt.**AWTEvent** [since 1.1]

public abstract class **AWTEvent** extends EventObject
{
    public static final long **ACTION_EVENT_MASK** ;
    public static final long **ADJUSTMENT_EVENT_MASK** ;
    public static final long **COMPONENT_EVENT_MASK** ;
    public static final long **CONTAINER_EVENT_MASK** ;
    public static final long **FOCUS_EVENT_MASK** ;
    public static final long **HIERARCHY_BOUNDS_EVENT_MASK** ;
    public static final long **HIERARCHY_EVENT_MASK** ;
    public static final long **INPUT_METHOD_EVENT_MASK** ;
    public static final long **INVOCATION_EVENT_MASK** ;
    public static final long **ITEM_EVENT_MASK** ;
    public static final long **KEY_EVENT_MASK** ;
    public static final long **MOUSE_EVENT_MASK** ;
    public static final long **MOUSE_MOTION_EVENT_MASK** ;
    public static final long **MOUSE_WHEEL_EVENT_MASK** ;
    public static final long **PAINT_EVENT_MASK** ;
    public static final int **RESERVED_ID_MAX** ;
    public static final long **TEXT_EVENT_MASK** ;
    public static final long **WINDOW_EVENT_MASK** ;
    public static final long **WINDOW_FOCUS_EVENT_MASK** ;
    public static final long **WINDOW_STATE_EVENT_MASK** ;
    protected boolean **consumed** ;
    protected int **id** ;
    // Constructors
    public **AWTEvent**(int id, Object source) ;
    public **AWTEvent**(Event event) ;
    // Static methods
    // Instance methods
    protected void **consume**() ;
    public int **getID**() ;
    protected boolean **isConsumed**() ;
    public String **paramString**() ;
    public void **setSource**(Object newSource) ; // Since 1.4
    public String **toString**() ;
}

---

java.awt.event.**AWTEventListener** [since 1.2]

---

public interface **AWTEventListener** implements EventListener
{
    // Instance methods
    public void **eventDispatched**(AWTEvent event) ;
}

---

java.awt.event.**AWTEventListenerProxy** [since 1.4]

---

public class **AWTEventListenerProxy** extends EventListenerProxy<AWTEventListener> implements AWTEventListener
{
    // Constructors
    public **AWTEventListenerProxy**(AWTEventListener listener, long eventMask) ;
    // Instance methods
    public void **eventDispatched**(AWTEvent event) ;
    public long **getEventMask**() ;
}

---

java.awt.**AWTEventMulticaster** [since 1.1]

---

public class **AWTEventMulticaster** implements MouseWheelListener, HierarchyBoundsListener, HierarchyListener, InputMethodListener, TextListener, AdjustmentListener, ItemListener, ActionListener, WindowStateListener, WindowFocusListener, WindowListener, MouseMotionListener, MouseListener, KeyListener, FocusListener, ContainerListener, ComponentListener
{
    protected final EventListener **a** ;
    protected final EventListener **b** ;
    // Constructors
    protected **AWTEventMulticaster**(EventListener b, EventListener a) ;
    // Static methods
    public static ComponentListener **add**(ComponentListener b, ComponentListener a) ;
    public static HierarchyListener **add**(HierarchyListener b, HierarchyListener a) ; // Since 1.3
    public static InputMethodListener **add**(InputMethodListener b, InputMethodListener a) ;
    public static TextListener **add**(TextListener b, TextListener a) ;
    public static AdjustmentListener **add**(AdjustmentListener b, AdjustmentListener a) ;

---

public static ActionListener **add**(ActionListener b, ActionListener a) ;
public static WindowFocusListener **add**(WindowFocusListener b, WindowFocusListener a) ; // Since 1.4
public static WindowStateListener **add**(WindowStateListener b, WindowStateListener a) ; // Since 1.4
public static WindowListener **add**(WindowListener b, WindowListener a) ;
public static MouseMotionListener **add**(MouseMotionListener b, MouseMotionListener a) ;
public static MouseWheelListener **add**(MouseWheelListener b, MouseWheelListener a) ; // Since 1.4
public static MouseListener **add**(MouseListener b, MouseListener a) ;
public static KeyListener **add**(KeyListener b, KeyListener a) ;
public static FocusListener **add**(FocusListener b, FocusListener a) ;
public static ContainerListener **add**(ContainerListener b, ContainerListener a) ;
public static ItemListener **add**(ItemListener b, ItemListener a) ;
public static HierarchyBoundsListener **add**(HierarchyBoundsListener b, HierarchyBoundsListener a) ; // Since 1.3
protected static EventListener **addInternal**(EventListener b, EventListener a) ;
public static T **getListeners**(Class<T> listenerType, EventListener l) ; // Since 1.4
public static MouseListener **remove**(MouseListener oldl, MouseListener l) ;
public static ItemListener **remove**(ItemListener oldl, ItemListener l) ;
public static ContainerListener **remove**(ContainerListener oldl, ContainerListener l) ;
public static FocusListener **remove**(FocusListener oldl, FocusListener l) ;
public static KeyListener **remove**(KeyListener oldl, KeyListener l) ;
public static ActionListener **remove**(ActionListener oldl, ActionListener l) ;
public static MouseMotionListener **remove**(MouseMotionListener oldl, MouseMotionListener l) ;
public static WindowListener **remove**(WindowListener oldl, WindowListener l) ;
public static WindowStateListener **remove**(WindowStateListener oldl, WindowStateListener l) ; // Since 1.4
public static ComponentListener **remove**(ComponentListener oldl, ComponentListener l) ;
public static AdjustmentListener **remove**(AdjustmentListener oldl, AdjustmentListener l) ;
public static InputMethodListener **remove**(InputMethodListener oldl, InputMethodListener l) ;
public static WindowFocusListener **remove**(WindowFocusListener oldl, WindowFocusListener l) ; // Since 1.4
public static MouseWheelListener **remove**(MouseWheelListener oldl, MouseWheelListener l) ; // Since 1.4
public static HierarchyBoundsListener **remove**(HierarchyBoundsListener oldl, HierarchyBoundsListener l) ; // Since 1.3
public static HierarchyListener **remove**(HierarchyListener oldl, HierarchyListener l) ; // Since 1.3
public static TextListener **remove**(TextListener oldl, TextListener l) ;
protected static EventListener **removeInternal**(EventListener oldl, EventListener l) ;
protected static void **save**(EventListener l, String k, ObjectOutputStream s) throws IOException ;
// Instance methods
public void **actionPerformed**(ActionEvent e) ;
public void **adjustmentValueChanged**(AdjustmentEvent e) ;
public void **ancestorMoved**(HierarchyEvent e) ; // Since 1.3
public void **ancestorResized**(HierarchyEvent e) ; // Since 1.3
public void **caretPositionChanged**(InputMethodEvent e) ;

```
        public void componentAdded(ContainerEvent e) ;
        public void componentHidden(ComponentEvent e) ;
        public void componentMoved(ComponentEvent e) ;
        public void componentRemoved(ContainerEvent e) ;
        public void componentResized(ComponentEvent e) ;
        public void componentShown(ComponentEvent e) ;
        public void focusGained(FocusEvent e) ;
        public void focusLost(FocusEvent e) ;
        public void hierarchyChanged(HierarchyEvent e) ; // Since 1.3
        public void inputMethodTextChanged(InputMethodEvent e) ;
        public void itemStateChanged(ItemEvent e) ;
        public void keyPressed(KeyEvent e) ;
        public void keyReleased(KeyEvent e) ;
        public void keyTyped(KeyEvent e) ;
        public void mouseClicked(MouseEvent e) ;
        public void mouseDragged(MouseEvent e) ;
        public void mouseEntered(MouseEvent e) ;
        public void mouseExited(MouseEvent e) ;
        public void mouseMoved(MouseEvent e) ;
        public void mousePressed(MouseEvent e) ;
        public void mouseReleased(MouseEvent e) ;
        public void mouseWheelMoved(MouseWheelEvent e) ; // Since 1.4
        protected EventListener remove(EventListener oldl) ;
        protected void saveInternal(String k, ObjectOutputStream s) throws IOException ;
        public void textValueChanged(TextEvent e) ;
        public void windowActivated(WindowEvent e) ;
        public void windowClosed(WindowEvent e) ;
        public void windowClosing(WindowEvent e) ;
        public void windowDeactivated(WindowEvent e) ;
        public void windowDeiconified(WindowEvent e) ;
        public void windowGainedFocus(WindowEvent e) ; // Since 1.4
        public void windowIconified(WindowEvent e) ;
        public void windowLostFocus(WindowEvent e) ; // Since 1.4
        public void windowOpened(WindowEvent e) ;
        public void windowStateChanged(WindowEvent e) ; // Since 1.4
}
```

java.awt.**AWTException**

```
public class AWTException extends Exception
{
    // Constructors
    public AWTException(String msg) ;
}
```

java.awt.**AWTKeyStroke** [since 1.4]

public class **AWTKeyStroke** implements Serializable
{
    // Constructors
    protected **AWTKeyStroke**(boolean onKeyRelease, int modifiers, int keyCode, char keyChar) ;
    protected **AWTKeyStroke**() ;
    // Static methods
    public static AWTKeyStroke **getAWTKeyStroke**(boolean onKeyRelease, int modifiers, int
        keyCode) ;
    public static AWTKeyStroke **getAWTKeyStroke**(int modifiers, int keyCode) ;
    public static AWTKeyStroke **getAWTKeyStroke**(char keyChar) ;
    public static AWTKeyStroke **getAWTKeyStroke**(String s) ;
    public static AWTKeyStroke **getAWTKeyStroke**(int modifiers, Character keyChar) ;
    public static AWTKeyStroke **getAWTKeyStrokeForEvent**(KeyEvent anEvent) ;
    protected static void **registerSubclass**(Class<?> subclass) ;
    // Instance methods
    public final boolean **equals**(Object anObject) ;
    public final char **getKeyChar**() ;
    public final int **getKeyCode**() ;
    public final int **getKeyEventType**() ;
    public final int **getModifiers**() ;
    public int **hashCode**() ;
    public final boolean **isOnKeyRelease**() ;
    protected Object **readResolve**() throws ObjectStreamException ;
    public String **toString**() ;
}

java.awt.**AWTPermission**

public final class **AWTPermission** extends BasicPermission
{
    // Constructors
    public **AWTPermission**(String actions, String name) ;
    public **AWTPermission**(String name) ;
}

javax.swing.text.**BadLocationException**

public class **BadLocationException** extends Exception
{
    // Constructors
    public **BadLocationException**(int offs, String s) ;
    // Instance methods
    public int **offsetRequested**() ;
}

java.awt.image.**BandCombineOp**

public class **BandCombineOp** implements RasterOp
{
    // Constructors
    public **BandCombineOp**(RenderingHints hints, float[][] matrix) ;
    // Instance methods
    public WritableRaster **createCompatibleDestRaster**(Raster src) ;
    public WritableRaster **filter**(WritableRaster dst, Raster src) ;
    public final Rectangle2D **getBounds2D**(Raster src) ;
    public final float **getMatrix**() ;
    public final Point2D **getPoint2D**(Point2D dstPt, Point2D srcPt) ;
    public final RenderingHints **getRenderingHints**() ;
}

javax.swing.plaf.basic.**BasicArrowButton**

public class **BasicArrowButton** extends JButton implements SwingConstants
{
    protected int **direction** ;
    // Constructors
    public **BasicArrowButton**(int direction) ;
    public **BasicArrowButton**(Color highlight, Color darkShadow, Color shadow, Color background, int
        direction) ;
    // Instance methods
    public int **getDirection**() ;
    public Dimension **getMaximumSize**() ;

```
    public Dimension getMinimumSize() ;
    public Dimension getPreferredSize() ;
    public boolean isFocusTraversable() ;
    public void paint(Graphics g) ;
    public void paintTriangle(boolean isEnabled, int direction, int size, int y, int x, Graphics g) ;
    public void setDirection(int direction) ;
}
```

javax.swing.plaf.basic.**BasicBorders**

public class **BasicBorders**
```
{
    // Constructors
    public BasicBorders() ;
    // Static methods
    public static Border getButtonBorder() ;
    public static Border getInternalFrameBorder() ;
    public static Border getMenuBarBorder() ;
    public static Border getProgressBarBorder() ;
    public static Border getRadioButtonBorder() ;
    public static Border getSplitPaneBorder() ;
    public static Border getSplitPaneDividerBorder() ; // Since 1.3
    public static Border getTextFieldBorder() ;
    public static Border getToggleButtonBorder() ;
}
```

javax.swing.plaf.basic.**BasicBorders.ButtonBorder**

public static class **BasicBorders.ButtonBorder** extends AbstractBorder implements UIResource
```
{
    protected Color darkShadow ;
    protected Color highlight ;
    protected Color lightHighlight ;
    protected Color shadow ;
    // Constructors
    public BasicBorders.ButtonBorder(Color lightHighlight, Color highlight, Color darkShadow, Color
        shadow) ;
    // Instance methods
    public Insets getBorderInsets(Insets insets, Component c) ;
    public void paintBorder(int height, int width, int y, int x, Graphics g, Component c) ;
}
```

javax.swing.plaf.basic.**BasicBorders.FieldBorder**

public static class **BasicBorders.FieldBorder** extends AbstractBorder implements UIResource
{
    protected Color **darkShadow** ;
    protected Color **highlight** ;
    protected Color **lightHighlight** ;
    protected Color **shadow** ;
    // Constructors
    public **BasicBorders.FieldBorder**(Color lightHighlight, Color highlight, Color darkShadow, Color
        shadow) ;
    // Instance methods
    public Insets **getBorderInsets**(Insets insets, Component c) ;
    public void **paintBorder**(int height, int width, int y, int x, Graphics g, Component c) ;
}

javax.swing.plaf.basic.**BasicBorders.MarginBorder**

public static class **BasicBorders.MarginBorder** extends AbstractBorder implements UIResource
{
    // Constructors
    public **BasicBorders.MarginBorder**() ;
    // Instance methods
    public Insets **getBorderInsets**(Insets insets, Component c) ;
}

javax.swing.plaf.basic.**BasicBorders.MenuBarBorder**

public static class **BasicBorders.MenuBarBorder** extends AbstractBorder implements UIResource
{
    // Constructors
    public **BasicBorders.MenuBarBorder**(Color highlight, Color shadow) ;
    // Instance methods
    public Insets **getBorderInsets**(Insets insets, Component c) ;
    public void **paintBorder**(int height, int width, int y, int x, Graphics g, Component c) ;
}

javax.swing.plaf.basic.**BasicBorders.RadioButtonBorder**

public static class **BasicBorders.RadioButtonBorder** extends BasicBorders.ButtonBorder
{
    // Constructors
    public **BasicBorders.RadioButtonBorder**(Color lightHighlight, Color highlight, Color darkShadow,
        Color shadow) ;
    // Instance methods
    public Insets **getBorderInsets**(Insets insets, Component c) ;
    public void **paintBorder**(int height, int width, int y, int x, Graphics g, Component c) ;
}

javax.swing.plaf.basic.**BasicBorders.RolloverButtonBorder** [since 1.4]

public static class **BasicBorders.RolloverButtonBorder** extends BasicBorders.ButtonBorder
{
    // Constructors
    public **BasicBorders.RolloverButtonBorder**(Color lightHighlight, Color highlight, Color
        darkShadow, Color shadow) ;
    // Instance methods
    public void **paintBorder**(int h, int w, int y, int x, Graphics g, Component c) ;
}

javax.swing.plaf.basic.**BasicBorders.SplitPaneBorder**

public static class **BasicBorders.SplitPaneBorder** implements UIResource, Border
{
    protected Color **highlight** ;
    protected Color **shadow** ;
    // Constructors
    public **BasicBorders.SplitPaneBorder**(Color shadow, Color highlight) ;
    // Instance methods
    public Insets **getBorderInsets**(Component c) ;
    public boolean **isBorderOpaque**() ;
    public void **paintBorder**(int height, int width, int y, int x, Graphics g, Component c) ;
}

javax.swing.plaf.basic.**BasicBorders.ToggleButtonBorder**

public static class **BasicBorders.ToggleButtonBorder** extends BasicBorders.ButtonBorder
{
    // Constructors
    public **BasicBorders.ToggleButtonBorder**(Color lightHighlight, Color highlight, Color
        darkShadow, Color shadow) ;
    // Instance methods
    public Insets **getBorderInsets**(Insets insets, Component c) ;
    public void **paintBorder**(int height, int width, int y, int x, Graphics g, Component c) ;
}

javax.swing.plaf.basic.**BasicButtonListener**

public class **BasicButtonListener** implements PropertyChangeListener, ChangeListener, FocusListener,
MouseMotionListener, MouseListener
{
    // Constructors
    public **BasicButtonListener**(AbstractButton b) ;
    // Static methods
    // Instance methods
    protected void **checkOpacity**(AbstractButton b) ;
    public void **focusGained**(FocusEvent e) ;
    public void **focusLost**(FocusEvent e) ;
    public void **installKeyboardActions**(JComponent c) ;
    public void **mouseClicked**(MouseEvent e) ;
    public void **mouseDragged**(MouseEvent e) ;
    public void **mouseEntered**(MouseEvent e) ;
    public void **mouseExited**(MouseEvent e) ;
    public void **mouseMoved**(MouseEvent e) ;
    public void **mousePressed**(MouseEvent e) ;
    public void **mouseReleased**(MouseEvent e) ;
    public void **propertyChange**(PropertyChangeEvent e) ;
    public void **stateChanged**(ChangeEvent e) ;
    public void **uninstallKeyboardActions**(JComponent c) ;
}

---

javax.swing.plaf.basic.**BasicButtonUI**

---

public class **BasicButtonUI** extends ButtonUI
{
    protected int **defaultTextIconGap** ;
    protected int **defaultTextShiftOffset** ;
    // Constructors
    public **BasicButtonUI**() ;
    // Static methods
    public static ComponentUI **createUI**(JComponent c) ;
    // Instance methods
    protected void **clearTextShiftOffset**() ;
    protected BasicButtonListener **createButtonListener**(AbstractButton b) ;
    public int **getBaseline**(int height, int width, JComponent c) ; // Since 1.6
    public Component.BaselineResizeBehavior **getBaselineResizeBehavior**(JComponent c) ; // Since 1.6
    public int **getDefaultTextIconGap**(AbstractButton b) ;
    public Dimension **getMaximumSize**(JComponent c) ;
    public Dimension **getMinimumSize**(JComponent c) ;
    public Dimension **getPreferredSize**(JComponent c) ;
    protected String **getPropertyPrefix**() ;
    protected int **getTextShiftOffset**() ;
    protected void **installDefaults**(AbstractButton b) ;
    protected void **installKeyboardActions**(AbstractButton b) ;
    protected void **installListeners**(AbstractButton b) ;
    public void **installUI**(JComponent c) ;
    public void **paint**(JComponent c, Graphics g) ;
    protected void **paintButtonPressed**(AbstractButton b, Graphics g) ;
    protected void **paintFocus**(Rectangle iconRect, Rectangle textRect, Rectangle viewRect,
        AbstractButton b, Graphics g) ;
    protected void **paintIcon**(Rectangle iconRect, JComponent c, Graphics g) ;
    protected void **paintText**(String text, Rectangle textRect, AbstractButton b, Graphics g) ; // Since 1.4
    protected void **paintText**(String text, Rectangle textRect, JComponent c, Graphics g) ;
    protected void **setTextShiftOffset**() ;
    protected void **uninstallDefaults**(AbstractButton b) ;
    protected void **uninstallKeyboardActions**(AbstractButton b) ;
    protected void **uninstallListeners**(AbstractButton b) ;
    public void **uninstallUI**(JComponent c) ;
}

javax.swing.plaf.basic.**BasicCheckBoxMenuItemUI**

public class **BasicCheckBoxMenuItemUI** extends BasicMenuItemUI
{
    // Constructors
    public **BasicCheckBoxMenuItemUI**() ;
    // Static methods
    public static ComponentUI **createUI**(JComponent c) ;
    // Instance methods
    protected String **getPropertyPrefix**() ;
    public void **processMouseEvent**(MenuSelectionManager manager, javax.swing.MenuElement[]
        path, MouseEvent e, JMenuItem item) ;
}

javax.swing.plaf.basic.**BasicCheckBoxUI**

public class **BasicCheckBoxUI** extends BasicRadioButtonUI
{
    // Constructors
    public **BasicCheckBoxUI**() ;
    // Static methods
    public static ComponentUI **createUI**(JComponent b) ;
    // Instance methods
    public String **getPropertyPrefix**() ;
}

javax.swing.plaf.basic.**BasicColorChooserUI**

public class **BasicColorChooserUI** extends ColorChooserUI
{
    protected JColorChooser **chooser** ;
    protected AbstractColorChooserPanel **defaultChoosers** ;
    protected ChangeListener **previewListener** ;
    protected PropertyChangeListener **propertyChangeListener** ;
    // Constructors
    public **BasicColorChooserUI**() ;
    // Static methods

```
    public static ComponentUI createUI(JComponent c) ;
    // Instance methods
    protected AbstractColorChooserPanel createDefaultChoosers() ;
    protected PropertyChangeListener createPropertyChangeListener() ;
    protected void installDefaults() ;
    protected void installListeners() ;
    protected void installPreviewPanel() ;
    public void installUI(JComponent c) ;
    protected void uninstallDefaultChoosers() ;
    protected void uninstallDefaults() ;
    protected void uninstallListeners() ;
    public void uninstallUI(JComponent c) ;
}
```

---

javax.swing.plaf.basic.**BasicComboBoxEditor**

```
public class BasicComboBoxEditor  implements FocusListener, ComboBoxEditor
{
    protected JTextField editor ;
    // Constructors
    public BasicComboBoxEditor() ;
    // Instance methods
    public void addActionListener(ActionListener l) ;
    protected JTextField createEditorComponent() ; // Since 1.6
    public void focusGained(FocusEvent e) ;
    public void focusLost(FocusEvent e) ;
    public Component getEditorComponent() ;
    public Object getItem() ;
    public void removeActionListener(ActionListener l) ;
    public void selectAll() ;
    public void setItem(Object anObject) ;
}
```

---

javax.swing.plaf.basic.**BasicComboBoxEditor.UIResource**

```
public static class BasicComboBoxEditor.UIResource extends BasicComboBoxEditor implements
UIResource
{
    // Constructors
    public BasicComboBoxEditor.UIResource() ;
}
```

javax.swing.plaf.basic.**BasicComboBoxRenderer**

public class **BasicComboBoxRenderer** extends JLabel implements Serializable, ListCellRenderer
{
    protected static Border **noFocusBorder** ;
    // Constructors
    public **BasicComboBoxRenderer**() ;
    // Static methods
    // Instance methods
    public Component **getListCellRendererComponent**(boolean cellHasFocus, boolean isSelected, int
        index, Object value, JList list) ;
    public Dimension **getPreferredSize**() ;
}

javax.swing.plaf.basic.**BasicComboBoxRenderer.UIResource**

public static class **BasicComboBoxRenderer.UIResource** extends BasicComboBoxRenderer implements
UIResource
{
    // Constructors
    public **BasicComboBoxRenderer.UIResource**() ;
}

javax.swing.plaf.basic.**BasicComboBoxUI**

public class **BasicComboBoxUI** extends ComboBoxUI
{
    protected JButton **arrowButton** ;
    protected Dimension **cachedMinimumSize** ;
    protected JComboBox **comboBox** ;
    protected CellRendererPane **currentValuePane** ;
    protected Component **editor** ;
    protected FocusListener **focusListener** ;
    protected boolean **hasFocus** ;
    protected boolean **isMinimumSizeDirty** ;
    protected ItemListener **itemListener** ;
    protected KeyListener **keyListener** ;

protected JList **listBox** ;
protected ListDataListener **listDataListener** ;
protected ComboPopup **popup** ;
protected KeyListener **popupKeyListener** ;
protected MouseListener **popupMouseListener** ;
protected MouseMotionListener **popupMouseMotionListener** ;
protected PropertyChangeListener **propertyChangeListener** ;
// Constructors
public **BasicComboBoxUI**() ;
// Static methods
public static ComponentUI **createUI**(JComponent c) ;
// Instance methods
public void **addEditor**() ;
public void **configureArrowButton**() ;
protected void **configureEditor**() ;
protected JButton **createArrowButton**() ;
protected ComboBoxEditor **createEditor**() ;
protected FocusListener **createFocusListener**() ;
protected ItemListener **createItemListener**() ;
protected KeyListener **createKeyListener**() ;
protected LayoutManager **createLayoutManager**() ;
protected ListDataListener **createListDataListener**() ;
protected ComboPopup **createPopup**() ;
protected PropertyChangeListener **createPropertyChangeListener**() ;
protected ListCellRenderer **createRenderer**() ;
public Accessible **getAccessibleChild**(int i, JComponent c) ;
public int **getAccessibleChildrenCount**(JComponent c) ;
public int **getBaseline**(int height, int width, JComponent c) ; // Since 1.6
public Component.BaselineResizeBehavior **getBaselineResizeBehavior**(JComponent c) ; // Since 1.6
protected Dimension **getDefaultSize**() ;
protected Dimension **getDisplaySize**() ;
protected Insets **getInsets**() ;
public Dimension **getMaximumSize**(JComponent c) ;
public Dimension **getMinimumSize**(JComponent c) ;
public Dimension **getPreferredSize**(JComponent c) ;
protected void **installComponents**() ;
protected void **installDefaults**() ;
protected void **installKeyboardActions**() ;
protected void **installListeners**() ;
public void **installUI**(JComponent c) ;
public boolean **isFocusTraversable**(JComboBox c) ;
protected boolean **isNavigationKey**(int keyCode) ;
public boolean **isPopupVisible**(JComboBox c) ;
public void **paint**(JComponent c, Graphics g) ;
public void **paintCurrentValue**(boolean hasFocus, Rectangle bounds, Graphics g) ;
public void **paintCurrentValueBackground**(boolean hasFocus, Rectangle bounds, Graphics g) ;

```
        protected Rectangle rectangleForCurrentValue() ;
        public void removeEditor() ;
        protected void selectNextPossibleValue() ;
        protected void selectPreviousPossibleValue() ;
        public void setPopupVisible(boolean v, JComboBox c) ;
        protected void toggleOpenClose() ;
        public void unconfigureArrowButton() ;
        protected void unconfigureEditor() ;
        protected void uninstallComponents() ;
        protected void uninstallDefaults() ;
        protected void uninstallKeyboardActions() ;
        protected void uninstallListeners() ;
        public void uninstallUI(JComponent c) ;
}
```

javax.swing.plaf.basic.**BasicComboPopup**

public class **BasicComboPopup** extends JPopupMenu implements ComboPopup
```
{
        protected static final int SCROLL_DOWN ;
        protected static final int SCROLL_UP ;
        protected Timer autoscrollTimer ;
        protected JComboBox comboBox ;
        protected boolean hasEntered ;
        protected boolean isAutoScrolling ;
        protected ItemListener itemListener ;
        protected KeyListener keyListener ;
        protected JList list ;
        protected ListDataListener listDataListener ;
        protected MouseListener listMouseListener ;
        protected MouseMotionListener listMouseMotionListener ;
        protected ListSelectionListener listSelectionListener ;
        protected MouseListener mouseListener ;
        protected MouseMotionListener mouseMotionListener ;
        protected PropertyChangeListener propertyChangeListener ;
        protected int scrollDirection ;
        protected JScrollPane scroller ;
        protected boolean valueIsAdjusting ;
        // Constructors
        public BasicComboPopup(JComboBox combo) ;
        // Instance methods
        protected void autoScrollDown() ;
        protected void autoScrollUp() ;
        protected Rectangle computePopupBounds(int ph, int pw, int py, int px) ;
```

```
protected void configureList() ;
protected void configurePopup() ;
protected void configureScroller() ;
protected MouseEvent convertMouseEvent(MouseEvent e) ;
protected ItemListener createItemListener() ;
protected KeyListener createKeyListener() ;
protected JList createList() ;
protected ListDataListener createListDataListener() ;
protected MouseListener createListMouseListener() ;
protected MouseMotionListener createListMouseMotionListener() ;
protected ListSelectionListener createListSelectionListener() ;
protected MouseListener createMouseListener() ;
protected MouseMotionListener createMouseMotionListener() ;
protected PropertyChangeListener createPropertyChangeListener() ;
protected JScrollPane createScroller() ;
protected void delegateFocus(MouseEvent e) ;
protected void firePopupMenuCanceled() ;
protected void firePopupMenuWillBecomeInvisible() ;
protected void firePopupMenuWillBecomeVisible() ;
public AccessibleContext getAccessibleContext() ; // Since 1.5
public KeyListener getKeyListener() ;
public JList getList() ;
public MouseListener getMouseListener() ;
public MouseMotionListener getMouseMotionListener() ;
protected int getPopupHeightForRowCount(int maxRowCount) ;
public void hide() ;
protected void installComboBoxListeners() ;
protected void installComboBoxModelListeners(ComboBoxModel model) ;
protected void installKeyboardActions() ;
protected void installListListeners() ;
public boolean isFocusTraversable() ;
public void show() ;
protected void startAutoScrolling(int direction) ;
protected void stopAutoScrolling() ;
protected void togglePopup() ;
protected void uninstallComboBoxModelListeners(ComboBoxModel model) ;
public void uninstallingUI() ;
protected void uninstallKeyboardActions() ;
protected void updateListBoxSelectionForEvent(boolean shouldScroll, MouseEvent anEvent) ;
}
```

javax.swing.plaf.basic.**BasicDesktopIconUI**

public class **BasicDesktopIconUI** extends DesktopIconUI
{
    protected JInternalFrame.JDesktopIcon **desktopIcon** ;
    protected JInternalFrame **frame** ;
    protected JComponent **iconPane** ;
    // Constructors
    public **BasicDesktopIconUI**() ;
    // Static methods
    public static ComponentUI **createUI**(JComponent c) ;
    // Instance methods
    protected MouseInputListener **createMouseInputListener**() ;
    public void **deiconize**() ;
    public Insets **getInsets**(JComponent c) ;
    public Dimension **getMaximumSize**(JComponent c) ;
    public Dimension **getMinimumSize**(JComponent c) ;
    public Dimension **getPreferredSize**(JComponent c) ;
    protected void **installComponents**() ;
    protected void **installDefaults**() ;
    protected void **installListeners**() ;
    public void **installUI**(JComponent c) ;
    protected void **uninstallComponents**() ;
    protected void **uninstallDefaults**() ;
    protected void **uninstallListeners**() ;
    public void **uninstallUI**(JComponent c) ;
}

javax.swing.plaf.basic.**BasicDesktopPaneUI**

public class **BasicDesktopPaneUI** extends DesktopPaneUI
{
    protected KeyStroke **closeKey** ;
    protected JDesktopPane **desktop** ;
    protected DesktopManager **desktopManager** ;
    protected KeyStroke **maximizeKey** ;
    protected KeyStroke **minimizeKey** ;
    protected KeyStroke **navigateKey** ;
    protected KeyStroke **navigateKey2** ;
    // Constructors

```
    public BasicDesktopPaneUI() ;
    // Static methods
    public static ComponentUI createUI(JComponent c) ;
    // Instance methods
    protected PropertyChangeListener createPropertyChangeListener() ; // Since 1.5
    public Dimension getMaximumSize(JComponent c) ;
    public Dimension getMinimumSize(JComponent c) ;
    public Dimension getPreferredSize(JComponent c) ;
    protected void installDefaults() ;
    protected void installDesktopManager() ;
    protected void installKeyboardActions() ;
    protected void installListeners() ; // Since 1.5
    public void installUI(JComponent c) ;
    public void paint(JComponent c, Graphics g) ;
    protected void registerKeyboardActions() ;
    protected void uninstallDefaults() ;
    protected void uninstallDesktopManager() ;
    protected void uninstallKeyboardActions() ;
    protected void uninstallListeners() ; // Since 1.5
    public void uninstallUI(JComponent c) ;
    protected void unregisterKeyboardActions() ;
}
```

---

javax.swing.plaf.basic.**BasicDirectoryModel**

---

public class **BasicDirectoryModel** extends AbstractListModel implements PropertyChangeListener
```
{
    // Constructors
    public BasicDirectoryModel(JFileChooser filechooser) ;
    // Instance methods
    public void addPropertyChangeListener(PropertyChangeListener listener) ; // Since 1.6
    public boolean contains(Object o) ;
    public void fireContentsChanged() ;
    protected void firePropertyChange(Object newValue, Object oldValue, String propertyName) ; //
        Since 1.6
    public Vector<File> getDirectories() ;
    public Object getElementAt(int index) ;
    public Vector<File> getFiles() ;
    public PropertyChangeListener getPropertyChangeListeners() ; // Since 1.6
    public int getSize() ;
    public int indexOf(Object o) ;
    public void intervalAdded(ListDataEvent e) ;
    public void intervalRemoved(ListDataEvent e) ;
    public void invalidateFileCache() ;
```

```
    protected boolean lt(File b, File a) ;
    public void propertyChange(PropertyChangeEvent e) ;
    public void removePropertyChangeListener(PropertyChangeListener listener) ; // Since 1.6
    public boolean renameFile(File newFile, File oldFile) ; // Since 1.4
    protected void sort(Vector<?> v) ;
    public void validateFileCache() ;
}
```

javax.swing.plaf.basic.**BasicEditorPaneUI**

```
public class BasicEditorPaneUI extends BasicTextUI
{
    // Constructors
    public BasicEditorPaneUI() ;
    // Static methods
    public static ComponentUI createUI(JComponent c) ;
    // Instance methods
    public EditorKit getEditorKit(JTextComponent tc) ;
    protected String getPropertyPrefix() ;
    public void installUI(JComponent c) ; // Since 1.5
    protected void propertyChange(PropertyChangeEvent evt) ;
    public void uninstallUI(JComponent c) ; // Since 1.5
}
```

javax.swing.plaf.basic.**BasicFileChooserUI**

```
public class BasicFileChooserUI extends FileChooserUI
{
    protected int cancelButtonMnemonic ;
    protected String cancelButtonText ;
    protected String cancelButtonToolTipText ;
    protected Icon computerIcon ;
    protected Icon detailsViewIcon ;
    protected Icon directoryIcon ;
    protected int directoryOpenButtonMnemonic ;
    protected String directoryOpenButtonText ;
    protected String directoryOpenButtonToolTipText ;
    protected Icon fileIcon ;
    protected Icon floppyDriveIcon ;
    protected Icon hardDriveIcon ;
    protected int helpButtonMnemonic ;
```

protected String **helpButtonText** ;
protected String **helpButtonToolTipText** ;
protected Icon **homeFolderIcon** ;
protected Icon **listViewIcon** ;
protected Icon **newFolderIcon** ;
protected int **openButtonMnemonic** ;
protected String **openButtonText** ;
protected String **openButtonToolTipText** ;
protected int **saveButtonMnemonic** ;
protected String **saveButtonText** ;
protected String **saveButtonToolTipText** ;
protected int **updateButtonMnemonic** ;
protected String **updateButtonText** ;
protected String **updateButtonToolTipText** ;
protected Icon **upFolderIcon** ;
protected Icon **viewMenuIcon** ;
// Constructors
public **BasicFileChooserUI**(JFileChooser b) ;
// Static methods
// Instance methods
public void **clearIconCache**() ;
protected MouseListener **createDoubleClickListener**(JList list, JFileChooser fc) ;
public ListSelectionListener **createListSelectionListener**(JFileChooser fc) ;
protected void **createModel**() ;
public PropertyChangeListener **createPropertyChangeListener**(JFileChooser fc) ;
public void **ensureFileIsVisible**(File f, JFileChooser fc) ;
public FileFilter **getAcceptAllFileFilter**(JFileChooser fc) ;
public JPanel **getAccessoryPanel**() ;
protected JButton **getApproveButton**(JFileChooser fc) ;
public int **getApproveButtonMnemonic**(JFileChooser fc) ;
public String **getApproveButtonText**(JFileChooser fc) ;
public String **getApproveButtonToolTipText**(JFileChooser fc) ;
public Action **getApproveSelectionAction**() ;
public Action **getCancelSelectionAction**() ;
public Action **getChangeToParentDirectoryAction**() ;
public String **getDialogTitle**(JFileChooser fc) ;
protected File **getDirectory**() ; // Since 1.4
public String **getDirectoryName**() ;
public JFileChooser **getFileChooser**() ;
public String **getFileName**() ;
public FileView **getFileView**(JFileChooser fc) ;
public Action **getGoHomeAction**() ;
public BasicDirectoryModel **getModel**() ;
public Action **getNewFolderAction**() ;
public Action **getUpdateAction**() ;
public void **installComponents**(JFileChooser fc) ;

```
        protected void installDefaults(JFileChooser fc) ;
        protected void installIcons(JFileChooser fc) ;
        protected void installListeners(JFileChooser fc) ;
        protected void installStrings(JFileChooser fc) ;
        public void installUI(JComponent c) ;
        protected boolean isDirectorySelected() ; // Since 1.4
        public void rescanCurrentDirectory(JFileChooser fc) ;
        protected void setDirectory(File f) ; // Since 1.4
        public void setDirectoryName(String dirname) ;
        protected void setDirectorySelected(boolean b) ; // Since 1.4
        public void setFileName(String filename) ;
        public void uninstallComponents(JFileChooser fc) ;
        protected void uninstallDefaults(JFileChooser fc) ;
        protected void uninstallIcons(JFileChooser fc) ;
        protected void uninstallListeners(JFileChooser fc) ;
        protected void uninstallStrings(JFileChooser fc) ;
        public void uninstallUI(JComponent c) ;
}
```

---

javax.swing.plaf.basic.**BasicFormattedTextFieldUI** [since 1.4]

```
public class BasicFormattedTextFieldUI extends BasicTextFieldUI
{
        // Constructors
        public BasicFormattedTextFieldUI() ;
        // Static methods
        public static ComponentUI createUI(JComponent c) ;
        // Instance methods
        protected String getPropertyPrefix() ;
}
```

---

javax.swing.plaf.basic.**BasicGraphicsUtils**

```
public class BasicGraphicsUtils
{
        // Constructors
        public BasicGraphicsUtils() ;
        // Static methods
        public static void drawBezel(Color lightHighlight, Color highlight, Color darkShadow, Color
                shadow, boolean isDefault, boolean isPressed, int h, int w, int y, int x, Graphics g) ;
        public static void drawDashedRect(int height, int width, int y, int x, Graphics g) ;
```

```
    public static void drawEtchedRect(Color lightHighlight, Color highlight, Color darkShadow, Color
        shadow, int h, int w, int y, int x, Graphics g) ;
    public static void drawGroove(Color highlight, Color shadow, int h, int w, int y, int x, Graphics g) ;
    public static void drawLoweredBezel(Color lightHighlight, Color highlight, Color darkShadow,
        Color shadow, int h, int w, int y, int x, Graphics g) ;
    public static void drawString(int y, int x, int underlinedChar, String text, Graphics g) ;
    public static void drawStringUnderlineCharAt(int y, int x, int underlinedIndex, String text,
        Graphics g) ; // Since 1.4
    public static Insets getEtchedInsets() ;
    public static Insets getGrooveInsets() ;
    public static Dimension getPreferredButtonSize(int textIconGap, AbstractButton b) ;
}
```

---

javax.swing.plaf.basic.**BasicHTML** [since 1.3]

```
public class BasicHTML
{
    public static final String documentBaseKey ;
    public static final String propertyKey ;
    // Constructors
    public BasicHTML() ;
    // Static methods
    public static View createHTMLView(String html, JComponent c) ;
    public static int getHTMLBaseline(int h, int w, View view) ; // Since 1.6
    public static boolean isHTMLString(String s) ;
    public static void updateRenderer(String text, JComponent c) ;
}
```

---

javax.swing.plaf.basic.**BasicIconFactory**

```
public class BasicIconFactory  implements Serializable
{
    // Constructors
    public BasicIconFactory() ;
    // Static methods
    public static Icon createEmptyFrameIcon() ;
    public static Icon getCheckBoxIcon() ;
    public static Icon getCheckBoxMenuItemIcon() ;
    public static Icon getMenuArrowIcon() ;
    public static Icon getMenuItemArrowIcon() ;
    public static Icon getMenuItemCheckIcon() ;
```

```
    public static Icon getRadioButtonIcon() ;
    public static Icon getRadioButtonMenuItemIcon() ;
}
```

javax.swing.plaf.basic.**BasicInternalFrameTitlePane**

public class **BasicInternalFrameTitlePane** extends JComponent
```
{
    protected static final String CLOSE_CMD ;
    protected static final String ICONIFY_CMD ;
    protected static final String MAXIMIZE_CMD ;
    protected static final String MOVE_CMD ;
    protected static final String RESTORE_CMD ;
    protected static final String SIZE_CMD ;
    protected Action closeAction ;
    protected JButton closeButton ;
    protected Icon closeIcon ;
    protected JInternalFrame frame ;
    protected JButton iconButton ;
    protected Icon iconIcon ;
    protected Action iconifyAction ;
    protected JButton maxButton ;
    protected Icon maxIcon ;
    protected Action maximizeAction ;
    protected JMenuBar menuBar ;
    protected Icon minIcon ;
    protected Action moveAction ;
    protected Color notSelectedTextColor ;
    protected Color notSelectedTitleColor ;
    protected PropertyChangeListener propertyChangeListener ;
    protected Action restoreAction ;
    protected Color selectedTextColor ;
    protected Color selectedTitleColor ;
    protected Action sizeAction ;
    protected JMenu windowMenu ;
    // Constructors
    public BasicInternalFrameTitlePane(JInternalFrame f) ;
    // Instance methods
    protected void addSubComponents() ;
    protected void addSystemMenuItems(JMenu systemMenu) ;
    protected void assembleSystemMenu() ;
    protected void createActions() ;
    protected void createButtons() ;
    protected LayoutManager createLayout() ;
```

```
        protected PropertyChangeListener createPropertyChangeListener() ;
        protected JMenu createSystemMenu() ;
        protected JMenuBar createSystemMenuBar() ;
        protected void enableActions() ;
        protected String getTitle(int availTextWidth, FontMetrics fm, String text) ;
        protected void installDefaults() ;
        protected void installListeners() ;
        protected void installTitlePane() ;
        public void paintComponent(Graphics g) ;
        protected void paintTitleBackground(Graphics g) ; // Since 1.4
        protected void postClosingEvent(JInternalFrame frame) ;
        protected void setButtonIcons() ;
        protected void showSystemMenu() ;
        protected void uninstallDefaults() ;
        protected void uninstallListeners() ;
}
```

javax.swing.plaf.basic.**BasicInternalFrameUI**

public class **BasicInternalFrameUI** extends InternalFrameUI
```
{
        protected MouseInputAdapter borderListener ;
        protected ComponentListener componentListener ;
        protected JComponent eastPane ;
        protected JInternalFrame frame ;
        protected MouseInputListener glassPaneDispatcher ;
        protected LayoutManager internalFrameLayout ;
        protected JComponent northPane ;
        protected KeyStroke openMenuKey ;
        protected PropertyChangeListener propertyChangeListener ;
        protected JComponent southPane ;
        protected BasicInternalFrameTitlePane titlePane ;
        protected JComponent westPane ;
        // Constructors
        public BasicInternalFrameUI(JInternalFrame b) ;
        // Static methods
        public static ComponentUI createUI(JComponent b) ;
        // Instance methods
        protected void activateFrame(JInternalFrame f) ;
        protected void closeFrame(JInternalFrame f) ;
        protected MouseInputAdapter createBorderListener(JInternalFrame w) ;
        protected ComponentListener createComponentListener() ;
        protected DesktopManager createDesktopManager() ;
        protected JComponent createEastPane(JInternalFrame w) ;
```

```
    protected MouseInputListener createGlassPaneDispatcher() ;
    protected void createInternalFrameListener() ;
    protected LayoutManager createLayoutManager() ;
    protected JComponent createNorthPane(JInternalFrame w) ;
    protected PropertyChangeListener createPropertyChangeListener() ;
    protected JComponent createSouthPane(JInternalFrame w) ;
    protected JComponent createWestPane(JInternalFrame w) ;
    protected void deactivateFrame(JInternalFrame f) ;
    protected void deiconifyFrame(JInternalFrame f) ;
    protected void deinstallMouseHandlers(JComponent c) ;
    protected DesktopManager getDesktopManager() ;
    public JComponent getEastPane() ;
    public Dimension getMaximumSize(JComponent x) ;
    public Dimension getMinimumSize(JComponent x) ;
    public JComponent getNorthPane() ;
    public Dimension getPreferredSize(JComponent x) ;
    public JComponent getSouthPane() ;
    public JComponent getWestPane() ;
    protected void iconifyFrame(JInternalFrame f) ;
    protected void installComponents() ;
    protected void installDefaults() ;
    protected void installKeyboardActions() ;
    protected void installListeners() ; // Since 1.3
    protected void installMouseHandlers(JComponent c) ;
    public void installUI(JComponent c) ;
    public final boolean isKeyBindingActive() ;
    protected final boolean isKeyBindingRegistered() ;
    protected void maximizeFrame(JInternalFrame f) ;
    protected void minimizeFrame(JInternalFrame f) ;
    protected void replacePane(JComponent newPane, JComponent currentPane) ;
    public void setEastPane(JComponent c) ;
    protected final void setKeyBindingActive(boolean b) ;
    protected final void setKeyBindingRegistered(boolean b) ;
    public void setNorthPane(JComponent c) ;
    public void setSouthPane(JComponent c) ;
    protected void setupMenuCloseKey() ;
    protected void setupMenuOpenKey() ;
    public void setWestPane(JComponent c) ;
    protected void uninstallComponents() ;
    protected void uninstallDefaults() ;
    protected void uninstallKeyboardActions() ;
    protected void uninstallListeners() ; // Since 1.3
    public void uninstallUI(JComponent c) ;
}
```

javax.swing.plaf.basic.**BasicLabelUI**

public class **BasicLabelUI** extends LabelUI implements PropertyChangeListener
{
    protected static BasicLabelUI **labelUI** ;
    // Constructors
    public **BasicLabelUI**() ;
    // Static methods
    public static ComponentUI **createUI**(JComponent c) ;
    // Instance methods
    public int **getBaseline**(int height, int width, JComponent c) ; // Since 1.6
    public Component.BaselineResizeBehavior **getBaselineResizeBehavior**(JComponent c) ; // Since 1.6
    public Dimension **getMaximumSize**(JComponent c) ;
    public Dimension **getMinimumSize**(JComponent c) ;
    public Dimension **getPreferredSize**(JComponent c) ;
    protected void **installComponents**(JLabel c) ;
    protected void **installDefaults**(JLabel c) ;
    protected void **installKeyboardActions**(JLabel l) ;
    protected void **installListeners**(JLabel c) ;
    public void **installUI**(JComponent c) ;
    protected String **layoutCL**(Rectangle textR, Rectangle iconR, Rectangle viewR, Icon icon, String
        text, FontMetrics fontMetrics, JLabel label) ;
    public void **paint**(JComponent c, Graphics g) ;
    protected void **paintDisabledText**(int textY, int textX, String s, Graphics g, JLabel l) ;
    protected void **paintEnabledText**(int textY, int textX, String s, Graphics g, JLabel l) ;
    public void **propertyChange**(PropertyChangeEvent e) ;
    protected void **uninstallComponents**(JLabel c) ;
    protected void **uninstallDefaults**(JLabel c) ;
    protected void **uninstallKeyboardActions**(JLabel c) ;
    protected void **uninstallListeners**(JLabel c) ;
    public void **uninstallUI**(JComponent c) ;
}

javax.swing.plaf.basic.**BasicListUI**

public class **BasicListUI** extends ListUI
{
    protected static final int **cellRendererChanged** ;
    protected static final int **fixedCellHeightChanged** ;
    protected static final int **fixedCellWidthChanged** ;
    protected static final int **fontChanged** ;

protected static final int **modelChanged** ;
protected static final int **prototypeCellValueChanged** ;
protected static final int **selectionModelChanged** ;
protected int **cellHeight** ;
protected int **cellHeights** ;
protected int **cellWidth** ;
protected FocusListener **focusListener** ;
protected JList **list** ;
protected ListDataListener **listDataListener** ;
protected ListSelectionListener **listSelectionListener** ;
protected MouseInputListener **mouseInputListener** ;
protected PropertyChangeListener **propertyChangeListener** ;
protected CellRendererPane **rendererPane** ;
protected int **updateLayoutStateNeeded** ;
// Constructors
public **BasicListUI**() ;
// Static methods
public static ComponentUI **createUI**(JComponent list) ;
// Instance methods
protected int **convertRowToY**(int row) ;
protected int **convertYToRow**(int y0) ;
protected FocusListener **createFocusListener**() ;
protected ListDataListener **createListDataListener**() ;
protected ListSelectionListener **createListSelectionListener**() ;
protected MouseInputListener **createMouseInputListener**() ;
protected PropertyChangeListener **createPropertyChangeListener**() ;
public int **getBaseline**(int height, int width, JComponent c) ; // Since 1.6
public Component.BaselineResizeBehavior **getBaselineResizeBehavior**(JComponent c) ; // Since 1.6
public Rectangle **getCellBounds**(int index2, int index1, JList list) ;
public Dimension **getPreferredSize**(JComponent c) ;
protected int **getRowHeight**(int row) ;
public Point **indexToLocation**(int index, JList list) ;
protected void **installDefaults**() ;
protected void **installKeyboardActions**() ;
protected void **installListeners**() ;
public void **installUI**(JComponent c) ;
public int **locationToIndex**(Point location, JList list) ;
protected void **maybeUpdateLayoutState**() ;
public void **paint**(JComponent c, Graphics g) ;
protected void **paintCell**(int leadIndex, ListSelectionModel selModel, ListModel dataModel,
    ListCellRenderer cellRenderer, Rectangle rowBounds, int row, Graphics g) ;
protected void **selectNextIndex**() ;
protected void **selectPreviousIndex**() ;
protected void **uninstallDefaults**() ;
protected void **uninstallKeyboardActions**() ;
protected void **uninstallListeners**() ;

```
    public void uninstallUI(JComponent c) ;
    protected void updateLayoutState() ;
}
```

---

javax.swing.plaf.basic.**BasicLookAndFeel**

```
public abstract class BasicLookAndFeel extends LookAndFeel implements Serializable
{
    // Constructors
    public BasicLookAndFeel() ;
    // Static methods
    // Instance methods
    protected Action createAudioAction(Object key) ; // Since 1.4
    protected ActionMap getAudioActionMap() ; // Since 1.4
    public UIDefaults getDefaults() ;
    protected void initClassDefaults(UIDefaults table) ;
    protected void initComponentDefaults(UIDefaults table) ;
    public void initialize() ;
    protected void initSystemColorDefaults(UIDefaults table) ;
    protected void loadSystemColors(boolean useNative, java.lang.String[] systemColors, UIDefaults
        table) ;
    protected void playSound(Action audioAction) ; // Since 1.4
    public void uninitialize() ;
}
```

---

javax.swing.plaf.basic.**BasicMenuBarUI**

```
public class BasicMenuBarUI extends MenuBarUI
{
    protected ChangeListener changeListener ;
    protected ContainerListener containerListener ;
    protected JMenuBar menuBar ;
    // Constructors
    public BasicMenuBarUI() ;
    // Static methods
    public static ComponentUI createUI(JComponent x) ;
    // Instance methods
    protected ChangeListener createChangeListener() ;
    protected ContainerListener createContainerListener() ;
    public Dimension getMaximumSize(JComponent c) ;
    public Dimension getMinimumSize(JComponent c) ;
```

```
        protected void installDefaults() ;
        protected void installKeyboardActions() ;
        protected void installListeners() ;
        public void installUI(JComponent c) ;
        protected void uninstallDefaults() ;
        protected void uninstallKeyboardActions() ;
        protected void uninstallListeners() ;
        public void uninstallUI(JComponent c) ;
}
```

javax.swing.plaf.basic.**BasicMenuItemUI**

```
public class BasicMenuItemUI extends MenuItemUI
{
        protected Font acceleratorFont ;
        protected Color acceleratorForeground ;
        protected Color acceleratorSelectionForeground ;
        protected Icon arrowIcon ;
        protected Icon checkIcon ;
        protected int defaultTextIconGap ;
        protected Color disabledForeground ;
        protected MenuDragMouseListener menuDragMouseListener ;
        protected JMenuItem menuItem ;
        protected MenuKeyListener menuKeyListener ;
        protected MouseInputListener mouseInputListener ;
        protected boolean oldBorderPainted ;
        protected PropertyChangeListener propertyChangeListener ;
        protected Color selectionBackground ;
        protected Color selectionForeground ;
        // Constructors
        public BasicMenuItemUI() ;
        // Static methods
        public static ComponentUI createUI(JComponent c) ;
        // Instance methods
        protected MenuDragMouseListener createMenuDragMouseListener(JComponent c) ;
        protected MenuKeyListener createMenuKeyListener(JComponent c) ;
        protected MouseInputListener createMouseInputListener(JComponent c) ;
        protected PropertyChangeListener createPropertyChangeListener(JComponent c) ; // Since 1.6
        protected void doClick(MenuSelectionManager msm) ; // Since 1.4
        public Dimension getMaximumSize(JComponent c) ;
        public Dimension getMinimumSize(JComponent c) ;
        public MenuElement getPath() ;
        protected Dimension getPreferredMenuItemSize(int defaultTextIconGap, Icon arrowIcon, Icon
            checkIcon, JComponent c) ;
```

```
        public Dimension getPreferredSize(JComponent c) ;
        protected String getPropertyPrefix() ;
        protected void installComponents(JMenuItem menuItem) ; // Since 1.3
        protected void installDefaults() ;
        protected void installKeyboardActions() ;
        protected void installListeners() ;
        public void installUI(JComponent c) ;
        public void paint(JComponent c, Graphics g) ;
        protected void paintBackground(Color bgColor, JMenuItem menuItem, Graphics g) ; // Since 1.4
        protected void paintMenuItem(int defaultTextIconGap, Color foreground, Color background, Icon
            arrowIcon, Icon checkIcon, JComponent c, Graphics g) ;
        protected void paintText(String text, Rectangle textRect, JMenuItem menuItem, Graphics g) ; //
            Since 1.4
        protected void uninstallComponents(JMenuItem menuItem) ; // Since 1.3
        protected void uninstallDefaults() ;
        protected void uninstallKeyboardActions() ;
        protected void uninstallListeners() ;
        public void uninstallUI(JComponent c) ;
        public void update(JComponent c, Graphics g) ;
}
```

---

javax.swing.plaf.basic.**BasicMenuUI**

```
public class BasicMenuUI extends BasicMenuItemUI
{
        protected ChangeListener changeListener ;
        protected MenuListener menuListener ;
        // Constructors
        public BasicMenuUI() ;
        // Static methods
        public static ComponentUI createUI(JComponent x) ;
        // Instance methods
        protected ChangeListener createChangeListener(JComponent c) ;
        protected MenuDragMouseListener createMenuDragMouseListener(JComponent c) ;
        protected MenuKeyListener createMenuKeyListener(JComponent c) ;
        protected MenuListener createMenuListener(JComponent c) ;
        protected MouseInputListener createMouseInputListener(JComponent c) ;
        protected PropertyChangeListener createPropertyChangeListener(JComponent c) ;
        public Dimension getMaximumSize(JComponent c) ;
        protected String getPropertyPrefix() ;
        protected void installDefaults() ;
        protected void installKeyboardActions() ;
        protected void installListeners() ;
        protected void setupPostTimer(JMenu menu) ;
```

```
        protected void uninstallDefaults() ;
        protected void uninstallKeyboardActions() ;
        protected void uninstallListeners() ;
}
```

javax.swing.plaf.basic.**BasicOptionPaneUI**

public class **BasicOptionPaneUI** extends OptionPaneUI
{
    public static final int **MinimumHeight** ;
    public static final int **MinimumWidth** ;
    protected boolean **hasCustomComponents** ;
    protected Component **initialFocusComponent** ;
    protected JComponent **inputComponent** ;
    protected Dimension **minimumSize** ;
    protected JOptionPane **optionPane** ;
    protected PropertyChangeListener **propertyChangeListener** ;
    // Constructors
    public **BasicOptionPaneUI**() ;
    // Static methods
    public static ComponentUI **createUI**(JComponent x) ;
    // Instance methods
    protected void **addButtonComponents**(int initialIndex, java.lang.Object[] buttons, Container
        container) ;
    protected void **addIcon**(Container top) ;
    protected void **addMessageComponents**(boolean internallyCreated, int maxll, Object msg,
        GridBagConstraints cons, Container container) ;
    protected void **burstStringInto**(int maxll, String d, Container c) ;
    public boolean **containsCustomComponents**(JOptionPane op) ;
    protected ActionListener **createButtonActionListener**(int buttonIndex) ;
    protected Container **createButtonArea**() ;
    protected LayoutManager **createLayoutManager**() ;
    protected Container **createMessageArea**() ;
    protected PropertyChangeListener **createPropertyChangeListener**() ;
    protected Container **createSeparator**() ;
    protected Object **getButtons**() ;
    protected Icon **getIcon**() ;
    protected Icon **getIconForType**(int messageType) ;
    protected int **getInitialValueIndex**() ;
    protected int **getMaxCharactersPerLineCount**() ;
    protected Object **getMessage**() ;
    public Dimension **getMinimumOptionPaneSize**() ;
    public Dimension **getPreferredSize**(JComponent c) ;
    protected boolean **getSizeButtonsToSameWidth**() ;

```
        protected void installComponents() ;
        protected void installDefaults() ;
        protected void installKeyboardActions() ;
        protected void installListeners() ;
        public void installUI(JComponent c) ;
        protected void resetInputValue() ;
        public void selectInitialValue(JOptionPane op) ;
        protected void uninstallComponents() ;
        protected void uninstallDefaults() ;
        protected void uninstallKeyboardActions() ;
        protected void uninstallListeners() ;
        public void uninstallUI(JComponent c) ;
}
```

javax.swing.plaf.basic.**BasicOptionPaneUI.ButtonAreaLayout**

public static class **BasicOptionPaneUI.ButtonAreaLayout** implements LayoutManager
{
        protected boolean **centersChildren** ;
        protected int **padding** ;
        protected boolean **syncAllWidths** ;
        // Constructors
        private **BasicOptionPaneUI.ButtonAreaLayout**(boolean reverseButtons, int orientation, int
            padding, boolean syncAllSizes) ;
        public **BasicOptionPaneUI.ButtonAreaLayout**(int padding, boolean syncAllWidths) ;
        // Instance methods
        public void **addLayoutComponent**(Component comp, String string) ;
        public boolean **getCentersChildren**() ;
        public int **getPadding**() ;
        public boolean **getSyncAllWidths**() ;
        public void **layoutContainer**(Container container) ;
        public Dimension **minimumLayoutSize**(Container c) ;
        public Dimension **preferredLayoutSize**(Container c) ;
        public void **removeLayoutComponent**(Component c) ;
        public void **setCentersChildren**(boolean newValue) ;
        public void **setPadding**(int newPadding) ;
        public void **setSyncAllWidths**(boolean newValue) ;
}

javax.swing.plaf.basic.**BasicPanelUI**

public class **BasicPanelUI** extends PanelUI
{
    // Constructors
    public **BasicPanelUI**() ;
    // Static methods
    public static ComponentUI **createUI**(JComponent c) ;
    // Instance methods
    public int **getBaseline**(int height, int width, JComponent c) ; // Since 1.6
    public Component.BaselineResizeBehavior **getBaselineResizeBehavior**(JComponent c) ; // Since 1.6
    protected void **installDefaults**(JPanel p) ;
    public void **installUI**(JComponent c) ;
    protected void **uninstallDefaults**(JPanel p) ;
    public void **uninstallUI**(JComponent c) ;
}

javax.swing.plaf.basic.**BasicPasswordFieldUI**

public class **BasicPasswordFieldUI** extends BasicTextFieldUI
{
    // Constructors
    public **BasicPasswordFieldUI**() ;
    // Static methods
    public static ComponentUI **createUI**(JComponent c) ;
    // Instance methods
    public View **create**(Element elem) ;
    protected String **getPropertyPrefix**() ;
    protected void **installDefaults**() ; // Since 1.6
}

javax.swing.plaf.basic.**BasicPopupMenuSeparatorUI**

public class **BasicPopupMenuSeparatorUI** extends BasicSeparatorUI
{
    // Constructors
    public **BasicPopupMenuSeparatorUI**() ;

```
    // Static methods
    public static ComponentUI createUI(JComponent c) ;
    // Instance methods
    public Dimension getPreferredSize(JComponent c) ;
    public void paint(JComponent c, Graphics g) ;
}
```

javax.swing.plaf.basic.**BasicPopupMenuUI**

```
public class BasicPopupMenuUI extends PopupMenuUI
{
    protected JPopupMenu popupMenu ;
    // Constructors
    public BasicPopupMenuUI() ;
    // Static methods
    public static ComponentUI createUI(JComponent x) ;
    // Instance methods
    public void installDefaults() ;
    protected void installKeyboardActions() ;
    protected void installListeners() ;
    public void installUI(JComponent c) ;
    public boolean isPopupTrigger(MouseEvent e) ;
    protected void uninstallDefaults() ;
    protected void uninstallKeyboardActions() ;
    protected void uninstallListeners() ;
    public void uninstallUI(JComponent c) ;
}
```

javax.swing.plaf.basic.**BasicProgressBarUI**

```
public class BasicProgressBarUI extends ProgressBarUI
{
    protected Rectangle boxRect ;
    protected ChangeListener changeListener ;
    protected JProgressBar progressBar ;
    // Constructors
    public BasicProgressBarUI() ;
    // Static methods
    public static ComponentUI createUI(JComponent x) ;
    // Instance methods
    protected int getAmountFull(int height, int width, Insets b) ;
```

```
    protected int getAnimationIndex() ; // Since 1.4
    public int getBaseline(int height, int width, JComponent c) ; // Since 1.6
    public Component.BaselineResizeBehavior getBaselineResizeBehavior(JComponent c) ; // Since 1.6
    protected Rectangle getBox(Rectangle r) ; // Since 1.4
    protected int getBoxLength(int otherDimension, int availableLength) ; // Since 1.5
    protected int getCellLength() ;
    protected int getCellSpacing() ;
    protected final int getFrameCount() ; // Since 1.6
    public Dimension getMaximumSize(JComponent c) ;
    public Dimension getMinimumSize(JComponent c) ;
    protected Dimension getPreferredInnerHorizontal() ;
    protected Dimension getPreferredInnerVertical() ;
    public Dimension getPreferredSize(JComponent c) ;
    protected Color getSelectionBackground() ;
    protected Color getSelectionForeground() ;
    protected Point getStringPlacement(int height, int width, int y, int x, String progressString, Graphics
        g) ;
    protected void incrementAnimationIndex() ; // Since 1.4
    protected void installDefaults() ;
    protected void installListeners() ;
    public void installUI(JComponent c) ;
    public void paint(JComponent c, Graphics g) ;
    protected void paintDeterminate(JComponent c, Graphics g) ; // Since 1.4
    protected void paintIndeterminate(JComponent c, Graphics g) ; // Since 1.4
    protected void paintString(Insets b, int amountFull, int height, int width, int y, int x, Graphics g) ;
    protected void setAnimationIndex(int newValue) ; // Since 1.4
    protected void setCellLength(int cellLen) ;
    protected void setCellSpacing(int cellSpace) ;
    protected void startAnimationTimer() ; // Since 1.4
    protected void stopAnimationTimer() ; // Since 1.4
    protected void uninstallDefaults() ;
    protected void uninstallListeners() ;
    public void uninstallUI(JComponent c) ;
}
```

javax.swing.plaf.basic.**BasicRadioButtonMenuItemUI**

public class **BasicRadioButtonMenuItemUI** extends BasicMenuItemUI
```
{
    // Constructors
    public BasicRadioButtonMenuItemUI() ;
    // Static methods
    public static ComponentUI createUI(JComponent b) ;
    // Instance methods
```

```
    protected String getPropertyPrefix() ;
    public void processMouseEvent(MenuSelectionManager manager, javax.swing.MenuElement[]
        path, MouseEvent e, JMenuItem item) ;
}
```

javax.swing.plaf.basic.**BasicRadioButtonUI**

```
public class BasicRadioButtonUI extends BasicToggleButtonUI
{
    protected Icon icon ;
    // Constructors
    public BasicRadioButtonUI() ;
    // Static methods
    public static ComponentUI createUI(JComponent b) ;
    // Instance methods
    public Icon getDefaultIcon() ;
    public Dimension getPreferredSize(JComponent c) ;
    protected String getPropertyPrefix() ;
    protected void installDefaults(AbstractButton b) ;
    public synchronized void paint(JComponent c, Graphics g) ;
    protected void paintFocus(Dimension size, Rectangle textRect, Graphics g) ;
    protected void uninstallDefaults(AbstractButton b) ;
}
```

javax.swing.plaf.basic.**BasicRootPaneUI** [since 1.3]

```
public class BasicRootPaneUI extends RootPaneUI implements PropertyChangeListener
{
    // Constructors
    public BasicRootPaneUI() ;
    // Static methods
    public static ComponentUI createUI(JComponent c) ;
    // Instance methods
    protected void installComponents(JRootPane root) ;
    protected void installDefaults(JRootPane c) ;
    protected void installKeyboardActions(JRootPane root) ;
    protected void installListeners(JRootPane root) ;
    public void installUI(JComponent c) ;
    public void propertyChange(PropertyChangeEvent e) ;
    protected void uninstallComponents(JRootPane root) ;
    protected void uninstallDefaults(JRootPane root) ;
```

```
    protected void uninstallKeyboardActions(JRootPane root) ;
    protected void uninstallListeners(JRootPane root) ;
    public void uninstallUI(JComponent c) ;
}
```

javax.swing.plaf.basic.**BasicScrollBarUI**

```
public class BasicScrollBarUI extends ScrollBarUI implements SwingConstants, LayoutManager
{
    protected static final int DECREASE_HIGHLIGHT ;
    protected static final int INCREASE_HIGHLIGHT ;
    protected static final int NO_HIGHLIGHT ;
    protected BasicScrollBarUI.ArrowButtonListener buttonListener ;
    protected JButton decrButton ;
    protected JButton incrButton ;
    protected boolean isDragging ;
    protected Dimension maximumThumbSize ;
    protected Dimension minimumThumbSize ;
    protected BasicScrollBarUI.ModelListener modelListener ;
    protected PropertyChangeListener propertyChangeListener ;
    protected JScrollBar scrollbar ;
    protected BasicScrollBarUI.ScrollListener scrollListener ;
    protected Timer scrollTimer ;
    protected Color thumbColor ;
    protected Color thumbDarkShadowColor ;
    protected Color thumbHighlightColor ;
    protected Color thumbLightShadowColor ;
    protected Rectangle thumbRect ;
    protected Color trackColor ;
    protected int trackHighlight ;
    protected Color trackHighlightColor ;
    protected BasicScrollBarUI.TrackListener trackListener ;
    protected Rectangle trackRect ;
    // Constructors
    public BasicScrollBarUI() ;
    // Static methods
    public static ComponentUI createUI(JComponent c) ;
    // Instance methods
    public void addLayoutComponent(Component child, String name) ;
    protected void configureScrollBarColors() ;
    protected BasicScrollBarUI.ArrowButtonListener createArrowButtonListener() ;
    protected JButton createDecreaseButton(int orientation) ;
    protected JButton createIncreaseButton(int orientation) ;
    protected BasicScrollBarUI.ModelListener createModelListener() ;
```

```
    protected PropertyChangeListener createPropertyChangeListener() ;
    protected BasicScrollBarUI.ScrollListener createScrollListener() ;
    protected BasicScrollBarUI.TrackListener createTrackListener() ;
    public Dimension getMaximumSize(JComponent c) ;
    protected Dimension getMaximumThumbSize() ;
    protected Dimension getMinimumThumbSize() ;
    public Dimension getPreferredSize(JComponent c) ;
    public boolean getSupportsAbsolutePositioning() ; // Since 1.5
    protected Rectangle getThumbBounds() ;
    protected Rectangle getTrackBounds() ;
    protected void installComponents() ;
    protected void installDefaults() ;
    protected void installKeyboardActions() ;
    protected void installListeners() ;
    public void installUI(JComponent c) ;
    public boolean isThumbRollover() ; // Since 1.5
    public void layoutContainer(Container scrollbarContainer) ;
    protected void layoutHScrollbar(JScrollBar sb) ;
    protected void layoutVScrollbar(JScrollBar sb) ;
    public Dimension minimumLayoutSize(Container scrollbarContainer) ;
    public void paint(JComponent c, Graphics g) ;
    protected void paintDecreaseHighlight(Graphics g) ;
    protected void paintIncreaseHighlight(Graphics g) ;
    protected void paintThumb(Rectangle thumbBounds, JComponent c, Graphics g) ;
    protected void paintTrack(Rectangle trackBounds, JComponent c, Graphics g) ;
    public Dimension preferredLayoutSize(Container scrollbarContainer) ;
    public void removeLayoutComponent(Component child) ;
    protected void scrollByBlock(int direction) ;
    protected void scrollByUnit(int direction) ;
    protected void setThumbBounds(int height, int width, int y, int x) ;
    protected void setThumbRollover(boolean active) ; // Since 1.5
    protected void uninstallComponents() ;
    protected void uninstallDefaults() ;
    protected void uninstallKeyboardActions() ;
    protected void uninstallListeners() ;
    public void uninstallUI(JComponent c) ;
}
```

javax.swing.plaf.basic.**BasicScrollPaneUI**

public class **BasicScrollPaneUI** extends ScrollPaneUI implements ScrollPaneConstants
{
    protected ChangeListener **hsbChangeListener** ;
    protected JScrollPane **scrollpane** ;

```
      protected PropertyChangeListener spPropertyChangeListener ;
      protected ChangeListener viewportChangeListener ;
      protected ChangeListener vsbChangeListener ;
      // Constructors
      public BasicScrollPaneUI() ;
      // Static methods
      public static ComponentUI createUI(JComponent x) ;
      // Instance methods
      protected ChangeListener createHSBChangeListener() ;
      protected MouseWheelListener createMouseWheelListener() ; // Since 1.4
      protected PropertyChangeListener createPropertyChangeListener() ;
      protected ChangeListener createViewportChangeListener() ;
      protected ChangeListener createVSBChangeListener() ;
      public int getBaseline(int height, int width, JComponent c) ; // Since 1.6
      public Component.BaselineResizeBehavior getBaselineResizeBehavior(JComponent c) ; // Since 1.6
      public Dimension getMaximumSize(JComponent c) ;
      protected void installDefaults(JScrollPane scrollpane) ;
      protected void installKeyboardActions(JScrollPane c) ;
      protected void installListeners(JScrollPane c) ;
      public void installUI(JComponent x) ;
      public void paint(JComponent c, Graphics g) ;
      protected void syncScrollPaneWithViewport() ;
      protected void uninstallDefaults(JScrollPane c) ;
      protected void uninstallKeyboardActions(JScrollPane c) ;
      protected void uninstallListeners(JComponent c) ;
      public void uninstallUI(JComponent c) ;
      protected void updateColumnHeader(PropertyChangeEvent e) ;
      protected void updateRowHeader(PropertyChangeEvent e) ;
      protected void updateScrollBarDisplayPolicy(PropertyChangeEvent e) ;
      protected void updateViewport(PropertyChangeEvent e) ;
}
```

javax.swing.plaf.basic.**BasicSeparatorUI**

```
public class BasicSeparatorUI extends SeparatorUI
{
      protected Color highlight ;
      protected Color shadow ;
      // Constructors
      public BasicSeparatorUI() ;
      // Static methods
      public static ComponentUI createUI(JComponent c) ;
      // Instance methods
      public Dimension getMaximumSize(JComponent c) ;
```

```
public Dimension getMinimumSize(JComponent c) ;
public Dimension getPreferredSize(JComponent c) ;
protected void installDefaults(JSeparator s) ;
protected void installListeners(JSeparator s) ;
public void installUI(JComponent c) ;
public void paint(JComponent c, Graphics g) ;
protected void uninstallDefaults(JSeparator s) ;
protected void uninstallListeners(JSeparator s) ;
public void uninstallUI(JComponent c) ;
}
```

javax.swing.plaf.basic.**BasicSliderUI**

```
public class BasicSliderUI extends SliderUI
{
    public static final int MAX_SCROLL ;
    public static final int MIN_SCROLL ;
    public static final int NEGATIVE_SCROLL ;
    public static final int POSITIVE_SCROLL ;
    protected ChangeListener changeListener ;
    protected ComponentListener componentListener ;
    protected Rectangle contentRect ;
    protected Insets focusInsets ;
    protected FocusListener focusListener ;
    protected Rectangle focusRect ;
    protected Insets insetCache ;
    protected Rectangle labelRect ;
    protected boolean leftToRightCache ;
    protected PropertyChangeListener propertyChangeListener ;
    protected BasicSliderUI.ScrollListener scrollListener ;
    protected Timer scrollTimer ;
    protected JSlider slider ;
    protected Rectangle thumbRect ;
    protected Rectangle tickRect ;
    protected int trackBuffer ;
    protected BasicSliderUI.TrackListener trackListener ;
    protected Rectangle trackRect ;
    // Constructors
    public BasicSliderUI(JSlider b) ;
    // Static methods
    public static ComponentUI createUI(JComponent b) ;
    // Instance methods
    protected void calculateContentRect() ;
    protected void calculateFocusRect() ;
```

protected void **calculateGeometry**() ;
protected void **calculateLabelRect**() ;
protected void **calculateThumbLocation**() ;
protected void **calculateThumbSize**() ;
protected void **calculateTickRect**() ;
protected void **calculateTrackBuffer**() ;
protected void **calculateTrackRect**() ;
protected ChangeListener **createChangeListener**(JSlider slider) ;
protected ComponentListener **createComponentListener**(JSlider slider) ;
protected FocusListener **createFocusListener**(JSlider slider) ;
protected PropertyChangeListener **createPropertyChangeListener**(JSlider slider) ;
protected BasicSliderUI.ScrollListener **createScrollListener**(JSlider slider) ;
protected BasicSliderUI.TrackListener **createTrackListener**(JSlider slider) ;
protected boolean **drawInverted**() ;
public int **getBaseline**(int height, int width, JComponent c) ; // Since 1.6
public Component.BaselineResizeBehavior **getBaselineResizeBehavior**(JComponent c) ; // Since 1.6
protected Color **getFocusColor**() ;
protected int **getHeightOfHighValueLabel**() ;
protected int **getHeightOfLowValueLabel**() ;
protected int **getHeightOfTallestLabel**() ;
protected Integer **getHighestValue**() ; // Since 1.6
protected Component **getHighestValueLabel**() ;
protected Color **getHighlightColor**() ;
protected Integer **getLowestValue**() ; // Since 1.6
protected Component **getLowestValueLabel**() ;
public Dimension **getMaximumSize**(JComponent c) ;
public Dimension **getMinimumHorizontalSize**() ;
public Dimension **getMinimumSize**(JComponent c) ;
public Dimension **getMinimumVerticalSize**() ;
public Dimension **getPreferredHorizontalSize**() ;
public Dimension **getPreferredSize**(JComponent c) ;
public Dimension **getPreferredVerticalSize**() ;
protected Color **getShadowColor**() ;
protected Dimension **getThumbSize**() ;
protected int **getTickLength**() ;
protected int **getWidthOfHighValueLabel**() ;
protected int **getWidthOfLowValueLabel**() ;
protected int **getWidthOfWidestLabel**() ;
protected void **installDefaults**(JSlider slider) ;
protected void **installKeyboardActions**(JSlider slider) ;
protected void **installListeners**(JSlider slider) ;
public void **installUI**(JComponent c) ;
protected boolean **isDragging**() ; // Since 1.5
protected boolean **labelsHaveSameBaselines**() ; // Since 1.6
public void **paint**(JComponent c, Graphics g) ;
public void **paintFocus**(Graphics g) ;

protected void **paintHorizontalLabel**(Component label, int value, Graphics g) ;
public void **paintLabels**(Graphics g) ;
protected void **paintMajorTickForHorizSlider**(int x, Rectangle tickBounds, Graphics g) ;
protected void **paintMajorTickForVertSlider**(int y, Rectangle tickBounds, Graphics g) ;
protected void **paintMinorTickForHorizSlider**(int x, Rectangle tickBounds, Graphics g) ;
protected void **paintMinorTickForVertSlider**(int y, Rectangle tickBounds, Graphics g) ;
public void **paintThumb**(Graphics g) ;
public void **paintTicks**(Graphics g) ;
public void **paintTrack**(Graphics g) ;
protected void **paintVerticalLabel**(Component label, int value, Graphics g) ;
protected void **recalculateIfInsetsChanged**() ;
protected void **recalculateIfOrientationChanged**() ;
public void **scrollByBlock**(int direction) ;
public void **scrollByUnit**(int direction) ;
protected void **scrollDueToClickInTrack**(int dir) ;
public void **setThumbLocation**(int y, int x) ;
protected void **uninstallKeyboardActions**(JSlider slider) ;
protected void **uninstallListeners**(JSlider slider) ;
public void **uninstallUI**(JComponent c) ;
public int **valueForXPosition**(int xPos) ;
public int **valueForYPosition**(int yPos) ;
protected int **xPositionForValue**(int value) ;
protected int **yPositionForValue**(int value) ;
protected int **yPositionForValue**(int trackHeight, int trackY, int value) ; // Since 1.6
}

---

javax.swing.plaf.basic.**BasicSpinnerUI** [since 1.4]

---

public class **BasicSpinnerUI** extends SpinnerUI
{
    protected JSpinner **spinner** ;
    // Constructors
    public **BasicSpinnerUI**() ;
    // Static methods
    public static ComponentUI **createUI**(JComponent c) ;
    // Instance methods
    protected JComponent **createEditor**() ;
    protected LayoutManager **createLayout**() ;
    protected Component **createNextButton**() ;
    protected Component **createPreviousButton**() ;
    protected PropertyChangeListener **createPropertyChangeListener**() ;
    public int **getBaseline**(int height, int width, JComponent c) ; // Since 1.6
    public Component.BaselineResizeBehavior **getBaselineResizeBehavior**(JComponent c) ; // Since 1.6
    protected void **installDefaults**() ;

```
    protected void installKeyboardActions() ; // Since 1.5
    protected void installListeners() ;
    protected void installNextButtonListeners(Component c) ; // Since 1.5
    protected void installPreviousButtonListeners(Component c) ; // Since 1.5
    public void installUI(JComponent c) ;
    protected void replaceEditor(JComponent newEditor, JComponent oldEditor) ;
    protected void uninstallDefaults() ;
    protected void uninstallListeners() ;
    public void uninstallUI(JComponent c) ;
}
```

javax.swing.plaf.basic.**BasicSplitPaneDivider**

```
public class BasicSplitPaneDivider extends Container implements PropertyChangeListener
{
    protected static final int ONE_TOUCH_OFFSET ;
    protected static final int ONE_TOUCH_SIZE ;
    protected int dividerSize ;
    protected BasicSplitPaneDivider.DragController dragger ;
    protected Component hiddenDivider ;
    protected JButton leftButton ;
    protected BasicSplitPaneDivider.MouseHandler mouseHandler ;
    protected int orientation ;
    protected JButton rightButton ;
    protected JSplitPane splitPane ;
    protected BasicSplitPaneUI splitPaneUI ;
    // Constructors
    public BasicSplitPaneDivider(BasicSplitPaneUI ui) ;
    // Instance methods
    protected JButton createLeftOneTouchButton() ;
    protected JButton createRightOneTouchButton() ;
    protected void dragDividerTo(int location) ;
    protected void finishDraggingTo(int location) ;
    public BasicSplitPaneUI getBasicSplitPaneUI() ;
    public Border getBorder() ; // Since 1.3
    public int getDividerSize() ;
    public Insets getInsets() ;
    public Dimension getMinimumSize() ;
    public Dimension getPreferredSize() ;
    public boolean isMouseOver() ; // Since 1.5
    protected void oneTouchExpandableChanged() ;
    public void paint(Graphics g) ;
    protected void prepareForDragging() ;
    public void propertyChange(PropertyChangeEvent e) ;
```

public void **setBasicSplitPaneUI**(BasicSplitPaneUI newUI) ;
public void **setBorder**(Border border) ; // Since 1.3
public void **setDividerSize**(int newSize) ;
protected void **setMouseOver**(boolean mouseOver) ; // Since 1.5
}

---

javax.swing.plaf.basic.**BasicSplitPaneUI**

---

public class **BasicSplitPaneUI** extends SplitPaneUI
{
    protected static int **KEYBOARD_DIVIDER_MOVE_OFFSET** ;
    protected static final String **NON_CONTINUOUS_DIVIDER** ;
    protected int **beginDragDividerLocation** ;
    protected BasicSplitPaneDivider **divider** ;
    protected KeyStroke **dividerResizeToggleKey** ;
    protected int **dividerSize** ;
    protected KeyStroke **downKey** ;
    protected boolean **draggingHW** ;
    protected KeyStroke **endKey** ;
    protected FocusListener **focusListener** ;
    protected KeyStroke **homeKey** ;
    protected ActionListener **keyboardDownRightListener** ;
    protected ActionListener **keyboardEndListener** ;
    protected ActionListener **keyboardHomeListener** ;
    protected ActionListener **keyboardResizeToggleListener** ;
    protected ActionListener **keyboardUpLeftListener** ;
    protected BasicSplitPaneUI.BasicHorizontalLayoutManager **layoutManager** ;
    protected KeyStroke **leftKey** ;
    protected Component **nonContinuousLayoutDivider** ;
    protected PropertyChangeListener **propertyChangeListener** ;
    protected KeyStroke **rightKey** ;
    protected JSplitPane **splitPane** ;
    protected KeyStroke **upKey** ;
    // Constructors
    public **BasicSplitPaneUI**() ;
    // Static methods
    public static ComponentUI **createUI**(JComponent x) ;
    // Instance methods
    public BasicSplitPaneDivider **createDefaultDivider**() ;
    protected Component **createDefaultNonContinuousLayoutDivider**() ;
    protected FocusListener **createFocusListener**() ;
    protected ActionListener **createKeyboardDownRightListener**() ;
    protected ActionListener **createKeyboardEndListener**() ;
    protected ActionListener **createKeyboardHomeListener**() ;

protected ActionListener **createKeyboardResizeToggleListener**() ;
protected ActionListener **createKeyboardUpLeftListener**() ;
protected PropertyChangeListener **createPropertyChangeListener**() ;
protected void **dragDividerTo**(int location) ;
protected void **finishDraggingTo**(int location) ;
public void **finishedPaintingChildren**(Graphics g, JSplitPane jc) ;
public BasicSplitPaneDivider **getDivider**() ;
protected int **getDividerBorderSize**() ;
public int **getDividerLocation**(JSplitPane jc) ;
public Insets **getInsets**(JComponent jc) ;
public int **getLastDragLocation**() ;
public int **getMaximumDividerLocation**(JSplitPane jc) ;
public Dimension **getMaximumSize**(JComponent jc) ;
public int **getMinimumDividerLocation**(JSplitPane jc) ;
public Dimension **getMinimumSize**(JComponent jc) ;
public Component **getNonContinuousLayoutDivider**() ;
public int **getOrientation**() ;
public Dimension **getPreferredSize**(JComponent jc) ;
public JSplitPane **getSplitPane**() ;
protected void **installDefaults**() ;
protected void **installKeyboardActions**() ;
protected void **installListeners**() ;
public void **installUI**(JComponent c) ;
public boolean **isContinuousLayout**() ;
public void **paint**(JComponent jc, Graphics g) ;
protected void **resetLayoutManager**() ;
public void **resetToPreferredSizes**(JSplitPane jc) ;
public void **setContinuousLayout**(boolean b) ;
public void **setDividerLocation**(int location, JSplitPane jc) ;
public void **setLastDragLocation**(int l) ;
protected void **setNonContinuousLayoutDivider**(boolean rememberSizes, Component newDivider)
   ;
protected void **setNonContinuousLayoutDivider**(Component newDivider) ;
public void **setOrientation**(int orientation) ;
protected void **startDragging**() ;
protected void **uninstallDefaults**() ;
protected void **uninstallKeyboardActions**() ;
protected void **uninstallListeners**() ;
public void **uninstallUI**(JComponent c) ;
}

java.awt.**BasicStroke**

public class **BasicStroke** implements Stroke
{
    public static final int **CAP_BUTT** ;
    public static final int **CAP_ROUND** ;
    public static final int **CAP_SQUARE** ;
    public static final int **JOIN_BEVEL** ;
    public static final int **JOIN_MITER** ;
    public static final int **JOIN_ROUND** ;
    // Constructors
    public **BasicStroke**() ;
    public **BasicStroke**(float width) ;
    public **BasicStroke**(int join, int cap, float width) ;
    public **BasicStroke**(float miterlimit, int join, int cap, float width) ;
    public **BasicStroke**(float dash_phase, float[] dash, float miterlimit, int join, int cap, float width) ;
    // Instance methods
    public Shape **createStrokedShape**(Shape s) ;
    public boolean **equals**(Object obj) ;
    public float **getDashArray**() ;
    public float **getDashPhase**() ;
    public int **getEndCap**() ;
    public int **getLineJoin**() ;
    public float **getLineWidth**() ;
    public float **getMiterLimit**() ;
    public int **hashCode**() ;
}

javax.swing.plaf.basic.**BasicTabbedPaneUI**

public class **BasicTabbedPaneUI** extends TabbedPaneUI implements SwingConstants
{
    protected transient Rectangle **calcRect** ;
    protected Insets **contentBorderInsets** ;
    protected Color **darkShadow** ;
    protected KeyStroke **downKey** ;
    protected Color **focus** ;
    protected FocusListener **focusListener** ;
    protected Color **highlight** ;
    protected KeyStroke **leftKey** ;

protected Color **lightHighlight** ;
protected int **maxTabHeight** ;
protected int **maxTabWidth** ;
protected MouseListener **mouseListener** ;
protected PropertyChangeListener **propertyChangeListener** ;
protected Rectangle **rects** ;
protected KeyStroke **rightKey** ;
protected int **runCount** ;
protected int **selectedRun** ;
protected Insets **selectedTabPadInsets** ;
protected Color **shadow** ;
protected Insets **tabAreaInsets** ;
protected ChangeListener **tabChangeListener** ;
protected Insets **tabInsets** ;
protected JTabbedPane **tabPane** ;
protected int **tabRunOverlay** ;
protected int **tabRuns** ;
protected int **textIconGap** ;
protected KeyStroke **upKey** ;
// Constructors
public **BasicTabbedPaneUI**() ;
// Static methods
public static ComponentUI **createUI**(JComponent c) ;
protected static void **rotateInsets**(int targetPlacement, Insets targetInsets, Insets topInsets) ;
// Instance methods
protected void **assureRectsCreated**(int tabCount) ;
protected int **calculateMaxTabHeight**(int tabPlacement) ;
protected int **calculateMaxTabWidth**(int tabPlacement) ;
protected int **calculateTabAreaHeight**(int maxTabHeight, int horizRunCount, int tabPlacement) ;
protected int **calculateTabAreaWidth**(int maxTabWidth, int vertRunCount, int tabPlacement) ;
protected int **calculateTabHeight**(int fontHeight, int tabIndex, int tabPlacement) ;
protected int **calculateTabWidth**(FontMetrics metrics, int tabIndex, int tabPlacement) ;
protected ChangeListener **createChangeListener**() ;
protected FocusListener **createFocusListener**() ;
protected LayoutManager **createLayoutManager**() ;
protected MouseListener **createMouseListener**() ;
protected PropertyChangeListener **createPropertyChangeListener**() ;
protected JButton **createScrollButton**(int direction) ; // Since 1.5
protected void **expandTabRunsArray**() ;
public int **getBaseline**(int height, int width, JComponent c) ; // Since 1.6
protected int **getBaseline**(int tab) ; // Since 1.6
protected int **getBaselineOffset**() ; // Since 1.6
public Component.BaselineResizeBehavior **getBaselineResizeBehavior**(JComponent c) ; // Since 1.6
protected Insets **getContentBorderInsets**(int tabPlacement) ;
protected int **getFocusIndex**() ; // Since 1.5
protected FontMetrics **getFontMetrics**() ;

protected Icon **getIconForTab**(int tabIndex) ;
public Dimension **getMaximumSize**(JComponent c) ;
public Dimension **getMinimumSize**(JComponent c) ;
protected int **getNextTabIndex**(int base) ;
protected int **getNextTabIndexInRun**(int base, int tabCount) ;
protected int **getNextTabRun**(int baseRun) ;
protected int **getPreviousTabIndex**(int base) ;
protected int **getPreviousTabIndexInRun**(int base, int tabCount) ;
protected int **getPreviousTabRun**(int baseRun) ;
protected int **getRolloverTab**() ; // Since 1.5
protected int **getRunForTab**(int tabIndex, int tabCount) ;
protected Insets **getSelectedTabPadInsets**(int tabPlacement) ;
protected Insets **getTabAreaInsets**(int tabPlacement) ;
protected Rectangle **getTabBounds**(Rectangle dest, int tabIndex) ; // Since 1.4
public Rectangle **getTabBounds**(int i, JTabbedPane pane) ;
protected Insets **getTabInsets**(int tabIndex, int tabPlacement) ;
protected int **getTabLabelShiftX**(boolean isSelected, int tabIndex, int tabPlacement) ;
protected int **getTabLabelShiftY**(boolean isSelected, int tabIndex, int tabPlacement) ;
public int **getTabRunCount**(JTabbedPane pane) ;
protected int **getTabRunIndent**(int run, int tabPlacement) ;
protected int **getTabRunOffset**(boolean forward, int tabIndex, int tabCount, int tabPlacement) ;
protected int **getTabRunOverlay**(int tabPlacement) ;
protected View **getTextViewForTab**(int tabIndex) ; // Since 1.4
protected Component **getVisibleComponent**() ;
protected void **installComponents**() ; // Since 1.4
protected void **installDefaults**() ;
protected void **installKeyboardActions**() ;
protected void **installListeners**() ;
public void **installUI**(JComponent c) ;
protected int **lastTabInRun**(int run, int tabCount) ;
protected void **layoutLabel**(boolean isSelected, Rectangle textRect, Rectangle iconRect, Rectangle
    tabRect, Icon icon, String title, int tabIndex, FontMetrics metrics, int tabPlacement) ;
protected void **navigateSelectedTab**(int direction) ;
public void **paint**(JComponent c, Graphics g) ;
protected void **paintContentBorder**(int selectedIndex, int tabPlacement, Graphics g) ;
protected void **paintContentBorderBottomEdge**(int h, int w, int y, int x, int selectedIndex, int
    tabPlacement, Graphics g) ;
protected void **paintContentBorderLeftEdge**(int h, int w, int y, int x, int selectedIndex, int
    tabPlacement, Graphics g) ;
protected void **paintContentBorderRightEdge**(int h, int w, int y, int x, int selectedIndex, int
    tabPlacement, Graphics g) ;
protected void **paintContentBorderTopEdge**(int h, int w, int y, int x, int selectedIndex, int
    tabPlacement, Graphics g) ;
protected void **paintFocusIndicator**(boolean isSelected, Rectangle textRect, Rectangle iconRect, int
    tabIndex, java.awt.Rectangle[] rects, int tabPlacement, Graphics g) ;

```
        protected void paintIcon(boolean isSelected, Rectangle iconRect, Icon icon, int tabIndex, int
            tabPlacement, Graphics g) ;
        protected void paintTab(Rectangle textRect, Rectangle iconRect, int tabIndex, java.awt.Rectangle[]
            rects, int tabPlacement, Graphics g) ;
        protected void paintTabArea(int selectedIndex, int tabPlacement, Graphics g) ; // Since 1.4
        protected void paintTabBackground(boolean isSelected, int h, int w, int y, int x, int tabIndex, int
            tabPlacement, Graphics g) ;
        protected void paintTabBorder(boolean isSelected, int h, int w, int y, int x, int tabIndex, int
            tabPlacement, Graphics g) ;
        protected void paintText(boolean isSelected, Rectangle textRect, String title, int tabIndex,
            FontMetrics metrics, Font font, int tabPlacement, Graphics g) ;
        protected void selectAdjacentRunTab(int offset, int tabIndex, int tabPlacement) ;
        protected void selectNextTab(int current) ;
        protected void selectNextTabInRun(int current) ;
        protected void selectPreviousTab(int current) ;
        protected void selectPreviousTabInRun(int current) ;
        protected void setRolloverTab(int index) ; // Since 1.5
        protected void setVisibleComponent(Component component) ;
        protected boolean shouldPadTabRun(int run, int tabPlacement) ;
        protected boolean shouldRotateTabRuns(int tabPlacement) ;
        public int tabForCoordinate(int y, int x, JTabbedPane pane) ;
        protected void uninstallComponents() ; // Since 1.4
        protected void uninstallDefaults() ;
        protected void uninstallKeyboardActions() ;
        protected void uninstallListeners() ;
        public void uninstallUI(JComponent c) ;
}
```

---

javax.swing.plaf.basic.**BasicTableHeaderUI**

```
public class BasicTableHeaderUI extends TableHeaderUI
{
        protected JTableHeader header ;
        protected MouseInputListener mouseInputListener ;
        protected CellRendererPane rendererPane ;
        // Constructors
        public BasicTableHeaderUI() ;
        // Static methods
        public static ComponentUI createUI(JComponent h) ;
        // Instance methods
        protected MouseInputListener createMouseInputListener() ;
        public int getBaseline(int height, int width, JComponent c) ; // Since 1.6
        public Dimension getMaximumSize(JComponent c) ;
        public Dimension getMinimumSize(JComponent c) ;
```

```
    public Dimension getPreferredSize(JComponent c) ;
    protected int getRolloverColumn() ; // Since 1.6
    protected void installDefaults() ;
    protected void installKeyboardActions() ;
    protected void installListeners() ;
    public void installUI(JComponent c) ;
    public void paint(JComponent c, Graphics g) ;
    protected void rolloverColumnUpdated(int newColumn, int oldColumn) ; // Since 1.6
    protected void uninstallDefaults() ;
    protected void uninstallKeyboardActions() ;
    protected void uninstallListeners() ;
    public void uninstallUI(JComponent c) ;
}
```

javax.swing.plaf.basic.**BasicTableUI**

```
public class BasicTableUI extends TableUI
{
    protected FocusListener focusListener ;
    protected KeyListener keyListener ;
    protected MouseInputListener mouseInputListener ;
    protected CellRendererPane rendererPane ;
    protected JTable table ;
    // Constructors
    public BasicTableUI() ;
    // Static methods
    public static ComponentUI createUI(JComponent c) ;
    // Instance methods
    protected FocusListener createFocusListener() ;
    protected KeyListener createKeyListener() ;
    protected MouseInputListener createMouseInputListener() ;
    public int getBaseline(int height, int width, JComponent c) ; // Since 1.6
    public Component.BaselineResizeBehavior getBaselineResizeBehavior(JComponent c) ; // Since 1.6
    public Dimension getMaximumSize(JComponent c) ;
    public Dimension getMinimumSize(JComponent c) ;
    public Dimension getPreferredSize(JComponent c) ;
    protected void installDefaults() ;
    protected void installKeyboardActions() ;
    protected void installListeners() ;
    public void installUI(JComponent c) ;
    public void paint(JComponent c, Graphics g) ;
    protected void uninstallDefaults() ;
    protected void uninstallKeyboardActions() ;
    protected void uninstallListeners() ;
```

```
        public void uninstallUI(JComponent c) ;
}
```

---

javax.swing.plaf.basic.**BasicTextAreaUI**

```
public class BasicTextAreaUI extends BasicTextUI
{
    // Constructors
    public BasicTextAreaUI() ;
    // Static methods
    public static ComponentUI createUI(JComponent ta) ;
    // Instance methods
    public View create(Element elem) ;
    public int getBaseline(int height, int width, JComponent c) ; // Since 1.6
    public Component.BaselineResizeBehavior getBaselineResizeBehavior(JComponent c) ; // Since 1.6
    public Dimension getMinimumSize(JComponent c) ; // Since 1.5
    public Dimension getPreferredSize(JComponent c) ; // Since 1.5
    protected String getPropertyPrefix() ;
    protected void installDefaults() ;
    protected void propertyChange(PropertyChangeEvent evt) ;
}
```

---

javax.swing.plaf.basic.**BasicTextFieldUI**

```
public class BasicTextFieldUI extends BasicTextUI
{
    // Constructors
    public BasicTextFieldUI() ;
    // Static methods
    public static ComponentUI createUI(JComponent c) ;
    // Instance methods
    public View create(Element elem) ;
    public int getBaseline(int height, int width, JComponent c) ; // Since 1.6
    public Component.BaselineResizeBehavior getBaselineResizeBehavior(JComponent c) ; // Since 1.6
    protected String getPropertyPrefix() ;
}
```

javax.swing.plaf.basic.**BasicTextPaneUI**

public class **BasicTextPaneUI** extends BasicEditorPaneUI
{
    // Constructors
    public **BasicTextPaneUI**() ;
    // Static methods
    public static ComponentUI **createUI**(JComponent c) ;
    // Instance methods
    protected String **getPropertyPrefix**() ;
    public void **installUI**(JComponent c) ;
    protected void **propertyChange**(PropertyChangeEvent evt) ;
}

javax.swing.plaf.basic.**BasicTextUI**

public abstract class **BasicTextUI** extends TextUI implements ViewFactory
{
    // Constructors
    public **BasicTextUI**() ;
    // Static methods
    // Instance methods
    public View **create**(int p1, int p0, Element elem) ;
    public View **create**(Element elem) ;
    protected Caret **createCaret**() ;
    protected Highlighter **createHighlighter**() ;
    protected Keymap **createKeymap**() ;
    public void **damageRange**(Position.Bias p1Bias, Position.Bias p0Bias, int p1, int p0,
        JTextComponent t) ;
    public void **damageRange**(int p1, int p0, JTextComponent tc) ;
    protected final JTextComponent **getComponent**() ;
    public EditorKit **getEditorKit**(JTextComponent tc) ;
    protected String **getKeymapName**() ;
    public Dimension **getMaximumSize**(JComponent c) ;
    public Dimension **getMinimumSize**(JComponent c) ;
    public int **getNextVisualPositionFrom**(javax.swing.text.Position.Bias[] biasRet, int direction,
        Position.Bias b, int pos, JTextComponent t) throws BadLocationException ;
    public Dimension **getPreferredSize**(JComponent c) ;
    protected abstract String **getPropertyPrefix**() ;
    public View **getRootView**(JTextComponent tc) ;

```
    public String getToolTipText(Point pt, JTextComponent t) ; // Since 1.4
    protected Rectangle getVisibleEditorRect() ;
    protected void installDefaults() ;
    protected void installKeyboardActions() ;
    protected void installListeners() ;
    public void installUI(JComponent c) ;
    protected void modelChanged() ;
    public Rectangle modelToView(Position.Bias bias, int pos, JTextComponent tc) throws
        BadLocationException ;
    public Rectangle modelToView(int pos, JTextComponent tc) throws BadLocationException ;
    public final void paint(JComponent c, Graphics g) ;
    protected void paintBackground(Graphics g) ;
    protected void paintSafely(Graphics g) ;
    protected void propertyChange(PropertyChangeEvent evt) ;
    protected final void setView(View v) ;
    protected void uninstallDefaults() ;
    protected void uninstallKeyboardActions() ;
    protected void uninstallListeners() ;
    public void uninstallUI(JComponent c) ;
    public void update(JComponent c, Graphics g) ;
    public int viewToModel(Point pt, JTextComponent tc) ;
    public int viewToModel(javax.swing.text.Position.Bias[] biasReturn, Point pt, JTextComponent tc) ;
}
```

javax.swing.plaf.basic.**BasicTextUI.BasicCaret**

```
public static class BasicTextUI.BasicCaret extends DefaultCaret implements UIResource
{
    // Constructors
    public BasicTextUI.BasicCaret() ;
}
```

javax.swing.plaf.basic.**BasicTextUI.BasicHighlighter**

```
public static class BasicTextUI.BasicHighlighter extends DefaultHighlighter implements UIResource
{
    // Constructors
    public BasicTextUI.BasicHighlighter() ;
}
```

javax.swing.plaf.basic.**BasicToggleButtonUI**

public class **BasicToggleButtonUI** extends BasicButtonUI
{
    // Constructors
    public **BasicToggleButtonUI**() ;
    // Static methods
    public static ComponentUI **createUI**(JComponent b) ;
    // Instance methods
    protected String **getPropertyPrefix**() ;
    protected int **getTextShiftOffset**() ;
    public void **paint**(JComponent c, Graphics g) ;
    protected void **paintIcon**(Rectangle iconRect, AbstractButton b, Graphics g) ;
}

javax.swing.plaf.basic.**BasicToolBarSeparatorUI**

public class **BasicToolBarSeparatorUI** extends BasicSeparatorUI
{
    // Constructors
    public **BasicToolBarSeparatorUI**() ;
    // Static methods
    public static ComponentUI **createUI**(JComponent c) ;
    // Instance methods
    public Dimension **getPreferredSize**(JComponent c) ;
    protected void **installDefaults**(JSeparator s) ;
    public void **paint**(JComponent c, Graphics g) ;
}

javax.swing.plaf.basic.**BasicToolBarUI**

public class **BasicToolBarUI** extends ToolBarUI implements SwingConstants
{
    protected String **constraintBeforeFloating** ;
    protected Color **dockingBorderColor** ;
    protected Color **dockingColor** ;
    protected MouseInputListener **dockingListener** ;

protected KeyStroke **downKey** ;
protected BasicToolBarUI.DragWindow **dragWindow** ;
protected Color **floatingBorderColor** ;
protected Color **floatingColor** ;
protected int **focusedCompIndex** ;
protected KeyStroke **leftKey** ;
protected PropertyChangeListener **propertyListener** ;
protected KeyStroke **rightKey** ;
protected JToolBar **toolBar** ;
protected ContainerListener **toolBarContListener** ;
protected FocusListener **toolBarFocusListener** ;
protected KeyStroke **upKey** ;
// Constructors
public **BasicToolBarUI**() ;
// Static methods
public static ComponentUI **createUI**(JComponent c) ;
// Instance methods
public boolean **canDock**(Point p, Component c) ;
protected MouseInputListener **createDockingListener**() ;
protected BasicToolBarUI.DragWindow **createDragWindow**(JToolBar toolbar) ;
protected JFrame **createFloatingFrame**(JToolBar toolbar) ;
protected RootPaneContainer **createFloatingWindow**(JToolBar toolbar) ; // Since 1.4
protected WindowListener **createFrameListener**() ;
protected Border **createNonRolloverBorder**() ; // Since 1.4
protected PropertyChangeListener **createPropertyListener**() ;
protected Border **createRolloverBorder**() ; // Since 1.4
protected ContainerListener **createToolBarContListener**() ;
protected FocusListener **createToolBarFocusListener**() ;
protected void **dragTo**(Point origin, Point position) ;
protected void **floatAt**(Point origin, Point position) ;
public Color **getDockingColor**() ;
public Color **getFloatingColor**() ;
protected Border **getNonRolloverBorder**(AbstractButton b) ; // Since 1.6
protected Border **getRolloverBorder**(AbstractButton b) ; // Since 1.6
protected void **installComponents**() ;
protected void **installDefaults**() ;
protected void **installKeyboardActions**() ;
protected void **installListeners**() ;
protected void **installNonRolloverBorders**(JComponent c) ; // Since 1.4
protected void **installNormalBorders**(JComponent c) ; // Since 1.4
protected void **installRolloverBorders**(JComponent c) ; // Since 1.4
public void **installUI**(JComponent c) ;
public boolean **isFloating**() ;
public boolean **isRolloverBorders**() ; // Since 1.4
protected void **navigateFocusedComp**(int direction) ;
protected void **paintDragWindow**(Graphics g) ; // Since 1.5

```
        protected void setBorderToNonRollover(Component c) ; // Since 1.4
        protected void setBorderToNormal(Component c) ; // Since 1.4
        protected void setBorderToRollover(Component c) ; // Since 1.4
        public void setDockingColor(Color c) ;
        public void setFloating(Point p, boolean b) ;
        public void setFloatingColor(Color c) ;
        public void setFloatingLocation(int y, int x) ;
        public void setOrientation(int orientation) ;
        public void setRolloverBorders(boolean rollover) ; // Since 1.4
        protected void uninstallComponents() ;
        protected void uninstallDefaults() ;
        protected void uninstallKeyboardActions() ;
        protected void uninstallListeners() ;
        public void uninstallUI(JComponent c) ;
}
```

---

javax.swing.plaf.basic.**BasicToolTipUI**

```
public class BasicToolTipUI extends ToolTipUI
{
        // Constructors
        public BasicToolTipUI() ;
        // Static methods
        public static ComponentUI createUI(JComponent c) ;
        // Instance methods
        public Dimension getMaximumSize(JComponent c) ;
        public Dimension getMinimumSize(JComponent c) ;
        public Dimension getPreferredSize(JComponent c) ;
        protected void installDefaults(JComponent c) ;
        protected void installListeners(JComponent c) ;
        public void installUI(JComponent c) ;
        public void paint(JComponent c, Graphics g) ;
        protected void uninstallDefaults(JComponent c) ;
        protected void uninstallListeners(JComponent c) ;
        public void uninstallUI(JComponent c) ;
}
```

---

javax.swing.plaf.basic.**BasicTreeUI**

```
public class BasicTreeUI extends TreeUI
{
```

protected transient TreeCellEditor **cellEditor** ;
protected transient Icon **collapsedIcon** ;
protected boolean **createdCellEditor** ;
protected boolean **createdRenderer** ;
protected transient TreeCellRenderer **currentCellRenderer** ;
protected int **depthOffset** ;
protected Hashtable<TreePath, Boolean> **drawingCache** ;
protected Component **editingComponent** ;
protected TreePath **editingPath** ;
protected int **editingRow** ;
protected boolean **editorHasDifferentSize** ;
protected transient Icon **expandedIcon** ;
protected boolean **largeModel** ;
protected int **lastSelectedRow** ;
protected int **leftChildIndent** ;
protected AbstractLayoutCache.NodeDimensions **nodeDimensions** ;
protected Dimension **preferredMinSize** ;
protected Dimension **preferredSize** ;
protected CellRendererPane **rendererPane** ;
protected int **rightChildIndent** ;
protected boolean **stopEditingInCompleteEditing** ;
protected int **totalChildIndent** ;
protected JTree **tree** ;
protected TreeModel **treeModel** ;
protected TreeSelectionModel **treeSelectionModel** ;
protected AbstractLayoutCache **treeState** ;
protected boolean **validCachedPreferredSize** ;
// Constructors
public **BasicTreeUI**() ;
// Static methods
public static ComponentUI **createUI**(JComponent x) ;
// Instance methods
public void **cancelEditing**(JTree tree) ;
protected void **checkForClickInExpandControl**(int mouseY, int mouseX, TreePath path) ;
protected void **completeEditing**() ;
protected void **completeEditing**(boolean messageTree, boolean messageCancel, boolean
    messageStop) ;
protected void **completeUIInstall**() ;
protected void **completeUIUninstall**() ;
protected void **configureLayoutCache**() ;
protected CellEditorListener **createCellEditorListener**() ;
protected CellRendererPane **createCellRendererPane**() ;
protected ComponentListener **createComponentListener**() ;
protected TreeCellEditor **createDefaultCellEditor**() ;
protected TreeCellRenderer **createDefaultCellRenderer**() ;
protected FocusListener **createFocusListener**() ;

protected KeyListener **createKeyListener**() ;
protected AbstractLayoutCache **createLayoutCache**() ;
protected MouseListener **createMouseListener**() ;
protected AbstractLayoutCache.NodeDimensions **createNodeDimensions**() ;
protected PropertyChangeListener **createPropertyChangeListener**() ;
protected PropertyChangeListener **createSelectionModelPropertyChangeListener**() ;
protected TreeExpansionListener **createTreeExpansionListener**() ;
protected TreeModelListener **createTreeModelListener**() ;
protected TreeSelectionListener **createTreeSelectionListener**() ;
protected void **drawCentered**(int y, int x, Icon icon, Graphics graphics, Component c) ;
protected void **drawDashedHorizontalLine**(int x2, int x1, int y, Graphics g) ;
protected void **drawDashedVerticalLine**(int y2, int y1, int x, Graphics g) ;
protected void **ensureRowsAreVisible**(int endRow, int beginRow) ;
public int **getBaseline**(int height, int width, JComponent c) ; // Since 1.6
public Component.BaselineResizeBehavior **getBaselineResizeBehavior**(JComponent c) ; // Since 1.6
protected TreeCellEditor **getCellEditor**() ;
protected TreeCellRenderer **getCellRenderer**() ;
public TreePath **getClosestPathForLocation**(int y, int x, JTree tree) ;
public Icon **getCollapsedIcon**() ;
public TreePath **getEditingPath**(JTree tree) ;
public Icon **getExpandedIcon**() ;
protected Color **getHashColor**() ;
protected int **getHorizontalLegBuffer**() ;
protected TreePath **getLastChildPath**(TreePath parent) ;
public int **getLeftChildIndent**() ;
public Dimension **getMaximumSize**(JComponent c) ;
public Dimension **getMinimumSize**(JComponent c) ;
protected TreeModel **getModel**() ;
public Rectangle **getPathBounds**(TreePath path, JTree tree) ;
public TreePath **getPathForRow**(int row, JTree tree) ;
public Dimension **getPreferredMinSize**() ;
public Dimension **getPreferredSize**(JComponent c) ;
public Dimension **getPreferredSize**(boolean checkConsistancy, JComponent c) ;
public int **getRightChildIndent**() ;
public int **getRowCount**(JTree tree) ;
public int **getRowForPath**(TreePath path, JTree tree) ;
protected int **getRowHeight**() ;
protected int **getRowX**(int depth, int row) ; // Since 1.5
protected TreeSelectionModel **getSelectionModel**() ;
protected boolean **getShowsRootHandles**() ;
protected int **getVerticalLegBuffer**() ;
protected void **handleExpandControlClick**(int mouseY, int mouseX, TreePath path) ;
protected void **installComponents**() ;
protected void **installDefaults**() ;
protected void **installKeyboardActions**() ;
protected void **installListeners**() ;

public void **installUI**(JComponent c) ;
protected boolean **isEditable**() ;
public boolean **isEditing**(JTree tree) ;
protected boolean **isLargeModel**() ;
protected boolean **isLeaf**(int row) ;
protected boolean **isLocationInExpandControl**(int mouseY, int mouseX, TreePath path) ;
protected boolean **isMultiSelectEvent**(MouseEvent event) ;
protected boolean **isRootVisible**() ;
protected boolean **isToggleEvent**(MouseEvent event) ;
protected boolean **isToggleSelectionEvent**(MouseEvent event) ;
public void **paint**(JComponent c, Graphics g) ;
protected void **paintExpandControl**(boolean isLeaf, boolean hasBeenExpanded, boolean
    isExpanded, int row, TreePath path, Rectangle bounds, Insets insets, Rectangle clipBounds,
    Graphics g) ;
protected void **paintHorizontalLine**(int right, int left, int y, JComponent c, Graphics g) ;
protected void **paintHorizontalPartOfLeg**(boolean isLeaf, boolean hasBeenExpanded, boolean
    isExpanded, int row, TreePath path, Rectangle bounds, Insets insets, Rectangle clipBounds,
    Graphics g) ;
protected void **paintRow**(boolean isLeaf, boolean hasBeenExpanded, boolean isExpanded, int row,
    TreePath path, Rectangle bounds, Insets insets, Rectangle clipBounds, Graphics g) ;
protected void **paintVerticalLine**(int bottom, int top, int x, JComponent c, Graphics g) ;
protected void **paintVerticalPartOfLeg**(TreePath path, Insets insets, Rectangle clipBounds, Graphics
    g) ;
protected void **pathWasCollapsed**(TreePath path) ;
protected void **pathWasExpanded**(TreePath path) ;
protected void **prepareForUIInstall**() ;
protected void **prepareForUIUninstall**() ;
protected void **selectPathForEvent**(MouseEvent event, TreePath path) ;
protected void **setCellEditor**(TreeCellEditor editor) ;
protected void **setCellRenderer**(TreeCellRenderer tcr) ;
public void **setCollapsedIcon**(Icon newG) ;
protected void **setEditable**(boolean newValue) ;
public void **setExpandedIcon**(Icon newG) ;
protected void **setHashColor**(Color color) ;
protected void **setLargeModel**(boolean largeModel) ;
public void **setLeftChildIndent**(int newAmount) ;
protected void **setModel**(TreeModel model) ;
public void **setPreferredMinSize**(Dimension newSize) ;
public void **setRightChildIndent**(int newAmount) ;
protected void **setRootVisible**(boolean newValue) ;
protected void **setRowHeight**(int rowHeight) ;
protected void **setSelectionModel**(TreeSelectionModel newLSM) ;
protected void **setShowsRootHandles**(boolean newValue) ;
protected boolean **shouldPaintExpandControl**(boolean isLeaf, boolean hasBeenExpanded, boolean
    isExpanded, int row, TreePath path) ;
protected boolean **startEditing**(MouseEvent event, TreePath path) ;

public void **startEditingAtPath**(TreePath path, JTree tree) ;
public boolean **stopEditing**(JTree tree) ;
protected void **toggleExpandState**(TreePath path) ;
protected void **uninstallComponents**() ;
protected void **uninstallDefaults**() ;
protected void **uninstallKeyboardActions**() ;
protected void **uninstallListeners**() ;
public void **uninstallUI**(JComponent c) ;
protected void **updateCachedPreferredSize**() ;
protected void **updateCellEditor**() ;
protected void **updateDepthOffset**() ;
protected void **updateExpandedDescendants**(TreePath path) ;
protected void **updateLayoutCacheExpandedNodes**() ;
protected void **updateRenderer**() ;
protected void **updateSize**() ;
}

---

javax.swing.plaf.basic.**BasicViewportUI**

---

public class **BasicViewportUI** extends ViewportUI
{
    // Constructors
    public **BasicViewportUI**() ;
    // Static methods
    public static ComponentUI **createUI**(JComponent c) ;
    // Instance methods
    protected void **installDefaults**(JComponent c) ;
    public void **installUI**(JComponent c) ;
    protected void **uninstallDefaults**(JComponent c) ;
    public void **uninstallUI**(JComponent c) ;
}

---

javax.swing.border.**BevelBorder**

---

public class **BevelBorder** extends AbstractBorder
{
    public static final int **LOWERED** ;
    public static final int **RAISED** ;
    protected int **bevelType** ;
    protected Color **highlightInner** ;
    protected Color **highlightOuter** ;

```
    protected Color shadowInner ;
    protected Color shadowOuter ;
    // Constructors
    public BevelBorder(Color shadowInnerColor, Color shadowOuterColor, Color highlightInnerColor,
        Color highlightOuterColor, int bevelType) ;
    public BevelBorder(Color shadow, Color highlight, int bevelType) ;
    public BevelBorder(int bevelType) ;
    // Instance methods
    public int getBevelType() ;
    public Insets getBorderInsets(Insets insets, Component c) ;
    public Color getHighlightInnerColor(Component c) ; // Since 1.3
    public Color getHighlightInnerColor() ; // Since 1.3
    public Color getHighlightOuterColor(Component c) ; // Since 1.3
    public Color getHighlightOuterColor() ; // Since 1.3
    public Color getShadowInnerColor(Component c) ; // Since 1.3
    public Color getShadowInnerColor() ; // Since 1.3
    public Color getShadowOuterColor() ; // Since 1.3
    public Color getShadowOuterColor(Component c) ; // Since 1.3
    public boolean isBorderOpaque() ;
    public void paintBorder(int height, int width, int y, int x, Graphics g, Component c) ;
    protected void paintLoweredBevel(int height, int width, int y, int x, Graphics g, Component c) ;
    protected void paintRaisedBevel(int height, int width, int y, int x, Graphics g, Component c) ;
}
```

---

javax.swing.text.html.**BlockView**

```
public class BlockView extends BoxView
{
    // Constructors
    public BlockView(int axis, Element elem) ;
    // Static methods
    // Instance methods
    protected SizeRequirements calculateMajorAxisRequirements(SizeRequirements r, int axis) ;
    protected SizeRequirements calculateMinorAxisRequirements(SizeRequirements r, int axis) ;
    public void changedUpdate(ViewFactory f, Shape a, DocumentEvent changes) ;
    public float getAlignment(int axis) ;
    public AttributeSet getAttributes() ;
    public float getMaximumSpan(int axis) ;
    public float getMinimumSpan(int axis) ;
    public float getPreferredSpan(int axis) ;
    public int getResizeWeight(int axis) ;
    protected StyleSheet getStyleSheet() ;
    protected void layoutMinorAxis(int[] spans, int[] offsets, int axis, int targetSpan) ;
    public void paint(Shape allocation, Graphics g) ;
```

```
    public void setParent(View parent) ;
    protected void setPropertiesFromAttributes() ;
}
```

java.awt.print.**Book**

```
public class Book  implements Pageable
{
    // Constructors
    public Book() ;
    // Instance methods
    public void append(int numPages, PageFormat page, Printable painter) ;
    public void append(PageFormat page, Printable painter) ;
    public int getNumberOfPages() ;
    public PageFormat getPageFormat(int pageIndex) throws IndexOutOfBoundsException ;
    public Printable getPrintable(int pageIndex) throws IndexOutOfBoundsException ;
    public void setPage(PageFormat page, Printable painter, int pageIndex) throws
        IndexOutOfBoundsException ;
}
```

javax.swing.border.**Border**

```
public interface Border
{
    // Instance methods
    public Insets getBorderInsets(Component c) ;
    public boolean isBorderOpaque() ;
    public void paintBorder(int height, int width, int y, int x, Graphics g, Component c) ;
}
```

javax.swing.**BorderFactory**

```
public class BorderFactory
{
    // Constructors
    private BorderFactory() ;
    // Static methods
    public static Border createBevelBorder(int type) ;
```

```
    public static Border createBevelBorder(Color shadow, Color highlight, int type) ;
    public static Border createBevelBorder(Color shadowInner, Color shadowOuter, Color
        highlightInner, Color highlightOuter, int type) ;
    public static CompoundBorder createCompoundBorder(Border insideBorder, Border
        outsideBorder) ;
    public static CompoundBorder createCompoundBorder() ;
    public static Border createEmptyBorder(int right, int bottom, int left, int top) ;
    public static Border createEmptyBorder() ;
    public static Border createEtchedBorder(Color shadow, Color highlight) ;
    public static Border createEtchedBorder() ;
    public static Border createEtchedBorder(Color shadow, Color highlight, int type) ; // Since 1.3
    public static Border createEtchedBorder(int type) ; // Since 1.3
    public static Border createLineBorder(int thickness, Color color) ;
    public static Border createLineBorder(Color color) ;
    public static Border createLoweredBevelBorder() ;
    public static MatteBorder createMatteBorder(Icon tileIcon, int right, int bottom, int left, int top) ;
    public static MatteBorder createMatteBorder(Color color, int right, int bottom, int left, int top) ;
    public static Border createRaisedBevelBorder() ;
    public static TitledBorder createTitledBorder(Color titleColor, Font titleFont, int titlePosition, int
        titleJustification, String title, Border border) ;
    public static TitledBorder createTitledBorder(Font titleFont, int titlePosition, int titleJustification,
        String title, Border border) ;
    public static TitledBorder createTitledBorder(int titlePosition, int titleJustification, String title,
        Border border) ;
    public static TitledBorder createTitledBorder(String title, Border border) ;
    public static TitledBorder createTitledBorder(Border border) ;
    public static TitledBorder createTitledBorder(String title) ;
}
```

java.awt.**BorderLayout** [since 1.0]

```
public class BorderLayout  implements Serializable, LayoutManager2
{
    public static final String AFTER_LAST_LINE ;
    public static final String AFTER_LINE_ENDS ;
    public static final String BEFORE_FIRST_LINE ;
    public static final String BEFORE_LINE_BEGINS ;
    public static final String CENTER ;
    public static final String EAST ;
    public static final String LINE_END ;
    public static final String LINE_START ;
    public static final String NORTH ;
    public static final String PAGE_END ;
    public static final String PAGE_START ;
```

```
    public static final String SOUTH ;
    public static final String WEST ;
    // Constructors
    public BorderLayout(int vgap, int hgap) ;
    public BorderLayout() ;
    // Instance methods
    public void addLayoutComponent(Object constraints, Component comp) ; // Since 1.1
    public void addLayoutComponent(Component comp, String name) ;
    public Object getConstraints(Component comp) ; // Since 1.5
    public int getHgap() ; // Since 1.1
    public float getLayoutAlignmentX(Container parent) ;
    public float getLayoutAlignmentY(Container parent) ;
    public Component getLayoutComponent(Object constraints) ; // Since 1.5
    public Component getLayoutComponent(Object constraints, Container target) ; // Since 1.5
    public int getVgap() ; // Since 1.1
    public void invalidateLayout(Container target) ;
    public void layoutContainer(Container target) ;
    public Dimension maximumLayoutSize(Container target) ;
    public Dimension minimumLayoutSize(Container target) ;
    public Dimension preferredLayoutSize(Container target) ;
    public void removeLayoutComponent(Component comp) ;
    public void setHgap(int hgap) ; // Since 1.1
    public void setVgap(int vgap) ; // Since 1.1
    public String toString() ;
}
```

---

javax.swing.plaf.**BorderUIResource**

```
public class BorderUIResource  implements Serializable, UIResource, Border
{
    // Constructors
    public BorderUIResource(Border delegate) ;
    // Static methods
    public static Border getBlackLineBorderUIResource() ;
    public static Border getEtchedBorderUIResource() ;
    public static Border getLoweredBevelBorderUIResource() ;
    public static Border getRaisedBevelBorderUIResource() ;
    // Instance methods
    public Insets getBorderInsets(Component c) ;
    public boolean isBorderOpaque() ;
    public void paintBorder(int height, int width, int y, int x, Graphics g, Component c) ;
}
```

javax.swing.plaf.**BorderUIResource.BevelBorderUIResource**

public static class **BorderUIResource.BevelBorderUIResource** extends BevelBorder implements UIResource
{
    // Constructors
    public **BorderUIResource.BevelBorderUIResource**(Color shadowInner, Color shadowOuter, Color
        highlightInner, Color highlightOuter, int bevelType) ;
    public **BorderUIResource.BevelBorderUIResource**(Color shadow, Color highlight, int bevelType)
        ;
    public **BorderUIResource.BevelBorderUIResource**(int bevelType) ;
}

javax.swing.plaf.**BorderUIResource.CompoundBorderUIResource**

public static class **BorderUIResource.CompoundBorderUIResource** extends CompoundBorder implements UIResource
{
    // Constructors
    public **BorderUIResource.CompoundBorderUIResource**(Border insideBorder, Border
        outsideBorder) ;
}

javax.swing.plaf.**BorderUIResource.EmptyBorderUIResource**

public static class **BorderUIResource.EmptyBorderUIResource** extends EmptyBorder implements UIResource
{
    // Constructors
    public **BorderUIResource.EmptyBorderUIResource**(Insets insets) ;
    public **BorderUIResource.EmptyBorderUIResource**(int right, int bottom, int left, int top) ;
}

javax.swing.plaf.**BorderUIResource.EtchedBorderUIResource**

public static class **BorderUIResource.EtchedBorderUIResource** extends EtchedBorder implements UIResource
{
    // Constructors
    public **BorderUIResource.EtchedBorderUIResource**(Color shadow, Color highlight, int etchType) ;
    public **BorderUIResource.EtchedBorderUIResource**(Color shadow, Color highlight) ;
    public **BorderUIResource.EtchedBorderUIResource**(int etchType) ;
    public **BorderUIResource.EtchedBorderUIResource**() ;
}

---

javax.swing.plaf.**BorderUIResource.LineBorderUIResource**

---

public static class **BorderUIResource.LineBorderUIResource** extends LineBorder implements UIResource
{
    // Constructors
    public **BorderUIResource.LineBorderUIResource**(int thickness, Color color) ;
    public **BorderUIResource.LineBorderUIResource**(Color color) ;
}

---

javax.swing.plaf.**BorderUIResource.MatteBorderUIResource**

---

public static class **BorderUIResource.MatteBorderUIResource** extends MatteBorder implements UIResource
{
    // Constructors
    public **BorderUIResource.MatteBorderUIResource**(Icon tileIcon) ;
    public **BorderUIResource.MatteBorderUIResource**(Icon tileIcon, int right, int bottom, int left, int top) ;
    public **BorderUIResource.MatteBorderUIResource**(Color color, int right, int bottom, int left, int top) ;
}

---

javax.swing.plaf.**BorderUIResource.TitledBorderUIResource**

---

public static class **BorderUIResource.TitledBorderUIResource** extends TitledBorder implements UIResource

```
{
    // Constructors
    public BorderUIResource.TitledBorderUIResource(Color titleColor, Font titleFont, int
        titlePosition, int titleJustification, String title, Border border) ;
    public BorderUIResource.TitledBorderUIResource(Font titleFont, int titlePosition, int
        titleJustification, String title, Border border) ;
    public BorderUIResource.TitledBorderUIResource(int titlePosition, int titleJustification, String
        title, Border border) ;
    public BorderUIResource.TitledBorderUIResource(String title, Border border) ;
    public BorderUIResource.TitledBorderUIResource(Border border) ;
    public BorderUIResource.TitledBorderUIResource(String title) ;
}
```

javax.swing.**BoundedRangeModel**

```
public interface BoundedRangeModel
{
    // Instance methods
    public void addChangeListener(ChangeListener x) ;
    public int getExtent() ;
    public int getMaximum() ;
    public int getMinimum() ;
    public int getValue() ;
    public boolean getValueIsAdjusting() ;
    public void removeChangeListener(ChangeListener x) ;
    public void setExtent(int newExtent) ;
    public void setMaximum(int newMaximum) ;
    public void setMinimum(int newMinimum) ;
    public void setRangeProperties(boolean adjusting, int max, int min, int extent, int value) ;
    public void setValue(int newValue) ;
    public void setValueIsAdjusting(boolean b) ;
}
```

javax.swing.**Box**

```
public class Box extends JComponent implements Accessible
{
    // Constructors
    public Box(int axis) ;
    // Static methods
    public static Component createGlue() ;
```

```
    public static Box createHorizontalBox() ;
    public static Component createHorizontalGlue() ;
    public static Component createHorizontalStrut(int width) ;
    public static Component createRigidArea(Dimension d) ;
    public static Box createVerticalBox() ;
    public static Component createVerticalGlue() ;
    public static Component createVerticalStrut(int height) ;
    // Instance methods
    public AccessibleContext getAccessibleContext() ;
    protected void paintComponent(Graphics g) ; // Since 1.6
    public void setLayout(LayoutManager l) ;
}
```

javax.swing.**Box.Filler**

public static class **Box.Filler** extends JComponent implements Accessible
```
{
    // Constructors
    public Box.Filler(Dimension max, Dimension pref, Dimension min) ;
    // Instance methods
    public void changeShape(Dimension max, Dimension pref, Dimension min) ;
    public AccessibleContext getAccessibleContext() ;
    protected void paintComponent(Graphics g) ; // Since 1.6
}
```

javax.swing.**BoxLayout**

public class **BoxLayout** implements Serializable, LayoutManager2
```
{
    public static final int LINE_AXIS ;
    public static final int PAGE_AXIS ;
    public static final int X_AXIS ;
    public static final int Y_AXIS ;
    // Constructors
    private BoxLayout(PrintStream dbg, int axis, Container target) ;
    public BoxLayout(int axis, Container target) ;
    // Instance methods
    public void addLayoutComponent(Component comp, String name) ;
    public void addLayoutComponent(Object constraints, Component comp) ;
    public final int getAxis() ; // Since 1.6
    public synchronized float getLayoutAlignmentX(Container target) ;
```

public synchronized float **getLayoutAlignmentY**(Container target) ;
public final Container **getTarget**() ; // Since 1.6
public synchronized void **invalidateLayout**(Container target) ;
public void **layoutContainer**(Container target) ;
public Dimension **maximumLayoutSize**(Container target) ;
public Dimension **minimumLayoutSize**(Container target) ;
public Dimension **preferredLayoutSize**(Container target) ;
public void **removeLayoutComponent**(Component comp) ;
}

javax.swing.text.**BoxView**

public class **BoxView** extends CompositeView
{
    // Constructors
    public **BoxView**(int axis, Element elem) ;
    // Instance methods
    protected void **baselineLayout**(int[] spans, int[] offsets, int axis, int targetSpan) ;
    protected SizeRequirements **baselineRequirements**(SizeRequirements r, int axis) ;
    protected SizeRequirements **calculateMajorAxisRequirements**(SizeRequirements r, int axis) ;
    protected SizeRequirements **calculateMinorAxisRequirements**(SizeRequirements r, int axis) ;
    protected void **childAllocation**(Rectangle alloc, int index) ;
    protected boolean **flipEastAndWestAtEnds**(Position.Bias bias, int position) ;
    protected void **forwardUpdate**(ViewFactory f, Shape a, DocumentEvent e,
        DocumentEvent.ElementChange ec) ; // Since 1.3
    public float **getAlignment**(int axis) ;
    public int **getAxis**() ; // Since 1.3
    public Shape **getChildAllocation**(Shape a, int index) ;
    public int **getHeight**() ;
    public float **getMaximumSpan**(int axis) ;
    public float **getMinimumSpan**(int axis) ;
    protected int **getOffset**(int childIndex, int axis) ;
    public float **getPreferredSpan**(int axis) ;
    public int **getResizeWeight**(int axis) ;
    protected int **getSpan**(int childIndex, int axis) ;
    protected View **getViewAtPoint**(Rectangle alloc, int y, int x) ;
    public int **getWidth**() ;
    protected boolean **isAfter**(Rectangle innerAlloc, int y, int x) ;
    protected boolean **isAllocationValid**() ;
    protected boolean **isBefore**(Rectangle innerAlloc, int y, int x) ;
    protected boolean **isLayoutValid**(int axis) ; // Since 1.4
    protected void **layout**(int height, int width) ;
    public void **layoutChanged**(int axis) ; // Since 1.3
    protected void **layoutMajorAxis**(int[] spans, int[] offsets, int axis, int targetSpan) ;

```
    protected void layoutMinorAxis(int[] spans, int[] offsets, int axis, int targetSpan) ;
    public Shape modelToView(Position.Bias b, Shape a, int pos) throws BadLocationException ;
    public void paint(Shape allocation, Graphics g) ;
    protected void paintChild(int index, Rectangle alloc, Graphics g) ;
    public void preferenceChanged(boolean height, boolean width, View child) ;
    public void replace(javax.swing.text.View[] elems, int length, int index) ;
    public void setAxis(int axis) ; // Since 1.3
    public void setSize(float height, float width) ;
    public int viewToModel(javax.swing.text.Position.Bias[] bias, Shape a, float y, float x) ;
}
```

java.awt.**BufferCapabilities** [since 1.4]

```
public class BufferCapabilities  implements Cloneable
{
    // Constructors
    public BufferCapabilities(BufferCapabilities.FlipContents flipContents, ImageCapabilities
        backCaps, ImageCapabilities frontCaps) ;
    // Instance methods
    public Object clone() ;
    public ImageCapabilities getBackBufferCapabilities() ;
    public BufferCapabilities.FlipContents getFlipContents() ;
    public ImageCapabilities getFrontBufferCapabilities() ;
    public boolean isFullScreenRequired() ;
    public boolean isMultiBufferAvailable() ;
    public boolean isPageFlipping() ;
}
```

java.awt.**BufferCapabilities.FlipContents** [since 1.4]

```
public static final class BufferCapabilities.FlipContents extends AttributeValue
{
    public static final BufferCapabilities.FlipContents BACKGROUND ;
    public static final BufferCapabilities.FlipContents COPIED ;
    public static final BufferCapabilities.FlipContents PRIOR ;
    public static final BufferCapabilities.FlipContents UNDEFINED ;
    // Constructors
    private BufferCapabilities.FlipContents(int type) ;
}
```

java.awt.image.**BufferedImage**

public class **BufferedImage** extends Image implements Transparency, WritableRenderedImage
{
    public static final int **TYPE_3BYTE_BGR** ;
    public static final int **TYPE_4BYTE_ABGR** ;
    public static final int **TYPE_4BYTE_ABGR_PRE** ;
    public static final int **TYPE_BYTE_BINARY** ;
    public static final int **TYPE_BYTE_GRAY** ;
    public static final int **TYPE_BYTE_INDEXED** ;
    public static final int **TYPE_CUSTOM** ;
    public static final int **TYPE_INT_ARGB** ;
    public static final int **TYPE_INT_ARGB_PRE** ;
    public static final int **TYPE_INT_BGR** ;
    public static final int **TYPE_INT_RGB** ;
    public static final int **TYPE_USHORT_555_RGB** ;
    public static final int **TYPE_USHORT_565_RGB** ;
    public static final int **TYPE_USHORT_GRAY** ;
    // Constructors
    public **BufferedImage**(Hashtable<?, ?> properties, boolean isRasterPremultiplied, WritableRaster
        raster, ColorModel cm) ;
    public **BufferedImage**(IndexColorModel cm, int imageType, int height, int width) ;
    public **BufferedImage**(int imageType, int height, int width) ;
    // Static methods
    // Instance methods
    public void **addTileObserver**(TileObserver to) ;
    public void **coerceData**(boolean isAlphaPremultiplied) ;
    public WritableRaster **copyData**(WritableRaster outRaster) ;
    public Graphics2D **createGraphics**() ;
    public WritableRaster **getAlphaRaster**() ;
    public ColorModel **getColorModel**() ;
    public Raster **getData**() ;
    public Raster **getData**(Rectangle rect) ;
    public Graphics **getGraphics**() ;
    public int **getHeight**(ImageObserver observer) ;
    public int **getHeight**() ;
    public int **getMinTileX**() ;
    public int **getMinTileY**() ;
    public int **getMinX**() ;
    public int **getMinY**() ;
    public int **getNumXTiles**() ;
    public int **getNumYTiles**() ;
    public Object **getProperty**(ImageObserver observer, String name) ;

```
    public Object getProperty(String name) ;
    public String getPropertyNames() ;
    public WritableRaster getRaster() ;
    public int getRGB(int scansize, int offset, int[] rgbArray, int h, int w, int startY, int startX) ;
    public int getRGB(int y, int x) ;
    public SampleModel getSampleModel() ;
    public ImageProducer getSource() ;
    public Vector<RenderedImage> getSources() ;
    public BufferedImage getSubimage(int h, int w, int y, int x) ;
    public Raster getTile(int tileY, int tileX) ;
    public int getTileGridXOffset() ;
    public int getTileGridYOffset() ;
    public int getTileHeight() ;
    public int getTileWidth() ;
    public int getTransparency() ; // Since 1.5
    public int getType() ;
    public int getWidth(ImageObserver observer) ;
    public int getWidth() ;
    public WritableRaster getWritableTile(int tileY, int tileX) ;
    public Point getWritableTileIndices() ;
    public boolean hasTileWriters() ;
    public boolean isAlphaPremultiplied() ;
    public boolean isTileWritable(int tileY, int tileX) ;
    public void releaseWritableTile(int tileY, int tileX) ;
    public void removeTileObserver(TileObserver to) ;
    public void setData(Raster r) ;
    public void setRGB(int scansize, int offset, int[] rgbArray, int h, int w, int startY, int startX) ;
    public synchronized void setRGB(int rgb, int y, int x) ;
    public String toString() ;
}
```

java.awt.image.**BufferedImageFilter**

public class **BufferedImageFilter** extends ImageFilter implements Cloneable
```
{
    // Constructors
    public BufferedImageFilter(BufferedImageOp op) ;
    // Instance methods
    public BufferedImageOp getBufferedImageOp() ;
    public void imageComplete(int status) ;
    public void setColorModel(ColorModel model) ;
    public void setDimensions(int height, int width) ;
    public void setPixels(int scansize, int off, int[] pixels, ColorModel model, int h, int w, int y, int x) ;
    public void setPixels(int scansize, int off, byte[] pixels, ColorModel model, int h, int w, int y, int x) ;
```

}

java.awt.image.**BufferedImageOp**

public interface **BufferedImageOp**
{
    // Instance methods
    public BufferedImage **createCompatibleDestImage**(ColorModel destCM, BufferedImage src) ;
    public BufferedImage **filter**(BufferedImage dest, BufferedImage src) ;
    public Rectangle2D **getBounds2D**(BufferedImage src) ;
    public Point2D **getPoint2D**(Point2D dstPt, Point2D srcPt) ;
    public RenderingHints **getRenderingHints**() ;
}

java.awt.image.**BufferStrategy** [since 1.4]

public abstract class **BufferStrategy**
{
    // Constructors
    public **BufferStrategy**() ;
    // Instance methods
    public abstract boolean **contentsLost**() ;
    public abstract boolean **contentsRestored**() ;
    public void **dispose**() ; // Since 1.6
    public abstract BufferCapabilities **getCapabilities**() ;
    public abstract Graphics **getDrawGraphics**() ;
    public abstract void **show**() ;
}

java.awt.**Button** [since 1.0]

public class **Button** extends Component implements Accessible
{
    // Constructors
    public **Button**(String label) ;
    public **Button**() ;
    // Static methods
    // Instance methods

```
    public synchronized void addActionListener(ActionListener l) ; // Since 1.1
    public void addNotify() ;
    public AccessibleContext getAccessibleContext() ; // Since 1.3
    public String getActionCommand() ;
    public synchronized ActionListener getActionListeners() ; // Since 1.4
    public String getLabel() ;
    public T getListeners(Class<T> listenerType) ; // Since 1.3
    protected String paramString() ;
    protected void processActionEvent(ActionEvent e) ; // Since 1.1
    protected void processEvent(AWTEvent e) ; // Since 1.1
    public synchronized void removeActionListener(ActionListener l) ; // Since 1.1
    public void setActionCommand(String command) ; // Since 1.1
    public void setLabel(String label) ;
}
```

---

javax.swing.**ButtonGroup**

```
public class ButtonGroup  implements Serializable
{
    protected Vector<AbstractButton> buttons ;
    // Constructors
    public ButtonGroup() ;
    // Instance methods
    public void add(AbstractButton b) ;
    public void clearSelection() ; // Since 1.6
    public int getButtonCount() ; // Since 1.3
    public Enumeration<AbstractButton> getElements() ;
    public ButtonModel getSelection() ;
    public boolean isSelected(ButtonModel m) ;
    public void remove(AbstractButton b) ;
    public void setSelected(boolean b, ButtonModel m) ;
}
```

---

javax.swing.**ButtonModel**

```
public interface ButtonModel  implements ItemSelectable
{
    // Instance methods
    public void addActionListener(ActionListener l) ;
    public void addChangeListener(ChangeListener l) ;
    public void addItemListener(ItemListener l) ;
```

```
    public String getActionCommand() ;
    public int getMnemonic() ;
    public boolean isArmed() ;
    public boolean isEnabled() ;
    public boolean isPressed() ;
    public boolean isRollover() ;
    public boolean isSelected() ;
    public void removeActionListener(ActionListener l) ;
    public void removeChangeListener(ChangeListener l) ;
    public void removeItemListener(ItemListener l) ;
    public void setActionCommand(String s) ;
    public void setArmed(boolean b) ;
    public void setEnabled(boolean b) ;
    public void setGroup(ButtonGroup group) ;
    public void setMnemonic(int key) ;
    public void setPressed(boolean b) ;
    public void setRollover(boolean b) ;
    public void setSelected(boolean b) ;
}
```

java.awt.peer.**ButtonPeer**

```
public interface ButtonPeer  implements ComponentPeer
{
    // Instance methods
    public void setLabel(String label) ;
}
```

javax.swing.plaf.**ButtonUI**

```
public abstract class ButtonUI extends ComponentUI
{
    // Constructors
    public ButtonUI() ;
}
```

---

java.awt.image.**ByteLookupTable**

public class **ByteLookupTable** extends LookupTable
{
    // Constructors
    public **ByteLookupTable**(byte[] data, int offset) ;
    public **ByteLookupTable**(byte[][] data, int offset) ;
    // Instance methods
    public final byte **getTable**() ;
    public byte **lookupPixel**(byte[] dst, byte[] src) ;
    public int **lookupPixel**(int[] dst, int[] src) ;
}

---

javax.swing.undo.**CannotRedoException**

public class **CannotRedoException** extends RuntimeException
{
    // Constructors
    public **CannotRedoException**() ;
}

---

javax.swing.undo.**CannotUndoException**

public class **CannotUndoException** extends RuntimeException
{
    // Constructors
    public **CannotUndoException**() ;
}

---

java.awt.**Canvas** [since 1.0]

public class **Canvas** extends Component implements Accessible
{
    // Constructors
    public **Canvas**(GraphicsConfiguration config) ;

```
    public Canvas() ;
    // Instance methods
    public void addNotify() ;
    public void createBufferStrategy(BufferCapabilities caps, int numBuffers) throws AWTException ;
        // Since 1.4
    public void createBufferStrategy(int numBuffers) ; // Since 1.4
    public AccessibleContext getAccessibleContext() ; // Since 1.3
    public BufferStrategy getBufferStrategy() ; // Since 1.4
    public void paint(Graphics g) ;
    public void update(Graphics g) ;
}
```

java.awt.**CardLayout** [since 1.0]

```
public class CardLayout  implements Serializable, LayoutManager2
{
    // Constructors
    public CardLayout(int vgap, int hgap) ;
    public CardLayout() ;
    // Instance methods
    public void addLayoutComponent(Object constraints, Component comp) ;
    public void addLayoutComponent(Component comp, String name) ;
    public void first(Container parent) ;
    public int getHgap() ; // Since 1.1
    public float getLayoutAlignmentX(Container parent) ;
    public float getLayoutAlignmentY(Container parent) ;
    public int getVgap() ;
    public void invalidateLayout(Container target) ;
    public void last(Container parent) ;
    public void layoutContainer(Container parent) ;
    public Dimension maximumLayoutSize(Container target) ;
    public Dimension minimumLayoutSize(Container parent) ;
    public void next(Container parent) ;
    public Dimension preferredLayoutSize(Container parent) ;
    public void previous(Container parent) ;
    public void removeLayoutComponent(Component comp) ;
    public void setHgap(int hgap) ; // Since 1.1
    public void setVgap(int vgap) ; // Since 1.1
    public void show(String name, Container parent) ;
    public String toString() ;
}
```

---

javax.swing.text.**Caret**

---

public interface **Caret**
{
    // Instance methods
    public void **addChangeListener**(ChangeListener l) ;
    public void **deinstall**(JTextComponent c) ;
    public int **getBlinkRate**() ;
    public int **getDot**() ;
    public Point **getMagicCaretPosition**() ;
    public int **getMark**() ;
    public void **install**(JTextComponent c) ;
    public boolean **isSelectionVisible**() ;
    public boolean **isVisible**() ;
    public void **moveDot**(int dot) ;
    public void **paint**(Graphics g) ;
    public void **removeChangeListener**(ChangeListener l) ;
    public void **setBlinkRate**(int rate) ;
    public void **setDot**(int dot) ;
    public void **setMagicCaretPosition**(Point p) ;
    public void **setSelectionVisible**(boolean v) ;
    public void **setVisible**(boolean v) ;
}

---

javax.swing.event.**CaretEvent**

---

public abstract class **CaretEvent** extends EventObject
{
    // Constructors
    public **CaretEvent**(Object source) ;
    // Instance methods
    public abstract int **getDot**() ;
    public abstract int **getMark**() ;
}

javax.swing.event.**CaretListener**

```
public interface CaretListener  implements EventListener
{
    // Instance methods
    public void caretUpdate(CaretEvent e) ;
}
```

javax.swing.**CellEditor**

```
public interface CellEditor
{
    // Instance methods
    public void addCellEditorListener(CellEditorListener l) ;
    public void cancelCellEditing() ;
    public Object getCellEditorValue() ;
    public boolean isCellEditable(EventObject anEvent) ;
    public void removeCellEditorListener(CellEditorListener l) ;
    public boolean shouldSelectCell(EventObject anEvent) ;
    public boolean stopCellEditing() ;
}
```

javax.swing.event.**CellEditorListener**

```
public interface CellEditorListener  implements EventListener
{
    // Instance methods
    public void editingCanceled(ChangeEvent e) ;
    public void editingStopped(ChangeEvent e) ;
}
```

javax.swing.**CellRendererPane**

```
public class CellRendererPane extends Container implements Accessible
{
```

```
    protected AccessibleContext accessibleContext ;
    // Constructors
    public CellRendererPane() ;
    // Instance methods
    protected void addImpl(int index, Object constraints, Component x) ;
    public AccessibleContext getAccessibleContext() ;
    public void invalidate() ;
    public void paint(Graphics g) ;
    public void paintComponent(Rectangle r, Container p, Component c, Graphics g) ;
    public void paintComponent(int h, int w, int y, int x, Container p, Component c, Graphics g) ;
    public void paintComponent(boolean shouldValidate, int h, int w, int y, int x, Container p,
        Component c, Graphics g) ;
    public void update(Graphics g) ;
}
```

---

javax.swing.text.**ChangedCharSetException**

```
public class ChangedCharSetException extends IOException
{
    // Constructors
    public ChangedCharSetException(boolean charSetKey, String charSetSpec) ;
    // Instance methods
    public String getCharSetSpec() ;
    public boolean keyEqualsCharSet() ;
}
```

---

javax.swing.event.**ChangeEvent**

```
public class ChangeEvent extends EventObject
{
    // Constructors
    public ChangeEvent(Object source) ;
}
```

---

javax.swing.event.**ChangeListener**

```
public interface ChangeListener  implements EventListener
{
```

```
    // Instance methods
    public void stateChanged(ChangeEvent e) ;
}
```

java.awt.**Checkbox** [since 1.0]

```
public class Checkbox extends Component implements Accessible, ItemSelectable
{
    // Constructors
    public Checkbox(boolean state, CheckboxGroup group, String label) ;
    public Checkbox(CheckboxGroup group, boolean state, String label) ;
    public Checkbox(boolean state, String label) ;
    public Checkbox(String label) ;
    public Checkbox() ;
    // Static methods
    // Instance methods
    public synchronized void addItemListener(ItemListener l) ; // Since 1.1
    public void addNotify() ;
    public AccessibleContext getAccessibleContext() ; // Since 1.3
    public CheckboxGroup getCheckboxGroup() ;
    public synchronized ItemListener getItemListeners() ; // Since 1.4
    public String getLabel() ;
    public T getListeners(Class<T> listenerType) ; // Since 1.3
    public Object getSelectedObjects() ;
    public boolean getState() ;
    protected String paramString() ;
    protected void processEvent(AWTEvent e) ; // Since 1.1
    protected void processItemEvent(ItemEvent e) ; // Since 1.1
    public synchronized void removeItemListener(ItemListener l) ; // Since 1.1
    public void setCheckboxGroup(CheckboxGroup g) ;
    public void setLabel(String label) ;
    public void setState(boolean state) ;
}
```

java.awt.**CheckboxGroup** [since 1.0]

```
public class CheckboxGroup  implements Serializable
{
    // Constructors
    public CheckboxGroup() ;
    // Instance methods
```

```
    public Checkbox getCurrent() ;
    public Checkbox getSelectedCheckbox() ; // Since 1.1
    public synchronized void setCurrent(Checkbox box) ;
    public void setSelectedCheckbox(Checkbox box) ; // Since 1.1
    public String toString() ;
}
```

---

java.awt.**CheckboxMenuItem** [since 1.0]

```
public class CheckboxMenuItem extends MenuItem implements Accessible, ItemSelectable
{
    // Constructors
    public CheckboxMenuItem(boolean state, String label) ;
    public CheckboxMenuItem(String label) ;
    public CheckboxMenuItem() ;
    // Static methods
    // Instance methods
    public synchronized void addItemListener(ItemListener l) ; // Since 1.1
    public void addNotify() ;
    public AccessibleContext getAccessibleContext() ; // Since 1.3
    public synchronized ItemListener getItemListeners() ; // Since 1.4
    public T getListeners(Class<T> listenerType) ; // Since 1.3
    public synchronized Object getSelectedObjects() ;
    public boolean getState() ;
    public String paramString() ;
    protected void processEvent(AWTEvent e) ; // Since 1.1
    protected void processItemEvent(ItemEvent e) ; // Since 1.1
    public synchronized void removeItemListener(ItemListener l) ; // Since 1.1
    public synchronized void setState(boolean b) ;
}
```

---

java.awt.peer.**CheckboxMenuItemPeer**

```
public interface CheckboxMenuItemPeer  implements MenuItemPeer
{
    // Instance methods
    public void setState(boolean t) ;
}
```

java.awt.peer.**CheckboxPeer**

public interface **CheckboxPeer** implements ComponentPeer
{
    // Instance methods
    public void **setCheckboxGroup**(CheckboxGroup g) ;
    public void **setLabel**(String label) ;
    public void **setState**(boolean state) ;
}

java.awt.**Choice** [since 1.0]

public class **Choice** extends Component implements Accessible, ItemSelectable
{
    // Constructors
    public **Choice**() ;
    // Instance methods
    public void **add**(String item) ; // Since 1.1
    public void **addItem**(String item) ;
    public synchronized void **addItemListener**(ItemListener l) ; // Since 1.1
    public void **addNotify**() ;
    public int **countItems**() ;
    public AccessibleContext **getAccessibleContext**() ; // Since 1.3
    public String **getItem**(int index) ;
    public int **getItemCount**() ; // Since 1.1
    public synchronized ItemListener **getItemListeners**() ; // Since 1.4
    public T **getListeners**(Class<T> listenerType) ; // Since 1.3
    public int **getSelectedIndex**() ;
    public synchronized String **getSelectedItem**() ;
    public synchronized Object **getSelectedObjects**() ;
    public void **insert**(int index, String item) ;
    protected String **paramString**() ;
    protected void **processEvent**(AWTEvent e) ; // Since 1.1
    protected void **processItemEvent**(ItemEvent e) ; // Since 1.1
    public void **remove**(int position) ; // Since 1.1
    public void **remove**(String item) ; // Since 1.1
    public void **removeAll**() ; // Since 1.1
    public synchronized void **removeItemListener**(ItemListener l) ; // Since 1.1
    public synchronized void **select**(int pos) ;
    public synchronized void **select**(String str) ;

}

---

java.awt.peer.**ChoicePeer**

---

public interface **ChoicePeer** implements ComponentPeer
{
    // Instance methods
    public void **add**(int index, String item) ;
    public void **addItem**(int index, String item) ;
    public void **remove**(int index) ;
    public void **removeAll**() ;
    public void **select**(int index) ;
}

---

java.awt.datatransfer.**Clipboard**

---

public class **Clipboard**
{
    protected Transferable **contents** ;
    protected ClipboardOwner **owner** ;
    // Constructors
    public **Clipboard**(String name) ;
    // Instance methods
    public synchronized void **addFlavorListener**(FlavorListener listener) ; // Since 1.5
    public DataFlavor **getAvailableDataFlavors**() ; // Since 1.5
    public synchronized Transferable **getContents**(Object requestor) ;
    public Object **getData**(DataFlavor flavor) throws UnsupportedFlavorException, IOException ; //
        Since 1.5
    public synchronized FlavorListener **getFlavorListeners**() ; // Since 1.5
    public String **getName**() ;
    public boolean **isDataFlavorAvailable**(DataFlavor flavor) ; // Since 1.5
    public synchronized void **removeFlavorListener**(FlavorListener listener) ; // Since 1.5
    public synchronized void **setContents**(ClipboardOwner owner, Transferable contents) ;
}

---

java.awt.datatransfer.**ClipboardOwner**

---

public interface **ClipboardOwner**

```
{
    // Instance methods
    public void lostOwnership(Transferable contents, Clipboard clipboard) ;
}
```

---

java.awt.**Color**

---

public class **Color** implements Serializable, Paint
```
{
    public static final Color BLACK ;
    public static final Color black ;
    public static final Color blue ;
    public static final Color BLUE ;
    public static final Color cyan ;
    public static final Color CYAN ;
    public static final Color darkGray ;
    public static final Color DARK_GRAY ;
    public static final Color gray ;
    public static final Color GRAY ;
    public static final Color GREEN ;
    public static final Color green ;
    public static final Color lightGray ;
    public static final Color LIGHT_GRAY ;
    public static final Color MAGENTA ;
    public static final Color magenta ;
    public static final Color orange ;
    public static final Color ORANGE ;
    public static final Color pink ;
    public static final Color PINK ;
    public static final Color red ;
    public static final Color RED ;
    public static final Color WHITE ;
    public static final Color white ;
    public static final Color YELLOW ;
    public static final Color yellow ;
    // Constructors
    public Color(float alpha, float[] components, ColorSpace cspace) ;
    public Color(float a, float b, float g, float r) ;
    public Color(float b, float g, float r) ;
    public Color(boolean hasalpha, int rgba) ;
    public Color(int rgb) ;
    public Color(int a, int b, int g, int r) ;
    public Color(int b, int g, int r) ;
    // Static methods
```

```
    public static Color decode(String nm) throws NumberFormatException ; // Since 1.1
    public static Color getColor(Color v, String nm) ; // Since 1.0
    public static Color getColor(int v, String nm) ; // Since 1.0
    public static Color getColor(String nm) ; // Since 1.0
    public static Color getHSBColor(float b, float s, float h) ; // Since 1.0
    public static int HSBtoRGB(float brightness, float saturation, float hue) ; // Since 1.0
    public static float RGBtoHSB(float[] hsbvals, int b, int g, int r) ; // Since 1.0
    // Instance methods
    public Color brighter() ; // Since 1.0
    public synchronized PaintContext createContext(RenderingHints hints, AffineTransform xform,
        Rectangle2D r2d, Rectangle r, ColorModel cm) ;
    public Color darker() ; // Since 1.0
    public boolean equals(Object obj) ; // Since 1.0
    public int getAlpha() ;
    public int getBlue() ;
    public float getColorComponents(float[] compArray) ;
    public float getColorComponents(float[] compArray, ColorSpace cspace) ;
    public ColorSpace getColorSpace() ;
    public float getComponents(float[] compArray) ;
    public float getComponents(float[] compArray, ColorSpace cspace) ;
    public int getGreen() ;
    public int getRed() ;
    public int getRGB() ; // Since 1.0
    public float getRGBColorComponents(float[] compArray) ;
    public float getRGBComponents(float[] compArray) ;
    public int getTransparency() ;
    public int hashCode() ; // Since 1.0
    public String toString() ;
}
```

---

javax.swing.colorchooser.**ColorChooserComponentFactory**

```
public class ColorChooserComponentFactory
{
    // Constructors
    private ColorChooserComponentFactory() ;
    // Static methods
    public static AbstractColorChooserPanel getDefaultChooserPanels() ;
    public static JComponent getPreviewPanel() ;
}
```

javax.swing.plaf.**ColorChooserUI**

public abstract class **ColorChooserUI** extends ComponentUI
{
    // Constructors
    public **ColorChooserUI**() ;
}

java.awt.image.**ColorModel**

public abstract class **ColorModel** implements Transparency
{
    protected int **pixel_bits** ;
    protected int **transferType** ;
    // Constructors
    protected **ColorModel**(int transferType, int transparency, boolean isAlphaPremultiplied, boolean
        hasAlpha, ColorSpace cspace, int[] bits, int pixel_bits) ;
    public **ColorModel**(int bits) ;
    // Static methods
    public static ColorModel **getRGBdefault**() ;
    // Instance methods
    public ColorModel **coerceData**(boolean isAlphaPremultiplied, WritableRaster raster) ;
    public SampleModel **createCompatibleSampleModel**(int h, int w) ;
    public WritableRaster **createCompatibleWritableRaster**(int h, int w) ;
    public boolean **equals**(Object obj) ;
    public void **finalize**() ;
    public int **getAlpha**(Object inData) ;
    public abstract int **getAlpha**(int pixel) ;
    public WritableRaster **getAlphaRaster**(WritableRaster raster) ;
    public abstract int **getBlue**(int pixel) ;
    public int **getBlue**(Object inData) ;
    public final ColorSpace **getColorSpace**() ;
    public int **getComponents**(int offset, int[] components, Object pixel) ;
    public int **getComponents**(int offset, int[] components, int pixel) ;
    public int **getComponentSize**(int componentIdx) ;
    public int **getComponentSize**() ;
    public int **getDataElement**(int normOffset, float[] normComponents) ; // Since 1.4
    public int **getDataElement**(int offset, int[] components) ;
    public Object **getDataElements**(Object pixel, int rgb) ;
    public Object **getDataElements**(Object obj, int normOffset, float[] normComponents) ; // Since 1.4

public Object **getDataElements**(Object obj, int offset, int[] components) ;
public int **getGreen**(Object inData) ;
public abstract int **getGreen**(int pixel) ;
public float **getNormalizedComponents**(int normOffset, float[] normComponents, Object pixel) ; // Since 1.4
public float **getNormalizedComponents**(int normOffset, float[] normComponents, int offset, int[] components) ;
public int **getNumColorComponents**() ;
public int **getNumComponents**() ;
public int **getPixelSize**() ;
public abstract int **getRed**(int pixel) ;
public int **getRed**(Object inData) ;
public int **getRGB**(int pixel) ;
public int **getRGB**(Object inData) ;
public final int **getTransferType**() ; // Since 1.3
public int **getTransparency**() ;
public int **getUnnormalizedComponents**(int offset, int[] components, int normOffset, float[] normComponents) ;
public final boolean **hasAlpha**() ;
public int **hashCode**() ;
public final boolean **isAlphaPremultiplied**() ;
public boolean **isCompatibleRaster**(Raster raster) ;
public boolean **isCompatibleSampleModel**(SampleModel sm) ;
public String **toString**() ;
}

javax.swing.colorchooser.**ColorSelectionModel**

public interface **ColorSelectionModel**
{
    // Instance methods
    public void **addChangeListener**(ChangeListener listener) ;
    public Color **getSelectedColor**() ;
    public void **removeChangeListener**(ChangeListener listener) ;
    public void **setSelectedColor**(Color color) ;
}

javax.swing.plaf.synth.**ColorType** [since 1.5]

public class **ColorType**
{

```
    public static final ColorType BACKGROUND ;
    public static final ColorType FOCUS ;
    public static final ColorType FOREGROUND ;
    public static final int MAX_COUNT ;
    public static final ColorType TEXT_BACKGROUND ;
    public static final ColorType TEXT_FOREGROUND ;
    // Constructors
    protected ColorType(String description) ;
    // Instance methods
    public final int getID() ;
    public String toString() ;
}
```

javax.swing.plaf.**ColorUIResource**

```
public class ColorUIResource extends Color implements UIResource
{
    // Constructors
    public ColorUIResource(Color c) ;
    public ColorUIResource(float b, float g, float r) ;
    public ColorUIResource(int rgb) ;
    public ColorUIResource(int b, int g, int r) ;
}
```

javax.swing.**ComboBoxEditor**

```
public interface ComboBoxEditor
{
    // Instance methods
    public void addActionListener(ActionListener l) ;
    public Component getEditorComponent() ;
    public Object getItem() ;
    public void removeActionListener(ActionListener l) ;
    public void selectAll() ;
    public void setItem(Object anObject) ;
}
```

javax.swing.**ComboBoxModel**

public interface **ComboBoxModel** implements ListModel
{
    // Instance methods
    public Object **getSelectedItem**() ;
    public void **setSelectedItem**(Object anItem) ;
}

javax.swing.plaf.**ComboBoxUI**

public abstract class **ComboBoxUI** extends ComponentUI
{
    // Constructors
    public **ComboBoxUI**() ;
    // Instance methods
    public abstract boolean **isFocusTraversable**(JComboBox c) ;
    public abstract boolean **isPopupVisible**(JComboBox c) ;
    public abstract void **setPopupVisible**(boolean v, JComboBox c) ;
}

javax.swing.plaf.basic.**ComboPopup**

public interface **ComboPopup**
{
    // Instance methods
    public KeyListener **getKeyListener**() ;
    public JList **getList**() ;
    public MouseListener **getMouseListener**() ;
    public MouseMotionListener **getMouseMotionListener**() ;
    public void **hide**() ;
    public boolean **isVisible**() ;
    public void **show**() ;
    public void **uninstallingUI**() ;
}

java.awt.**Component**

public abstract class **Component** implements Serializable, MenuContainer, ImageObserver
{
    public static final float **BOTTOM_ALIGNMENT** ;
    public static final float **CENTER_ALIGNMENT** ;
    public static final float **LEFT_ALIGNMENT** ;
    public static final float **RIGHT_ALIGNMENT** ;
    public static final float **TOP_ALIGNMENT** ;
    // Constructors
    protected **Component**() ;
    // Static methods
    // Instance methods
    public boolean **action**(Object what, Event evt) ;
    public void **add**(PopupMenu popup) ; // Since 1.1
    public synchronized void **addComponentListener**(ComponentListener l) ; // Since 1.1
    public synchronized void **addFocusListener**(FocusListener l) ; // Since 1.1
    public void **addHierarchyBoundsListener**(HierarchyBoundsListener l) ; // Since 1.3
    public void **addHierarchyListener**(HierarchyListener l) ; // Since 1.3
    public synchronized void **addInputMethodListener**(InputMethodListener l) ; // Since 1.2
    public synchronized void **addKeyListener**(KeyListener l) ; // Since 1.1
    public synchronized void **addMouseListener**(MouseListener l) ; // Since 1.1
    public synchronized void **addMouseMotionListener**(MouseMotionListener l) ; // Since 1.1
    public synchronized void **addMouseWheelListener**(MouseWheelListener l) ; // Since 1.4
    public void **addNotify**() ; // Since 1.0
    public void **addPropertyChangeListener**(PropertyChangeListener listener, String propertyName) ;
    public void **addPropertyChangeListener**(PropertyChangeListener listener) ;
    public void **applyComponentOrientation**(ComponentOrientation orientation) ; // Since 1.4
    public boolean **areFocusTraversalKeysSet**(int id) ; // Since 1.4
    public Rectangle **bounds**() ;
    public int **checkImage**(ImageObserver observer, Image image) ; // Since 1.0
    public int **checkImage**(ImageObserver observer, int height, int width, Image image) ; // Since 1.0
    protected AWTEvent **coalesceEvents**(AWTEvent newEvent, AWTEvent existingEvent) ;
    public boolean **contains**(int y, int x) ; // Since 1.1
    public boolean **contains**(Point p) ; // Since 1.1
    public Image **createImage**(ImageProducer producer) ; // Since 1.0
    public Image **createImage**(int height, int width) ; // Since 1.0
    public VolatileImage **createVolatileImage**(ImageCapabilities caps, int height, int width) throws
        AWTException ; // Since 1.4
    public VolatileImage **createVolatileImage**(int height, int width) ; // Since 1.4
    public void **deliverEvent**(Event e) ;
    public void **disable**() ;
    protected final void **disableEvents**(long eventsToDisable) ; // Since 1.1

public final void **dispatchEvent**(AWTEvent e) ;
public void **doLayout**() ;
public void **enable**() ;
public void **enable**(boolean b) ;
protected final void **enableEvents**(long eventsToEnable) ; // Since 1.1
public void **enableInputMethods**(boolean enable) ; // Since 1.2
public void **firePropertyChange**(double newValue, double oldValue, String propertyName) ; // Since 1.5
protected void **firePropertyChange**(Object newValue, Object oldValue, String propertyName) ;
public void **firePropertyChange**(float newValue, float oldValue, String propertyName) ; // Since 1.5
protected void **firePropertyChange**(int newValue, int oldValue, String propertyName) ; // Since 1.4
public void **firePropertyChange**(long newValue, long oldValue, String propertyName) ; // Since 1.5
public void **firePropertyChange**(short newValue, short oldValue, String propertyName) ; // Since 1.5
public void **firePropertyChange**(byte newValue, byte oldValue, String propertyName) ; // Since 1.5
protected void **firePropertyChange**(boolean newValue, boolean oldValue, String propertyName) ; // Since 1.4
public void **firePropertyChange**(char newValue, char oldValue, String propertyName) ; // Since 1.5
public AccessibleContext **getAccessibleContext**() ; // Since 1.3
public float **getAlignmentX**() ;
public float **getAlignmentY**() ;
public Color **getBackground**() ; // Since 1.0
public int **getBaseline**(int height, int width) ; // Since 1.6
public Component.BaselineResizeBehavior **getBaselineResizeBehavior**() ; // Since 1.6
public Rectangle **getBounds**(Rectangle rv) ;
public Rectangle **getBounds**() ;
public ColorModel **getColorModel**() ; // Since 1.0
public Component **getComponentAt**(Point p) ; // Since 1.1
public Component **getComponentAt**(int y, int x) ; // Since 1.0
public synchronized ComponentListener **getComponentListeners**() ; // Since 1.4
public ComponentOrientation **getComponentOrientation**() ;
public Cursor **getCursor**() ; // Since 1.1
public synchronized DropTarget **getDropTarget**() ;
public Container **getFocusCycleRootAncestor**() ; // Since 1.4
public synchronized FocusListener **getFocusListeners**() ; // Since 1.4
public Set<AWTKeyStroke> **getFocusTraversalKeys**(int id) ; // Since 1.4
public boolean **getFocusTraversalKeysEnabled**() ; // Since 1.4
public Font **getFont**() ; // Since 1.0
public FontMetrics **getFontMetrics**(Font font) ; // Since 1.0
public Color **getForeground**() ; // Since 1.0
public Graphics **getGraphics**() ; // Since 1.0
public GraphicsConfiguration **getGraphicsConfiguration**() ; // Since 1.3
public int **getHeight**() ; // Since 1.2
public synchronized HierarchyBoundsListener **getHierarchyBoundsListeners**() ; // Since 1.4
public synchronized HierarchyListener **getHierarchyListeners**() ; // Since 1.4
public boolean **getIgnoreRepaint**() ; // Since 1.4

public InputContext **getInputContext**() ; // Since 1.2
public synchronized InputMethodListener **getInputMethodListeners**() ; // Since 1.4
public InputMethodRequests **getInputMethodRequests**() ; // Since 1.2
public synchronized KeyListener **getKeyListeners**() ; // Since 1.4
public T **getListeners**(Class<T> listenerType) ; // Since 1.3
public Locale **getLocale**() ; // Since 1.1
public Point **getLocation**(Point rv) ;
public Point **getLocation**() ; // Since 1.1
public Point **getLocationOnScreen**() ;
public Dimension **getMaximumSize**() ;
public Dimension **getMinimumSize**() ;
public synchronized MouseListener **getMouseListeners**() ; // Since 1.4
public synchronized MouseMotionListener **getMouseMotionListeners**() ; // Since 1.4
public Point **getMousePosition**() throws HeadlessException ; // Since 1.5
public synchronized MouseWheelListener **getMouseWheelListeners**() ; // Since 1.4
public String **getName**() ; // Since 1.1
public Container **getParent**() ; // Since 1.0
public ComponentPeer **getPeer**() ;
public Dimension **getPreferredSize**() ;
public PropertyChangeListener **getPropertyChangeListeners**(String propertyName) ; // Since 1.4
public PropertyChangeListener **getPropertyChangeListeners**() ; // Since 1.4
public Dimension **getSize**() ; // Since 1.1
public Dimension **getSize**(Dimension rv) ;
public Toolkit **getToolkit**() ; // Since 1.0
public final Object **getTreeLock**() ;
public int **getWidth**() ; // Since 1.2
public int **getX**() ; // Since 1.2
public int **getY**() ; // Since 1.2
public boolean **gotFocus**(Object what, Event evt) ;
public boolean **handleEvent**(Event evt) ;
public boolean **hasFocus**() ; // Since 1.2
public void **hide**() ;
public boolean **imageUpdate**(int h, int w, int y, int x, int infoflags, Image img) ; // Since 1.0
public boolean **inside**(int y, int x) ;
public void **invalidate**() ; // Since 1.0
public boolean **isBackgroundSet**() ; // Since 1.4
public boolean **isCursorSet**() ; // Since 1.4
public boolean **isDisplayable**() ; // Since 1.2
public boolean **isDoubleBuffered**() ;
public boolean **isEnabled**() ; // Since 1.0
public boolean **isFocusable**() ; // Since 1.4
public boolean **isFocusCycleRoot**(Container container) ; // Since 1.4
public boolean **isFocusOwner**() ; // Since 1.4
public boolean **isFocusTraversable**() ; // Since 1.1
public boolean **isFontSet**() ; // Since 1.4
public boolean **isForegroundSet**() ; // Since 1.4

public boolean **isLightweight**() ; // Since 1.2
public boolean **isMaximumSizeSet**() ; // Since 1.5
public boolean **isMinimumSizeSet**() ; // Since 1.5
public boolean **isOpaque**() ; // Since 1.2
public boolean **isPreferredSizeSet**() ; // Since 1.5
public boolean **isShowing**() ; // Since 1.0
public boolean **isValid**() ; // Since 1.0
public boolean **isVisible**() ; // Since 1.0
public boolean **keyDown**(int key, Event evt) ;
public boolean **keyUp**(int key, Event evt) ;
public void **layout**() ;
public void **list**(PrintWriter out) ; // Since 1.1
public void **list**() ; // Since 1.0
public void **list**(PrintStream out) ; // Since 1.0
public void **list**(int indent, PrintStream out) ; // Since 1.0
public void **list**(int indent, PrintWriter out) ; // Since 1.1
public Component **locate**(int y, int x) ;
public Point **location**() ;
public boolean **lostFocus**(Object what, Event evt) ;
public Dimension **minimumSize**() ;
public boolean **mouseDown**(int y, int x, Event evt) ;
public boolean **mouseDrag**(int y, int x, Event evt) ;
public boolean **mouseEnter**(int y, int x, Event evt) ;
public boolean **mouseExit**(int y, int x, Event evt) ;
public boolean **mouseMove**(int y, int x, Event evt) ;
public boolean **mouseUp**(int y, int x, Event evt) ;
public void **move**(int y, int x) ;
public void **nextFocus**() ;
public void **paint**(Graphics g) ; // Since 1.0
public void **paintAll**(Graphics g) ; // Since 1.0
protected String **paramString**() ; // Since 1.0
public boolean **postEvent**(Event e) ;
public Dimension **preferredSize**() ;
public boolean **prepareImage**(ImageObserver observer, int height, int width, Image image) ; // Since 1.0
public boolean **prepareImage**(ImageObserver observer, Image image) ; // Since 1.0
public void **print**(Graphics g) ; // Since 1.0
public void **printAll**(Graphics g) ; // Since 1.0
protected void **processComponentEvent**(ComponentEvent e) ; // Since 1.1
protected void **processEvent**(AWTEvent e) ; // Since 1.1
protected void **processFocusEvent**(FocusEvent e) ; // Since 1.1
protected void **processHierarchyBoundsEvent**(HierarchyEvent e) ; // Since 1.3
protected void **processHierarchyEvent**(HierarchyEvent e) ; // Since 1.3
protected void **processInputMethodEvent**(InputMethodEvent e) ; // Since 1.2
protected void **processKeyEvent**(KeyEvent e) ; // Since 1.1
protected void **processMouseEvent**(MouseEvent e) ; // Since 1.1

protected void **processMouseMotionEvent**(MouseEvent e) ; // Since 1.1

protected void **processMouseWheelEvent**(MouseWheelEvent e) ; // Since 1.4

public void **remove**(MenuComponent popup) ; // Since 1.1

public synchronized void **removeComponentListener**(ComponentListener l) ; // Since 1.1

public synchronized void **removeFocusListener**(FocusListener l) ; // Since 1.1

public void **removeHierarchyBoundsListener**(HierarchyBoundsListener l) ; // Since 1.3

public void **removeHierarchyListener**(HierarchyListener l) ; // Since 1.3

public synchronized void **removeInputMethodListener**(InputMethodListener l) ; // Since 1.2

public synchronized void **removeKeyListener**(KeyListener l) ; // Since 1.1

public synchronized void **removeMouseListener**(MouseListener l) ; // Since 1.1

public synchronized void **removeMouseMotionListener**(MouseMotionListener l) ; // Since 1.1

public synchronized void **removeMouseWheelListener**(MouseWheelListener l) ; // Since 1.4

public void **removeNotify**() ; // Since 1.0

public void **removePropertyChangeListener**(PropertyChangeListener listener) ;

public void **removePropertyChangeListener**(PropertyChangeListener listener, String
    propertyName) ;

public void **repaint**(long tm) ; // Since 1.0

public void **repaint**(int height, int width, int y, int x, long tm) ; // Since 1.0

public void **repaint**(int height, int width, int y, int x) ; // Since 1.0

public void **repaint**() ; // Since 1.0

protected boolean **requestFocus**(boolean temporary) ; // Since 1.4

public void **requestFocus**() ; // Since 1.0

public boolean **requestFocusInWindow**() ; // Since 1.4

protected boolean **requestFocusInWindow**(boolean temporary) ; // Since 1.4

public void **reshape**(int height, int width, int y, int x) ;

public void **resize**(int height, int width) ;

public void **resize**(Dimension d) ;

public void **setBackground**(Color c) ; // Since 1.0

public void **setBounds**(int height, int width, int y, int x) ; // Since 1.1

public void **setBounds**(Rectangle r) ; // Since 1.1

public void **setComponentOrientation**(ComponentOrientation o) ;

public void **setCursor**(Cursor cursor) ; // Since 1.1

public synchronized void **setDropTarget**(DropTarget dt) ;

public void **setEnabled**(boolean b) ; // Since 1.1

public void **setFocusable**(boolean focusable) ; // Since 1.4

public void **setFocusTraversalKeys**(Set<?> keystrokes, int id) ; // Since 1.4

public void **setFocusTraversalKeysEnabled**(boolean focusTraversalKeysEnabled) ; // Since 1.4

public void **setFont**(Font f) ; // Since 1.0

public void **setForeground**(Color c) ; // Since 1.0

public void **setIgnoreRepaint**(boolean ignoreRepaint) ; // Since 1.4

public void **setLocale**(Locale l) ; // Since 1.1

public void **setLocation**(int y, int x) ; // Since 1.1

public void **setLocation**(Point p) ; // Since 1.1

public void **setMaximumSize**(Dimension maximumSize) ; // Since 1.5

public void **setMinimumSize**(Dimension minimumSize) ; // Since 1.5

public void **setName**(String name) ; // Since 1.1

```
    public void setPreferredSize(Dimension preferredSize) ; // Since 1.5
    public void setSize(Dimension d) ; // Since 1.1
    public void setSize(int height, int width) ; // Since 1.1
    public void setVisible(boolean b) ; // Since 1.1
    public void show(boolean b) ;
    public void show() ;
    public Dimension size() ;
    public String toString() ; // Since 1.0
    public void transferFocus() ; // Since 1.1
    public void transferFocusBackward() ; // Since 1.4
    public void transferFocusUpCycle() ; // Since 1.4
    public void update(Graphics g) ; // Since 1.0
    public void validate() ; // Since 1.0
}
```

java.awt.**Component.BaselineResizeBehavior** [since 1.6]

```
public static final class Component.BaselineResizeBehavior extends
Enum<Component.BaselineResizeBehavior>
{
    // Constructors
    private Component.BaselineResizeBehavior() ;
    // Static methods
    public static Component.BaselineResizeBehavior valueOf(String name) ;
    public static final Component.BaselineResizeBehavior values() ;
}
```

java.awt.event.**ComponentAdapter** [since 1.1]

```
public abstract class ComponentAdapter  implements ComponentListener
{
    // Constructors
    public ComponentAdapter() ;
    // Instance methods
    public void componentHidden(ComponentEvent e) ;
    public void componentMoved(ComponentEvent e) ;
    public void componentResized(ComponentEvent e) ;
    public void componentShown(ComponentEvent e) ;
}
```

java.awt.image.**ComponentColorModel**

public class **ComponentColorModel** extends ColorModel
{
    // Constructors
    public **ComponentColorModel**(int transferType, int transparency, boolean isAlphaPremultiplied,
        boolean hasAlpha, ColorSpace colorSpace) ;
    public **ComponentColorModel**(int transferType, int transparency, boolean isAlphaPremultiplied,
        boolean hasAlpha, int[] bits, ColorSpace colorSpace) ;
    // Static methods
    // Instance methods
    public ColorModel **coerceData**(boolean isAlphaPremultiplied, WritableRaster raster) ;
    public SampleModel **createCompatibleSampleModel**(int h, int w) ;
    public WritableRaster **createCompatibleWritableRaster**(int h, int w) ;
    public boolean **equals**(Object obj) ;
    public int **getAlpha**(int pixel) ;
    public int **getAlpha**(Object inData) ;
    public WritableRaster **getAlphaRaster**(WritableRaster raster) ;
    public int **getBlue**(int pixel) ;
    public int **getBlue**(Object inData) ;
    public int **getComponents**(int offset, int[] components, int pixel) ;
    public int **getComponents**(int offset, int[] components, Object pixel) ;
    public int **getDataElement**(int normOffset, float[] normComponents) ; // Since 1.4
    public int **getDataElement**(int offset, int[] components) ;
    public Object **getDataElements**(Object pixel, int rgb) ;
    public Object **getDataElements**(Object obj, int normOffset, float[] normComponents) ; // Since 1.4
    public Object **getDataElements**(Object obj, int offset, int[] components) ;
    public int **getGreen**(int pixel) ;
    public int **getGreen**(Object inData) ;
    public float **getNormalizedComponents**(int normOffset, float[] normComponents, Object pixel) ; //
        Since 1.4
    public float **getNormalizedComponents**(int normOffset, float[] normComponents, int offset, int[]
        components) ;
    public int **getRed**(Object inData) ;
    public int **getRed**(int pixel) ;
    public int **getRGB**(int pixel) ;
    public int **getRGB**(Object inData) ;
    public int **getUnnormalizedComponents**(int offset, int[] components, int normOffset, float[]
        normComponents) ;
    public boolean **isCompatibleRaster**(Raster raster) ;
    public boolean **isCompatibleSampleModel**(SampleModel sm) ;
}

java.awt.event.**ComponentEvent** [since 1.1]

public class **ComponentEvent** extends AWTEvent
{
    public static final int **COMPONENT_FIRST** ;
    public static final int **COMPONENT_HIDDEN** ;
    public static final int **COMPONENT_LAST** ;
    public static final int **COMPONENT_MOVED** ;
    public static final int **COMPONENT_RESIZED** ;
    public static final int **COMPONENT_SHOWN** ;
    // Constructors
    public **ComponentEvent**(int id, Component source) ;
    // Instance methods
    public Component **getComponent**() ;
    public String **paramString**() ;
}

javax.swing.**ComponentInputMap** [since 1.3]

public class **ComponentInputMap** extends InputMap
{
    // Constructors
    public **ComponentInputMap**(JComponent component) ;
    // Instance methods
    public void **clear**() ;
    public JComponent **getComponent**() ;
    public void **put**(Object actionMapKey, KeyStroke keyStroke) ;
    public void **remove**(KeyStroke key) ;
    public void **setParent**(InputMap map) ;
}

javax.swing.plaf.**ComponentInputMapUIResource** [since 1.3]

public class **ComponentInputMapUIResource** extends ComponentInputMap implements UIResource
{
    // Constructors
    public **ComponentInputMapUIResource**(JComponent component) ;
}

java.awt.event.**ComponentListener** [since 1.1]

public interface **ComponentListener** implements EventListener
{
    // Instance methods
    public void **componentHidden**(ComponentEvent e) ;
    public void **componentMoved**(ComponentEvent e) ;
    public void **componentResized**(ComponentEvent e) ;
    public void **componentShown**(ComponentEvent e) ;
}

java.awt.**ComponentOrientation**

public final class **ComponentOrientation** implements Serializable
{
    public static final ComponentOrientation **LEFT_TO_RIGHT** ;
    public static final ComponentOrientation **RIGHT_TO_LEFT** ;
    public static final ComponentOrientation **UNKNOWN** ;
    // Constructors
    private **ComponentOrientation**(int value) ;
    // Static methods
    public static ComponentOrientation **getOrientation**(ResourceBundle bdl) ;
    public static ComponentOrientation **getOrientation**(Locale locale) ;
    // Instance methods
    public boolean **isHorizontal**() ;
    public boolean **isLeftToRight**() ;
}

java.awt.peer.**ComponentPeer**

public interface **ComponentPeer**
{
    public static final int **DEFAULT_OPERATION** ;
    public static final int **NO_EMBEDDED_CHECK** ;
    public static final int **RESET_OPERATION** ;
    public static final int **SET_BOUNDS** ;
    public static final int **SET_CLIENT_SIZE** ;

public static final int **SET_LOCATION** ;
public static final int **SET_SIZE** ;
// Instance methods
public void **applyShape**(Region shape) ; // Since 1.7
public boolean **canDetermineObscurity**() ;
public int **checkImage**(ImageObserver o, int h, int w, Image img) ;
public void **coalescePaintEvent**(PaintEvent e) ;
public void **createBuffers**(BufferCapabilities caps, int numBuffers) throws AWTException ;
public Image **createImage**(int height, int width) ;
public Image **createImage**(ImageProducer producer) ;
public VolatileImage **createVolatileImage**(int height, int width) ;
public void **destroyBuffers**() ;
public void **disable**() ;
public void **dispose**() ;
public void **enable**() ;
public void **flip**(BufferCapabilities.FlipContents flipAction) ;
public Image **getBackBuffer**() ;
public Rectangle **getBounds**() ;
public ColorModel **getColorModel**() ;
public FontMetrics **getFontMetrics**(Font font) ;
public Graphics **getGraphics**() ;
public GraphicsConfiguration **getGraphicsConfiguration**() ;
public Point **getLocationOnScreen**() ;
public Dimension **getMinimumSize**() ;
public Dimension **getPreferredSize**() ;
public Toolkit **getToolkit**() ;
public void **handleEvent**(AWTEvent e) ;
public boolean **handlesWheelScrolling**() ;
public void **hide**() ;
public boolean **isFocusable**() ;
public boolean **isObscured**() ;
public boolean **isReparentSupported**() ; // Since 1.5
public void **layout**() ;
public Dimension **minimumSize**() ;
public void **paint**(Graphics g) ;
public Dimension **preferredSize**() ;
public boolean **prepareImage**(ImageObserver o, int h, int w, Image img) ;
public void **print**(Graphics g) ;
public void **repaint**(int height, int width, int y, int x, long tm) ;
public void **reparent**(ContainerPeer newContainer) ; // Since 1.5
public boolean **requestFocus**(CausedFocusEvent.Cause cause, long time, boolean
    focusedWindowChangeAllowed, boolean temporary, Component lightweightChild) ;
public void **reshape**(int height, int width, int y, int x) ;
public void **setBackground**(Color c) ;
public void **setBounds**(int op, int height, int width, int y, int x) ;
public void **setEnabled**(boolean b) ;

```
    public void setFont(Font f) ;
    public void setForeground(Color c) ;
    public void setVisible(boolean b) ;
    public void show() ;
    public void updateCursorImmediately() ;
}
```

javax.swing.plaf.**ComponentUI**

```
public abstract class ComponentUI
{
    // Constructors
    public ComponentUI() ;
    // Static methods
    public static ComponentUI createUI(JComponent c) ;
    // Instance methods
    public boolean contains(int y, int x, JComponent c) ;
    public Accessible getAccessibleChild(int i, JComponent c) ;
    public int getAccessibleChildrenCount(JComponent c) ;
    public int getBaseline(int height, int width, JComponent c) ; // Since 1.6
    public Component.BaselineResizeBehavior getBaselineResizeBehavior(JComponent c) ; // Since 1.6
    public Dimension getMaximumSize(JComponent c) ;
    public Dimension getMinimumSize(JComponent c) ;
    public Dimension getPreferredSize(JComponent c) ;
    public void installUI(JComponent c) ;
    public void paint(JComponent c, Graphics g) ;
    public void uninstallUI(JComponent c) ;
    public void update(JComponent c, Graphics g) ;
}
```

javax.swing.text.**ComponentView**

```
public class ComponentView extends View
{
    // Constructors
    public ComponentView(Element elem) ;
    // Instance methods
    protected Component createComponent() ;
    public float getAlignment(int axis) ;
    public final Component getComponent() ;
    public float getMaximumSpan(int axis) ;
```

```
    public float getMinimumSpan(int axis) ;
    public float getPreferredSpan(int axis) ;
    public Shape modelToView(Position.Bias b, Shape a, int pos) throws BadLocationException ;
    public void paint(Shape a, Graphics g) ;
    public void setParent(View p) ;
    public int viewToModel(javax.swing.text.Position.Bias[] bias, Shape a, float y, float x) ;
}
```

java.awt.**Composite**

```
public interface Composite
{
    // Instance methods
    public CompositeContext createContext(RenderingHints hints, ColorModel dstColorModel,
        ColorModel srcColorModel) ;
}
```

java.awt.**CompositeContext**

```
public interface CompositeContext
{
    // Instance methods
    public void compose(WritableRaster dstOut, Raster dstIn, Raster src) ;
    public void dispose() ;
}
```

javax.swing.text.**CompositeView**

```
public abstract class CompositeView extends View
{
    // Constructors
    public CompositeView(Element elem) ;
    // Instance methods
    protected abstract void childAllocation(Rectangle a, int index) ;
    protected boolean flipEastAndWestAtEnds(Position.Bias bias, int position) ;
    protected short getBottomInset() ;
    public Shape getChildAllocation(Shape a, int index) ;
    protected Rectangle getInsideAllocation(Shape a) ;
```

protected short **getLeftInset**() ;
protected int **getNextEastWestVisualPositionFrom**(javax.swing.text.Position.Bias[] biasRet, int direction, Shape a, Position.Bias b, int pos) throws BadLocationException ;
protected int **getNextNorthSouthVisualPositionFrom**(javax.swing.text.Position.Bias[] biasRet, int direction, Shape a, Position.Bias b, int pos) throws BadLocationException ;
public int **getNextVisualPositionFrom**(javax.swing.text.Position.Bias[] biasRet, int direction, Shape a, Position.Bias b, int pos) throws BadLocationException ;
protected short **getRightInset**() ;
protected short **getTopInset**() ;
public View **getView**(int n) ;
protected abstract View **getViewAtPoint**(Rectangle alloc, int y, int x) ;
protected View **getViewAtPosition**(Rectangle a, int pos) ;
public int **getViewCount**() ;
public int **getViewIndex**(Position.Bias b, int pos) ; // Since 1.3
protected int **getViewIndexAtPosition**(int pos) ;
protected abstract boolean **isAfter**(Rectangle alloc, int y, int x) ;
protected abstract boolean **isBefore**(Rectangle alloc, int y, int x) ;
protected void **loadChildren**(ViewFactory f) ;
public Shape **modelToView**(Shape a, Position.Bias b1, int p1, Position.Bias b0, int p0) throws BadLocationException ;
public Shape **modelToView**(Position.Bias b, Shape a, int pos) throws BadLocationException ;
public void **replace**(javax.swing.text.View[] views, int length, int offset) ;
protected void **setInsets**(short right, short bottom, short left, short top) ;
protected void **setParagraphInsets**(AttributeSet attr) ;
public void **setParent**(View parent) ;
public int **viewToModel**(javax.swing.text.Position.Bias[] bias, Shape a, float y, float x) ;
}

---

javax.swing.border.**CompoundBorder**

---

public class **CompoundBorder** extends AbstractBorder
{
    protected Border **insideBorder** ;
    protected Border **outsideBorder** ;
    // Constructors
    public **CompoundBorder**(Border insideBorder, Border outsideBorder) ;
    public **CompoundBorder**() ;
    // Instance methods
    public Insets **getBorderInsets**(Insets insets, Component c) ;
    public Border **getInsideBorder**() ;
    public Border **getOutsideBorder**() ;
    public boolean **isBorderOpaque**() ;
    public void **paintBorder**(int height, int width, int y, int x, Graphics g, Component c) ;
}

---

javax.swing.undo.**CompoundEdit**

public class **CompoundEdit** extends AbstractUndoableEdit
{
    protected Vector<UndoableEdit> **edits** ;
    // Constructors
    public **CompoundEdit**() ;
    // Instance methods
    public boolean **addEdit**(UndoableEdit anEdit) ;
    public boolean **canRedo**() ;
    public boolean **canUndo**() ;
    public void **die**() ;
    public void **end**() ;
    public String **getPresentationName**() ;
    public String **getRedoPresentationName**() ;
    public String **getUndoPresentationName**() ;
    public boolean **isInProgress**() ;
    public boolean **isSignificant**() ;
    protected UndoableEdit **lastEdit**() ;
    public void **redo**() throws CannotRedoException ;
    public String **toString**() ;
    public void **undo**() throws CannotUndoException ;
}

---

java.awt.**Container** [since 1.0]

public class **Container** extends Component
{
    // Constructors
    public **Container**() ;
    // Static methods
    // Instance methods
    public void **add**(Object constraints, Component comp) ; // Since 1.1
    public void **add**(int index, Object constraints, Component comp) ;
    public Component **add**(int index, Component comp) ;
    public Component **add**(Component comp, String name) ;
    public Component **add**(Component comp) ;
    public synchronized void **addContainerListener**(ContainerListener l) ;
    protected void **addImpl**(int index, Object constraints, Component comp) ; // Since 1.1
    public void **addNotify**() ;

public void **addPropertyChangeListener**(PropertyChangeListener listener) ;
public void **addPropertyChangeListener**(PropertyChangeListener listener, String propertyName) ;
public void **applyComponentOrientation**(ComponentOrientation o) ; // Since 1.4
public boolean **areFocusTraversalKeysSet**(int id) ; // Since 1.4
public int **countComponents**() ;
public void **deliverEvent**(Event e) ;
public void **doLayout**() ; // Since 1.1
public Component **findComponentAt**(Point p) ; // Since 1.2
public Component **findComponentAt**(int y, int x) ; // Since 1.2
public float **getAlignmentX**() ;
public float **getAlignmentY**() ;
public Component **getComponent**(int n) ;
public Component **getComponentAt**(Point p) ; // Since 1.1
public Component **getComponentAt**(int y, int x) ; // Since 1.1
public int **getComponentCount**() ; // Since 1.1
public Component **getComponents**() ;
public int **getComponentZOrder**(Component comp) ; // Since 1.5
public synchronized ContainerListener **getContainerListeners**() ; // Since 1.4
public Set<AWTKeyStroke> **getFocusTraversalKeys**(int id) ; // Since 1.4
public FocusTraversalPolicy **getFocusTraversalPolicy**() ; // Since 1.4
public Insets **getInsets**() ; // Since 1.1
public LayoutManager **getLayout**() ;
public T **getListeners**(Class<T> listenerType) ; // Since 1.3
public Dimension **getMaximumSize**() ;
public Dimension **getMinimumSize**() ; // Since 1.1
public Point **getMousePosition**(boolean allowChildren) throws HeadlessException ; // Since 1.5
public Dimension **getPreferredSize**() ;
public Insets **insets**() ;
public void **invalidate**() ;
public boolean **isAncestorOf**(Component c) ; // Since 1.1
public boolean **isFocusCycleRoot**() ; // Since 1.4
public boolean **isFocusCycleRoot**(Container container) ; // Since 1.4
public final boolean **isFocusTraversalPolicyProvider**() ; // Since 1.5
public boolean **isFocusTraversalPolicySet**() ; // Since 1.4
public void **layout**() ;
public void **list**(int indent, PrintStream out) ; // Since 1.0
public void **list**(int indent, PrintWriter out) ; // Since 1.1
public Component **locate**(int y, int x) ;
public Dimension **minimumSize**() ;
public void **paint**(Graphics g) ;
public void **paintComponents**(Graphics g) ;
protected String **paramString**() ;
public Dimension **preferredSize**() ;
public void **print**(Graphics g) ;
public void **printComponents**(Graphics g) ;
protected void **processContainerEvent**(ContainerEvent e) ;

```
        protected void processEvent(AWTEvent e) ;
        public void remove(Component comp) ;
        public void remove(int index) ; // Since 1.1
        public void removeAll() ;
        public synchronized void removeContainerListener(ContainerListener l) ;
        public void removeNotify() ;
        public void setComponentZOrder(int index, Component comp) ; // Since 1.5
        public void setFocusCycleRoot(boolean focusCycleRoot) ; // Since 1.4
        public void setFocusTraversalKeys(Set<?> keystrokes, int id) ; // Since 1.4
        public void setFocusTraversalPolicy(FocusTraversalPolicy policy) ; // Since 1.4
        public final void setFocusTraversalPolicyProvider(boolean provider) ; // Since 1.5
        public void setFont(Font f) ; // Since 1.0
        public void setLayout(LayoutManager mgr) ;
        public void transferFocusDownCycle() ; // Since 1.4
        public void update(Graphics g) ;
        public void validate() ;
        protected void validateTree() ;
}
```

---

java.awt.event.**ContainerAdapter** [since 1.1]

```
public abstract class ContainerAdapter  implements ContainerListener
{
    // Constructors
    public ContainerAdapter() ;
    // Instance methods
    public void componentAdded(ContainerEvent e) ;
    public void componentRemoved(ContainerEvent e) ;
}
```

---

java.awt.event.**ContainerEvent** [since 1.1]

```
public class ContainerEvent extends ComponentEvent
{
    public static final int COMPONENT_ADDED ;
    public static final int COMPONENT_REMOVED ;
    public static final int CONTAINER_FIRST ;
    public static final int CONTAINER_LAST ;
    // Constructors
    public ContainerEvent(Component child, int id, Component source) ;
    // Instance methods
```

```
     public Component getChild() ;
     public Container getContainer() ;
     public String paramString() ;
}
```

java.awt.event.**ContainerListener** [since 1.1]

```
public interface ContainerListener  implements EventListener
{
     // Instance methods
     public void componentAdded(ContainerEvent e) ;
     public void componentRemoved(ContainerEvent e) ;
}
```

java.awt.**ContainerOrderFocusTraversalPolicy** [since 1.4]

```
public class ContainerOrderFocusTraversalPolicy extends FocusTraversalPolicy implements
Serializable
{
     // Constructors
     public ContainerOrderFocusTraversalPolicy() ;
     // Instance methods
     protected boolean accept(Component aComponent) ;
     public Component getComponentAfter(Component aComponent, Container aContainer) ;
     public Component getComponentBefore(Component aComponent, Container aContainer) ;
     public Component getDefaultComponent(Container aContainer) ;
     public Component getFirstComponent(Container aContainer) ;
     public boolean getImplicitDownCycleTraversal() ;
     public Component getLastComponent(Container aContainer) ;
     public void setImplicitDownCycleTraversal(boolean implicitDownCycleTraversal) ;
}
```

java.awt.peer.**ContainerPeer**

```
public interface ContainerPeer  implements ComponentPeer
{
     // Instance methods
     public void beginLayout() ;
```

```
    public void beginValidate() ;
    public void endLayout() ;
    public void endValidate() ;
    public Insets getInsets() ;
    public Insets insets() ;
    public boolean isPaintPending() ;
    public boolean isRestackSupported() ; // Since 1.5
    public void restack() ; // Since 1.5
}
```

javax.swing.text.html.parser.**ContentModel**

```
public final class ContentModel  implements Serializable
{
    public Object content ;
    public ContentModel next ;
    public int type ;
    // Constructors
    public ContentModel(ContentModel next, Object content, int type) ;
    public ContentModel(ContentModel content, int type) ;
    public ContentModel(Element content) ;
    public ContentModel() ;
    // Instance methods
    public boolean empty() ;
    public Element first() ;
    public boolean first(Object token) ;
    public void getElements(Vector<Element> elemVec) ;
    public String toString() ;
}
```

java.awt.image.**ConvolveOp**

```
public class ConvolveOp  implements RasterOp, BufferedImageOp
{
    public static final int EDGE_NO_OP ;
    public static final int EDGE_ZERO_FILL ;
    // Constructors
    public ConvolveOp(Kernel kernel) ;
    public ConvolveOp(RenderingHints hints, int edgeCondition, Kernel kernel) ;
    // Instance methods
    public BufferedImage createCompatibleDestImage(ColorModel destCM, BufferedImage src) ;
```

```
        public WritableRaster createCompatibleDestRaster(Raster src) ;
        public final BufferedImage filter(BufferedImage dst, BufferedImage src) ;
        public final WritableRaster filter(WritableRaster dst, Raster src) ;
        public final Rectangle2D getBounds2D(Raster src) ;
        public final Rectangle2D getBounds2D(BufferedImage src) ;
        public int getEdgeCondition() ;
        public final Kernel getKernel() ;
        public final Point2D getPoint2D(Point2D dstPt, Point2D srcPt) ;
        public final RenderingHints getRenderingHints() ;
}
```

java.awt.image.**CropImageFilter**

```
public class CropImageFilter extends ImageFilter
{
        // Constructors
        public CropImageFilter(int h, int w, int y, int x) ;
        // Instance methods
        public void setDimensions(int h, int w) ;
        public void setPixels(int scansize, int off, int[] pixels, ColorModel model, int h, int w, int y, int x) ;
        public void setPixels(int scansize, int off, byte[] pixels, ColorModel model, int h, int w, int y, int x) ;
        public void setProperties(Hashtable<?, ?> props) ;
}
```

javax.swing.text.html.**CSS**

```
public class CSS  implements Serializable
{
        // Constructors
        public CSS() ;
        // Static methods
        public static CSS.Attribute getAllAttributeKeys() ;
        public static final CSS.Attribute getAttribute(String name) ;
        // Instance methods
}
```

javax.swing.text.html.**CSS.Attribute**

public static final class **CSS.Attribute**
{
    public static final CSS.Attribute **BACKGROUND** ;
    public static final CSS.Attribute **BACKGROUND_ATTACHMENT** ;
    public static final CSS.Attribute **BACKGROUND_COLOR** ;
    public static final CSS.Attribute **BACKGROUND_IMAGE** ;
    public static final CSS.Attribute **BACKGROUND_POSITION** ;
    public static final CSS.Attribute **BACKGROUND_REPEAT** ;
    public static final CSS.Attribute **BORDER** ;
    public static final CSS.Attribute **BORDER_BOTTOM** ;
    public static final CSS.Attribute **BORDER_BOTTOM_COLOR** ;
    public static final CSS.Attribute **BORDER_BOTTOM_STYLE** ;
    public static final CSS.Attribute **BORDER_BOTTOM_WIDTH** ;
    public static final CSS.Attribute **BORDER_COLOR** ;
    public static final CSS.Attribute **BORDER_LEFT** ;
    public static final CSS.Attribute **BORDER_LEFT_COLOR** ;
    public static final CSS.Attribute **BORDER_LEFT_STYLE** ;
    public static final CSS.Attribute **BORDER_LEFT_WIDTH** ;
    public static final CSS.Attribute **BORDER_RIGHT** ;
    public static final CSS.Attribute **BORDER_RIGHT_COLOR** ;
    public static final CSS.Attribute **BORDER_RIGHT_STYLE** ;
    public static final CSS.Attribute **BORDER_RIGHT_WIDTH** ;
    public static final CSS.Attribute **BORDER_STYLE** ;
    public static final CSS.Attribute **BORDER_TOP** ;
    public static final CSS.Attribute **BORDER_TOP_COLOR** ;
    public static final CSS.Attribute **BORDER_TOP_STYLE** ;
    public static final CSS.Attribute **BORDER_TOP_WIDTH** ;
    public static final CSS.Attribute **BORDER_WIDTH** ;
    public static final CSS.Attribute **CLEAR** ;
    public static final CSS.Attribute **COLOR** ;
    public static final CSS.Attribute **DISPLAY** ;
    public static final CSS.Attribute **FLOAT** ;
    public static final CSS.Attribute **FONT** ;
    public static final CSS.Attribute **FONT_FAMILY** ;
    public static final CSS.Attribute **FONT_SIZE** ;
    public static final CSS.Attribute **FONT_STYLE** ;
    public static final CSS.Attribute **FONT_VARIANT** ;
    public static final CSS.Attribute **FONT_WEIGHT** ;
    public static final CSS.Attribute **HEIGHT** ;
    public static final CSS.Attribute **LETTER_SPACING** ;
    public static final CSS.Attribute **LINE_HEIGHT** ;

```
public static final CSS.Attribute LIST_STYLE ;
public static final CSS.Attribute LIST_STYLE_IMAGE ;
public static final CSS.Attribute LIST_STYLE_POSITION ;
public static final CSS.Attribute LIST_STYLE_TYPE ;
public static final CSS.Attribute MARGIN ;
public static final CSS.Attribute MARGIN_BOTTOM ;
public static final CSS.Attribute MARGIN_LEFT ;
public static final CSS.Attribute MARGIN_RIGHT ;
public static final CSS.Attribute MARGIN_TOP ;
public static final CSS.Attribute PADDING ;
public static final CSS.Attribute PADDING_BOTTOM ;
public static final CSS.Attribute PADDING_LEFT ;
public static final CSS.Attribute PADDING_RIGHT ;
public static final CSS.Attribute PADDING_TOP ;
public static final CSS.Attribute TEXT_ALIGN ;
public static final CSS.Attribute TEXT_DECORATION ;
public static final CSS.Attribute TEXT_INDENT ;
public static final CSS.Attribute TEXT_TRANSFORM ;
public static final CSS.Attribute VERTICAL_ALIGN ;
public static final CSS.Attribute WHITE_SPACE ;
public static final CSS.Attribute WIDTH ;
public static final CSS.Attribute WORD_SPACING ;
// Constructors
private CSS.Attribute(boolean inherited, String defaultValue, String name) ;
// Instance methods
public String getDefaultValue() ;
public boolean isInherited() ;
public String toString() ;
}
```

---

java.awt.geom.**CubicCurve2D** [since 1.2]

```
public abstract class CubicCurve2D  implements Cloneable, Shape
{
    // Constructors
    protected CubicCurve2D() ;
    // Static methods
    public static double getFlatness(double y2, double x2, double ctrly2, double ctrlx2, double ctrly1,
        double ctrlx1, double y1, double x1) ; // Since 1.2
    public static double getFlatness(int offset, double[] coords) ; // Since 1.2
    public static double getFlatnessSq(int offset, double[] coords) ; // Since 1.2
    public static double getFlatnessSq(double y2, double x2, double ctrly2, double ctrlx2, double ctrly1,
        double ctrlx1, double y1, double x1) ; // Since 1.2
    public static int solveCubic(double[] res, double[] eqn) ; // Since 1.3
```

```
public static int solveCubic(double[] eqn) ; // Since 1.2
public static void subdivide(int rightoff, double[] right, int leftoff, double[] left, int srcoff, double[]
    src) ; // Since 1.2
public static void subdivide(CubicCurve2D right, CubicCurve2D left, CubicCurve2D src) ; // Since
    1.2
// Instance methods
public Object clone() ; // Since 1.2
public boolean contains(double y, double x) ; // Since 1.2
public boolean contains(Point2D p) ; // Since 1.2
public boolean contains(Rectangle2D r) ; // Since 1.2
public boolean contains(double h, double w, double y, double x) ; // Since 1.2
public Rectangle getBounds() ; // Since 1.2
public abstract Point2D getCtrlP1() ; // Since 1.2
public abstract Point2D getCtrlP2() ; // Since 1.2
public abstract double getCtrlX1() ; // Since 1.2
public abstract double getCtrlX2() ; // Since 1.2
public abstract double getCtrlY1() ; // Since 1.2
public abstract double getCtrlY2() ; // Since 1.2
public double getFlatness() ; // Since 1.2
public double getFlatnessSq() ; // Since 1.2
public abstract Point2D getP1() ; // Since 1.2
public abstract Point2D getP2() ; // Since 1.2
public PathIterator getPathIterator(double flatness, AffineTransform at) ; // Since 1.2
public PathIterator getPathIterator(AffineTransform at) ; // Since 1.2
public abstract double getX1() ; // Since 1.2
public abstract double getX2() ; // Since 1.2
public abstract double getY1() ; // Since 1.2
public abstract double getY2() ; // Since 1.2
public boolean intersects(Rectangle2D r) ; // Since 1.2
public boolean intersects(double h, double w, double y, double x) ; // Since 1.2
public void setCurve(int offset, double[] coords) ; // Since 1.2
public void setCurve(CubicCurve2D c) ; // Since 1.2
public void setCurve(int offset, java.awt.geom.Point2D[] pts) ; // Since 1.2
public void setCurve(Point2D p2, Point2D cp2, Point2D cp1, Point2D p1) ; // Since 1.2
public abstract void setCurve(double y2, double x2, double ctrly2, double ctrlx2, double ctrly1,
    double ctrlx1, double y1, double x1) ; // Since 1.2
public void subdivide(CubicCurve2D right, CubicCurve2D left) ; // Since 1.2
}
```

---

java.awt.geom.**CubicCurve2D.Double** [since 1.2]

```
public static class CubicCurve2D.Double extends CubicCurve2D implements Serializable
{
    public double ctrlx1 ;
```

```
    public double ctrlx2 ;
    public double ctrly1 ;
    public double ctrly2 ;
    public double x1 ;
    public double x2 ;
    public double y1 ;
    public double y2 ;
    // Constructors
    public CubicCurve2D.Double(double y2, double x2, double ctrly2, double ctrlx2, double ctrly1,
        double ctrlx1, double y1, double x1) ;
    public CubicCurve2D.Double() ;
    // Instance methods
    public Rectangle2D getBounds2D() ; // Since 1.2
    public Point2D getCtrlP1() ; // Since 1.2
    public Point2D getCtrlP2() ; // Since 1.2
    public double getCtrlX1() ; // Since 1.2
    public double getCtrlX2() ; // Since 1.2
    public double getCtrlY1() ; // Since 1.2
    public double getCtrlY2() ; // Since 1.2
    public Point2D getP1() ; // Since 1.2
    public Point2D getP2() ; // Since 1.2
    public double getX1() ; // Since 1.2
    public double getX2() ; // Since 1.2
    public double getY1() ; // Since 1.2
    public double getY2() ; // Since 1.2
    public void setCurve(double y2, double x2, double ctrly2, double ctrlx2, double ctrly1, double ctrlx1,
        double y1, double x1) ; // Since 1.2
}
```

---

java.awt.geom.**CubicCurve2D.Float** [since 1.2]

```
public static class CubicCurve2D.Float extends CubicCurve2D implements Serializable
{
    public float ctrlx1 ;
    public float ctrlx2 ;
    public float ctrly1 ;
    public float ctrly2 ;
    public float x1 ;
    public float x2 ;
    public float y1 ;
    public float y2 ;
    // Constructors
    public CubicCurve2D.Float(float y2, float x2, float ctrly2, float ctrlx2, float ctrly1, float ctrlx1, float
        y1, float x1) ;
```

```
    public CubicCurve2D.Float() ;
    // Instance methods
    public Rectangle2D getBounds2D() ; // Since 1.2
    public Point2D getCtrlP1() ; // Since 1.2
    public Point2D getCtrlP2() ; // Since 1.2
    public double getCtrlX1() ; // Since 1.2
    public double getCtrlX2() ; // Since 1.2
    public double getCtrlY1() ; // Since 1.2
    public double getCtrlY2() ; // Since 1.2
    public Point2D getP1() ; // Since 1.2
    public Point2D getP2() ; // Since 1.2
    public double getX1() ; // Since 1.2
    public double getX2() ; // Since 1.2
    public double getY1() ; // Since 1.2
    public double getY2() ; // Since 1.2
    public void setCurve(double y2, double x2, double ctrly2, double ctrlx2, double ctrly1, double ctrlx1,
        double y1, double x1) ; // Since 1.2
    public void setCurve(float y2, float x2, float ctrly2, float ctrlx2, float ctrly1, float ctrlx1, float y1,
        float x1) ; // Since 1.2
}
```

java.awt.**Cursor**

```
public class Cursor  implements Serializable
{
    public static final int CROSSHAIR_CURSOR ;
    public static final int CUSTOM_CURSOR ;
    public static final int DEFAULT_CURSOR ;
    public static final int E_RESIZE_CURSOR ;
    public static final int HAND_CURSOR ;
    public static final int MOVE_CURSOR ;
    public static final int NE_RESIZE_CURSOR ;
    public static final int NW_RESIZE_CURSOR ;
    public static final int N_RESIZE_CURSOR ;
    protected static Cursor predefined ;
    public static final int SE_RESIZE_CURSOR ;
    public static final int SW_RESIZE_CURSOR ;
    public static final int S_RESIZE_CURSOR ;
    public static final int TEXT_CURSOR ;
    public static final int WAIT_CURSOR ;
    public static final int W_RESIZE_CURSOR ;
    protected String name ;
    // Constructors
    protected Cursor(String name) ;
```

```
    public Cursor(int type) ;
    // Static methods
    public static Cursor getDefaultCursor() ;
    public static Cursor getPredefinedCursor(int type) ;
    public static Cursor getSystemCustomCursor(String name) throws AWTException,
        HeadlessException ;
    // Instance methods
    public String getName() ; // Since 1.2
    public int getType() ;
    public String toString() ; // Since 1.2
}
```

java.awt.image.**DataBufferDouble** [since 1.4]

```
public final class DataBufferDouble extends DataBuffer
{
    // Constructors
    public DataBufferDouble(int[] offsets, int size, double[][] dataArray) ;
    public DataBufferDouble(int size, double[][] dataArray) ;
    public DataBufferDouble(int offset, int size, double[] dataArray) ;
    public DataBufferDouble(int size, double[] dataArray) ;
    public DataBufferDouble(int numBanks, int size) ;
    public DataBufferDouble(int size) ;
    // Instance methods
    public double getBankData() ;
    public double getData() ;
    public double getData(int bank) ;
    public int getElem(int i) ;
    public int getElem(int i, int bank) ;
    public double getElemDouble(int i, int bank) ;
    public double getElemDouble(int i) ;
    public float getElemFloat(int i) ;
    public float getElemFloat(int i, int bank) ;
    public void setElem(int val, int i, int bank) ;
    public void setElem(int val, int i) ;
    public void setElemDouble(double val, int i) ;
    public void setElemDouble(double val, int i, int bank) ;
    public void setElemFloat(float val, int i) ;
    public void setElemFloat(float val, int i, int bank) ;
}
```

java.awt.image.**DataBufferFloat** [since 1.4]

public final class **DataBufferFloat** extends DataBuffer
{
    // Constructors
    public **DataBufferFloat**(int[] offsets, int size, float[][] dataArray) ;
    public **DataBufferFloat**(int size, float[][] dataArray) ;
    public **DataBufferFloat**(int offset, int size, float[] dataArray) ;
    public **DataBufferFloat**(int size, float[] dataArray) ;
    public **DataBufferFloat**(int numBanks, int size) ;
    public **DataBufferFloat**(int size) ;
    // Instance methods
    public float **getBankData**() ;
    public float **getData**() ;
    public float **getData**(int bank) ;
    public int **getElem**(int i) ;
    public int **getElem**(int i, int bank) ;
    public double **getElemDouble**(int i, int bank) ;
    public double **getElemDouble**(int i) ;
    public float **getElemFloat**(int i) ;
    public float **getElemFloat**(int i, int bank) ;
    public void **setElem**(int val, int i, int bank) ;
    public void **setElem**(int val, int i) ;
    public void **setElemDouble**(double val, int i) ;
    public void **setElemDouble**(double val, int i, int bank) ;
    public void **setElemFloat**(float val, int i) ;
    public void **setElemFloat**(float val, int i, int bank) ;
}

java.awt.datatransfer.**DataFlavor**

public class **DataFlavor** implements Cloneable, Externalizable
{
    public static final DataFlavor **imageFlavor** ;
    public static final DataFlavor **javaFileListFlavor** ;
    public static final String **javaJVMLocalObjectMimeType** ;
    public static final String **javaRemoteObjectMimeType** ;
    public static final String **javaSerializedObjectMimeType** ;
    public static final DataFlavor **plainTextFlavor** ;
    public static final DataFlavor **stringFlavor** ;

```
// Constructors
public DataFlavor(String mimeType) ;
public DataFlavor(ClassLoader classLoader, String humanPresentableName, String mimeType) ;
public DataFlavor(String humanPresentableName, String mimeType) ;
public DataFlavor(String humanPresentableName, Class<?> representationClass) ;
private DataFlavor(String humanPresentableName, Class representationClass,
    MimeTypeParameterList params, String subType, String primaryType) ;
public DataFlavor() ;
// Static methods
public static final DataFlavor getTextPlainUnicodeFlavor() ; // Since 1.3
public static final DataFlavor selectBestTextFlavor(java.awt.datatransfer.DataFlavor[]
    availableFlavors) ; // Since 1.3
protected static final Class<?> tryToLoadClass(ClassLoader fallback, String className) throws
    ClassNotFoundException ;
// Instance methods
public Object clone() throws CloneNotSupportedException ;
public boolean equals(String s) ;
public boolean equals(DataFlavor that) ;
public boolean equals(Object o) ;
public final Class<?> getDefaultRepresentationClass() ;
public final String getDefaultRepresentationClassAsString() ;
public String getHumanPresentableName() ;
public String getMimeType() ;
public String getParameter(String paramName) ;
public String getPrimaryType() ;
public Reader getReaderForText(Transferable transferable) throws UnsupportedFlavorException,
    IOException ; // Since 1.3
public Class<?> getRepresentationClass() ;
public String getSubType() ;
public int hashCode() ;
public boolean isFlavorJavaFileListType() ;
public boolean isFlavorRemoteObjectType() ;
public boolean isFlavorSerializedObjectType() ;
public boolean isFlavorTextType() ; // Since 1.4
public boolean isMimeTypeEqual(String mimeType) ;
public final boolean isMimeTypeEqual(DataFlavor dataFlavor) ;
public boolean isMimeTypeSerializedObject() ;
public boolean isRepresentationClassByteBuffer() ; // Since 1.4
public boolean isRepresentationClassCharBuffer() ; // Since 1.4
public boolean isRepresentationClassInputStream() ;
public boolean isRepresentationClassReader() ; // Since 1.4
public boolean isRepresentationClassRemote() ;
public boolean isRepresentationClassSerializable() ;
public boolean match(DataFlavor that) ; // Since 1.3
protected String normalizeMimeType(String mimeType) ;
protected String normalizeMimeTypeParameter(String parameterValue, String parameterName) ;
```

```
    public synchronized void readExternal(ObjectInput is) throws IOException,
        ClassNotFoundException ;
    public void setHumanPresentableName(String humanPresentableName) ;
    public String toString() ;
    public synchronized void writeExternal(ObjectOutput os) throws IOException ;
}
```

javax.swing.text.**DateFormatter** [since 1.4]

```
public class DateFormatter extends InternationalFormatter
{
    // Constructors
    public DateFormatter(DateFormat format) ;
    public DateFormatter() ;
    // Instance methods
    public void setFormat(DateFormat format) ;
}
```

javax.swing.**DebugGraphics**

```
public class DebugGraphics extends Graphics
{
    public static final int BUFFERED_OPTION ;
    public static final int FLASH_OPTION ;
    public static final int LOG_OPTION ;
    public static final int NONE_OPTION ;
    // Constructors
    public DebugGraphics(Graphics graphics) ;
    public DebugGraphics(JComponent component, Graphics graphics) ;
    public DebugGraphics() ;
    // Static methods
    public static Color flashColor() ;
    public static int flashCount() ;
    public static int flashTime() ;
    public static PrintStream logStream() ;
    public static void setFlashColor(Color flashColor) ;
    public static void setFlashCount(int flashCount) ;
    public static void setFlashTime(int flashTime) ;
    public static void setLogStream(PrintStream stream) ;
    // Instance methods
    public void clearRect(int height, int width, int y, int x) ;
```

public void **clipRect**(int height, int width, int y, int x) ;
public void **copyArea**(int destY, int destX, int height, int width, int y, int x) ;
public Graphics **create**() ;
public Graphics **create**(int height, int width, int y, int x) ;
public void **dispose**() ;
public void **draw3DRect**(boolean raised, int height, int width, int y, int x) ;
public void **drawArc**(int arcAngle, int startAngle, int height, int width, int y, int x) ;
public void **drawBytes**(int y, int x, int length, int offset, byte[] data) ;
public void **drawChars**(int y, int x, int length, int offset, char[] data) ;
public boolean **drawImage**(ImageObserver observer, Color bgcolor, int height, int width, int y, int x,
    Image img) ;
public boolean **drawImage**(ImageObserver observer, Color bgcolor, int y, int x, Image img) ;
public boolean **drawImage**(ImageObserver observer, int sy2, int sx2, int sy1, int sx1, int dy2, int dx2,
    int dy1, int dx1, Image img) ;
public boolean **drawImage**(ImageObserver observer, Color bgcolor, int sy2, int sx2, int sy1, int sx1,
    int dy2, int dx2, int dy1, int dx1, Image img) ;
public boolean **drawImage**(ImageObserver observer, int height, int width, int y, int x, Image img) ;
public boolean **drawImage**(ImageObserver observer, int y, int x, Image img) ;
public void **drawLine**(int y2, int x2, int y1, int x1) ;
public void **drawOval**(int height, int width, int y, int x) ;
public void **drawPolygon**(int nPoints, int[] yPoints, int[] xPoints) ;
public void **drawPolyline**(int nPoints, int[] yPoints, int[] xPoints) ;
public void **drawRect**(int height, int width, int y, int x) ;
public void **drawRoundRect**(int arcHeight, int arcWidth, int height, int width, int y, int x) ;
public void **drawString**(int y, int x, String aString) ;
public void **drawString**(int y, int x, AttributedCharacterIterator iterator) ;
public void **fill3DRect**(boolean raised, int height, int width, int y, int x) ;
public void **fillArc**(int arcAngle, int startAngle, int height, int width, int y, int x) ;
public void **fillOval**(int height, int width, int y, int x) ;
public void **fillPolygon**(int nPoints, int[] yPoints, int[] xPoints) ;
public void **fillRect**(int height, int width, int y, int x) ;
public void **fillRoundRect**(int arcHeight, int arcWidth, int height, int width, int y, int x) ;
public Shape **getClip**() ;
public Rectangle **getClipBounds**() ;
public Color **getColor**() ;
public int **getDebugOptions**() ;
public Font **getFont**() ;
public FontMetrics **getFontMetrics**() ;
public FontMetrics **getFontMetrics**(Font f) ;
public boolean **isDrawingBuffer**() ;
public void **setClip**(int height, int width, int y, int x) ;
public void **setClip**(Shape clip) ;
public void **setColor**(Color aColor) ;
public void **setDebugOptions**(int options) ;
public void **setFont**(Font aFont) ;
public void **setPaintMode**() ;

```
        public void setXORMode(Color aColor) ;
        public void translate(int y, int x) ;
}
```

```
public class DefaultBoundedRangeModel  implements Serializable, BoundedRangeModel
{
        protected transient ChangeEvent changeEvent ;
        protected EventListenerList listenerList ;
        // Constructors
        public DefaultBoundedRangeModel(int max, int min, int extent, int value) ;
        public DefaultBoundedRangeModel() ;
        // Instance methods
        public void addChangeListener(ChangeListener l) ;
        protected void fireStateChanged() ;
        public ChangeListener getChangeListeners() ; // Since 1.4
        public int getExtent() ;
        public T getListeners(Class<T> listenerType) ; // Since 1.3
        public int getMaximum() ;
        public int getMinimum() ;
        public int getValue() ;
        public boolean getValueIsAdjusting() ;
        public void removeChangeListener(ChangeListener l) ;
        public void setExtent(int n) ;
        public void setMaximum(int n) ;
        public void setMinimum(int n) ;
        public void setRangeProperties(boolean adjusting, int newMax, int newMin, int newExtent, int
            newValue) ;
        public void setValue(int n) ;
        public void setValueIsAdjusting(boolean b) ;
        public String toString() ;
}
```

```
public class DefaultButtonModel  implements Serializable, ButtonModel
{
        public static final int ARMED ;
        public static final int ENABLED ;
        public static final int PRESSED ;
```

```
        public static final int ROLLOVER ;
        public static final int SELECTED ;
        protected String actionCommand ;
        protected transient ChangeEvent changeEvent ;
        protected ButtonGroup group ;
        protected EventListenerList listenerList ;
        protected int mnemonic ;
        protected int stateMask ;
        // Constructors
        public DefaultButtonModel() ;
        // Instance methods
        public void addActionListener(ActionListener l) ;
        public void addChangeListener(ChangeListener l) ;
        public void addItemListener(ItemListener l) ;
        protected void fireActionPerformed(ActionEvent e) ;
        protected void fireItemStateChanged(ItemEvent e) ;
        protected void fireStateChanged() ;
        public String getActionCommand() ;
        public ActionListener getActionListeners() ; // Since 1.4
        public ChangeListener getChangeListeners() ; // Since 1.4
        public ButtonGroup getGroup() ; // Since 1.3
        public ItemListener getItemListeners() ; // Since 1.4
        public T getListeners(Class<T> listenerType) ; // Since 1.3
        public int getMnemonic() ;
        public Object getSelectedObjects() ;
        public boolean isArmed() ;
        public boolean isEnabled() ;
        public boolean isPressed() ;
        public boolean isRollover() ;
        public boolean isSelected() ;
        public void removeActionListener(ActionListener l) ;
        public void removeChangeListener(ChangeListener l) ;
        public void removeItemListener(ItemListener l) ;
        public void setActionCommand(String actionCommand) ;
        public void setArmed(boolean b) ;
        public void setEnabled(boolean b) ;
        public void setGroup(ButtonGroup group) ;
        public void setMnemonic(int key) ;
        public void setPressed(boolean b) ;
        public void setRollover(boolean b) ;
        public void setSelected(boolean b) ;
}
```

javax.swing.text.**DefaultCaret**

public class **DefaultCaret** extends Rectangle implements MouseMotionListener, MouseListener, FocusListener, Caret
{
    public static final int **ALWAYS_UPDATE** ;
    public static final int **NEVER_UPDATE** ;
    public static final int **UPDATE_WHEN_ON_EDT** ;
    protected transient ChangeEvent **changeEvent** ;
    protected EventListenerList **listenerList** ;
    // Constructors
    public **DefaultCaret**() ;
    // Instance methods
    public void **addChangeListener**(ChangeListener l) ;
    protected void **adjustVisibility**(Rectangle nloc) ;
    protected synchronized void **damage**(Rectangle r) ;
    public void **deinstall**(JTextComponent c) ;
    public boolean **equals**(Object obj) ;
    protected void **fireStateChanged**() ;
    public void **focusGained**(FocusEvent e) ;
    public void **focusLost**(FocusEvent e) ;
    public int **getBlinkRate**() ;
    public ChangeListener **getChangeListeners**() ; // Since 1.4
    protected final JTextComponent **getComponent**() ;
    public int **getDot**() ;
    public Position.Bias **getDotBias**() ; // Since 1.6
    public T **getListeners**(Class<T> listenerType) ; // Since 1.3
    public Point **getMagicCaretPosition**() ;
    public int **getMark**() ;
    public Position.Bias **getMarkBias**() ; // Since 1.6
    protected Highlighter.HighlightPainter **getSelectionPainter**() ;
    public int **getUpdatePolicy**() ; // Since 1.5
    public void **install**(JTextComponent c) ;
    public boolean **isActive**() ; // Since 1.5
    public boolean **isSelectionVisible**() ;
    public boolean **isVisible**() ;
    public void **mouseClicked**(MouseEvent e) ;
    public void **mouseDragged**(MouseEvent e) ;
    public void **mouseEntered**(MouseEvent e) ;
    public void **mouseExited**(MouseEvent e) ;
    public void **mouseMoved**(MouseEvent e) ;
    public void **mousePressed**(MouseEvent e) ;
    public void **mouseReleased**(MouseEvent e) ;

    protected void **moveCaret**(MouseEvent e) ;
    public void **moveDot**(int dot) ;
    public void **moveDot**(Position.Bias dotBias, int dot) ; // Since 1.6
    public void **paint**(Graphics g) ;
    protected void **positionCaret**(MouseEvent e) ;
    public void **removeChangeListener**(ChangeListener l) ;
    protected final synchronized void **repaint**() ;
    public void **setBlinkRate**(int rate) ;
    public void **setDot**(Position.Bias dotBias, int dot) ; // Since 1.6
    public void **setDot**(int dot) ;
    public void **setMagicCaretPosition**(Point p) ;
    public void **setSelectionVisible**(boolean vis) ;
    public void **setUpdatePolicy**(int policy) ; // Since 1.5
    public void **setVisible**(boolean e) ;
    public String **toString**() ;
}

---

javax.swing.**DefaultCellEditor**

---

public class **DefaultCellEditor** extends AbstractCellEditor implements TreeCellEditor, TableCellEditor
{
    protected int **clickCountToStart** ;
    protected DefaultCellEditor.EditorDelegate **delegate** ;
    protected JComponent **editorComponent** ;
    // Constructors
    public **DefaultCellEditor**(JComboBox comboBox) ;
    public **DefaultCellEditor**(JCheckBox checkBox) ;
    public **DefaultCellEditor**(JTextField textField) ;
    // Instance methods
    public void **cancelCellEditing**() ;
    public Object **getCellEditorValue**() ;
    public int **getClickCountToStart**() ;
    public Component **getComponent**() ;
    public Component **getTableCellEditorComponent**(int column, int row, boolean isSelected, Object
        value, JTable table) ;
    public Component **getTreeCellEditorComponent**(int row, boolean leaf, boolean expanded, boolean
        isSelected, Object value, JTree tree) ;
    public boolean **isCellEditable**(EventObject anEvent) ;
    public void **setClickCountToStart**(int count) ;
    public boolean **shouldSelectCell**(EventObject anEvent) ;
    public boolean **stopCellEditing**() ;
}

javax.swing.colorchooser.**DefaultColorSelectionModel**

public class **DefaultColorSelectionModel** implements Serializable, ColorSelectionModel
{
    protected transient ChangeEvent **changeEvent** ;
    protected EventListenerList **listenerList** ;
    // Constructors
    public **DefaultColorSelectionModel**(Color color) ;
    public **DefaultColorSelectionModel**() ;
    // Instance methods
    public void **addChangeListener**(ChangeListener l) ;
    protected void **fireStateChanged**() ;
    public ChangeListener **getChangeListeners**() ; // Since 1.4
    public Color **getSelectedColor**() ;
    public void **removeChangeListener**(ChangeListener l) ;
    public void **setSelectedColor**(Color color) ;
}

javax.swing.**DefaultComboBoxModel**

public class **DefaultComboBoxModel** extends AbstractListModel implements Serializable, MutableComboBoxModel
{
    // Constructors
    public **DefaultComboBoxModel**(Vector<?> v) ;
    public **DefaultComboBoxModel**(java.lang.Object[] items) ;
    public **DefaultComboBoxModel**() ;
    // Instance methods
    public void **addElement**(Object anObject) ;
    public Object **getElementAt**(int index) ;
    public int **getIndexOf**(Object anObject) ;
    public Object **getSelectedItem**() ;
    public int **getSize**() ;
    public void **insertElementAt**(int index, Object anObject) ;
    public void **removeAllElements**() ;
    public void **removeElement**(Object anObject) ;
    public void **removeElementAt**(int index) ;
    public void **setSelectedItem**(Object anObject) ;
}

javax.swing.**DefaultDesktopManager**

public class **DefaultDesktopManager** implements Serializable, DesktopManager
{
    // Constructors
    public **DefaultDesktopManager**() ;
    // Instance methods
    public void **activateFrame**(JInternalFrame f) ;
    public void **beginDraggingFrame**(JComponent f) ;
    public void **beginResizingFrame**(int direction, JComponent f) ;
    public void **closeFrame**(JInternalFrame f) ;
    public void **deactivateFrame**(JInternalFrame f) ;
    public void **deiconifyFrame**(JInternalFrame f) ;
    public void **dragFrame**(int newY, int newX, JComponent f) ;
    public void **endDraggingFrame**(JComponent f) ;
    public void **endResizingFrame**(JComponent f) ;
    protected Rectangle **getBoundsForIconOf**(JInternalFrame f) ;
    protected Rectangle **getPreviousBounds**(JInternalFrame f) ;
    public void **iconifyFrame**(JInternalFrame f) ;
    public void **maximizeFrame**(JInternalFrame f) ;
    public void **minimizeFrame**(JInternalFrame f) ;
    public void **openFrame**(JInternalFrame f) ;
    protected void **removeIconFor**(JInternalFrame f) ;
    public void **resizeFrame**(int newHeight, int newWidth, int newY, int newX, JComponent f) ;
    public void **setBoundsForFrame**(int newHeight, int newWidth, int newY, int newX, JComponent f) ;
    protected void **setPreviousBounds**(Rectangle r, JInternalFrame f) ;
    protected void **setWasIcon**(Boolean value, JInternalFrame f) ;
    protected boolean **wasIcon**(JInternalFrame f) ;
}

javax.swing.text.**DefaultEditorKit**

public class **DefaultEditorKit** extends EditorKit
{
    public static final String **backwardAction** ;
    public static final String **beepAction** ;
    public static final String **beginAction** ;
    public static final String **beginLineAction** ;
    public static final String **beginParagraphAction** ;
    public static final String **beginWordAction** ;

```
public static final String copyAction ;
public static final String cutAction ;
public static final String defaultKeyTypedAction ;
public static final String deleteNextCharAction ;
public static final String deleteNextWordAction ;
public static final String deletePrevCharAction ;
public static final String deletePrevWordAction ;
public static final String downAction ;
public static final String endAction ;
public static final String endLineAction ;
public static final String EndOfLineStringProperty ;
public static final String endParagraphAction ;
public static final String endWordAction ;
public static final String forwardAction ;
public static final String insertBreakAction ;
public static final String insertContentAction ;
public static final String insertTabAction ;
public static final String nextWordAction ;
public static final String pageDownAction ;
public static final String pageUpAction ;
public static final String pasteAction ;
public static final String previousWordAction ;
public static final String readOnlyAction ;
public static final String selectAllAction ;
public static final String selectionBackwardAction ;
public static final String selectionBeginAction ;
public static final String selectionBeginLineAction ;
public static final String selectionBeginParagraphAction ;
public static final String selectionBeginWordAction ;
public static final String selectionDownAction ;
public static final String selectionEndAction ;
public static final String selectionEndLineAction ;
public static final String selectionEndParagraphAction ;
public static final String selectionEndWordAction ;
public static final String selectionForwardAction ;
public static final String selectionNextWordAction ;
public static final String selectionPreviousWordAction ;
public static final String selectionUpAction ;
public static final String selectLineAction ;
public static final String selectParagraphAction ;
public static final String selectWordAction ;
public static final String upAction ;
public static final String writableAction ;
// Constructors
public DefaultEditorKit() ;
// Instance methods
```

```
    public Caret createCaret() ;
    public Document createDefaultDocument() ;
    public Action getActions() ;
    public String getContentType() ;
    public ViewFactory getViewFactory() ;
    public void read(int pos, Document doc, InputStream in) throws IOException, BadLocationException
        ;
    public void read(int pos, Document doc, Reader in) throws IOException, BadLocationException ;
    public void write(int len, int pos, Document doc, OutputStream out) throws IOException,
        BadLocationException ;
    public void write(int len, int pos, Document doc, Writer out) throws IOException,
        BadLocationException ;
}
```

javax.swing.text.**DefaultEditorKit.BeepAction**

```
public static class DefaultEditorKit.BeepAction extends TextAction
{
    // Constructors
    public DefaultEditorKit.BeepAction() ;
    // Instance methods
    public void actionPerformed(ActionEvent e) ;
}
```

javax.swing.text.**DefaultEditorKit.CopyAction**

```
public static class DefaultEditorKit.CopyAction extends TextAction
{
    // Constructors
    public DefaultEditorKit.CopyAction() ;
    // Instance methods
    public void actionPerformed(ActionEvent e) ;
}
```

javax.swing.text.**DefaultEditorKit.CutAction**

```
public static class DefaultEditorKit.CutAction extends TextAction
{
```

```
    // Constructors
    public DefaultEditorKit.CutAction() ;
    // Instance methods
    public void actionPerformed(ActionEvent e) ;
}
```

---

javax.swing.text.**DefaultEditorKit.DefaultKeyTypedAction**

public static class **DefaultEditorKit.DefaultKeyTypedAction** extends TextAction
```
{
    // Constructors
    public DefaultEditorKit.DefaultKeyTypedAction() ;
    // Instance methods
    public void actionPerformed(ActionEvent e) ;
}
```

---

javax.swing.text.**DefaultEditorKit.InsertBreakAction**

public static class **DefaultEditorKit.InsertBreakAction** extends TextAction
```
{
    // Constructors
    public DefaultEditorKit.InsertBreakAction() ;
    // Instance methods
    public void actionPerformed(ActionEvent e) ;
}
```

---

javax.swing.text.**DefaultEditorKit.InsertContentAction**

public static class **DefaultEditorKit.InsertContentAction** extends TextAction
```
{
    // Constructors
    public DefaultEditorKit.InsertContentAction() ;
    // Instance methods
    public void actionPerformed(ActionEvent e) ;
}
```

javax.swing.text.**DefaultEditorKit.InsertTabAction**

public static class **DefaultEditorKit.InsertTabAction** extends TextAction
{
    // Constructors
    public **DefaultEditorKit.InsertTabAction**() ;
    // Instance methods
    public void **actionPerformed**(ActionEvent e) ;
}

javax.swing.text.**DefaultEditorKit.PasteAction**

public static class **DefaultEditorKit.PasteAction** extends TextAction
{
    // Constructors
    public **DefaultEditorKit.PasteAction**() ;
    // Instance methods
    public void **actionPerformed**(ActionEvent e) ;
}

javax.swing.**DefaultFocusManager**

public class **DefaultFocusManager** extends FocusManager
{
    // Constructors
    public **DefaultFocusManager**() ;
    // Instance methods
    public boolean **compareTabOrder**(Component b, Component a) ;
    public Component **getComponentAfter**(Component aComponent, Container aContainer) ;
    public Component **getComponentBefore**(Component aComponent, Container aContainer) ;
    public Component **getFirstComponent**(Container aContainer) ;
    public Component **getLastComponent**(Container aContainer) ;
}

---

java.awt.**DefaultFocusTraversalPolicy** [since 1.4]

---

public class **DefaultFocusTraversalPolicy** extends ContainerOrderFocusTraversalPolicy
{
    // Constructors
    public **DefaultFocusTraversalPolicy**() ;
    // Instance methods
    protected boolean **accept**(Component aComponent) ;
}

---

javax.swing.text.**DefaultFormatter** [since 1.4]

---

public class **DefaultFormatter** extends JFormattedTextField.AbstractFormatter implements Serializable, Cloneable
{
    // Constructors
    public **DefaultFormatter**() ;
    // Instance methods
    public Object **clone**() throws CloneNotSupportedException ;
    public boolean **getAllowsInvalid**() ;
    public boolean **getCommitsOnValidEdit**() ;
    protected DocumentFilter **getDocumentFilter**() ;
    protected NavigationFilter **getNavigationFilter**() ;
    public boolean **getOverwriteMode**() ;
    public Class<?> **getValueClass**() ;
    public void **install**(JFormattedTextField ftf) ;
    public void **setAllowsInvalid**(boolean allowsInvalid) ;
    public void **setCommitsOnValidEdit**(boolean commit) ;
    public void **setOverwriteMode**(boolean overwriteMode) ;
    public void **setValueClass**(Class<?> valueClass) ;
    public Object **stringToValue**(String string) throws ParseException ;
    public String **valueToString**(Object value) throws ParseException ;
}

---

javax.swing.text.**DefaultFormatterFactory** [since 1.4]

---

public class **DefaultFormatterFactory** extends JFormattedTextField.AbstractFormatterFactory implements Serializable
{
    // Constructors
    public **DefaultFormatterFactory**(JFormattedTextField.AbstractFormatter nullFormat,
        JFormattedTextField.AbstractFormatter editFormat, JFormattedTextField.AbstractFormatter
        displayFormat, JFormattedTextField.AbstractFormatter defaultFormat) ;
    public **DefaultFormatterFactory**(JFormattedTextField.AbstractFormatter editFormat,
        JFormattedTextField.AbstractFormatter displayFormat, JFormattedTextField.AbstractFormatter
        defaultFormat) ;
    public **DefaultFormatterFactory**(JFormattedTextField.AbstractFormatter displayFormat,
        JFormattedTextField.AbstractFormatter defaultFormat) ;
    public **DefaultFormatterFactory**(JFormattedTextField.AbstractFormatter defaultFormat) ;
    public **DefaultFormatterFactory**() ;
    // Instance methods
    public JFormattedTextField.AbstractFormatter **getDefaultFormatter**() ;
    public JFormattedTextField.AbstractFormatter **getDisplayFormatter**() ;
    public JFormattedTextField.AbstractFormatter **getEditFormatter**() ;
    public JFormattedTextField.AbstractFormatter **getFormatter**(JFormattedTextField source) ;
    public JFormattedTextField.AbstractFormatter **getNullFormatter**() ;
    public void **setDefaultFormatter**(JFormattedTextField.AbstractFormatter atf) ;
    public void **setDisplayFormatter**(JFormattedTextField.AbstractFormatter atf) ;
    public void **setEditFormatter**(JFormattedTextField.AbstractFormatter atf) ;
    public void **setNullFormatter**(JFormattedTextField.AbstractFormatter atf) ;
}

---

javax.swing.text.**DefaultHighlighter**

---

public class **DefaultHighlighter** extends LayeredHighlighter
{
    public static final LayeredHighlighter.LayerPainter **DefaultPainter** ;
    // Constructors
    public **DefaultHighlighter**() ;
    // Instance methods
    public Object **addHighlight**(Highlighter.HighlightPainter p, int p1, int p0) throws
        BadLocationException ;
    public void **changeHighlight**(int p1, int p0, Object tag) throws BadLocationException ;
    public void **deinstall**(JTextComponent c) ;
    public boolean **getDrawsLayeredHighlights**() ;
    public Highlighter.Highlight **getHighlights**() ;
    public void **install**(JTextComponent c) ;
    public void **paint**(Graphics g) ;
    public void **paintLayeredHighlights**(View view, JTextComponent editor, Shape viewBounds, int p1,
        int p0, Graphics g) ;

```
    public void removeAllHighlights() ;
    public void removeHighlight(Object tag) ;
    public void setDrawsLayeredHighlights(boolean newValue) ;
}
```

---

javax.swing.text.**DefaultHighlighter.DefaultHighlightPainter**

```
public static class DefaultHighlighter.DefaultHighlightPainter extends
LayeredHighlighter.LayerPainter
{
    // Constructors
    public DefaultHighlighter.DefaultHighlightPainter(Color c) ;
    // Instance methods
    public Color getColor() ;
    public void paint(JTextComponent c, Shape bounds, int offs1, int offs0, Graphics g) ;
    public Shape paintLayer(View view, JTextComponent c, Shape bounds, int offs1, int offs0, Graphics
        g) ;
}
```

---

java.awt.**DefaultKeyboardFocusManager** [since 1.4]

```
public class DefaultKeyboardFocusManager extends KeyboardFocusManager
{
    // Constructors
    public DefaultKeyboardFocusManager() ;
    // Static methods
    // Instance methods
    protected synchronized void dequeueKeyEvents(Component untilFocused, long after) ;
    protected synchronized void discardKeyEvents(Component comp) ;
    public boolean dispatchEvent(AWTEvent e) ;
    public boolean dispatchKeyEvent(KeyEvent e) ;
    public void downFocusCycle(Container aContainer) ;
    protected synchronized void enqueueKeyEvents(Component untilFocused, long after) ;
    public void focusNextComponent(Component aComponent) ;
    public void focusPreviousComponent(Component aComponent) ;
    public boolean postProcessKeyEvent(KeyEvent e) ;
    public void processKeyEvent(KeyEvent e, Component focusedComponent) ;
    public void upFocusCycle(Component aComponent) ;
}
```

javax.swing.**DefaultListCellRenderer**

public class **DefaultListCellRenderer** extends JLabel implements Serializable, ListCellRenderer
{
    protected static Border **noFocusBorder** ;
    // Constructors
    public **DefaultListCellRenderer**() ;
    // Static methods
    // Instance methods
    public void **firePropertyChange**(boolean newValue, boolean oldValue, String propertyName) ;
    protected void **firePropertyChange**(Object newValue, Object oldValue, String propertyName) ;
    public void **firePropertyChange**(byte newValue, byte oldValue, String propertyName) ;
    public void **firePropertyChange**(char newValue, char oldValue, String propertyName) ;
    public void **firePropertyChange**(short newValue, short oldValue, String propertyName) ;
    public void **firePropertyChange**(int newValue, int oldValue, String propertyName) ;
    public void **firePropertyChange**(long newValue, long oldValue, String propertyName) ;
    public void **firePropertyChange**(float newValue, float oldValue, String propertyName) ;
    public void **firePropertyChange**(double newValue, double oldValue, String propertyName) ;
    public Component **getListCellRendererComponent**(boolean cellHasFocus, boolean isSelected, int
        index, Object value, JList list) ;
    public void **invalidate**() ; // Since 1.5
    public boolean **isOpaque**() ; // Since 1.5
    public void **repaint**(int height, int width, int y, int x, long tm) ;
    public void **repaint**() ; // Since 1.5
    public void **repaint**(Rectangle r) ;
    public void **revalidate**() ;
    public void **validate**() ;
}

javax.swing.**DefaultListCellRenderer.UIResource**

public static class **DefaultListCellRenderer.UIResource** extends DefaultListCellRenderer implements
UIResource
{
    // Constructors
    public **DefaultListCellRenderer.UIResource**() ;
}

javax.swing.**DefaultListModel**

public class **DefaultListModel** extends AbstractListModel
{
    // Constructors
    public **DefaultListModel**() ;
    // Instance methods
    public void **add**(Object element, int index) ;
    public void **addElement**(Object obj) ;
    public int **capacity**() ;
    public void **clear**() ;
    public boolean **contains**(Object elem) ;
    public void **copyInto**(java.lang.Object[] anArray) ;
    public Object **elementAt**(int index) ;
    public Enumeration<?> **elements**() ;
    public void **ensureCapacity**(int minCapacity) ;
    public Object **firstElement**() ;
    public Object **get**(int index) ;
    public Object **getElementAt**(int index) ;
    public int **getSize**() ;
    public int **indexOf**(Object elem) ;
    public int **indexOf**(int index, Object elem) ;
    public void **insertElementAt**(int index, Object obj) ;
    public boolean **isEmpty**() ;
    public Object **lastElement**() ;
    public int **lastIndexOf**(Object elem) ;
    public int **lastIndexOf**(int index, Object elem) ;
    public Object **remove**(int index) ;
    public void **removeAllElements**() ;
    public boolean **removeElement**(Object obj) ;
    public void **removeElementAt**(int index) ;
    public void **removeRange**(int toIndex, int fromIndex) ;
    public Object **set**(Object element, int index) ;
    public void **setElementAt**(int index, Object obj) ;
    public void **setSize**(int newSize) ;
    public int **size**() ;
    public Object **toArray**() ;
    public String **toString**() ;
    public void **trimToSize**() ;
}

---

javax.swing.**DefaultListSelectionModel**

---

public class **DefaultListSelectionModel** implements Serializable, Cloneable, ListSelectionModel
{
    protected boolean **leadAnchorNotificationEnabled** ;
    protected EventListenerList **listenerList** ;
    // Constructors
    public **DefaultListSelectionModel**() ;
    // Instance methods
    public void **addListSelectionListener**(ListSelectionListener l) ;
    public void **addSelectionInterval**(int index1, int index0) ;
    public void **clearSelection**() ;
    public Object **clone**() throws CloneNotSupportedException ;
    protected void **fireValueChanged**(boolean isAdjusting, int lastIndex, int firstIndex) ;
    protected void **fireValueChanged**(int lastIndex, int firstIndex) ;
    protected void **fireValueChanged**(boolean isAdjusting) ;
    public int **getAnchorSelectionIndex**() ;
    public int **getLeadSelectionIndex**() ;
    public T **getListeners**(Class<T> listenerType) ; // Since 1.3
    public ListSelectionListener **getListSelectionListeners**() ; // Since 1.4
    public int **getMaxSelectionIndex**() ;
    public int **getMinSelectionIndex**() ;
    public int **getSelectionMode**() ;
    public boolean **getValueIsAdjusting**() ;
    public void **insertIndexInterval**(boolean before, int length, int index) ;
    public boolean **isLeadAnchorNotificationEnabled**() ;
    public boolean **isSelectedIndex**(int index) ;
    public boolean **isSelectionEmpty**() ;
    public void **moveLeadSelectionIndex**(int leadIndex) ; // Since 1.5
    public void **removeIndexInterval**(int index1, int index0) ;
    public void **removeListSelectionListener**(ListSelectionListener l) ;
    public void **removeSelectionInterval**(int index1, int index0) ;
    public void **setAnchorSelectionIndex**(int anchorIndex) ;
    public void **setLeadAnchorNotificationEnabled**(boolean flag) ;
    public void **setLeadSelectionIndex**(int leadIndex) ;
    public void **setSelectionInterval**(int index1, int index0) ;
    public void **setSelectionMode**(int selectionMode) ;
    public void **setValueIsAdjusting**(boolean isAdjusting) ;
    public String **toString**() ;
}

---

javax.swing.plaf.basic.**DefaultMenuLayout**

---

public class **DefaultMenuLayout** extends BoxLayout implements UIResource
{
    // Constructors
    public **DefaultMenuLayout**(int axis, Container target) ;
    // Instance methods
    public Dimension **preferredLayoutSize**(Container target) ;
}

---

javax.swing.plaf.metal.**DefaultMetalTheme**

---

public class **DefaultMetalTheme** extends MetalTheme
{
    // Constructors
    public **DefaultMetalTheme**() ;
    // Static methods
    // Instance methods
    public FontUIResource **getControlTextFont**() ;
    public FontUIResource **getMenuTextFont**() ;
    public String **getName**() ;
    protected ColorUIResource **getPrimary1**() ;
    protected ColorUIResource **getPrimary2**() ;
    protected ColorUIResource **getPrimary3**() ;
    protected ColorUIResource **getSecondary1**() ;
    protected ColorUIResource **getSecondary2**() ;
    protected ColorUIResource **getSecondary3**() ;
    public FontUIResource **getSubTextFont**() ;
    public FontUIResource **getSystemTextFont**() ;
    public FontUIResource **getUserTextFont**() ;
    public FontUIResource **getWindowTitleFont**() ;
}

---

javax.swing.tree.**DefaultMutableTreeNode**

---

public class **DefaultMutableTreeNode** implements Serializable, MutableTreeNode, Cloneable
{

```
public static final Enumeration<TreeNode> EMPTY_ENUMERATION ;
protected boolean allowsChildren ;
protected Vector children ;
protected MutableTreeNode parent ;
protected transient Object userObject ;
// Constructors
public DefaultMutableTreeNode(boolean allowsChildren, Object userObject) ;
public DefaultMutableTreeNode(Object userObject) ;
public DefaultMutableTreeNode() ;
// Instance methods
public void add(MutableTreeNode newChild) ;
public Enumeration breadthFirstEnumeration() ;
public Enumeration children() ;
public Object clone() ;
public Enumeration depthFirstEnumeration() ;
public boolean getAllowsChildren() ;
public TreeNode getChildAfter(TreeNode aChild) ;
public TreeNode getChildAt(int index) ;
public TreeNode getChildBefore(TreeNode aChild) ;
public int getChildCount() ;
public int getDepth() ;
public TreeNode getFirstChild() ;
public DefaultMutableTreeNode getFirstLeaf() ;
public int getIndex(TreeNode aChild) ;
public TreeNode getLastChild() ;
public DefaultMutableTreeNode getLastLeaf() ;
public int getLeafCount() ;
public int getLevel() ;
public DefaultMutableTreeNode getNextLeaf() ;
public DefaultMutableTreeNode getNextNode() ;
public DefaultMutableTreeNode getNextSibling() ;
public TreeNode getParent() ;
public TreeNode getPath() ;
protected TreeNode getPathToRoot(int depth, TreeNode aNode) ;
public DefaultMutableTreeNode getPreviousLeaf() ;
public DefaultMutableTreeNode getPreviousNode() ;
public DefaultMutableTreeNode getPreviousSibling() ;
public TreeNode getRoot() ;
public TreeNode getSharedAncestor(DefaultMutableTreeNode aNode) ;
public int getSiblingCount() ;
public Object getUserObject() ;
public Object getUserObjectPath() ;
public void insert(int childIndex, MutableTreeNode newChild) ;
public boolean isLeaf() ;
public boolean isNodeAncestor(TreeNode anotherNode) ;
public boolean isNodeChild(TreeNode aNode) ;
```

```
public boolean isNodeDescendant(DefaultMutableTreeNode anotherNode) ;
public boolean isNodeRelated(DefaultMutableTreeNode aNode) ;
public boolean isNodeSibling(TreeNode anotherNode) ;
public boolean isRoot() ;
public Enumeration pathFromAncestorEnumeration(TreeNode ancestor) ;
public Enumeration postorderEnumeration() ;
public Enumeration preorderEnumeration() ;
public void remove(int childIndex) ;
public void remove(MutableTreeNode aChild) ;
public void removeAllChildren() ;
public void removeFromParent() ;
public void setAllowsChildren(boolean allows) ;
public void setParent(MutableTreeNode newParent) ;
public void setUserObject(Object userObject) ;
public String toString() ;
}
```

javax.swing.**DefaultRowSorter<M, I>** [since 1.6]

```
public abstract class DefaultRowSorter<M, I> extends RowSorter<M>
{
    // Constructors
    public DefaultRowSorter() ;
    // Instance methods
    public void allRowsChanged() ;
    public int convertRowIndexToModel(int index) ;
    public int convertRowIndexToView(int index) ;
    public Comparator<?> getComparator(int column) ;
    public int getMaxSortKeys() ;
    public final M getModel() ;
    public int getModelRowCount() ;
    protected final DefaultRowSorter.ModelWrapper<M, I> getModelWrapper() ;
    public RowFilter<?, ?> getRowFilter() ;
    public List<?> getSortKeys() ;
    public boolean getSortsOnUpdates() ;
    public int getViewRowCount() ;
    public boolean isSortable(int column) ;
    public void modelStructureChanged() ;
    public void rowsDeleted(int endRow, int firstRow) ;
    public void rowsInserted(int endRow, int firstRow) ;
    public void rowsUpdated(int column, int endRow, int firstRow) ;
    public void rowsUpdated(int endRow, int firstRow) ;
    public void setComparator(Comparator<?> comparator, int column) ;
    public void setMaxSortKeys(int max) ;
```

```
        protected final void setModelWrapper(DefaultRowSorter.ModelWrapper<M, I> modelWrapper) ;
        public void setRowFilter(RowFilter<?, ?> filter) ;
        public void setSortable(boolean sortable, int column) ;
        public void setSortKeys(List<?> sortKeys) ;
        public void setSortsOnUpdates(boolean sortsOnUpdates) ;
        public void sort() ;
        public void toggleSortOrder(int column) ;
        protected boolean useToString(int column) ;
}
```

javax.swing.**DefaultSingleSelectionModel**

```
public class DefaultSingleSelectionModel  implements Serializable, SingleSelectionModel
{
        protected transient ChangeEvent changeEvent ;
        protected EventListenerList listenerList ;
        // Constructors
        public DefaultSingleSelectionModel() ;
        // Instance methods
        public void addChangeListener(ChangeListener l) ;
        public void clearSelection() ;
        protected void fireStateChanged() ;
        public ChangeListener getChangeListeners() ; // Since 1.4
        public T getListeners(Class<T> listenerType) ; // Since 1.3
        public int getSelectedIndex() ;
        public boolean isSelected() ;
        public void removeChangeListener(ChangeListener l) ;
        public void setSelectedIndex(int index) ;
}
```

javax.swing.text.**DefaultStyledDocument**

```
public class DefaultStyledDocument extends AbstractDocument implements StyledDocument
{
        public static final int BUFFER_SIZE_DEFAULT ;
        protected DefaultStyledDocument.ElementBuffer buffer ;
        // Constructors
        public DefaultStyledDocument() ;
        public DefaultStyledDocument(StyleContext styles) ;
        public DefaultStyledDocument(StyleContext styles, AbstractDocument.Content c) ;
        // Instance methods
```

```
    public void addDocumentListener(DocumentListener listener) ;
    public Style addStyle(Style parent, String nm) ;
    protected void create(javax.swing.text.DefaultStyledDocument.ElementSpec[] data) ;
    protected AbstractDocument.AbstractElement createDefaultRoot() ;
    public Color getBackground(AttributeSet attr) ;
    public Element getCharacterElement(int pos) ;
    public Element getDefaultRootElement() ;
    public Font getFont(AttributeSet attr) ;
    public Color getForeground(AttributeSet attr) ;
    public Style getLogicalStyle(int p) ;
    public Element getParagraphElement(int pos) ;
    public Style getStyle(String nm) ;
    public Enumeration<?> getStyleNames() ;
    protected void insert(javax.swing.text.DefaultStyledDocument.ElementSpec[] data, int offset) throws
        BadLocationException ;
    protected void insertUpdate(AttributeSet attr, AbstractDocument.DefaultDocumentEvent chng) ;
    public void removeDocumentListener(DocumentListener listener) ;
    public void removeElement(Element elem) ; // Since 1.7
    public void removeStyle(String nm) ;
    protected void removeUpdate(AbstractDocument.DefaultDocumentEvent chng) ;
    public void setCharacterAttributes(boolean replace, AttributeSet s, int length, int offset) ;
    public void setLogicalStyle(Style s, int pos) ;
    public void setParagraphAttributes(boolean replace, AttributeSet s, int length, int offset) ;
    protected void styleChanged(Style style) ;
}
```

javax.swing.text.**DefaultStyledDocument.AttributeUndoableEdit**

```
public static class DefaultStyledDocument.AttributeUndoableEdit extends AbstractUndoableEdit
{
    protected AttributeSet copy ;
    protected Element element ;
    protected boolean isReplacing ;
    protected AttributeSet newAttributes ;
    // Constructors
    public DefaultStyledDocument.AttributeUndoableEdit(boolean isReplacing, AttributeSet
        newAttributes, Element element) ;
    // Instance methods
    public void redo() throws CannotRedoException ;
    public void undo() throws CannotUndoException ;
}
```

---

javax.swing.text.**DefaultStyledDocument.ElementSpec**

---

public static class **DefaultStyledDocument.ElementSpec**
{
    public static final short **ContentType** ;
    public static final short **EndTagType** ;
    public static final short **JoinFractureDirection** ;
    public static final short **JoinNextDirection** ;
    public static final short **JoinPreviousDirection** ;
    public static final short **OriginateDirection** ;
    public static final short **StartTagType** ;
    // Constructors
    public **DefaultStyledDocument.ElementSpec**(int len, int offs, char[] txt, short type, AttributeSet a) ;
    public **DefaultStyledDocument.ElementSpec**(int len, short type, AttributeSet a) ;
    public **DefaultStyledDocument.ElementSpec**(short type, AttributeSet a) ;
    // Instance methods
    public char **getArray**() ;
    public AttributeSet **getAttributes**() ;
    public short **getDirection**() ;
    public int **getLength**() ;
    public int **getOffset**() ;
    public short **getType**() ;
    public void **setDirection**(short direction) ;
    public void **setType**(short type) ;
    public String **toString**() ;
}

---

javax.swing.table.**DefaultTableCellRenderer**

---

public class **DefaultTableCellRenderer** extends JLabel implements Serializable, TableCellRenderer
{
    protected static Border **noFocusBorder** ;
    // Constructors
    public **DefaultTableCellRenderer**() ;
    // Static methods
    // Instance methods
    public void **firePropertyChange**(boolean newValue, boolean oldValue, String propertyName) ;
    protected void **firePropertyChange**(Object newValue, Object oldValue, String propertyName) ;
    public Component **getTableCellRendererComponent**(int column, int row, boolean hasFocus,
        boolean isSelected, Object value, JTable table) ;

```
    public void invalidate() ; // Since 1.5
    public boolean isOpaque() ;
    public void repaint() ; // Since 1.5
    public void repaint(Rectangle r) ;
    public void repaint(int height, int width, int y, int x, long tm) ;
    public void revalidate() ;
    public void setBackground(Color c) ;
    public void setForeground(Color c) ;
    protected void setValue(Object value) ;
    public void updateUI() ;
    public void validate() ;
}
```

javax.swing.table.**DefaultTableCellRenderer.UIResource**

```
public static class DefaultTableCellRenderer.UIResource extends DefaultTableCellRenderer
implements UIResource
{
    // Constructors
    public DefaultTableCellRenderer.UIResource() ;
}
```

javax.swing.table.**DefaultTableColumnModel**

```
public class DefaultTableColumnModel  implements Serializable, ListSelectionListener,
PropertyChangeListener, TableColumnModel
{
    protected transient ChangeEvent changeEvent ;
    protected int columnMargin ;
    protected boolean columnSelectionAllowed ;
    protected EventListenerList listenerList ;
    protected ListSelectionModel selectionModel ;
    protected Vector<TableColumn> tableColumns ;
    protected int totalColumnWidth ;
    // Constructors
    public DefaultTableColumnModel() ;
    // Instance methods
    public void addColumn(TableColumn aColumn) ;
    public void addColumnModelListener(TableColumnModelListener x) ;
    protected ListSelectionModel createSelectionModel() ;
    protected void fireColumnAdded(TableColumnModelEvent e) ;
```

```
    protected void fireColumnMarginChanged() ;
    protected void fireColumnMoved(TableColumnModelEvent e) ;
    protected void fireColumnRemoved(TableColumnModelEvent e) ;
    protected void fireColumnSelectionChanged(ListSelectionEvent e) ;
    public TableColumn getColumn(int columnIndex) ;
    public int getColumnCount() ;
    public int getColumnIndex(Object identifier) ;
    public int getColumnIndexAtX(int x) ;
    public int getColumnMargin() ;
    public TableColumnModelListener getColumnModelListeners() ; // Since 1.4
    public Enumeration<TableColumn> getColumns() ;
    public boolean getColumnSelectionAllowed() ;
    public T getListeners(Class<T> listenerType) ; // Since 1.3
    public int getSelectedColumnCount() ;
    public int getSelectedColumns() ;
    public ListSelectionModel getSelectionModel() ;
    public int getTotalColumnWidth() ;
    public void moveColumn(int newIndex, int columnIndex) ;
    public void propertyChange(PropertyChangeEvent evt) ;
    protected void recalcWidthCache() ;
    public void removeColumn(TableColumn column) ;
    public void removeColumnModelListener(TableColumnModelListener x) ;
    public void setColumnMargin(int newMargin) ;
    public void setColumnSelectionAllowed(boolean flag) ;
    public void setSelectionModel(ListSelectionModel newModel) ;
    public void valueChanged(ListSelectionEvent e) ;
}
```

javax.swing.table.**DefaultTableModel**

public class **DefaultTableModel** extends AbstractTableModel implements Serializable
```
{
    protected Vector columnIdentifiers ;
    protected Vector dataVector ;
    // Constructors
    public DefaultTableModel(java.lang.Object[] columnNames, java.lang.Object[][] data) ;
    public DefaultTableModel(Vector columnNames, Vector data) ;
    public DefaultTableModel(int rowCount, java.lang.Object[] columnNames) ;
    public DefaultTableModel(int rowCount, Vector columnNames) ;
    public DefaultTableModel(int columnCount, int rowCount) ;
    public DefaultTableModel() ;
    // Static methods
    protected static Vector convertToVector(java.lang.Object[][] anArray) ;
    protected static Vector convertToVector(java.lang.Object[] anArray) ;
```

```
    // Instance methods
    public void addColumn(Object columnName) ;
    public void addColumn(Vector columnData, Object columnName) ;
    public void addColumn(java.lang.Object[] columnData, Object columnName) ;
    public void addRow(java.lang.Object[] rowData) ;
    public void addRow(Vector rowData) ;
    public int getColumnCount() ;
    public String getColumnName(int column) ;
    public Vector getDataVector() ;
    public int getRowCount() ;
    public Object getValueAt(int column, int row) ;
    public void insertRow(java.lang.Object[] rowData, int row) ;
    public void insertRow(Vector rowData, int row) ;
    public boolean isCellEditable(int column, int row) ;
    public void moveRow(int to, int end, int start) ;
    public void newDataAvailable(TableModelEvent event) ;
    public void newRowsAdded(TableModelEvent e) ;
    public void removeRow(int row) ;
    public void rowsRemoved(TableModelEvent event) ;
    public void setColumnCount(int columnCount) ; // Since 1.3
    public void setColumnIdentifiers(Vector columnIdentifiers) ;
    public void setColumnIdentifiers(java.lang.Object[] newIdentifiers) ;
    public void setDataVector(java.lang.Object[] columnIdentifiers, java.lang.Object[][] dataVector) ;
    public void setDataVector(Vector columnIdentifiers, Vector dataVector) ;
    public void setNumRows(int rowCount) ;
    public void setRowCount(int rowCount) ; // Since 1.3
    public void setValueAt(int column, int row, Object aValue) ;
}
```

javax.swing.text.**DefaultTextUI**

```
public abstract class DefaultTextUI extends BasicTextUI
{
    // Constructors
    public DefaultTextUI() ;
}
```

javax.swing.tree.**DefaultTreeCellEditor**

```
public class DefaultTreeCellEditor  implements TreeSelectionListener, TreeCellEditor, ActionListener
{
```

```
    protected Color borderSelectionColor ;
    protected boolean canEdit ;
    protected transient Component editingComponent ;
    protected Container editingContainer ;
    protected transient Icon editingIcon ;
    protected Font font ;
    protected transient TreePath lastPath ;
    protected transient int lastRow ;
    protected transient int offset ;
    protected TreeCellEditor realEditor ;
    protected DefaultTreeCellRenderer renderer ;
    protected transient Timer timer ;
    protected transient JTree tree ;
    // Constructors
    public DefaultTreeCellEditor(TreeCellEditor editor, DefaultTreeCellRenderer renderer, JTree tree) ;
    public DefaultTreeCellEditor(DefaultTreeCellRenderer renderer, JTree tree) ;
    // Instance methods
    public void actionPerformed(ActionEvent e) ;
    public void addCellEditorListener(CellEditorListener l) ;
    public void cancelCellEditing() ;
    protected boolean canEditImmediately(EventObject event) ;
    protected Container createContainer() ;
    protected TreeCellEditor createTreeCellEditor() ;
    protected void determineOffset(int row, boolean leaf, boolean expanded, boolean isSelected, Object
        value, JTree tree) ;
    public Color getBorderSelectionColor() ;
    public CellEditorListener getCellEditorListeners() ; // Since 1.4
    public Object getCellEditorValue() ;
    public Font getFont() ;
    public Component getTreeCellEditorComponent(int row, boolean leaf, boolean expanded, boolean
        isSelected, Object value, JTree tree) ;
    protected boolean inHitRegion(int y, int x) ;
    public boolean isCellEditable(EventObject event) ;
    protected void prepareForEditing() ;
    public void removeCellEditorListener(CellEditorListener l) ;
    public void setBorderSelectionColor(Color newColor) ;
    public void setFont(Font font) ;
    protected void setTree(JTree newTree) ;
    public boolean shouldSelectCell(EventObject event) ;
    protected boolean shouldStartEditingTimer(EventObject event) ;
    protected void startEditingTimer() ;
    public boolean stopCellEditing() ;
    public void valueChanged(TreeSelectionEvent e) ;
}
```

javax.swing.tree.**DefaultTreeCellRenderer**

public class **DefaultTreeCellRenderer** extends JLabel implements TreeCellRenderer
{
    protected Color **backgroundNonSelectionColor** ;
    protected Color **backgroundSelectionColor** ;
    protected Color **borderSelectionColor** ;
    protected transient Icon **closedIcon** ;
    protected boolean **hasFocus** ;
    protected transient Icon **leafIcon** ;
    protected transient Icon **openIcon** ;
    protected boolean **selected** ;
    protected Color **textNonSelectionColor** ;
    protected Color **textSelectionColor** ;
    // Constructors
    public **DefaultTreeCellRenderer**() ;
    // Instance methods
    public void **firePropertyChange**(boolean newValue, boolean oldValue, String propertyName) ;
    protected void **firePropertyChange**(Object newValue, Object oldValue, String propertyName) ;
    public void **firePropertyChange**(byte newValue, byte oldValue, String propertyName) ;
    public void **firePropertyChange**(char newValue, char oldValue, String propertyName) ;
    public void **firePropertyChange**(short newValue, short oldValue, String propertyName) ;
    public void **firePropertyChange**(int newValue, int oldValue, String propertyName) ;
    public void **firePropertyChange**(long newValue, long oldValue, String propertyName) ;
    public void **firePropertyChange**(float newValue, float oldValue, String propertyName) ;
    public void **firePropertyChange**(double newValue, double oldValue, String propertyName) ;
    public Color **getBackgroundNonSelectionColor**() ;
    public Color **getBackgroundSelectionColor**() ;
    public Color **getBorderSelectionColor**() ;
    public Icon **getClosedIcon**() ;
    public Icon **getDefaultClosedIcon**() ;
    public Icon **getDefaultLeafIcon**() ;
    public Icon **getDefaultOpenIcon**() ;
    public Font **getFont**() ;
    public Icon **getLeafIcon**() ;
    public Icon **getOpenIcon**() ;
    public Dimension **getPreferredSize**() ;
    public Color **getTextNonSelectionColor**() ;
    public Color **getTextSelectionColor**() ;
    public Component **getTreeCellRendererComponent**(boolean hasFocus, int row, boolean leaf,
        boolean expanded, boolean sel, Object value, JTree tree) ;
    public void **invalidate**() ; // Since 1.5
    public void **paint**(Graphics g) ;
    public void **repaint**(int height, int width, int y, int x, long tm) ;

```
    public void repaint(Rectangle r) ;
    public void repaint() ; // Since 1.5
    public void revalidate() ;
    public void setBackground(Color color) ;
    public void setBackgroundNonSelectionColor(Color newColor) ;
    public void setBackgroundSelectionColor(Color newColor) ;
    public void setBorderSelectionColor(Color newColor) ;
    public void setClosedIcon(Icon newIcon) ;
    public void setFont(Font font) ;
    public void setLeafIcon(Icon newIcon) ;
    public void setOpenIcon(Icon newIcon) ;
    public void setTextNonSelectionColor(Color newColor) ;
    public void setTextSelectionColor(Color newColor) ;
    public void updateUI() ; // Since 1.7
    public void validate() ;
}
```

javax.swing.tree.**DefaultTreeModel**

```
public class DefaultTreeModel  implements TreeModel, Serializable
{
    protected boolean asksAllowsChildren ;
    protected EventListenerList listenerList ;
    protected TreeNode root ;
    // Constructors
    public DefaultTreeModel(boolean asksAllowsChildren, TreeNode root) ;
    public DefaultTreeModel(TreeNode root) ;
    // Instance methods
    public void addTreeModelListener(TreeModelListener l) ;
    public boolean asksAllowsChildren() ;
    protected void fireTreeNodesChanged(java.lang.Object[] children, int[] childIndices,
        java.lang.Object[] path, Object source) ;
    protected void fireTreeNodesInserted(java.lang.Object[] children, int[] childIndices,
        java.lang.Object[] path, Object source) ;
    protected void fireTreeNodesRemoved(java.lang.Object[] children, int[] childIndices,
        java.lang.Object[] path, Object source) ;
    protected void fireTreeStructureChanged(java.lang.Object[] children, int[] childIndices,
        java.lang.Object[] path, Object source) ;
    public Object getChild(int index, Object parent) ;
    public int getChildCount(Object parent) ;
    public int getIndexOfChild(Object child, Object parent) ;
    public T getListeners(Class<T> listenerType) ; // Since 1.3
    public TreeNode getPathToRoot(TreeNode aNode) ;
    protected TreeNode getPathToRoot(int depth, TreeNode aNode) ;
```

```
    public Object getRoot() ;
    public TreeModelListener getTreeModelListeners() ; // Since 1.4
    public void insertNodeInto(int index, MutableTreeNode parent, MutableTreeNode newChild) ;
    public boolean isLeaf(Object node) ;
    public void nodeChanged(TreeNode node) ;
    public void nodesChanged(int[] childIndices, TreeNode node) ;
    public void nodeStructureChanged(TreeNode node) ;
    public void nodesWereInserted(int[] childIndices, TreeNode node) ;
    public void nodesWereRemoved(java.lang.Object[] removedChildren, int[] childIndices, TreeNode
        node) ;
    public void reload() ;
    public void reload(TreeNode node) ;
    public void removeNodeFromParent(MutableTreeNode node) ;
    public void removeTreeModelListener(TreeModelListener l) ;
    public void setAsksAllowsChildren(boolean newValue) ;
    public void setRoot(TreeNode root) ;
    public void valueForPathChanged(Object newValue, TreePath path) ;
}
```

---

javax.swing.tree.**DefaultTreeSelectionModel**

```
public class DefaultTreeSelectionModel  implements TreeSelectionModel, Serializable, Cloneable
{
    public static final String SELECTION_MODE_PROPERTY ;
    protected SwingPropertyChangeSupport changeSupport ;
    protected int leadIndex ;
    protected TreePath leadPath ;
    protected int leadRow ;
    protected EventListenerList listenerList ;
    protected DefaultListSelectionModel listSelectionModel ;
    protected transient RowMapper rowMapper ;
    protected TreePath selection ;
    protected int selectionMode ;
    // Constructors
    public DefaultTreeSelectionModel() ;
    // Instance methods
    public synchronized void addPropertyChangeListener(PropertyChangeListener listener) ;
    public void addSelectionPath(TreePath path) ;
    public void addSelectionPaths(javax.swing.tree.TreePath[] paths) ;
    public void addTreeSelectionListener(TreeSelectionListener x) ;
    protected boolean arePathsContiguous(javax.swing.tree.TreePath[] paths) ;
    protected boolean canPathsBeAdded(javax.swing.tree.TreePath[] paths) ;
    protected boolean canPathsBeRemoved(javax.swing.tree.TreePath[] paths) ;
    public void clearSelection() ;
```

```
        public Object clone() throws CloneNotSupportedException ;
        protected void fireValueChanged(TreeSelectionEvent e) ;
        public TreePath getLeadSelectionPath() ;
        public int getLeadSelectionRow() ;
        public T getListeners(Class<T> listenerType) ; // Since 1.3
        public int getMaxSelectionRow() ;
        public int getMinSelectionRow() ;
        public PropertyChangeListener getPropertyChangeListeners() ; // Since 1.4
        public RowMapper getRowMapper() ;
        public int getSelectionCount() ;
        public int getSelectionMode() ;
        public TreePath getSelectionPath() ;
        public TreePath getSelectionPaths() ;
        public int getSelectionRows() ;
        public TreeSelectionListener getTreeSelectionListeners() ; // Since 1.4
        protected void insureRowContinuity() ;
        protected void insureUniqueness() ;
        public boolean isPathSelected(TreePath path) ;
        public boolean isRowSelected(int row) ;
        public boolean isSelectionEmpty() ;
        protected void notifyPathChange(TreePath oldLeadSelection, Vector<PathPlaceHolder>
            changedPaths) ;
        public synchronized void removePropertyChangeListener(PropertyChangeListener listener) ;
        public void removeSelectionPath(TreePath path) ;
        public void removeSelectionPaths(javax.swing.tree.TreePath[] paths) ;
        public void removeTreeSelectionListener(TreeSelectionListener x) ;
        public void resetRowSelection() ;
        public void setRowMapper(RowMapper newMapper) ;
        public void setSelectionMode(int mode) ;
        public void setSelectionPath(TreePath path) ;
        public void setSelectionPaths(javax.swing.tree.TreePath[] pPaths) ;
        public String toString() ;
        protected void updateLeadIndex() ;
}
```

java.awt.**Desktop** [since 1.6]

```
public class Desktop
{
    // Constructors
    private Desktop() ;
    // Static methods
    public static synchronized Desktop getDesktop() ;
    public static boolean isDesktopSupported() ;
```

```
    // Instance methods
    public void browse(URI uri) throws IOException ;
    public void edit(File file) throws IOException ;
    public boolean isSupported(Desktop.Action action) ;
    public void mail() throws IOException ;
    public void mail(URI mailtoURI) throws IOException ;
    public void open(File file) throws IOException ;
    public void print(File file) throws IOException ;
}
```

java.awt.**Desktop.Action** [since 1.6]

```
public static final class Desktop.Action extends Enum<Desktop.Action>
{
    // Constructors
    private Desktop.Action() ;
    // Static methods
    public static Desktop.Action valueOf(String name) ;
    public static final Desktop.Action values() ;
}
```

javax.swing.plaf.**DesktopIconUI**

```
public abstract class DesktopIconUI extends ComponentUI
{
    // Constructors
    public DesktopIconUI() ;
}
```

javax.swing.**DesktopManager**

```
public interface DesktopManager
{
    // Instance methods
    public void activateFrame(JInternalFrame f) ;
    public void beginDraggingFrame(JComponent f) ;
    public void beginResizingFrame(int direction, JComponent f) ;
    public void closeFrame(JInternalFrame f) ;
```

```
    public void deactivateFrame(JInternalFrame f) ;
    public void deiconifyFrame(JInternalFrame f) ;
    public void dragFrame(int newY, int newX, JComponent f) ;
    public void endDraggingFrame(JComponent f) ;
    public void endResizingFrame(JComponent f) ;
    public void iconifyFrame(JInternalFrame f) ;
    public void maximizeFrame(JInternalFrame f) ;
    public void minimizeFrame(JInternalFrame f) ;
    public void openFrame(JInternalFrame f) ;
    public void resizeFrame(int newHeight, int newWidth, int newY, int newX, JComponent f) ;
    public void setBoundsForFrame(int newHeight, int newWidth, int newY, int newX, JComponent f) ;
}
```

javax.swing.plaf.**DesktopPaneUI**

```
public abstract class DesktopPaneUI extends ComponentUI
{
    // Constructors
    public DesktopPaneUI() ;
}
```

java.awt.peer.**DesktopPeer**

```
public interface DesktopPeer
{
    // Instance methods
    public void browse(URI url) throws IOException ;
    public void edit(File file) throws IOException ;
    public boolean isSupported(Desktop.Action action) ;
    public void mail(URI mailtoURL) throws IOException ;
    public void open(File file) throws IOException ;
    public void print(File file) throws IOException ;
}
```

java.awt.**Dialog** [since 1.0]

```
public class Dialog extends Window
{
```

```
        public static final Dialog.ModalityType DEFAULT_MODALITY_TYPE ;
        // Constructors
        public Dialog(GraphicsConfiguration gc, Dialog.ModalityType modalityType, String title, Window
            owner) ;
        public Dialog(Dialog.ModalityType modalityType, String title, Window owner) ;
        public Dialog(Dialog.ModalityType modalityType, Window owner) ;
        public Dialog(String title, Window owner) ;
        public Dialog(Window owner) ;
        public Dialog(GraphicsConfiguration gc, boolean modal, String title, Dialog owner) ;
        public Dialog(boolean modal, String title, Dialog owner) ;
        public Dialog(String title, Dialog owner) ;
        public Dialog(Dialog owner) ;
        public Dialog(GraphicsConfiguration gc, boolean modal, String title, Frame owner) ;
        public Dialog(boolean modal, String title, Frame owner) ;
        public Dialog(String title, Frame owner) ;
        public Dialog(boolean modal, Frame owner) ;
        public Dialog(Frame owner) ;
        // Static methods
        // Instance methods
        public void addNotify() ;
        public AccessibleContext getAccessibleContext() ; // Since 1.3
        public Dialog.ModalityType getModalityType() ; // Since 1.6
        public String getTitle() ;
        public void hide() ;
        public boolean isModal() ;
        public boolean isResizable() ;
        public boolean isUndecorated() ; // Since 1.4
        protected String paramString() ;
        public void setModal(boolean modal) ; // Since 1.1
        public void setModalityType(Dialog.ModalityType type) ; // Since 1.6
        public void setResizable(boolean resizable) ;
        public void setTitle(String title) ;
        public void setUndecorated(boolean undecorated) ; // Since 1.4
        public void setVisible(boolean b) ;
        public void show() ;
        public void toBack() ;
}
```

java.awt.**Dialog.ModalExclusionType** [since 1.6]

```
public static final class Dialog.ModalExclusionType extends Enum<Dialog.ModalExclusionType>
{
        // Constructors
        private Dialog.ModalExclusionType() ;
```

```
    // Static methods
    public static Dialog.ModalExclusionType valueOf(String name) ;
    public static final Dialog.ModalExclusionType values() ;
}
```

---

java.awt.**Dialog.ModalityType** [since 1.6]

```
public static final class Dialog.ModalityType extends Enum<Dialog.ModalityType>
{
    // Constructors
    private Dialog.ModalityType() ;
    // Static methods
    public static Dialog.ModalityType valueOf(String name) ;
    public static final Dialog.ModalityType values() ;
}
```

---

java.awt.peer.**DialogPeer**

```
public interface DialogPeer  implements WindowPeer
{
    // Instance methods
    public void blockWindows(List<Window> windows) ;
    public void setResizable(boolean resizeable) ;
    public void setTitle(String title) ;
}
```

---

java.awt.**Dimension** [since 1.0]

```
public class Dimension extends Dimension2D implements Serializable
{
    public int height ;
    public int width ;
    // Constructors
    public Dimension(int height, int width) ;
    public Dimension(Dimension d) ;
    public Dimension() ;
    // Static methods
    // Instance methods
```

```
    public boolean equals(Object obj) ;
    public double getHeight() ; // Since 1.2
    public Dimension getSize() ; // Since 1.1
    public double getWidth() ; // Since 1.2
    public int hashCode() ;
    public void setSize(double height, double width) ; // Since 1.2
    public void setSize(Dimension d) ; // Since 1.1
    public void setSize(int height, int width) ; // Since 1.1
    public String toString() ;
}
```

java.awt.geom.**Dimension2D** [since 1.2]

```
public abstract class Dimension2D  implements Cloneable
{
    // Constructors
    protected Dimension2D() ;
    // Instance methods
    public Object clone() ; // Since 1.2
    public abstract double getHeight() ; // Since 1.2
    public abstract double getWidth() ; // Since 1.2
    public void setSize(Dimension2D d) ; // Since 1.2
    public abstract void setSize(double height, double width) ; // Since 1.2
}
```

javax.swing.plaf.**DimensionUIResource**

```
public class DimensionUIResource extends Dimension implements UIResource
{
    // Constructors
    public DimensionUIResource(int height, int width) ;
}
```

java.awt.image.**DirectColorModel**

```
public class DirectColorModel extends PackedColorModel
{
    // Constructors
```

public **DirectColorModel**(int transferType, boolean isAlphaPremultiplied, int amask, int bmask, int gmask, int rmask, int bits, ColorSpace space) ;
public **DirectColorModel**(int amask, int bmask, int gmask, int rmask, int bits) ;
public **DirectColorModel**(int bmask, int gmask, int rmask, int bits) ;
// Instance methods
public final ColorModel **coerceData**(boolean isAlphaPremultiplied, WritableRaster raster) ;
public final WritableRaster **createCompatibleWritableRaster**(int h, int w) ;
public final int **getAlpha**(int pixel) ;
public int **getAlpha**(Object inData) ;
public final int **getAlphaMask**() ;
public final int **getBlue**(int pixel) ;
public int **getBlue**(Object inData) ;
public final int **getBlueMask**() ;
public final int **getComponents**(int offset, int[] components, int pixel) ;
public final int **getComponents**(int offset, int[] components, Object pixel) ;
public int **getDataElement**(int offset, int[] components) ;
public Object **getDataElements**(Object pixel, int rgb) ;
public Object **getDataElements**(Object obj, int offset, int[] components) ;
public int **getGreen**(Object inData) ;
public final int **getGreen**(int pixel) ;
public final int **getGreenMask**() ;
public int **getRed**(Object inData) ;
public final int **getRed**(int pixel) ;
public final int **getRedMask**() ;
public final int **getRGB**(int pixel) ;
public int **getRGB**(Object inData) ;
public boolean **isCompatibleRaster**(Raster raster) ;
public String **toString**() ;
}

---

java.awt.**DisplayMode** [since 1.4]

---

public final class **DisplayMode**
{
    public static final int **BIT_DEPTH_MULTI** ;
    public static final int **REFRESH_RATE_UNKNOWN** ;
    // Constructors
    public **DisplayMode**(int refreshRate, int bitDepth, int height, int width) ;
    // Instance methods
    public boolean **equals**(Object dm) ;
    public boolean **equals**(DisplayMode dm) ;
    public int **getBitDepth**() ;
    public int **getHeight**() ;
    public int **getRefreshRate**() ;

```
    public int getWidth() ;
    public int hashCode() ;
}
```

---

java.awt.dnd.**DnDConstants** [since 1.2]

```
public final class DnDConstants
{
    public static final int ACTION_COPY ;
    public static final int ACTION_COPY_OR_MOVE ;
    public static final int ACTION_LINK ;
    public static final int ACTION_MOVE ;
    public static final int ACTION_NONE ;
    public static final int ACTION_REFERENCE ;
    // Constructors
    private DnDConstants() ;
}
```

---

javax.swing.text.**Document**

```
public interface Document
{
    public static final String StreamDescriptionProperty ;
    public static final String TitleProperty ;
    // Instance methods
    public void addDocumentListener(DocumentListener listener) ;
    public void addUndoableEditListener(UndoableEditListener listener) ;
    public Position createPosition(int offs) throws BadLocationException ;
    public Element getDefaultRootElement() ;
    public Position getEndPosition() ;
    public int getLength() ;
    public Object getProperty(Object key) ;
    public Element getRootElements() ;
    public Position getStartPosition() ;
    public void getText(Segment txt, int length, int offset) throws BadLocationException ;
    public String getText(int length, int offset) throws BadLocationException ;
    public void insertString(AttributeSet a, String str, int offset) throws BadLocationException ;
    public void putProperty(Object value, Object key) ;
    public void remove(int len, int offs) throws BadLocationException ;
    public void removeDocumentListener(DocumentListener listener) ;
    public void removeUndoableEditListener(UndoableEditListener listener) ;
```

```
        public void render(Runnable r) ;
}
```

```
public interface DocumentEvent
{
    // Instance methods
    public DocumentEvent.ElementChange getChange(Element elem) ;
    public Document getDocument() ;
    public int getLength() ;
    public int getOffset() ;
    public DocumentEvent.EventType getType() ;
}
```

```
public static interface DocumentEvent.ElementChange
{
    // Instance methods
    public Element getChildrenAdded() ;
    public Element getChildrenRemoved() ;
    public Element getElement() ;
    public int getIndex() ;
}
```

```
public static final class DocumentEvent.EventType
{
    public static final DocumentEvent.EventType CHANGE ;
    public static final DocumentEvent.EventType INSERT ;
    public static final DocumentEvent.EventType REMOVE ;
    // Constructors
    private DocumentEvent.EventType(String s) ;
    // Instance methods
    public String toString() ;
}
```

javax.swing.text.**DocumentFilter** [since 1.4]

public class **DocumentFilter**
{
    // Constructors
    public **DocumentFilter**() ;
    // Instance methods
    public void **insertString**(AttributeSet attr, String string, int offset, DocumentFilter.FilterBypass fb)
        throws BadLocationException ;
    public void **remove**(int length, int offset, DocumentFilter.FilterBypass fb) throws
        BadLocationException ;
    public void **replace**(AttributeSet attrs, String text, int length, int offset, DocumentFilter.FilterBypass
        fb) throws BadLocationException ;
}

javax.swing.text.**DocumentFilter.FilterBypass** [since 1.4]

public abstract static class **DocumentFilter.FilterBypass**
{
    // Constructors
    public **DocumentFilter.FilterBypass**() ;
    // Instance methods
    public abstract Document **getDocument**() ;
    public abstract void **insertString**(AttributeSet attr, String string, int offset) throws
        BadLocationException ;
    public abstract void **remove**(int length, int offset) throws BadLocationException ;
    public abstract void **replace**(AttributeSet attrs, String string, int length, int offset) throws
        BadLocationException ;
}

javax.swing.event.**DocumentListener**

public interface **DocumentListener** implements EventListener
{
    // Instance methods
    public void **changedUpdate**(DocumentEvent e) ;
    public void **insertUpdate**(DocumentEvent e) ;

```
    public void removeUpdate(DocumentEvent e) ;
}
```

javax.swing.text.html.parser.**DocumentParser**

```
public class DocumentParser extends Parser
{
    // Constructors
    public DocumentParser(DTD dtd) ;
    // Instance methods
    protected void handleComment(char[] text) ;
    protected void handleEmptyTag(TagElement tag) throws ChangedCharSetException ;
    protected void handleEndTag(TagElement tag) ;
    protected void handleError(String errorMsg, int ln) ;
    protected void handleStartTag(TagElement tag) ;
    protected void handleText(char[] data) ;
    public void parse(boolean ignoreCharSet, HTMLEditorKit.ParserCallback callback, Reader in)
        throws IOException ;
}
```

java.awt.dnd.**DragGestureEvent**

```
public class DragGestureEvent extends EventObject
{
    // Constructors
    public DragGestureEvent(List<?> evs, Point ori, int act, DragGestureRecognizer dgr) ;
    // Instance methods
    public Component getComponent() ;
    public int getDragAction() ;
    public Point getDragOrigin() ;
    public DragSource getDragSource() ;
    public DragGestureRecognizer getSourceAsDragGestureRecognizer() ;
    public InputEvent getTriggerEvent() ;
    public Iterator<InputEvent> iterator() ;
    public void startDrag(Transferable transferable, Cursor dragCursor) throws
        InvalidDnDOperationException ; // Since 1.4
    public void startDrag(DragSourceListener dsl, Transferable transferable, Cursor dragCursor) throws
        InvalidDnDOperationException ;
    public void startDrag(DragSourceListener dsl, Transferable transferable, Point imageOffset, Image
        dragImage, Cursor dragCursor) throws InvalidDnDOperationException ;
    public Object toArray() ;
```

```
        public Object toArray(java.lang.Object[] array) ;
}
```

---

java.awt.dnd.**DragGestureListener**

```
public interface DragGestureListener  implements EventListener
{
    // Instance methods
    public void dragGestureRecognized(DragGestureEvent dge) ;
}
```

---

java.awt.dnd.**DragGestureRecognizer**

```
public abstract class DragGestureRecognizer  implements Serializable
{
    protected Component component ;
    protected transient DragGestureListener dragGestureListener ;
    protected DragSource dragSource ;
    protected ArrayList<InputEvent> events ;
    protected int sourceActions ;
    // Constructors
    protected DragGestureRecognizer(DragSource ds) ;
    protected DragGestureRecognizer(Component c, DragSource ds) ;
    protected DragGestureRecognizer(int sa, Component c, DragSource ds) ;
    protected DragGestureRecognizer(DragGestureListener dgl, int sa, Component c, DragSource ds) ;
    // Instance methods
    public synchronized void addDragGestureListener(DragGestureListener dgl) throws
        TooManyListenersException ;
    protected synchronized void appendEvent(InputEvent awtie) ;
    protected synchronized void fireDragGestureRecognized(Point p, int dragAction) ;
    public synchronized Component getComponent() ;
    public DragSource getDragSource() ;
    public synchronized int getSourceActions() ;
    public InputEvent getTriggerEvent() ;
    protected abstract void registerListeners() ;
    public synchronized void removeDragGestureListener(DragGestureListener dgl) ;
    public void resetRecognizer() ;
    public synchronized void setComponent(Component c) ;
    public synchronized void setSourceActions(int actions) ;
    protected abstract void unregisterListeners() ;
}
```

---

javax.swing.plaf.basic.**DragRecognitionSupport.BeforeDrag**

public static interface **DragRecognitionSupport.BeforeDrag**
{
    // Instance methods
    public void **dragStarting**(MouseEvent me) ;
}

java.awt.dnd.**DragSource** [since 1.2]

public class **DragSource** implements Serializable
{
    public static final Cursor **DefaultCopyDrop** ;
    public static final Cursor **DefaultCopyNoDrop** ;
    public static final Cursor **DefaultLinkDrop** ;
    public static final Cursor **DefaultLinkNoDrop** ;
    public static final Cursor **DefaultMoveDrop** ;
    public static final Cursor **DefaultMoveNoDrop** ;
    // Constructors
    public **DragSource**() ;
    // Static methods
    public static DragSource **getDefaultDragSource**() ;
    public static int **getDragThreshold**() ; // Since 1.5
    public static boolean **isDragImageSupported**() ;
    // Instance methods
    public void **addDragSourceListener**(DragSourceListener dsl) ; // Since 1.4
    public void **addDragSourceMotionListener**(DragSourceMotionListener dsml) ; // Since 1.4
    public DragGestureRecognizer **createDefaultDragGestureRecognizer**(DragGestureListener dgl, int
        actions, Component c) ;
    public T **createDragGestureRecognizer**(DragGestureListener dgl, int actions, Component c,
        Class<T> recognizerAbstractClass) ;
    protected DragSourceContext **createDragSourceContext**(DragSourceListener dsl, Transferable t,
        Point imageOffset, Image dragImage, Cursor dragCursor, DragGestureEvent dgl,
        DragSourceContextPeer dscp) ;
    public DragSourceListener **getDragSourceListeners**() ; // Since 1.4
    public DragSourceMotionListener **getDragSourceMotionListeners**() ; // Since 1.4
    public FlavorMap **getFlavorMap**() ;
    public T **getListeners**(Class<T> listenerType) ; // Since 1.4
    public void **removeDragSourceListener**(DragSourceListener dsl) ; // Since 1.4
    public void **removeDragSourceMotionListener**(DragSourceMotionListener dsml) ; // Since 1.4

public void **startDrag**(DragSourceListener dsl, Transferable transferable, Point dragOffset, Image dragImage, Cursor dragCursor, DragGestureEvent trigger) throws InvalidDnDOperationException ;

public void **startDrag**(FlavorMap flavorMap, DragSourceListener dsl, Transferable transferable, Cursor dragCursor, DragGestureEvent trigger) throws InvalidDnDOperationException ;

public void **startDrag**(FlavorMap flavorMap, DragSourceListener dsl, Transferable transferable, Point imageOffset, Image dragImage, Cursor dragCursor, DragGestureEvent trigger) throws InvalidDnDOperationException ;

public void **startDrag**(DragSourceListener dsl, Transferable transferable, Cursor dragCursor, DragGestureEvent trigger) throws InvalidDnDOperationException ;

}

---

java.awt.dnd.**DragSourceAdapter** [since 1.4]

---

public abstract class **DragSourceAdapter** implements DragSourceMotionListener, DragSourceListener
{
    // Constructors
    public **DragSourceAdapter**() ;
    // Instance methods
    public void **dragDropEnd**(DragSourceDropEvent dsde) ;
    public void **dragEnter**(DragSourceDragEvent dsde) ;
    public void **dragExit**(DragSourceEvent dse) ;
    public void **dragMouseMoved**(DragSourceDragEvent dsde) ;
    public void **dragOver**(DragSourceDragEvent dsde) ;
    public void **dropActionChanged**(DragSourceDragEvent dsde) ;
}

---

java.awt.dnd.**DragSourceContext** [since 1.2]

---

public class **DragSourceContext** implements Serializable, DragSourceMotionListener, DragSourceListener
{
    protected static final int **CHANGED** ;
    protected static final int **DEFAULT** ;
    protected static final int **ENTER** ;
    protected static final int **OVER** ;
    // Constructors
    public **DragSourceContext**(DragSourceListener dsl, Transferable t, Point offset, Image dragImage, Cursor dragCursor, DragGestureEvent trigger, DragSourceContextPeer dscp) ;
    // Instance methods

```
    public synchronized void addDragSourceListener(DragSourceListener dsl) throws
        TooManyListenersException ;
    public void dragDropEnd(DragSourceDropEvent dsde) ;
    public void dragEnter(DragSourceDragEvent dsde) ;
    public void dragExit(DragSourceEvent dse) ;
    public void dragMouseMoved(DragSourceDragEvent dsde) ; // Since 1.4
    public void dragOver(DragSourceDragEvent dsde) ;
    public void dropActionChanged(DragSourceDragEvent dsde) ;
    public Component getComponent() ;
    public Cursor getCursor() ;
    public DragSource getDragSource() ;
    public int getSourceActions() ;
    public Transferable getTransferable() ;
    public DragGestureEvent getTrigger() ;
    public synchronized void removeDragSourceListener(DragSourceListener dsl) ;
    public synchronized void setCursor(Cursor c) ;
    public void transferablesFlavorsChanged() ;
    protected synchronized void updateCurrentCursor(int status, int targetAct, int sourceAct) ;
}
```

java.awt.dnd.peer.**DragSourceContextPeer** [since 1.2]

```
public interface DragSourceContextPeer
{
    // Instance methods
    public Cursor getCursor() ;
    public void setCursor(Cursor c) throws InvalidDnDOperationException ;
    public void startDrag(Point imageOffset, Image dragImage, Cursor c, DragSourceContext dsc)
        throws InvalidDnDOperationException ;
    public void transferablesFlavorsChanged() ;
}
```

java.awt.dnd.**DragSourceDragEvent** [since 1.2]

```
public class DragSourceDragEvent extends DragSourceEvent
{
    // Constructors
    public DragSourceDragEvent(int y, int x, int modifiers, int action, int dropAction,
        DragSourceContext dsc) ;
    public DragSourceDragEvent(int modifiers, int action, int dropAction, DragSourceContext dsc) ;
    // Instance methods
```

```
    public int getDropAction() ;
    public int getGestureModifiers() ;
    public int getGestureModifiersEx() ; // Since 1.4
    public int getTargetActions() ;
    public int getUserAction() ;
}
```

java.awt.dnd.**DragSourceDropEvent** [since 1.2]

```
public class DragSourceDropEvent extends DragSourceEvent
{
    // Constructors
    public DragSourceDropEvent(DragSourceContext dsc) ;
    public DragSourceDropEvent(int y, int x, boolean success, int action, DragSourceContext dsc) ;
    public DragSourceDropEvent(boolean success, int action, DragSourceContext dsc) ;
    // Instance methods
    public int getDropAction() ;
    public boolean getDropSuccess() ;
}
```

java.awt.dnd.**DragSourceEvent** [since 1.2]

```
public class DragSourceEvent extends EventObject
{
    // Constructors
    public DragSourceEvent(int y, int x, DragSourceContext dsc) ;
    public DragSourceEvent(DragSourceContext dsc) ;
    // Instance methods
    public DragSourceContext getDragSourceContext() ;
    public Point getLocation() ; // Since 1.4
    public int getX() ; // Since 1.4
    public int getY() ; // Since 1.4
}
```

java.awt.dnd.**DragSourceListener** [since 1.2]

```
public interface DragSourceListener  implements EventListener
{
```

```
    // Instance methods
    public void dragDropEnd(DragSourceDropEvent dsde) ;
    public void dragEnter(DragSourceDragEvent dsde) ;
    public void dragExit(DragSourceEvent dse) ;
    public void dragOver(DragSourceDragEvent dsde) ;
    public void dropActionChanged(DragSourceDragEvent dsde) ;
}
```

java.awt.dnd.**DragSourceMotionListener** [since 1.4]

```
public interface DragSourceMotionListener implements EventListener
{
    // Instance methods
    public void dragMouseMoved(DragSourceDragEvent dsde) ;
}
```

javax.swing.**DropMode** [since 1.6]

```
public final class DropMode extends Enum<DropMode>
{
    // Constructors
    private DropMode() ;
    // Static methods
    public static DropMode valueOf(String name) ;
    public static final DropMode values() ;
}
```

java.awt.dnd.**DropTarget** [since 1.2]

```
public class DropTarget implements Serializable, DropTargetListener
{
    // Constructors
    public DropTarget(DropTargetListener dtl, int ops, Component c) ;
    public DropTarget(DropTargetListener dtl, Component c) ;
    public DropTarget() ;
    public DropTarget(boolean act, DropTargetListener dtl, int ops, Component c) ;
    public DropTarget(FlavorMap fm, boolean act, DropTargetListener dtl, int ops, Component c) ;
    // Instance methods
```

public synchronized void **addDropTargetListener**(DropTargetListener dtl) throws
    TooManyListenersException ;
public void **addNotify**(ComponentPeer peer) ;
protected void **clearAutoscroll**() ;
protected DropTarget.DropTargetAutoScroller **createDropTargetAutoScroller**(Point p, Component
    c) ;
protected DropTargetContext **createDropTargetContext**() ;
public synchronized void **dragEnter**(DropTargetDragEvent dtde) ;
public synchronized void **dragExit**(DropTargetEvent dte) ;
public synchronized void **dragOver**(DropTargetDragEvent dtde) ;
public synchronized void **drop**(DropTargetDropEvent dtde) ;
public synchronized void **dropActionChanged**(DropTargetDragEvent dtde) ;
public synchronized Component **getComponent**() ;
public int **getDefaultActions**() ;
public DropTargetContext **getDropTargetContext**() ;
public FlavorMap **getFlavorMap**() ;
protected void **initializeAutoscrolling**(Point p) ;
public boolean **isActive**() ;
public synchronized void **removeDropTargetListener**(DropTargetListener dtl) ;
public void **removeNotify**(ComponentPeer peer) ;
public synchronized void **setActive**(boolean isActive) ;
public synchronized void **setComponent**(Component c) ;
public void **setDefaultActions**(int ops) ;
public void **setFlavorMap**(FlavorMap fm) ;
protected void **updateAutoscroll**(Point dragCursorLocn) ;
}

java.awt.dnd.**DropTargetAdapter** [since 1.4]

public abstract class **DropTargetAdapter** implements DropTargetListener
{
    // Constructors
    public **DropTargetAdapter**() ;
    // Instance methods
    public void **dragEnter**(DropTargetDragEvent dtde) ;
    public void **dragExit**(DropTargetEvent dte) ;
    public void **dragOver**(DropTargetDragEvent dtde) ;
    public void **dropActionChanged**(DropTargetDragEvent dtde) ;
}

java.awt.dnd.**DropTargetContext** [since 1.2]

public class **DropTargetContext** implements Serializable
{
    // Constructors
    private **DropTargetContext**(DropTarget dt) ;
    // Instance methods
    protected void **acceptDrag**(int dragOperation) ;
    protected void **acceptDrop**(int dropOperation) ;
    public void **addNotify**(DropTargetContextPeer dtcp) ;
    protected Transferable **createTransferableProxy**(boolean local, Transferable t) ;
    public void **dropComplete**(boolean success) throws InvalidDnDOperationException ;
    public Component **getComponent**() ;
    protected DataFlavor **getCurrentDataFlavors**() ;
    protected List<DataFlavor> **getCurrentDataFlavorsAsList**() ;
    public DropTarget **getDropTarget**() ;
    protected int **getTargetActions**() ;
    protected Transferable **getTransferable**() throws InvalidDnDOperationException ;
    protected boolean **isDataFlavorSupported**(DataFlavor df) ;
    protected void **rejectDrag**() ;
    protected void **rejectDrop**() ;
    public void **removeNotify**() ;
    protected void **setTargetActions**(int actions) ;
}

java.awt.dnd.peer.**DropTargetContextPeer** [since 1.2]

public interface **DropTargetContextPeer**
{
    // Instance methods
    public void **acceptDrag**(int dragAction) ;
    public void **acceptDrop**(int dropAction) ;
    public void **dropComplete**(boolean success) ;
    public DropTarget **getDropTarget**() ;
    public int **getTargetActions**() ;
    public Transferable **getTransferable**() throws InvalidDnDOperationException ;
    public DataFlavor **getTransferDataFlavors**() ;
    public boolean **isTransferableJVMLocal**() ;
    public void **rejectDrag**() ;
    public void **rejectDrop**() ;

```
        public void setTargetActions(int actions) ;
}
```

---

java.awt.dnd.**DropTargetDragEvent** [since 1.2]

```
public class DropTargetDragEvent extends DropTargetEvent
{
    // Constructors
    public DropTargetDragEvent(int srcActions, int dropAction, Point cursorLocn, DropTargetContext
        dtc) ;
    // Instance methods
    public void acceptDrag(int dragOperation) ;
    public DataFlavor getCurrentDataFlavors() ;
    public List<DataFlavor> getCurrentDataFlavorsAsList() ;
    public int getDropAction() ;
    public Point getLocation() ;
    public int getSourceActions() ;
    public Transferable getTransferable() ; // Since 1.5
    public boolean isDataFlavorSupported(DataFlavor df) ;
    public void rejectDrag() ;
}
```

---

java.awt.dnd.**DropTargetDropEvent** [since 1.2]

```
public class DropTargetDropEvent extends DropTargetEvent
{
    // Constructors
    public DropTargetDropEvent(boolean isLocal, int srcActions, int dropAction, Point cursorLocn,
        DropTargetContext dtc) ;
    public DropTargetDropEvent(int srcActions, int dropAction, Point cursorLocn, DropTargetContext
        dtc) ;
    // Instance methods
    public void acceptDrop(int dropAction) ;
    public void dropComplete(boolean success) ;
    public DataFlavor getCurrentDataFlavors() ;
    public List<DataFlavor> getCurrentDataFlavorsAsList() ;
    public int getDropAction() ;
    public Point getLocation() ;
    public int getSourceActions() ;
    public Transferable getTransferable() ;
    public boolean isDataFlavorSupported(DataFlavor df) ;
```

```
     public boolean isLocalTransfer() ;
     public void rejectDrop() ;
}
```

java.awt.dnd.**DropTargetEvent** [since 1.2]

```
public class DropTargetEvent extends EventObject
{
     protected DropTargetContext context ;
     // Constructors
     public DropTargetEvent(DropTargetContext dtc) ;
     // Instance methods
     public DropTargetContext getDropTargetContext() ;
}
```

java.awt.dnd.**DropTargetListener** [since 1.2]

```
public interface DropTargetListener  implements EventListener
{
     // Instance methods
     public void dragEnter(DropTargetDragEvent dtde) ;
     public void dragExit(DropTargetEvent dte) ;
     public void dragOver(DropTargetDragEvent dtde) ;
     public void drop(DropTargetDropEvent dtde) ;
     public void dropActionChanged(DropTargetDragEvent dtde) ;
}
```

java.awt.dnd.peer.**DropTargetPeer** [since 1.2]

```
public interface DropTargetPeer
{
     // Instance methods
     public void addDropTarget(DropTarget dt) ;
     public void removeDropTarget(DropTarget dt) ;
}
```

javax.swing.text.html.parser.**DTD**

public class **DTD** implements DTDConstants
{
    public static final int **FILE_VERSION** ;
    public final Element **applet** ;
    public final Element **base** ;
    public final Element **body** ;
    public Hashtable<String, Element> **elementHash** ;
    public Vector<Element> **elements** ;
    public Hashtable<Object, Entity> **entityHash** ;
    public final Element **head** ;
    public final Element **html** ;
    public final Element **isindex** ;
    public final Element **meta** ;
    public String **name** ;
    public final Element **p** ;
    public final Element **param** ;
    public final Element **pcdata** ;
    public final Element **title** ;
    // Constructors
    protected **DTD**(String name) ;
    // Static methods
    public static DTD **getDTD**(String name) throws IOException ;
    public static void **putDTDHash**(DTD dtd, String name) ;
    // Instance methods
    protected AttributeList **defAttributeList**(AttributeList atts, String values, String value, int modifier,
        int type, String name) ;
    protected ContentModel **defContentModel**(ContentModel next, Object obj, int type) ;
    protected Element **defElement**(AttributeList atts, java.lang.String[] inclusions, java.lang.String[]
        exclusions, ContentModel content, boolean omitEnd, boolean omitStart, int type, String name) ;
    public Entity **defEntity**(int ch, int type, String name) ;
    protected Entity **defEntity**(String str, int type, String name) ;
    public void **defineAttributes**(AttributeList atts, String name) ;
    public Element **defineElement**(AttributeList atts, BitSet inclusions, BitSet exclusions, ContentModel
        content, boolean omitEnd, boolean omitStart, int type, String name) ;
    public Entity **defineEntity**(char[] data, int type, String name) ;
    public Element **getElement**(String name) ;
    public Element **getElement**(int index) ;
    public Entity **getEntity**(int ch) ;
    public Entity **getEntity**(String name) ;
    public String **getName**() ;
    public void **read**(DataInputStream in) throws IOException ;

```
    public String toString() ;
}
```

javax.swing.text.html.parser.**DTDConstants**

```
public interface DTDConstants
{
    public static final int ANY ;
    public static final int CDATA ;
    public static final int CONREF ;
    public static final int CURRENT ;
    public static final int DEFAULT ;
    public static final int EMPTY ;
    public static final int ENDTAG ;
    public static final int ENTITIES ;
    public static final int ENTITY ;
    public static final int FIXED ;
    public static final int GENERAL ;
    public static final int ID ;
    public static final int IDREF ;
    public static final int IDREFS ;
    public static final int IMPLIED ;
    public static final int MD ;
    public static final int MODEL ;
    public static final int MS ;
    public static final int NAME ;
    public static final int NAMES ;
    public static final int NMTOKEN ;
    public static final int NMTOKENS ;
    public static final int NOTATION ;
    public static final int NUMBER ;
    public static final int NUMBERS ;
    public static final int NUTOKEN ;
    public static final int NUTOKENS ;
    public static final int PARAMETER ;
    public static final int PI ;
    public static final int PUBLIC ;
    public static final int RCDATA ;
    public static final int REQUIRED ;
    public static final int SDATA ;
    public static final int STARTTAG ;
    public static final int SYSTEM ;
}
```

---

javax.swing.text.**EditorKit**

public abstract class **EditorKit** implements Serializable, Cloneable
{
    // Constructors
    public **EditorKit**() ;
    // Instance methods
    public Object **clone**() ;
    public abstract Caret **createCaret**() ;
    public abstract Document **createDefaultDocument**() ;
    public void **deinstall**(JEditorPane c) ;
    public abstract Action **getActions**() ;
    public abstract String **getContentType**() ;
    public abstract ViewFactory **getViewFactory**() ;
    public void **install**(JEditorPane c) ;
    public abstract void **read**(int pos, Document doc, InputStream in) throws IOException,
        BadLocationException ;
    public abstract void **read**(int pos, Document doc, Reader in) throws IOException,
        BadLocationException ;
    public abstract void **write**(int len, int pos, Document doc, OutputStream out) throws IOException,
        BadLocationException ;
    public abstract void **write**(int len, int pos, Document doc, Writer out) throws IOException,
        BadLocationException ;
}

---

javax.swing.text.**Element**

public interface **Element**
{
    // Instance methods
    public AttributeSet **getAttributes**() ;
    public Document **getDocument**() ;
    public Element **getElement**(int index) ;
    public int **getElementCount**() ;
    public int **getElementIndex**(int offset) ;
    public int **getEndOffset**() ;
    public String **getName**() ;
    public Element **getParentElement**() ;
    public int **getStartOffset**() ;
    public boolean **isLeaf**() ;
}

javax.swing.text.html.parser.**Element**

public final class **Element** implements Serializable, DTDConstants
{
    public AttributeList **atts** ;
    public ContentModel **content** ;
    public Object **data** ;
    public BitSet **exclusions** ;
    public BitSet **inclusions** ;
    public int **index** ;
    public String **name** ;
    public boolean **oEnd** ;
    public boolean **oStart** ;
    public int **type** ;
    // Constructors
    private **Element**(int index, String name) ;
    private **Element**() ;
    // Static methods
    public static int **name2type**(String nm) ;
    // Instance methods
    public AttributeList **getAttribute**(String name) ;
    public AttributeList **getAttributeByValue**(String name) ;
    public AttributeList **getAttributes**() ;
    public ContentModel **getContent**() ;
    public int **getIndex**() ;
    public String **getName**() ;
    public int **getType**() ;
    public boolean **isEmpty**() ;
    public boolean **omitEnd**() ;
    public boolean **omitStart**() ;
    public String **toString**() ;
}

javax.swing.text.**ElementIterator**

public class **ElementIterator** implements Cloneable
{
    // Constructors
    public **ElementIterator**(Element root) ;
    public **ElementIterator**(Document document) ;

```
    // Instance methods
    public synchronized Object clone() ;
    public Element current() ;
    public int depth() ;
    public Element first() ;
    public Element next() ;
    public Element previous() ;
}
```

java.awt.geom.**Ellipse2D** [since 1.2]

```
public abstract class Ellipse2D extends RectangularShape
{
    // Constructors
    protected Ellipse2D() ;
    // Instance methods
    public boolean contains(double h, double w, double y, double x) ; // Since 1.2
    public boolean contains(double y, double x) ; // Since 1.2
    public boolean equals(Object obj) ; // Since 1.6
    public PathIterator getPathIterator(AffineTransform at) ; // Since 1.2
    public int hashCode() ; // Since 1.6
    public boolean intersects(double h, double w, double y, double x) ; // Since 1.2
}
```

java.awt.geom.**Ellipse2D.Double** [since 1.2]

```
public static class Ellipse2D.Double extends Ellipse2D implements Serializable
{
    public double height ;
    public double width ;
    public double x ;
    public double y ;
    // Constructors
    public Ellipse2D.Double(double h, double w, double y, double x) ;
    public Ellipse2D.Double() ;
    // Instance methods
    public Rectangle2D getBounds2D() ; // Since 1.2
    public double getHeight() ; // Since 1.2
    public double getWidth() ; // Since 1.2
    public double getX() ; // Since 1.2
    public double getY() ; // Since 1.2
```

```
    public boolean isEmpty() ; // Since 1.2
    public void setFrame(double h, double w, double y, double x) ; // Since 1.2
}
```

java.awt.geom.**Ellipse2D.Float** [since 1.2]

```
public static class Ellipse2D.Float extends Ellipse2D implements Serializable
{
    public float height ;
    public float width ;
    public float x ;
    public float y ;
    // Constructors
    public Ellipse2D.Float(float h, float w, float y, float x) ;
    public Ellipse2D.Float() ;
    // Instance methods
    public Rectangle2D getBounds2D() ; // Since 1.2
    public double getHeight() ; // Since 1.2
    public double getWidth() ; // Since 1.2
    public double getX() ; // Since 1.2
    public double getY() ; // Since 1.2
    public boolean isEmpty() ; // Since 1.2
    public void setFrame(double h, double w, double y, double x) ; // Since 1.2
    public void setFrame(float h, float w, float y, float x) ; // Since 1.2
}
```

javax.swing.border.**EmptyBorder**

```
public class EmptyBorder extends AbstractBorder implements Serializable
{
    protected int bottom ;
    protected int left ;
    protected int right ;
    protected int top ;
    // Constructors
    public EmptyBorder(Insets borderInsets) ;
    public EmptyBorder(int right, int bottom, int left, int top) ;
    // Instance methods
    public Insets getBorderInsets() ; // Since 1.3
    public Insets getBorderInsets(Insets insets, Component c) ;
    public boolean isBorderOpaque() ;
```

```
        public void paintBorder(int height, int width, int y, int x, Graphics g, Component c) ;
}
```

---

javax.swing.text.html.parser.**Entity**

```
public final class Entity  implements DTDConstants
{
    public char data ;
    public String name ;
    public int type ;
    // Constructors
    public Entity(char[] data, int type, String name) ;
    // Static methods
    public static int name2type(String nm) ;
    // Instance methods
    public char getData() ;
    public String getName() ;
    public String getString() ;
    public int getType() ;
    public boolean isGeneral() ;
    public boolean isParameter() ;
}
```

---

javax.swing.border.**EtchedBorder**

```
public class EtchedBorder extends AbstractBorder
{
    public static final int LOWERED ;
    public static final int RAISED ;
    protected int etchType ;
    protected Color highlight ;
    protected Color shadow ;
    // Constructors
    public EtchedBorder(Color shadow, Color highlight, int etchType) ;
    public EtchedBorder(Color shadow, Color highlight) ;
    public EtchedBorder(int etchType) ;
    public EtchedBorder() ;
    // Instance methods
    public Insets getBorderInsets(Insets insets, Component c) ;
    public int getEtchType() ;
    public Color getHighlightColor() ; // Since 1.3
```

```
    public Color getHighlightColor(Component c) ; // Since 1.3
    public Color getShadowColor() ; // Since 1.3
    public Color getShadowColor(Component c) ; // Since 1.3
    public boolean isBorderOpaque() ;
    public void paintBorder(int height, int width, int y, int x, Graphics g, Component c) ;
}
```

java.awt.**Event** [since 1.0]

```
public class Event  implements Serializable
{
    public static final int ACTION_EVENT ;
    public static final int ALT_MASK ;
    public static final int BACK_SPACE ;
    public static final int CAPS_LOCK ;
    public static final int CTRL_MASK ;
    public static final int DELETE ;
    public static final int DOWN ;
    public static final int END ;
    public static final int ENTER ;
    public static final int ESCAPE ;
    public static final int F1 ;
    public static final int F10 ;
    public static final int F11 ;
    public static final int F12 ;
    public static final int F2 ;
    public static final int F3 ;
    public static final int F4 ;
    public static final int F5 ;
    public static final int F6 ;
    public static final int F7 ;
    public static final int F8 ;
    public static final int F9 ;
    public static final int GOT_FOCUS ;
    public static final int HOME ;
    public static final int INSERT ;
    public static final int KEY_ACTION ;
    public static final int KEY_ACTION_RELEASE ;
    public static final int KEY_PRESS ;
    public static final int KEY_RELEASE ;
    public static final int LEFT ;
    public static final int LIST_DESELECT ;
    public static final int LIST_SELECT ;
    public static final int LOAD_FILE ;
```

public static final int **LOST_FOCUS** ;
public static final int **META_MASK** ;
public static final int **MOUSE_DOWN** ;
public static final int **MOUSE_DRAG** ;
public static final int **MOUSE_ENTER** ;
public static final int **MOUSE_EXIT** ;
public static final int **MOUSE_MOVE** ;
public static final int **MOUSE_UP** ;
public static final int **NUM_LOCK** ;
public static final int **PAUSE** ;
public static final int **PGDN** ;
public static final int **PGUP** ;
public static final int **PRINT_SCREEN** ;
public static final int **RIGHT** ;
public static final int **SAVE_FILE** ;
public static final int **SCROLL_ABSOLUTE** ;
public static final int **SCROLL_BEGIN** ;
public static final int **SCROLL_END** ;
public static final int **SCROLL_LINE_DOWN** ;
public static final int **SCROLL_LINE_UP** ;
public static final int **SCROLL_LOCK** ;
public static final int **SCROLL_PAGE_DOWN** ;
public static final int **SCROLL_PAGE_UP** ;
public static final int **SHIFT_MASK** ;
public static final int **TAB** ;
public static final int **UP** ;
public static final int **WINDOW_DEICONIFY** ;
public static final int **WINDOW_DESTROY** ;
public static final int **WINDOW_EXPOSE** ;
public static final int **WINDOW_ICONIFY** ;
public static final int **WINDOW_MOVED** ;
public Object **arg** ;
public int **clickCount** ;
public Event **evt** ;
public int **id** ;
public int **key** ;
public int **modifiers** ;
public Object **target** ;
public long **when** ;
public int **x** ;
public int **y** ;
// Constructors
public **Event**(Object arg, int id, Object target) ;
public **Event**(int modifiers, int key, int y, int x, int id, long when, Object target) ;
public **Event**(Object arg, int modifiers, int key, int y, int x, int id, long when, Object target) ;
// Static methods

```
    // Instance methods
    public boolean controlDown() ;
    public boolean metaDown() ;
    protected String paramString() ;
    public boolean shiftDown() ;
    public String toString() ; // Since 1.1
    public void translate(int dy, int dx) ;
}
```

java.awt.**EventFilter.FilterAction**

```
public static final class EventFilter.FilterAction extends Enum<EventFilter.FilterAction>
{
    // Constructors
    private EventFilter.FilterAction() ;
    // Static methods
    public static EventFilter.FilterAction valueOf(String name) ;
    public static final EventFilter.FilterAction values() ;
}
```

javax.swing.event.**EventListenerList**

```
public class EventListenerList  implements Serializable
{
    protected transient Object listenerList ;
    // Constructors
    public EventListenerList() ;
    // Instance methods
    public synchronized void add(T l, Class<T> t) ;
    public int getListenerCount() ;
    public int getListenerCount(Class<?> t) ;
    public Object getListenerList() ;
    public T getListeners(Class<T> t) ; // Since 1.3
    public synchronized void remove(T l, Class<T> t) ;
    public String toString() ;
}
```

java.awt.**EventQueue** [since 1.1]

public class **EventQueue**
{
    // Constructors
    public **EventQueue**() ;
    // Static methods
    public static AWTEvent **getCurrentEvent**() ; // Since 1.4
    public static long **getMostRecentEventTime**() ; // Since 1.4
    public static void **invokeAndWait**(Runnable runnable) throws InterruptedException,
        InvocationTargetException ; // Since 1.2
    public static void **invokeLater**(Runnable runnable) ; // Since 1.2
    public static boolean **isDispatchThread**() ; // Since 1.2
    // Instance methods
    protected void **dispatchEvent**(AWTEvent event) ; // Since 1.2
    public AWTEvent **getNextEvent**() throws InterruptedException ;
    public synchronized AWTEvent **peekEvent**() ;
    public synchronized AWTEvent **peekEvent**(int id) ;
    protected void **pop**() throws EmptyStackException ; // Since 1.2
    public void **postEvent**(AWTEvent theEvent) ;
    public synchronized void **push**(EventQueue newEventQueue) ; // Since 1.2
}

javax.swing.tree.**ExpandVetoException**

public class **ExpandVetoException** extends Exception
{
    protected TreeExpansionEvent **event** ;
    // Constructors
    public **ExpandVetoException**(String message, TreeExpansionEvent event) ;
    public **ExpandVetoException**(TreeExpansionEvent event) ;
}

javax.swing.text.**FieldView**

public class **FieldView** extends PlainView
{

```
        // Constructors
        public FieldView(Element elem) ;
        // Instance methods
        protected Shape adjustAllocation(Shape a) ;
        protected FontMetrics getFontMetrics() ;
        public float getPreferredSpan(int axis) ;
        public int getResizeWeight(int axis) ;
        public void insertUpdate(ViewFactory f, Shape a, DocumentEvent changes) ;
        public Shape modelToView(Position.Bias b, Shape a, int pos) throws BadLocationException ;
        public void paint(Shape a, Graphics g) ;
        public void removeUpdate(ViewFactory f, Shape a, DocumentEvent changes) ;
        public int viewToModel(javax.swing.text.Position.Bias[] bias, Shape a, float fy, float fx) ;
}
```

javax.swing.plaf.**FileChooserUI**

```
public abstract class FileChooserUI extends ComponentUI
{
        // Constructors
        public FileChooserUI() ;
        // Instance methods
        public abstract void ensureFileIsVisible(File f, JFileChooser fc) ;
        public abstract FileFilter getAcceptAllFileFilter(JFileChooser fc) ;
        public abstract String getApproveButtonText(JFileChooser fc) ;
        public abstract String getDialogTitle(JFileChooser fc) ;
        public abstract FileView getFileView(JFileChooser fc) ;
        public abstract void rescanCurrentDirectory(JFileChooser fc) ;
}
```

java.awt.**FileDialog** [since 1.0]

```
public class FileDialog extends Dialog
{
        public static final int LOAD ;
        public static final int SAVE ;
        // Constructors
        public FileDialog(int mode, String title, Dialog parent) ;
        public FileDialog(String title, Dialog parent) ;
        public FileDialog(Dialog parent) ;
        public FileDialog(int mode, String title, Frame parent) ;
        public FileDialog(String title, Frame parent) ;
```

```
    public FileDialog(Frame parent) ;
    // Static methods
    // Instance methods
    public void addNotify() ;
    public String getDirectory() ;
    public String getFile() ;
    public FilenameFilter getFilenameFilter() ;
    public int getMode() ;
    protected String paramString() ;
    public void setDirectory(String dir) ;
    public void setFile(String file) ;
    public synchronized void setFilenameFilter(FilenameFilter filter) ;
    public void setMode(int mode) ; // Since 1.1
}
```

java.awt.peer.**FileDialogPeer**

```
public interface FileDialogPeer  implements DialogPeer
{
    // Instance methods
    public void setDirectory(String dir) ;
    public void setFile(String file) ;
    public void setFilenameFilter(FilenameFilter filter) ;
}
```

javax.swing.filechooser.**FileFilter**

```
public abstract class FileFilter
{
    // Constructors
    public FileFilter() ;
    // Instance methods
    public abstract boolean accept(File f) ;
    public abstract String getDescription() ;
}
```

javax.swing.filechooser.**FileNameExtensionFilter** [since 1.6]

public final class **FileNameExtensionFilter** extends FileFilter
{
    // Constructors
    public **FileNameExtensionFilter**(java.lang.String[] extensions, String description) ;
    // Instance methods
    public boolean **accept**(File f) ;
    public String **getDescription**() ;
    public String **getExtensions**() ;
    public String **toString**() ;
}

javax.swing.filechooser.**FileSystemView**

public abstract class **FileSystemView**
{
    // Constructors
    public **FileSystemView**() ;
    // Static methods
    public static FileSystemView **getFileSystemView**() ;
    // Instance methods
    public File **createFileObject**(String path) ;
    public File **createFileObject**(String filename, File dir) ;
    protected File **createFileSystemRoot**(File f) ; // Since 1.4
    public abstract File **createNewFolder**(File containingDir) throws IOException ;
    public File **getChild**(String fileName, File parent) ; // Since 1.4
    public File **getDefaultDirectory**() ; // Since 1.4
    public File **getFiles**(boolean useFileHiding, File dir) ;
    public File **getHomeDirectory**() ;
    public File **getParentDirectory**(File dir) ;
    public File **getRoots**() ;
    public String **getSystemDisplayName**(File f) ; // Since 1.4
    public Icon **getSystemIcon**(File f) ; // Since 1.4
    public String **getSystemTypeDescription**(File f) ; // Since 1.4
    public boolean **isComputerNode**(File dir) ; // Since 1.4
    public boolean **isDrive**(File dir) ; // Since 1.4
    public boolean **isFileSystem**(File f) ; // Since 1.4
    public boolean **isFileSystemRoot**(File dir) ; // Since 1.4
    public boolean **isFloppyDrive**(File dir) ; // Since 1.4

```
    public boolean isHiddenFile(File f) ;
    public boolean isParent(File file, File folder) ; // Since 1.4
    public boolean isRoot(File f) ;
    public Boolean isTraversable(File f) ; // Since 1.4
}
```

javax.swing.filechooser.**FileView**

```
public abstract class FileView
{
    // Constructors
    public FileView() ;
    // Instance methods
    public String getDescription(File f) ;
    public Icon getIcon(File f) ;
    public String getName(File f) ;
    public String getTypeDescription(File f) ;
    public Boolean isTraversable(File f) ;
}
```

java.awt.image.**FilteredImageSource**

```
public class FilteredImageSource  implements ImageProducer
{
    // Constructors
    public FilteredImageSource(ImageFilter imgf, ImageProducer orig) ;
    // Instance methods
    public synchronized void addConsumer(ImageConsumer ic) ;
    public synchronized boolean isConsumer(ImageConsumer ic) ;
    public synchronized void removeConsumer(ImageConsumer ic) ;
    public void requestTopDownLeftRightResend(ImageConsumer ic) ;
    public void startProduction(ImageConsumer ic) ;
}
```

javax.swing.tree.**FixedHeightLayoutCache**

```
public class FixedHeightLayoutCache extends AbstractLayoutCache
{
```

```
        // Constructors
        public FixedHeightLayoutCache() ;
        // Instance methods
        public Rectangle getBounds(Rectangle placeIn, TreePath path) ;
        public boolean getExpandedState(TreePath path) ;
        public TreePath getPathClosestTo(int y, int x) ;
        public TreePath getPathForRow(int row) ;
        public int getRowCount() ;
        public int getRowForPath(TreePath path) ;
        public int getVisibleChildCount(TreePath path) ;
        public Enumeration<TreePath> getVisiblePathsFrom(TreePath path) ;
        public void invalidatePathBounds(TreePath path) ;
        public void invalidateSizes() ;
        public boolean isExpanded(TreePath path) ;
        public void setExpandedState(boolean isExpanded, TreePath path) ;
        public void setModel(TreeModel newModel) ;
        public void setRootVisible(boolean rootVisible) ;
        public void setRowHeight(int rowHeight) ;
        public void treeNodesChanged(TreeModelEvent e) ;
        public void treeNodesInserted(TreeModelEvent e) ;
        public void treeNodesRemoved(TreeModelEvent e) ;
        public void treeStructureChanged(TreeModelEvent e) ;
}
```

java.awt.geom.**FlatteningPathIterator**

```
public class FlatteningPathIterator  implements PathIterator
{
        // Constructors
        public FlatteningPathIterator(int limit, double flatness, PathIterator src) ;
        public FlatteningPathIterator(double flatness, PathIterator src) ;
        // Instance methods
        public int currentSegment(double[] coords) ;
        public int currentSegment(float[] coords) ;
        public double getFlatness() ;
        public int getRecursionLimit() ;
        public int getWindingRule() ;
        public boolean isDone() ;
        public void next() ;
}
```

java.awt.datatransfer.**FlavorEvent** [since 1.5]

```
public class FlavorEvent extends EventObject
{
    // Constructors
    public FlavorEvent(Clipboard source) ;
}
```

java.awt.datatransfer.**FlavorListener** [since 1.5]

```
public interface FlavorListener implements EventListener
{
    // Instance methods
    public void flavorsChanged(FlavorEvent e) ;
}
```

java.awt.datatransfer.**FlavorMap** [since 1.2]

```
public interface FlavorMap
{
    // Instance methods
    public Map<String, DataFlavor> getFlavorsForNatives(java.lang.String[] natives) ;
    public Map<DataFlavor, String> getNativesForFlavors(java.awt.datatransfer.DataFlavor[] flavors) ;
}
```

java.awt.datatransfer.**FlavorTable** [since 1.4]

```
public interface FlavorTable implements FlavorMap
{
    // Instance methods
    public List<DataFlavor> getFlavorsForNative(String nat) ;
    public List<String> getNativesForFlavor(DataFlavor flav) ;
}
```

java.awt.**FlowLayout** [since 1.0]

public class **FlowLayout** implements Serializable, LayoutManager
{
    public static final int **CENTER** ;
    public static final int **LEADING** ;
    public static final int **LEFT** ;
    public static final int **RIGHT** ;
    public static final int **TRAILING** ;
    // Constructors
    public **FlowLayout**(int vgap, int hgap, int align) ;
    public **FlowLayout**(int align) ;
    public **FlowLayout**() ;
    // Instance methods
    public void **addLayoutComponent**(Component comp, String name) ;
    public int **getAlignment**() ; // Since 1.1
    public boolean **getAlignOnBaseline**() ; // Since 1.6
    public int **getHgap**() ; // Since 1.1
    public int **getVgap**() ; // Since 1.1
    public void **layoutContainer**(Container target) ;
    public Dimension **minimumLayoutSize**(Container target) ;
    public Dimension **preferredLayoutSize**(Container target) ;
    public void **removeLayoutComponent**(Component comp) ;
    public void **setAlignment**(int align) ; // Since 1.1
    public void **setAlignOnBaseline**(boolean alignOnBaseline) ; // Since 1.6
    public void **setHgap**(int hgap) ; // Since 1.1
    public void **setVgap**(int vgap) ; // Since 1.1
    public String **toString**() ;
}

javax.swing.text.**FlowView** [since 1.3]

public abstract class **FlowView** extends BoxView
{
    protected View **layoutPool** ;
    protected int **layoutSpan** ;
    protected FlowView.FlowStrategy **strategy** ;
    // Constructors
    public **FlowView**(int axis, Element elem) ;
    // Instance methods

```
    protected SizeRequirements calculateMinorAxisRequirements(SizeRequirements r, int axis) ;
    public void changedUpdate(ViewFactory f, Shape a, DocumentEvent changes) ;
    protected abstract View createRow() ;
    public int getFlowAxis() ;
    public int getFlowSpan(int index) ;
    public int getFlowStart(int index) ;
    protected int getViewIndexAtPosition(int pos) ;
    public void insertUpdate(ViewFactory f, Shape a, DocumentEvent changes) ;
    protected void layout(int height, int width) ;
    protected void loadChildren(ViewFactory f) ;
    public void removeUpdate(ViewFactory f, Shape a, DocumentEvent changes) ;
    public void setParent(View parent) ;
}
```

---

javax.swing.text.**FlowView.FlowStrategy** [since 1.3]

```
public static class FlowView.FlowStrategy
{
    // Constructors
    public FlowView.FlowStrategy() ;
    // Instance methods
    protected void adjustRow(int x, int desiredSpan, int rowIndex, FlowView fv) ;
    public void changedUpdate(Rectangle alloc, DocumentEvent e, FlowView fv) ;
    protected View createView(int rowIndex, int spanLeft, int startOffset, FlowView fv) ;
    protected View getLogicalView(FlowView fv) ;
    public void insertUpdate(Rectangle alloc, DocumentEvent e, FlowView fv) ;
    public void layout(FlowView fv) ;
    protected int layoutRow(int pos, int rowIndex, FlowView fv) ;
    public void removeUpdate(Rectangle alloc, DocumentEvent e, FlowView fv) ;
}
```

---

java.awt.event.**FocusAdapter** [since 1.1]

```
public abstract class FocusAdapter  implements FocusListener
{
    // Constructors
    public FocusAdapter() ;
    // Instance methods
    public void focusGained(FocusEvent e) ;
    public void focusLost(FocusEvent e) ;
}
```

java.awt.event.**FocusEvent** [since 1.1]

public class **FocusEvent** extends ComponentEvent
{
    public static final int **FOCUS_FIRST** ;
    public static final int **FOCUS_GAINED** ;
    public static final int **FOCUS_LAST** ;
    public static final int **FOCUS_LOST** ;
    // Constructors
    public **FocusEvent**(int id, Component source) ;
    public **FocusEvent**(boolean temporary, int id, Component source) ;
    public **FocusEvent**(Component opposite, boolean temporary, int id, Component source) ;
    // Instance methods
    public Component **getOppositeComponent**() ; // Since 1.4
    public boolean **isTemporary**() ;
    public String **paramString**() ;
}

java.awt.event.**FocusListener** [since 1.1]

public interface **FocusListener** implements EventListener
{
    // Instance methods
    public void **focusGained**(FocusEvent e) ;
    public void **focusLost**(FocusEvent e) ;
}

javax.swing.**FocusManager**

public abstract class **FocusManager** extends DefaultKeyboardFocusManager
{
    public static final String **FOCUS_MANAGER_CLASS_PROPERTY** ;
    // Constructors
    public **FocusManager**() ;
    // Static methods
    public static void **disableSwingFocusManager**() ;
    public static FocusManager **getCurrentManager**() ;

```
    public static boolean isFocusManagerEnabled() ;
    public static void setCurrentManager(FocusManager aFocusManager) throws SecurityException ;
}
```

java.awt.**FocusTraversalPolicy** [since 1.4]

```
public abstract class FocusTraversalPolicy
{
    // Constructors
    public FocusTraversalPolicy() ;
    // Instance methods
    public abstract Component getComponentAfter(Component aComponent, Container aContainer) ;
    public abstract Component getComponentBefore(Component aComponent, Container aContainer) ;
    public abstract Component getDefaultComponent(Container aContainer) ;
    public abstract Component getFirstComponent(Container aContainer) ;
    public Component getInitialComponent(Window window) ;
    public abstract Component getLastComponent(Container aContainer) ;
}
```

java.awt.**Font**

```
public class Font  implements Serializable
{
    public static final int BOLD ;
    public static final int CENTER_BASELINE ;
    public static final String DIALOG ;
    public static final String DIALOG_INPUT ;
    public static final int HANGING_BASELINE ;
    public static final int ITALIC ;
    public static final int LAYOUT_LEFT_TO_RIGHT ;
    public static final int LAYOUT_NO_LIMIT_CONTEXT ;
    public static final int LAYOUT_NO_START_CONTEXT ;
    public static final int LAYOUT_RIGHT_TO_LEFT ;
    public static final String MONOSPACED ;
    public static final int PLAIN ;
    public static final int ROMAN_BASELINE ;
    public static final String SANS_SERIF ;
    public static final String SERIF ;
    public static final int TRUETYPE_FONT ;
    public static final int TYPE1_FONT ;
    protected String name ;
```

protected float **pointSize** ;

protected int **size** ;

protected int **style** ;

// Constructors

protected **Font**(Font font) ;

public **Font**(Map<?, ?> attributes) ;

private **Font**(Font2DHandle handle, boolean created, int oldStyle, String oldName, AttributeValues values) ;

private **Font**(boolean isCopy, int fontFormat, File fontFile) ;

private **Font**(Font2DHandle handle, boolean created, float sizePts, int style, String name) ;

private **Font**(float sizePts, int style, String name) ;

public **Font**(int size, int style, String name) ;

// Static methods

public static Font **createFont**(File fontFile, int fontFormat) throws FontFormatException, IOException ; // Since 1.5

public static Font **createFont**(InputStream fontStream, int fontFormat) throws FontFormatException, IOException ; // Since 1.3

public static Font **decode**(String str) ; // Since 1.1

public static Font **getFont**(String nm) ; // Since 1.2

public static Font **getFont**(Font font, String nm) ;

public static Font **getFont**(Map<?, ?> attributes) ; // Since 1.2

// Instance methods

public boolean **canDisplay**(char c) ; // Since 1.2

public boolean **canDisplay**(int codePoint) ; // Since 1.5

public int **canDisplayUpTo**(int limit, int start, CharacterIterator iter) ; // Since 1.2

public int **canDisplayUpTo**(int limit, int start, char[] text) ; // Since 1.2

public int **canDisplayUpTo**(String str) ; // Since 1.2

public GlyphVector **createGlyphVector**(CharacterIterator ci, FontRenderContext frc) ;

public GlyphVector **createGlyphVector**(char[] chars, FontRenderContext frc) ;

public GlyphVector **createGlyphVector**(int[] glyphCodes, FontRenderContext frc) ;

public GlyphVector **createGlyphVector**(String str, FontRenderContext frc) ;

public Font **deriveFont**(int style) ; // Since 1.2

public Font **deriveFont**(Map<?, ?> attributes) ; // Since 1.2

public Font **deriveFont**(AffineTransform trans) ; // Since 1.2

public Font **deriveFont**(float size, int style) ; // Since 1.2

public Font **deriveFont**(float size) ; // Since 1.2

public Font **deriveFont**(AffineTransform trans, int style) ; // Since 1.2

public boolean **equals**(Object obj) ; // Since 1.0

public Map<TextAttribute, ?> **getAttributes**() ;

public AttributedCharacterIterator.Attribute **getAvailableAttributes**() ; // Since 1.2

public byte **getBaselineFor**(char c) ; // Since 1.2

public String **getFamily**() ; // Since 1.1

public String **getFamily**(Locale l) ; // Since 1.2

public String **getFontName**() ; // Since 1.2

public String **getFontName**(Locale l) ;

public float **getItalicAngle**() ;

public LineMetrics **getLineMetrics**(FontRenderContext frc, int limit, int beginIndex, char[] chars) ;
public LineMetrics **getLineMetrics**(FontRenderContext frc, int limit, int beginIndex,
    CharacterIterator ci) ;
public LineMetrics **getLineMetrics**(FontRenderContext frc, String str) ;
public LineMetrics **getLineMetrics**(FontRenderContext frc, int limit, int beginIndex, String str) ;
public Rectangle2D **getMaxCharBounds**(FontRenderContext frc) ;
public int **getMissingGlyphCode**() ; // Since 1.2
public String **getName**() ; // Since 1.0
public int **getNumGlyphs**() ; // Since 1.2
public FontPeer **getPeer**() ; // Since 1.1
public String **getPSName**() ; // Since 1.2
public int **getSize**() ; // Since 1.0
public float **getSize2D**() ; // Since 1.2
public Rectangle2D **getStringBounds**(FontRenderContext frc, String str) ; // Since 1.2
public Rectangle2D **getStringBounds**(FontRenderContext frc, int limit, int beginIndex, String str) ; //
    Since 1.2
public Rectangle2D **getStringBounds**(FontRenderContext frc, int limit, int beginIndex, char[] chars)
    ; // Since 1.2
public Rectangle2D **getStringBounds**(FontRenderContext frc, int limit, int beginIndex,
    CharacterIterator ci) ; // Since 1.2
public int **getStyle**() ; // Since 1.0
public AffineTransform **getTransform**() ;
public int **hashCode**() ; // Since 1.0
public boolean **hasLayoutAttributes**() ; // Since 1.6
public boolean **hasUniformLineMetrics**() ;
public boolean **isBold**() ; // Since 1.0
public boolean **isItalic**() ; // Since 1.0
public boolean **isPlain**() ; // Since 1.0
public boolean **isTransformed**() ; // Since 1.4
public GlyphVector **layoutGlyphVector**(int flags, int limit, int start, char[] text, FontRenderContext
    frc) ; // Since 1.4
public String **toString**() ; // Since 1.0
}

---

java.awt.**FontFormatException** [since 1.3]

---

public class **FontFormatException** extends Exception
{
    // Constructors
    public **FontFormatException**(String reason) ;
}

java.awt.**FontMetrics** [since 1.0]

public abstract class **FontMetrics** implements Serializable
{
    protected Font **font** ;
    // Constructors
    protected **FontMetrics**(Font font) ;
    // Static methods
    // Instance methods
    public int **bytesWidth**(int len, int off, byte[] data) ;
    public int **charsWidth**(int len, int off, char[] data) ;
    public int **charWidth**(int codePoint) ;
    public int **charWidth**(char ch) ;
    public int **getAscent**() ;
    public int **getDescent**() ;
    public Font **getFont**() ;
    public FontRenderContext **getFontRenderContext**() ; // Since 1.6
    public int **getHeight**() ;
    public int **getLeading**() ;
    public LineMetrics **getLineMetrics**(Graphics context, int limit, int beginIndex, CharacterIterator ci) ;
    public LineMetrics **getLineMetrics**(Graphics context, int limit, int beginIndex, char[] chars) ;
    public LineMetrics **getLineMetrics**(Graphics context, int limit, int beginIndex, String str) ;
    public LineMetrics **getLineMetrics**(Graphics context, String str) ;
    public int **getMaxAdvance**() ;
    public int **getMaxAscent**() ;
    public Rectangle2D **getMaxCharBounds**(Graphics context) ;
    public int **getMaxDecent**() ;
    public int **getMaxDescent**() ;
    public Rectangle2D **getStringBounds**(Graphics context, String str) ;
    public Rectangle2D **getStringBounds**(Graphics context, int limit, int beginIndex, CharacterIterator
        ci) ;
    public Rectangle2D **getStringBounds**(Graphics context, int limit, int beginIndex, char[] chars) ;
    public Rectangle2D **getStringBounds**(Graphics context, int limit, int beginIndex, String str) ;
    public int **getWidths**() ;
    public boolean **hasUniformLineMetrics**() ;
    public int **stringWidth**(String str) ;
    public String **toString**() ; // Since 1.0.
}

java.awt.font.**FontRenderContext**

public class **FontRenderContext**
{
    // Constructors
    public **FontRenderContext**(Object fmHint, Object aaHint, AffineTransform tx) ;
    public **FontRenderContext**(boolean usesFractionalMetrics, boolean isAntiAliased, AffineTransform
        tx) ;
    protected **FontRenderContext**() ;
    // Instance methods
    public boolean **equals**(FontRenderContext rhs) ; // Since 1.4
    public boolean **equals**(Object obj) ;
    public Object **getAntiAliasingHint**() ; // Since 1.6
    public Object **getFractionalMetricsHint**() ; // Since 1.6
    public AffineTransform **getTransform**() ;
    public int **getTransformType**() ; // Since 1.6
    public int **hashCode**() ;
    public boolean **isAntiAliased**() ;
    public boolean **isTransformed**() ; // Since 1.6
    public boolean **usesFractionalMetrics**() ;
}

javax.swing.plaf.**FontUIResource**

public class **FontUIResource** extends Font implements UIResource
{
    // Constructors
    public **FontUIResource**(Font font) ;
    public **FontUIResource**(int size, int style, String name) ;
}

javax.swing.text.html.**FormSubmitEvent** [since 1.5]

public class **FormSubmitEvent** extends HTMLFrameHyperlinkEvent
{
    // Constructors

```
    private FormSubmitEvent(String data, FormSubmitEvent.MethodType method, String targetFrame,
        Element sourceElement, URL targetURL, HyperlinkEvent.EventType type, Object source) ;
    // Instance methods
    public String getData() ;
    public FormSubmitEvent.MethodType getMethod() ;
}
```

---

javax.swing.text.html.**FormSubmitEvent.MethodType** [since 1.5]

```
public static final class FormSubmitEvent.MethodType extends
Enum<FormSubmitEvent.MethodType>
{
    // Constructors
    private FormSubmitEvent.MethodType() ;
    // Static methods
    public static FormSubmitEvent.MethodType valueOf(String name) ;
    public static final FormSubmitEvent.MethodType values() ;
}
```

---

javax.swing.text.html.**FormView**

```
public class FormView extends ComponentView implements ActionListener
{
    public static final String RESET ;
    public static final String SUBMIT ;
    // Constructors
    public FormView(Element elem) ;
    // Instance methods
    public void actionPerformed(ActionEvent evt) ;
    protected Component createComponent() ;
    public float getMaximumSpan(int axis) ;
    protected void imageSubmit(String imageData) ;
    protected void submitData(String data) ;
}
```

---

java.awt.**Frame** [since 1.0]

```
public class Frame extends Window implements MenuContainer
```

```
{
    public static final int CROSSHAIR_CURSOR ;
    public static final int DEFAULT_CURSOR ;
    public static final int E_RESIZE_CURSOR ;
    public static final int HAND_CURSOR ;
    public static final int ICONIFIED ;
    public static final int MAXIMIZED_BOTH ;
    public static final int MAXIMIZED_HORIZ ;
    public static final int MAXIMIZED_VERT ;
    public static final int MOVE_CURSOR ;
    public static final int NE_RESIZE_CURSOR ;
    public static final int NORMAL ;
    public static final int NW_RESIZE_CURSOR ;
    public static final int N_RESIZE_CURSOR ;
    public static final int SE_RESIZE_CURSOR ;
    public static final int SW_RESIZE_CURSOR ;
    public static final int S_RESIZE_CURSOR ;
    public static final int TEXT_CURSOR ;
    public static final int WAIT_CURSOR ;
    public static final int W_RESIZE_CURSOR ;
    // Constructors
    public Frame(GraphicsConfiguration gc, String title) ;
    public Frame(String title) ;
    public Frame(GraphicsConfiguration gc) ;
    public Frame() ;
    // Static methods
    public static Frame getFrames() ; // Since 1.2
    // Instance methods
    public void addNotify() ;
    public AccessibleContext getAccessibleContext() ; // Since 1.3
    public int getCursorType() ;
    public synchronized int getExtendedState() ; // Since 1.4
    public Image getIconImage() ;
    public Rectangle getMaximizedBounds() ; // Since 1.4
    public MenuBar getMenuBar() ;
    public synchronized int getState() ;
    public String getTitle() ;
    public boolean isResizable() ;
    public boolean isUndecorated() ; // Since 1.4
    protected String paramString() ;
    public void remove(MenuComponent m) ;
    public void removeNotify() ;
    public void setCursor(int cursorType) ;
    public synchronized void setExtendedState(int state) ; // Since 1.4
    public void setIconImage(Image image) ;
    public synchronized void setMaximizedBounds(Rectangle bounds) ; // Since 1.4
```

```
    public void setMenuBar(MenuBar mb) ;
    public void setResizable(boolean resizable) ;
    public synchronized void setState(int state) ;
    public void setTitle(String title) ;
    public void setUndecorated(boolean undecorated) ; // Since 1.4
}
```

java.awt.peer.**FramePeer**

```
public interface FramePeer  implements WindowPeer
{
    // Instance methods
    public Rectangle getBoundsPrivate() ;
    public int getState() ;
    public void setBoundsPrivate(int height, int width, int y, int x) ;
    public void setMaximizedBounds(Rectangle bounds) ;
    public void setMenuBar(MenuBar mb) ;
    public void setResizable(boolean resizeable) ;
    public void setState(int state) ;
    public void setTitle(String title) ;
}
```

javax.swing.text.**GapContent**

```
public class GapContent extends GapVector implements Serializable, AbstractDocument.Content
{
    // Constructors
    public GapContent(int initialLength) ;
    public GapContent() ;
    // Instance methods
    protected Object allocateArray(int len) ;
    public Position createPosition(int offset) throws BadLocationException ;
    protected int getArrayLength() ;
    public void getChars(Segment chars, int len, int where) throws BadLocationException ;
    protected Vector getPositionsInRange(int length, int offset, Vector v) ;
    public String getString(int len, int where) throws BadLocationException ;
    public UndoableEdit insertString(String str, int where) throws BadLocationException ;
    public int length() ;
    public UndoableEdit remove(int nitems, int where) throws BadLocationException ;
    protected void resetMarksAtZero() ;
    protected void shiftEnd(int newSize) ;
```

```
    protected void shiftGap(int newGapStart) ;
    protected void shiftGapEndUp(int newGapEnd) ;
    protected void shiftGapStartDown(int newGapStart) ;
    protected void updateUndoPositions(int length, int offset, Vector positions) ;
}
```

---

java.awt.geom.**GeneralPath** [since 1.2]

```
public final class GeneralPath extends Path2D.Float
{
    // Constructors
    private GeneralPath(int numCoords, float[] pointCoords, int numTypes, byte[] pointTypes, int
        windingRule) ;
    public GeneralPath(Shape s) ;
    public GeneralPath(int initialCapacity, int rule) ;
    public GeneralPath(int rule) ;
    public GeneralPath() ;
}
```

---

java.awt.font.**GlyphJustificationInfo**

```
public final class GlyphJustificationInfo
{
    public static final int PRIORITY_INTERCHAR ;
    public static final int PRIORITY_KASHIDA ;
    public static final int PRIORITY_NONE ;
    public static final int PRIORITY_WHITESPACE ;
    public final boolean growAbsorb ;
    public final float growLeftLimit ;
    public final int growPriority ;
    public final float growRightLimit ;
    public final boolean shrinkAbsorb ;
    public final float shrinkLeftLimit ;
    public final int shrinkPriority ;
    public final float shrinkRightLimit ;
    public final float weight ;
    // Constructors
    public GlyphJustificationInfo(float shrinkRightLimit, float shrinkLeftLimit, int shrinkPriority,
        boolean shrinkAbsorb, float growRightLimit, float growLeftLimit, int growPriority, boolean
        growAbsorb, float weight) ;
    // Static methods
```

}

---

java.awt.font.**GlyphMetrics**

---

public final class **GlyphMetrics**
{
    public static final byte **COMBINING** ;
    public static final byte **COMPONENT** ;
    public static final byte **LIGATURE** ;
    public static final byte **STANDARD** ;
    public static final byte **WHITESPACE** ;
    // Constructors
    public **GlyphMetrics**(byte glyphType, Rectangle2D bounds, float advanceY, float advanceX,
        boolean horizontal) ;
    public **GlyphMetrics**(byte glyphType, Rectangle2D bounds, float advance) ;
    // Instance methods
    public float **getAdvance**() ;
    public float **getAdvanceX**() ; // Since 1.4
    public float **getAdvanceY**() ; // Since 1.4
    public Rectangle2D **getBounds2D**() ;
    public float **getLSB**() ;
    public float **getRSB**() ;
    public int **getType**() ;
    public boolean **isCombining**() ;
    public boolean **isComponent**() ;
    public boolean **isLigature**() ;
    public boolean **isStandard**() ;
    public boolean **isWhitespace**() ;
}

---

java.awt.font.**GlyphVector**

---

public abstract class **GlyphVector** implements Cloneable
{
    public static final int **FLAG_COMPLEX_GLYPHS** ;
    public static final int **FLAG_HAS_POSITION_ADJUSTMENTS** ;
    public static final int **FLAG_HAS_TRANSFORMS** ;
    public static final int **FLAG_MASK** ;
    public static final int **FLAG_RUN_RTL** ;
    // Constructors
    public **GlyphVector**() ;

```
    // Instance methods
    public abstract boolean equals(GlyphVector set) ;
    public abstract Font getFont() ;
    public abstract FontRenderContext getFontRenderContext() ;
    public int getGlyphCharIndex(int glyphIndex) ; // Since 1.4
    public int getGlyphCharIndices(int[] codeReturn, int numEntries, int beginGlyphIndex) ; // Since
        1.4
    public abstract int getGlyphCode(int glyphIndex) ;
    public abstract int getGlyphCodes(int[] codeReturn, int numEntries, int beginGlyphIndex) ;
    public abstract GlyphJustificationInfo getGlyphJustificationInfo(int glyphIndex) ;
    public abstract Shape getGlyphLogicalBounds(int glyphIndex) ;
    public abstract GlyphMetrics getGlyphMetrics(int glyphIndex) ;
    public abstract Shape getGlyphOutline(int glyphIndex) ;
    public Shape getGlyphOutline(float y, float x, int glyphIndex) ; // Since 1.4
    public Rectangle getGlyphPixelBounds(float y, float x, FontRenderContext renderFRC, int index) ;
        // Since 1.4
    public abstract Point2D getGlyphPosition(int glyphIndex) ;
    public abstract float getGlyphPositions(float[] positionReturn, int numEntries, int beginGlyphIndex)
        ;
    public abstract AffineTransform getGlyphTransform(int glyphIndex) ;
    public abstract Shape getGlyphVisualBounds(int glyphIndex) ;
    public int getLayoutFlags() ; // Since 1.4
    public abstract Rectangle2D getLogicalBounds() ;
    public abstract int getNumGlyphs() ;
    public abstract Shape getOutline(float y, float x) ;
    public abstract Shape getOutline() ;
    public Rectangle getPixelBounds(float y, float x, FontRenderContext renderFRC) ; // Since 1.4
    public abstract Rectangle2D getVisualBounds() ;
    public abstract void performDefaultLayout() ;
    public abstract void setGlyphPosition(Point2D newPos, int glyphIndex) ;
    public abstract void setGlyphTransform(AffineTransform newTX, int glyphIndex) ;
}
```

---

javax.swing.text.**GlyphView** [since 1.3]

```
public class GlyphView extends View implements Cloneable, TabableView
{
    // Constructors
    public GlyphView(Element elem) ;
    // Instance methods
    public View breakView(float len, float pos, int p0, int axis) ;
    public void changedUpdate(ViewFactory f, Shape a, DocumentEvent e) ;
    protected void checkPainter() ;
    protected final Object clone() ;
```

```
    public View createFragment(int p1, int p0) ;
    public float getAlignment(int axis) ;
    public Color getBackground() ;
    public int getBreakWeight(float len, float pos, int axis) ;
    public int getEndOffset() ;
    public Font getFont() ;
    public Color getForeground() ;
    public GlyphView.GlyphPainter getGlyphPainter() ;
    public float getMinimumSpan(int axis) ;
    public int getNextVisualPositionFrom(javax.swing.text.Position.Bias[] biasRet, int direction, Shape
        a, Position.Bias b, int pos) throws BadLocationException ;
    public float getPartialSpan(int p1, int p0) ;
    public float getPreferredSpan(int axis) ;
    public int getStartOffset() ;
    public float getTabbedSpan(TabExpander e, float x) ;
    public TabExpander getTabExpander() ;
    public Segment getText(int p1, int p0) ;
    public void insertUpdate(ViewFactory f, Shape a, DocumentEvent e) ;
    public boolean isStrikeThrough() ;
    public boolean isSubscript() ;
    public boolean isSuperscript() ;
    public boolean isUnderline() ;
    public Shape modelToView(Position.Bias b, Shape a, int pos) throws BadLocationException ;
    public void paint(Shape a, Graphics g) ;
    public void removeUpdate(ViewFactory f, Shape a, DocumentEvent e) ;
    public void setGlyphPainter(GlyphView.GlyphPainter p) ;
    public int viewToModel(javax.swing.text.Position.Bias[] biasReturn, Shape a, float y, float x) ;
}
```

javax.swing.text.**GlyphView.GlyphPainter** [since 1.3]

```
public abstract static class GlyphView.GlyphPainter
{
    // Constructors
    public GlyphView.GlyphPainter() ;
    // Instance methods
    public abstract float getAscent(GlyphView v) ;
    public abstract int getBoundedPosition(float len, float x, int p0, GlyphView v) ;
    public abstract float getDescent(GlyphView v) ;
    public abstract float getHeight(GlyphView v) ;
    public int getNextVisualPositionFrom(javax.swing.text.Position.Bias[] biasRet, int direction, Shape
        a, Position.Bias b, int pos, GlyphView v) throws BadLocationException ;
    public GlyphView.GlyphPainter getPainter(int p1, int p0, GlyphView v) ;
    public abstract float getSpan(float x, TabExpander e, int p1, int p0, GlyphView v) ;
```

public abstract Shape **modelToView**(Shape a, Position.Bias bias, int pos, GlyphView v) throws
    BadLocationException ;
public abstract void **paint**(int p1, int p0, Shape a, Graphics g, GlyphView v) ;
public abstract int **viewToModel**(javax.swing.text.Position.Bias[] biasReturn, Shape a, float y, float
    x, GlyphView v) ;
}

---

java.awt.**GradientPaint**

public class **GradientPaint** implements Paint
{
    // Constructors
    public **GradientPaint**(boolean cyclic, Color color2, Point2D pt2, Color color1, Point2D pt1) ;
    public **GradientPaint**(boolean cyclic, Color color2, float y2, float x2, Color color1, float y1, float x1)
        ;
    public **GradientPaint**(Color color2, Point2D pt2, Color color1, Point2D pt1) ;
    public **GradientPaint**(Color color2, float y2, float x2, Color color1, float y1, float x1) ;
    // Instance methods
    public PaintContext **createContext**(RenderingHints hints, AffineTransform xform, Rectangle2D
        userBounds, Rectangle deviceBounds, ColorModel cm) ;
    public Color **getColor1**() ;
    public Color **getColor2**() ;
    public Point2D **getPoint1**() ;
    public Point2D **getPoint2**() ;
    public int **getTransparency**() ;
    public boolean **isCyclic**() ;
}

---

java.awt.font.**GraphicAttribute**

public abstract class **GraphicAttribute**
{
    public static final int **BOTTOM_ALIGNMENT** ;
    public static final int **CENTER_BASELINE** ;
    public static final int **HANGING_BASELINE** ;
    public static final int **ROMAN_BASELINE** ;
    public static final int **TOP_ALIGNMENT** ;
    // Constructors
    protected **GraphicAttribute**(int alignment) ;
    // Instance methods
    public abstract void **draw**(float y, float x, Graphics2D graphics) ;

```
public abstract float getAdvance() ;
public final int getAlignment() ;
public abstract float getAscent() ;
public Rectangle2D getBounds() ;
public abstract float getDescent() ;
public GlyphJustificationInfo getJustificationInfo() ;
public Shape getOutline(AffineTransform tx) ; // Since 1.6
}
```

java.awt.**Graphics** [since 1.0]

public abstract class **Graphics**
{
    // Constructors
    protected **Graphics**() ;
    // Instance methods
    public abstract void **clearRect**(int height, int width, int y, int x) ;
    public abstract void **clipRect**(int height, int width, int y, int x) ;
    public abstract void **copyArea**(int dy, int dx, int height, int width, int y, int x) ;
    public Graphics **create**(int height, int width, int y, int x) ;
    public abstract Graphics **create**() ;
    public abstract void **dispose**() ;
    public void **draw3DRect**(boolean raised, int height, int width, int y, int x) ;
    public abstract void **drawArc**(int arcAngle, int startAngle, int height, int width, int y, int x) ;
    public void **drawBytes**(int y, int x, int length, int offset, byte[] data) ;
    public void **drawChars**(int y, int x, int length, int offset, char[] data) ;
    public abstract boolean **drawImage**(ImageObserver observer, Color bgcolor, int sy2, int sx2, int sy1, int sx1, int dy2, int dx2, int dy1, int dx1, Image img) ; // Since 1.1
    public abstract boolean **drawImage**(ImageObserver observer, int y, int x, Image img) ;
    public abstract boolean **drawImage**(ImageObserver observer, Color bgcolor, int height, int width, int y, int x, Image img) ;
    public abstract boolean **drawImage**(ImageObserver observer, int height, int width, int y, int x, Image img) ;
    public abstract boolean **drawImage**(ImageObserver observer, Color bgcolor, int y, int x, Image img) ;
    public abstract boolean **drawImage**(ImageObserver observer, int sy2, int sx2, int sy1, int sx1, int dy2, int dx2, int dy1, int dx1, Image img) ; // Since 1.1
    public abstract void **drawLine**(int y2, int x2, int y1, int x1) ;
    public abstract void **drawOval**(int height, int width, int y, int x) ;
    public abstract void **drawPolygon**(int nPoints, int[] yPoints, int[] xPoints) ;
    public void **drawPolygon**(Polygon p) ;
    public abstract void **drawPolyline**(int nPoints, int[] yPoints, int[] xPoints) ; // Since 1.1
    public void **drawRect**(int height, int width, int y, int x) ;
    public abstract void **drawRoundRect**(int arcHeight, int arcWidth, int height, int width, int y, int x) ;
    public abstract void **drawString**(int y, int x, String str) ;

```
    public abstract void drawString(int y, int x, AttributedCharacterIterator iterator) ;
    public void fill3DRect(boolean raised, int height, int width, int y, int x) ;
    public abstract void fillArc(int arcAngle, int startAngle, int height, int width, int y, int x) ;
    public abstract void fillOval(int height, int width, int y, int x) ;
    public abstract void fillPolygon(int nPoints, int[] yPoints, int[] xPoints) ;
    public void fillPolygon(Polygon p) ;
    public abstract void fillRect(int height, int width, int y, int x) ;
    public abstract void fillRoundRect(int arcHeight, int arcWidth, int height, int width, int y, int x) ;
    public void finalize() ;
    public abstract Shape getClip() ; // Since 1.1
    public abstract Rectangle getClipBounds() ; // Since 1.1
    public Rectangle getClipBounds(Rectangle r) ;
    public Rectangle getClipRect() ;
    public abstract Color getColor() ;
    public abstract Font getFont() ;
    public abstract FontMetrics getFontMetrics(Font f) ;
    public FontMetrics getFontMetrics() ;
    public boolean hitClip(int height, int width, int y, int x) ;
    public abstract void setClip(Shape clip) ; // Since 1.1
    public abstract void setClip(int height, int width, int y, int x) ; // Since 1.1
    public abstract void setColor(Color c) ;
    public abstract void setFont(Font font) ;
    public abstract void setPaintMode() ;
    public abstract void setXORMode(Color c1) ;
    public String toString() ;
    public abstract void translate(int y, int x) ;
}
```

---

java.awt.**Graphics2D**

```
public abstract class Graphics2D extends Graphics
{
    // Constructors
    protected Graphics2D() ;
    // Instance methods
    public abstract void addRenderingHints(Map<?, ?> hints) ;
    public abstract void clip(Shape s) ;
    public abstract void draw(Shape s) ;
    public void draw3DRect(boolean raised, int height, int width, int y, int x) ;
    public abstract void drawGlyphVector(float y, float x, GlyphVector g) ;
    public abstract boolean drawImage(ImageObserver obs, AffineTransform xform, Image img) ;
    public abstract void drawImage(int y, int x, BufferedImageOp op, BufferedImage img) ;
    public abstract void drawRenderableImage(AffineTransform xform, RenderableImage img) ;
    public abstract void drawRenderedImage(AffineTransform xform, RenderedImage img) ;
```

```
        public abstract void drawString(float y, float x, AttributedCharacterIterator iterator) ;
        public abstract void drawString(int y, int x, AttributedCharacterIterator iterator) ;
        public abstract void drawString(float y, float x, String str) ;
        public abstract void drawString(int y, int x, String str) ; // Since 1.0
        public abstract void fill(Shape s) ;
        public void fill3DRect(boolean raised, int height, int width, int y, int x) ;
        public abstract Color getBackground() ;
        public abstract Composite getComposite() ;
        public abstract GraphicsConfiguration getDeviceConfiguration() ;
        public abstract FontRenderContext getFontRenderContext() ; // Since 1.2
        public abstract Paint getPaint() ;
        public abstract Object getRenderingHint(RenderingHints.Key hintKey) ;
        public abstract RenderingHints getRenderingHints() ;
        public abstract Stroke getStroke() ;
        public abstract AffineTransform getTransform() ;
        public abstract boolean hit(boolean onStroke, Shape s, Rectangle rect) ;
        public abstract void rotate(double y, double x, double theta) ;
        public abstract void rotate(double theta) ;
        public abstract void scale(double sy, double sx) ;
        public abstract void setBackground(Color color) ;
        public abstract void setComposite(Composite comp) ;
        public abstract void setPaint(Paint paint) ;
        public abstract void setRenderingHint(Object hintValue, RenderingHints.Key hintKey) ;
        public abstract void setRenderingHints(Map<?, ?> hints) ;
        public abstract void setStroke(Stroke s) ;
        public abstract void setTransform(AffineTransform Tx) ;
        public abstract void shear(double shy, double shx) ;
        public abstract void transform(AffineTransform Tx) ;
        public abstract void translate(int y, int x) ; // Since 1.0
        public abstract void translate(double ty, double tx) ;
}
```

java.awt.**GraphicsConfigTemplate** [since 1.2]

```
public abstract class GraphicsConfigTemplate  implements Serializable
{
        public static final int PREFERRED ;
        public static final int REQUIRED ;
        public static final int UNNECESSARY ;
        // Constructors
        public GraphicsConfigTemplate() ;
        // Instance methods
        public abstract GraphicsConfiguration getBestConfiguration(java.awt.GraphicsConfiguration[] gc) ;
        public abstract boolean isGraphicsConfigSupported(GraphicsConfiguration gc) ;
```

}

---

java.awt.**GraphicsConfiguration**

---

public abstract class **GraphicsConfiguration**
{
    // Constructors
    protected **GraphicsConfiguration**() ;
    // Instance methods
    public BufferedImage **createCompatibleImage**(int height, int width) ;
    public BufferedImage **createCompatibleImage**(int transparency, int height, int width) ;
    public VolatileImage **createCompatibleVolatileImage**(int transparency, ImageCapabilities caps, int
        height, int width) throws AWTException ; // Since 1.5
    public VolatileImage **createCompatibleVolatileImage**(int transparency, int height, int width) ; //
        Since 1.5
    public VolatileImage **createCompatibleVolatileImage**(ImageCapabilities caps, int height, int width)
        throws AWTException ; // Since 1.4
    public VolatileImage **createCompatibleVolatileImage**(int height, int width) ; // Since 1.4
    public abstract Rectangle **getBounds**() ; // Since 1.3
    public BufferCapabilities **getBufferCapabilities**() ; // Since 1.4
    public abstract ColorModel **getColorModel**() ;
    public abstract ColorModel **getColorModel**(int transparency) ;
    public abstract AffineTransform **getDefaultTransform**() ;
    public abstract GraphicsDevice **getDevice**() ;
    public ImageCapabilities **getImageCapabilities**() ; // Since 1.4
    public abstract AffineTransform **getNormalizingTransform**() ;
}

---

java.awt.**GraphicsDevice**

---

public abstract class **GraphicsDevice**
{
    public static final int **TYPE_IMAGE_BUFFER** ;
    public static final int **TYPE_PRINTER** ;
    public static final int **TYPE_RASTER_SCREEN** ;
    // Constructors
    protected **GraphicsDevice**() ;
    // Instance methods
    public int **getAvailableAcceleratedMemory**() ; // Since 1.4
    public GraphicsConfiguration **getBestConfiguration**(GraphicsConfigTemplate gct) ;
    public abstract GraphicsConfiguration **getConfigurations**() ;

```
    public abstract GraphicsConfiguration getDefaultConfiguration() ;
    public DisplayMode getDisplayMode() ; // Since 1.4
    public DisplayMode getDisplayModes() ; // Since 1.4
    public Window getFullScreenWindow() ; // Since 1.4
    public abstract String getIDstring() ;
    public abstract int getType() ;
    public boolean isDisplayChangeSupported() ; // Since 1.4
    public boolean isFullScreenSupported() ; // Since 1.4
    public void setDisplayMode(DisplayMode dm) ; // Since 1.4
    public void setFullScreenWindow(Window w) ; // Since 1.4
}
```

java.awt.**GraphicsEnvironment**

public abstract class **GraphicsEnvironment**
{
    // Constructors
    protected **GraphicsEnvironment**() ;
    // Static methods
    public static synchronized GraphicsEnvironment **getLocalGraphicsEnvironment**() ;
    public static boolean **isHeadless**() ; // Since 1.4
    // Instance methods
    public abstract Graphics2D **createGraphics**(BufferedImage img) ;
    public abstract Font **getAllFonts**() ; // Since 1.2
    public abstract String **getAvailableFontFamilyNames**(Locale l) ; // Since 1.2
    public abstract String **getAvailableFontFamilyNames**() ; // Since 1.2
    public Point **getCenterPoint**() throws HeadlessException ; // Since 1.4
    public abstract GraphicsDevice **getDefaultScreenDevice**() throws HeadlessException ;
    public Rectangle **getMaximumWindowBounds**() throws HeadlessException ; // Since 1.4
    public abstract GraphicsDevice **getScreenDevices**() throws HeadlessException ;
    public boolean **isHeadlessInstance**() ; // Since 1.4
    public void **preferLocaleFonts**() ; // Since 1.5
    public void **preferProportionalFonts**() ; // Since 1.5
    public boolean **registerFont**(Font font) ; // Since 1.6
}

javax.swing.**GrayFilter**

public class **GrayFilter** extends RGBImageFilter
{
    // Constructors

```
    public GrayFilter(int p, boolean b) ;
    // Static methods
    public static Image createDisabledImage(Image i) ;
    // Instance methods
    public int filterRGB(int rgb, int y, int x) ;
}
```

java.awt.**GridBagConstraints** [since 1.0]

public class **GridBagConstraints** implements Serializable, Cloneable
{
    public static final int **ABOVE_BASELINE** ;
    public static final int **ABOVE_BASELINE_LEADING** ;
    public static final int **ABOVE_BASELINE_TRAILING** ;
    public static final int **BASELINE** ;
    public static final int **BASELINE_LEADING** ;
    public static final int **BASELINE_TRAILING** ;
    public static final int **BELOW_BASELINE** ;
    public static final int **BELOW_BASELINE_LEADING** ;
    public static final int **BELOW_BASELINE_TRAILING** ;
    public static final int **BOTH** ;
    public static final int **CENTER** ;
    public static final int **EAST** ;
    public static final int **FIRST_LINE_END** ;
    public static final int **FIRST_LINE_START** ;
    public static final int **HORIZONTAL** ;
    public static final int **LAST_LINE_END** ;
    public static final int **LAST_LINE_START** ;
    public static final int **LINE_END** ;
    public static final int **LINE_START** ;
    public static final int **NONE** ;
    public static final int **NORTH** ;
    public static final int **NORTHEAST** ;
    public static final int **NORTHWEST** ;
    public static final int **PAGE_END** ;
    public static final int **PAGE_START** ;
    public static final int **RELATIVE** ;
    public static final int **REMAINDER** ;
    public static final int **SOUTH** ;
    public static final int **SOUTHEAST** ;
    public static final int **SOUTHWEST** ;
    public static final int **VERTICAL** ;
    public static final int **WEST** ;
    public int **anchor** ;

```
    public int fill ;
    public int gridheight ;
    public int gridwidth ;
    public int gridx ;
    public int gridy ;
    public Insets insets ;
    public int ipadx ;
    public int ipady ;
    public double weightx ;
    public double weighty ;
    // Constructors
    public GridBagConstraints(int ipady, int ipadx, Insets insets, int fill, int anchor, double weighty,
        double weightx, int gridheight, int gridwidth, int gridy, int gridx) ;
    public GridBagConstraints() ;
    // Instance methods
    public Object clone() ;
}
```

java.awt.**GridBagLayout** [since 1.0]

```
public class GridBagLayout  implements Serializable, LayoutManager2
{
    protected static final int MAXGRIDSIZE ;
    protected static final int MINSIZE ;
    protected static final int PREFERREDSIZE ;
    public double columnWeights ;
    public int columnWidths ;
    protected Hashtable<Component, GridBagConstraints> comptable ;
    protected GridBagConstraints defaultConstraints ;
    protected GridBagLayoutInfo layoutInfo ;
    public int rowHeights ;
    public double rowWeights ;
    // Constructors
    public GridBagLayout() ;
    // Instance methods
    public void addLayoutComponent(Object constraints, Component comp) ;
    public void addLayoutComponent(Component comp, String name) ;
    protected void adjustForGravity(Rectangle r, GridBagConstraints constraints) ; // Since 1.4
    protected void AdjustForGravity(Rectangle r, GridBagConstraints constraints) ;
    protected void ArrangeGrid(Container parent) ;
    protected void arrangeGrid(Container parent) ; // Since 1.4
    public GridBagConstraints getConstraints(Component comp) ;
    public float getLayoutAlignmentX(Container parent) ;
    public float getLayoutAlignmentY(Container parent) ;
```

```
    public int getLayoutDimensions() ; // Since 1.1
    protected GridBagLayoutInfo GetLayoutInfo(int sizeflag, Container parent) ;
    protected GridBagLayoutInfo getLayoutInfo(int sizeflag, Container parent) ; // Since 1.4
    public Point getLayoutOrigin() ; // Since 1.1
    public double getLayoutWeights() ; // Since 1.1
    protected Dimension GetMinSize(GridBagLayoutInfo info, Container parent) ;
    protected Dimension getMinSize(GridBagLayoutInfo info, Container parent) ; // Since 1.4
    public void invalidateLayout(Container target) ;
    public void layoutContainer(Container parent) ;
    public Point location(int y, int x) ; // Since 1.1
    protected GridBagConstraints lookupConstraints(Component comp) ;
    public Dimension maximumLayoutSize(Container target) ;
    public Dimension minimumLayoutSize(Container parent) ;
    public Dimension preferredLayoutSize(Container parent) ;
    public void removeLayoutComponent(Component comp) ;
    public void setConstraints(GridBagConstraints constraints, Component comp) ;
    public String toString() ;
}
```

---

java.awt.**GridBagLayoutInfo** [since 1.6]

```
public class GridBagLayoutInfo  implements Serializable
{
    // Constructors
    private GridBagLayoutInfo(int height, int width) ;
    // Instance methods
}
```

---

java.awt.**GridLayout** [since 1.0]

```
public class GridLayout  implements Serializable, LayoutManager
{
    // Constructors
    public GridLayout(int vgap, int hgap, int cols, int rows) ;
    public GridLayout(int cols, int rows) ;
    public GridLayout() ;
    // Instance methods
    public void addLayoutComponent(Component comp, String name) ;
    public int getColumns() ; // Since 1.1
    public int getHgap() ; // Since 1.1
    public int getRows() ; // Since 1.1
```

```
    public int getVgap() ; // Since 1.1
    public void layoutContainer(Container parent) ;
    public Dimension minimumLayoutSize(Container parent) ;
    public Dimension preferredLayoutSize(Container parent) ;
    public void removeLayoutComponent(Component comp) ;
    public void setColumns(int cols) ; // Since 1.1
    public void setHgap(int hgap) ; // Since 1.1
    public void setRows(int rows) ; // Since 1.1
    public void setVgap(int vgap) ; // Since 1.1
    public String toString() ;
}
```

---

javax.swing.**GroupLayout** [since 1.6]

---

public class **GroupLayout** implements LayoutManager2
```
{
    public static final int DEFAULT_SIZE ;
    public static final int PREFERRED_SIZE ;
    // Constructors
    public GroupLayout(Container host) ;
    // Static methods
    // Instance methods
    public void addLayoutComponent(Object constraints, Component component) ;
    public void addLayoutComponent(Component component, String name) ;
    public GroupLayout.ParallelGroup createBaselineGroup(boolean anchorBaselineToTop, boolean
        resizable) ;
    public GroupLayout.ParallelGroup createParallelGroup(GroupLayout.Alignment alignment) ;
    public GroupLayout.ParallelGroup createParallelGroup() ;
    public GroupLayout.ParallelGroup createParallelGroup(boolean resizable, GroupLayout.Alignment
        alignment) ;
    public GroupLayout.SequentialGroup createSequentialGroup() ;
    public boolean getAutoCreateContainerGaps() ;
    public boolean getAutoCreateGaps() ;
    public boolean getHonorsVisibility() ;
    public float getLayoutAlignmentX(Container parent) ;
    public float getLayoutAlignmentY(Container parent) ;
    public LayoutStyle getLayoutStyle() ;
    public void invalidateLayout(Container parent) ;
    public void layoutContainer(Container parent) ;
    public void linkSize(java.awt.Component[] components) ;
    public void linkSize(java.awt.Component[] components, int axis) ;
    public Dimension maximumLayoutSize(Container parent) ;
    public Dimension minimumLayoutSize(Container parent) ;
    public Dimension preferredLayoutSize(Container parent) ;
```

```
    public void removeLayoutComponent(Component component) ;
    public void replace(Component newComponent, Component existingComponent) ;
    public void setAutoCreateContainerGaps(boolean autoCreateContainerPadding) ;
    public void setAutoCreateGaps(boolean autoCreatePadding) ;
    public void setHonorsVisibility(Boolean honorsVisibility, Component component) ;
    public void setHonorsVisibility(boolean honorsVisibility) ;
    public void setHorizontalGroup(GroupLayout.Group group) ;
    public void setLayoutStyle(LayoutStyle layoutStyle) ;
    public void setVerticalGroup(GroupLayout.Group group) ;
    public String toString() ;
}
```

javax.swing.**GroupLayout.Alignment** [since 1.6]

```
public static final class GroupLayout.Alignment extends Enum<GroupLayout.Alignment>
{
    // Constructors
    private GroupLayout.Alignment() ;
    // Static methods
    public static GroupLayout.Alignment valueOf(String name) ;
    public static final GroupLayout.Alignment values() ;
}
```

java.awt.**HeadlessException** [since 1.4]

```
public class HeadlessException extends UnsupportedOperationException
{
    // Constructors
    public HeadlessException(String msg) ;
    public HeadlessException() ;
    // Instance methods
    public String getMessage() ;
}
```

java.awt.event.**HierarchyBoundsAdapter** [since 1.3]

```
public abstract class HierarchyBoundsAdapter  implements HierarchyBoundsListener
{
```

```
    // Constructors
    public HierarchyBoundsAdapter() ;
    // Instance methods
    public void ancestorMoved(HierarchyEvent e) ;
    public void ancestorResized(HierarchyEvent e) ;
}
```

java.awt.event.**HierarchyBoundsListener** [since 1.3]

```
public interface HierarchyBoundsListener  implements EventListener
{
    // Instance methods
    public void ancestorMoved(HierarchyEvent e) ;
    public void ancestorResized(HierarchyEvent e) ;
}
```

java.awt.event.**HierarchyEvent** [since 1.3]

```
public class HierarchyEvent extends AWTEvent
{
    public static final int ANCESTOR_MOVED ;
    public static final int ANCESTOR_RESIZED ;
    public static final int DISPLAYABILITY_CHANGED ;
    public static final int HIERARCHY_CHANGED ;
    public static final int HIERARCHY_FIRST ;
    public static final int HIERARCHY_LAST ;
    public static final int PARENT_CHANGED ;
    public static final int SHOWING_CHANGED ;
    // Constructors
    public HierarchyEvent(long changeFlags, Container changedParent, Component changed, int id,
        Component source) ;
    public HierarchyEvent(Container changedParent, Component changed, int id, Component source) ;
    // Instance methods
    public Component getChanged() ;
    public Container getChangedParent() ;
    public long getChangeFlags() ;
    public Component getComponent() ;
    public String paramString() ;
}
```

java.awt.event.**HierarchyListener** [since 1.3]

public interface **HierarchyListener** implements EventListener
{
    // Instance methods
    public void **hierarchyChanged**(HierarchyEvent e) ;
}

javax.swing.text.**Highlighter**

public interface **Highlighter**
{
    // Instance methods
    public Object **addHighlight**(Highlighter.HighlightPainter p, int p1, int p0) throws
        BadLocationException ;
    public void **changeHighlight**(int p1, int p0, Object tag) throws BadLocationException ;
    public void **deinstall**(JTextComponent c) ;
    public Highlighter.Highlight **getHighlights**() ;
    public void **install**(JTextComponent c) ;
    public void **paint**(Graphics g) ;
    public void **removeAllHighlights**() ;
    public void **removeHighlight**(Object tag) ;
}

javax.swing.text.**Highlighter.Highlight**

public static interface **Highlighter.Highlight**
{
    // Instance methods
    public int **getEndOffset**() ;
    public Highlighter.HighlightPainter **getPainter**() ;
    public int **getStartOffset**() ;
}

javax.swing.text.**Highlighter.HighlightPainter**

public static interface **Highlighter.HighlightPainter**
{
    // Instance methods
    public void **paint**(JTextComponent c, Shape bounds, int p1, int p0, Graphics g) ;
}

javax.swing.text.html.**HTML**

public class **HTML**
{
    public static final String **NULL_ATTRIBUTE_VALUE** ;
    // Constructors
    public **HTML**() ;
    // Static methods
    public static HTML.Attribute **getAllAttributeKeys**() ;
    public static HTML.Tag **getAllTags**() ;
    public static HTML.Attribute **getAttributeKey**(String attName) ;
    public static int **getIntegerAttributeValue**(int def, HTML.Attribute key, AttributeSet attr) ;
    public static HTML.Tag **getTag**(String tagName) ;
}

javax.swing.text.html.**HTML.Attribute**

public static final class **HTML.Attribute**
{
    public static final HTML.Attribute **ACTION** ;
    public static final HTML.Attribute **ALIGN** ;
    public static final HTML.Attribute **ALINK** ;
    public static final HTML.Attribute **ALT** ;
    public static final HTML.Attribute **ARCHIVE** ;
    public static final HTML.Attribute **BACKGROUND** ;
    public static final HTML.Attribute **BGCOLOR** ;
    public static final HTML.Attribute **BORDER** ;
    public static final HTML.Attribute **CELLPADDING** ;
    public static final HTML.Attribute **CELLSPACING** ;

public static final HTML.Attribute **CHECKED** ;
public static final HTML.Attribute **CLASS** ;
public static final HTML.Attribute **CLASSID** ;
public static final HTML.Attribute **CLEAR** ;
public static final HTML.Attribute **CODE** ;
public static final HTML.Attribute **CODEBASE** ;
public static final HTML.Attribute **CODETYPE** ;
public static final HTML.Attribute **COLOR** ;
public static final HTML.Attribute **COLS** ;
public static final HTML.Attribute **COLSPAN** ;
public static final HTML.Attribute **COMMENT** ;
public static final HTML.Attribute **COMPACT** ;
public static final HTML.Attribute **CONTENT** ;
public static final HTML.Attribute **COORDS** ;
public static final HTML.Attribute **DATA** ;
public static final HTML.Attribute **DECLARE** ;
public static final HTML.Attribute **DIR** ;
public static final HTML.Attribute **DUMMY** ;
public static final HTML.Attribute **ENCTYPE** ;
public static final HTML.Attribute **ENDTAG** ;
public static final HTML.Attribute **FACE** ;
public static final HTML.Attribute **FRAMEBORDER** ;
public static final HTML.Attribute **HALIGN** ;
public static final HTML.Attribute **HEIGHT** ;
public static final HTML.Attribute **HREF** ;
public static final HTML.Attribute **HSPACE** ;
public static final HTML.Attribute **HTTPEQUIV** ;
public static final HTML.Attribute **ID** ;
public static final HTML.Attribute **ISMAP** ;
public static final HTML.Attribute **LANG** ;
public static final HTML.Attribute **LANGUAGE** ;
public static final HTML.Attribute **LINK** ;
public static final HTML.Attribute **LOWSRC** ;
public static final HTML.Attribute **MARGINHEIGHT** ;
public static final HTML.Attribute **MARGINWIDTH** ;
public static final HTML.Attribute **MAXLENGTH** ;
public static final HTML.Attribute **METHOD** ;
public static final HTML.Attribute **MULTIPLE** ;
public static final HTML.Attribute **N** ;
public static final HTML.Attribute **NAME** ;
public static final HTML.Attribute **NOHREF** ;
public static final HTML.Attribute **NORESIZE** ;
public static final HTML.Attribute **NOSHADE** ;
public static final HTML.Attribute **NOWRAP** ;
public static final HTML.Attribute **PROMPT** ;
public static final HTML.Attribute **REL** ;

public static final HTML.Attribute **REV** ;
public static final HTML.Attribute **ROWS** ;
public static final HTML.Attribute **ROWSPAN** ;
public static final HTML.Attribute **SCROLLING** ;
public static final HTML.Attribute **SELECTED** ;
public static final HTML.Attribute **SHAPE** ;
public static final HTML.Attribute **SHAPES** ;
public static final HTML.Attribute **SIZE** ;
public static final HTML.Attribute **SRC** ;
public static final HTML.Attribute **STANDBY** ;
public static final HTML.Attribute **START** ;
public static final HTML.Attribute **STYLE** ;
public static final HTML.Attribute **TARGET** ;
public static final HTML.Attribute **TEXT** ;
public static final HTML.Attribute **TITLE** ;
public static final HTML.Attribute **TYPE** ;
public static final HTML.Attribute **USEMAP** ;
public static final HTML.Attribute **VALIGN** ;
public static final HTML.Attribute **VALUE** ;
public static final HTML.Attribute **VALUETYPE** ;
public static final HTML.Attribute **VERSION** ;
public static final HTML.Attribute **VLINK** ;
public static final HTML.Attribute **VSPACE** ;
public static final HTML.Attribute **WIDTH** ;
// Constructors
private **HTML.Attribute**(String id) ;
// Instance methods
public String **toString**() ;
}

javax.swing.text.html.**HTML.Tag**

public static class **HTML.Tag**
{
    public static final HTML.Tag **A** ;
    public static final HTML.Tag **ADDRESS** ;
    public static final HTML.Tag **APPLET** ;
    public static final HTML.Tag **AREA** ;
    public static final HTML.Tag **B** ;
    public static final HTML.Tag **BASE** ;
    public static final HTML.Tag **BASEFONT** ;
    public static final HTML.Tag **BIG** ;
    public static final HTML.Tag **BLOCKQUOTE** ;
    public static final HTML.Tag **BODY** ;

public static final HTML.Tag **BR** ;
public static final HTML.Tag **CAPTION** ;
public static final HTML.Tag **CENTER** ;
public static final HTML.Tag **CITE** ;
public static final HTML.Tag **CODE** ;
public static final HTML.Tag **COMMENT** ;
public static final HTML.Tag **CONTENT** ;
public static final HTML.Tag **DD** ;
public static final HTML.Tag **DFN** ;
public static final HTML.Tag **DIR** ;
public static final HTML.Tag **DIV** ;
public static final HTML.Tag **DL** ;
public static final HTML.Tag **DT** ;
public static final HTML.Tag **EM** ;
public static final HTML.Tag **FONT** ;
public static final HTML.Tag **FORM** ;
public static final HTML.Tag **FRAME** ;
public static final HTML.Tag **FRAMESET** ;
public static final HTML.Tag **H1** ;
public static final HTML.Tag **H2** ;
public static final HTML.Tag **H3** ;
public static final HTML.Tag **H4** ;
public static final HTML.Tag **H5** ;
public static final HTML.Tag **H6** ;
public static final HTML.Tag **HEAD** ;
public static final HTML.Tag **HR** ;
public static final HTML.Tag **HTML** ;
public static final HTML.Tag **I** ;
public static final HTML.Tag **IMG** ;
public static final HTML.Tag **IMPLIED** ;
public static final HTML.Tag **INPUT** ;
public static final HTML.Tag **ISINDEX** ;
public static final HTML.Tag **KBD** ;
public static final HTML.Tag **LI** ;
public static final HTML.Tag **LINK** ;
public static final HTML.Tag **MAP** ;
public static final HTML.Tag **MENU** ;
public static final HTML.Tag **META** ;
public static final HTML.Tag **NOFRAMES** ;
public static final HTML.Tag **OBJECT** ;
public static final HTML.Tag **OL** ;
public static final HTML.Tag **OPTION** ;
public static final HTML.Tag **P** ;
public static final HTML.Tag **PARAM** ;
public static final HTML.Tag **PRE** ;
public static final HTML.Tag **S** ;

```
    public static final HTML.Tag SAMP ;
    public static final HTML.Tag SCRIPT ;
    public static final HTML.Tag SELECT ;
    public static final HTML.Tag SMALL ;
    public static final HTML.Tag SPAN ;
    public static final HTML.Tag STRIKE ;
    public static final HTML.Tag STRONG ;
    public static final HTML.Tag STYLE ;
    public static final HTML.Tag SUB ;
    public static final HTML.Tag SUP ;
    public static final HTML.Tag TABLE ;
    public static final HTML.Tag TD ;
    public static final HTML.Tag TEXTAREA ;
    public static final HTML.Tag TH ;
    public static final HTML.Tag TITLE ;
    public static final HTML.Tag TR ;
    public static final HTML.Tag TT ;
    public static final HTML.Tag U ;
    public static final HTML.Tag UL ;
    public static final HTML.Tag VAR ;
    // Constructors
    protected HTML.Tag(boolean isBlock, boolean causesBreak, String id) ;
    protected HTML.Tag(String id) ;
    public HTML.Tag() ;
    // Instance methods
    public boolean breaksFlow() ;
    public boolean isBlock() ;
    public boolean isPreformatted() ;
    public String toString() ;
}
```

---

javax.swing.text.html.**HTML.UnknownTag**

```
public static class HTML.UnknownTag extends HTML.Tag implements Serializable
{
    // Constructors
    public HTML.UnknownTag(String id) ;
    // Instance methods
    public boolean equals(Object obj) ;
    public int hashCode() ;
}
```

javax.swing.text.html.**HTMLDocument**

public class **HTMLDocument** extends DefaultStyledDocument
{
    public static final String **AdditionalComments** ;
    // Constructors
    public **HTMLDocument**(StyleSheet styles, AbstractDocument.Content c) ;
    public **HTMLDocument**(StyleSheet styles) ;
    public **HTMLDocument**() ;
    // Static methods
    // Instance methods
    protected void **create**(javax.swing.text.DefaultStyledDocument.ElementSpec[] data) ;
    protected Element **createBranchElement**(AttributeSet a, Element parent) ;
    protected AbstractDocument.AbstractElement **createDefaultRoot**() ;
    protected Element **createLeafElement**(int p1, int p0, AttributeSet a, Element parent) ;
    protected void **fireChangedUpdate**(DocumentEvent e) ;
    protected void **fireUndoableEditUpdate**(UndoableEditEvent e) ;
    public URL **getBase**() ;
    public Element **getElement**(Object value, Object attribute, Element e) ; // Since 1.3
    public Element **getElement**(String id) ; // Since 1.3
    public HTMLDocument.Iterator **getIterator**(HTML.Tag t) ;
    public HTMLEditorKit.Parser **getParser**() ; // Since 1.3
    public boolean **getPreservesUnknownTags**() ;
    public HTMLEditorKit.ParserCallback **getReader**(int pos) ;
    public HTMLEditorKit.ParserCallback **getReader**(HTML.Tag insertTag, int pushDepth, int
        popDepth, int pos) ;
    public StyleSheet **getStyleSheet**() ;
    public int **getTokenThreshold**() ;
    protected void **insert**(javax.swing.text.DefaultStyledDocument.ElementSpec[] data, int offset) throws
        BadLocationException ;
    public void **insertAfterEnd**(String htmlText, Element elem) throws BadLocationException,
        IOException ; // Since 1.3
    public void **insertAfterStart**(String htmlText, Element elem) throws BadLocationException,
        IOException ; // Since 1.3
    public void **insertBeforeEnd**(String htmlText, Element elem) throws BadLocationException,
        IOException ; // Since 1.3
    public void **insertBeforeStart**(String htmlText, Element elem) throws BadLocationException,
        IOException ; // Since 1.3
    protected void **insertUpdate**(AttributeSet attr, AbstractDocument.DefaultDocumentEvent chng) ;
    public void **processHTMLFrameHyperlinkEvent**(HTMLFrameHyperlinkEvent e) ;
    public void **setBase**(URL u) ;
    public void **setInnerHTML**(String htmlText, Element elem) throws BadLocationException,
        IOException ; // Since 1.3

public void **setOuterHTML**(String htmlText, Element elem) throws BadLocationException,
    IOException ; // Since 1.3
public void **setParagraphAttributes**(boolean replace, AttributeSet s, int length, int offset) ;
public void **setParser**(HTMLEditorKit.Parser parser) ; // Since 1.3
public void **setPreservesUnknownTags**(boolean preservesTags) ;
public void **setTokenThreshold**(int n) ;
}

---

javax.swing.text.html.**HTMLDocument.Iterator**

---

public abstract static class **HTMLDocument.Iterator**
{
    // Constructors
    public **HTMLDocument.Iterator**() ;
    // Instance methods
    public abstract AttributeSet **getAttributes**() ;
    public abstract int **getEndOffset**() ;
    public abstract int **getStartOffset**() ;
    public abstract HTML.Tag **getTag**() ;
    public abstract boolean **isValid**() ;
    public abstract void **next**() ;
}

---

javax.swing.text.html.**HTMLEditorKit**

---

public class **HTMLEditorKit** extends StyledEditorKit implements Accessible
{
    public static final String **BOLD_ACTION** ;
    public static final String **COLOR_ACTION** ;
    public static final String **DEFAULT_CSS** ;
    public static final String **FONT_CHANGE_BIGGER** ;
    public static final String **FONT_CHANGE_SMALLER** ;
    public static final String **IMG_ALIGN_BOTTOM** ;
    public static final String **IMG_ALIGN_MIDDLE** ;
    public static final String **IMG_ALIGN_TOP** ;
    public static final String **IMG_BORDER** ;
    public static final String **ITALIC_ACTION** ;
    public static final String **LOGICAL_STYLE_ACTION** ;
    public static final String **PARA_INDENT_LEFT** ;
    public static final String **PARA_INDENT_RIGHT** ;
    // Constructors

```
public HTMLEditorKit() ;
// Static methods
// Instance methods
public Object clone() ;
public Document createDefaultDocument() ;
protected void createInputAttributes(MutableAttributeSet set, Element element) ;
public void deinstall(JEditorPane c) ;
public AccessibleContext getAccessibleContext() ; // Since 1.4
public Action getActions() ;
public String getContentType() ;
public Cursor getDefaultCursor() ; // Since 1.3
public MutableAttributeSet getInputAttributes() ;
public Cursor getLinkCursor() ; // Since 1.3
protected HTMLEditorKit.Parser getParser() ;
public StyleSheet getStyleSheet() ;
public ViewFactory getViewFactory() ;
public void insertHTML(HTML.Tag insertTag, int pushDepth, int popDepth, String html, int offset,
    HTMLDocument doc) throws BadLocationException, IOException ;
public void install(JEditorPane c) ;
public boolean isAutoFormSubmission() ; // Since 1.5
public void read(int pos, Document doc, Reader in) throws IOException, BadLocationException ;
public void setAutoFormSubmission(boolean isAuto) ; // Since 1.5
public void setDefaultCursor(Cursor cursor) ; // Since 1.3
public void setLinkCursor(Cursor cursor) ; // Since 1.3
public void setStyleSheet(StyleSheet s) ;
public void write(int len, int pos, Document doc, Writer out) throws IOException,
    BadLocationException ;
}
```

---

javax.swing.text.html.**HTMLEditorKit.HTMLFactory**

```
public static class HTMLEditorKit.HTMLFactory  implements ViewFactory
{
    // Constructors
    public HTMLEditorKit.HTMLFactory() ;
    // Instance methods
    public View create(Element elem) ;
}
```

---

javax.swing.text.html.**HTMLEditorKit.HTMLTextAction**

---

public abstract static class **HTMLEditorKit.HTMLTextAction** extends
StyledEditorKit.StyledTextAction
{
    // Constructors
    public **HTMLEditorKit.HTMLTextAction**(String name) ;
    // Instance methods
    protected int **elementCountToTag**(HTML.Tag tag, int offset, HTMLDocument doc) ;
    protected Element **findElementMatchingTag**(HTML.Tag tag, int offset, HTMLDocument doc) ;
    protected Element **getElementsAt**(int offset, HTMLDocument doc) ;
    protected HTMLDocument **getHTMLDocument**(JEditorPane e) ;
    protected HTMLEditorKit **getHTMLEditorKit**(JEditorPane e) ;
}

---

javax.swing.text.html.**HTMLEditorKit.InsertHTMLTextAction**

---

public static class **HTMLEditorKit.InsertHTMLTextAction** extends
HTMLEditorKit.HTMLTextAction
{
    protected HTML.Tag **addTag** ;
    protected HTML.Tag **alternateAddTag** ;
    protected HTML.Tag **alternateParentTag** ;
    protected String **html** ;
    protected HTML.Tag **parentTag** ;
    // Constructors
    private **HTMLEditorKit.InsertHTMLTextAction**(boolean adjustSelection, HTML.Tag
        alternateAddTag, HTML.Tag alternateParentTag, HTML.Tag addTag, HTML.Tag parentTag,
        String html, String name) ;
    public **HTMLEditorKit.InsertHTMLTextAction**(HTML.Tag alternateAddTag, HTML.Tag
        alternateParentTag, HTML.Tag addTag, HTML.Tag parentTag, String html, String name) ;
    public **HTMLEditorKit.InsertHTMLTextAction**(HTML.Tag addTag, HTML.Tag parentTag,
        String html, String name) ;
    // Instance methods
    public void **actionPerformed**(ActionEvent ae) ;
    protected void **insertAtBoundary**(HTML.Tag addTag, HTML.Tag parentTag, String html, Element
        insertElement, int offset, HTMLDocument doc, JEditorPane editor) ; // Since 1.3
    protected void **insertAtBoundry**(HTML.Tag addTag, HTML.Tag parentTag, String html, Element
        insertElement, int offset, HTMLDocument doc, JEditorPane editor) ;

```
    protected void insertHTML(HTML.Tag addTag, int pushDepth, int popDepth, String html, int offset,
        HTMLDocument doc, JEditorPane editor) ;
}
```

---

javax.swing.text.html.**HTMLEditorKit.LinkController**

```
public static class HTMLEditorKit.LinkController extends MouseAdapter implements Serializable,
MouseMotionListener
{
    // Constructors
    public HTMLEditorKit.LinkController() ;
    // Instance methods
    protected void activateLink(JEditorPane editor, int pos) ;
    public void mouseClicked(MouseEvent e) ;
    public void mouseDragged(MouseEvent e) ;
    public void mouseMoved(MouseEvent e) ;
}
```

---

javax.swing.text.html.**HTMLEditorKit.Parser**

```
public abstract static class HTMLEditorKit.Parser
{
    // Constructors
    public HTMLEditorKit.Parser() ;
    // Instance methods
    public abstract void parse(boolean ignoreCharSet, HTMLEditorKit.ParserCallback cb, Reader r)
        throws IOException ;
}
```

---

javax.swing.text.html.**HTMLEditorKit.ParserCallback**

```
public static class HTMLEditorKit.ParserCallback
{
    public static final Object IMPLIED ;
    // Constructors
    public HTMLEditorKit.ParserCallback() ;
    // Instance methods
    public void flush() throws BadLocationException ;
```

```
    public void handleComment(int pos, char[] data) ;
    public void handleEndOfLineString(String eol) ; // Since 1.3
    public void handleEndTag(int pos, HTML.Tag t) ;
    public void handleError(int pos, String errorMsg) ;
    public void handleSimpleTag(int pos, MutableAttributeSet a, HTML.Tag t) ;
    public void handleStartTag(int pos, MutableAttributeSet a, HTML.Tag t) ;
    public void handleText(int pos, char[] data) ;
}
```

javax.swing.text.html.**HTMLFrameHyperlinkEvent**

public class **HTMLFrameHyperlinkEvent** extends HyperlinkEvent
{
    // Constructors
    public **HTMLFrameHyperlinkEvent**(String targetFrame, InputEvent inputEvent, Element
        sourceElement, String desc, URL targetURL, HyperlinkEvent.EventType type, Object source) ;
    public **HTMLFrameHyperlinkEvent**(String targetFrame, Element sourceElement, String desc, URL
        targetURL, HyperlinkEvent.EventType type, Object source) ;
    public **HTMLFrameHyperlinkEvent**(String targetFrame, Element sourceElement, URL targetURL,
        HyperlinkEvent.EventType type, Object source) ;
    public **HTMLFrameHyperlinkEvent**(String targetFrame, String desc, URL targetURL,
        HyperlinkEvent.EventType type, Object source) ;
    public **HTMLFrameHyperlinkEvent**(String targetFrame, URL targetURL,
        HyperlinkEvent.EventType type, Object source) ;
    // Instance methods
    public String **getTarget**() ;
}

javax.swing.text.html.**HTMLWriter**

public class **HTMLWriter** extends AbstractWriter
{
    // Constructors
    public **HTMLWriter**(int len, int pos, HTMLDocument doc, Writer w) ;
    public **HTMLWriter**(HTMLDocument doc, Writer w) ;
    // Static methods
    // Instance methods
    protected void **closeOutUnwantedEmbeddedTags**(AttributeSet attr) throws IOException ;
    protected void **comment**(Element elem) throws BadLocationException, IOException ;
    protected void **emptyTag**(Element elem) throws BadLocationException, IOException ;
    protected void **endTag**(Element elem) throws IOException ;

protected boolean **isBlockTag**(AttributeSet attr) ;
protected boolean **matchNameAttribute**(HTML.Tag tag, AttributeSet attr) ;
protected void **output**(int length, int start, char[] chars) throws IOException ; // Since 1.3
protected void **selectContent**(AttributeSet attr) throws IOException ;
protected void **startTag**(Element elem) throws IOException, BadLocationException ;
protected boolean **synthesizedElement**(Element elem) ;
protected void **text**(Element elem) throws BadLocationException, IOException ;
protected void **textAreaContent**(AttributeSet attr) throws BadLocationException, IOException ;
public void **write**() throws IOException, BadLocationException ;
protected void **writeAttributes**(AttributeSet attr) throws IOException ;
protected void **writeEmbeddedTags**(AttributeSet attr) throws IOException ;
protected void **writeLineSeparator**() throws IOException ; // Since 1.3
protected void **writeOption**(Option option) throws IOException ;
}

javax.swing.event.**HyperlinkEvent**

public class **HyperlinkEvent** extends EventObject
{
    // Constructors
    public **HyperlinkEvent**(InputEvent inputEvent, Element sourceElement, String desc, URL u,
        HyperlinkEvent.EventType type, Object source) ;
    public **HyperlinkEvent**(Element sourceElement, String desc, URL u, HyperlinkEvent.EventType
        type, Object source) ;
    public **HyperlinkEvent**(String desc, URL u, HyperlinkEvent.EventType type, Object source) ;
    public **HyperlinkEvent**(URL u, HyperlinkEvent.EventType type, Object source) ;
    // Instance methods
    public String **getDescription**() ;
    public HyperlinkEvent.EventType **getEventType**() ;
    public InputEvent **getInputEvent**() ; // Since 1.7
    public Element **getSourceElement**() ; // Since 1.4
    public URL **getURL**() ;
}

javax.swing.event.**HyperlinkEvent.EventType**

public static final class **HyperlinkEvent.EventType**
{
    public static final HyperlinkEvent.EventType **ACTIVATED** ;
    public static final HyperlinkEvent.EventType **ENTERED** ;
    public static final HyperlinkEvent.EventType **EXITED** ;

```
    // Constructors
    private HyperlinkEvent.EventType(String s) ;
    // Instance methods
    public String toString() ;
}
```

---

javax.swing.event.**HyperlinkListener**

```
public interface HyperlinkListener  implements EventListener
{
    // Instance methods
    public void hyperlinkUpdate(HyperlinkEvent e) ;
}
```

---

javax.swing.**Icon**

```
public interface Icon
{
    // Instance methods
    public int getIconHeight() ;
    public int getIconWidth() ;
    public void paintIcon(int y, int x, Graphics g, Component c) ;
}
```

---

javax.swing.plaf.**IconUIResource**

```
public class IconUIResource  implements Serializable, UIResource, Icon
{
    // Constructors
    public IconUIResource(Icon delegate) ;
    // Instance methods
    public int getIconHeight() ;
    public int getIconWidth() ;
    public void paintIcon(int y, int x, Graphics g, Component c) ;
}
```

---

javax.swing.text.**IconView**

---

public class **IconView** extends View
{
    // Constructors
    public **IconView**(Element elem) ;
    // Instance methods
    public float **getAlignment**(int axis) ;
    public float **getPreferredSpan**(int axis) ;
    public Shape **modelToView**(Position.Bias b, Shape a, int pos) throws BadLocationException ;
    public void **paint**(Shape a, Graphics g) ;
    public int **viewToModel**(javax.swing.text.Position.Bias[] bias, Shape a, float y, float x) ;
}

---

java.awt.**IllegalComponentStateException**

---

public class **IllegalComponentStateException** extends IllegalStateException
{
    // Constructors
    public **IllegalComponentStateException**(String s) ;
    public **IllegalComponentStateException**() ;
}

---

java.awt.geom.**IllegalPathStateException**

---

public class **IllegalPathStateException** extends RuntimeException
{
    // Constructors
    public **IllegalPathStateException**(String s) ;
    public **IllegalPathStateException**() ;
}

---

java.awt.**Image** [since 1.0]

---

public abstract class **Image**

```
{
    public static final int SCALE_AREA_AVERAGING ;
    public static final int SCALE_DEFAULT ;
    public static final int SCALE_FAST ;
    public static final int SCALE_REPLICATE ;
    public static final int SCALE_SMOOTH ;
    public static final Object UndefinedProperty ;
    protected float accelerationPriority ;
    // Constructors
    public Image() ;
    // Instance methods
    public void flush() ;
    public float getAccelerationPriority() ; // Since 1.5
    public ImageCapabilities getCapabilities(GraphicsConfiguration gc) ; // Since 1.5
    public abstract Graphics getGraphics() ;
    public abstract int getHeight(ImageObserver observer) ;
    public abstract Object getProperty(ImageObserver observer, String name) ;
    public Image getScaledInstance(int hints, int height, int width) ; // Since 1.1
    public abstract ImageProducer getSource() ;
    public abstract int getWidth(ImageObserver observer) ;
    public void setAccelerationPriority(float priority) ; // Since 1.5
}
```

java.awt.**ImageCapabilities** [since 1.4]

public class **ImageCapabilities** implements Cloneable
```
{
    // Constructors
    public ImageCapabilities(boolean accelerated) ;
    // Instance methods
    public Object clone() ;
    public boolean isAccelerated() ;
    public boolean isTrueVolatile() ;
}
```

java.awt.image.**ImageConsumer**

public interface **ImageConsumer**
```
{
    public static final int COMPLETESCANLINES ;
    public static final int IMAGEABORTED ;
```

```
     public static final int IMAGEERROR ;
     public static final int RANDOMPIXELORDER ;
     public static final int SINGLEFRAME ;
     public static final int SINGLEFRAMEDONE ;
     public static final int SINGLEPASS ;
     public static final int STATICIMAGEDONE ;
     public static final int TOPDOWNLEFTRIGHT ;
     // Instance methods
     public void imageComplete(int status) ;
     public void setColorModel(ColorModel model) ;
     public void setDimensions(int height, int width) ;
     public void setHints(int hintflags) ;
     public void setPixels(int scansize, int off, int[] pixels, ColorModel model, int h, int w, int y, int x) ;
     public void setPixels(int scansize, int off, byte[] pixels, ColorModel model, int h, int w, int y, int x) ;
     public void setProperties(Hashtable<?, ?> props) ;
}
```

java.awt.image.**ImageFilter**

```
public class ImageFilter  implements Cloneable, ImageConsumer
{
     protected ImageConsumer consumer ;
     // Constructors
     public ImageFilter() ;
     // Instance methods
     public Object clone() ;
     public ImageFilter getFilterInstance(ImageConsumer ic) ;
     public void imageComplete(int status) ;
     public void resendTopDownLeftRight(ImageProducer ip) ;
     public void setColorModel(ColorModel model) ;
     public void setDimensions(int height, int width) ;
     public void setHints(int hints) ;
     public void setPixels(int scansize, int off, int[] pixels, ColorModel model, int h, int w, int y, int x) ;
     public void setPixels(int scansize, int off, byte[] pixels, ColorModel model, int h, int w, int y, int x) ;
     public void setProperties(Hashtable<?, ?> props) ;
}
```

java.awt.font.**ImageGraphicAttribute**

```
public final class ImageGraphicAttribute extends GraphicAttribute
{
```

```
    // Constructors
    public ImageGraphicAttribute(float originY, float originX, int alignment, Image image) ;
    public ImageGraphicAttribute(int alignment, Image image) ;
    // Instance methods
    public void draw(float y, float x, Graphics2D graphics) ;
    public boolean equals(ImageGraphicAttribute rhs) ;
    public boolean equals(Object rhs) ;
    public float getAdvance() ;
    public float getAscent() ;
    public Rectangle2D getBounds() ;
    public float getDescent() ;
    public int hashCode() ;
}
```

javax.swing.**ImageIcon**

```
public class ImageIcon  implements Accessible, Serializable, Icon
{
    protected static final Component component ;
    protected static final MediaTracker tracker ;
    // Constructors
    public ImageIcon() ;
    public ImageIcon(byte[] imageData) ;
    public ImageIcon(String description, byte[] imageData) ;
    public ImageIcon(Image image) ;
    public ImageIcon(String description, Image image) ;
    public ImageIcon(URL location) ;
    public ImageIcon(String description, URL location) ;
    public ImageIcon(String filename) ;
    public ImageIcon(String description, String filename) ;
    // Instance methods
    public AccessibleContext getAccessibleContext() ; // Since 1.3
    public String getDescription() ;
    public int getIconHeight() ;
    public int getIconWidth() ;
    public Image getImage() ;
    public int getImageLoadStatus() ;
    public ImageObserver getImageObserver() ;
    protected void loadImage(Image image) ;
    public synchronized void paintIcon(int y, int x, Graphics g, Component c) ;
    public void setDescription(String description) ;
    public void setImage(Image image) ;
    public void setImageObserver(ImageObserver observer) ;
    public String toString() ;
```

}

---

java.awt.image.**ImageObserver**

---

public interface **ImageObserver**
{
    public static final int **ABORT** ;
    public static final int **ALLBITS** ;
    public static final int **ERROR** ;
    public static final int **FRAMEBITS** ;
    public static final int **HEIGHT** ;
    public static final int **PROPERTIES** ;
    public static final int **SOMEBITS** ;
    public static final int **WIDTH** ;
    // Instance methods
    public boolean **imageUpdate**(int height, int width, int y, int x, int infoflags, Image img) ;
}

---

java.awt.image.**ImageProducer**

---

public interface **ImageProducer**
{
    // Instance methods
    public void **addConsumer**(ImageConsumer ic) ;
    public boolean **isConsumer**(ImageConsumer ic) ;
    public void **removeConsumer**(ImageConsumer ic) ;
    public void **requestTopDownLeftRightResend**(ImageConsumer ic) ;
    public void **startProduction**(ImageConsumer ic) ;
}

---

javax.swing.text.html.**ImageView** [since 1.4]

---

public class **ImageView** extends View
{
    // Constructors
    public **ImageView**(Element elem) ;
    // Instance methods
    public void **changedUpdate**(ViewFactory f, Shape a, DocumentEvent e) ;

```
    public float getAlignment(int axis) ;
    public String getAltText() ;
    public AttributeSet getAttributes() ;
    public Image getImage() ;
    public URL getImageURL() ;
    public Icon getLoadingImageIcon() ;
    public boolean getLoadsSynchronously() ;
    public Icon getNoImageIcon() ;
    public float getPreferredSpan(int axis) ;
    protected StyleSheet getStyleSheet() ;
    public String getToolTipText(Shape allocation, float y, float x) ;
    public Shape modelToView(Position.Bias b, Shape a, int pos) throws BadLocationException ;
    public void paint(Shape a, Graphics g) ;
    public void setLoadsSynchronously(boolean newValue) ;
    public void setParent(View parent) ;
    protected void setPropertiesFromAttributes() ;
    public void setSize(float height, float width) ;
    public int viewToModel(javax.swing.text.Position.Bias[] bias, Shape a, float y, float x) ;
}
```

java.awt.image.**ImagingOpException**

```
public class ImagingOpException extends RuntimeException
{
    // Constructors
    public ImagingOpException(String s) ;
}
```

java.awt.image.**IndexColorModel**

```
public class IndexColorModel extends ColorModel
{
    // Constructors
    public IndexColorModel(BigInteger validBits, int transferType, int start, int[] cmap, int size, int bits)
        ;
    public IndexColorModel(int transferType, int trans, boolean hasalpha, int start, int[] cmap, int size,
        int bits) ;
    public IndexColorModel(int trans, boolean hasalpha, int start, byte[] cmap, int size, int bits) ;
    public IndexColorModel(boolean hasalpha, int start, byte[] cmap, int size, int bits) ;
    public IndexColorModel(byte[] a, byte[] b, byte[] g, byte[] r, int size, int bits) ;
    public IndexColorModel(int trans, byte[] b, byte[] g, byte[] r, int size, int bits) ;
```

public **IndexColorModel**(byte[] b, byte[] g, byte[] r, int size, int bits) ;
// Static methods
// Instance methods
public BufferedImage **convertToIntDiscrete**(boolean forceARGB, Raster raster) ;
public SampleModel **createCompatibleSampleModel**(int h, int w) ;
public WritableRaster **createCompatibleWritableRaster**(int h, int w) ;
public void **finalize**() ;
public final int **getAlpha**(int pixel) ;
public final void **getAlphas**(byte[] a) ;
public final int **getBlue**(int pixel) ;
public final void **getBlues**(byte[] b) ;
public int **getComponents**(int offset, int[] components, int pixel) ;
public int **getComponents**(int offset, int[] components, Object pixel) ;
public int **getComponentSize**() ;
public int **getDataElement**(int offset, int[] components) ;
public synchronized Object **getDataElements**(Object pixel, int rgb) ;
public Object **getDataElements**(Object pixel, int offset, int[] components) ;
public final int **getGreen**(int pixel) ;
public final void **getGreens**(byte[] g) ;
public final int **getMapSize**() ;
public final int **getRed**(int pixel) ;
public final void **getReds**(byte[] r) ;
public final int **getRGB**(int pixel) ;
public final void **getRGBs**(int[] rgb) ;
public int **getTransparency**() ;
public final int **getTransparentPixel**() ;
public BigInteger **getValidPixels**() ; // Since 1.3
public boolean **isCompatibleRaster**(Raster raster) ;
public boolean **isCompatibleSampleModel**(SampleModel sm) ;
public boolean **isValid**(int pixel) ; // Since 1.3
public boolean **isValid**() ; // Since 1.3
public String **toString**() ;
}

---

javax.swing.text.html.**InlineView**

---

public class **InlineView** extends LabelView
{
    // Constructors
    public **InlineView**(Element elem) ;
    // Instance methods
    public View **breakView**(float len, float pos, int offset, int axis) ; // Since 1.5
    public void **changedUpdate**(ViewFactory f, Shape a, DocumentEvent e) ;
    public AttributeSet **getAttributes**() ;

```
    public int getBreakWeight(float len, float pos, int axis) ;
    protected StyleSheet getStyleSheet() ;
    public void insertUpdate(ViewFactory f, Shape a, DocumentEvent e) ; // Since 1.5
    public void removeUpdate(ViewFactory f, Shape a, DocumentEvent e) ; // Since 1.5
    protected void setPropertiesFromAttributes() ;
}
```

java.awt.im.**InputContext** [since 1.2]

```
public class InputContext
{
    // Constructors
    protected InputContext() ;
    // Static methods
    public static InputContext getInstance() ;
    // Instance methods
    public void dispatchEvent(AWTEvent event) ;
    public void dispose() ;
    public void endComposition() ;
    public Object getInputMethodControlObject() ;
    public Locale getLocale() ; // Since 1.3
    public boolean isCompositionEnabled() ; // Since 1.3
    public void reconvert() ; // Since 1.3
    public void removeNotify(Component client) ;
    public boolean selectInputMethod(Locale locale) ;
    public void setCharacterSubsets(java.lang.Character.Subset[] subsets) ;
    public void setCompositionEnabled(boolean enable) ; // Since 1.3
}
```

java.awt.event.**InputEvent** [since 1.1]

```
public abstract class InputEvent extends ComponentEvent
{
    public static final int ALT_DOWN_MASK ;
    public static final int ALT_GRAPH_DOWN_MASK ;
    public static final int ALT_GRAPH_MASK ;
    public static final int ALT_MASK ;
    public static final int BUTTON1_DOWN_MASK ;
    public static final int BUTTON1_MASK ;
    public static final int BUTTON2_DOWN_MASK ;
    public static final int BUTTON2_MASK ;
```

```
    public static final int BUTTON3_DOWN_MASK ;
    public static final int BUTTON3_MASK ;
    public static final int CTRL_DOWN_MASK ;
    public static final int CTRL_MASK ;
    public static final int META_DOWN_MASK ;
    public static final int META_MASK ;
    public static final int SHIFT_DOWN_MASK ;
    public static final int SHIFT_MASK ;
    // Constructors
    private InputEvent(int modifiers, long when, int id, Component source) ;
    // Static methods
    public static String getModifiersExText(int modifiers) ; // Since 1.4
    // Instance methods
    public void consume() ;
    public int getModifiers() ;
    public int getModifiersEx() ; // Since 1.4
    public long getWhen() ;
    public boolean isAltDown() ;
    public boolean isAltGraphDown() ;
    public boolean isConsumed() ;
    public boolean isControlDown() ;
    public boolean isMetaDown() ;
    public boolean isShiftDown() ;
}
```

---

javax.swing.**InputMap** [since 1.3]

```
public class InputMap  implements Serializable
{
    // Constructors
    public InputMap() ;
    // Instance methods
    public KeyStroke allKeys() ;
    public void clear() ;
    public Object get(KeyStroke keyStroke) ;
    public InputMap getParent() ;
    public KeyStroke keys() ;
    public void put(Object actionMapKey, KeyStroke keyStroke) ;
    public void remove(KeyStroke key) ;
    public void setParent(InputMap map) ;
    public int size() ;
}
```

---

javax.swing.plaf.**InputMapUIResource** [since 1.3]

---

public class **InputMapUIResource** extends InputMap implements UIResource
{
    // Constructors
    public **InputMapUIResource**() ;
}

---

java.awt.im.spi.**InputMethod** [since 1.3]

---

public interface **InputMethod**
{
    // Instance methods
    public void **activate**() ;
    public void **deactivate**(boolean isTemporary) ;
    public void **dispatchEvent**(AWTEvent event) ;
    public void **dispose**() ;
    public void **endComposition**() ;
    public Object **getControlObject**() ;
    public Locale **getLocale**() ;
    public void **hideWindows**() ;
    public boolean **isCompositionEnabled**() ;
    public void **notifyClientWindowChange**(Rectangle bounds) ;
    public void **reconvert**() ;
    public void **removeNotify**() ;
    public void **setCharacterSubsets**(java.lang.Character.Subset[] subsets) ;
    public void **setCompositionEnabled**(boolean enable) ;
    public void **setInputMethodContext**(InputMethodContext context) ;
    public boolean **setLocale**(Locale locale) ;
}

---

java.awt.im.spi.**InputMethodContext** [since 1.3]

---

public interface **InputMethodContext** implements InputMethodRequests
{
    // Instance methods
    public JFrame **createInputMethodJFrame**(boolean attachToInputContext, String title) ; // Since 1.4
    public Window **createInputMethodWindow**(boolean attachToInputContext, String title) ;

```
    public void dispatchInputMethodEvent(TextHitInfo visiblePosition, TextHitInfo caret, int
        committedCharacterCount, AttributedCharacterIterator text, int id) ;
    public void enableClientWindowNotification(boolean enable, InputMethod inputMethod) ;
}
```

---

java.awt.im.spi.**InputMethodDescriptor** [since 1.3]

```
public interface InputMethodDescriptor
{
    // Instance methods
    public InputMethod createInputMethod() throws Exception ;
    public Locale getAvailableLocales() throws AWTException ;
    public String getInputMethodDisplayName(Locale displayLanguage, Locale inputLocale) ;
    public Image getInputMethodIcon(Locale inputLocale) ;
    public boolean hasDynamicLocaleList() ;
}
```

---

java.awt.event.**InputMethodEvent** [since 1.2]

```
public class InputMethodEvent extends AWTEvent
{
    public static final int CARET_POSITION_CHANGED ;
    public static final int INPUT_METHOD_FIRST ;
    public static final int INPUT_METHOD_LAST ;
    public static final int INPUT_METHOD_TEXT_CHANGED ;
    // Constructors
    public InputMethodEvent(TextHitInfo visiblePosition, TextHitInfo caret, int id, Component source)
        ;
    public InputMethodEvent(TextHitInfo visiblePosition, TextHitInfo caret, int
        committedCharacterCount, AttributedCharacterIterator text, int id, Component source) ;
    public InputMethodEvent(TextHitInfo visiblePosition, TextHitInfo caret, int
        committedCharacterCount, AttributedCharacterIterator text, long when, int id, Component source)
        ;
    // Instance methods
    public void consume() ;
    public TextHitInfo getCaret() ;
    public int getCommittedCharacterCount() ;
    public AttributedCharacterIterator getText() ;
    public TextHitInfo getVisiblePosition() ;
    public long getWhen() ; // Since 1.4
    public boolean isConsumed() ;
```

```
        public String paramString() ;
}
```

---

java.awt.im.**InputMethodHighlight** [since 1.2]

```
public class InputMethodHighlight
{
    public static final int CONVERTED_TEXT ;
    public static final int RAW_TEXT ;
    public static final InputMethodHighlight SELECTED_CONVERTED_TEXT_HIGHLIGHT ;
    public static final InputMethodHighlight SELECTED_RAW_TEXT_HIGHLIGHT ;
    public static final InputMethodHighlight UNSELECTED_CONVERTED_TEXT_HIGHLIGHT ;
    public static final InputMethodHighlight UNSELECTED_RAW_TEXT_HIGHLIGHT ;
    // Constructors
    public InputMethodHighlight(Map<TextAttribute, ?> style, int variation, int state, boolean selected)
        ;
    public InputMethodHighlight(int variation, int state, boolean selected) ;
    public InputMethodHighlight(int state, boolean selected) ;
    // Instance methods
    public int getState() ;
    public Map<TextAttribute, ?> getStyle() ; // Since 1.3
    public int getVariation() ;
    public boolean isSelected() ;
}
```

---

java.awt.event.**InputMethodListener** [since 1.2]

```
public interface InputMethodListener  implements EventListener
{
    // Instance methods
    public void caretPositionChanged(InputMethodEvent event) ;
    public void inputMethodTextChanged(InputMethodEvent event) ;
}
```

---

java.awt.im.**InputMethodRequests** [since 1.2]

```
public interface InputMethodRequests
{
```

// Instance methods
public AttributedCharacterIterator
    cancelLatestCommittedText(java.text.AttributedCharacterIterator.Attribute[] attributes) ;
public AttributedCharacterIterator
    getCommittedText(java.text.AttributedCharacterIterator.Attribute[] attributes, int endIndex, int
    beginIndex) ;
public int **getCommittedTextLength**() ;
public int **getInsertPositionOffset**() ;
public TextHitInfo **getLocationOffset**(int y, int x) ;
public AttributedCharacterIterator **getSelectedText**(java.text.AttributedCharacterIterator.Attribute[]
    attributes) ;
public Rectangle **getTextLocation**(TextHitInfo offset) ;
}

---

java.awt.im.**InputSubset** [since 1.2]

---

public final class **InputSubset** extends Character.Subset
{
    public static final InputSubset **FULLWIDTH_DIGITS** ;
    public static final InputSubset **FULLWIDTH_LATIN** ;
    public static final InputSubset **HALFWIDTH_KATAKANA** ;
    public static final InputSubset **HANJA** ;
    public static final InputSubset **KANJI** ;
    public static final InputSubset **LATIN** ;
    public static final InputSubset **LATIN_DIGITS** ;
    public static final InputSubset **SIMPLIFIED_HANZI** ;
    public static final InputSubset **TRADITIONAL_HANZI** ;
    // Constructors
    private **InputSubset**(String name) ;
}

---

javax.swing.**InputVerifier** [since 1.3]

---

public abstract class **InputVerifier**
{
    // Constructors
    public **InputVerifier**() ;
    // Instance methods
    public boolean **shouldYieldFocus**(JComponent input) ;
    public abstract boolean **verify**(JComponent input) ;
}

java.awt.**Insets** [since 1.0]

public class **Insets** implements Serializable, Cloneable
{
    public int **bottom** ;
    public int **left** ;
    public int **right** ;
    public int **top** ;
    // Constructors
    public **Insets**(int right, int bottom, int left, int top) ;
    // Static methods
    // Instance methods
    public Object **clone**() ;
    public boolean **equals**(Object obj) ; // Since 1.1
    public int **hashCode**() ;
    public void **set**(int right, int bottom, int left, int top) ; // Since 1.5
    public String **toString**() ;
}

javax.swing.plaf.**InsetsUIResource**

public class **InsetsUIResource** extends Insets implements UIResource
{
    // Constructors
    public **InsetsUIResource**(int right, int bottom, int left, int top) ;
}

javax.swing.event.**InternalFrameAdapter**

public abstract class **InternalFrameAdapter** implements InternalFrameListener
{
    // Constructors
    public **InternalFrameAdapter**() ;
    // Instance methods
    public void **internalFrameActivated**(InternalFrameEvent e) ;
    public void **internalFrameClosed**(InternalFrameEvent e) ;
    public void **internalFrameClosing**(InternalFrameEvent e) ;

```
    public void internalFrameDeactivated(InternalFrameEvent e) ;
    public void internalFrameDeiconified(InternalFrameEvent e) ;
    public void internalFrameIconified(InternalFrameEvent e) ;
    public void internalFrameOpened(InternalFrameEvent e) ;
}
```

javax.swing.event.**InternalFrameEvent**

```
public class InternalFrameEvent extends AWTEvent
{
    public static final int INTERNAL_FRAME_ACTIVATED ;
    public static final int INTERNAL_FRAME_CLOSED ;
    public static final int INTERNAL_FRAME_CLOSING ;
    public static final int INTERNAL_FRAME_DEACTIVATED ;
    public static final int INTERNAL_FRAME_DEICONIFIED ;
    public static final int INTERNAL_FRAME_FIRST ;
    public static final int INTERNAL_FRAME_ICONIFIED ;
    public static final int INTERNAL_FRAME_LAST ;
    public static final int INTERNAL_FRAME_OPENED ;
    // Constructors
    public InternalFrameEvent(int id, JInternalFrame source) ;
    // Instance methods
    public JInternalFrame getInternalFrame() ; // Since 1.3
    public String paramString() ;
}
```

javax.swing.**InternalFrameFocusTraversalPolicy** [since 1.4]

```
public abstract class InternalFrameFocusTraversalPolicy extends FocusTraversalPolicy
{
    // Constructors
    public InternalFrameFocusTraversalPolicy() ;
    // Instance methods
    public Component getInitialComponent(JInternalFrame frame) ;
}
```

javax.swing.event.**InternalFrameListener**

public interface **InternalFrameListener** implements EventListener
{
    // Instance methods
    public void **internalFrameActivated**(InternalFrameEvent e) ;
    public void **internalFrameClosed**(InternalFrameEvent e) ;
    public void **internalFrameClosing**(InternalFrameEvent e) ;
    public void **internalFrameDeactivated**(InternalFrameEvent e) ;
    public void **internalFrameDeiconified**(InternalFrameEvent e) ;
    public void **internalFrameIconified**(InternalFrameEvent e) ;
    public void **internalFrameOpened**(InternalFrameEvent e) ;
}

javax.swing.plaf.**InternalFrameUI**

public abstract class **InternalFrameUI** extends ComponentUI
{
    // Constructors
    public **InternalFrameUI**() ;
}

javax.swing.text.**InternationalFormatter** [since 1.4]

public class **InternationalFormatter** extends DefaultFormatter
{
    // Constructors
    public **InternationalFormatter**(Format format) ;
    public **InternationalFormatter**() ;
    // Instance methods
    public Object **clone**() throws CloneNotSupportedException ;
    protected Action **getActions**() ;
    public Format.Field **getFields**(int offset) ;
    public Format **getFormat**() ;
    public Comparable **getMaximum**() ;
    public Comparable **getMinimum**() ;
    public void **install**(JFormattedTextField ftf) ;

```
    public void setFormat(Format format) ;
    public void setMaximum(Comparable max) ;
    public void setMinimum(Comparable minimum) ;
    public Object stringToValue(String text) throws ParseException ;
    public String valueToString(Object value) throws ParseException ;
}
```

java.awt.dnd.**InvalidDnDOperationException** [since 1.2]

```
public class InvalidDnDOperationException extends IllegalStateException
{
    // Constructors
    public InvalidDnDOperationException(String msg) ;
    public InvalidDnDOperationException() ;
}
```

java.awt.event.**InvocationEvent** [since 1.2]

```
public class InvocationEvent extends AWTEvent implements ActiveEvent
{
    public static final int INVOCATION_DEFAULT ;
    public static final int INVOCATION_FIRST ;
    public static final int INVOCATION_LAST ;
    protected boolean catchExceptions ;
    protected Object notifier ;
    protected Runnable runnable ;
    // Constructors
    protected InvocationEvent(boolean catchThrowables, Object notifier, Runnable runnable, int id,
        Object source) ;
    public InvocationEvent(boolean catchThrowables, Object notifier, Runnable runnable, Object
        source) ;
    public InvocationEvent(Runnable runnable, Object source) ;
    // Instance methods
    public void dispatch() ;
    public Exception getException() ;
    public Throwable getThrowable() ; // Since 1.5
    public long getWhen() ; // Since 1.4
    public String paramString() ;
}
```

java.awt.event.**ItemEvent** [since 1.1]

public class **ItemEvent** extends AWTEvent
{
    public static final int **DESELECTED** ;
    public static final int **ITEM_FIRST** ;
    public static final int **ITEM_LAST** ;
    public static final int **ITEM_STATE_CHANGED** ;
    public static final int **SELECTED** ;
    // Constructors
    public **ItemEvent**(int stateChange, Object item, int id, ItemSelectable source) ;
    // Instance methods
    public Object **getItem**() ;
    public ItemSelectable **getItemSelectable**() ;
    public int **getStateChange**() ;
    public String **paramString**() ;
}

java.awt.event.**ItemListener** [since 1.1]

public interface **ItemListener** implements EventListener
{
    // Instance methods
    public void **itemStateChanged**(ItemEvent e) ;
}

java.awt.**ItemSelectable**

public interface **ItemSelectable**
{
    // Instance methods
    public void **addItemListener**(ItemListener l) ;
    public Object **getSelectedObjects**() ;
    public void **removeItemListener**(ItemListener l) ;
}

javax.swing.**JApplet**

public class **JApplet** extends Applet implements TransferHandler.HasGetTransferHandler, RootPaneContainer, Accessible
{
    protected AccessibleContext **accessibleContext** ;
    protected JRootPane **rootPane** ;
    protected boolean **rootPaneCheckingEnabled** ;
    // Constructors
    public **JApplet**() ;
    // Instance methods
    protected void **addImpl**(int index, Object constraints, Component comp) ;
    protected JRootPane **createRootPane**() ;
    public AccessibleContext **getAccessibleContext**() ;
    public Container **getContentPane**() ;
    public Component **getGlassPane**() ;
    public Graphics **getGraphics**() ; // Since 1.6
    public JMenuBar **getJMenuBar**() ;
    public JLayeredPane **getLayeredPane**() ;
    public JRootPane **getRootPane**() ;
    public TransferHandler **getTransferHandler**() ; // Since 1.6
    protected boolean **isRootPaneCheckingEnabled**() ;
    protected String **paramString**() ;
    public void **remove**(Component comp) ;
    public void **repaint**(int height, int width, int y, int x, long time) ; // Since 1.6
    public void **setContentPane**(Container contentPane) ;
    public void **setGlassPane**(Component glassPane) ;
    public void **setJMenuBar**(JMenuBar menuBar) ;
    public void **setLayeredPane**(JLayeredPane layeredPane) ;
    public void **setLayout**(LayoutManager manager) ;
    protected void **setRootPane**(JRootPane root) ;
    protected void **setRootPaneCheckingEnabled**(boolean enabled) ;
    public void **setTransferHandler**(TransferHandler newHandler) ; // Since 1.6
    public void **update**(Graphics g) ;
}

javax.swing.**JButton**

public class **JButton** extends AbstractButton implements Accessible
{

```
    // Constructors
    public JButton(Icon icon, String text) ;
    public JButton(Action a) ;
    public JButton(String text) ;
    public JButton(Icon icon) ;
    public JButton() ;
    // Instance methods
    public AccessibleContext getAccessibleContext() ;
    public String getUIClassID() ;
    public boolean isDefaultButton() ;
    public boolean isDefaultCapable() ;
    protected String paramString() ;
    public void removeNotify() ;
    public void setDefaultCapable(boolean defaultCapable) ;
    public void updateUI() ;
}
```

---

javax.swing.**JCheckBox**

```
public class JCheckBox extends JToggleButton implements Accessible
{
    public static final String BORDER_PAINTED_FLAT_CHANGED_PROPERTY ;
    // Constructors
    public JCheckBox(boolean selected, Icon icon, String text) ;
    public JCheckBox(Icon icon, String text) ;
    public JCheckBox(boolean selected, String text) ;
    public JCheckBox(Action a) ;
    public JCheckBox(String text) ;
    public JCheckBox(boolean selected, Icon icon) ;
    public JCheckBox(Icon icon) ;
    public JCheckBox() ;
    // Instance methods
    public AccessibleContext getAccessibleContext() ;
    public String getUIClassID() ;
    public boolean isBorderPaintedFlat() ; // Since 1.3
    protected String paramString() ;
    public void setBorderPaintedFlat(boolean b) ; // Since 1.3
    public void updateUI() ;
}
```

---

javax.swing.**JCheckBoxMenuItem**

---

public class **JCheckBoxMenuItem** extends JMenuItem implements Accessible, SwingConstants
{
    // Constructors
    public **JCheckBoxMenuItem**(boolean b, Icon icon, String text) ;
    public **JCheckBoxMenuItem**(boolean b, String text) ;
    public **JCheckBoxMenuItem**(Icon icon, String text) ;
    public **JCheckBoxMenuItem**(Action a) ;
    public **JCheckBoxMenuItem**(String text) ;
    public **JCheckBoxMenuItem**(Icon icon) ;
    public **JCheckBoxMenuItem**() ;
    // Instance methods
    public AccessibleContext **getAccessibleContext**() ;
    public Object **getSelectedObjects**() ;
    public boolean **getState**() ;
    public String **getUIClassID**() ;
    protected String **paramString**() ;
    public synchronized void **setState**(boolean b) ;
}

---

javax.swing.**JColorChooser**

---

public class **JColorChooser** extends JComponent implements Accessible
{
    public static final String **CHOOSER_PANELS_PROPERTY** ;
    public static final String **PREVIEW_PANEL_PROPERTY** ;
    public static final String **SELECTION_MODEL_PROPERTY** ;
    protected AccessibleContext **accessibleContext** ;
    // Constructors
    public **JColorChooser**(ColorSelectionModel model) ;
    public **JColorChooser**(Color initialColor) ;
    public **JColorChooser**() ;
    // Static methods
    public static JDialog **createDialog**(ActionListener cancelListener, ActionListener okListener,
        JColorChooser chooserPane, boolean modal, String title, Component c) throws
        HeadlessException ;
    public static Color **showDialog**(Color initialColor, String title, Component component) throws
        HeadlessException ;
    // Instance methods

public void **addChooserPanel**(AbstractColorChooserPanel panel) ;
public AccessibleContext **getAccessibleContext**() ;
public AbstractColorChooserPanel **getChooserPanels**() ;
public Color **getColor**() ;
public boolean **getDragEnabled**() ; // Since 1.4
public JComponent **getPreviewPanel**() ;
public ColorSelectionModel **getSelectionModel**() ;
public ColorChooserUI **getUI**() ;
public String **getUIClassID**() ;
protected String **paramString**() ;
public AbstractColorChooserPanel **removeChooserPanel**(AbstractColorChooserPanel panel) ;
public void **setChooserPanels**(javax.swing.colorchooser.AbstractColorChooserPanel[] panels) ;
public void **setColor**(Color color) ;
public void **setColor**(int b, int g, int r) ;
public void **setColor**(int c) ;
public void **setDragEnabled**(boolean b) ; // Since 1.4
public void **setPreviewPanel**(JComponent preview) ;
public void **setSelectionModel**(ColorSelectionModel newModel) ;
public void **setUI**(ColorChooserUI ui) ;
public void **updateUI**() ;
}

---

javax.swing.**JComboBox**

---

public class **JComboBox** extends JComponent implements Accessible, ActionListener, ListDataListener, ItemSelectable
{
    protected String **actionCommand** ;
    protected ComboBoxModel **dataModel** ;
    protected ComboBoxEditor **editor** ;
    protected boolean **isEditable** ;
    protected JComboBox.KeySelectionManager **keySelectionManager** ;
    protected boolean **lightWeightPopupEnabled** ;
    protected int **maximumRowCount** ;
    protected ListCellRenderer **renderer** ;
    protected Object **selectedItemReminder** ;
    // Constructors
    public **JComboBox**() ;
    public **JComboBox**(Vector<?> items) ;
    public **JComboBox**(java.lang.Object[] items) ;
    public **JComboBox**(ComboBoxModel aModel) ;
    // Instance methods
    public void **actionPerformed**(ActionEvent e) ;
    protected void **actionPropertyChanged**(String propertyName, Action action) ; // Since 1.6

---

public void **addActionListener**(ActionListener l) ;
public void **addItem**(Object anObject) ;
public void **addItemListener**(ItemListener aListener) ;
public void **addPopupMenuListener**(PopupMenuListener l) ; // Since 1.4
public void **configureEditor**(Object anItem, ComboBoxEditor anEditor) ;
protected void **configurePropertiesFromAction**(Action a) ; // Since 1.3
public void **contentsChanged**(ListDataEvent e) ;
protected PropertyChangeListener **createActionPropertyChangeListener**(Action a) ; // Since 1.3
protected JComboBox.KeySelectionManager **createDefaultKeySelectionManager**() ;
protected void **fireActionEvent**() ;
protected void **fireItemStateChanged**(ItemEvent e) ;
public void **firePopupMenuCanceled**() ; // Since 1.4
public void **firePopupMenuWillBecomeInvisible**() ; // Since 1.4
public void **firePopupMenuWillBecomeVisible**() ; // Since 1.4
public AccessibleContext **getAccessibleContext**() ;
public Action **getAction**() ; // Since 1.3
public String **getActionCommand**() ;
public ActionListener **getActionListeners**() ; // Since 1.4
public ComboBoxEditor **getEditor**() ;
public Object **getItemAt**(int index) ;
public int **getItemCount**() ;
public ItemListener **getItemListeners**() ; // Since 1.4
public JComboBox.KeySelectionManager **getKeySelectionManager**() ;
public int **getMaximumRowCount**() ;
public ComboBoxModel **getModel**() ;
public PopupMenuListener **getPopupMenuListeners**() ; // Since 1.4
public Object **getPrototypeDisplayValue**() ; // Since 1.4
public ListCellRenderer **getRenderer**() ;
public int **getSelectedIndex**() ;
public Object **getSelectedItem**() ;
public Object **getSelectedObjects**() ;
public ComboBoxUI **getUI**() ;
public String **getUIClassID**() ;
public void **hidePopup**() ;
public void **insertItemAt**(int index, Object anObject) ;
protected void **installAncestorListener**() ;
public void **intervalAdded**(ListDataEvent e) ;
public void **intervalRemoved**(ListDataEvent e) ;
public boolean **isEditable**() ;
public boolean **isLightWeightPopupEnabled**() ;
public boolean **isPopupVisible**() ;
protected String **paramString**() ;
public void **processKeyEvent**(KeyEvent e) ;
public void **removeActionListener**(ActionListener l) ;
public void **removeAllItems**() ;
public void **removeItem**(Object anObject) ;

```
    public void removeItemAt(int anIndex) ;
    public void removeItemListener(ItemListener aListener) ;
    public void removePopupMenuListener(PopupMenuListener l) ; // Since 1.4
    protected void selectedItemChanged() ;
    public boolean selectWithKeyChar(char keyChar) ;
    public void setAction(Action a) ; // Since 1.3
    public void setActionCommand(String aCommand) ;
    public void setEditable(boolean aFlag) ;
    public void setEditor(ComboBoxEditor anEditor) ;
    public void setEnabled(boolean b) ;
    public void setKeySelectionManager(JComboBox.KeySelectionManager aManager) ;
    public void setLightWeightPopupEnabled(boolean aFlag) ;
    public void setMaximumRowCount(int count) ;
    public void setModel(ComboBoxModel aModel) ;
    public void setPopupVisible(boolean v) ;
    public void setPrototypeDisplayValue(Object prototypeDisplayValue) ; // Since 1.4
    public void setRenderer(ListCellRenderer aRenderer) ;
    public void setSelectedIndex(int anIndex) ;
    public void setSelectedItem(Object anObject) ;
    public void setUI(ComboBoxUI ui) ;
    public void showPopup() ;
    public void updateUI() ;
}
```

javax.swing.**JComboBox.KeySelectionManager**

```
public static interface JComboBox.KeySelectionManager
{
    // Instance methods
    public int selectionForKey(ComboBoxModel aModel, char aKey) ;
}
```

javax.swing.**JComponent**

```
public abstract class JComponent extends Container implements
TransferHandler.HasGetTransferHandler, Serializable
{
    public static final String TOOL_TIP_TEXT_KEY ;
    public static final int UNDEFINED_CONDITION ;
    public static final int WHEN_ANCESTOR_OF_FOCUSED_COMPONENT ;
    public static final int WHEN_FOCUSED ;
```

public static final int **WHEN_IN_FOCUSED_WINDOW** ;
protected AccessibleContext **accessibleContext** ;
protected EventListenerList **listenerList** ;
protected transient ComponentUI **ui** ;
// Constructors
public **JComponent**() ;
// Static methods
public static Locale **getDefaultLocale**() ; // Since 1.4
public static boolean **isLightweightComponent**(Component c) ;
public static void **setDefaultLocale**(Locale l) ; // Since 1.4
// Instance methods
public void **addAncestorListener**(AncestorListener listener) ;
public void **addNotify**() ;
public synchronized void **addVetoableChangeListener**(VetoableChangeListener listener) ;
public void **computeVisibleRect**(Rectangle visibleRect) ;
public boolean **contains**(int y, int x) ;
public JToolTip **createToolTip**() ;
public void **disable**() ;
public void **enable**() ;
public void **firePropertyChange**(int newValue, int oldValue, String propertyName) ;
public void **firePropertyChange**(boolean newValue, boolean oldValue, String propertyName) ;
public void **firePropertyChange**(char newValue, char oldValue, String propertyName) ;
protected void **fireVetoableChange**(Object newValue, Object oldValue, String propertyName)
    throws PropertyVetoException ;
public AccessibleContext **getAccessibleContext**() ;
public ActionListener **getActionForKeyStroke**(KeyStroke aKeyStroke) ;
public final ActionMap **getActionMap**() ; // Since 1.3
public float **getAlignmentX**() ;
public float **getAlignmentY**() ;
public AncestorListener **getAncestorListeners**() ; // Since 1.4
public boolean **getAutoscrolls**() ;
public int **getBaseline**(int height, int width) ; // Since 1.6
public Component.BaselineResizeBehavior **getBaselineResizeBehavior**() ; // Since 1.6
public Border **getBorder**() ;
public Rectangle **getBounds**(Rectangle rv) ;
public final Object **getClientProperty**(Object key) ;
protected Graphics **getComponentGraphics**(Graphics g) ;
public JPopupMenu **getComponentPopupMenu**() ; // Since 1.5
public int **getConditionForKeyStroke**(KeyStroke aKeyStroke) ;
public int **getDebugGraphicsOptions**() ;
public FontMetrics **getFontMetrics**(Font font) ; // Since 1.5
public Graphics **getGraphics**() ;
public int **getHeight**() ;
public boolean **getInheritsPopupMenu**() ; // Since 1.5
public final InputMap **getInputMap**(int condition) ; // Since 1.3
public final InputMap **getInputMap**() ; // Since 1.3

public InputVerifier **getInputVerifier**() ; // Since 1.3
public Insets **getInsets**() ;
public Insets **getInsets**(Insets insets) ;
public T **getListeners**(Class<T> listenerType) ; // Since 1.3
public Point **getLocation**(Point rv) ;
public Dimension **getMaximumSize**() ;
public Dimension **getMinimumSize**() ;
public Component **getNextFocusableComponent**() ;
public Point **getPopupLocation**(MouseEvent event) ; // Since 1.5
public Dimension **getPreferredSize**() ;
public KeyStroke **getRegisteredKeyStrokes**() ;
public JRootPane **getRootPane**() ;
public Dimension **getSize**(Dimension rv) ;
public Point **getToolTipLocation**(MouseEvent event) ;
public String **getToolTipText**() ;
public String **getToolTipText**(MouseEvent event) ;
public Container **getTopLevelAncestor**() ;
public TransferHandler **getTransferHandler**() ; // Since 1.4
public String **getUIClassID**() ;
public boolean **getVerifyInputWhenFocusTarget**() ; // Since 1.3
public synchronized VetoableChangeListener **getVetoableChangeListeners**() ; // Since 1.4
public Rectangle **getVisibleRect**() ;
public int **getWidth**() ;
public int **getX**() ;
public int **getY**() ;
public void **grabFocus**() ;
public boolean **isDoubleBuffered**() ;
public boolean **isManagingFocus**() ;
public boolean **isOpaque**() ;
public boolean **isOptimizedDrawingEnabled**() ;
public final boolean **isPaintingForPrint**() ; // Since 1.6
public boolean **isPaintingTile**() ;
public boolean **isRequestFocusEnabled**() ;
public boolean **isValidateRoot**() ;
public void **paint**(Graphics g) ;
protected void **paintBorder**(Graphics g) ;
protected void **paintChildren**(Graphics g) ;
protected void **paintComponent**(Graphics g) ;
public void **paintImmediately**(Rectangle r) ;
public void **paintImmediately**(int h, int w, int y, int x) ;
protected String **paramString**() ;
public void **print**(Graphics g) ;
public void **printAll**(Graphics g) ;
protected void **printBorder**(Graphics g) ; // Since 1.3
protected void **printChildren**(Graphics g) ; // Since 1.3
protected void **printComponent**(Graphics g) ; // Since 1.3

protected void **processComponentKeyEvent**(KeyEvent e) ;

protected boolean **processKeyBinding**(boolean pressed, int condition, KeyEvent e, KeyStroke ks) ; // Since 1.3

protected void **processKeyEvent**(KeyEvent e) ;

protected void **processMouseEvent**(MouseEvent e) ; // Since 1.5

protected void **processMouseMotionEvent**(MouseEvent e) ;

public final void **putClientProperty**(Object value, Object key) ;

public void **registerKeyboardAction**(int aCondition, KeyStroke aKeyStroke, ActionListener anAction) ;

public void **registerKeyboardAction**(int aCondition, KeyStroke aKeyStroke, String aCommand, ActionListener anAction) ;

public void **removeAncestorListener**(AncestorListener listener) ;

public void **removeNotify**() ;

public synchronized void **removeVetoableChangeListener**(VetoableChangeListener listener) ;

public void **repaint**(int height, int width, int y, int x, long tm) ;

public void **repaint**(Rectangle r) ;

public boolean **requestDefaultFocus**() ;

public void **requestFocus**() ; // Since 1.4

public boolean **requestFocus**(boolean temporary) ; // Since 1.4

public boolean **requestFocusInWindow**() ; // Since 1.4

protected boolean **requestFocusInWindow**(boolean temporary) ; // Since 1.4

public void **resetKeyboardActions**() ;

public void **reshape**(int h, int w, int y, int x) ;

public void **revalidate**() ;

public void **scrollRectToVisible**(Rectangle aRect) ;

public final void **setActionMap**(ActionMap am) ; // Since 1.3

public void **setAlignmentX**(float alignmentX) ;

public void **setAlignmentY**(float alignmentY) ;

public void **setAutoscrolls**(boolean autoscrolls) ;

public void **setBackground**(Color bg) ;

public void **setBorder**(Border border) ;

public void **setComponentPopupMenu**(JPopupMenu popup) ; // Since 1.5

public void **setDebugGraphicsOptions**(int debugOptions) ;

public void **setDoubleBuffered**(boolean aFlag) ;

public void **setEnabled**(boolean enabled) ;

public void **setFocusTraversalKeys**(Set<?> keystrokes, int id) ; // Since 1.5

public void **setFont**(Font font) ;

public void **setForeground**(Color fg) ;

public void **setInheritsPopupMenu**(boolean value) ; // Since 1.5

public final void **setInputMap**(InputMap map, int condition) ; // Since 1.3

public void **setInputVerifier**(InputVerifier inputVerifier) ; // Since 1.3

public void **setMaximumSize**(Dimension maximumSize) ;

public void **setMinimumSize**(Dimension minimumSize) ;

public void **setNextFocusableComponent**(Component aComponent) ;

public void **setOpaque**(boolean isOpaque) ;

public void **setPreferredSize**(Dimension preferredSize) ;

```
    public void setRequestFocusEnabled(boolean requestFocusEnabled) ;
    public void setToolTipText(String text) ;
    public void setTransferHandler(TransferHandler newHandler) ; // Since 1.4
    protected void setUI(ComponentUI newUI) ;
    public void setVerifyInputWhenFocusTarget(boolean verifyInputWhenFocusTarget) ; // Since 1.3
    public void setVisible(boolean aFlag) ;
    public void unregisterKeyboardAction(KeyStroke aKeyStroke) ;
    public void update(Graphics g) ;
    public void updateUI() ;
}
```

javax.swing.**JDesktopPane**

public class **JDesktopPane** extends JLayeredPane implements Accessible
```
{
    public static final int LIVE_DRAG_MODE ;
    public static final int OUTLINE_DRAG_MODE ;
    // Constructors
    public JDesktopPane() ;
    // Instance methods
    protected void addImpl(int index, Object constraints, Component comp) ; // Since 1.6
    public AccessibleContext getAccessibleContext() ;
    public JInternalFrame getAllFrames() ;
    public JInternalFrame getAllFramesInLayer(int layer) ;
    public DesktopManager getDesktopManager() ;
    public int getDragMode() ; // Since 1.3
    public JInternalFrame getSelectedFrame() ; // Since 1.3
    public DesktopPaneUI getUI() ;
    public String getUIClassID() ;
    protected String paramString() ;
    public void remove(int index) ; // Since 1.6
    public void removeAll() ; // Since 1.6
    public JInternalFrame selectFrame(boolean forward) ; // Since 1.6
    public void setComponentZOrder(int index, Component comp) ; // Since 1.6
    public void setDesktopManager(DesktopManager d) ;
    public void setDragMode(int dragMode) ; // Since 1.3
    public void setSelectedFrame(JInternalFrame f) ; // Since 1.3
    public void setUI(DesktopPaneUI ui) ;
    public void updateUI() ;
}
```

javax.swing.**JDialog**

public class **JDialog** extends Dialog implements TransferHandler.HasGetTransferHandler, RootPaneContainer, Accessible, WindowConstants
{
    protected AccessibleContext **accessibleContext** ;
    protected JRootPane **rootPane** ;
    protected boolean **rootPaneCheckingEnabled** ;
    // Constructors
    public **JDialog**(GraphicsConfiguration gc, Dialog.ModalityType modalityType, String title, Window
        owner) ;
    public **JDialog**(Dialog.ModalityType modalityType, String title, Window owner) ;
    public **JDialog**(String title, Window owner) ;
    public **JDialog**(Dialog.ModalityType modalityType, Window owner) ;
    public **JDialog**(Window owner) ;
    public **JDialog**(GraphicsConfiguration gc, boolean modal, String title, Dialog owner) ;
    public **JDialog**(boolean modal, String title, Dialog owner) ;
    public **JDialog**(String title, Dialog owner) ;
    public **JDialog**(boolean modal, Dialog owner) ;
    public **JDialog**(Dialog owner) ;
    public **JDialog**(GraphicsConfiguration gc, boolean modal, String title, Frame owner) ;
    public **JDialog**(boolean modal, String title, Frame owner) ;
    public **JDialog**(String title, Frame owner) ;
    public **JDialog**(boolean modal, Frame owner) ;
    public **JDialog**(Frame owner) ;
    public **JDialog**() ;
    // Static methods
    public static boolean **isDefaultLookAndFeelDecorated**() ; // Since 1.4
    public static void **setDefaultLookAndFeelDecorated**(boolean defaultLookAndFeelDecorated) ; //
        Since 1.4
    // Instance methods
    protected void **addImpl**(int index, Object constraints, Component comp) ;
    protected JRootPane **createRootPane**() ;
    protected void **dialogInit**() ;
    public AccessibleContext **getAccessibleContext**() ;
    public Container **getContentPane**() ;
    public int **getDefaultCloseOperation**() ;
    public Component **getGlassPane**() ;
    public Graphics **getGraphics**() ; // Since 1.6
    public JMenuBar **getJMenuBar**() ;
    public JLayeredPane **getLayeredPane**() ;
    public JRootPane **getRootPane**() ;
    public TransferHandler **getTransferHandler**() ; // Since 1.6

```
    protected boolean isRootPaneCheckingEnabled() ;
    protected String paramString() ;
    protected void processWindowEvent(WindowEvent e) ;
    public void remove(Component comp) ;
    public void repaint(int height, int width, int y, int x, long time) ; // Since 1.6
    public void setContentPane(Container contentPane) ;
    public void setDefaultCloseOperation(int operation) ;
    public void setGlassPane(Component glassPane) ;
    public void setJMenuBar(JMenuBar menu) ;
    public void setLayeredPane(JLayeredPane layeredPane) ;
    public void setLayout(LayoutManager manager) ;
    protected void setRootPane(JRootPane root) ;
    protected void setRootPaneCheckingEnabled(boolean enabled) ;
    public void setTransferHandler(TransferHandler newHandler) ; // Since 1.6
    public void update(Graphics g) ;
}
```

---

javax.swing.**JEditorPane**

```
public class JEditorPane extends JTextComponent
{
    public static final String HONOR_DISPLAY_PROPERTIES ;
    public static final String W3C_LENGTH_UNITS ;
    // Constructors
    public JEditorPane(String text, String type) ;
    public JEditorPane(String url) ;
    public JEditorPane(URL initialPage) ;
    public JEditorPane() ;
    // Static methods
    public static EditorKit createEditorKitForContentType(String type) ;
    public static String getEditorKitClassNameForContentType(String type) ; // Since 1.3
    public static void registerEditorKitForContentType(String classname, String type) ;
    public static void registerEditorKitForContentType(ClassLoader loader, String classname, String
        type) ;
    // Instance methods
    public synchronized void addHyperlinkListener(HyperlinkListener listener) ;
    protected EditorKit createDefaultEditorKit() ;
    public void fireHyperlinkUpdate(HyperlinkEvent e) ;
    public AccessibleContext getAccessibleContext() ;
    public final String getContentType() ;
    public EditorKit getEditorKit() ;
    public EditorKit getEditorKitForContentType(String type) ;
    public synchronized HyperlinkListener getHyperlinkListeners() ; // Since 1.4
    public URL getPage() ;
```

```
    public Dimension getPreferredSize() ;
    public boolean getScrollableTracksViewportHeight() ;
    public boolean getScrollableTracksViewportWidth() ;
    protected InputStream getStream(URL page) throws IOException ;
    public String getText() ;
    public String getUIClassID() ;
    protected String paramString() ;
    public void read(Object desc, InputStream in) throws IOException ;
    public synchronized void removeHyperlinkListener(HyperlinkListener listener) ;
    public void replaceSelection(String content) ;
    public void scrollToReference(String reference) ;
    public final void setContentType(String type) ;
    public void setEditorKit(EditorKit kit) ;
    public void setEditorKitForContentType(EditorKit k, String type) ;
    public void setPage(URL page) throws IOException ;
    public void setPage(String url) throws IOException ;
    public void setText(String t) ;
}
```

javax.swing.**JFileChooser**

public class **JFileChooser** extends JComponent implements Accessible
{
    public static final String **ACCEPT_ALL_FILE_FILTER_USED_CHANGED_PROPERTY** ;
    public static final String **ACCESSORY_CHANGED_PROPERTY** ;
    public static final String **APPROVE_BUTTON_MNEMONIC_CHANGED_PROPERTY** ;
    public static final String **APPROVE_BUTTON_TEXT_CHANGED_PROPERTY** ;
    public static final String **APPROVE_BUTTON_TOOL_TIP_TEXT_CHANGED_PROPERTY** ;
    public static final int **APPROVE_OPTION** ;
    public static final String **APPROVE_SELECTION** ;
    public static final int **CANCEL_OPTION** ;
    public static final String **CANCEL_SELECTION** ;
    public static final String **CHOOSABLE_FILE_FILTER_CHANGED_PROPERTY** ;
    public static final String **CONTROL_BUTTONS_ARE_SHOWN_CHANGED_PROPERTY** ;
    public static final int **CUSTOM_DIALOG** ;
    public static final String **DIALOG_TITLE_CHANGED_PROPERTY** ;
    public static final String **DIALOG_TYPE_CHANGED_PROPERTY** ;
    public static final int **DIRECTORIES_ONLY** ;
    public static final String **DIRECTORY_CHANGED_PROPERTY** ;
    public static final int **ERROR_OPTION** ;
    public static final int **FILES_AND_DIRECTORIES** ;
    public static final int **FILES_ONLY** ;
    public static final String **FILE_FILTER_CHANGED_PROPERTY** ;
    public static final String **FILE_HIDING_CHANGED_PROPERTY** ;

public static final String **FILE_SELECTION_MODE_CHANGED_PROPERTY** ;
public static final String **FILE_SYSTEM_VIEW_CHANGED_PROPERTY** ;
public static final String **FILE_VIEW_CHANGED_PROPERTY** ;
public static final String **MULTI_SELECTION_ENABLED_CHANGED_PROPERTY** ;
public static final int **OPEN_DIALOG** ;
public static final int **SAVE_DIALOG** ;
public static final String **SELECTED_FILES_CHANGED_PROPERTY** ;
public static final String **SELECTED_FILE_CHANGED_PROPERTY** ;
protected AccessibleContext **accessibleContext** ;
// Constructors
public **JFileChooser**(FileSystemView fsv, String currentDirectoryPath) ;
public **JFileChooser**(FileSystemView fsv, File currentDirectory) ;
public **JFileChooser**(FileSystemView fsv) ;
public **JFileChooser**(File currentDirectory) ;
public **JFileChooser**(String currentDirectoryPath) ;
public **JFileChooser**() ;
// Instance methods
public boolean **accept**(File f) ;
public void **addActionListener**(ActionListener l) ;
public void **addChoosableFileFilter**(FileFilter filter) ;
public void **approveSelection**() ;
public void **cancelSelection**() ;
public void **changeToParentDirectory**() ;
protected JDialog **createDialog**(Component parent) throws HeadlessException ; // Since 1.4
public void **ensureFileIsVisible**(File f) ;
protected void **fireActionPerformed**(String command) ;
public FileFilter **getAcceptAllFileFilter**() ;
public AccessibleContext **getAccessibleContext**() ;
public JComponent **getAccessory**() ;
public ActionListener **getActionListeners**() ; // Since 1.4
public int **getApproveButtonMnemonic**() ;
public String **getApproveButtonText**() ;
public String **getApproveButtonToolTipText**() ;
public FileFilter **getChoosableFileFilters**() ;
public boolean **getControlButtonsAreShown**() ; // Since 1.3
public File **getCurrentDirectory**() ;
public String **getDescription**(File f) ;
public String **getDialogTitle**() ;
public int **getDialogType**() ;
public boolean **getDragEnabled**() ; // Since 1.4
public FileFilter **getFileFilter**() ;
public int **getFileSelectionMode**() ;
public FileSystemView **getFileSystemView**() ;
public FileView **getFileView**() ;
public Icon **getIcon**(File f) ;
public String **getName**(File f) ;

```
    public File getSelectedFile() ;
    public File getSelectedFiles() ;
    public String getTypeDescription(File f) ;
    public FileChooserUI getUI() ;
    public String getUIClassID() ;
    public boolean isAcceptAllFileFilterUsed() ; // Since 1.3
    public boolean isDirectorySelectionEnabled() ;
    public boolean isFileHidingEnabled() ;
    public boolean isFileSelectionEnabled() ;
    public boolean isMultiSelectionEnabled() ;
    public boolean isTraversable(File f) ;
    protected String paramString() ;
    public void removeActionListener(ActionListener l) ;
    public boolean removeChoosableFileFilter(FileFilter f) ;
    public void rescanCurrentDirectory() ;
    public void resetChoosableFileFilters() ;
    public void setAcceptAllFileFilterUsed(boolean b) ; // Since 1.3
    public void setAccessory(JComponent newAccessory) ;
    public void setApproveButtonMnemonic(int mnemonic) ;
    public void setApproveButtonMnemonic(char mnemonic) ;
    public void setApproveButtonText(String approveButtonText) ;
    public void setApproveButtonToolTipText(String toolTipText) ;
    public void setControlButtonsAreShown(boolean b) ; // Since 1.3
    public void setCurrentDirectory(File dir) ;
    public void setDialogTitle(String dialogTitle) ;
    public void setDialogType(int dialogType) ;
    public void setDragEnabled(boolean b) ; // Since 1.4
    public void setFileFilter(FileFilter filter) ;
    public void setFileHidingEnabled(boolean b) ;
    public void setFileSelectionMode(int mode) ;
    public void setFileSystemView(FileSystemView fsv) ;
    public void setFileView(FileView fileView) ;
    public void setMultiSelectionEnabled(boolean b) ;
    public void setSelectedFile(File file) ;
    public void setSelectedFiles(java.io.File[] selectedFiles) ;
    protected void setup(FileSystemView view) ;
    public int showDialog(String approveButtonText, Component parent) throws HeadlessException ;
    public int showOpenDialog(Component parent) throws HeadlessException ;
    public int showSaveDialog(Component parent) throws HeadlessException ;
    public void updateUI() ;
}
```

javax.swing.**JFormattedTextField** [since 1.4]

public class **JFormattedTextField** extends JTextField
{
    public static final int **COMMIT** ;
    public static final int **COMMIT_OR_REVERT** ;
    public static final int **PERSIST** ;
    public static final int **REVERT** ;
    // Constructors
    public **JFormattedTextField**(Object currentValue, JFormattedTextField.AbstractFormatterFactory
        factory) ;
    public **JFormattedTextField**(JFormattedTextField.AbstractFormatterFactory factory) ;
    public **JFormattedTextField**(JFormattedTextField.AbstractFormatter formatter) ;
    public **JFormattedTextField**(Format format) ;
    public **JFormattedTextField**(Object value) ;
    public **JFormattedTextField**() ;
    // Instance methods
    public void **commitEdit**() throws ParseException ;
    public Action **getActions**() ;
    public int **getFocusLostBehavior**() ;
    public JFormattedTextField.AbstractFormatter **getFormatter**() ;
    public JFormattedTextField.AbstractFormatterFactory **getFormatterFactory**() ;
    public String **getUIClassID**() ;
    public Object **getValue**() ;
    protected void **invalidEdit**() ;
    public boolean **isEditValid**() ;
    protected void **processFocusEvent**(FocusEvent e) ;
    protected void **processInputMethodEvent**(InputMethodEvent e) ;
    public void **setDocument**(Document doc) ;
    public void **setFocusLostBehavior**(int behavior) ;
    protected void **setFormatter**(JFormattedTextField.AbstractFormatter format) ;
    public void **setFormatterFactory**(JFormattedTextField.AbstractFormatterFactory tf) ;
    public void **setValue**(Object value) ;
}

javax.swing.**JFormattedTextField.AbstractFormatter** [since 1.4]

public abstract static class **JFormattedTextField.AbstractFormatter** implements Serializable
{
    // Constructors

public **JFormattedTextField.AbstractFormatter**() ;
// Instance methods
protected Object **clone**() throws CloneNotSupportedException ;
protected Action **getActions**() ;
protected DocumentFilter **getDocumentFilter**() ;
protected JFormattedTextField **getFormattedTextField**() ;
protected NavigationFilter **getNavigationFilter**() ;
public void **install**(JFormattedTextField ftf) ;
protected void **invalidEdit**() ;
protected void **setEditValid**(boolean valid) ;
public abstract Object **stringToValue**(String text) throws ParseException ;
public void **uninstall**() ;
public abstract String **valueToString**(Object value) throws ParseException ;
}

---

javax.swing.**JFormattedTextField.AbstractFormatterFactory** [since 1.4]

---

public abstract static class **JFormattedTextField.AbstractFormatterFactory**
{
    // Constructors
    public **JFormattedTextField.AbstractFormatterFactory**() ;
    // Instance methods
    public abstract JFormattedTextField.AbstractFormatter **getFormatter**(JFormattedTextField tf) ;
}

---

javax.swing.**JFrame**

---

public class **JFrame** extends Frame implements TransferHandler.HasGetTransferHandler,
RootPaneContainer, Accessible, WindowConstants
{
    public static final int **EXIT_ON_CLOSE** ;
    protected AccessibleContext **accessibleContext** ;
    protected JRootPane **rootPane** ;
    protected boolean **rootPaneCheckingEnabled** ;
    // Constructors
    public **JFrame**(GraphicsConfiguration gc, String title) ;
    public **JFrame**(String title) ;
    public **JFrame**(GraphicsConfiguration gc) ;
    public **JFrame**() ;
    // Static methods
    public static boolean **isDefaultLookAndFeelDecorated**() ; // Since 1.4

public static void **setDefaultLookAndFeelDecorated**(boolean defaultLookAndFeelDecorated) ; // Since 1.4
// Instance methods
protected void **addImpl**(int index, Object constraints, Component comp) ;
protected JRootPane **createRootPane**() ;
protected void **frameInit**() ;
public AccessibleContext **getAccessibleContext**() ;
public Container **getContentPane**() ;
public int **getDefaultCloseOperation**() ;
public Component **getGlassPane**() ;
public Graphics **getGraphics**() ; // Since 1.6
public JMenuBar **getJMenuBar**() ;
public JLayeredPane **getLayeredPane**() ;
public JRootPane **getRootPane**() ;
public TransferHandler **getTransferHandler**() ; // Since 1.6
protected boolean **isRootPaneCheckingEnabled**() ;
protected String **paramString**() ;
protected void **processWindowEvent**(WindowEvent e) ;
public void **remove**(Component comp) ;
public void **repaint**(int height, int width, int y, int x, long time) ; // Since 1.6
public void **setContentPane**(Container contentPane) ;
public void **setDefaultCloseOperation**(int operation) ;
public void **setGlassPane**(Component glassPane) ;
public void **setIconImage**(Image image) ;
public void **setJMenuBar**(JMenuBar menubar) ;
public void **setLayeredPane**(JLayeredPane layeredPane) ;
public void **setLayout**(LayoutManager manager) ;
protected void **setRootPane**(JRootPane root) ;
protected void **setRootPaneCheckingEnabled**(boolean enabled) ;
public void **setTransferHandler**(TransferHandler newHandler) ; // Since 1.6
public void **update**(Graphics g) ;
}

---

javax.swing.**JInternalFrame**

---

public class **JInternalFrame** extends JComponent implements RootPaneContainer, WindowConstants, Accessible
{
    public static final String **CONTENT_PANE_PROPERTY** ;
    public static final String **FRAME_ICON_PROPERTY** ;
    public static final String **GLASS_PANE_PROPERTY** ;
    public static final String **IS_CLOSED_PROPERTY** ;
    public static final String **IS_ICON_PROPERTY** ;
    public static final String **IS_MAXIMUM_PROPERTY** ;

public static final String **IS_SELECTED_PROPERTY** ;
public static final String **LAYERED_PANE_PROPERTY** ;
public static final String **MENU_BAR_PROPERTY** ;
public static final String **ROOT_PANE_PROPERTY** ;
public static final String **TITLE_PROPERTY** ;
protected boolean **closable** ;
protected JInternalFrame.JDesktopIcon **desktopIcon** ;
protected Icon **frameIcon** ;
protected boolean **iconable** ;
protected boolean **isClosed** ;
protected boolean **isIcon** ;
protected boolean **isMaximum** ;
protected boolean **isSelected** ;
protected boolean **maximizable** ;
protected boolean **resizable** ;
protected JRootPane **rootPane** ;
protected boolean **rootPaneCheckingEnabled** ;
protected String **title** ;
// Constructors
public **JInternalFrame**(boolean iconifiable, boolean maximizable, boolean closable, boolean
    resizable, String title) ;
public **JInternalFrame**(boolean maximizable, boolean closable, boolean resizable, String title) ;
public **JInternalFrame**(boolean closable, boolean resizable, String title) ;
public **JInternalFrame**(boolean resizable, String title) ;
public **JInternalFrame**(String title) ;
public **JInternalFrame**() ;
// Static methods
// Instance methods
protected void **addImpl**(int index, Object constraints, Component comp) ;
public void **addInternalFrameListener**(InternalFrameListener l) ;
protected JRootPane **createRootPane**() ;
public void **dispose**() ;
public void **doDefaultCloseAction**() ; // Since 1.3
protected void **fireInternalFrameEvent**(int id) ;
public AccessibleContext **getAccessibleContext**() ;
public Container **getContentPane**() ;
public int **getDefaultCloseOperation**() ;
public JInternalFrame.JDesktopIcon **getDesktopIcon**() ;
public JDesktopPane **getDesktopPane**() ;
public final Container **getFocusCycleRootAncestor**() ; // Since 1.4
public Component **getFocusOwner**() ; // Since 1.3
public Icon **getFrameIcon**() ;
public Component **getGlassPane**() ;
public InternalFrameListener **getInternalFrameListeners**() ; // Since 1.4
public JMenuBar **getJMenuBar**() ;
public Cursor **getLastCursor**() ; // Since 1.6

public int **getLayer**() ;
public JLayeredPane **getLayeredPane**() ;
public JMenuBar **getMenuBar**() ;
public Component **getMostRecentFocusOwner**() ; // Since 1.4
public Rectangle **getNormalBounds**() ; // Since 1.3
public JRootPane **getRootPane**() ;
public String **getTitle**() ;
public InternalFrameUI **getUI**() ;
public String **getUIClassID**() ;
public final String **getWarningString**() ;
public void **hide**() ;
public boolean **isClosable**() ;
public boolean **isClosed**() ;
public final boolean **isFocusCycleRoot**() ; // Since 1.4
public boolean **isIcon**() ;
public boolean **isIconifiable**() ;
public boolean **isMaximizable**() ;
public boolean **isMaximum**() ;
public boolean **isResizable**() ;
protected boolean **isRootPaneCheckingEnabled**() ;
public boolean **isSelected**() ;
public void **moveToBack**() ;
public void **moveToFront**() ;
public void **pack**() ;
protected void **paintComponent**(Graphics g) ;
protected String **paramString**() ;
public void **remove**(Component comp) ;
public void **removeInternalFrameListener**(InternalFrameListener l) ;
public void **reshape**(int height, int width, int y, int x) ;
public void **restoreSubcomponentFocus**() ; // Since 1.3
public void **setClosable**(boolean b) ;
public void **setClosed**(boolean b) throws PropertyVetoException ;
public void **setContentPane**(Container c) ;
public void **setCursor**(Cursor cursor) ; // Since 1.6
public void **setDefaultCloseOperation**(int operation) ;
public void **setDesktopIcon**(JInternalFrame.JDesktopIcon d) ;
public final void **setFocusCycleRoot**(boolean focusCycleRoot) ; // Since 1.4
public void **setFrameIcon**(Icon icon) ;
public void **setGlassPane**(Component glass) ;
public void **setIcon**(boolean b) throws PropertyVetoException ;
public void **setIconifiable**(boolean b) ;
public void **setJMenuBar**(JMenuBar m) ;
public void **setLayer**(Integer layer) ;
public void **setLayer**(int layer) ; // Since 1.3
public void **setLayeredPane**(JLayeredPane layered) ;
public void **setLayout**(LayoutManager manager) ;

```
    public void setMaximizable(boolean b) ;
    public void setMaximum(boolean b) throws PropertyVetoException ;
    public void setMenuBar(JMenuBar m) ;
    public void setNormalBounds(Rectangle r) ; // Since 1.3
    public void setResizable(boolean b) ;
    protected void setRootPane(JRootPane root) ;
    protected void setRootPaneCheckingEnabled(boolean enabled) ;
    public void setSelected(boolean selected) throws PropertyVetoException ;
    public void setTitle(String title) ;
    public void setUI(InternalFrameUI ui) ;
    public void show() ;
    public void toBack() ;
    public void toFront() ;
    public void updateUI() ;
}
```

javax.swing.**JInternalFrame.JDesktopIcon**

```
public static class JInternalFrame.JDesktopIcon extends JComponent implements Accessible
{
    // Constructors
    public JInternalFrame.JDesktopIcon(JInternalFrame f) ;
    // Instance methods
    public AccessibleContext getAccessibleContext() ;
    public JDesktopPane getDesktopPane() ;
    public JInternalFrame getInternalFrame() ;
    public DesktopIconUI getUI() ;
    public String getUIClassID() ;
    public void setInternalFrame(JInternalFrame f) ;
    public void setUI(DesktopIconUI ui) ;
    public void updateUI() ;
}
```

javax.swing.**JLabel**

```
public class JLabel extends JComponent implements Accessible, SwingConstants
{
    protected Component labelFor ;
    // Constructors
    public JLabel() ;
    public JLabel(Icon image) ;
```

```
      public JLabel(int horizontalAlignment, Icon image) ;
      public JLabel(String text) ;
      public JLabel(int horizontalAlignment, String text) ;
      public JLabel(int horizontalAlignment, Icon icon, String text) ;
      // Instance methods
      protected int checkHorizontalKey(String message, int key) ;
      protected int checkVerticalKey(String message, int key) ;
      public AccessibleContext getAccessibleContext() ;
      public Icon getDisabledIcon() ;
      public int getDisplayedMnemonic() ;
      public int getDisplayedMnemonicIndex() ; // Since 1.4
      public int getHorizontalAlignment() ;
      public int getHorizontalTextPosition() ;
      public Icon getIcon() ;
      public int getIconTextGap() ;
      public Component getLabelFor() ;
      public String getText() ;
      public LabelUI getUI() ;
      public String getUIClassID() ;
      public int getVerticalAlignment() ;
      public int getVerticalTextPosition() ;
      public boolean imageUpdate(int h, int w, int y, int x, int infoflags, Image img) ;
      protected String paramString() ;
      public void setDisabledIcon(Icon disabledIcon) ;
      public void setDisplayedMnemonic(char aChar) ;
      public void setDisplayedMnemonic(int key) ;
      public void setDisplayedMnemonicIndex(int index) throws IllegalArgumentException ; // Since 1.4
      public void setHorizontalAlignment(int alignment) ;
      public void setHorizontalTextPosition(int textPosition) ;
      public void setIcon(Icon icon) ;
      public void setIconTextGap(int iconTextGap) ;
      public void setLabelFor(Component c) ;
      public void setText(String text) ;
      public void setUI(LabelUI ui) ;
      public void setVerticalAlignment(int alignment) ;
      public void setVerticalTextPosition(int textPosition) ;
      public void updateUI() ;
}
```

---

javax.swing.**JLayeredPane**

```
public class JLayeredPane extends JComponent implements Accessible
{
      public static final Integer DEFAULT_LAYER ;
```

```
    public static final Integer DRAG_LAYER ;
    public static final Integer FRAME_CONTENT_LAYER ;
    public static final String LAYER_PROPERTY ;
    public static final Integer MODAL_LAYER ;
    public static final Integer PALETTE_LAYER ;
    public static final Integer POPUP_LAYER ;
    // Constructors
    public JLayeredPane() ;
    // Static methods
    public static int getLayer(JComponent c) ;
    public static JLayeredPane getLayeredPaneAbove(Component c) ;
    public static void putLayer(int layer, JComponent c) ;
    // Instance methods
    protected void addImpl(int index, Object constraints, Component comp) ;
    public AccessibleContext getAccessibleContext() ;
    public int getComponentCountInLayer(int layer) ;
    public Component getComponentsInLayer(int layer) ;
    protected Hashtable<Component, Integer> getComponentToLayer() ;
    public int getIndexOf(Component c) ;
    public int getLayer(Component c) ;
    protected Integer getObjectForLayer(int layer) ;
    public int getPosition(Component c) ;
    public int highestLayer() ;
    protected int insertIndexForLayer(int position, int layer) ;
    public boolean isOptimizedDrawingEnabled() ;
    public int lowestLayer() ;
    public void moveToBack(Component c) ;
    public void moveToFront(Component c) ;
    public void paint(Graphics g) ;
    protected String paramString() ;
    public void remove(int index) ;
    public void removeAll() ; // Since 1.5
    public void setLayer(int layer, Component c) ;
    public void setLayer(int position, int layer, Component c) ;
    public void setPosition(int position, Component c) ;
}
```

javax.swing.**JList**

```
public class JList extends JComponent implements Accessible, Scrollable
{
    public static final int HORIZONTAL_WRAP ;
    public static final int VERTICAL ;
    public static final int VERTICAL_WRAP ;
```

```
// Constructors
public JList() ;
public JList(Vector<?> listData) ;
public JList(java.lang.Object[] listData) ;
public JList(ListModel dataModel) ;
// Instance methods
public void addListSelectionListener(ListSelectionListener listener) ;
public void addSelectionInterval(int lead, int anchor) ;
public void clearSelection() ;
protected ListSelectionModel createSelectionModel() ;
public void ensureIndexIsVisible(int index) ;
protected void fireSelectionValueChanged(boolean isAdjusting, int lastIndex, int firstIndex) ;
public AccessibleContext getAccessibleContext() ;
public int getAnchorSelectionIndex() ;
public Rectangle getCellBounds(int index1, int index0) ;
public ListCellRenderer getCellRenderer() ;
public boolean getDragEnabled() ; // Since 1.4
public final JList.DropLocation getDropLocation() ; // Since 1.6
public final DropMode getDropMode() ; // Since 1.6
public int getFirstVisibleIndex() ;
public int getFixedCellHeight() ;
public int getFixedCellWidth() ;
public int getLastVisibleIndex() ;
public int getLayoutOrientation() ; // Since 1.4
public int getLeadSelectionIndex() ;
public ListSelectionListener getListSelectionListeners() ; // Since 1.4
public int getMaxSelectionIndex() ;
public int getMinSelectionIndex() ;
public ListModel getModel() ;
public int getNextMatch(Position.Bias bias, int startIndex, String prefix) ; // Since 1.4
public Dimension getPreferredScrollableViewportSize() ;
public Object getPrototypeCellValue() ;
public int getScrollableBlockIncrement(int direction, int orientation, Rectangle visibleRect) ;
public boolean getScrollableTracksViewportHeight() ;
public boolean getScrollableTracksViewportWidth() ;
public int getScrollableUnitIncrement(int direction, int orientation, Rectangle visibleRect) ;
public int getSelectedIndex() ;
public int getSelectedIndices() ;
public Object getSelectedValue() ;
public Object getSelectedValues() ;
public Color getSelectionBackground() ;
public Color getSelectionForeground() ;
public int getSelectionMode() ;
public ListSelectionModel getSelectionModel() ;
public String getToolTipText(MouseEvent event) ;
public ListUI getUI() ;
```

```
    public String getUIClassID() ;
    public boolean getValueIsAdjusting() ;
    public int getVisibleRowCount() ;
    public Point indexToLocation(int index) ;
    public boolean isSelectedIndex(int index) ;
    public boolean isSelectionEmpty() ;
    public int locationToIndex(Point location) ;
    protected String paramString() ;
    public void removeListSelectionListener(ListSelectionListener listener) ;
    public void removeSelectionInterval(int index1, int index0) ;
    public void setCellRenderer(ListCellRenderer cellRenderer) ;
    public void setDragEnabled(boolean b) ; // Since 1.4
    public final void setDropMode(DropMode dropMode) ; // Since 1.6
    public void setFixedCellHeight(int height) ;
    public void setFixedCellWidth(int width) ;
    public void setLayoutOrientation(int layoutOrientation) ; // Since 1.4
    public void setListData(Vector<?> listData) ;
    public void setListData(java.lang.Object[] listData) ;
    public void setModel(ListModel model) ;
    public void setPrototypeCellValue(Object prototypeCellValue) ;
    public void setSelectedIndex(int index) ;
    public void setSelectedIndices(int[] indices) ;
    public void setSelectedValue(boolean shouldScroll, Object anObject) ;
    public void setSelectionBackground(Color selectionBackground) ;
    public void setSelectionForeground(Color selectionForeground) ;
    public void setSelectionInterval(int lead, int anchor) ;
    public void setSelectionMode(int selectionMode) ;
    public void setSelectionModel(ListSelectionModel selectionModel) ;
    public void setUI(ListUI ui) ;
    public void setValueIsAdjusting(boolean b) ;
    public void setVisibleRowCount(int visibleRowCount) ;
    public void updateUI() ;
}
```

---

javax.swing.**JList.DropLocation** [since 1.6]

```
public static final class JList.DropLocation extends TransferHandler.DropLocation
{
    // Constructors
    private JList.DropLocation(boolean isInsert, int index, Point p) ;
    // Instance methods
    public int getIndex() ;
    public boolean isInsert() ;
    public String toString() ;
```

}

javax.swing.**JMenu**

public class **JMenu** extends JMenuItem implements MenuElement, Accessible
{
    protected JMenu.WinListener **popupListener** ;
    // Constructors
    public **JMenu**(boolean b, String s) ;
    public **JMenu**(Action a) ;
    public **JMenu**(String s) ;
    public **JMenu**() ;
    // Instance methods
    public Component **add**(Component c) ;
    public JMenuItem **add**(JMenuItem menuItem) ;
    public Component **add**(int index, Component c) ;
    public JMenuItem **add**(String s) ;
    public JMenuItem **add**(Action a) ;
    public void **addMenuListener**(MenuListener l) ;
    public void **addSeparator**() ;
    public void **applyComponentOrientation**(ComponentOrientation o) ; // Since 1.4
    protected PropertyChangeListener **createActionChangeListener**(JMenuItem b) ;
    protected JMenuItem **createActionComponent**(Action a) ; // Since 1.3
    protected JMenu.WinListener **createWinListener**(JPopupMenu p) ;
    public void **doClick**(int pressTime) ;
    protected void **fireMenuCanceled**() ;
    protected void **fireMenuDeselected**() ;
    protected void **fireMenuSelected**() ;
    public AccessibleContext **getAccessibleContext**() ;
    public Component **getComponent**() ;
    public int **getDelay**() ;
    public JMenuItem **getItem**(int pos) ;
    public int **getItemCount**() ;
    public Component **getMenuComponent**(int n) ;
    public int **getMenuComponentCount**() ;
    public Component **getMenuComponents**() ;
    public MenuListener **getMenuListeners**() ; // Since 1.4
    public JPopupMenu **getPopupMenu**() ;
    protected Point **getPopupMenuOrigin**() ; // Since 1.3
    public MenuElement **getSubElements**() ;
    public String **getUIClassID**() ;
    public JMenuItem **insert**(int pos, Action a) ;
    public void **insert**(int pos, String s) ;
    public JMenuItem **insert**(int pos, JMenuItem mi) ;

```
        public void insertSeparator(int index) ;
        public boolean isMenuComponent(Component c) ;
        public boolean isPopupMenuVisible() ;
        public boolean isSelected() ;
        public boolean isTearOff() ;
        public boolean isTopLevelMenu() ;
        public void menuSelectionChanged(boolean isIncluded) ;
        protected String paramString() ;
        protected void processKeyEvent(KeyEvent evt) ;
        public void remove(Component c) ;
        public void remove(int pos) ;
        public void remove(JMenuItem item) ;
        public void removeAll() ;
        public void removeMenuListener(MenuListener l) ;
        public void setAccelerator(KeyStroke keyStroke) ;
        public void setComponentOrientation(ComponentOrientation o) ;
        public void setDelay(int d) ;
        public void setMenuLocation(int y, int x) ;
        public void setModel(ButtonModel newModel) ;
        public void setPopupMenuVisible(boolean b) ;
        public void setSelected(boolean b) ;
        public void updateUI() ;
}
```

javax.swing.**JMenuBar**

```
public class JMenuBar extends JComponent implements MenuElement, Accessible
{
    // Constructors
    public JMenuBar() ;
    // Static methods
    // Instance methods
    public JMenu add(JMenu c) ;
    public void addNotify() ;
    public AccessibleContext getAccessibleContext() ;
    public Component getComponent() ;
    public Component getComponentAtIndex(int i) ;
    public int getComponentIndex(Component c) ;
    public JMenu getHelpMenu() ;
    public Insets getMargin() ;
    public JMenu getMenu(int index) ;
    public int getMenuCount() ;
    public SingleSelectionModel getSelectionModel() ;
    public MenuElement getSubElements() ;
```

public MenuBarUI **getUI**() ;
public String **getUIClassID**() ;
public boolean **isBorderPainted**() ;
public boolean **isSelected**() ;
public void **menuSelectionChanged**(boolean isIncluded) ;
protected void **paintBorder**(Graphics g) ;
protected String **paramString**() ;
protected boolean **processKeyBinding**(boolean pressed, int condition, KeyEvent e, KeyStroke ks) ; //
    Since 1.3
public void **processKeyEvent**(MenuSelectionManager manager, javax.swing.MenuElement[] path,
    KeyEvent e) ;
public void **processMouseEvent**(MenuSelectionManager manager, javax.swing.MenuElement[]
    path, MouseEvent event) ;
public void **removeNotify**() ;
public void **setBorderPainted**(boolean b) ;
public void **setHelpMenu**(JMenu menu) ;
public void **setMargin**(Insets m) ;
public void **setSelected**(Component sel) ;
public void **setSelectionModel**(SingleSelectionModel model) ;
public void **setUI**(MenuBarUI ui) ;
public void **updateUI**() ;
}

javax.swing.**JMenuItem**

public class **JMenuItem** extends AbstractButton implements MenuElement, Accessible
{
    // Constructors
    public **JMenuItem**(int mnemonic, String text) ;
    public **JMenuItem**(Icon icon, String text) ;
    public **JMenuItem**(Action a) ;
    public **JMenuItem**(String text) ;
    public **JMenuItem**(Icon icon) ;
    public **JMenuItem**() ;
    // Instance methods
    protected void **actionPropertyChanged**(String propertyName, Action action) ; // Since 1.6
    public void **addMenuDragMouseListener**(MenuDragMouseListener l) ;
    public void **addMenuKeyListener**(MenuKeyListener l) ;
    protected void **configurePropertiesFromAction**(Action a) ; // Since 1.3
    protected void **fireMenuDragMouseDragged**(MenuDragMouseEvent event) ;
    protected void **fireMenuDragMouseEntered**(MenuDragMouseEvent event) ;
    protected void **fireMenuDragMouseExited**(MenuDragMouseEvent event) ;
    protected void **fireMenuDragMouseReleased**(MenuDragMouseEvent event) ;
    protected void **fireMenuKeyPressed**(MenuKeyEvent event) ;

```
        protected void fireMenuKeyReleased(MenuKeyEvent event) ;
        protected void fireMenuKeyTyped(MenuKeyEvent event) ;
        public KeyStroke getAccelerator() ;
        public AccessibleContext getAccessibleContext() ;
        public Component getComponent() ;
        public MenuDragMouseListener getMenuDragMouseListeners() ; // Since 1.4
        public MenuKeyListener getMenuKeyListeners() ; // Since 1.4
        public MenuElement getSubElements() ;
        public String getUIClassID() ;
        protected void init(Icon icon, String text) ;
        public boolean isArmed() ;
        public void menuSelectionChanged(boolean isIncluded) ;
        protected String paramString() ;
        public void processKeyEvent(MenuSelectionManager manager, javax.swing.MenuElement[] path,
            KeyEvent e) ;
        public void processMenuDragMouseEvent(MenuDragMouseEvent e) ;
        public void processMenuKeyEvent(MenuKeyEvent e) ;
        public void processMouseEvent(MenuSelectionManager manager, javax.swing.MenuElement[]
            path, MouseEvent e) ;
        public void removeMenuDragMouseListener(MenuDragMouseListener l) ;
        public void removeMenuKeyListener(MenuKeyListener l) ;
        public void setAccelerator(KeyStroke keyStroke) ;
        public void setArmed(boolean b) ;
        public void setEnabled(boolean b) ;
        public void setModel(ButtonModel newModel) ;
        public void setUI(MenuItemUI ui) ;
        public void updateUI() ;
}
```

---

java.awt.**JobAttributes** [since 1.3]

```
public final class JobAttributes  implements Cloneable
{
        // Constructors
        public JobAttributes(JobAttributes.SidesType sides, String printer, int[][] pageRanges,
            JobAttributes.MultipleDocumentHandlingType multipleDocumentHandling, int minPage, int
            maxPage, String fileName, JobAttributes.DialogType dialog, JobAttributes.DestinationType
            destination, JobAttributes.DefaultSelectionType defaultSelection, int copies) ;
        public JobAttributes(JobAttributes obj) ;
        public JobAttributes() ;
        // Instance methods
        public Object clone() ;
        public boolean equals(Object obj) ;
        public int getCopies() ;
```

```
    public JobAttributes.DefaultSelectionType getDefaultSelection() ;
    public JobAttributes.DestinationType getDestination() ;
    public JobAttributes.DialogType getDialog() ;
    public String getFileName() ;
    public int getFromPage() ;
    public int getMaxPage() ;
    public int getMinPage() ;
    public JobAttributes.MultipleDocumentHandlingType getMultipleDocumentHandling() ;
    public int getPageRanges() ;
    public String getPrinter() ;
    public JobAttributes.SidesType getSides() ;
    public int getToPage() ;
    public int hashCode() ;
    public void set(JobAttributes obj) ;
    public void setCopies(int copies) ;
    public void setCopiesToDefault() ;
    public void setDefaultSelection(JobAttributes.DefaultSelectionType defaultSelection) ;
    public void setDestination(JobAttributes.DestinationType destination) ;
    public void setDialog(JobAttributes.DialogType dialog) ;
    public void setFileName(String fileName) ;
    public void setFromPage(int fromPage) ;
    public void setMaxPage(int maxPage) ;
    public void setMinPage(int minPage) ;
    public void setMultipleDocumentHandling(JobAttributes.MultipleDocumentHandlingType
        multipleDocumentHandling) ;
    public void setMultipleDocumentHandlingToDefault() ;
    public void setPageRanges(int[][] pageRanges) ;
    public void setPrinter(String printer) ;
    public void setSides(JobAttributes.SidesType sides) ;
    public void setSidesToDefault() ;
    public void setToPage(int toPage) ;
    public String toString() ;
}
```

java.awt.**JobAttributes.DefaultSelectionType** [since 1.3]

```
public static final class JobAttributes.DefaultSelectionType extends AttributeValue
{
    public static final JobAttributes.DefaultSelectionType ALL ;
    public static final JobAttributes.DefaultSelectionType RANGE ;
    public static final JobAttributes.DefaultSelectionType SELECTION ;
    // Constructors
    private JobAttributes.DefaultSelectionType(int type) ;
}
```

java.awt.**JobAttributes.DestinationType** [since 1.3]

public static final class **JobAttributes.DestinationType** extends AttributeValue
{
    public static final JobAttributes.DestinationType **FILE** ;
    public static final JobAttributes.DestinationType **PRINTER** ;
    // Constructors
    private **JobAttributes.DestinationType**(int type) ;
}

java.awt.**JobAttributes.DialogType** [since 1.3]

public static final class **JobAttributes.DialogType** extends AttributeValue
{
    public static final JobAttributes.DialogType **COMMON** ;
    public static final JobAttributes.DialogType **NATIVE** ;
    public static final JobAttributes.DialogType **NONE** ;
    // Constructors
    private **JobAttributes.DialogType**(int type) ;
}

java.awt.**JobAttributes.MultipleDocumentHandlingType** [since 1.3]

public static final class **JobAttributes.MultipleDocumentHandlingType** extends AttributeValue
{
    public static final JobAttributes.MultipleDocumentHandlingType
        SEPARATE_DOCUMENTS_COLLATED_COPIES ;
    public static final JobAttributes.MultipleDocumentHandlingType
        SEPARATE_DOCUMENTS_UNCOLLATED_COPIES ;
    // Constructors
    private **JobAttributes.MultipleDocumentHandlingType**(int type) ;
}

java.awt.**JobAttributes.SidesType** [since 1.3]

public static final class **JobAttributes.SidesType** extends AttributeValue
{
    public static final JobAttributes.SidesType **ONE_SIDED** ;
    public static final JobAttributes.SidesType **TWO_SIDED_LONG_EDGE** ;
    public static final JobAttributes.SidesType **TWO_SIDED_SHORT_EDGE** ;
    // Constructors
    private **JobAttributes.SidesType**(int type) ;
}

javax.swing.**JOptionPane**

public class **JOptionPane** extends JComponent implements Accessible
{
    public static final int **CANCEL_OPTION** ;
    public static final int **CLOSED_OPTION** ;
    public static final int **DEFAULT_OPTION** ;
    public static final int **ERROR_MESSAGE** ;
    public static final String **ICON_PROPERTY** ;
    public static final int **INFORMATION_MESSAGE** ;
    public static final String **INITIAL_SELECTION_VALUE_PROPERTY** ;
    public static final String **INITIAL_VALUE_PROPERTY** ;
    public static final String **INPUT_VALUE_PROPERTY** ;
    public static final String **MESSAGE_PROPERTY** ;
    public static final String **MESSAGE_TYPE_PROPERTY** ;
    public static final int **NO_OPTION** ;
    public static final int **OK_CANCEL_OPTION** ;
    public static final int **OK_OPTION** ;
    public static final String **OPTIONS_PROPERTY** ;
    public static final String **OPTION_TYPE_PROPERTY** ;
    public static final int **PLAIN_MESSAGE** ;
    public static final int **QUESTION_MESSAGE** ;
    public static final String **SELECTION_VALUES_PROPERTY** ;
    public static final Object **UNINITIALIZED_VALUE** ;
    public static final String **VALUE_PROPERTY** ;
    public static final String **WANTS_INPUT_PROPERTY** ;
    public static final int **WARNING_MESSAGE** ;
    public static final int **YES_NO_CANCEL_OPTION** ;
    public static final int **YES_NO_OPTION** ;

public static final int **YES_OPTION** ;
protected transient Icon **icon** ;
protected transient Object **initialSelectionValue** ;
protected transient Object **initialValue** ;
protected transient Object **inputValue** ;
protected transient Object **message** ;
protected int **messageType** ;
protected transient Object **options** ;
protected int **optionType** ;
protected transient Object **selectionValues** ;
protected transient Object **value** ;
protected boolean **wantsInput** ;
// Constructors
public **JOptionPane**(Object initialValue, java.lang.Object[] options, Icon icon, int optionType, int messageType, Object message) ;
public **JOptionPane**(java.lang.Object[] options, Icon icon, int optionType, int messageType, Object message) ;
public **JOptionPane**(Icon icon, int optionType, int messageType, Object message) ;
public **JOptionPane**(int optionType, int messageType, Object message) ;
public **JOptionPane**(int messageType, Object message) ;
public **JOptionPane**(Object message) ;
public **JOptionPane**() ;
// Static methods
public static JDesktopPane **getDesktopPaneForComponent**(Component parentComponent) ;
public static Frame **getFrameForComponent**(Component parentComponent) throws HeadlessException ;
public static Frame **getRootFrame**() throws HeadlessException ;
public static void **setRootFrame**(Frame newRootFrame) ;
public static int **showConfirmDialog**(int optionType, String title, Object message, Component parentComponent) throws HeadlessException ;
public static int **showConfirmDialog**(Object message, Component parentComponent) throws HeadlessException ;
public static int **showConfirmDialog**(Icon icon, int messageType, int optionType, String title, Object message, Component parentComponent) throws HeadlessException ;
public static int **showConfirmDialog**(int messageType, int optionType, String title, Object message, Component parentComponent) throws HeadlessException ;
public static String **showInputDialog**(Object message, Component parentComponent) throws HeadlessException ;
public static String **showInputDialog**(Object initialSelectionValue, Object message) ; // Since 1.4
public static String **showInputDialog**(int messageType, String title, Object message, Component parentComponent) throws HeadlessException ;
public static Object **showInputDialog**(Object initialSelectionValue, java.lang.Object[] selectionValues, Icon icon, int messageType, String title, Object message, Component parentComponent) throws HeadlessException ;
public static String **showInputDialog**(Object message) throws HeadlessException ;

public static String **showInputDialog**(Object initialSelectionValue, Object message, Component
parentComponent) ; // Since 1.4
public static int **showInternalConfirmDialog**(Object message, Component parentComponent) ;
public static int **showInternalConfirmDialog**(int optionType, String title, Object message,
Component parentComponent) ;
public static int **showInternalConfirmDialog**(int messageType, int optionType, String title, Object
message, Component parentComponent) ;
public static int **showInternalConfirmDialog**(Icon icon, int messageType, int optionType, String
title, Object message, Component parentComponent) ;
public static Object **showInternalInputDialog**(Object initialSelectionValue, java.lang.Object[]
selectionValues, Icon icon, int messageType, String title, Object message, Component
parentComponent) ;
public static String **showInternalInputDialog**(Object message, Component parentComponent) ;
public static String **showInternalInputDialog**(int messageType, String title, Object message,
Component parentComponent) ;
public static void **showInternalMessageDialog**(Object message, Component parentComponent) ;
public static void **showInternalMessageDialog**(int messageType, String title, Object message,
Component parentComponent) ;
public static void **showInternalMessageDialog**(Icon icon, int messageType, String title, Object
message, Component parentComponent) ;
public static int **showInternalOptionDialog**(Object initialValue, java.lang.Object[] options, Icon
icon, int messageType, int optionType, String title, Object message, Component
parentComponent) ;
public static void **showMessageDialog**(Object message, Component parentComponent) throws
HeadlessException ;
public static void **showMessageDialog**(int messageType, String title, Object message, Component
parentComponent) throws HeadlessException ;
public static void **showMessageDialog**(Icon icon, int messageType, String title, Object message,
Component parentComponent) throws HeadlessException ;
public static int **showOptionDialog**(Object initialValue, java.lang.Object[] options, Icon icon, int
messageType, int optionType, String title, Object message, Component parentComponent) throws
HeadlessException ;
// Instance methods
public JDialog **createDialog**(String title, Component parentComponent) throws HeadlessException ;
public JDialog **createDialog**(String title) throws HeadlessException ; // Since 1.6
public JInternalFrame **createInternalFrame**(String title, Component parentComponent) ;
public AccessibleContext **getAccessibleContext**() ;
public Icon **getIcon**() ;
public Object **getInitialSelectionValue**() ;
public Object **getInitialValue**() ;
public Object **getInputValue**() ;
public int **getMaxCharactersPerLineCount**() ;
public Object **getMessage**() ;
public int **getMessageType**() ;
public Object **getOptions**() ;
public int **getOptionType**() ;

```
    public Object getSelectionValues() ;
    public OptionPaneUI getUI() ;
    public String getUIClassID() ;
    public Object getValue() ;
    public boolean getWantsInput() ;
    protected String paramString() ;
    public void selectInitialValue() ;
    public void setIcon(Icon newIcon) ;
    public void setInitialSelectionValue(Object newValue) ;
    public void setInitialValue(Object newInitialValue) ;
    public void setInputValue(Object newValue) ;
    public void setMessage(Object newMessage) ;
    public void setMessageType(int newType) ;
    public void setOptions(java.lang.Object[] newOptions) ;
    public void setOptionType(int newType) ;
    public void setSelectionValues(java.lang.Object[] newValues) ;
    public void setUI(OptionPaneUI ui) ;
    public void setValue(Object newValue) ;
    public void setWantsInput(boolean newValue) ;
    public void updateUI() ;
}
```

javax.swing.**JPanel**

```
public class JPanel extends JComponent implements Accessible
{
    // Constructors
    public JPanel() ;
    public JPanel(boolean isDoubleBuffered) ;
    public JPanel(LayoutManager layout) ;
    public JPanel(boolean isDoubleBuffered, LayoutManager layout) ;
    // Instance methods
    public AccessibleContext getAccessibleContext() ;
    public PanelUI getUI() ; // Since 1.4
    public String getUIClassID() ;
    protected String paramString() ;
    public void setUI(PanelUI ui) ; // Since 1.4
    public void updateUI() ;
}
```

---

javax.swing.**JPasswordField**

---

public class **JPasswordField** extends JTextField
{
    // Constructors
    public **JPasswordField**(int columns, String txt, Document doc) ;
    public **JPasswordField**(int columns, String text) ;
    public **JPasswordField**(int columns) ;
    public **JPasswordField**(String text) ;
    public **JPasswordField**() ;
    // Instance methods
    public void **copy**() ;
    public void **cut**() ;
    public boolean **echoCharIsSet**() ;
    public AccessibleContext **getAccessibleContext**() ;
    public char **getEchoChar**() ;
    public char **getPassword**() ;
    public String **getText**(int len, int offs) throws BadLocationException ;
    public String **getText**() ;
    public String **getUIClassID**() ;
    protected String **paramString**() ;
    public void **setEchoChar**(char c) ;
    public void **updateUI**() ; // Since 1.6
}

---

javax.swing.**JPopupMenu**

---

public class **JPopupMenu** extends JComponent implements MenuElement, Accessible
{
    // Constructors
    public **JPopupMenu**(String label) ;
    public **JPopupMenu**() ;
    // Static methods
    public static boolean **getDefaultLightWeightPopupEnabled**() ;
    public static void **setDefaultLightWeightPopupEnabled**(boolean aFlag) ;
    // Instance methods
    public JMenuItem **add**(JMenuItem menuItem) ;
    public JMenuItem **add**(Action a) ;
    public JMenuItem **add**(String s) ;
    public void **addMenuKeyListener**(MenuKeyListener l) ; // Since 1.5

---

public void **addPopupMenuListener**(PopupMenuListener l) ;
public void **addSeparator**() ;
protected PropertyChangeListener **createActionChangeListener**(JMenuItem b) ;
protected JMenuItem **createActionComponent**(Action a) ; // Since 1.3
protected void **firePopupMenuCanceled**() ;
protected void **firePopupMenuWillBecomeInvisible**() ;
protected void **firePopupMenuWillBecomeVisible**() ;
public AccessibleContext **getAccessibleContext**() ;
public Component **getComponent**() ;
public Component **getComponentAtIndex**(int i) ;
public int **getComponentIndex**(Component c) ;
public Component **getInvoker**() ;
public String **getLabel**() ;
public Insets **getMargin**() ;
public MenuKeyListener **getMenuKeyListeners**() ; // Since 1.5
public PopupMenuListener **getPopupMenuListeners**() ; // Since 1.4
public SingleSelectionModel **getSelectionModel**() ;
public MenuElement **getSubElements**() ;
public PopupMenuUI **getUI**() ;
public String **getUIClassID**() ;
public void **insert**(int index, Component component) ;
public void **insert**(int index, Action a) ;
public boolean **isBorderPainted**() ;
public boolean **isLightWeightPopupEnabled**() ;
public boolean **isPopupTrigger**(MouseEvent e) ; // Since 1.3
public boolean **isVisible**() ;
public void **menuSelectionChanged**(boolean isIncluded) ;
public void **pack**() ;
protected void **paintBorder**(Graphics g) ;
protected String **paramString**() ;
protected void **processFocusEvent**(FocusEvent evt) ;
public void **processKeyEvent**(MenuSelectionManager manager, javax.swing.MenuElement[] path,
   KeyEvent e) ;
protected void **processKeyEvent**(KeyEvent evt) ;
public void **processMouseEvent**(MenuSelectionManager manager, javax.swing.MenuElement[]
   path, MouseEvent event) ;
public void **remove**(int pos) ;
public void **removeMenuKeyListener**(MenuKeyListener l) ; // Since 1.5
public void **removePopupMenuListener**(PopupMenuListener l) ;
public void **setBorderPainted**(boolean b) ;
public void **setInvoker**(Component invoker) ;
public void **setLabel**(String label) ;
public void **setLightWeightPopupEnabled**(boolean aFlag) ;
public void **setLocation**(int y, int x) ;
public void **setPopupSize**(int height, int width) ;
public void **setPopupSize**(Dimension d) ;

```
    public void setSelected(Component sel) ;
    public void setSelectionModel(SingleSelectionModel model) ;
    public void setUI(PopupMenuUI ui) ;
    public void setVisible(boolean b) ;
    public void show(int y, int x, Component invoker) ;
    public void updateUI() ;
}
```

javax.swing.**JPopupMenu.Separator**

```
public static class JPopupMenu.Separator extends JSeparator
{
    // Constructors
    public JPopupMenu.Separator() ;
    // Instance methods
    public String getUIClassID() ;
}
```

javax.swing.**JProgressBar**

```
public class JProgressBar extends JComponent implements Accessible, SwingConstants
{
    protected transient ChangeEvent changeEvent ;
    protected ChangeListener changeListener ;
    protected BoundedRangeModel model ;
    protected int orientation ;
    protected boolean paintBorder ;
    protected boolean paintString ;
    protected String progressString ;
    // Constructors
    public JProgressBar(BoundedRangeModel newModel) ;
    public JProgressBar(int max, int min, int orient) ;
    public JProgressBar(int max, int min) ;
    public JProgressBar(int orient) ;
    public JProgressBar() ;
    // Instance methods
    public void addChangeListener(ChangeListener l) ;
    protected ChangeListener createChangeListener() ;
    protected void fireStateChanged() ;
    public AccessibleContext getAccessibleContext() ;
    public ChangeListener getChangeListeners() ; // Since 1.4
```

```
    public int getMaximum() ;
    public int getMinimum() ;
    public BoundedRangeModel getModel() ;
    public int getOrientation() ;
    public double getPercentComplete() ;
    public String getString() ;
    public ProgressBarUI getUI() ;
    public String getUIClassID() ;
    public int getValue() ;
    public boolean isBorderPainted() ;
    public boolean isIndeterminate() ; // Since 1.4
    public boolean isStringPainted() ;
    protected void paintBorder(Graphics g) ;
    protected String paramString() ;
    public void removeChangeListener(ChangeListener l) ;
    public void setBorderPainted(boolean b) ;
    public void setIndeterminate(boolean newValue) ; // Since 1.4
    public void setMaximum(int n) ;
    public void setMinimum(int n) ;
    public void setModel(BoundedRangeModel newModel) ;
    public void setOrientation(int newOrientation) ;
    public void setString(String s) ;
    public void setStringPainted(boolean b) ;
    public void setUI(ProgressBarUI ui) ;
    public void setValue(int n) ;
    public void updateUI() ;
}
```

javax.swing.**JRadioButton**

```
public class JRadioButton extends JToggleButton implements Accessible
{
    // Constructors
    public JRadioButton(boolean selected, Icon icon, String text) ;
    public JRadioButton(Icon icon, String text) ;
    public JRadioButton(boolean selected, String text) ;
    public JRadioButton(String text) ;
    public JRadioButton(boolean selected, Icon icon) ;
    public JRadioButton(Action a) ;
    public JRadioButton(Icon icon) ;
    public JRadioButton() ;
    // Instance methods
    public AccessibleContext getAccessibleContext() ;
    public String getUIClassID() ;
```

```
    protected String paramString() ;
    public void updateUI() ;
}
```

---

javax.swing.**JRadioButtonMenuItem**

---

public class **JRadioButtonMenuItem** extends JMenuItem implements Accessible
```
{
    // Constructors
    public JRadioButtonMenuItem(boolean selected, Icon icon, String text) ;
    public JRadioButtonMenuItem(boolean selected, Icon icon) ;
    public JRadioButtonMenuItem(boolean selected, String text) ;
    public JRadioButtonMenuItem(Icon icon, String text) ;
    public JRadioButtonMenuItem(Action a) ;
    public JRadioButtonMenuItem(String text) ;
    public JRadioButtonMenuItem(Icon icon) ;
    public JRadioButtonMenuItem() ;
    // Instance methods
    public AccessibleContext getAccessibleContext() ;
    public String getUIClassID() ;
    protected String paramString() ;
}
```

---

javax.swing.**JRootPane**

---

public class **JRootPane** extends JComponent implements Accessible
```
{
    public static final int COLOR_CHOOSER_DIALOG ;
    public static final int ERROR_DIALOG ;
    public static final int FILE_CHOOSER_DIALOG ;
    public static final int FRAME ;
    public static final int INFORMATION_DIALOG ;
    public static final int NONE ;
    public static final int PLAIN_DIALOG ;
    public static final int QUESTION_DIALOG ;
    public static final int WARNING_DIALOG ;
    protected Container contentPane ;
    protected JButton defaultButton ;
    protected JRootPane.DefaultAction defaultPressAction ;
    protected JRootPane.DefaultAction defaultReleaseAction ;
    protected Component glassPane ;
```

```
    protected JLayeredPane layeredPane ;
    protected JMenuBar menuBar ;
    // Constructors
    public JRootPane() ;
    // Instance methods
    protected void addImpl(int index, Object constraints, Component comp) ;
    public void addNotify() ;
    protected Container createContentPane() ;
    protected Component createGlassPane() ;
    protected JLayeredPane createLayeredPane() ;
    protected LayoutManager createRootLayout() ;
    public AccessibleContext getAccessibleContext() ;
    public Container getContentPane() ;
    public JButton getDefaultButton() ;
    public Component getGlassPane() ;
    public JMenuBar getJMenuBar() ;
    public JLayeredPane getLayeredPane() ;
    public JMenuBar getMenuBar() ;
    public RootPaneUI getUI() ; // Since 1.3
    public String getUIClassID() ;
    public int getWindowDecorationStyle() ; // Since 1.4
    public boolean isOptimizedDrawingEnabled() ;
    public boolean isValidateRoot() ;
    protected String paramString() ;
    public void removeNotify() ;
    public void setContentPane(Container content) ;
    public void setDefaultButton(JButton defaultButton) ;
    public void setDoubleBuffered(boolean aFlag) ; // Since 1.6
    public void setGlassPane(Component glass) ;
    public void setJMenuBar(JMenuBar menu) ;
    public void setLayeredPane(JLayeredPane layered) ;
    public void setMenuBar(JMenuBar menu) ;
    public void setUI(RootPaneUI ui) ; // Since 1.3
    public void setWindowDecorationStyle(int windowDecorationStyle) ; // Since 1.4
    public void updateUI() ;
}
```

javax.swing.**JScrollBar**

public class **JScrollBar** extends JComponent implements Accessible, Adjustable
```
{
    protected int blockIncrement ;
    protected BoundedRangeModel model ;
    protected int orientation ;
```

```
    protected int unitIncrement ;
    // Constructors
    public JScrollBar() ;
    public JScrollBar(int orientation) ;
    public JScrollBar(int max, int min, int extent, int value, int orientation) ;
    // Instance methods
    public void addAdjustmentListener(AdjustmentListener l) ;
    protected void fireAdjustmentValueChanged(int value, int type, int id) ;
    public AccessibleContext getAccessibleContext() ;
    public AdjustmentListener getAdjustmentListeners() ; // Since 1.4
    public int getBlockIncrement() ;
    public int getBlockIncrement(int direction) ;
    public int getMaximum() ;
    public Dimension getMaximumSize() ;
    public int getMinimum() ;
    public Dimension getMinimumSize() ;
    public BoundedRangeModel getModel() ;
    public int getOrientation() ;
    public ScrollBarUI getUI() ;
    public String getUIClassID() ;
    public int getUnitIncrement() ;
    public int getUnitIncrement(int direction) ;
    public int getValue() ;
    public boolean getValueIsAdjusting() ;
    public int getVisibleAmount() ;
    protected String paramString() ;
    public void removeAdjustmentListener(AdjustmentListener l) ;
    public void setBlockIncrement(int blockIncrement) ;
    public void setEnabled(boolean x) ;
    public void setMaximum(int maximum) ;
    public void setMinimum(int minimum) ;
    public void setModel(BoundedRangeModel newModel) ;
    public void setOrientation(int orientation) ;
    public void setUI(ScrollBarUI ui) ; // Since 1.4
    public void setUnitIncrement(int unitIncrement) ;
    public void setValue(int value) ;
    public void setValueIsAdjusting(boolean b) ;
    public void setValues(int newMax, int newMin, int newExtent, int newValue) ;
    public void setVisibleAmount(int extent) ;
    public void updateUI() ;
}
```

javax.swing.**JScrollPane**

public class **JScrollPane** extends JComponent implements Accessible, ScrollPaneConstants
{
    protected JViewport **columnHeader** ;
    protected JScrollBar **horizontalScrollBar** ;
    protected int **horizontalScrollBarPolicy** ;
    protected Component **lowerLeft** ;
    protected Component **lowerRight** ;
    protected JViewport **rowHeader** ;
    protected Component **upperLeft** ;
    protected Component **upperRight** ;
    protected JScrollBar **verticalScrollBar** ;
    protected int **verticalScrollBarPolicy** ;
    protected JViewport **viewport** ;
    // Constructors
    public **JScrollPane**() ;
    public **JScrollPane**(int hsbPolicy, int vsbPolicy) ;
    public **JScrollPane**(Component view) ;
    public **JScrollPane**(int hsbPolicy, int vsbPolicy, Component view) ;
    // Instance methods
    public JScrollBar **createHorizontalScrollBar**() ;
    public JScrollBar **createVerticalScrollBar**() ;
    protected JViewport **createViewport**() ;
    public AccessibleContext **getAccessibleContext**() ;
    public JViewport **getColumnHeader**() ;
    public Component **getCorner**(String key) ;
    public JScrollBar **getHorizontalScrollBar**() ;
    public int **getHorizontalScrollBarPolicy**() ;
    public JViewport **getRowHeader**() ;
    public ScrollPaneUI **getUI**() ;
    public String **getUIClassID**() ;
    public JScrollBar **getVerticalScrollBar**() ;
    public int **getVerticalScrollBarPolicy**() ;
    public JViewport **getViewport**() ;
    public Border **getViewportBorder**() ;
    public Rectangle **getViewportBorderBounds**() ;
    public boolean **isValidateRoot**() ;
    public boolean **isWheelScrollingEnabled**() ; // Since 1.4
    protected String **paramString**() ;
    public void **setColumnHeader**(JViewport columnHeader) ;
    public void **setColumnHeaderView**(Component view) ;
    public void **setComponentOrientation**(ComponentOrientation co) ;

```
    public void setCorner(Component corner, String key) ;
    public void setHorizontalScrollBar(JScrollBar horizontalScrollBar) ;
    public void setHorizontalScrollBarPolicy(int policy) ;
    public void setLayout(LayoutManager layout) ;
    public void setRowHeader(JViewport rowHeader) ;
    public void setRowHeaderView(Component view) ;
    public void setUI(ScrollPaneUI ui) ;
    public void setVerticalScrollBar(JScrollBar verticalScrollBar) ;
    public void setVerticalScrollBarPolicy(int policy) ;
    public void setViewport(JViewport viewport) ;
    public void setViewportBorder(Border viewportBorder) ;
    public void setViewportView(Component view) ;
    public void setWheelScrollingEnabled(boolean handleWheel) ; // Since 1.4
    public void updateUI() ;
}
```

---

javax.swing.**JSeparator**

```
public class JSeparator extends JComponent implements Accessible, SwingConstants
{
    // Constructors
    public JSeparator(int orientation) ;
    public JSeparator() ;
    // Instance methods
    public AccessibleContext getAccessibleContext() ;
    public int getOrientation() ;
    public SeparatorUI getUI() ;
    public String getUIClassID() ;
    protected String paramString() ;
    public void setOrientation(int orientation) ;
    public void setUI(SeparatorUI ui) ;
    public void updateUI() ;
}
```

---

javax.swing.**JSlider**

```
public class JSlider extends JComponent implements Accessible, SwingConstants
{
    protected transient ChangeEvent changeEvent ;
    protected ChangeListener changeListener ;
    protected int majorTickSpacing ;
```

protected int **minorTickSpacing** ;
protected int **orientation** ;
protected BoundedRangeModel **sliderModel** ;
protected boolean **snapToTicks** ;
// Constructors
public **JSlider**(BoundedRangeModel brm) ;
public **JSlider**(int value, int max, int min, int orientation) ;
public **JSlider**(int value, int max, int min) ;
public **JSlider**(int max, int min) ;
public **JSlider**(int orientation) ;
public **JSlider**() ;
// Instance methods
public void **addChangeListener**(ChangeListener l) ;
protected ChangeListener **createChangeListener**() ;
public Hashtable **createStandardLabels**(int start, int increment) ;
public Hashtable **createStandardLabels**(int increment) ;
protected void **fireStateChanged**() ;
public AccessibleContext **getAccessibleContext**() ;
public ChangeListener **getChangeListeners**() ; // Since 1.4
public int **getExtent**() ;
public boolean **getInverted**() ;
public Dictionary **getLabelTable**() ;
public int **getMajorTickSpacing**() ;
public int **getMaximum**() ;
public int **getMinimum**() ;
public int **getMinorTickSpacing**() ;
public BoundedRangeModel **getModel**() ;
public int **getOrientation**() ;
public boolean **getPaintLabels**() ;
public boolean **getPaintTicks**() ;
public boolean **getPaintTrack**() ;
public boolean **getSnapToTicks**() ;
public SliderUI **getUI**() ;
public String **getUIClassID**() ;
public int **getValue**() ;
public boolean **getValueIsAdjusting**() ;
protected String **paramString**() ;
public void **removeChangeListener**(ChangeListener l) ;
public void **setExtent**(int extent) ;
public void **setFont**(Font font) ; // Since 1.6
public void **setInverted**(boolean b) ;
public void **setLabelTable**(Dictionary labels) ;
public void **setMajorTickSpacing**(int n) ;
public void **setMaximum**(int maximum) ;
public void **setMinimum**(int minimum) ;
public void **setMinorTickSpacing**(int n) ;

```
        public void setModel(BoundedRangeModel newModel) ;
        public void setOrientation(int orientation) ;
        public void setPaintLabels(boolean b) ;
        public void setPaintTicks(boolean b) ;
        public void setPaintTrack(boolean b) ;
        public void setSnapToTicks(boolean b) ;
        public void setUI(SliderUI ui) ;
        public void setValue(int n) ;
        public void setValueIsAdjusting(boolean b) ;
        protected void updateLabelUIs() ;
        public void updateUI() ;
}
```

javax.swing.**JSpinner** [since 1.4]

```
public class JSpinner extends JComponent implements Accessible
{
        // Constructors
        public JSpinner() ;
        public JSpinner(SpinnerModel model) ;
        // Instance methods
        public void addChangeListener(ChangeListener listener) ;
        public void commitEdit() throws ParseException ;
        protected JComponent createEditor(SpinnerModel model) ;
        protected void fireStateChanged() ;
        public AccessibleContext getAccessibleContext() ; // Since 1.5
        public ChangeListener getChangeListeners() ; // Since 1.4
        public JComponent getEditor() ;
        public SpinnerModel getModel() ;
        public Object getNextValue() ;
        public Object getPreviousValue() ;
        public SpinnerUI getUI() ;
        public String getUIClassID() ;
        public Object getValue() ;
        public void removeChangeListener(ChangeListener listener) ;
        public void setEditor(JComponent editor) ;
        public void setModel(SpinnerModel model) ;
        public void setUI(SpinnerUI ui) ;
        public void setValue(Object value) ;
        public void updateUI() ;
}
```

javax.swing.**JSpinner.DateEditor** [since 1.4]

public static class **JSpinner.DateEditor** extends JSpinner.DefaultEditor
{
    // Constructors
    private **JSpinner.DateEditor**(DateFormat format, JSpinner spinner) ;
    public **JSpinner.DateEditor**(String dateFormatPattern, JSpinner spinner) ;
    public **JSpinner.DateEditor**(JSpinner spinner) ;
    // Static methods
    // Instance methods
    public SimpleDateFormat **getFormat**() ;
    public SpinnerDateModel **getModel**() ;
}

javax.swing.**JSpinner.DefaultEditor** [since 1.4]

public static class **JSpinner.DefaultEditor** extends JPanel implements LayoutManager, PropertyChangeListener, ChangeListener
{
    // Constructors
    public **JSpinner.DefaultEditor**(JSpinner spinner) ;
    // Instance methods
    public void **addLayoutComponent**(Component child, String name) ;
    public void **commitEdit**() throws ParseException ;
    public void **dismiss**(JSpinner spinner) ;
    public int **getBaseline**(int height, int width) ; // Since 1.6
    public Component.BaselineResizeBehavior **getBaselineResizeBehavior**() ; // Since 1.6
    public JSpinner **getSpinner**() ;
    public JFormattedTextField **getTextField**() ;
    public void **layoutContainer**(Container parent) ;
    public Dimension **minimumLayoutSize**(Container parent) ;
    public Dimension **preferredLayoutSize**(Container parent) ;
    public void **propertyChange**(PropertyChangeEvent e) ;
    public void **removeLayoutComponent**(Component child) ;
    public void **stateChanged**(ChangeEvent e) ;
}

javax.swing.**JSpinner.ListEditor** [since 1.4]

public static class **JSpinner.ListEditor** extends JSpinner.DefaultEditor
{
    // Constructors
    public **JSpinner.ListEditor**(JSpinner spinner) ;
    // Instance methods
    public SpinnerListModel **getModel**() ;
}

javax.swing.**JSpinner.NumberEditor** [since 1.4]

public static class **JSpinner.NumberEditor** extends JSpinner.DefaultEditor
{
    // Constructors
    private **JSpinner.NumberEditor**(DecimalFormat format, JSpinner spinner) ;
    public **JSpinner.NumberEditor**(String decimalFormatPattern, JSpinner spinner) ;
    public **JSpinner.NumberEditor**(JSpinner spinner) ;
    // Static methods
    // Instance methods
    public DecimalFormat **getFormat**() ;
    public SpinnerNumberModel **getModel**() ;
}

javax.swing.**JSplitPane**

public class **JSplitPane** extends JComponent implements Accessible
{
    public static final String **BOTTOM** ;
    public static final String **CONTINUOUS_LAYOUT_PROPERTY** ;
    public static final String **DIVIDER** ;
    public static final String **DIVIDER_LOCATION_PROPERTY** ;
    public static final String **DIVIDER_SIZE_PROPERTY** ;
    public static final int **HORIZONTAL_SPLIT** ;
    public static final String **LAST_DIVIDER_LOCATION_PROPERTY** ;
    public static final String **LEFT** ;
    public static final String **ONE_TOUCH_EXPANDABLE_PROPERTY** ;

public static final String **ORIENTATION_PROPERTY** ;
public static final String **RESIZE_WEIGHT_PROPERTY** ;
public static final String **RIGHT** ;
public static final String **TOP** ;
public static final int **VERTICAL_SPLIT** ;
protected boolean **continuousLayout** ;
protected int **dividerSize** ;
protected int **lastDividerLocation** ;
protected Component **leftComponent** ;
protected boolean **oneTouchExpandable** ;
protected int **orientation** ;
protected Component **rightComponent** ;
// Constructors
public **JSplitPane**(Component newRightComponent, Component newLeftComponent, boolean
    newContinuousLayout, int newOrientation) ;
public **JSplitPane**(Component newRightComponent, Component newLeftComponent, int
    newOrientation) ;
public **JSplitPane**(boolean newContinuousLayout, int newOrientation) ;
public **JSplitPane**(int newOrientation) ;
public **JSplitPane**() ;
// Instance methods
protected void **addImpl**(int index, Object constraints, Component comp) ;
public AccessibleContext **getAccessibleContext**() ;
public Component **getBottomComponent**() ;
public int **getDividerLocation**() ;
public int **getDividerSize**() ;
public int **getLastDividerLocation**() ;
public Component **getLeftComponent**() ;
public int **getMaximumDividerLocation**() ;
public int **getMinimumDividerLocation**() ;
public int **getOrientation**() ;
public double **getResizeWeight**() ; // Since 1.3
public Component **getRightComponent**() ;
public Component **getTopComponent**() ;
public SplitPaneUI **getUI**() ;
public String **getUIClassID**() ;
public boolean **isContinuousLayout**() ;
public boolean **isOneTouchExpandable**() ;
public boolean **isValidateRoot**() ;
protected void **paintChildren**(Graphics g) ;
protected String **paramString**() ;
public void **remove**(Component component) ;
public void **remove**(int index) ;
public void **removeAll**() ;
public void **resetToPreferredSizes**() ;
public void **setBottomComponent**(Component comp) ;

```
    public void setContinuousLayout(boolean newContinuousLayout) ;
    public void setDividerLocation(int location) ;
    public void setDividerLocation(double proportionalLocation) ;
    public void setDividerSize(int newSize) ;
    public void setLastDividerLocation(int newLastLocation) ;
    public void setLeftComponent(Component comp) ;
    public void setOneTouchExpandable(boolean newValue) ;
    public void setOrientation(int orientation) ;
    public void setResizeWeight(double value) ; // Since 1.3
    public void setRightComponent(Component comp) ;
    public void setTopComponent(Component comp) ;
    public void setUI(SplitPaneUI ui) ;
    public void updateUI() ;
}
```

javax.swing.**JTabbedPane**

```
public class JTabbedPane extends JComponent implements SwingConstants, Accessible, Serializable
{
    public static final int SCROLL_TAB_LAYOUT ;
    public static final int WRAP_TAB_LAYOUT ;
    protected transient ChangeEvent changeEvent ;
    protected ChangeListener changeListener ;
    protected SingleSelectionModel model ;
    protected int tabPlacement ;
    // Constructors
    public JTabbedPane(int tabLayoutPolicy, int tabPlacement) ;
    public JTabbedPane(int tabPlacement) ;
    public JTabbedPane() ;
    // Instance methods
    public Component add(Component component, String title) ;
    public Component add(int index, Component component) ;
    public void add(int index, Object constraints, Component component) ;
    public void add(Object constraints, Component component) ;
    public Component add(Component component) ;
    public void addChangeListener(ChangeListener l) ;
    public void addTab(String tip, Component component, Icon icon, String title) ;
    public void addTab(Component component, String title) ;
    public void addTab(Component component, Icon icon, String title) ;
    protected ChangeListener createChangeListener() ;
    protected void fireStateChanged() ;
    public AccessibleContext getAccessibleContext() ;
    public Color getBackgroundAt(int index) ;
    public Rectangle getBoundsAt(int index) ;
```

public ChangeListener **getChangeListeners**() ; // Since 1.4
public Component **getComponentAt**(int index) ;
public Icon **getDisabledIconAt**(int index) ;
public int **getDisplayedMnemonicIndexAt**(int tabIndex) ; // Since 1.4
public Color **getForegroundAt**(int index) ;
public Icon **getIconAt**(int index) ;
public int **getMnemonicAt**(int tabIndex) ; // Since 1.4
public SingleSelectionModel **getModel**() ;
public Component **getSelectedComponent**() ;
public int **getSelectedIndex**() ;
public Component **getTabComponentAt**(int index) ; // Since 1.6
public int **getTabCount**() ;
public int **getTabLayoutPolicy**() ; // Since 1.4
public int **getTabPlacement**() ;
public int **getTabRunCount**() ;
public String **getTitleAt**(int index) ;
public String **getToolTipText**(MouseEvent event) ;
public String **getToolTipTextAt**(int index) ; // Since 1.3
public TabbedPaneUI **getUI**() ;
public String **getUIClassID**() ;
public int **indexAtLocation**(int y, int x) ; // Since 1.4
public int **indexOfComponent**(Component component) ;
public int **indexOfTab**(String title) ;
public int **indexOfTab**(Icon icon) ;
public int **indexOfTabComponent**(Component tabComponent) ; // Since 1.6
public void **insertTab**(int index, String tip, Component component, Icon icon, String title) ;
public boolean **isEnabledAt**(int index) ;
protected String **paramString**() ;
public void **remove**(Component component) ;
public void **remove**(int index) ;
public void **removeAll**() ;
public void **removeChangeListener**(ChangeListener l) ;
public void **removeTabAt**(int index) ;
public void **setBackgroundAt**(Color background, int index) ;
public void **setComponentAt**(Component component, int index) ;
public void **setDisabledIconAt**(Icon disabledIcon, int index) ;
public void **setDisplayedMnemonicIndexAt**(int mnemonicIndex, int tabIndex) ; // Since 1.4
public void **setEnabledAt**(boolean enabled, int index) ;
public void **setForegroundAt**(Color foreground, int index) ;
public void **setIconAt**(Icon icon, int index) ;
public void **setMnemonicAt**(int mnemonic, int tabIndex) ; // Since 1.4
public void **setModel**(SingleSelectionModel model) ;
public void **setSelectedComponent**(Component c) ;
public void **setSelectedIndex**(int index) ;
public void **setTabComponentAt**(Component component, int index) ; // Since 1.6
public void **setTabLayoutPolicy**(int tabLayoutPolicy) ; // Since 1.4

```
    public void setTabPlacement(int tabPlacement) ;
    public void setTitleAt(String title, int index) ;
    public void setToolTipTextAt(String toolTipText, int index) ; // Since 1.3
    public void setUI(TabbedPaneUI ui) ;
    public void updateUI() ;
}
```

---

javax.swing.**JTable**

---

public class **JTable** extends JComponent implements RowSorterListener, Accessible, CellEditorListener, ListSelectionListener, TableColumnModelListener, Scrollable, TableModelListener

```
{
    public static final int AUTO_RESIZE_ALL_COLUMNS ;
    public static final int AUTO_RESIZE_LAST_COLUMN ;
    public static final int AUTO_RESIZE_NEXT_COLUMN ;
    public static final int AUTO_RESIZE_OFF ;
    public static final int AUTO_RESIZE_SUBSEQUENT_COLUMNS ;
    protected boolean autoCreateColumnsFromModel ;
    protected int autoResizeMode ;
    protected transient TableCellEditor cellEditor ;
    protected boolean cellSelectionEnabled ;
    protected TableColumnModel columnModel ;
    protected TableModel dataModel ;
    protected transient Hashtable defaultEditorsByColumnClass ;
    protected transient Hashtable defaultRenderersByColumnClass ;
    protected transient int editingColumn ;
    protected transient int editingRow ;
    protected transient Component editorComp ;
    protected Color gridColor ;
    protected Dimension preferredViewportSize ;
    protected int rowHeight ;
    protected int rowMargin ;
    protected boolean rowSelectionAllowed ;
    protected Color selectionBackground ;
    protected Color selectionForeground ;
    protected ListSelectionModel selectionModel ;
    protected boolean showHorizontalLines ;
    protected boolean showVerticalLines ;
    protected JTableHeader tableHeader ;
    // Constructors
    public JTable(java.lang.Object[] columnNames, java.lang.Object[][] rowData) ;
    public JTable(Vector columnNames, Vector rowData) ;
    public JTable(int numColumns, int numRows) ;
    public JTable(ListSelectionModel sm, TableColumnModel cm, TableModel dm) ;
```

public **JTable**(TableColumnModel cm, TableModel dm) ;
public **JTable**(TableModel dm) ;
public **JTable**() ;
// Static methods
public static JScrollPane **createScrollPaneForTable**(JTable aTable) ;
// Instance methods
public void **addColumn**(TableColumn aColumn) ;
public void **addColumnSelectionInterval**(int index1, int index0) ;
public void **addNotify**() ;
public void **addRowSelectionInterval**(int index1, int index0) ;
public void **changeSelection**(boolean extend, boolean toggle, int columnIndex, int rowIndex) ; // Since 1.3
public void **clearSelection**() ;
public void **columnAdded**(TableColumnModelEvent e) ;
public int **columnAtPoint**(Point point) ;
public void **columnMarginChanged**(ChangeEvent e) ;
public void **columnMoved**(TableColumnModelEvent e) ;
public void **columnRemoved**(TableColumnModelEvent e) ;
public void **columnSelectionChanged**(ListSelectionEvent e) ;
protected void **configureEnclosingScrollPane**() ;
public int **convertColumnIndexToModel**(int viewColumnIndex) ;
public int **convertColumnIndexToView**(int modelColumnIndex) ;
public int **convertRowIndexToModel**(int viewRowIndex) ; // Since 1.6
public int **convertRowIndexToView**(int modelRowIndex) ; // Since 1.6
protected TableColumnModel **createDefaultColumnModel**() ;
public void **createDefaultColumnsFromModel**() ;
protected TableModel **createDefaultDataModel**() ;
protected void **createDefaultEditors**() ;
protected void **createDefaultRenderers**() ;
protected ListSelectionModel **createDefaultSelectionModel**() ;
protected JTableHeader **createDefaultTableHeader**() ;
public void **doLayout**() ;
public boolean **editCellAt**(EventObject e, int column, int row) ;
public boolean **editCellAt**(int column, int row) ;
public void **editingCanceled**(ChangeEvent e) ;
public void **editingStopped**(ChangeEvent e) ;
public AccessibleContext **getAccessibleContext**() ;
public boolean **getAutoCreateColumnsFromModel**() ;
public boolean **getAutoCreateRowSorter**() ; // Since 1.6
public int **getAutoResizeMode**() ;
public TableCellEditor **getCellEditor**(int column, int row) ;
public TableCellEditor **getCellEditor**() ;
public Rectangle **getCellRect**(boolean includeSpacing, int column, int row) ;
public TableCellRenderer **getCellRenderer**(int column, int row) ;
public boolean **getCellSelectionEnabled**() ;
public TableColumn **getColumn**(Object identifier) ;

public Class<?> **getColumnClass**(int column) ;
public int **getColumnCount**() ;
public TableColumnModel **getColumnModel**() ;
public String **getColumnName**(int column) ;
public boolean **getColumnSelectionAllowed**() ;
public TableCellEditor **getDefaultEditor**(Class<?> columnClass) ;
public TableCellRenderer **getDefaultRenderer**(Class<?> columnClass) ;
public boolean **getDragEnabled**() ; // Since 1.4
public final JTable.DropLocation **getDropLocation**() ; // Since 1.6
public final DropMode **getDropMode**() ; // Since 1.6
public int **getEditingColumn**() ;
public int **getEditingRow**() ;
public Component **getEditorComponent**() ;
public boolean **getFillsViewportHeight**() ; // Since 1.6
public Color **getGridColor**() ;
public Dimension **getIntercellSpacing**() ;
public TableModel **getModel**() ;
public Dimension **getPreferredScrollableViewportSize**() ;
public Printable **getPrintable**(MessageFormat footerFormat, MessageFormat headerFormat,
    JTable.PrintMode printMode) ; // Since 1.5
public int **getRowCount**() ;
public int **getRowHeight**(int row) ; // Since 1.3
public int **getRowHeight**() ;
public int **getRowMargin**() ;
public boolean **getRowSelectionAllowed**() ;
public RowSorter<?> **getRowSorter**() ; // Since 1.6
public int **getScrollableBlockIncrement**(int direction, int orientation, Rectangle visibleRect) ;
public boolean **getScrollableTracksViewportHeight**() ;
public boolean **getScrollableTracksViewportWidth**() ;
public int **getScrollableUnitIncrement**(int direction, int orientation, Rectangle visibleRect) ;
public int **getSelectedColumn**() ;
public int **getSelectedColumnCount**() ;
public int **getSelectedColumns**() ;
public int **getSelectedRow**() ;
public int **getSelectedRowCount**() ;
public int **getSelectedRows**() ;
public Color **getSelectionBackground**() ;
public Color **getSelectionForeground**() ;
public ListSelectionModel **getSelectionModel**() ;
public boolean **getShowHorizontalLines**() ;
public boolean **getShowVerticalLines**() ;
public boolean **getSurrendersFocusOnKeystroke**() ; // Since 1.4
public JTableHeader **getTableHeader**() ;
public String **getToolTipText**(MouseEvent event) ;
public TableUI **getUI**() ;
public String **getUIClassID**() ;

public boolean **getUpdateSelectionOnSort**() ; // Since 1.6
public Object **getValueAt**(int column, int row) ;
protected void **initializeLocalVars**() ;
public boolean **isCellEditable**(int column, int row) ;
public boolean **isCellSelected**(int column, int row) ;
public boolean **isColumnSelected**(int column) ;
public boolean **isEditing**() ;
public boolean **isRowSelected**(int row) ;
public void **moveColumn**(int targetColumn, int column) ;
protected String **paramString**() ;
public Component **prepareEditor**(int column, int row, TableCellEditor editor) ;
public Component **prepareRenderer**(int column, int row, TableCellRenderer renderer) ;
public boolean **print**(JTable.PrintMode printMode) throws PrinterException ; // Since 1.5
public boolean **print**() throws PrinterException ; // Since 1.5
public boolean **print**(PrintService service, boolean interactive, PrintRequestAttributeSet attr, boolean
    showPrintDialog, MessageFormat footerFormat, MessageFormat headerFormat,
    JTable.PrintMode printMode) throws PrinterException, HeadlessException ; // Since 1.6
public boolean **print**(MessageFormat footerFormat, MessageFormat headerFormat, JTable.PrintMode
    printMode) throws PrinterException ; // Since 1.5
public boolean **print**(boolean interactive, PrintRequestAttributeSet attr, boolean showPrintDialog,
    MessageFormat footerFormat, MessageFormat headerFormat, JTable.PrintMode printMode)
    throws PrinterException, HeadlessException ; // Since 1.5
protected boolean **processKeyBinding**(boolean pressed, int condition, KeyEvent e, KeyStroke ks) ;
public void **removeColumn**(TableColumn aColumn) ;
public void **removeColumnSelectionInterval**(int index1, int index0) ;
public void **removeEditor**() ;
public void **removeNotify**() ;
public void **removeRowSelectionInterval**(int index1, int index0) ;
protected void **resizeAndRepaint**() ;
public int **rowAtPoint**(Point point) ;
public void **selectAll**() ;
public void **setAutoCreateColumnsFromModel**(boolean autoCreateColumnsFromModel) ;
public void **setAutoCreateRowSorter**(boolean autoCreateRowSorter) ; // Since 1.6
public void **setAutoResizeMode**(int mode) ;
public void **setCellEditor**(TableCellEditor anEditor) ;
public void **setCellSelectionEnabled**(boolean cellSelectionEnabled) ;
public void **setColumnModel**(TableColumnModel columnModel) ;
public void **setColumnSelectionAllowed**(boolean columnSelectionAllowed) ;
public void **setColumnSelectionInterval**(int index1, int index0) ;
public void **setDefaultEditor**(TableCellEditor editor, Class<?> columnClass) ;
public void **setDefaultRenderer**(TableCellRenderer renderer, Class<?> columnClass) ;
public void **setDragEnabled**(boolean b) ; // Since 1.4
public final void **setDropMode**(DropMode dropMode) ; // Since 1.6
public void **setEditingColumn**(int aColumn) ;
public void **setEditingRow**(int aRow) ;
public void **setFillsViewportHeight**(boolean fillsViewportHeight) ; // Since 1.6

```
        public void setGridColor(Color gridColor) ;
        public void setIntercellSpacing(Dimension intercellSpacing) ;
        public void setModel(TableModel dataModel) ;
        public void setPreferredScrollableViewportSize(Dimension size) ;
        public void setRowHeight(int rowHeight) ;
        public void setRowHeight(int rowHeight, int row) ; // Since 1.3
        public void setRowMargin(int rowMargin) ;
        public void setRowSelectionAllowed(boolean rowSelectionAllowed) ;
        public void setRowSelectionInterval(int index1, int index0) ;
        public void setRowSorter(RowSorter<?> sorter) ; // Since 1.6
        public void setSelectionBackground(Color selectionBackground) ;
        public void setSelectionForeground(Color selectionForeground) ;
        public void setSelectionMode(int selectionMode) ;
        public void setSelectionModel(ListSelectionModel newModel) ;
        public void setShowGrid(boolean showGrid) ;
        public void setShowHorizontalLines(boolean showHorizontalLines) ;
        public void setShowVerticalLines(boolean showVerticalLines) ;
        public void setSurrendersFocusOnKeystroke(boolean surrendersFocusOnKeystroke) ; // Since 1.4
        public void setTableHeader(JTableHeader tableHeader) ;
        public void setUI(TableUI ui) ;
        public void setUpdateSelectionOnSort(boolean update) ; // Since 1.6
        public void setValueAt(int column, int row, Object aValue) ;
        public void sizeColumnsToFit(boolean lastColumnOnly) ;
        public void sizeColumnsToFit(int resizingColumn) ;
        public void sorterChanged(RowSorterEvent e) ; // Since 1.6
        public void tableChanged(TableModelEvent e) ;
        protected void unconfigureEnclosingScrollPane() ; // Since 1.3
        public void updateUI() ;
        public void valueChanged(ListSelectionEvent e) ;
}
```

---

javax.swing.**JTable.DropLocation** [since 1.6]

---

public static final class **JTable.DropLocation** extends TransferHandler.DropLocation
```
{
        // Constructors
        private JTable.DropLocation(boolean isInsertCol, boolean isInsertRow, int col, int row, Point p) ;
        // Instance methods
        public int getColumn() ;
        public int getRow() ;
        public boolean isInsertColumn() ;
        public boolean isInsertRow() ;
        public String toString() ;
}
```

javax.swing.**JTable.PrintMode** [since 1.5]

public static final class **JTable.PrintMode** extends Enum<JTable.PrintMode>
{
    // Constructors
    private **JTable.PrintMode**() ;
    // Static methods
    public static JTable.PrintMode **valueOf**(String name) ;
    public static final JTable.PrintMode **values**() ;
}

javax.swing.table.**JTableHeader**

public class **JTableHeader** extends JComponent implements Accessible, TableColumnModelListener
{
    protected TableColumnModel **columnModel** ;
    protected transient TableColumn **draggedColumn** ;
    protected transient int **draggedDistance** ;
    protected boolean **reorderingAllowed** ;
    protected boolean **resizingAllowed** ;
    protected transient TableColumn **resizingColumn** ;
    protected JTable **table** ;
    protected boolean **updateTableInRealTime** ;
    // Constructors
    public **JTableHeader**(TableColumnModel cm) ;
    public **JTableHeader**() ;
    // Instance methods
    public void **columnAdded**(TableColumnModelEvent e) ;
    public int **columnAtPoint**(Point point) ;
    public void **columnMarginChanged**(ChangeEvent e) ;
    public void **columnMoved**(TableColumnModelEvent e) ;
    public void **columnRemoved**(TableColumnModelEvent e) ;
    public void **columnSelectionChanged**(ListSelectionEvent e) ;
    protected TableColumnModel **createDefaultColumnModel**() ;
    protected TableCellRenderer **createDefaultRenderer**() ; // Since 1.3
    public AccessibleContext **getAccessibleContext**() ;
    public TableColumnModel **getColumnModel**() ;
    public TableCellRenderer **getDefaultRenderer**() ; // Since 1.3
    public TableColumn **getDraggedColumn**() ;
    public int **getDraggedDistance**() ;

```
        public Rectangle getHeaderRect(int column) ;
        public boolean getReorderingAllowed() ;
        public boolean getResizingAllowed() ;
        public TableColumn getResizingColumn() ;
        public JTable getTable() ;
        public String getToolTipText(MouseEvent event) ;
        public TableHeaderUI getUI() ;
        public String getUIClassID() ;
        public boolean getUpdateTableInRealTime() ;
        protected void initializeLocalVars() ;
        protected String paramString() ;
        public void resizeAndRepaint() ;
        public void setColumnModel(TableColumnModel columnModel) ;
        public void setDefaultRenderer(TableCellRenderer defaultRenderer) ; // Since 1.3
        public void setDraggedColumn(TableColumn aColumn) ;
        public void setDraggedDistance(int distance) ;
        public void setReorderingAllowed(boolean reorderingAllowed) ;
        public void setResizingAllowed(boolean resizingAllowed) ;
        public void setResizingColumn(TableColumn aColumn) ;
        public void setTable(JTable table) ;
        public void setUI(TableHeaderUI ui) ;
        public void setUpdateTableInRealTime(boolean flag) ;
        public void updateUI() ;
}
```

---

javax.swing.**JTextArea**

```
public class JTextArea extends JTextComponent
{
        // Constructors
        public JTextArea(int columns, int rows, String text, Document doc) ;
        public JTextArea(Document doc) ;
        public JTextArea(int columns, int rows, String text) ;
        public JTextArea(int columns, int rows) ;
        public JTextArea(String text) ;
        public JTextArea() ;
        // Instance methods
        public void append(String str) ;
        protected Document createDefaultModel() ;
        public AccessibleContext getAccessibleContext() ;
        public int getColumns() ;
        protected int getColumnWidth() ;
        public int getLineCount() ;
        public int getLineEndOffset(int line) throws BadLocationException ;
```

```
    public int getLineOfOffset(int offset) throws BadLocationException ;
    public int getLineStartOffset(int line) throws BadLocationException ;
    public boolean getLineWrap() ;
    public Dimension getPreferredScrollableViewportSize() ;
    public Dimension getPreferredSize() ;
    protected int getRowHeight() ;
    public int getRows() ;
    public boolean getScrollableTracksViewportWidth() ;
    public int getScrollableUnitIncrement(int direction, int orientation, Rectangle visibleRect) ;
    public int getTabSize() ;
    public String getUIClassID() ;
    public boolean getWrapStyleWord() ;
    public void insert(int pos, String str) ;
    protected String paramString() ;
    public void replaceRange(int end, int start, String str) ;
    public void setColumns(int columns) ;
    public void setFont(Font f) ;
    public void setLineWrap(boolean wrap) ;
    public void setRows(int rows) ;
    public void setTabSize(int size) ;
    public void setWrapStyleWord(boolean word) ;
}
```

javax.swing.text.**JTextComponent**

public abstract class **JTextComponent** extends JComponent implements Accessible, Scrollable
```
{
    public static final String DEFAULT_KEYMAP ;
    public static final String FOCUS_ACCELERATOR_KEY ;
    // Constructors
    public JTextComponent() ;
    // Static methods
    public static Keymap addKeymap(Keymap parent, String nm) ;
    public static Keymap getKeymap(String nm) ;
    public static void loadKeymap(javax.swing.Action[] actions,
        javax.swing.text.JTextComponent.KeyBinding[] bindings, Keymap map) ;
    public static Keymap removeKeymap(String nm) ;
    // Instance methods
    public void addCaretListener(CaretListener listener) ;
    public void addInputMethodListener(InputMethodListener l) ;
    public void copy() ;
    public void cut() ;
    protected void fireCaretUpdate(CaretEvent e) ;
    public AccessibleContext getAccessibleContext() ;
```

public Action **getActions**() ;
public Caret **getCaret**() ;
public Color **getCaretColor**() ;
public CaretListener **getCaretListeners**() ; // Since 1.4
public int **getCaretPosition**() ;
public Color **getDisabledTextColor**() ;
public Document **getDocument**() ;
public boolean **getDragEnabled**() ; // Since 1.4
public final JTextComponent.DropLocation **getDropLocation**() ; // Since 1.6
public final DropMode **getDropMode**() ; // Since 1.6
public char **getFocusAccelerator**() ;
public Highlighter **getHighlighter**() ;
public InputMethodRequests **getInputMethodRequests**() ;
public Keymap **getKeymap**() ;
public Insets **getMargin**() ;
public NavigationFilter **getNavigationFilter**() ; // Since 1.4
public Dimension **getPreferredScrollableViewportSize**() ;
public Printable **getPrintable**(MessageFormat footerFormat, MessageFormat headerFormat) ; // Since 1.6
public int **getScrollableBlockIncrement**(int direction, int orientation, Rectangle visibleRect) ;
public boolean **getScrollableTracksViewportHeight**() ;
public boolean **getScrollableTracksViewportWidth**() ;
public int **getScrollableUnitIncrement**(int direction, int orientation, Rectangle visibleRect) ;
public String **getSelectedText**() ;
public Color **getSelectedTextColor**() ;
public Color **getSelectionColor**() ;
public int **getSelectionEnd**() ;
public int **getSelectionStart**() ;
public String **getText**(int len, int offs) throws BadLocationException ;
public String **getText**() ;
public String **getToolTipText**(MouseEvent event) ;
public TextUI **getUI**() ;
public boolean **isEditable**() ;
public Rectangle **modelToView**(int pos) throws BadLocationException ;
public void **moveCaretPosition**(int pos) ;
protected String **paramString**() ;
public void **paste**() ;
public boolean **print**(MessageFormat footerFormat, MessageFormat headerFormat) throws PrinterException ; // Since 1.6
public boolean **print**(boolean interactive, PrintRequestAttributeSet attributes, PrintService service, boolean showPrintDialog, MessageFormat footerFormat, MessageFormat headerFormat) throws PrinterException ; // Since 1.6
public boolean **print**() throws PrinterException ; // Since 1.6
protected void **processInputMethodEvent**(InputMethodEvent e) ;
public void **read**(Object desc, Reader in) throws IOException ;
public void **removeCaretListener**(CaretListener listener) ;

```
        public void removeNotify() ;
        public void replaceSelection(String content) ;
        public void select(int selectionEnd, int selectionStart) ;
        public void selectAll() ;
        public void setCaret(Caret c) ;
        public void setCaretColor(Color c) ;
        public void setCaretPosition(int position) ;
        public void setComponentOrientation(ComponentOrientation o) ;
        public void setDisabledTextColor(Color c) ;
        public void setDocument(Document doc) ;
        public void setDragEnabled(boolean b) ; // Since 1.4
        public final void setDropMode(DropMode dropMode) ; // Since 1.6
        public void setEditable(boolean b) ;
        public void setFocusAccelerator(char aKey) ;
        public void setHighlighter(Highlighter h) ;
        public void setKeymap(Keymap map) ;
        public void setMargin(Insets m) ;
        public void setNavigationFilter(NavigationFilter filter) ; // Since 1.4
        public void setSelectedTextColor(Color c) ;
        public void setSelectionColor(Color c) ;
        public void setSelectionEnd(int selectionEnd) ;
        public void setSelectionStart(int selectionStart) ;
        public void setText(String t) ;
        public void setUI(TextUI ui) ;
        public void updateUI() ;
        public int viewToModel(Point pt) ;
        public void write(Writer out) throws IOException ;
}
```

javax.swing.text.**JTextComponent.DropLocation** [since 1.6]

```
public static final class JTextComponent.DropLocation extends TransferHandler.DropLocation
{
        // Constructors
        private JTextComponent.DropLocation(Position.Bias bias, int index, Point p) ;
        // Instance methods
        public Position.Bias getBias() ;
        public int getIndex() ;
        public String toString() ;
}
```

---

javax.swing.text.**JTextComponent.KeyBinding**

---

public static class **JTextComponent.KeyBinding**
{
    public String **actionName** ;
    public KeyStroke **key** ;
    // Constructors
    public **JTextComponent.KeyBinding**(String actionName, KeyStroke key) ;
}

---

javax.swing.**JTextField**

---

public class **JTextField** extends JTextComponent implements SwingConstants
{
    public static final String **notifyAction** ;
    // Constructors
    public **JTextField**(int columns, String text, Document doc) ;
    public **JTextField**(int columns, String text) ;
    public **JTextField**(int columns) ;
    public **JTextField**(String text) ;
    public **JTextField**() ;
    // Instance methods
    protected void **actionPropertyChanged**(String propertyName, Action action) ; // Since 1.6
    public synchronized void **addActionListener**(ActionListener l) ;
    protected void **configurePropertiesFromAction**(Action a) ; // Since 1.3
    protected PropertyChangeListener **createActionPropertyChangeListener**(Action a) ; // Since 1.3
    protected Document **createDefaultModel**() ;
    protected void **fireActionPerformed**() ;
    public AccessibleContext **getAccessibleContext**() ;
    public Action **getAction**() ; // Since 1.3
    public synchronized ActionListener **getActionListeners**() ; // Since 1.4
    public Action **getActions**() ;
    public int **getColumns**() ;
    protected int **getColumnWidth**() ;
    public int **getHorizontalAlignment**() ;
    public BoundedRangeModel **getHorizontalVisibility**() ;
    public Dimension **getPreferredSize**() ;
    public int **getScrollOffset**() ;
    public String **getUIClassID**() ;
    public boolean **isValidateRoot**() ;

```
    protected String paramString() ;
    public void postActionEvent() ;
    public synchronized void removeActionListener(ActionListener l) ;
    public void scrollRectToVisible(Rectangle r) ;
    public void setAction(Action a) ; // Since 1.3
    public void setActionCommand(String command) ;
    public void setColumns(int columns) ;
    public void setDocument(Document doc) ;
    public void setFont(Font f) ;
    public void setHorizontalAlignment(int alignment) ;
    public void setScrollOffset(int scrollOffset) ;
}
```

javax.swing.**JTextPane**

```
public class JTextPane extends JEditorPane
{
    // Constructors
    public JTextPane(StyledDocument doc) ;
    public JTextPane() ;
    // Instance methods
    public Style addStyle(Style parent, String nm) ;
    protected EditorKit createDefaultEditorKit() ;
    public AttributeSet getCharacterAttributes() ;
    public MutableAttributeSet getInputAttributes() ;
    public Style getLogicalStyle() ;
    public AttributeSet getParagraphAttributes() ;
    public Style getStyle(String nm) ;
    public StyledDocument getStyledDocument() ;
    protected final StyledEditorKit getStyledEditorKit() ;
    public String getUIClassID() ;
    public void insertComponent(Component c) ;
    public void insertIcon(Icon g) ;
    protected String paramString() ;
    public void removeStyle(String nm) ;
    public void replaceSelection(String content) ;
    public void setCharacterAttributes(boolean replace, AttributeSet attr) ;
    public void setDocument(Document doc) ;
    public final void setEditorKit(EditorKit kit) ;
    public void setLogicalStyle(Style s) ;
    public void setParagraphAttributes(boolean replace, AttributeSet attr) ;
    public void setStyledDocument(StyledDocument doc) ;
}
```

javax.swing.**JToggleButton**

public class **JToggleButton** extends AbstractButton implements Accessible
{
    // Constructors
    public **JToggleButton**(boolean selected, Icon icon, String text) ;
    public **JToggleButton**(Icon icon, String text) ;
    public **JToggleButton**(Action a) ;
    public **JToggleButton**(boolean selected, String text) ;
    public **JToggleButton**(String text) ;
    public **JToggleButton**(boolean selected, Icon icon) ;
    public **JToggleButton**(Icon icon) ;
    public **JToggleButton**() ;
    // Instance methods
    public AccessibleContext **getAccessibleContext**() ;
    public String **getUIClassID**() ;
    protected String **paramString**() ;
    public void **updateUI**() ;
}

javax.swing.**JToggleButton.ToggleButtonModel**

public static class **JToggleButton.ToggleButtonModel** extends DefaultButtonModel
{
    // Constructors
    public **JToggleButton.ToggleButtonModel**() ;
    // Instance methods
    public boolean **isSelected**() ;
    public void **setPressed**(boolean b) ;
    public void **setSelected**(boolean b) ;
}

javax.swing.**JToolBar**

public class **JToolBar** extends JComponent implements Accessible, SwingConstants
{
    // Constructors
    public **JToolBar**(int orientation, String name) ;

```
    public JToolBar(String name) ;
    public JToolBar(int orientation) ;
    public JToolBar() ;
    // Instance methods
    public JButton add(Action a) ;
    protected void addImpl(int index, Object constraints, Component comp) ;
    public void addSeparator() ;
    public void addSeparator(Dimension size) ;
    protected PropertyChangeListener createActionChangeListener(JButton b) ;
    protected JButton createActionComponent(Action a) ; // Since 1.3
    public AccessibleContext getAccessibleContext() ;
    public Component getComponentAtIndex(int i) ;
    public int getComponentIndex(Component c) ;
    public Insets getMargin() ;
    public int getOrientation() ;
    public ToolBarUI getUI() ;
    public String getUIClassID() ;
    public boolean isBorderPainted() ;
    public boolean isFloatable() ;
    public boolean isRollover() ; // Since 1.4
    protected void paintBorder(Graphics g) ;
    protected String paramString() ;
    public void setBorderPainted(boolean b) ;
    public void setFloatable(boolean b) ;
    public void setLayout(LayoutManager mgr) ;
    public void setMargin(Insets m) ;
    public void setOrientation(int o) ;
    public void setRollover(boolean rollover) ; // Since 1.4
    public void setUI(ToolBarUI ui) ;
    public void updateUI() ;
}
```

javax.swing.**JToolBar.Separator**

```
public static class JToolBar.Separator extends JSeparator
{
    // Constructors
    public JToolBar.Separator(Dimension size) ;
    public JToolBar.Separator() ;
    // Instance methods
    public Dimension getMaximumSize() ;
    public Dimension getMinimumSize() ;
    public Dimension getPreferredSize() ;
    public Dimension getSeparatorSize() ;
```

```
    public String getUIClassID() ;
    public void setSeparatorSize(Dimension size) ;
}
```

javax.swing.**JToolTip**

```
public class JToolTip extends JComponent implements Accessible
{
    // Constructors
    public JToolTip() ;
    // Instance methods
    public AccessibleContext getAccessibleContext() ;
    public JComponent getComponent() ;
    public String getTipText() ;
    public ToolTipUI getUI() ;
    public String getUIClassID() ;
    protected String paramString() ;
    public void setComponent(JComponent c) ;
    public void setTipText(String tipText) ;
    public void updateUI() ;
}
```

javax.swing.**JTree**

```
public class JTree extends JComponent implements Accessible, Scrollable
{
    public static final String ANCHOR_SELECTION_PATH_PROPERTY ;
    public static final String CELL_EDITOR_PROPERTY ;
    public static final String CELL_RENDERER_PROPERTY ;
    public static final String EDITABLE_PROPERTY ;
    public static final String EXPANDS_SELECTED_PATHS_PROPERTY ;
    public static final String INVOKES_STOP_CELL_EDITING_PROPERTY ;
    public static final String LARGE_MODEL_PROPERTY ;
    public static final String LEAD_SELECTION_PATH_PROPERTY ;
    public static final String ROOT_VISIBLE_PROPERTY ;
    public static final String ROW_HEIGHT_PROPERTY ;
    public static final String SCROLLS_ON_EXPAND_PROPERTY ;
    public static final String SELECTION_MODEL_PROPERTY ;
    public static final String SHOWS_ROOT_HANDLES_PROPERTY ;
    public static final String TOGGLE_CLICK_COUNT_PROPERTY ;
    public static final String TREE_MODEL_PROPERTY ;
```

public static final String **VISIBLE_ROW_COUNT_PROPERTY** ;
protected transient TreeCellEditor **cellEditor** ;
protected transient TreeCellRenderer **cellRenderer** ;
protected boolean **editable** ;
protected boolean **invokesStopCellEditing** ;
protected boolean **largeModel** ;
protected boolean **rootVisible** ;
protected int **rowHeight** ;
protected boolean **scrollsOnExpand** ;
protected transient TreeSelectionModel **selectionModel** ;
protected transient JTree.TreeSelectionRedirector **selectionRedirector** ;
protected boolean **showsRootHandles** ;
protected int **toggleClickCount** ;
protected transient TreeModel **treeModel** ;
protected transient TreeModelListener **treeModelListener** ;
protected int **visibleRowCount** ;
// Constructors
public **JTree**(TreeModel newModel) ;
public **JTree**(boolean asksAllowsChildren, TreeNode root) ;
public **JTree**(TreeNode root) ;
public **JTree**(Hashtable<?, ?> value) ;
public **JTree**(Vector<?> value) ;
public **JTree**(java.lang.Object[] value) ;
public **JTree**() ;
// Static methods
protected static TreeModel **createTreeModel**(Object value) ;
protected static TreeModel **getDefaultTreeModel**() ;
// Instance methods
public void **addSelectionInterval**(int index1, int index0) ;
public void **addSelectionPath**(TreePath path) ;
public void **addSelectionPaths**(javax.swing.tree.TreePath[] paths) ;
public void **addSelectionRow**(int row) ;
public void **addSelectionRows**(int[] rows) ;
public void **addTreeExpansionListener**(TreeExpansionListener tel) ;
public void **addTreeSelectionListener**(TreeSelectionListener tsl) ;
public void **addTreeWillExpandListener**(TreeWillExpandListener tel) ;
public void **cancelEditing**() ;
public void **clearSelection**() ;
protected void **clearToggledPaths**() ;
public void **collapsePath**(TreePath path) ;
public void **collapseRow**(int row) ;
public String **convertValueToText**(boolean hasFocus, int row, boolean leaf, boolean expanded,
    boolean selected, Object value) ;
protected TreeModelListener **createTreeModelListener**() ;
public void **expandPath**(TreePath path) ;
public void **expandRow**(int row) ;

public void **fireTreeCollapsed**(TreePath path) ;
public void **fireTreeExpanded**(TreePath path) ;
public void **fireTreeWillCollapse**(TreePath path) throws ExpandVetoException ;
public void **fireTreeWillExpand**(TreePath path) throws ExpandVetoException ;
protected void **fireValueChanged**(TreeSelectionEvent e) ;
public AccessibleContext **getAccessibleContext**() ;
public TreePath **getAnchorSelectionPath**() ; // Since 1.3
public TreeCellEditor **getCellEditor**() ;
public TreeCellRenderer **getCellRenderer**() ;
public TreePath **getClosestPathForLocation**(int y, int x) ;
public int **getClosestRowForLocation**(int y, int x) ;
protected Enumeration<TreePath> **getDescendantToggledPaths**(TreePath parent) ;
public boolean **getDragEnabled**() ; // Since 1.4
public final JTree.DropLocation **getDropLocation**() ; // Since 1.6
public final DropMode **getDropMode**() ; // Since 1.6
public TreePath **getEditingPath**() ;
public Enumeration<TreePath> **getExpandedDescendants**(TreePath parent) ;
public boolean **getExpandsSelectedPaths**() ; // Since 1.3
public boolean **getInvokesStopCellEditing**() ;
public Object **getLastSelectedPathComponent**() ;
public TreePath **getLeadSelectionPath**() ;
public int **getLeadSelectionRow**() ;
public int **getMaxSelectionRow**() ;
public int **getMinSelectionRow**() ;
public TreeModel **getModel**() ;
public TreePath **getNextMatch**(Position.Bias bias, int startingRow, String prefix) ; // Since 1.4
protected TreePath **getPathBetweenRows**(int index1, int index0) ;
public Rectangle **getPathBounds**(TreePath path) ;
public TreePath **getPathForLocation**(int y, int x) ;
public TreePath **getPathForRow**(int row) ;
public Dimension **getPreferredScrollableViewportSize**() ;
public Rectangle **getRowBounds**(int row) ;
public int **getRowCount**() ;
public int **getRowForLocation**(int y, int x) ;
public int **getRowForPath**(TreePath path) ;
public int **getRowHeight**() ;
public int **getScrollableBlockIncrement**(int direction, int orientation, Rectangle visibleRect) ;
public boolean **getScrollableTracksViewportHeight**() ;
public boolean **getScrollableTracksViewportWidth**() ;
public int **getScrollableUnitIncrement**(int direction, int orientation, Rectangle visibleRect) ;
public boolean **getScrollsOnExpand**() ;
public int **getSelectionCount**() ;
public TreeSelectionModel **getSelectionModel**() ;
public TreePath **getSelectionPath**() ;
public TreePath **getSelectionPaths**() ;
public int **getSelectionRows**() ;

public boolean **getShowsRootHandles**() ;
public int **getToggleClickCount**() ; // Since 1.3
public String **getToolTipText**(MouseEvent event) ;
public TreeExpansionListener **getTreeExpansionListeners**() ; // Since 1.4
public TreeSelectionListener **getTreeSelectionListeners**() ; // Since 1.4
public TreeWillExpandListener **getTreeWillExpandListeners**() ; // Since 1.4
public TreeUI **getUI**() ;
public String **getUIClassID**() ;
public int **getVisibleRowCount**() ;
public boolean **hasBeenExpanded**(TreePath path) ;
public boolean **isCollapsed**(TreePath path) ;
public boolean **isCollapsed**(int row) ;
public boolean **isEditable**() ;
public boolean **isEditing**() ;
public boolean **isExpanded**(int row) ;
public boolean **isExpanded**(TreePath path) ;
public boolean **isFixedRowHeight**() ;
public boolean **isLargeModel**() ;
public boolean **isPathEditable**(TreePath path) ;
public boolean **isPathSelected**(TreePath path) ;
public boolean **isRootVisible**() ;
public boolean **isRowSelected**(int row) ;
public boolean **isSelectionEmpty**() ;
public boolean **isVisible**(TreePath path) ;
public void **makeVisible**(TreePath path) ;
protected String **paramString**() ;
protected boolean **removeDescendantSelectedPaths**(boolean includePath, TreePath path) ; // Since 1.3
protected void **removeDescendantToggledPaths**(Enumeration<TreePath> toRemove) ;
public void **removeSelectionInterval**(int index1, int index0) ;
public void **removeSelectionPath**(TreePath path) ;
public void **removeSelectionPaths**(javax.swing.tree.TreePath[] paths) ;
public void **removeSelectionRow**(int row) ;
public void **removeSelectionRows**(int[] rows) ;
public void **removeTreeExpansionListener**(TreeExpansionListener tel) ;
public void **removeTreeSelectionListener**(TreeSelectionListener tsl) ;
public void **removeTreeWillExpandListener**(TreeWillExpandListener tel) ;
public void **scrollPathToVisible**(TreePath path) ;
public void **scrollRowToVisible**(int row) ;
public void **setAnchorSelectionPath**(TreePath newPath) ; // Since 1.3
public void **setCellEditor**(TreeCellEditor cellEditor) ;
public void **setCellRenderer**(TreeCellRenderer x) ;
public void **setDragEnabled**(boolean b) ; // Since 1.4
public final void **setDropMode**(DropMode dropMode) ; // Since 1.6
public void **setEditable**(boolean flag) ;
protected void **setExpandedState**(boolean state, TreePath path) ;

```
    public void setExpandsSelectedPaths(boolean newValue) ; // Since 1.3
    public void setInvokesStopCellEditing(boolean newValue) ;
    public void setLargeModel(boolean newValue) ;
    public void setLeadSelectionPath(TreePath newPath) ; // Since 1.3
    public void setModel(TreeModel newModel) ;
    public void setRootVisible(boolean rootVisible) ;
    public void setRowHeight(int rowHeight) ;
    public void setScrollsOnExpand(boolean newValue) ;
    public void setSelectionInterval(int index1, int index0) ;
    public void setSelectionModel(TreeSelectionModel selectionModel) ;
    public void setSelectionPath(TreePath path) ;
    public void setSelectionPaths(javax.swing.tree.TreePath[] paths) ;
    public void setSelectionRow(int row) ;
    public void setSelectionRows(int[] rows) ;
    public void setShowsRootHandles(boolean newValue) ;
    public void setToggleClickCount(int clickCount) ; // Since 1.3
    public void setUI(TreeUI ui) ;
    public void setVisibleRowCount(int newCount) ;
    public void startEditingAtPath(TreePath path) ;
    public boolean stopEditing() ;
    public void treeDidChange() ;
    public void updateUI() ;
}
```

---

javax.swing.**JTree.DropLocation** [since 1.6]

```
public static final class JTree.DropLocation extends TransferHandler.DropLocation
{
    // Constructors
    private JTree.DropLocation(int index, TreePath path, Point p) ;
    // Instance methods
    public int getChildIndex() ;
    public TreePath getPath() ;
    public String toString() ;
}
```

---

javax.swing.**JTree.DynamicUtilTreeNode**

```
public static class JTree.DynamicUtilTreeNode extends DefaultMutableTreeNode
{
    protected Object childValue ;
```

```
    protected boolean hasChildren ;
    protected boolean loadedChildren ;
    // Constructors
    public JTree.DynamicUtilTreeNode(Object children, Object value) ;
    // Static methods
    public static void createChildren(Object children, DefaultMutableTreeNode parent) ;
    // Instance methods
    public Enumeration children() ;
    public TreeNode getChildAt(int index) ;
    public int getChildCount() ;
    public boolean isLeaf() ;
    protected void loadChildren() ;
}
```

javax.swing.**JViewport**

public class **JViewport** extends JComponent implements Accessible
```
{
    public static final int BACKINGSTORE_SCROLL_MODE ;
    public static final int BLIT_SCROLL_MODE ;
    public static final int SIMPLE_SCROLL_MODE ;
    protected boolean backingStore ;
    protected transient Image backingStoreImage ;
    protected boolean isViewSizeSet ;
    protected Point lastPaintPosition ;
    protected boolean scrollUnderway ;
    // Constructors
    public JViewport() ;
    // Instance methods
    public void addChangeListener(ChangeListener l) ;
    protected void addImpl(int index, Object constraints, Component child) ;
    protected boolean computeBlit(Rectangle blitPaint, Dimension blitSize, Point blitTo, Point blitFrom,
        int dy, int dx) ;
    protected LayoutManager createLayoutManager() ;
    protected JViewport.ViewListener createViewListener() ;
    protected void firePropertyChange(Object newValue, Object oldValue, String propertyName) ;
    protected void fireStateChanged() ;
    public AccessibleContext getAccessibleContext() ;
    public ChangeListener getChangeListeners() ; // Since 1.4
    public Dimension getExtentSize() ;
    public final Insets getInsets(Insets insets) ;
    public final Insets getInsets() ;
    public int getScrollMode() ; // Since 1.3
    public ViewportUI getUI() ; // Since 1.3
```

```
    public String getUIClassID() ;
    public Component getView() ;
    public Point getViewPosition() ;
    public Rectangle getViewRect() ;
    public Dimension getViewSize() ;
    public boolean isBackingStoreEnabled() ;
    public boolean isOptimizedDrawingEnabled() ;
    public void paint(Graphics g) ;
    protected String paramString() ;
    public void remove(Component child) ;
    public void removeChangeListener(ChangeListener l) ;
    public void repaint(int h, int w, int y, int x, long tm) ;
    public void reshape(int h, int w, int y, int x) ;
    public void scrollRectToVisible(Rectangle contentRect) ;
    public void setBackingStoreEnabled(boolean enabled) ;
    public final void setBorder(Border border) ;
    public void setExtentSize(Dimension newExtent) ;
    public void setScrollMode(int mode) ; // Since 1.3
    public void setUI(ViewportUI ui) ; // Since 1.3
    public void setView(Component view) ;
    public void setViewPosition(Point p) ;
    public void setViewSize(Dimension newSize) ;
    public Point toViewCoordinates(Point p) ;
    public Dimension toViewCoordinates(Dimension size) ;
    public void updateUI() ;
}
```

javax.swing.**JWindow**

public class **JWindow** extends Window implements TransferHandler.HasGetTransferHandler, RootPaneContainer, Accessible

```
{
    protected AccessibleContext accessibleContext ;
    protected JRootPane rootPane ;
    protected boolean rootPaneCheckingEnabled ;
    // Constructors
    public JWindow(GraphicsConfiguration gc, Window owner) ;
    public JWindow(Window owner) ;
    public JWindow(Frame owner) ;
    public JWindow(GraphicsConfiguration gc) ;
    public JWindow() ;
    // Instance methods
    protected void addImpl(int index, Object constraints, Component comp) ;
    protected JRootPane createRootPane() ;
```

```
    public AccessibleContext getAccessibleContext() ;
    public Container getContentPane() ;
    public Component getGlassPane() ;
    public Graphics getGraphics() ; // Since 1.6
    public JLayeredPane getLayeredPane() ;
    public JRootPane getRootPane() ;
    public TransferHandler getTransferHandler() ; // Since 1.6
    protected boolean isRootPaneCheckingEnabled() ;
    protected String paramString() ;
    public void remove(Component comp) ;
    public void repaint(int height, int width, int y, int x, long time) ; // Since 1.6
    public void setContentPane(Container contentPane) ;
    public void setGlassPane(Component glassPane) ;
    public void setLayeredPane(JLayeredPane layeredPane) ;
    public void setLayout(LayoutManager manager) ;
    protected void setRootPane(JRootPane root) ;
    protected void setRootPaneCheckingEnabled(boolean enabled) ;
    public void setTransferHandler(TransferHandler newHandler) ; // Since 1.6
    public void update(Graphics g) ;
    protected void windowInit() ;
}
```

java.awt.image.**Kernel**

```
public class Kernel  implements Cloneable
{
    // Constructors
    public Kernel(float[] data, int height, int width) ;
    // Static methods
    // Instance methods
    public Object clone() ;
    public final int getHeight() ;
    public final float getKernelData(float[] data) ;
    public final int getWidth() ;
    public final int getXOrigin() ;
    public final int getYOrigin() ;
}
```

java.awt.event.**KeyAdapter** [since 1.1]

public abstract class **KeyAdapter** implements KeyListener
{
    // Constructors
    public **KeyAdapter**() ;
    // Instance methods
    public void **keyPressed**(KeyEvent e) ;
    public void **keyReleased**(KeyEvent e) ;
    public void **keyTyped**(KeyEvent e) ;
}

java.awt.**KeyboardFocusManager** [since 1.4]

public abstract class **KeyboardFocusManager** implements KeyEventPostProcessor, KeyEventDispatcher
{
    public static final int **BACKWARD_TRAVERSAL_KEYS** ;
    public static final int **DOWN_CYCLE_TRAVERSAL_KEYS** ;
    public static final int **FORWARD_TRAVERSAL_KEYS** ;
    public static final int **UP_CYCLE_TRAVERSAL_KEYS** ;
    // Constructors
    public **KeyboardFocusManager**() ;
    // Static methods
    public static KeyboardFocusManager **getCurrentKeyboardFocusManager**() ;
    public static void **setCurrentKeyboardFocusManager**(KeyboardFocusManager newManager)
        throws SecurityException ;
    // Instance methods
    public void **addKeyEventDispatcher**(KeyEventDispatcher dispatcher) ;
    public void **addKeyEventPostProcessor**(KeyEventPostProcessor processor) ;
    public void **addPropertyChangeListener**(PropertyChangeListener listener) ;
    public void **addPropertyChangeListener**(PropertyChangeListener listener, String propertyName) ;
    public void **addVetoableChangeListener**(VetoableChangeListener listener) ;
    public void **addVetoableChangeListener**(VetoableChangeListener listener, String propertyName) ;
    public void **clearGlobalFocusOwner**() ;
    protected abstract void **dequeueKeyEvents**(Component untilFocused, long after) ;
    protected abstract void **discardKeyEvents**(Component comp) ;
    public abstract boolean **dispatchEvent**(AWTEvent e) ;
    public abstract boolean **dispatchKeyEvent**(KeyEvent e) ;
    public abstract void **downFocusCycle**(Container aContainer) ;

public final void **downFocusCycle**() ;
protected abstract void **enqueueKeyEvents**(Component untilFocused, long after) ;
protected void **firePropertyChange**(Object newValue, Object oldValue, String propertyName) ;
protected void **fireVetoableChange**(Object newValue, Object oldValue, String propertyName)
    throws PropertyVetoException ;
public abstract void **focusNextComponent**(Component aComponent) ;
public final void **focusNextComponent**() ;
public abstract void **focusPreviousComponent**(Component aComponent) ;
public final void **focusPreviousComponent**() ;
public Window **getActiveWindow**() ;
public Container **getCurrentFocusCycleRoot**() ;
public Set<AWTKeyStroke> **getDefaultFocusTraversalKeys**(int id) ;
public synchronized FocusTraversalPolicy **getDefaultFocusTraversalPolicy**() ;
public Window **getFocusedWindow**() ;
public Component **getFocusOwner**() ;
protected Window **getGlobalActiveWindow**() throws SecurityException ;
protected Container **getGlobalCurrentFocusCycleRoot**() throws SecurityException ;
protected Window **getGlobalFocusedWindow**() throws SecurityException ;
protected Component **getGlobalFocusOwner**() throws SecurityException ;
protected Component **getGlobalPermanentFocusOwner**() throws SecurityException ;
protected synchronized List<KeyEventDispatcher> **getKeyEventDispatchers**() ;
protected List<KeyEventPostProcessor> **getKeyEventPostProcessors**() ;
public Component **getPermanentFocusOwner**() ;
public synchronized PropertyChangeListener **getPropertyChangeListeners**() ; // Since 1.4
public synchronized PropertyChangeListener **getPropertyChangeListeners**(String propertyName) ;
    // Since 1.4
public synchronized VetoableChangeListener **getVetoableChangeListeners**(String propertyName) ;
    // Since 1.4
public synchronized VetoableChangeListener **getVetoableChangeListeners**() ; // Since 1.4
public abstract boolean **postProcessKeyEvent**(KeyEvent e) ;
public abstract void **processKeyEvent**(KeyEvent e, Component focusedComponent) ;
public final void **redispatchEvent**(AWTEvent e, Component target) ;
public void **removeKeyEventDispatcher**(KeyEventDispatcher dispatcher) ;
public void **removeKeyEventPostProcessor**(KeyEventPostProcessor processor) ;
public void **removePropertyChangeListener**(PropertyChangeListener listener, String
    propertyName) ;
public void **removePropertyChangeListener**(PropertyChangeListener listener) ;
public void **removeVetoableChangeListener**(VetoableChangeListener listener, String
    propertyName) ;
public void **removeVetoableChangeListener**(VetoableChangeListener listener) ;
public void **setDefaultFocusTraversalKeys**(Set<?> keystrokes, int id) ;
public void **setDefaultFocusTraversalPolicy**(FocusTraversalPolicy defaultPolicy) ;
protected void **setGlobalActiveWindow**(Window activeWindow) ;
public void **setGlobalCurrentFocusCycleRoot**(Container newFocusCycleRoot) ;
protected void **setGlobalFocusedWindow**(Window focusedWindow) ;
protected void **setGlobalFocusOwner**(Component focusOwner) ;

```
    protected void setGlobalPermanentFocusOwner(Component permanentFocusOwner) ;
    public final void upFocusCycle() ;
    public abstract void upFocusCycle(Component aComponent) ;
}
```

---

java.awt.peer.**KeyboardFocusManagerPeer**

```
public interface KeyboardFocusManagerPeer
{
    // Instance methods
    public void clearGlobalFocusOwner(Window activeWindow) ;
    public Window getCurrentFocusedWindow() ;
    public Component getCurrentFocusOwner() ;
    public void setCurrentFocusOwner(Component comp) ;
}
```

---

java.awt.event.**KeyEvent** [since 1.1]

```
public class KeyEvent extends InputEvent
{
    public static final char CHAR_UNDEFINED ;
    public static final int KEY_FIRST ;
    public static final int KEY_LAST ;
    public static final int KEY_LOCATION_LEFT ;
    public static final int KEY_LOCATION_NUMPAD ;
    public static final int KEY_LOCATION_RIGHT ;
    public static final int KEY_LOCATION_STANDARD ;
    public static final int KEY_LOCATION_UNKNOWN ;
    public static final int KEY_PRESSED ;
    public static final int KEY_RELEASED ;
    public static final int KEY_TYPED ;
    public static final int VK_0 ;
    public static final int VK_1 ;
    public static final int VK_2 ;
    public static final int VK_3 ;
    public static final int VK_4 ;
    public static final int VK_5 ;
    public static final int VK_6 ;
    public static final int VK_7 ;
    public static final int VK_8 ;
    public static final int VK_9 ;
```

---

public static final int **VK_A** ;
public static final int **VK_ACCEPT** ;
public static final int **VK_ADD** ;
public static final int **VK_AGAIN** ;
public static final int **VK_ALL_CANDIDATES** ;
public static final int **VK_ALPHANUMERIC** ;
public static final int **VK_ALT** ;
public static final int **VK_ALT_GRAPH** ;
public static final int **VK_AMPERSAND** ;
public static final int **VK_ASTERISK** ;
public static final int **VK_AT** ;
public static final int **VK_B** ;
public static final int **VK_BACK_QUOTE** ;
public static final int **VK_BACK_SLASH** ;
public static final int **VK_BACK_SPACE** ;
public static final int **VK_BEGIN** ;
public static final int **VK_BRACELEFT** ;
public static final int **VK_BRACERIGHT** ;
public static final int **VK_C** ;
public static final int **VK_CANCEL** ;
public static final int **VK_CAPS_LOCK** ;
public static final int **VK_CIRCUMFLEX** ;
public static final int **VK_CLEAR** ;
public static final int **VK_CLOSE_BRACKET** ;
public static final int **VK_CODE_INPUT** ;
public static final int **VK_COLON** ;
public static final int **VK_COMMA** ;
public static final int **VK_COMPOSE** ;
public static final int **VK_CONTEXT_MENU** ;
public static final int **VK_CONTROL** ;
public static final int **VK_CONVERT** ;
public static final int **VK_COPY** ;
public static final int **VK_CUT** ;
public static final int **VK_D** ;
public static final int **VK_DEAD_ABOVEDOT** ;
public static final int **VK_DEAD_ABOVERING** ;
public static final int **VK_DEAD_ACUTE** ;
public static final int **VK_DEAD_BREVE** ;
public static final int **VK_DEAD_CARON** ;
public static final int **VK_DEAD_CEDILLA** ;
public static final int **VK_DEAD_CIRCUMFLEX** ;
public static final int **VK_DEAD_DIAERESIS** ;
public static final int **VK_DEAD_DOUBLEACUTE** ;
public static final int **VK_DEAD_GRAVE** ;
public static final int **VK_DEAD_IOTA** ;
public static final int **VK_DEAD_MACRON** ;

```
public static final int VK_DEAD_OGONEK ;
public static final int VK_DEAD_SEMIVOICED_SOUND ;
public static final int VK_DEAD_TILDE ;
public static final int VK_DEAD_VOICED_SOUND ;
public static final int VK_DECIMAL ;
public static final int VK_DELETE ;
public static final int VK_DIVIDE ;
public static final int VK_DOLLAR ;
public static final int VK_DOWN ;
public static final int VK_E ;
public static final int VK_END ;
public static final int VK_ENTER ;
public static final int VK_EQUALS ;
public static final int VK_ESCAPE ;
public static final int VK_EURO_SIGN ;
public static final int VK_EXCLAMATION_MARK ;
public static final int VK_F ;
public static final int VK_F1 ;
public static final int VK_F10 ;
public static final int VK_F11 ;
public static final int VK_F12 ;
public static final int VK_F13 ;
public static final int VK_F14 ;
public static final int VK_F15 ;
public static final int VK_F16 ;
public static final int VK_F17 ;
public static final int VK_F18 ;
public static final int VK_F19 ;
public static final int VK_F2 ;
public static final int VK_F20 ;
public static final int VK_F21 ;
public static final int VK_F22 ;
public static final int VK_F23 ;
public static final int VK_F24 ;
public static final int VK_F3 ;
public static final int VK_F4 ;
public static final int VK_F5 ;
public static final int VK_F6 ;
public static final int VK_F7 ;
public static final int VK_F8 ;
public static final int VK_F9 ;
public static final int VK_FINAL ;
public static final int VK_FIND ;
public static final int VK_FULL_WIDTH ;
public static final int VK_G ;
public static final int VK_GREATER ;
```

public static final int **VK_H** ;
public static final int **VK_HALF_WIDTH** ;
public static final int **VK_HELP** ;
public static final int **VK_HIRAGANA** ;
public static final int **VK_HOME** ;
public static final int **VK_I** ;
public static final int **VK_INPUT_METHOD_ON_OFF** ;
public static final int **VK_INSERT** ;
public static final int **VK_INVERTED_EXCLAMATION_MARK** ;
public static final int **VK_J** ;
public static final int **VK_JAPANESE_HIRAGANA** ;
public static final int **VK_JAPANESE_KATAKANA** ;
public static final int **VK_JAPANESE_ROMAN** ;
public static final int **VK_K** ;
public static final int **VK_KANA** ;
public static final int **VK_KANA_LOCK** ;
public static final int **VK_KANJI** ;
public static final int **VK_KATAKANA** ;
public static final int **VK_KP_DOWN** ;
public static final int **VK_KP_LEFT** ;
public static final int **VK_KP_RIGHT** ;
public static final int **VK_KP_UP** ;
public static final int **VK_L** ;
public static final int **VK_LEFT** ;
public static final int **VK_LEFT_PARENTHESIS** ;
public static final int **VK_LESS** ;
public static final int **VK_M** ;
public static final int **VK_META** ;
public static final int **VK_MINUS** ;
public static final int **VK_MODECHANGE** ;
public static final int **VK_MULTIPLY** ;
public static final int **VK_N** ;
public static final int **VK_NONCONVERT** ;
public static final int **VK_NUMBER_SIGN** ;
public static final int **VK_NUMPAD0** ;
public static final int **VK_NUMPAD1** ;
public static final int **VK_NUMPAD2** ;
public static final int **VK_NUMPAD3** ;
public static final int **VK_NUMPAD4** ;
public static final int **VK_NUMPAD5** ;
public static final int **VK_NUMPAD6** ;
public static final int **VK_NUMPAD7** ;
public static final int **VK_NUMPAD8** ;
public static final int **VK_NUMPAD9** ;
public static final int **VK_NUM_LOCK** ;
public static final int **VK_O** ;

public static final int **VK_OPEN_BRACKET** ;
public static final int **VK_P** ;
public static final int **VK_PAGE_DOWN** ;
public static final int **VK_PAGE_UP** ;
public static final int **VK_PASTE** ;
public static final int **VK_PAUSE** ;
public static final int **VK_PERIOD** ;
public static final int **VK_PLUS** ;
public static final int **VK_PREVIOUS_CANDIDATE** ;
public static final int **VK_PRINTSCREEN** ;
public static final int **VK_PROPS** ;
public static final int **VK_Q** ;
public static final int **VK_QUOTE** ;
public static final int **VK_QUOTEDBL** ;
public static final int **VK_R** ;
public static final int **VK_RIGHT** ;
public static final int **VK_RIGHT_PARENTHESIS** ;
public static final int **VK_ROMAN_CHARACTERS** ;
public static final int **VK_S** ;
public static final int **VK_SCROLL_LOCK** ;
public static final int **VK_SEMICOLON** ;
public static final int **VK_SEPARATER** ;
public static final int **VK_SEPARATOR** ;
public static final int **VK_SHIFT** ;
public static final int **VK_SLASH** ;
public static final int **VK_SPACE** ;
public static final int **VK_STOP** ;
public static final int **VK_SUBTRACT** ;
public static final int **VK_T** ;
public static final int **VK_TAB** ;
public static final int **VK_U** ;
public static final int **VK_UNDEFINED** ;
public static final int **VK_UNDERSCORE** ;
public static final int **VK_UNDO** ;
public static final int **VK_UP** ;
public static final int **VK_V** ;
public static final int **VK_W** ;
public static final int **VK_WINDOWS** ;
public static final int **VK_X** ;
public static final int **VK_Y** ;
public static final int **VK_Z** ;
// Constructors
public **KeyEvent**(int keyCode, int modifiers, long when, int id, Component source) ;
public **KeyEvent**(char keyChar, int keyCode, int modifiers, long when, int id, Component source) ;
public **KeyEvent**(int keyLocation, char keyChar, int keyCode, int modifiers, long when, int id,
    Component source) ;

```
    private KeyEvent(boolean isProxyActive, int keyLocation, char keyChar, int keyCode, int modifiers,
        long when, int id, Component source) ;
    // Static methods
    public static String getKeyModifiersText(int modifiers) ;
    public static String getKeyText(int keyCode) ;
    // Instance methods
    public char getKeyChar() ;
    public int getKeyCode() ;
    public int getKeyLocation() ; // Since 1.4
    public boolean isActionKey() ;
    public String paramString() ;
    public void setKeyChar(char keyChar) ;
    public void setKeyCode(int keyCode) ;
    public void setModifiers(int modifiers) ;
}
```

java.awt.**KeyEventDispatcher** [since 1.4]

```
public interface KeyEventDispatcher
{
    // Instance methods
    public boolean dispatchKeyEvent(KeyEvent e) ;
}
```

java.awt.**KeyEventPostProcessor** [since 1.4]

```
public interface KeyEventPostProcessor
{
    // Instance methods
    public boolean postProcessKeyEvent(KeyEvent e) ;
}
```

java.awt.event.**KeyListener** [since 1.1]

```
public interface KeyListener  implements EventListener
{
    // Instance methods
    public void keyPressed(KeyEvent e) ;
```

```
    public void keyReleased(KeyEvent e) ;
    public void keyTyped(KeyEvent e) ;
}
```

javax.swing.text.**Keymap**

```
public interface Keymap
{
    // Instance methods
    public void addActionForKeyStroke(Action a, KeyStroke key) ;
    public Action getAction(KeyStroke key) ;
    public Action getBoundActions() ;
    public KeyStroke getBoundKeyStrokes() ;
    public Action getDefaultAction() ;
    public KeyStroke getKeyStrokesForAction(Action a) ;
    public String getName() ;
    public Keymap getResolveParent() ;
    public boolean isLocallyDefined(KeyStroke key) ;
    public void removeBindings() ;
    public void removeKeyStrokeBinding(KeyStroke keys) ;
    public void setDefaultAction(Action a) ;
    public void setResolveParent(Keymap parent) ;
}
```

javax.swing.**KeyStroke**

```
public class KeyStroke extends AWTKeyStroke
{
    // Constructors
    private KeyStroke(boolean onKeyRelease, int modifiers, int keyCode, char keyChar) ;
    private KeyStroke() ;
    // Static methods
    public static KeyStroke getKeyStroke(String s) ;
    public static KeyStroke getKeyStroke(int modifiers, int keyCode) ;
    public static KeyStroke getKeyStroke(boolean onKeyRelease, int modifiers, int keyCode) ;
    public static KeyStroke getKeyStroke(int modifiers, Character keyChar) ; // Since 1.3
    public static KeyStroke getKeyStroke(boolean onKeyRelease, char keyChar) ;
    public static KeyStroke getKeyStroke(char keyChar) ;
    public static KeyStroke getKeyStrokeForEvent(KeyEvent anEvent) ;
}
```

java.awt.**Label** [since 1.0]

public class **Label** extends Component implements Accessible
{
    public static final int **CENTER** ;
    public static final int **LEFT** ;
    public static final int **RIGHT** ;
    // Constructors
    public **Label**(int alignment, String text) ;
    public **Label**(String text) ;
    public **Label**() ;
    // Static methods
    // Instance methods
    public void **addNotify**() ;
    public AccessibleContext **getAccessibleContext**() ; // Since 1.3
    public int **getAlignment**() ;
    public String **getText**() ;
    protected String **paramString**() ;
    public synchronized void **setAlignment**(int alignment) ;
    public void **setText**(String text) ;
}

java.awt.peer.**LabelPeer**

public interface **LabelPeer** implements ComponentPeer
{
    // Instance methods
    public void **setAlignment**(int alignment) ;
    public void **setText**(String label) ;
}

javax.swing.plaf.**LabelUI**

public abstract class **LabelUI** extends ComponentUI
{
    // Constructors
    public **LabelUI**() ;
}

javax.swing.text.**LabelView**

public class **LabelView** extends GlyphView implements TabableView
{
    // Constructors
    public **LabelView**(Element elem) ;
    // Instance methods
    public void **changedUpdate**(ViewFactory f, Shape a, DocumentEvent e) ;
    public Color **getBackground**() ; // Since 1.3
    public Font **getFont**() ;
    protected FontMetrics **getFontMetrics**() ;
    public Color **getForeground**() ; // Since 1.3
    public boolean **isStrikeThrough**() ; // Since 1.3
    public boolean **isSubscript**() ; // Since 1.3
    public boolean **isSuperscript**() ; // Since 1.3
    public boolean **isUnderline**() ; // Since 1.3
    protected void **setBackground**(Color bg) ; // Since 1.5
    protected void **setPropertiesFromAttributes**() ;
    protected void **setStrikeThrough**(boolean s) ;
    protected void **setSubscript**(boolean s) ;
    protected void **setSuperscript**(boolean s) ;
    protected void **setUnderline**(boolean u) ;
}

javax.swing.text.**LayeredHighlighter**

public abstract class **LayeredHighlighter** implements Highlighter
{
    // Constructors
    public **LayeredHighlighter**() ;
    // Instance methods
    public abstract void **paintLayeredHighlights**(View view, JTextComponent editor, Shape
        viewBounds, int p1, int p0, Graphics g) ;
}

---

javax.swing.text.**LayeredHighlighter.LayerPainter**

---

public abstract static class **LayeredHighlighter.LayerPainter** implements Highlighter.HighlightPainter
{
    // Constructors
    public **LayeredHighlighter.LayerPainter**() ;
    // Instance methods
    public abstract Shape **paintLayer**(View view, JTextComponent editor, Shape viewBounds, int p1, int
        p0, Graphics g) ;
}

---

javax.swing.**LayoutFocusTraversalPolicy** [since 1.4]

---

public class **LayoutFocusTraversalPolicy** extends SortingFocusTraversalPolicy implements Serializable
{
    // Constructors
    private **LayoutFocusTraversalPolicy**(Comparator c) ;
    public **LayoutFocusTraversalPolicy**() ;
    // Instance methods
    protected boolean **accept**(Component aComponent) ;
    public Component **getComponentAfter**(Component aComponent, Container aContainer) ;
    public Component **getComponentBefore**(Component aComponent, Container aContainer) ;
    public Component **getFirstComponent**(Container aContainer) ;
    public Component **getLastComponent**(Container aContainer) ;
}

---

java.awt.**LayoutManager**

---

public interface **LayoutManager**
{
    // Instance methods
    public void **addLayoutComponent**(Component comp, String name) ;
    public void **layoutContainer**(Container parent) ;
    public Dimension **minimumLayoutSize**(Container parent) ;
    public Dimension **preferredLayoutSize**(Container parent) ;
    public void **removeLayoutComponent**(Component comp) ;
}

java.awt.**LayoutManager2**

public interface **LayoutManager2** implements LayoutManager
{
    // Instance methods
    public void **addLayoutComponent**(Object constraints, Component comp) ;
    public float **getLayoutAlignmentX**(Container target) ;
    public float **getLayoutAlignmentY**(Container target) ;
    public void **invalidateLayout**(Container target) ;
    public Dimension **maximumLayoutSize**(Container target) ;
}

java.awt.font.**LayoutPath** [since 1.6]

public abstract class **LayoutPath**
{
    // Constructors
    public **LayoutPath**() ;
    // Instance methods
    public abstract void **pathToPoint**(Point2D point, boolean preceding, Point2D location) ; // Since 1.6
    public abstract boolean **pointToPath**(Point2D location, Point2D point) ; // Since 1.6
}

javax.swing.text.**LayoutQueue** [since 1.3]

public class **LayoutQueue**
{
    // Constructors
    public **LayoutQueue**() ;
    // Static methods
    public static LayoutQueue **getDefaultQueue**() ;
    public static void **setDefaultQueue**(LayoutQueue q) ;
    // Instance methods
    public synchronized void **addTask**(Runnable task) ;
    protected synchronized Runnable **waitForWork**() ;
}

---

javax.swing.**LayoutStyle** [since 1.6]

---

public abstract class **LayoutStyle**
{
    // Constructors
    public **LayoutStyle**() ;
    // Static methods
    public static LayoutStyle **getInstance**() ;
    public static void **setInstance**(LayoutStyle style) ;
    // Instance methods
    public abstract int **getContainerGap**(Container parent, int position, JComponent component) ;
    public abstract int **getPreferredGap**(Container parent, int position,
        LayoutStyle.ComponentPlacement type, JComponent component2, JComponent component1) ; //
        Since 1.6
}

---

javax.swing.**LayoutStyle.ComponentPlacement** [since 1.6]

---

public static final class **LayoutStyle.ComponentPlacement** extends
Enum<LayoutStyle.ComponentPlacement>
{
    // Constructors
    private **LayoutStyle.ComponentPlacement**() ;
    // Static methods
    public static LayoutStyle.ComponentPlacement **valueOf**(String name) ;
    public static final LayoutStyle.ComponentPlacement **values**() ;
}

---

java.awt.geom.**Line2D** [since 1.2]

---

public abstract class **Line2D** implements Cloneable, Shape
{
    // Constructors
    protected **Line2D**() ;
    // Static methods
    public static boolean **linesIntersect**(double y4, double x4, double y3, double x3, double y2, double
        x2, double y1, double x1) ; // Since 1.2

public static double **ptLineDist**(double py, double px, double y2, double x2, double y1, double x1) ; // Since 1.2

public static double **ptLineDistSq**(double py, double px, double y2, double x2, double y1, double x1) ; // Since 1.2

public static double **ptSegDist**(double py, double px, double y2, double x2, double y1, double x1) ; // Since 1.2

public static double **ptSegDistSq**(double py, double px, double y2, double x2, double y1, double x1) ; // Since 1.2

public static int **relativeCCW**(double py, double px, double y2, double x2, double y1, double x1) ; // Since 1.2

// Instance methods

public Object **clone**() ; // Since 1.2

public boolean **contains**(double y, double x) ; // Since 1.2

public boolean **contains**(Point2D p) ; // Since 1.2

public boolean **contains**(double h, double w, double y, double x) ; // Since 1.2

public boolean **contains**(Rectangle2D r) ; // Since 1.2

public Rectangle **getBounds**() ; // Since 1.2

public abstract Point2D **getP1**() ; // Since 1.2

public abstract Point2D **getP2**() ; // Since 1.2

public PathIterator **getPathIterator**(AffineTransform at) ; // Since 1.2

public PathIterator **getPathIterator**(double flatness, AffineTransform at) ; // Since 1.2

public abstract double **getX1**() ; // Since 1.2

public abstract double **getX2**() ; // Since 1.2

public abstract double **getY1**() ; // Since 1.2

public abstract double **getY2**() ; // Since 1.2

public boolean **intersects**(Rectangle2D r) ; // Since 1.2

public boolean **intersects**(double h, double w, double y, double x) ; // Since 1.2

public boolean **intersectsLine**(double y2, double x2, double y1, double x1) ; // Since 1.2

public boolean **intersectsLine**(Line2D l) ; // Since 1.2

public double **ptLineDist**(double py, double px) ; // Since 1.2

public double **ptLineDist**(Point2D pt) ; // Since 1.2

public double **ptLineDistSq**(Point2D pt) ; // Since 1.2

public double **ptLineDistSq**(double py, double px) ; // Since 1.2

public double **ptSegDist**(double py, double px) ; // Since 1.2

public double **ptSegDist**(Point2D pt) ; // Since 1.2

public double **ptSegDistSq**(Point2D pt) ; // Since 1.2

public double **ptSegDistSq**(double py, double px) ; // Since 1.2

public int **relativeCCW**(double py, double px) ; // Since 1.2

public int **relativeCCW**(Point2D p) ; // Since 1.2

public void **setLine**(Point2D p2, Point2D p1) ; // Since 1.2

public abstract void **setLine**(double y2, double x2, double y1, double x1) ; // Since 1.2

public void **setLine**(Line2D l) ; // Since 1.2

}

java.awt.geom.**Line2D.Double** [since 1.2]

public static class **Line2D.Double** extends Line2D implements Serializable
{
    public double **x1** ;
    public double **x2** ;
    public double **y1** ;
    public double **y2** ;
    // Constructors
    public **Line2D.Double**(Point2D p2, Point2D p1) ;
    public **Line2D.Double**(double y2, double x2, double y1, double x1) ;
    public **Line2D.Double**() ;
    // Instance methods
    public Rectangle2D **getBounds2D**() ; // Since 1.2
    public Point2D **getP1**() ; // Since 1.2
    public Point2D **getP2**() ; // Since 1.2
    public double **getX1**() ; // Since 1.2
    public double **getX2**() ; // Since 1.2
    public double **getY1**() ; // Since 1.2
    public double **getY2**() ; // Since 1.2
    public void **setLine**(double y2, double x2, double y1, double x1) ; // Since 1.2
}

java.awt.geom.**Line2D.Float** [since 1.2]

public static class **Line2D.Float** extends Line2D implements Serializable
{
    public float **x1** ;
    public float **x2** ;
    public float **y1** ;
    public float **y2** ;
    // Constructors
    public **Line2D.Float**(Point2D p2, Point2D p1) ;
    public **Line2D.Float**(float y2, float x2, float y1, float x1) ;
    public **Line2D.Float**() ;
    // Instance methods
    public Rectangle2D **getBounds2D**() ; // Since 1.2
    public Point2D **getP1**() ; // Since 1.2
    public Point2D **getP2**() ; // Since 1.2
    public double **getX1**() ; // Since 1.2

```
    public double getX2() ; // Since 1.2
    public double getY1() ; // Since 1.2
    public double getY2() ; // Since 1.2
    public void setLine(float y2, float x2, float y1, float x1) ; // Since 1.2
    public void setLine(double y2, double x2, double y1, double x1) ; // Since 1.2
}
```

---

java.awt.**LinearGradientPaint** [since 1.6]

```
public final class LinearGradientPaint extends MultipleGradientPaint
{
    // Constructors
    public LinearGradientPaint(AffineTransform gradientTransform,
        MultipleGradientPaint.ColorSpaceType colorSpace, MultipleGradientPaint.CycleMethod
        cycleMethod, java.awt.Color[] colors, float[] fractions, Point2D end, Point2D start) ;
    public LinearGradientPaint(MultipleGradientPaint.CycleMethod cycleMethod, java.awt.Color[]
        colors, float[] fractions, Point2D end, Point2D start) ;
    public LinearGradientPaint(java.awt.Color[] colors, float[] fractions, Point2D end, Point2D start) ;
    public LinearGradientPaint(MultipleGradientPaint.CycleMethod cycleMethod, java.awt.Color[]
        colors, float[] fractions, float endY, float endX, float startY, float startX) ;
    public LinearGradientPaint(java.awt.Color[] colors, float[] fractions, float endY, float endX, float
        startY, float startX) ;
    // Instance methods
    public PaintContext createContext(RenderingHints hints, AffineTransform transform, Rectangle2D
        userBounds, Rectangle deviceBounds, ColorModel cm) ;
    public Point2D getEndPoint() ;
    public Point2D getStartPoint() ;
}
```

---

javax.swing.border.**LineBorder**

```
public class LineBorder extends AbstractBorder
{
    protected Color lineColor ;
    protected boolean roundedCorners ;
    protected int thickness ;
    // Constructors
    public LineBorder(boolean roundedCorners, int thickness, Color color) ;
    public LineBorder(int thickness, Color color) ;
    public LineBorder(Color color) ;
    // Static methods
```

---

public static Border **createBlackLineBorder**() ;
public static Border **createGrayLineBorder**() ;
// Instance methods
public Insets **getBorderInsets**(Insets insets, Component c) ;
public Color **getLineColor**() ;
public boolean **getRoundedCorners**() ; // Since 1.3
public int **getThickness**() ;
public boolean **isBorderOpaque**() ;
public void **paintBorder**(int height, int width, int y, int x, Graphics g, Component c) ;
}

---

java.awt.font.**LineBreakMeasurer**

---

public final class **LineBreakMeasurer**
{
    // Constructors
    public **LineBreakMeasurer**(FontRenderContext frc, BreakIterator breakIter,
        AttributedCharacterIterator text) ;
    public **LineBreakMeasurer**(FontRenderContext frc, AttributedCharacterIterator text) ;
    // Instance methods
    public void **deleteChar**(int deletePos, AttributedCharacterIterator newParagraph) ;
    public int **getPosition**() ;
    public void **insertChar**(int insertPos, AttributedCharacterIterator newParagraph) ;
    public TextLayout **nextLayout**(boolean requireNextWord, int offsetLimit, float wrappingWidth) ;
    public TextLayout **nextLayout**(float wrappingWidth) ;
    public int **nextOffset**(boolean requireNextWord, int offsetLimit, float wrappingWidth) ;
    public int **nextOffset**(float wrappingWidth) ;
    public void **setPosition**(int newPosition) ;
}

---

java.awt.font.**LineMetrics**

---

public abstract class **LineMetrics**
{
    // Constructors
    public **LineMetrics**() ;
    // Instance methods
    public abstract float **getAscent**() ;
    public abstract int **getBaselineIndex**() ;
    public abstract float **getBaselineOffsets**() ;
    public abstract float **getDescent**() ;

```
    public abstract float getHeight() ;
    public abstract float getLeading() ;
    public abstract int getNumChars() ;
    public abstract float getStrikethroughOffset() ;
    public abstract float getStrikethroughThickness() ;
    public abstract float getUnderlineOffset() ;
    public abstract float getUnderlineThickness() ;
}
```

java.awt.**List** [since 1.0]

```
public class List extends Component implements Accessible, ItemSelectable
{
    // Constructors
    public List(boolean multipleMode, int rows) ;
    public List(int rows) ;
    public List() ;
    // Instance methods
    public void add(String item) ; // Since 1.1
    public void add(int index, String item) ; // Since 1.1
    public synchronized void addActionListener(ActionListener l) ; // Since 1.1
    public synchronized void addItem(int index, String item) ;
    public void addItem(String item) ;
    public synchronized void addItemListener(ItemListener l) ; // Since 1.1
    public void addNotify() ;
    public boolean allowsMultipleSelections() ;
    public synchronized void clear() ;
    public int countItems() ;
    public void delItem(int position) ;
    public synchronized void delItems(int end, int start) ;
    public synchronized void deselect(int index) ;
    public AccessibleContext getAccessibleContext() ; // Since 1.3
    public synchronized ActionListener getActionListeners() ; // Since 1.4
    public String getItem(int index) ;
    public int getItemCount() ; // Since 1.1
    public synchronized ItemListener getItemListeners() ; // Since 1.4
    public synchronized String getItems() ; // Since 1.1
    public T getListeners(Class<T> listenerType) ; // Since 1.3
    public Dimension getMinimumSize() ; // Since 1.1
    public Dimension getMinimumSize(int rows) ; // Since 1.1
    public Dimension getPreferredSize(int rows) ; // Since 1.1
    public Dimension getPreferredSize() ; // Since 1.1
    public int getRows() ;
    public synchronized int getSelectedIndex() ;
```

```
    public synchronized int getSelectedIndexes() ;
    public synchronized String getSelectedItem() ;
    public synchronized String getSelectedItems() ;
    public Object getSelectedObjects() ;
    public int getVisibleIndex() ;
    public boolean isIndexSelected(int index) ; // Since 1.1
    public boolean isMultipleMode() ; // Since 1.1
    public boolean isSelected(int index) ;
    public synchronized void makeVisible(int index) ;
    public Dimension minimumSize(int rows) ;
    public Dimension minimumSize() ;
    protected String paramString() ;
    public Dimension preferredSize() ;
    public Dimension preferredSize(int rows) ;
    protected void processActionEvent(ActionEvent e) ; // Since 1.1
    protected void processEvent(AWTEvent e) ; // Since 1.1
    protected void processItemEvent(ItemEvent e) ; // Since 1.1
    public void remove(int position) ; // Since 1.1
    public synchronized void remove(String item) ; // Since 1.1
    public synchronized void removeActionListener(ActionListener l) ; // Since 1.1
    public void removeAll() ; // Since 1.1
    public synchronized void removeItemListener(ItemListener l) ; // Since 1.1
    public void removeNotify() ;
    public synchronized void replaceItem(int index, String newValue) ;
    public void select(int index) ;
    public void setMultipleMode(boolean b) ; // Since 1.1
    public synchronized void setMultipleSelections(boolean b) ;
}
```

---

javax.swing.**ListCellRenderer**

```
public interface ListCellRenderer
{
    // Instance methods
    public Component getListCellRendererComponent(boolean cellHasFocus, boolean isSelected, int
        index, Object value, JList list) ;
}
```

javax.swing.event.**ListDataEvent**

public class **ListDataEvent** extends EventObject
{
    public static final int **CONTENTS_CHANGED** ;
    public static final int **INTERVAL_ADDED** ;
    public static final int **INTERVAL_REMOVED** ;
    // Constructors
    public **ListDataEvent**(int index1, int index0, int type, Object source) ;
    // Instance methods
    public int **getIndex0**() ;
    public int **getIndex1**() ;
    public int **getType**() ;
    public String **toString**() ; // Since 1.4
}

javax.swing.event.**ListDataListener**

public interface **ListDataListener** implements EventListener
{
    // Instance methods
    public void **contentsChanged**(ListDataEvent e) ;
    public void **intervalAdded**(ListDataEvent e) ;
    public void **intervalRemoved**(ListDataEvent e) ;
}

javax.swing.**ListModel**

public interface **ListModel**
{
    // Instance methods
    public void **addListDataListener**(ListDataListener l) ;
    public Object **getElementAt**(int index) ;
    public int **getSize**() ;
    public void **removeListDataListener**(ListDataListener l) ;
}

java.awt.peer.**ListPeer**

public interface **ListPeer** implements ComponentPeer
{
    // Instance methods
    public void **add**(int index, String item) ;
    public void **addItem**(int index, String item) ;
    public void **clear**() ;
    public void **delItems**(int end, int start) ;
    public void **deselect**(int index) ;
    public Dimension **getMinimumSize**(int rows) ;
    public Dimension **getPreferredSize**(int rows) ;
    public int **getSelectedIndexes**() ;
    public void **makeVisible**(int index) ;
    public Dimension **minimumSize**(int v) ;
    public Dimension **preferredSize**(int v) ;
    public void **removeAll**() ;
    public void **select**(int index) ;
    public void **setMultipleMode**(boolean b) ;
    public void **setMultipleSelections**(boolean v) ;
}

javax.swing.event.**ListSelectionEvent**

public class **ListSelectionEvent** extends EventObject
{
    // Constructors
    public **ListSelectionEvent**(boolean isAdjusting, int lastIndex, int firstIndex, Object source) ;
    // Instance methods
    public int **getFirstIndex**() ;
    public int **getLastIndex**() ;
    public boolean **getValueIsAdjusting**() ;
    public String **toString**() ;
}

javax.swing.event.**ListSelectionListener**

public interface **ListSelectionListener** implements EventListener

```
{
    // Instance methods
    public void valueChanged(ListSelectionEvent e) ;
}
```

---

javax.swing.**ListSelectionModel**

```
public interface ListSelectionModel
{
    public static final int MULTIPLE_INTERVAL_SELECTION ;
    public static final int SINGLE_INTERVAL_SELECTION ;
    public static final int SINGLE_SELECTION ;
    // Instance methods
    public void addListSelectionListener(ListSelectionListener x) ;
    public void addSelectionInterval(int index1, int index0) ;
    public void clearSelection() ;
    public int getAnchorSelectionIndex() ;
    public int getLeadSelectionIndex() ;
    public int getMaxSelectionIndex() ;
    public int getMinSelectionIndex() ;
    public int getSelectionMode() ;
    public boolean getValueIsAdjusting() ;
    public void insertIndexInterval(boolean before, int length, int index) ;
    public boolean isSelectedIndex(int index) ;
    public boolean isSelectionEmpty() ;
    public void removeIndexInterval(int index1, int index0) ;
    public void removeListSelectionListener(ListSelectionListener x) ;
    public void removeSelectionInterval(int index1, int index0) ;
    public void setAnchorSelectionIndex(int index) ;
    public void setLeadSelectionIndex(int index) ;
    public void setSelectionInterval(int index1, int index0) ;
    public void setSelectionMode(int selectionMode) ;
    public void setValueIsAdjusting(boolean valueIsAdjusting) ;
}
```

---

javax.swing.plaf.**ListUI**

```
public abstract class ListUI extends ComponentUI
{
    // Constructors
    public ListUI() ;
```

```
    // Instance methods
    public abstract Rectangle getCellBounds(int index2, int index1, JList list) ;
    public abstract Point indexToLocation(int index, JList list) ;
    public abstract int locationToIndex(Point location, JList list) ;
}
```

---

javax.swing.text.html.**ListView**

```
public class ListView extends BlockView
{
    // Constructors
    public ListView(Element elem) ;
    // Instance methods
    public float getAlignment(int axis) ;
    public void paint(Shape allocation, Graphics g) ;
    protected void paintChild(int index, Rectangle alloc, Graphics g) ;
    protected void setPropertiesFromAttributes() ;
}
```

---

javax.swing.**LookAndFeel**

```
public abstract class LookAndFeel
{
    // Constructors
    public LookAndFeel() ;
    // Static methods
    public static Object getDesktopPropertyValue(Object fallbackValue, String systemPropertyName) ;
        // Since 1.4
    public static void installBorder(String defaultBorderName, JComponent c) ;
    public static void installColors(String defaultFgName, String defaultBgName, JComponent c) ;
    public static void installColorsAndFont(String defaultFontName, String defaultFgName, String
        defaultBgName, JComponent c) ;
    public static void installProperty(Object propertyValue, String propertyName, JComponent c) ; //
        Since 1.5
    public static void loadKeyBindings(java.lang.Object[] keys, InputMap retMap) ; // Since 1.3
    public static ComponentInputMap makeComponentInputMap(java.lang.Object[] keys, JComponent
        c) ; // Since 1.3
    public static Object makeIcon(String gifFile, Class<?> baseClass) ;
    public static InputMap makeInputMap(java.lang.Object[] keys) ; // Since 1.3
    public static JTextComponent.KeyBinding makeKeyBindings(java.lang.Object[] keyBindingList) ;
    public static void uninstallBorder(JComponent c) ;
```

```
    // Instance methods
    public UIDefaults getDefaults() ;
    public abstract String getDescription() ;
    public Icon getDisabledIcon(Icon icon, JComponent component) ; // Since 1.5
    public Icon getDisabledSelectedIcon(Icon icon, JComponent component) ; // Since 1.5
    public abstract String getID() ;
    public LayoutStyle getLayoutStyle() ; // Since 1.6
    public abstract String getName() ;
    public boolean getSupportsWindowDecorations() ; // Since 1.4
    public void initialize() ;
    public abstract boolean isNativeLookAndFeel() ;
    public abstract boolean isSupportedLookAndFeel() ;
    public void provideErrorFeedback(Component component) ; // Since 1.4
    public String toString() ;
    public void uninitialize() ;
}
```

java.awt.image.**LookupOp**

```
public class LookupOp  implements RasterOp, BufferedImageOp
{
    // Constructors
    public LookupOp(RenderingHints hints, LookupTable lookup) ;
    // Instance methods
    public BufferedImage createCompatibleDestImage(ColorModel destCM, BufferedImage src) ;
    public WritableRaster createCompatibleDestRaster(Raster src) ;
    public final BufferedImage filter(BufferedImage dst, BufferedImage src) ;
    public final WritableRaster filter(WritableRaster dst, Raster src) ;
    public final Rectangle2D getBounds2D(Raster src) ;
    public final Rectangle2D getBounds2D(BufferedImage src) ;
    public final Point2D getPoint2D(Point2D dstPt, Point2D srcPt) ;
    public final RenderingHints getRenderingHints() ;
    public final LookupTable getTable() ;
}
```

java.awt.image.**LookupTable**

```
public abstract class LookupTable
{
    // Constructors
    protected LookupTable(int numComponents, int offset) ;
```

```
    // Instance methods
    public int getNumComponents() ;
    public int getOffset() ;
    public abstract int lookupPixel(int[] dest, int[] src) ;
}
```

```
public class MaskFormatter extends DefaultFormatter
{
    // Constructors
    public MaskFormatter(String mask) ;
    public MaskFormatter() ;
    // Instance methods
    public String getInvalidCharacters() ;
    public String getMask() ;
    public String getPlaceholder() ;
    public char getPlaceholderCharacter() ;
    public String getValidCharacters() ;
    public boolean getValueContainsLiteralCharacters() ;
    public void install(JFormattedTextField ftf) ;
    public void setInvalidCharacters(String invalidCharacters) ;
    public void setMask(String mask) throws ParseException ;
    public void setPlaceholder(String placeholder) ;
    public void setPlaceholderCharacter(char placeholder) ;
    public void setValidCharacters(String validCharacters) ;
    public void setValueContainsLiteralCharacters(boolean containsLiteralChars) ;
    public Object stringToValue(String value) throws ParseException ;
    public String valueToString(Object value) throws ParseException ;
}
```

```
public class MatteBorder extends EmptyBorder
{
    protected Color color ;
    protected Icon tileIcon ;
    // Constructors
    public MatteBorder(Icon tileIcon) ;
    public MatteBorder(Icon tileIcon, Insets borderInsets) ;
    public MatteBorder(Icon tileIcon, int right, int bottom, int left, int top) ;
```

public **MatteBorder**(Color matteColor, Insets borderInsets) ;
public **MatteBorder**(Color matteColor, int right, int bottom, int left, int top) ;
// Instance methods
public Insets **getBorderInsets**() ; // Since 1.3
public Insets **getBorderInsets**(Insets insets, Component c) ; // Since 1.3
public Color **getMatteColor**() ; // Since 1.3
public Icon **getTileIcon**() ; // Since 1.3
public boolean **isBorderOpaque**() ;
public void **paintBorder**(int height, int width, int y, int x, Graphics g, Component c) ;
}

---

java.awt.**MediaTracker** [since 1.0]

---

public class **MediaTracker** implements Serializable
{
    public static final int **ABORTED** ;
    public static final int **COMPLETE** ;
    public static final int **ERRORED** ;
    public static final int **LOADING** ;
    // Constructors
    public **MediaTracker**(Component comp) ;
    // Instance methods
    public void **addImage**(int id, Image image) ;
    public synchronized void **addImage**(int h, int w, int id, Image image) ;
    public boolean **checkAll**() ;
    public boolean **checkAll**(boolean load) ;
    public boolean **checkID**(int id) ;
    public boolean **checkID**(boolean load, int id) ;
    public synchronized Object **getErrorsAny**() ;
    public synchronized Object **getErrorsID**(int id) ;
    public synchronized boolean **isErrorAny**() ;
    public synchronized boolean **isErrorID**(int id) ;
    public synchronized void **removeImage**(int height, int width, int id, Image image) ; // Since 1.1
    public synchronized void **removeImage**(int id, Image image) ; // Since 1.1
    public synchronized void **removeImage**(Image image) ; // Since 1.1
    public int **statusAll**(boolean load) ;
    public int **statusID**(boolean load, int id) ;
    public synchronized boolean **waitForAll**(long ms) throws InterruptedException ;
    public void **waitForAll**() throws InterruptedException ;
    public synchronized boolean **waitForID**(long ms, int id) throws InterruptedException ;
    public void **waitForID**(int id) throws InterruptedException ;
}

java.awt.image.**MemoryImageSource**

public class **MemoryImageSource** implements ImageProducer
{
    // Constructors
    public **MemoryImageSource**(Hashtable<?, ?> props, int scan, int off, int[] pix, int h, int w) ;
    public **MemoryImageSource**(int scan, int off, int[] pix, int h, int w) ;
    public **MemoryImageSource**(Hashtable<?, ?> props, int scan, int off, int[] pix, ColorModel cm, int
        h, int w) ;
    public **MemoryImageSource**(int scan, int off, int[] pix, ColorModel cm, int h, int w) ;
    public **MemoryImageSource**(Hashtable<?, ?> props, int scan, int off, byte[] pix, ColorModel cm, int
        h, int w) ;
    public **MemoryImageSource**(int scan, int off, byte[] pix, ColorModel cm, int h, int w) ;
    // Instance methods
    public synchronized void **addConsumer**(ImageConsumer ic) ;
    public synchronized boolean **isConsumer**(ImageConsumer ic) ;
    public void **newPixels**() ;
    public synchronized void **newPixels**(int h, int w, int y, int x) ;
    public synchronized void **newPixels**(boolean framenotify, int h, int w, int y, int x) ;
    public synchronized void **newPixels**(int scansize, int offset, ColorModel newmodel, byte[] newpix) ;
    public synchronized void **newPixels**(int scansize, int offset, ColorModel newmodel, int[] newpix) ;
    public synchronized void **removeConsumer**(ImageConsumer ic) ;
    public void **requestTopDownLeftRightResend**(ImageConsumer ic) ;
    public synchronized void **setAnimated**(boolean animated) ;
    public synchronized void **setFullBufferUpdates**(boolean fullbuffers) ;
    public void **startProduction**(ImageConsumer ic) ;
}

java.awt.**Menu** [since 1.0]

public class **Menu** extends MenuItem implements Accessible, MenuContainer
{
    // Constructors
    public **Menu**(boolean tearOff, String label) ;
    public **Menu**(String label) ;
    public **Menu**() ;
    // Static methods
    // Instance methods
    public MenuItem **add**(MenuItem mi) ;
    public void **add**(String label) ;
    public void **addNotify**() ;

```
    public void addSeparator() ;
    public int countItems() ;
    public AccessibleContext getAccessibleContext() ; // Since 1.3
    public MenuItem getItem(int index) ;
    public int getItemCount() ; // Since 1.1
    public void insert(int index, MenuItem menuitem) ; // Since 1.1
    public void insert(int index, String label) ; // Since 1.1
    public void insertSeparator(int index) ; // Since 1.1
    public boolean isTearOff() ;
    public String paramString() ;
    public void remove(MenuComponent item) ;
    public void remove(int index) ;
    public void removeAll() ; // Since 1.0.
    public void removeNotify() ;
}
```

java.awt.**MenuBar** [since 1.0]

```
public class MenuBar extends MenuComponent implements Accessible, MenuContainer
{
    // Constructors
    public MenuBar() ;
    // Static methods
    // Instance methods
    public Menu add(Menu m) ;
    public void addNotify() ;
    public int countMenus() ;
    public void deleteShortcut(MenuShortcut s) ; // Since 1.1
    public AccessibleContext getAccessibleContext() ; // Since 1.3
    public Menu getHelpMenu() ;
    public Menu getMenu(int i) ;
    public int getMenuCount() ; // Since 1.1
    public MenuItem getShortcutMenuItem(MenuShortcut s) ; // Since 1.1
    public void remove(int index) ;
    public void remove(MenuComponent m) ;
    public void removeNotify() ;
    public void setHelpMenu(Menu m) ;
    public synchronized Enumeration<MenuShortcut> shortcuts() ; // Since 1.1
}
```

java.awt.peer.**MenuBarPeer**

public interface **MenuBarPeer** implements MenuComponentPeer
{
    // Instance methods
    public void **addHelpMenu**(Menu m) ;
    public void **addMenu**(Menu m) ;
    public void **delMenu**(int index) ;
}

javax.swing.plaf.**MenuBarUI**

public abstract class **MenuBarUI** extends ComponentUI
{
    // Constructors
    public **MenuBarUI**() ;
}

java.awt.**MenuComponent** [since 1.0]

public abstract class **MenuComponent** implements Serializable
{
    // Constructors
    public **MenuComponent**() ;
    // Static methods
    // Instance methods
    public final void **dispatchEvent**(AWTEvent e) ;
    public AccessibleContext **getAccessibleContext**() ; // Since 1.3
    public Font **getFont**() ;
    public String **getName**() ; // Since 1.1
    public MenuContainer **getParent**() ;
    public MenuComponentPeer **getPeer**() ;
    protected final Object **getTreeLock**() ;
    protected String **paramString**() ;
    public boolean **postEvent**(Event evt) ;
    protected void **processEvent**(AWTEvent e) ; // Since 1.1
    public void **removeNotify**() ;

```
    public void setFont(Font f) ;
    public void setName(String name) ; // Since 1.1
    public String toString() ;
}
```

---

java.awt.peer.**MenuComponentPeer**

```
public interface MenuComponentPeer
{
    // Instance methods
    public void dispose() ;
    public void setFont(Font f) ;
}
```

---

java.awt.**MenuContainer**

```
public interface MenuContainer
{
    // Instance methods
    public Font getFont() ;
    public boolean postEvent(Event evt) ;
    public void remove(MenuComponent comp) ;
}
```

---

javax.swing.event.**MenuDragMouseEvent**

```
public class MenuDragMouseEvent extends MouseEvent
{
    // Constructors
    public MenuDragMouseEvent(MenuSelectionManager m, javax.swing.MenuElement[] p, boolean
        popupTrigger, int clickCount, int yAbs, int xAbs, int y, int x, int modifiers, long when, int id,
        Component source) ;
    public MenuDragMouseEvent(MenuSelectionManager m, javax.swing.MenuElement[] p, boolean
        popupTrigger, int clickCount, int y, int x, int modifiers, long when, int id, Component source) ;
    // Instance methods
    public MenuSelectionManager getMenuSelectionManager() ;
    public MenuElement getPath() ;
}
```

---

javax.swing.event.**MenuDragMouseListener**

public interface **MenuDragMouseListener** implements EventListener
{
    // Instance methods
    public void **menuDragMouseDragged**(MenuDragMouseEvent e) ;
    public void **menuDragMouseEntered**(MenuDragMouseEvent e) ;
    public void **menuDragMouseExited**(MenuDragMouseEvent e) ;
    public void **menuDragMouseReleased**(MenuDragMouseEvent e) ;
}

---

javax.swing.**MenuElement**

public interface **MenuElement**
{
    // Instance methods
    public Component **getComponent**() ;
    public MenuElement **getSubElements**() ;
    public void **menuSelectionChanged**(boolean isIncluded) ;
    public void **processKeyEvent**(MenuSelectionManager manager, javax.swing.MenuElement[] path,
        KeyEvent event) ;
    public void **processMouseEvent**(MenuSelectionManager manager, javax.swing.MenuElement[]
        path, MouseEvent event) ;
}

---

javax.swing.event.**MenuEvent**

public class **MenuEvent** extends EventObject
{
    // Constructors
    public **MenuEvent**(Object source) ;
}

java.awt.**MenuItem**

public class **MenuItem** extends MenuComponent implements Accessible
{
    // Constructors
    public **MenuItem**(MenuShortcut s, String label) ;
    public **MenuItem**(String label) ;
    public **MenuItem**() ;
    // Static methods
    // Instance methods
    public synchronized void **addActionListener**(ActionListener l) ; // Since 1.1
    public void **addNotify**() ;
    public void **deleteShortcut**() ; // Since 1.1
    public synchronized void **disable**() ;
    protected final void **disableEvents**(long eventsToDisable) ; // Since 1.1
    public void **enable**(boolean b) ;
    public synchronized void **enable**() ;
    protected final void **enableEvents**(long eventsToEnable) ; // Since 1.1
    public AccessibleContext **getAccessibleContext**() ; // Since 1.3
    public String **getActionCommand**() ; // Since 1.1
    public synchronized ActionListener **getActionListeners**() ; // Since 1.4
    public String **getLabel**() ; // Since 1.0
    public T **getListeners**(Class<T> listenerType) ; // Since 1.3
    public MenuShortcut **getShortcut**() ; // Since 1.1
    public boolean **isEnabled**() ; // Since 1.0
    public String **paramString**() ;
    protected void **processActionEvent**(ActionEvent e) ; // Since 1.1
    protected void **processEvent**(AWTEvent e) ; // Since 1.1
    public synchronized void **removeActionListener**(ActionListener l) ; // Since 1.1
    public void **setActionCommand**(String command) ; // Since 1.1
    public synchronized void **setEnabled**(boolean b) ; // Since 1.1
    public synchronized void **setLabel**(String label) ; // Since 1.0
    public void **setShortcut**(MenuShortcut s) ; // Since 1.1
}

java.awt.peer.**MenuItemPeer**

public interface **MenuItemPeer** implements MenuComponentPeer
{
    // Instance methods

```
    public void disable() ;
    public void enable() ;
    public void setEnabled(boolean b) ;
    public void setLabel(String label) ;
}
```

javax.swing.plaf.**MenuItemUI**

```
public abstract class MenuItemUI extends ButtonUI
{
    // Constructors
    public MenuItemUI() ;
}
```

javax.swing.event.**MenuKeyEvent**

```
public class MenuKeyEvent extends KeyEvent
{
    // Constructors
    public MenuKeyEvent(MenuSelectionManager m, javax.swing.MenuElement[] p, char keyChar, int
        keyCode, int modifiers, long when, int id, Component source) ;
    // Instance methods
    public MenuSelectionManager getMenuSelectionManager() ;
    public MenuElement getPath() ;
}
```

javax.swing.event.**MenuKeyListener**

```
public interface MenuKeyListener  implements EventListener
{
    // Instance methods
    public void menuKeyPressed(MenuKeyEvent e) ;
    public void menuKeyReleased(MenuKeyEvent e) ;
    public void menuKeyTyped(MenuKeyEvent e) ;
}
```

javax.swing.event.**MenuListener**

public interface **MenuListener** implements EventListener
{
    // Instance methods
    public void **menuCanceled**(MenuEvent e) ;
    public void **menuDeselected**(MenuEvent e) ;
    public void **menuSelected**(MenuEvent e) ;
}

java.awt.peer.**MenuPeer**

public interface **MenuPeer** implements MenuItemPeer
{
    // Instance methods
    public void **addItem**(MenuItem item) ;
    public void **addSeparator**() ;
    public void **delItem**(int index) ;
}

javax.swing.**MenuSelectionManager**

public class **MenuSelectionManager**
{
    protected transient ChangeEvent **changeEvent** ;
    protected EventListenerList **listenerList** ;
    // Constructors
    public **MenuSelectionManager**() ;
    // Static methods
    public static MenuSelectionManager **defaultManager**() ;
    // Instance methods
    public void **addChangeListener**(ChangeListener l) ;
    public void **clearSelectedPath**() ;
    public Component **componentForPoint**(Point sourcePoint, Component source) ;
    protected void **fireStateChanged**() ;
    public ChangeListener **getChangeListeners**() ; // Since 1.4
    public MenuElement **getSelectedPath**() ;

```
    public boolean isComponentPartOfCurrentMenu(Component c) ;
    public void processKeyEvent(KeyEvent e) ;
    public void processMouseEvent(MouseEvent event) ;
    public void removeChangeListener(ChangeListener l) ;
    public void setSelectedPath(javax.swing.MenuElement[] path) ;
}
```

java.awt.**MenuShortcut** [since 1.1]

```
public class MenuShortcut  implements Serializable
{
    // Constructors
    public MenuShortcut(boolean useShiftModifier, int key) ;
    public MenuShortcut(int key) ;
    // Instance methods
    public boolean equals(Object obj) ; // Since 1.2
    public boolean equals(MenuShortcut s) ; // Since 1.1
    public int getKey() ; // Since 1.1
    public int hashCode() ; // Since 1.2
    protected String paramString() ; // Since 1.1
    public String toString() ; // Since 1.1
    public boolean usesShiftModifier() ; // Since 1.1
}
```

javax.swing.plaf.metal.**MetalBorders**

```
public class MetalBorders
{
    // Constructors
    public MetalBorders() ;
    // Static methods
    public static Border getButtonBorder() ; // Since 1.3
    public static Border getDesktopIconBorder() ; // Since 1.3
    public static Border getTextBorder() ; // Since 1.3
    public static Border getTextFieldBorder() ; // Since 1.3
    public static Border getToggleButtonBorder() ; // Since 1.3
}
```

javax.swing.plaf.metal.**MetalBorders.ButtonBorder**

public static class **MetalBorders.ButtonBorder** extends AbstractBorder implements UIResource
{
    protected static Insets **borderInsets** ;
    // Constructors
    public **MetalBorders.ButtonBorder**() ;
    // Instance methods
    public Insets **getBorderInsets**(Insets newInsets, Component c) ;
    public void **paintBorder**(int h, int w, int y, int x, Graphics g, Component c) ;
}

javax.swing.plaf.metal.**MetalBorders.Flush3DBorder**

public static class **MetalBorders.Flush3DBorder** extends AbstractBorder implements UIResource
{
    // Constructors
    public **MetalBorders.Flush3DBorder**() ;
    // Instance methods
    public Insets **getBorderInsets**(Insets newInsets, Component c) ;
    public void **paintBorder**(int h, int w, int y, int x, Graphics g, Component c) ;
}

javax.swing.plaf.metal.**MetalBorders.InternalFrameBorder**

public static class **MetalBorders.InternalFrameBorder** extends AbstractBorder implements UIResource
{
    // Constructors
    public **MetalBorders.InternalFrameBorder**() ;
    // Instance methods
    public Insets **getBorderInsets**(Insets newInsets, Component c) ;
    public void **paintBorder**(int h, int w, int y, int x, Graphics g, Component c) ;
}

javax.swing.plaf.metal.**MetalBorders.MenuBarBorder**

public static class **MetalBorders.MenuBarBorder** extends AbstractBorder implements UIResource
{
    protected static Insets **borderInsets** ;
    // Constructors
    public **MetalBorders.MenuBarBorder**() ;
    // Instance methods
    public Insets **getBorderInsets**(Insets newInsets, Component c) ;
    public void **paintBorder**(int h, int w, int y, int x, Graphics g, Component c) ;
}

javax.swing.plaf.metal.**MetalBorders.MenuItemBorder**

public static class **MetalBorders.MenuItemBorder** extends AbstractBorder implements UIResource
{
    protected static Insets **borderInsets** ;
    // Constructors
    public **MetalBorders.MenuItemBorder**() ;
    // Instance methods
    public Insets **getBorderInsets**(Insets newInsets, Component c) ;
    public void **paintBorder**(int h, int w, int y, int x, Graphics g, Component c) ;
}

javax.swing.plaf.metal.**MetalBorders.OptionDialogBorder**

public static class **MetalBorders.OptionDialogBorder** extends AbstractBorder implements UIResource
{
    // Constructors
    public **MetalBorders.OptionDialogBorder**() ;
    // Instance methods
    public Insets **getBorderInsets**(Insets newInsets, Component c) ;
    public void **paintBorder**(int h, int w, int y, int x, Graphics g, Component c) ;
}

javax.swing.plaf.metal.**MetalBorders.PaletteBorder** [since 1.3]

public static class **MetalBorders.PaletteBorder** extends AbstractBorder implements UIResource
{
    // Constructors
    public **MetalBorders.PaletteBorder**() ;
    // Instance methods
    public Insets **getBorderInsets**(Insets newInsets, Component c) ;
    public void **paintBorder**(int h, int w, int y, int x, Graphics g, Component c) ;
}

javax.swing.plaf.metal.**MetalBorders.PopupMenuBorder**

public static class **MetalBorders.PopupMenuBorder** extends AbstractBorder implements UIResource
{
    protected static Insets **borderInsets** ;
    // Constructors
    public **MetalBorders.PopupMenuBorder**() ;
    // Instance methods
    public Insets **getBorderInsets**(Insets newInsets, Component c) ;
    public void **paintBorder**(int h, int w, int y, int x, Graphics g, Component c) ;
}

javax.swing.plaf.metal.**MetalBorders.RolloverButtonBorder**

public static class **MetalBorders.RolloverButtonBorder** extends MetalBorders.ButtonBorder
{
    // Constructors
    public **MetalBorders.RolloverButtonBorder**() ;
    // Instance methods
    public void **paintBorder**(int h, int w, int y, int x, Graphics g, Component c) ;
}

javax.swing.plaf.metal.**MetalBorders.ScrollPaneBorder**

public static class **MetalBorders.ScrollPaneBorder** extends AbstractBorder implements UIResource
{
    // Constructors
    public **MetalBorders.ScrollPaneBorder**() ;
    // Instance methods
    public Insets **getBorderInsets**(Insets insets, Component c) ;
    public void **paintBorder**(int h, int w, int y, int x, Graphics g, Component c) ;
}

javax.swing.plaf.metal.**MetalBorders.TableHeaderBorder** [since 1.3]

public static class **MetalBorders.TableHeaderBorder** extends AbstractBorder
{
    protected Insets **editorBorderInsets** ;
    // Constructors
    public **MetalBorders.TableHeaderBorder**() ;
    // Instance methods
    public Insets **getBorderInsets**(Insets insets, Component c) ;
    public void **paintBorder**(int h, int w, int y, int x, Graphics g, Component c) ;
}

javax.swing.plaf.metal.**MetalBorders.TextFieldBorder**

public static class **MetalBorders.TextFieldBorder** extends MetalBorders.Flush3DBorder
{
    // Constructors
    public **MetalBorders.TextFieldBorder**() ;
    // Instance methods
    public void **paintBorder**(int h, int w, int y, int x, Graphics g, Component c) ;
}

javax.swing.plaf.metal.**MetalBorders.ToggleButtonBorder** [since 1.3]

public static class **MetalBorders.ToggleButtonBorder** extends MetalBorders.ButtonBorder
{
    // Constructors
    public **MetalBorders.ToggleButtonBorder**() ;
    // Instance methods
    public void **paintBorder**(int h, int w, int y, int x, Graphics g, Component c) ;
}

javax.swing.plaf.metal.**MetalBorders.ToolBarBorder**

public static class **MetalBorders.ToolBarBorder** extends AbstractBorder implements SwingConstants, UIResource
{
    protected MetalBumps **bumps** ;
    // Constructors
    public **MetalBorders.ToolBarBorder**() ;
    // Instance methods
    public Insets **getBorderInsets**(Insets newInsets, Component c) ;
    public void **paintBorder**(int h, int w, int y, int x, Graphics g, Component c) ;
}

javax.swing.plaf.metal.**MetalButtonUI**

public class **MetalButtonUI** extends BasicButtonUI
{
    protected Color **disabledTextColor** ;
    protected Color **focusColor** ;
    protected Color **selectColor** ;
    // Constructors
    public **MetalButtonUI**() ;
    // Static methods
    public static ComponentUI **createUI**(JComponent c) ;
    // Instance methods
    protected BasicButtonListener **createButtonListener**(AbstractButton b) ;
    protected Color **getDisabledTextColor**() ;

```
    protected Color getFocusColor() ;
    protected Color getSelectColor() ;
    public void installDefaults(AbstractButton b) ;
    protected void paintButtonPressed(AbstractButton b, Graphics g) ;
    protected void paintFocus(Rectangle iconRect, Rectangle textRect, Rectangle viewRect,
        AbstractButton b, Graphics g) ;
    protected void paintText(String text, Rectangle textRect, JComponent c, Graphics g) ;
    public void uninstallDefaults(AbstractButton b) ;
    public void update(JComponent c, Graphics g) ; // Since 1.5
}
```

javax.swing.plaf.metal.**MetalCheckBoxIcon**

```
public class MetalCheckBoxIcon  implements Serializable, UIResource, Icon
{
    // Constructors
    public MetalCheckBoxIcon() ;
    // Instance methods
    protected void drawCheck(int y, int x, Graphics g, Component c) ;
    protected int getControlSize() ;
    public int getIconHeight() ;
    public int getIconWidth() ;
    public void paintIcon(int y, int x, Graphics g, Component c) ;
}
```

javax.swing.plaf.metal.**MetalCheckBoxUI**

```
public class MetalCheckBoxUI extends MetalRadioButtonUI
{
    // Constructors
    public MetalCheckBoxUI() ;
    // Static methods
    public static ComponentUI createUI(JComponent b) ;
    // Instance methods
    public String getPropertyPrefix() ;
    public void installDefaults(AbstractButton b) ;
    protected void uninstallDefaults(AbstractButton b) ;
}
```

---

javax.swing.plaf.metal.**MetalComboBoxButton**

---

public class **MetalComboBoxButton** extends JButton
{
    protected JComboBox **comboBox** ;
    protected Icon **comboIcon** ;
    protected boolean **iconOnly** ;
    protected JList **listBox** ;
    protected CellRendererPane **rendererPane** ;
    // Constructors
    public **MetalComboBoxButton**(JList list, CellRendererPane pane, boolean onlyIcon, Icon i,
        JComboBox cb) ;
    public **MetalComboBoxButton**(JList list, CellRendererPane pane, Icon i, JComboBox cb) ;
    private **MetalComboBoxButton**() ;
    // Instance methods
    public final JComboBox **getComboBox**() ;
    public final Icon **getComboIcon**() ;
    public Dimension **getMinimumSize**() ;
    public boolean **isFocusTraversable**() ;
    public final boolean **isIconOnly**() ;
    public void **paintComponent**(Graphics g) ;
    public final void **setComboBox**(JComboBox cb) ;
    public final void **setComboIcon**(Icon i) ;
    public void **setEnabled**(boolean enabled) ;
    public final void **setIconOnly**(boolean isIconOnly) ;
}

---

javax.swing.plaf.metal.**MetalComboBoxEditor**

---

public class **MetalComboBoxEditor** extends BasicComboBoxEditor
{
    protected static Insets **editorBorderInsets** ;
    // Constructors
    public **MetalComboBoxEditor**() ;
}

javax.swing.plaf.metal.**MetalComboBoxEditor.UIResource**

public static class **MetalComboBoxEditor.UIResource** extends MetalComboBoxEditor implements
UIResource
{
    // Constructors
    public **MetalComboBoxEditor.UIResource**() ;
}

javax.swing.plaf.metal.**MetalComboBoxIcon**

public class **MetalComboBoxIcon** implements Serializable, Icon
{
    // Constructors
    public **MetalComboBoxIcon**() ;
    // Instance methods
    public int **getIconHeight**() ;
    public int **getIconWidth**() ;
    public void **paintIcon**(int y, int x, Graphics g, Component c) ;
}

javax.swing.plaf.metal.**MetalComboBoxUI**

public class **MetalComboBoxUI** extends BasicComboBoxUI
{
    // Constructors
    public **MetalComboBoxUI**() ;
    // Static methods
    public static ComponentUI **createUI**(JComponent c) ;
    // Instance methods
    public void **configureEditor**() ;
    protected JButton **createArrowButton**() ;
    protected ComboBoxEditor **createEditor**() ;
    protected LayoutManager **createLayoutManager**() ;
    protected ComboPopup **createPopup**() ;
    public PropertyChangeListener **createPropertyChangeListener**() ;
    protected void **editablePropertyChanged**(PropertyChangeEvent e) ;

public int **getBaseline**(int height, int width, JComponent c) ; // Since 1.6
public Dimension **getMinimumSize**(JComponent c) ;
public void **layoutComboBox**(MetalComboBoxUI.MetalComboBoxLayoutManager manager,
    Container parent) ;
public void **paint**(JComponent c, Graphics g) ;
public void **paintCurrentValue**(boolean hasFocus, Rectangle bounds, Graphics g) ; // Since 1.5
public void **paintCurrentValueBackground**(boolean hasFocus, Rectangle bounds, Graphics g) ; //
    Since 1.5
protected void **removeListeners**() ;
public void **unconfigureEditor**() ;
}

---

javax.swing.plaf.metal.**MetalDesktopIconUI**

---

public class **MetalDesktopIconUI** extends BasicDesktopIconUI
{
    // Constructors
    public **MetalDesktopIconUI**() ;
    // Static methods
    public static ComponentUI **createUI**(JComponent c) ;
    // Instance methods
    public Dimension **getMaximumSize**(JComponent c) ;
    public Dimension **getMinimumSize**(JComponent c) ;
    public Dimension **getPreferredSize**(JComponent c) ;
    protected void **installComponents**() ;
    protected void **installDefaults**() ;
    protected void **installListeners**() ;
    protected void **uninstallComponents**() ;
    protected void **uninstallListeners**() ;
}

---

javax.swing.plaf.metal.**MetalFileChooserUI**

---

public class **MetalFileChooserUI** extends BasicFileChooserUI
{
    // Constructors
    public **MetalFileChooserUI**(JFileChooser filechooser) ;
    // Static methods
    public static ComponentUI **createUI**(JComponent c) ;
    // Instance methods
    protected void **addControlButtons**() ;

```
    protected ActionMap createActionMap() ;
    protected JPanel createDetailsView(JFileChooser fc) ;
    protected MetalFileChooserUI.DirectoryComboBoxModel
        createDirectoryComboBoxModel(JFileChooser fc) ;
    protected MetalFileChooserUI.DirectoryComboBoxRenderer
        createDirectoryComboBoxRenderer(JFileChooser fc) ;
    protected MetalFileChooserUI.FilterComboBoxModel createFilterComboBoxModel() ;
    protected MetalFileChooserUI.FilterComboBoxRenderer createFilterComboBoxRenderer() ;
    protected JPanel createList(JFileChooser fc) ;
    public ListSelectionListener createListSelectionListener(JFileChooser fc) ;
    public PropertyChangeListener createPropertyChangeListener(JFileChooser fc) ;
    public void ensureFileIsVisible(File f, JFileChooser fc) ;
    protected ActionMap getActionMap() ;
    protected JButton getApproveButton(JFileChooser fc) ;
    protected JPanel getBottomPanel() ;
    protected JPanel getButtonPanel() ;
    public String getDirectoryName() ;
    public String getFileName() ;
    public Dimension getMaximumSize(JComponent c) ;
    public Dimension getMinimumSize(JComponent c) ;
    public Dimension getPreferredSize(JComponent c) ;
    public void installComponents(JFileChooser fc) ;
    protected void installListeners(JFileChooser fc) ;
    protected void installStrings(JFileChooser fc) ;
    public void installUI(JComponent c) ;
    protected void removeControlButtons() ;
    public void rescanCurrentDirectory(JFileChooser fc) ;
    public void setDirectoryName(String dirname) ;
    protected void setDirectorySelected(boolean directorySelected) ; // Since 1.4
    public void setFileName(String filename) ;
    public void uninstallComponents(JFileChooser fc) ;
    public void uninstallUI(JComponent c) ;
    public void valueChanged(ListSelectionEvent e) ;
}
```

javax.swing.plaf.metal.**MetalIconFactory**

```
public class MetalIconFactory  implements Serializable
{
    public static final boolean DARK ;
    public static final boolean LIGHT ;
    // Constructors
    public MetalIconFactory() ;
    // Static methods
```

```
    public static Icon getCheckBoxIcon() ; // Since 1.3
    public static Icon getCheckBoxMenuItemIcon() ;
    public static Icon getFileChooserDetailViewIcon() ;
    public static Icon getFileChooserHomeFolderIcon() ;
    public static Icon getFileChooserListViewIcon() ;
    public static Icon getFileChooserNewFolderIcon() ;
    public static Icon getFileChooserUpFolderIcon() ;
    public static Icon getHorizontalSliderThumbIcon() ;
    public static Icon getInternalFrameAltMaximizeIcon(int size) ;
    public static Icon getInternalFrameCloseIcon(int size) ;
    public static Icon getInternalFrameDefaultMenuIcon() ;
    public static Icon getInternalFrameMaximizeIcon(int size) ;
    public static Icon getInternalFrameMinimizeIcon(int size) ;
    public static Icon getMenuArrowIcon() ;
    public static Icon getMenuItemArrowIcon() ;
    public static Icon getMenuItemCheckIcon() ;
    public static Icon getRadioButtonIcon() ;
    public static Icon getRadioButtonMenuItemIcon() ;
    public static Icon getTreeComputerIcon() ;
    public static Icon getTreeControlIcon(boolean isCollapsed) ;
    public static Icon getTreeFloppyDriveIcon() ;
    public static Icon getTreeFolderIcon() ;
    public static Icon getTreeHardDriveIcon() ;
    public static Icon getTreeLeafIcon() ;
    public static Icon getVerticalSliderThumbIcon() ;
}
```

---

javax.swing.plaf.metal.**MetalIconFactory.FileIcon16**

```
public static class MetalIconFactory.FileIcon16  implements Serializable, Icon
{
    // Constructors
    public MetalIconFactory.FileIcon16() ;
    // Instance methods
    public int getAdditionalHeight() ;
    public int getIconHeight() ;
    public int getIconWidth() ;
    public int getShift() ;
    public void paintIcon(int y, int x, Graphics g, Component c) ;
}
```

javax.swing.plaf.metal.**MetalIconFactory.FolderIcon16**

public static class **MetalIconFactory.FolderIcon16** implements Serializable, Icon
{
    // Constructors
    public **MetalIconFactory.FolderIcon16**() ;
    // Instance methods
    public int **getAdditionalHeight**() ;
    public int **getIconHeight**() ;
    public int **getIconWidth**() ;
    public int **getShift**() ;
    public void **paintIcon**(int y, int x, Graphics g, Component c) ;
}

javax.swing.plaf.metal.**MetalIconFactory.PaletteCloseIcon** [since 1.3]

public static class **MetalIconFactory.PaletteCloseIcon** implements Serializable, UIResource, Icon
{
    // Constructors
    public **MetalIconFactory.PaletteCloseIcon**() ;
    // Instance methods
    public int **getIconHeight**() ;
    public int **getIconWidth**() ;
    public void **paintIcon**(int y, int x, Graphics g, Component c) ;
}

javax.swing.plaf.metal.**MetalIconFactory.TreeControlIcon**

public static class **MetalIconFactory.TreeControlIcon** implements Serializable, Icon
{
    protected boolean **isLight** ;
    // Constructors
    public **MetalIconFactory.TreeControlIcon**(boolean isCollapsed) ;
    // Instance methods
    public int **getIconHeight**() ;
    public int **getIconWidth**() ;
    public void **paintIcon**(int y, int x, Graphics g, Component c) ;

```
        public void paintMe(int y, int x, Graphics g, Component c) ;
}
```

```
public static class MetalIconFactory.TreeFolderIcon extends MetalIconFactory.FolderIcon16
{
    // Constructors
    public MetalIconFactory.TreeFolderIcon() ;
    // Instance methods
    public int getAdditionalHeight() ;
    public int getShift() ;
}
```

```
public static class MetalIconFactory.TreeLeafIcon extends MetalIconFactory.FileIcon16
{
    // Constructors
    public MetalIconFactory.TreeLeafIcon() ;
    // Instance methods
    public int getAdditionalHeight() ;
    public int getShift() ;
}
```

```
public class MetalInternalFrameTitlePane extends BasicInternalFrameTitlePane
{
    protected boolean isPalette ;
    protected Icon paletteCloseIcon ;
    protected int paletteTitleHeight ;
    // Constructors
    public MetalInternalFrameTitlePane(JInternalFrame f) ;
    // Instance methods
    public void addNotify() ;
    protected void addSubComponents() ;
    protected void addSystemMenuItems(JMenu systemMenu) ;
```

```
    protected void assembleSystemMenu() ;
    protected void createButtons() ;
    protected LayoutManager createLayout() ;
    protected PropertyChangeListener createPropertyChangeListener() ;
    protected void installDefaults() ;
    public void paintComponent(Graphics g) ;
    public void paintPalette(Graphics g) ;
    public void setPalette(boolean b) ;
    protected void showSystemMenu() ;
    protected void uninstallDefaults() ;
}
```

javax.swing.plaf.metal.**MetalInternalFrameUI**

```
public class MetalInternalFrameUI extends BasicInternalFrameUI
{
    protected static String IS_PALETTE ;
    // Constructors
    public MetalInternalFrameUI(JInternalFrame b) ;
    // Static methods
    public static ComponentUI createUI(JComponent c) ;
    // Instance methods
    protected MouseInputAdapter createBorderListener(JInternalFrame w) ; // Since 1.6
    protected JComponent createNorthPane(JInternalFrame w) ;
    protected void installKeyboardActions() ;
    protected void installListeners() ;
    public void installUI(JComponent c) ;
    public void setPalette(boolean isPalette) ;
    protected void uninstallComponents() ;
    protected void uninstallKeyboardActions() ;
    protected void uninstallListeners() ;
    public void uninstallUI(JComponent c) ;
}
```

javax.swing.plaf.metal.**MetalLabelUI**

```
public class MetalLabelUI extends BasicLabelUI
{
    protected static MetalLabelUI metalLabelUI ;
    // Constructors
    public MetalLabelUI() ;
```

```
    // Static methods
    public static ComponentUI createUI(JComponent c) ;
    // Instance methods
    protected void paintDisabledText(int textY, int textX, String s, Graphics g, JLabel l) ;
}
```

javax.swing.plaf.metal.**MetalLookAndFeel**

```
public class MetalLookAndFeel extends BasicLookAndFeel
{
    // Constructors
    public MetalLookAndFeel() ;
    // Static methods
    public static ColorUIResource getAcceleratorForeground() ;
    public static ColorUIResource getAcceleratorSelectedForeground() ;
    public static ColorUIResource getBlack() ;
    public static ColorUIResource getControl() ;
    public static ColorUIResource getControlDarkShadow() ;
    public static ColorUIResource getControlDisabled() ;
    public static ColorUIResource getControlHighlight() ;
    public static ColorUIResource getControlInfo() ;
    public static ColorUIResource getControlShadow() ;
    public static ColorUIResource getControlTextColor() ;
    public static FontUIResource getControlTextFont() ;
    public static MetalTheme getCurrentTheme() ; // Since 1.5
    public static ColorUIResource getDesktopColor() ;
    public static ColorUIResource getFocusColor() ;
    public static ColorUIResource getHighlightedTextColor() ;
    public static ColorUIResource getInactiveControlTextColor() ;
    public static ColorUIResource getInactiveSystemTextColor() ;
    public static ColorUIResource getMenuBackground() ;
    public static ColorUIResource getMenuDisabledForeground() ;
    public static ColorUIResource getMenuForeground() ;
    public static ColorUIResource getMenuSelectedBackground() ;
    public static ColorUIResource getMenuSelectedForeground() ;
    public static FontUIResource getMenuTextFont() ;
    public static ColorUIResource getPrimaryControl() ;
    public static ColorUIResource getPrimaryControlDarkShadow() ;
    public static ColorUIResource getPrimaryControlHighlight() ;
    public static ColorUIResource getPrimaryControlInfo() ;
    public static ColorUIResource getPrimaryControlShadow() ;
    public static ColorUIResource getSeparatorBackground() ;
    public static ColorUIResource getSeparatorForeground() ;
    public static FontUIResource getSubTextFont() ;
```

public static ColorUIResource **getSystemTextColor**() ;
public static FontUIResource **getSystemTextFont**() ;
public static ColorUIResource **getTextHighlightColor**() ;
public static ColorUIResource **getUserTextColor**() ;
public static FontUIResource **getUserTextFont**() ;
public static ColorUIResource **getWhite**() ;
public static ColorUIResource **getWindowBackground**() ;
public static ColorUIResource **getWindowTitleBackground**() ;
public static FontUIResource **getWindowTitleFont**() ;
public static ColorUIResource **getWindowTitleForeground**() ;
public static ColorUIResource **getWindowTitleInactiveBackground**() ;
public static ColorUIResource **getWindowTitleInactiveForeground**() ;
public static void **setCurrentTheme**(MetalTheme theme) ;
// Instance methods
protected void **createDefaultTheme**() ;
public UIDefaults **getDefaults**() ;
public String **getDescription**() ;
public Icon **getDisabledIcon**(Icon icon, JComponent component) ; // Since 1.5
public Icon **getDisabledSelectedIcon**(Icon icon, JComponent component) ; // Since 1.5
public String **getID**() ;
public LayoutStyle **getLayoutStyle**() ; // Since 1.6
public String **getName**() ;
public boolean **getSupportsWindowDecorations**() ; // Since 1.4
protected void **initClassDefaults**(UIDefaults table) ;
protected void **initComponentDefaults**(UIDefaults table) ;
protected void **initSystemColorDefaults**(UIDefaults table) ;
public boolean **isNativeLookAndFeel**() ;
public boolean **isSupportedLookAndFeel**() ;
public void **provideErrorFeedback**(Component component) ; // Since 1.4
}

---

javax.swing.plaf.metal.**MetalMenuBarUI** [since 1.5]

---

public class **MetalMenuBarUI** extends BasicMenuBarUI
{
    // Constructors
    public **MetalMenuBarUI**() ;
    // Static methods
    public static ComponentUI **createUI**(JComponent x) ;
    // Instance methods
    public void **installUI**(JComponent c) ;
    public void **uninstallUI**(JComponent c) ;
    public void **update**(JComponent c, Graphics g) ; // Since 1.5
}

javax.swing.plaf.metal.**MetalPopupMenuSeparatorUI**

public class **MetalPopupMenuSeparatorUI** extends MetalSeparatorUI
{
    // Constructors
    public **MetalPopupMenuSeparatorUI**() ;
    // Static methods
    public static ComponentUI **createUI**(JComponent c) ;
    // Instance methods
    public Dimension **getPreferredSize**(JComponent c) ;
    public void **paint**(JComponent c, Graphics g) ;
}

javax.swing.plaf.metal.**MetalProgressBarUI**

public class **MetalProgressBarUI** extends BasicProgressBarUI
{
    // Constructors
    public **MetalProgressBarUI**() ;
    // Static methods
    public static ComponentUI **createUI**(JComponent c) ;
    // Instance methods
    public void **paintDeterminate**(JComponent c, Graphics g) ; // Since 1.4
    public void **paintIndeterminate**(JComponent c, Graphics g) ; // Since 1.4
}

javax.swing.plaf.metal.**MetalRadioButtonUI**

public class **MetalRadioButtonUI** extends BasicRadioButtonUI
{
    protected Color **disabledTextColor** ;
    protected Color **focusColor** ;
    protected Color **selectColor** ;
    // Constructors
    public **MetalRadioButtonUI**() ;
    // Static methods
    public static ComponentUI **createUI**(JComponent c) ;

// Instance methods
protected Color **getDisabledTextColor**() ;
protected Color **getFocusColor**() ;
protected Color **getSelectColor**() ;
public void **installDefaults**(AbstractButton b) ;
public synchronized void **paint**(JComponent c, Graphics g) ;
protected void **paintFocus**(Dimension d, Rectangle t, Graphics g) ;
protected void **uninstallDefaults**(AbstractButton b) ;
}

---

javax.swing.plaf.metal.**MetalRootPaneUI** [since 1.4]

---

public class **MetalRootPaneUI** extends BasicRootPaneUI
{
    // Constructors
    public **MetalRootPaneUI**() ;
    // Static methods
    public static ComponentUI **createUI**(JComponent c) ;
    // Instance methods
    public void **installUI**(JComponent c) ;
    public void **propertyChange**(PropertyChangeEvent e) ;
    public void **uninstallUI**(JComponent c) ;
}

---

javax.swing.plaf.metal.**MetalScrollBarUI**

---

public class **MetalScrollBarUI** extends BasicScrollBarUI
{
    public static final String **FREE_STANDING_PROP** ;
    protected MetalBumps **bumps** ;
    protected MetalScrollButton **decreaseButton** ;
    protected MetalScrollButton **increaseButton** ;
    protected boolean **isFreeStanding** ;
    protected int **scrollBarWidth** ;
    // Constructors
    public **MetalScrollBarUI**() ;
    // Static methods
    public static ComponentUI **createUI**(JComponent c) ;
    // Instance methods
    protected void **configureScrollBarColors**() ;
    protected JButton **createDecreaseButton**(int orientation) ;

```
     protected JButton createIncreaseButton(int orientation) ;
     protected PropertyChangeListener createPropertyChangeListener() ;
     protected Dimension getMinimumThumbSize() ;
     public Dimension getPreferredSize(JComponent c) ;
     protected void installDefaults() ;
     protected void installListeners() ;
     protected void paintThumb(Rectangle thumbBounds, JComponent c, Graphics g) ;
     protected void paintTrack(Rectangle trackBounds, JComponent c, Graphics g) ;
     protected void setThumbBounds(int height, int width, int y, int x) ;
}
```

---

javax.swing.plaf.metal.**MetalScrollButton**

```
public class MetalScrollButton extends BasicArrowButton
{
     // Constructors
     public MetalScrollButton(boolean freeStanding, int width, int direction) ;
     // Instance methods
     public int getButtonWidth() ;
     public Dimension getMaximumSize() ;
     public Dimension getMinimumSize() ;
     public Dimension getPreferredSize() ;
     public void paint(Graphics g) ;
     public void setFreeStanding(boolean freeStanding) ;
}
```

---

javax.swing.plaf.metal.**MetalScrollPaneUI**

```
public class MetalScrollPaneUI extends BasicScrollPaneUI
{
     // Constructors
     public MetalScrollPaneUI() ;
     // Static methods
     public static ComponentUI createUI(JComponent x) ;
     // Instance methods
     protected PropertyChangeListener createScrollBarSwapListener() ;
     public void installListeners(JScrollPane scrollPane) ;
     public void installUI(JComponent c) ;
     public void uninstallListeners(JScrollPane scrollPane) ;
     public void uninstallUI(JComponent c) ;
}
```

---

javax.swing.plaf.metal.**MetalSeparatorUI**

---

public class **MetalSeparatorUI** extends BasicSeparatorUI
{
    // Constructors
    public **MetalSeparatorUI**() ;
    // Static methods
    public static ComponentUI **createUI**(JComponent c) ;
    // Instance methods
    public Dimension **getPreferredSize**(JComponent c) ;
    protected void **installDefaults**(JSeparator s) ;
    public void **paint**(JComponent c, Graphics g) ;
}

---

javax.swing.plaf.metal.**MetalSliderUI**

---

public class **MetalSliderUI** extends BasicSliderUI
{
    protected static Color **darkShadowColor** ;
    protected static Color **highlightColor** ;
    protected static Icon **horizThumbIcon** ;
    protected static Color **thumbColor** ;
    protected static int **tickLength** ;
    protected static int **trackWidth** ;
    protected static Icon **vertThumbIcon** ;
    protected boolean **filledSlider** ;
    protected final String **SLIDER_FILL** ;
    protected final int **TICK_BUFFER** ;
    // Constructors
    public **MetalSliderUI**() ;
    // Static methods
    public static ComponentUI **createUI**(JComponent c) ;
    // Instance methods
    protected PropertyChangeListener **createPropertyChangeListener**(JSlider slider) ;
    protected int **getThumbOverhang**() ;
    protected Dimension **getThumbSize**() ;
    public int **getTickLength**() ;
    protected int **getTrackLength**() ;
    protected int **getTrackWidth**() ;
    public void **installUI**(JComponent c) ;

```
    public void paintFocus(Graphics g) ;
    protected void paintMajorTickForHorizSlider(int x, Rectangle tickBounds, Graphics g) ;
    protected void paintMajorTickForVertSlider(int y, Rectangle tickBounds, Graphics g) ;
    protected void paintMinorTickForHorizSlider(int x, Rectangle tickBounds, Graphics g) ;
    protected void paintMinorTickForVertSlider(int y, Rectangle tickBounds, Graphics g) ;
    public void paintThumb(Graphics g) ;
    public void paintTrack(Graphics g) ;
    protected void scrollDueToClickInTrack(int dir) ;
}
```

javax.swing.plaf.metal.**MetalSplitPaneUI**

public class **MetalSplitPaneUI** extends BasicSplitPaneUI
```
{
    // Constructors
    public MetalSplitPaneUI() ;
    // Static methods
    public static ComponentUI createUI(JComponent x) ;
    // Instance methods
    public BasicSplitPaneDivider createDefaultDivider() ;
}
```

javax.swing.plaf.metal.**MetalTabbedPaneUI**

public class **MetalTabbedPaneUI** extends BasicTabbedPaneUI
```
{
    protected int minTabWidth ;
    protected Color selectColor ;
    protected Color selectHighlight ;
    protected Color tabAreaBackground ;
    // Constructors
    public MetalTabbedPaneUI() ;
    // Static methods
    public static ComponentUI createUI(JComponent x) ;
    // Instance methods
    protected int calculateMaxTabHeight(int tabPlacement) ;
    protected LayoutManager createLayoutManager() ;
    protected int getBaselineOffset() ; // Since 1.6
    protected Color getColorForGap(int y, int x, int currentRun) ;
    protected int getTabLabelShiftX(boolean isSelected, int tabIndex, int tabPlacement) ;
    protected int getTabLabelShiftY(boolean isSelected, int tabIndex, int tabPlacement) ;
```

```
    protected int getTabRunOverlay(int tabPlacement) ;
    protected void installDefaults() ;
    public void paint(JComponent c, Graphics g) ;
    protected void paintBottomTabBorder(boolean isSelected, int rght, int btm, int h, int w, int y, int x,
        Graphics g, int tabIndex) ;
    protected void paintContentBorderBottomEdge(int h, int w, int y, int x, int selectedIndex, int
        tabPlacement, Graphics g) ;
    protected void paintContentBorderLeftEdge(int h, int w, int y, int x, int selectedIndex, int
        tabPlacement, Graphics g) ;
    protected void paintContentBorderRightEdge(int h, int w, int y, int x, int selectedIndex, int
        tabPlacement, Graphics g) ;
    protected void paintContentBorderTopEdge(int h, int w, int y, int x, int selectedIndex, int
        tabPlacement, Graphics g) ;
    protected void paintFocusIndicator(boolean isSelected, Rectangle textRect, Rectangle iconRect, int
        tabIndex, java.awt.Rectangle[] rects, int tabPlacement, Graphics g) ;
    protected void paintHighlightBelowTab() ;
    protected void paintLeftTabBorder(boolean isSelected, int rght, int btm, int h, int w, int y, int x,
        Graphics g, int tabIndex) ;
    protected void paintRightTabBorder(boolean isSelected, int rght, int btm, int h, int w, int y, int x,
        Graphics g, int tabIndex) ;
    protected void paintTabBackground(boolean isSelected, int h, int w, int y, int x, int tabIndex, int
        tabPlacement, Graphics g) ;
    protected void paintTabBorder(boolean isSelected, int h, int w, int y, int x, int tabIndex, int
        tabPlacement, Graphics g) ;
    protected void paintTopTabBorder(boolean isSelected, int rght, int btm, int h, int w, int y, int x,
        Graphics g, int tabIndex) ;
    protected boolean shouldFillGap(int y, int x, int tabIndex, int currentRun) ;
    protected boolean shouldPadTabRun(int run, int tabPlacement) ;
    protected boolean shouldRotateTabRuns(int selectedRun, int tabPlacement) ;
    public void update(JComponent c, Graphics g) ;
}
```

---

javax.swing.plaf.metal.**MetalTextFieldUI**

```
public class MetalTextFieldUI extends BasicTextFieldUI
{
    // Constructors
    public MetalTextFieldUI() ;
    // Static methods
    public static ComponentUI createUI(JComponent c) ;
    // Instance methods
    public void propertyChange(PropertyChangeEvent evt) ;
}
```

javax.swing.plaf.metal.**MetalTheme**

public abstract class **MetalTheme**
{
    // Constructors
    public **MetalTheme**() ;
    // Instance methods
    public void **addCustomEntriesToTable**(UIDefaults table) ;
    public ColorUIResource **getAcceleratorForeground**() ;
    public ColorUIResource **getAcceleratorSelectedForeground**() ;
    protected ColorUIResource **getBlack**() ;
    public ColorUIResource **getControl**() ;
    public ColorUIResource **getControlDarkShadow**() ;
    public ColorUIResource **getControlDisabled**() ;
    public ColorUIResource **getControlHighlight**() ;
    public ColorUIResource **getControlInfo**() ;
    public ColorUIResource **getControlShadow**() ;
    public ColorUIResource **getControlTextColor**() ;
    public abstract FontUIResource **getControlTextFont**() ;
    public ColorUIResource **getDesktopColor**() ;
    public ColorUIResource **getFocusColor**() ;
    public ColorUIResource **getHighlightedTextColor**() ;
    public ColorUIResource **getInactiveControlTextColor**() ;
    public ColorUIResource **getInactiveSystemTextColor**() ;
    public ColorUIResource **getMenuBackground**() ;
    public ColorUIResource **getMenuDisabledForeground**() ;
    public ColorUIResource **getMenuForeground**() ;
    public ColorUIResource **getMenuSelectedBackground**() ;
    public ColorUIResource **getMenuSelectedForeground**() ;
    public abstract FontUIResource **getMenuTextFont**() ;
    public abstract String **getName**() ;
    protected abstract ColorUIResource **getPrimary1**() ;
    protected abstract ColorUIResource **getPrimary2**() ;
    protected abstract ColorUIResource **getPrimary3**() ;
    public ColorUIResource **getPrimaryControl**() ;
    public ColorUIResource **getPrimaryControlDarkShadow**() ;
    public ColorUIResource **getPrimaryControlHighlight**() ;
    public ColorUIResource **getPrimaryControlInfo**() ;
    public ColorUIResource **getPrimaryControlShadow**() ;
    protected abstract ColorUIResource **getSecondary1**() ;
    protected abstract ColorUIResource **getSecondary2**() ;
    protected abstract ColorUIResource **getSecondary3**() ;
    public ColorUIResource **getSeparatorBackground**() ;
    public ColorUIResource **getSeparatorForeground**() ;

```
    public abstract FontUIResource getSubTextFont() ;
    public ColorUIResource getSystemTextColor() ;
    public abstract FontUIResource getSystemTextFont() ;
    public ColorUIResource getTextHighlightColor() ;
    public ColorUIResource getUserTextColor() ;
    public abstract FontUIResource getUserTextFont() ;
    protected ColorUIResource getWhite() ;
    public ColorUIResource getWindowBackground() ;
    public ColorUIResource getWindowTitleBackground() ;
    public abstract FontUIResource getWindowTitleFont() ;
    public ColorUIResource getWindowTitleForeground() ;
    public ColorUIResource getWindowTitleInactiveBackground() ;
    public ColorUIResource getWindowTitleInactiveForeground() ;
}
```

---

javax.swing.plaf.metal.**MetalToggleButtonUI**

```
public class MetalToggleButtonUI extends BasicToggleButtonUI
{
    protected Color disabledTextColor ;
    protected Color focusColor ;
    protected Color selectColor ;
    // Constructors
    public MetalToggleButtonUI() ;
    // Static methods
    public static ComponentUI createUI(JComponent b) ;
    // Instance methods
    protected Color getDisabledTextColor() ;
    protected Color getFocusColor() ;
    protected Color getSelectColor() ;
    public void installDefaults(AbstractButton b) ;
    protected void paintButtonPressed(AbstractButton b, Graphics g) ;
    protected void paintFocus(Rectangle iconRect, Rectangle textRect, Rectangle viewRect,
        AbstractButton b, Graphics g) ;
    protected void paintIcon(Rectangle iconRect, AbstractButton b, Graphics g) ; // Since 1.5
    protected void paintText(String text, Rectangle textRect, JComponent c, Graphics g) ;
    protected void uninstallDefaults(AbstractButton b) ;
    public void update(JComponent c, Graphics g) ; // Since 1.5
}
```

javax.swing.plaf.metal.**MetalToolBarUI**

public class **MetalToolBarUI** extends BasicToolBarUI
{
    protected ContainerListener **contListener** ;
    protected PropertyChangeListener **rolloverListener** ;
    // Constructors
    public **MetalToolBarUI**() ;
    // Static methods
    public static ComponentUI **createUI**(JComponent c) ;
    // Instance methods
    protected ContainerListener **createContainerListener**() ;
    protected MouseInputListener **createDockingListener**() ;
    protected Border **createNonRolloverBorder**() ;
    protected Border **createRolloverBorder**() ;
    protected PropertyChangeListener **createRolloverListener**() ;
    protected void **installListeners**() ;
    public void **installUI**(JComponent c) ;
    protected void **setBorderToNonRollover**(Component c) ;
    protected void **setDragOffset**(Point p) ;
    protected void **uninstallListeners**() ;
    public void **uninstallUI**(JComponent c) ;
    public void **update**(JComponent c, Graphics g) ; // Since 1.5
}

javax.swing.plaf.metal.**MetalToolTipUI**

public class **MetalToolTipUI** extends BasicToolTipUI
{
    public static final int **padSpaceBetweenStrings** ;
    // Constructors
    public **MetalToolTipUI**() ;
    // Static methods
    public static ComponentUI **createUI**(JComponent c) ;
    // Instance methods
    public String **getAcceleratorString**() ;
    public Dimension **getPreferredSize**(JComponent c) ;
    public void **installUI**(JComponent c) ;
    protected boolean **isAcceleratorHidden**() ;
    public void **paint**(JComponent c, Graphics g) ;

```
        public void uninstallUI(JComponent c) ;
}
```

---

javax.swing.plaf.metal.**MetalTreeUI**

```
public class MetalTreeUI extends BasicTreeUI
{
    // Constructors
    public MetalTreeUI() ;
    // Static methods
    public static ComponentUI createUI(JComponent x) ;
    // Instance methods
    protected void decodeLineStyle(Object lineStyleFlag) ;
    protected int getHorizontalLegBuffer() ;
    public void installUI(JComponent c) ;
    protected boolean isLocationInExpandControl(int mouseY, int mouseX, int rowLevel, int row) ;
    public void paint(JComponent c, Graphics g) ;
    protected void paintHorizontalPartOfLeg(boolean isLeaf, boolean hasBeenExpanded, boolean
        isExpanded, int row, TreePath path, Rectangle bounds, Insets insets, Rectangle clipBounds,
        Graphics g) ;
    protected void paintHorizontalSeparators(JComponent c, Graphics g) ;
    protected void paintVerticalPartOfLeg(TreePath path, Insets insets, Rectangle clipBounds, Graphics
        g) ;
    public void uninstallUI(JComponent c) ;
}
```

---

java.awt.datatransfer.**MimeTypeParseException** [since 1.3]

```
public class MimeTypeParseException extends Exception
{
    // Constructors
    public MimeTypeParseException(String s) ;
    public MimeTypeParseException() ;
}
```

---

javax.swing.text.html.**MinimalHTMLWriter**

```
public class MinimalHTMLWriter extends AbstractWriter
```

```
{
    // Constructors
    public MinimalHTMLWriter(int len, int pos, StyledDocument doc, Writer w) ;
    public MinimalHTMLWriter(StyledDocument doc, Writer w) ;
    // Instance methods
    protected void endFontTag() throws IOException ;
    protected boolean inFontTag() ;
    protected boolean isText(Element elem) ;
    protected void startFontTag(String style) throws IOException ;
    protected void text(Element elem) throws IOException, BadLocationException ;
    public void write() throws IOException, BadLocationException ;
    protected void writeAttributes(AttributeSet attr) throws IOException ;
    protected void writeBody() throws IOException, BadLocationException ;
    protected void writeComponent(Element elem) throws IOException ;
    protected void writeContent(boolean needsIndenting, Element elem) throws IOException,
        BadLocationException ;
    protected void writeEndParagraph() throws IOException ;
    protected void writeEndTag(String endTag) throws IOException ;
    protected void writeHeader() throws IOException ;
    protected void writeHTMLTags(AttributeSet attr) throws IOException ;
    protected void writeImage(Element elem) throws IOException ;
    protected void writeLeaf(Element elem) throws IOException ;
    protected void writeNonHTMLAttributes(AttributeSet attr) throws IOException ;
    protected void writeStartParagraph(Element elem) throws IOException ;
    protected void writeStartTag(String tag) throws IOException ;
    protected void writeStyles() throws IOException ;
}
```

java.awt.event.**MouseAdapter** [since 1.1]

public abstract class **MouseAdapter** implements MouseMotionListener, MouseWheelListener, MouseListener

```
{
    // Constructors
    public MouseAdapter() ;
    // Instance methods
    public void mouseClicked(MouseEvent e) ;
    public void mouseDragged(MouseEvent e) ; // Since 1.6
    public void mouseEntered(MouseEvent e) ;
    public void mouseExited(MouseEvent e) ;
    public void mouseMoved(MouseEvent e) ; // Since 1.6
    public void mousePressed(MouseEvent e) ;
    public void mouseReleased(MouseEvent e) ;
    public void mouseWheelMoved(MouseWheelEvent e) ; // Since 1.6
```

}

---

java.awt.dnd.**MouseDragGestureRecognizer**

---

public abstract class **MouseDragGestureRecognizer** extends DragGestureRecognizer implements
MouseMotionListener, MouseListener
{
    // Constructors
    protected **MouseDragGestureRecognizer**(DragSource ds) ;
    protected **MouseDragGestureRecognizer**(Component c, DragSource ds) ;
    protected **MouseDragGestureRecognizer**(int act, Component c, DragSource ds) ;
    protected **MouseDragGestureRecognizer**(DragGestureListener dgl, int act, Component c,
        DragSource ds) ;
    // Instance methods
    public void **mouseClicked**(MouseEvent e) ;
    public void **mouseDragged**(MouseEvent e) ;
    public void **mouseEntered**(MouseEvent e) ;
    public void **mouseExited**(MouseEvent e) ;
    public void **mouseMoved**(MouseEvent e) ;
    public void **mousePressed**(MouseEvent e) ;
    public void **mouseReleased**(MouseEvent e) ;
    protected void **registerListeners**() ;
    protected void **unregisterListeners**() ;
}

---

java.awt.event.**MouseEvent** [since 1.1]

---

public class **MouseEvent** extends InputEvent
{
    public static final int **BUTTON1** ;
    public static final int **BUTTON2** ;
    public static final int **BUTTON3** ;
    public static final int **MOUSE_CLICKED** ;
    public static final int **MOUSE_DRAGGED** ;
    public static final int **MOUSE_ENTERED** ;
    public static final int **MOUSE_EXITED** ;
    public static final int **MOUSE_FIRST** ;
    public static final int **MOUSE_LAST** ;
    public static final int **MOUSE_MOVED** ;
    public static final int **MOUSE_PRESSED** ;
    public static final int **MOUSE_RELEASED** ;

```
    public static final int MOUSE_WHEEL ;
    public static final int NOBUTTON ;
    // Constructors
    public MouseEvent(int button, boolean popupTrigger, int clickCount, int yAbs, int xAbs, int y, int x,
        int modifiers, long when, int id, Component source) ;
    public MouseEvent(boolean popupTrigger, int clickCount, int y, int x, int modifiers, long when, int
        id, Component source) ;
    public MouseEvent(int button, boolean popupTrigger, int clickCount, int y, int x, int modifiers, long
        when, int id, Component source) ;
    // Static methods
    public static String getMouseModifiersText(int modifiers) ; // Since 1.4
    // Instance methods
    public int getButton() ; // Since 1.4
    public int getClickCount() ;
    public Point getLocationOnScreen() ; // Since 1.6
    public Point getPoint() ;
    public int getX() ;
    public int getXOnScreen() ; // Since 1.6
    public int getY() ;
    public int getYOnScreen() ; // Since 1.6
    public boolean isPopupTrigger() ;
    public String paramString() ;
    public synchronized void translatePoint(int y, int x) ;
}
```

---

java.awt.**MouseInfo** [since 1.5]

```
public class MouseInfo
{
    // Constructors
    private MouseInfo() ;
    // Static methods
    public static int getNumberOfButtons() throws HeadlessException ; // Since 1.5
    public static PointerInfo getPointerInfo() throws HeadlessException ; // Since 1.5
}
```

---

java.awt.peer.**MouseInfoPeer**

```
public interface MouseInfoPeer
{
    // Instance methods
```

```
    public int fillPointWithCoords(Point point) ;
    public boolean isWindowUnderMouse(Window w) ;
}
```

---

javax.swing.event.**MouseInputAdapter**

---

public abstract class **MouseInputAdapter** extends MouseAdapter implements MouseInputListener
```
{
    // Constructors
    public MouseInputAdapter() ;
}
```

---

java.awt.event.**MouseListener** [since 1.1]

---

public interface **MouseListener** implements EventListener
```
{
    // Instance methods
    public void mouseClicked(MouseEvent e) ;
    public void mouseEntered(MouseEvent e) ;
    public void mouseExited(MouseEvent e) ;
    public void mousePressed(MouseEvent e) ;
    public void mouseReleased(MouseEvent e) ;
}
```

---

java.awt.event.**MouseMotionAdapter** [since 1.1]

---

public abstract class **MouseMotionAdapter** implements MouseMotionListener
```
{
    // Constructors
    public MouseMotionAdapter() ;
    // Instance methods
    public void mouseDragged(MouseEvent e) ;
    public void mouseMoved(MouseEvent e) ;
}
```

java.awt.event.**MouseMotionListener** [since 1.1]

public interface **MouseMotionListener** implements EventListener
{
    // Instance methods
    public void **mouseDragged**(MouseEvent e) ;
    public void **mouseMoved**(MouseEvent e) ;
}

java.awt.event.**MouseWheelEvent** [since 1.4]

public class **MouseWheelEvent** extends MouseEvent
{
    public static final int **WHEEL_BLOCK_SCROLL** ;
    public static final int **WHEEL_UNIT_SCROLL** ;
    // Constructors
    public **MouseWheelEvent**(double preciseWheelRotation, int wheelRotation, int scrollAmount, int
        scrollType, boolean popupTrigger, int clickCount, int yAbs, int xAbs, int y, int x, int modifiers,
        long when, int id, Component source) ;
    public **MouseWheelEvent**(int wheelRotation, int scrollAmount, int scrollType, boolean
        popupTrigger, int clickCount, int yAbs, int xAbs, int y, int x, int modifiers, long when, int id,
        Component source) ;
    public **MouseWheelEvent**(int wheelRotation, int scrollAmount, int scrollType, boolean
        popupTrigger, int clickCount, int y, int x, int modifiers, long when, int id, Component source) ;
    // Instance methods
    public double **getPreciseWheelRotation**() ; // Since 1.7
    public int **getScrollAmount**() ;
    public int **getScrollType**() ;
    public int **getUnitsToScroll**() ;
    public int **getWheelRotation**() ;
    public String **paramString**() ;
}

java.awt.event.**MouseWheelListener** [since 1.4]

public interface **MouseWheelListener** implements EventListener
{

```
        // Instance methods
        public void mouseWheelMoved(MouseWheelEvent e) ;
}
```

---

javax.swing.plaf.multi.**MultiButtonUI**

```
public class MultiButtonUI extends ButtonUI
{
        protected Vector uis ;
        // Constructors
        public MultiButtonUI() ;
        // Static methods
        public static ComponentUI createUI(JComponent a) ;
        // Instance methods
        public boolean contains(int c, int b, JComponent a) ;
        public Accessible getAccessibleChild(int b, JComponent a) ;
        public int getAccessibleChildrenCount(JComponent a) ;
        public Dimension getMaximumSize(JComponent a) ;
        public Dimension getMinimumSize(JComponent a) ;
        public Dimension getPreferredSize(JComponent a) ;
        public ComponentUI getUIs() ;
        public void installUI(JComponent a) ;
        public void paint(JComponent b, Graphics a) ;
        public void uninstallUI(JComponent a) ;
        public void update(JComponent b, Graphics a) ;
}
```

---

javax.swing.plaf.multi.**MultiColorChooserUI**

```
public class MultiColorChooserUI extends ColorChooserUI
{
        protected Vector uis ;
        // Constructors
        public MultiColorChooserUI() ;
        // Static methods
        public static ComponentUI createUI(JComponent a) ;
        // Instance methods
        public boolean contains(int c, int b, JComponent a) ;
        public Accessible getAccessibleChild(int b, JComponent a) ;
        public int getAccessibleChildrenCount(JComponent a) ;
        public Dimension getMaximumSize(JComponent a) ;
```

```
    public Dimension getMinimumSize(JComponent a) ;
    public Dimension getPreferredSize(JComponent a) ;
    public ComponentUI getUIs() ;
    public void installUI(JComponent a) ;
    public void paint(JComponent b, Graphics a) ;
    public void uninstallUI(JComponent a) ;
    public void update(JComponent b, Graphics a) ;
}
```

javax.swing.plaf.multi.**MultiComboBoxUI**

```
public class MultiComboBoxUI extends ComboBoxUI
{
    protected Vector uis ;
    // Constructors
    public MultiComboBoxUI() ;
    // Static methods
    public static ComponentUI createUI(JComponent a) ;
    // Instance methods
    public boolean contains(int c, int b, JComponent a) ;
    public Accessible getAccessibleChild(int b, JComponent a) ;
    public int getAccessibleChildrenCount(JComponent a) ;
    public Dimension getMaximumSize(JComponent a) ;
    public Dimension getMinimumSize(JComponent a) ;
    public Dimension getPreferredSize(JComponent a) ;
    public ComponentUI getUIs() ;
    public void installUI(JComponent a) ;
    public boolean isFocusTraversable(JComboBox a) ;
    public boolean isPopupVisible(JComboBox a) ;
    public void paint(JComponent b, Graphics a) ;
    public void setPopupVisible(boolean b, JComboBox a) ;
    public void uninstallUI(JComponent a) ;
    public void update(JComponent b, Graphics a) ;
}
```

javax.swing.plaf.multi.**MultiDesktopIconUI**

```
public class MultiDesktopIconUI extends DesktopIconUI
{
    protected Vector uis ;
    // Constructors
```

```
    public MultiDesktopIconUI() ;
    // Static methods
    public static ComponentUI createUI(JComponent a) ;
    // Instance methods
    public boolean contains(int c, int b, JComponent a) ;
    public Accessible getAccessibleChild(int b, JComponent a) ;
    public int getAccessibleChildrenCount(JComponent a) ;
    public Dimension getMaximumSize(JComponent a) ;
    public Dimension getMinimumSize(JComponent a) ;
    public Dimension getPreferredSize(JComponent a) ;
    public ComponentUI getUIs() ;
    public void installUI(JComponent a) ;
    public void paint(JComponent b, Graphics a) ;
    public void uninstallUI(JComponent a) ;
    public void update(JComponent b, Graphics a) ;
}
```

javax.swing.plaf.multi.**MultiDesktopPaneUI**

```
public class MultiDesktopPaneUI extends DesktopPaneUI
{
    protected Vector uis ;
    // Constructors
    public MultiDesktopPaneUI() ;
    // Static methods
    public static ComponentUI createUI(JComponent a) ;
    // Instance methods
    public boolean contains(int c, int b, JComponent a) ;
    public Accessible getAccessibleChild(int b, JComponent a) ;
    public int getAccessibleChildrenCount(JComponent a) ;
    public Dimension getMaximumSize(JComponent a) ;
    public Dimension getMinimumSize(JComponent a) ;
    public Dimension getPreferredSize(JComponent a) ;
    public ComponentUI getUIs() ;
    public void installUI(JComponent a) ;
    public void paint(JComponent b, Graphics a) ;
    public void uninstallUI(JComponent a) ;
    public void update(JComponent b, Graphics a) ;
}
```

javax.swing.plaf.multi.**MultiFileChooserUI**

public class **MultiFileChooserUI** extends FileChooserUI
{
    protected Vector **uis** ;
    // Constructors
    public **MultiFileChooserUI**() ;
    // Static methods
    public static ComponentUI **createUI**(JComponent a) ;
    // Instance methods
    public boolean **contains**(int c, int b, JComponent a) ;
    public void **ensureFileIsVisible**(File b, JFileChooser a) ;
    public FileFilter **getAcceptAllFileFilter**(JFileChooser a) ;
    public Accessible **getAccessibleChild**(int b, JComponent a) ;
    public int **getAccessibleChildrenCount**(JComponent a) ;
    public String **getApproveButtonText**(JFileChooser a) ;
    public String **getDialogTitle**(JFileChooser a) ;
    public FileView **getFileView**(JFileChooser a) ;
    public Dimension **getMaximumSize**(JComponent a) ;
    public Dimension **getMinimumSize**(JComponent a) ;
    public Dimension **getPreferredSize**(JComponent a) ;
    public ComponentUI **getUIs**() ;
    public void **installUI**(JComponent a) ;
    public void **paint**(JComponent b, Graphics a) ;
    public void **rescanCurrentDirectory**(JFileChooser a) ;
    public void **uninstallUI**(JComponent a) ;
    public void **update**(JComponent b, Graphics a) ;
}

javax.swing.plaf.multi.**MultiInternalFrameUI**

public class **MultiInternalFrameUI** extends InternalFrameUI
{
    protected Vector **uis** ;
    // Constructors
    public **MultiInternalFrameUI**() ;
    // Static methods
    public static ComponentUI **createUI**(JComponent a) ;
    // Instance methods
    public boolean **contains**(int c, int b, JComponent a) ;

```
        public Accessible getAccessibleChild(int b, JComponent a) ;
        public int getAccessibleChildrenCount(JComponent a) ;
        public Dimension getMaximumSize(JComponent a) ;
        public Dimension getMinimumSize(JComponent a) ;
        public Dimension getPreferredSize(JComponent a) ;
        public ComponentUI getUIs() ;
        public void installUI(JComponent a) ;
        public void paint(JComponent b, Graphics a) ;
        public void uninstallUI(JComponent a) ;
        public void update(JComponent b, Graphics a) ;
}
```

javax.swing.plaf.multi.**MultiLabelUI**

```
public class MultiLabelUI extends LabelUI
{
        protected Vector uis ;
        // Constructors
        public MultiLabelUI() ;
        // Static methods
        public static ComponentUI createUI(JComponent a) ;
        // Instance methods
        public boolean contains(int c, int b, JComponent a) ;
        public Accessible getAccessibleChild(int b, JComponent a) ;
        public int getAccessibleChildrenCount(JComponent a) ;
        public Dimension getMaximumSize(JComponent a) ;
        public Dimension getMinimumSize(JComponent a) ;
        public Dimension getPreferredSize(JComponent a) ;
        public ComponentUI getUIs() ;
        public void installUI(JComponent a) ;
        public void paint(JComponent b, Graphics a) ;
        public void uninstallUI(JComponent a) ;
        public void update(JComponent b, Graphics a) ;
}
```

javax.swing.plaf.multi.**MultiListUI**

```
public class MultiListUI extends ListUI
{
        protected Vector uis ;
        // Constructors
```

```
    public MultiListUI() ;
    // Static methods
    public static ComponentUI createUI(JComponent a) ;
    // Instance methods
    public boolean contains(int c, int b, JComponent a) ;
    public Accessible getAccessibleChild(int b, JComponent a) ;
    public int getAccessibleChildrenCount(JComponent a) ;
    public Rectangle getCellBounds(int c, int b, JList a) ;
    public Dimension getMaximumSize(JComponent a) ;
    public Dimension getMinimumSize(JComponent a) ;
    public Dimension getPreferredSize(JComponent a) ;
    public ComponentUI getUIs() ;
    public Point indexToLocation(int b, JList a) ;
    public void installUI(JComponent a) ;
    public int locationToIndex(Point b, JList a) ;
    public void paint(JComponent b, Graphics a) ;
    public void uninstallUI(JComponent a) ;
    public void update(JComponent b, Graphics a) ;
}
```

---

javax.swing.plaf.multi.**MultiLookAndFeel**

```
public class MultiLookAndFeel extends LookAndFeel
{
    // Constructors
    public MultiLookAndFeel() ;
    // Static methods
    public static ComponentUI createUIs(JComponent target, Vector uis, ComponentUI mui) ;
    protected static ComponentUI uisToArray(Vector uis) ;
    // Instance methods
    public UIDefaults getDefaults() ;
    public String getDescription() ;
    public String getID() ;
    public String getName() ;
    public boolean isNativeLookAndFeel() ;
    public boolean isSupportedLookAndFeel() ;
}
```

javax.swing.plaf.multi.**MultiMenuBarUI**

public class **MultiMenuBarUI** extends MenuBarUI
{
    protected Vector **uis** ;
    // Constructors
    public **MultiMenuBarUI**() ;
    // Static methods
    public static ComponentUI **createUI**(JComponent a) ;
    // Instance methods
    public boolean **contains**(int c, int b, JComponent a) ;
    public Accessible **getAccessibleChild**(int b, JComponent a) ;
    public int **getAccessibleChildrenCount**(JComponent a) ;
    public Dimension **getMaximumSize**(JComponent a) ;
    public Dimension **getMinimumSize**(JComponent a) ;
    public Dimension **getPreferredSize**(JComponent a) ;
    public ComponentUI **getUIs**() ;
    public void **installUI**(JComponent a) ;
    public void **paint**(JComponent b, Graphics a) ;
    public void **uninstallUI**(JComponent a) ;
    public void **update**(JComponent b, Graphics a) ;
}

javax.swing.plaf.multi.**MultiMenuItemUI**

public class **MultiMenuItemUI** extends MenuItemUI
{
    protected Vector **uis** ;
    // Constructors
    public **MultiMenuItemUI**() ;
    // Static methods
    public static ComponentUI **createUI**(JComponent a) ;
    // Instance methods
    public boolean **contains**(int c, int b, JComponent a) ;
    public Accessible **getAccessibleChild**(int b, JComponent a) ;
    public int **getAccessibleChildrenCount**(JComponent a) ;
    public Dimension **getMaximumSize**(JComponent a) ;
    public Dimension **getMinimumSize**(JComponent a) ;
    public Dimension **getPreferredSize**(JComponent a) ;
    public ComponentUI **getUIs**() ;

```
    public void installUI(JComponent a) ;
    public void paint(JComponent b, Graphics a) ;
    public void uninstallUI(JComponent a) ;
    public void update(JComponent b, Graphics a) ;
}
```

---

javax.swing.plaf.multi.**MultiOptionPaneUI**

```
public class MultiOptionPaneUI extends OptionPaneUI
{
    protected Vector uis ;
    // Constructors
    public MultiOptionPaneUI() ;
    // Static methods
    public static ComponentUI createUI(JComponent a) ;
    // Instance methods
    public boolean contains(int c, int b, JComponent a) ;
    public boolean containsCustomComponents(JOptionPane a) ;
    public Accessible getAccessibleChild(int b, JComponent a) ;
    public int getAccessibleChildrenCount(JComponent a) ;
    public Dimension getMaximumSize(JComponent a) ;
    public Dimension getMinimumSize(JComponent a) ;
    public Dimension getPreferredSize(JComponent a) ;
    public ComponentUI getUIs() ;
    public void installUI(JComponent a) ;
    public void paint(JComponent b, Graphics a) ;
    public void selectInitialValue(JOptionPane a) ;
    public void uninstallUI(JComponent a) ;
    public void update(JComponent b, Graphics a) ;
}
```

---

javax.swing.plaf.multi.**MultiPanelUI**

```
public class MultiPanelUI extends PanelUI
{
    protected Vector uis ;
    // Constructors
    public MultiPanelUI() ;
    // Static methods
    public static ComponentUI createUI(JComponent a) ;
    // Instance methods
```

```
    public boolean contains(int c, int b, JComponent a) ;
    public Accessible getAccessibleChild(int b, JComponent a) ;
    public int getAccessibleChildrenCount(JComponent a) ;
    public Dimension getMaximumSize(JComponent a) ;
    public Dimension getMinimumSize(JComponent a) ;
    public Dimension getPreferredSize(JComponent a) ;
    public ComponentUI getUIs() ;
    public void installUI(JComponent a) ;
    public void paint(JComponent b, Graphics a) ;
    public void uninstallUI(JComponent a) ;
    public void update(JComponent b, Graphics a) ;
}
```

---

java.awt.**MultipleGradientPaint** [since 1.6]

```
public abstract class MultipleGradientPaint  implements Paint
{
    // Constructors
    private MultipleGradientPaint(AffineTransform gradientTransform,
        MultipleGradientPaint.ColorSpaceType colorSpace, MultipleGradientPaint.CycleMethod
        cycleMethod, java.awt.Color[] colors, float[] fractions) ;
    // Instance methods
    public final Color getColors() ;
    public final MultipleGradientPaint.ColorSpaceType getColorSpace() ;
    public final MultipleGradientPaint.CycleMethod getCycleMethod() ;
    public final float getFractions() ;
    public final AffineTransform getTransform() ;
    public final int getTransparency() ;
}
```

---

java.awt.**MultipleGradientPaint.ColorSpaceType** [since 1.6]

```
public static final class MultipleGradientPaint.ColorSpaceType extends
Enum<MultipleGradientPaint.ColorSpaceType>
{
    // Constructors
    private MultipleGradientPaint.ColorSpaceType() ;
    // Static methods
    public static MultipleGradientPaint.ColorSpaceType valueOf(String name) ;
    public static final MultipleGradientPaint.ColorSpaceType values() ;
}
```

java.awt.**MultipleGradientPaint.CycleMethod** [since 1.6]

public static final class **MultipleGradientPaint.CycleMethod** extends
Enum<MultipleGradientPaint.CycleMethod>
{
    // Constructors
    private **MultipleGradientPaint.CycleMethod**() ;
    // Static methods
    public static MultipleGradientPaint.CycleMethod **valueOf**(String name) ;
    public static final MultipleGradientPaint.CycleMethod **values**() ;
}

java.awt.font.**MultipleMaster**

public interface **MultipleMaster**
{
    // Instance methods
    public Font **deriveMMFont**(float italicAngle, float typicalXHeight, float typicalCapHeight, float
        avgStemWidth, float[] glyphWidths) ;
    public Font **deriveMMFont**(float[] axes) ;
    public float **getDesignAxisDefaults**() ;
    public String **getDesignAxisNames**() ;
    public float **getDesignAxisRanges**() ;
    public int **getNumDesignAxes**() ;
}

javax.swing.plaf.multi.**MultiPopupMenuUI**

public class **MultiPopupMenuUI** extends PopupMenuUI
{
    protected Vector **uis** ;
    // Constructors
    public **MultiPopupMenuUI**() ;
    // Static methods
    public static ComponentUI **createUI**(JComponent a) ;
    // Instance methods
    public boolean **contains**(int c, int b, JComponent a) ;

```
    public Accessible getAccessibleChild(int b, JComponent a) ;
    public int getAccessibleChildrenCount(JComponent a) ;
    public Dimension getMaximumSize(JComponent a) ;
    public Dimension getMinimumSize(JComponent a) ;
    public Popup getPopup(int c, int b, JPopupMenu a) ; // Since 1.4
    public Dimension getPreferredSize(JComponent a) ;
    public ComponentUI getUIs() ;
    public void installUI(JComponent a) ;
    public boolean isPopupTrigger(MouseEvent a) ; // Since 1.3
    public void paint(JComponent b, Graphics a) ;
    public void uninstallUI(JComponent a) ;
    public void update(JComponent b, Graphics a) ;
}
```

javax.swing.plaf.multi.**MultiProgressBarUI**

public class **MultiProgressBarUI** extends ProgressBarUI
```
{
    protected Vector uis ;
    // Constructors
    public MultiProgressBarUI() ;
    // Static methods
    public static ComponentUI createUI(JComponent a) ;
    // Instance methods
    public boolean contains(int c, int b, JComponent a) ;
    public Accessible getAccessibleChild(int b, JComponent a) ;
    public int getAccessibleChildrenCount(JComponent a) ;
    public Dimension getMaximumSize(JComponent a) ;
    public Dimension getMinimumSize(JComponent a) ;
    public Dimension getPreferredSize(JComponent a) ;
    public ComponentUI getUIs() ;
    public void installUI(JComponent a) ;
    public void paint(JComponent b, Graphics a) ;
    public void uninstallUI(JComponent a) ;
    public void update(JComponent b, Graphics a) ;
}
```

javax.swing.plaf.multi.**MultiRootPaneUI** [since 1.4]

public class **MultiRootPaneUI** extends RootPaneUI
```
{
```

```
        protected Vector uis ;
        // Constructors
        public MultiRootPaneUI() ;
        // Static methods
        public static ComponentUI createUI(JComponent a) ;
        // Instance methods
        public boolean contains(int c, int b, JComponent a) ;
        public Accessible getAccessibleChild(int b, JComponent a) ;
        public int getAccessibleChildrenCount(JComponent a) ;
        public Dimension getMaximumSize(JComponent a) ;
        public Dimension getMinimumSize(JComponent a) ;
        public Dimension getPreferredSize(JComponent a) ;
        public ComponentUI getUIs() ;
        public void installUI(JComponent a) ;
        public void paint(JComponent b, Graphics a) ;
        public void uninstallUI(JComponent a) ;
        public void update(JComponent b, Graphics a) ;
}
```

javax.swing.plaf.multi.**MultiScrollBarUI**

```
public class MultiScrollBarUI extends ScrollBarUI
{
        protected Vector uis ;
        // Constructors
        public MultiScrollBarUI() ;
        // Static methods
        public static ComponentUI createUI(JComponent a) ;
        // Instance methods
        public boolean contains(int c, int b, JComponent a) ;
        public Accessible getAccessibleChild(int b, JComponent a) ;
        public int getAccessibleChildrenCount(JComponent a) ;
        public Dimension getMaximumSize(JComponent a) ;
        public Dimension getMinimumSize(JComponent a) ;
        public Dimension getPreferredSize(JComponent a) ;
        public ComponentUI getUIs() ;
        public void installUI(JComponent a) ;
        public void paint(JComponent b, Graphics a) ;
        public void uninstallUI(JComponent a) ;
        public void update(JComponent b, Graphics a) ;
}
```

javax.swing.plaf.multi.**MultiScrollPaneUI**

public class **MultiScrollPaneUI** extends ScrollPaneUI
{
    protected Vector **uis** ;
    // Constructors
    public **MultiScrollPaneUI**() ;
    // Static methods
    public static ComponentUI **createUI**(JComponent a) ;
    // Instance methods
    public boolean **contains**(int c, int b, JComponent a) ;
    public Accessible **getAccessibleChild**(int b, JComponent a) ;
    public int **getAccessibleChildrenCount**(JComponent a) ;
    public Dimension **getMaximumSize**(JComponent a) ;
    public Dimension **getMinimumSize**(JComponent a) ;
    public Dimension **getPreferredSize**(JComponent a) ;
    public ComponentUI **getUIs**() ;
    public void **installUI**(JComponent a) ;
    public void **paint**(JComponent b, Graphics a) ;
    public void **uninstallUI**(JComponent a) ;
    public void **update**(JComponent b, Graphics a) ;
}

javax.swing.plaf.multi.**MultiSeparatorUI**

public class **MultiSeparatorUI** extends SeparatorUI
{
    protected Vector **uis** ;
    // Constructors
    public **MultiSeparatorUI**() ;
    // Static methods
    public static ComponentUI **createUI**(JComponent a) ;
    // Instance methods
    public boolean **contains**(int c, int b, JComponent a) ;
    public Accessible **getAccessibleChild**(int b, JComponent a) ;
    public int **getAccessibleChildrenCount**(JComponent a) ;
    public Dimension **getMaximumSize**(JComponent a) ;
    public Dimension **getMinimumSize**(JComponent a) ;
    public Dimension **getPreferredSize**(JComponent a) ;
    public ComponentUI **getUIs**() ;

```
    public void installUI(JComponent a) ;
    public void paint(JComponent b, Graphics a) ;
    public void uninstallUI(JComponent a) ;
    public void update(JComponent b, Graphics a) ;
}
```

javax.swing.plaf.multi.**MultiSliderUI**

```
public class MultiSliderUI extends SliderUI
{
    protected Vector uis ;
    // Constructors
    public MultiSliderUI() ;
    // Static methods
    public static ComponentUI createUI(JComponent a) ;
    // Instance methods
    public boolean contains(int c, int b, JComponent a) ;
    public Accessible getAccessibleChild(int b, JComponent a) ;
    public int getAccessibleChildrenCount(JComponent a) ;
    public Dimension getMaximumSize(JComponent a) ;
    public Dimension getMinimumSize(JComponent a) ;
    public Dimension getPreferredSize(JComponent a) ;
    public ComponentUI getUIs() ;
    public void installUI(JComponent a) ;
    public void paint(JComponent b, Graphics a) ;
    public void uninstallUI(JComponent a) ;
    public void update(JComponent b, Graphics a) ;
}
```

javax.swing.plaf.multi.**MultiSpinnerUI** [since 1.4]

```
public class MultiSpinnerUI extends SpinnerUI
{
    protected Vector uis ;
    // Constructors
    public MultiSpinnerUI() ;
    // Static methods
    public static ComponentUI createUI(JComponent a) ;
    // Instance methods
    public boolean contains(int c, int b, JComponent a) ;
    public Accessible getAccessibleChild(int b, JComponent a) ;
```

```
    public int getAccessibleChildrenCount(JComponent a) ;
    public Dimension getMaximumSize(JComponent a) ;
    public Dimension getMinimumSize(JComponent a) ;
    public Dimension getPreferredSize(JComponent a) ;
    public ComponentUI getUIs() ;
    public void installUI(JComponent a) ;
    public void paint(JComponent b, Graphics a) ;
    public void uninstallUI(JComponent a) ;
    public void update(JComponent b, Graphics a) ;
}
```

javax.swing.plaf.multi.**MultiSplitPaneUI**

```
public class MultiSplitPaneUI extends SplitPaneUI
{
    protected Vector uis ;
    // Constructors
    public MultiSplitPaneUI() ;
    // Static methods
    public static ComponentUI createUI(JComponent a) ;
    // Instance methods
    public boolean contains(int c, int b, JComponent a) ;
    public void finishedPaintingChildren(Graphics b, JSplitPane a) ;
    public Accessible getAccessibleChild(int b, JComponent a) ;
    public int getAccessibleChildrenCount(JComponent a) ;
    public int getDividerLocation(JSplitPane a) ;
    public int getMaximumDividerLocation(JSplitPane a) ;
    public Dimension getMaximumSize(JComponent a) ;
    public int getMinimumDividerLocation(JSplitPane a) ;
    public Dimension getMinimumSize(JComponent a) ;
    public Dimension getPreferredSize(JComponent a) ;
    public ComponentUI getUIs() ;
    public void installUI(JComponent a) ;
    public void paint(JComponent b, Graphics a) ;
    public void resetToPreferredSizes(JSplitPane a) ;
    public void setDividerLocation(int b, JSplitPane a) ;
    public void uninstallUI(JComponent a) ;
    public void update(JComponent b, Graphics a) ;
}
```

javax.swing.plaf.multi.**MultiTabbedPaneUI**

public class **MultiTabbedPaneUI** extends TabbedPaneUI
{
    protected Vector **uis** ;
    // Constructors
    public **MultiTabbedPaneUI**() ;
    // Static methods
    public static ComponentUI **createUI**(JComponent a) ;
    // Instance methods
    public boolean **contains**(int c, int b, JComponent a) ;
    public Accessible **getAccessibleChild**(int b, JComponent a) ;
    public int **getAccessibleChildrenCount**(JComponent a) ;
    public Dimension **getMaximumSize**(JComponent a) ;
    public Dimension **getMinimumSize**(JComponent a) ;
    public Dimension **getPreferredSize**(JComponent a) ;
    public Rectangle **getTabBounds**(int b, JTabbedPane a) ;
    public int **getTabRunCount**(JTabbedPane a) ;
    public ComponentUI **getUIs**() ;
    public void **installUI**(JComponent a) ;
    public void **paint**(JComponent b, Graphics a) ;
    public int **tabForCoordinate**(int c, int b, JTabbedPane a) ;
    public void **uninstallUI**(JComponent a) ;
    public void **update**(JComponent b, Graphics a) ;
}

javax.swing.plaf.multi.**MultiTableHeaderUI**

public class **MultiTableHeaderUI** extends TableHeaderUI
{
    protected Vector **uis** ;
    // Constructors
    public **MultiTableHeaderUI**() ;
    // Static methods
    public static ComponentUI **createUI**(JComponent a) ;
    // Instance methods
    public boolean **contains**(int c, int b, JComponent a) ;
    public Accessible **getAccessibleChild**(int b, JComponent a) ;
    public int **getAccessibleChildrenCount**(JComponent a) ;
    public Dimension **getMaximumSize**(JComponent a) ;

```
    public Dimension getMinimumSize(JComponent a) ;
    public Dimension getPreferredSize(JComponent a) ;
    public ComponentUI getUIs() ;
    public void installUI(JComponent a) ;
    public void paint(JComponent b, Graphics a) ;
    public void uninstallUI(JComponent a) ;
    public void update(JComponent b, Graphics a) ;
}
```

javax.swing.plaf.multi.**MultiTableUI**

```
public class MultiTableUI extends TableUI
{
    protected Vector uis ;
    // Constructors
    public MultiTableUI() ;
    // Static methods
    public static ComponentUI createUI(JComponent a) ;
    // Instance methods
    public boolean contains(int c, int b, JComponent a) ;
    public Accessible getAccessibleChild(int b, JComponent a) ;
    public int getAccessibleChildrenCount(JComponent a) ;
    public Dimension getMaximumSize(JComponent a) ;
    public Dimension getMinimumSize(JComponent a) ;
    public Dimension getPreferredSize(JComponent a) ;
    public ComponentUI getUIs() ;
    public void installUI(JComponent a) ;
    public void paint(JComponent b, Graphics a) ;
    public void uninstallUI(JComponent a) ;
    public void update(JComponent b, Graphics a) ;
}
```

javax.swing.plaf.multi.**MultiTextUI**

```
public class MultiTextUI extends TextUI
{
    protected Vector uis ;
    // Constructors
    public MultiTextUI() ;
    // Static methods
    public static ComponentUI createUI(JComponent a) ;
```

```
// Instance methods
public boolean contains(int c, int b, JComponent a) ;
public void damageRange(Position.Bias e, Position.Bias d, int c, int b, JTextComponent a) ;
public void damageRange(int c, int b, JTextComponent a) ;
public Accessible getAccessibleChild(int b, JComponent a) ;
public int getAccessibleChildrenCount(JComponent a) ;
public EditorKit getEditorKit(JTextComponent a) ;
public Dimension getMaximumSize(JComponent a) ;
public Dimension getMinimumSize(JComponent a) ;
public int getNextVisualPositionFrom(javax.swing.text.Position.Bias[] e, int d, Position.Bias c, int
    b, JTextComponent a) throws BadLocationException ;
public Dimension getPreferredSize(JComponent a) ;
public View getRootView(JTextComponent a) ;
public String getToolTipText(Point b, JTextComponent a) ; // Since 1.4
public ComponentUI getUIs() ;
public void installUI(JComponent a) ;
public Rectangle modelToView(int b, JTextComponent a) throws BadLocationException ;
public Rectangle modelToView(Position.Bias c, int b, JTextComponent a) throws
    BadLocationException ;
public void paint(JComponent b, Graphics a) ;
public void uninstallUI(JComponent a) ;
public void update(JComponent b, Graphics a) ;
public int viewToModel(javax.swing.text.Position.Bias[] c, Point b, JTextComponent a) ;
public int viewToModel(Point b, JTextComponent a) ;
}
```

javax.swing.plaf.multi.**MultiToolBarUI**

```
public class MultiToolBarUI extends ToolBarUI
{
    protected Vector uis ;
    // Constructors
    public MultiToolBarUI() ;
    // Static methods
    public static ComponentUI createUI(JComponent a) ;
    // Instance methods
    public boolean contains(int c, int b, JComponent a) ;
    public Accessible getAccessibleChild(int b, JComponent a) ;
    public int getAccessibleChildrenCount(JComponent a) ;
    public Dimension getMaximumSize(JComponent a) ;
    public Dimension getMinimumSize(JComponent a) ;
    public Dimension getPreferredSize(JComponent a) ;
    public ComponentUI getUIs() ;
    public void installUI(JComponent a) ;
```

```
    public void paint(JComponent b, Graphics a) ;
    public void uninstallUI(JComponent a) ;
    public void update(JComponent b, Graphics a) ;
}
```

javax.swing.plaf.multi.**MultiToolTipUI**

```
public class MultiToolTipUI extends ToolTipUI
{
    protected Vector uis ;
    // Constructors
    public MultiToolTipUI() ;
    // Static methods
    public static ComponentUI createUI(JComponent a) ;
    // Instance methods
    public boolean contains(int c, int b, JComponent a) ;
    public Accessible getAccessibleChild(int b, JComponent a) ;
    public int getAccessibleChildrenCount(JComponent a) ;
    public Dimension getMaximumSize(JComponent a) ;
    public Dimension getMinimumSize(JComponent a) ;
    public Dimension getPreferredSize(JComponent a) ;
    public ComponentUI getUIs() ;
    public void installUI(JComponent a) ;
    public void paint(JComponent b, Graphics a) ;
    public void uninstallUI(JComponent a) ;
    public void update(JComponent b, Graphics a) ;
}
```

javax.swing.plaf.multi.**MultiTreeUI**

```
public class MultiTreeUI extends TreeUI
{
    protected Vector uis ;
    // Constructors
    public MultiTreeUI() ;
    // Static methods
    public static ComponentUI createUI(JComponent a) ;
    // Instance methods
    public void cancelEditing(JTree a) ;
    public boolean contains(int c, int b, JComponent a) ;
    public Accessible getAccessibleChild(int b, JComponent a) ;
```

```
        public int getAccessibleChildrenCount(JComponent a) ;
        public TreePath getClosestPathForLocation(int c, int b, JTree a) ;
        public TreePath getEditingPath(JTree a) ;
        public Dimension getMaximumSize(JComponent a) ;
        public Dimension getMinimumSize(JComponent a) ;
        public Rectangle getPathBounds(TreePath b, JTree a) ;
        public TreePath getPathForRow(int b, JTree a) ;
        public Dimension getPreferredSize(JComponent a) ;
        public int getRowCount(JTree a) ;
        public int getRowForPath(TreePath b, JTree a) ;
        public ComponentUI getUIs() ;
        public void installUI(JComponent a) ;
        public boolean isEditing(JTree a) ;
        public void paint(JComponent b, Graphics a) ;
        public void startEditingAtPath(TreePath b, JTree a) ;
        public boolean stopEditing(JTree a) ;
        public void uninstallUI(JComponent a) ;
        public void update(JComponent b, Graphics a) ;
}
```

---

javax.swing.plaf.multi.**MultiViewportUI**

```
public class MultiViewportUI extends ViewportUI
{
        protected Vector uis ;
        // Constructors
        public MultiViewportUI() ;
        // Static methods
        public static ComponentUI createUI(JComponent a) ;
        // Instance methods
        public boolean contains(int c, int b, JComponent a) ;
        public Accessible getAccessibleChild(int b, JComponent a) ;
        public int getAccessibleChildrenCount(JComponent a) ;
        public Dimension getMaximumSize(JComponent a) ;
        public Dimension getMinimumSize(JComponent a) ;
        public Dimension getPreferredSize(JComponent a) ;
        public ComponentUI getUIs() ;
        public void installUI(JComponent a) ;
        public void paint(JComponent b, Graphics a) ;
        public void uninstallUI(JComponent a) ;
        public void update(JComponent b, Graphics a) ;
}
```

javax.swing.text.**MutableAttributeSet**

public interface **MutableAttributeSet** implements AttributeSet
{
    // Instance methods
    public void **addAttribute**(Object value, Object name) ;
    public void **addAttributes**(AttributeSet attributes) ;
    public void **removeAttribute**(Object name) ;
    public void **removeAttributes**(AttributeSet attributes) ;
    public void **removeAttributes**(Enumeration<?> names) ;
    public void **setResolveParent**(AttributeSet parent) ;
}

javax.swing.**MutableComboBoxModel**

public interface **MutableComboBoxModel** implements ComboBoxModel
{
    // Instance methods
    public void **addElement**(Object obj) ;
    public void **insertElementAt**(int index, Object obj) ;
    public void **removeElement**(Object obj) ;
    public void **removeElementAt**(int index) ;
}

javax.swing.tree.**MutableTreeNode**

public interface **MutableTreeNode** implements TreeNode
{
    // Instance methods
    public void **insert**(int index, MutableTreeNode child) ;
    public void **remove**(MutableTreeNode node) ;
    public void **remove**(int index) ;
    public void **removeFromParent**() ;
    public void **setParent**(MutableTreeNode newParent) ;
    public void **setUserObject**(Object object) ;
}

javax.swing.text.**NavigationFilter** [since 1.4]

public class **NavigationFilter**
{
    // Constructors
    public **NavigationFilter**() ;
    // Instance methods
    public int **getNextVisualPositionFrom**(javax.swing.text.Position.Bias[] biasRet, int direction,
        Position.Bias bias, int pos, JTextComponent text) throws BadLocationException ;
    public void **moveDot**(Position.Bias bias, int dot, NavigationFilter.FilterBypass fb) ;
    public void **setDot**(Position.Bias bias, int dot, NavigationFilter.FilterBypass fb) ;
}

javax.swing.text.**NavigationFilter.FilterBypass** [since 1.4]

public abstract static class **NavigationFilter.FilterBypass**
{
    // Constructors
    public **NavigationFilter.FilterBypass**() ;
    // Instance methods
    public abstract Caret **getCaret**() ;
    public abstract void **moveDot**(Position.Bias bias, int dot) ;
    public abstract void **setDot**(Position.Bias bias, int dot) ;
}

java.awt.geom.**NoninvertibleTransformException**

public class **NoninvertibleTransformException** extends Exception
{
    // Constructors
    public **NoninvertibleTransformException**(String s) ;
}

javax.swing.text.**NumberFormatter** [since 1.4]

public class **NumberFormatter** extends InternationalFormatter
{
    // Constructors
    public **NumberFormatter**(NumberFormat format) ;
    public **NumberFormatter**() ;
    // Instance methods
    public void **setFormat**(Format format) ;
}

java.awt.font.**NumericShaper** [since 1.4]

public final class **NumericShaper** implements Serializable
{
    public static final int **ALL_RANGES** ;
    public static final int **ARABIC** ;
    public static final int **BENGALI** ;
    public static final int **DEVANAGARI** ;
    public static final int **EASTERN_ARABIC** ;
    public static final int **ETHIOPIC** ;
    public static final int **EUROPEAN** ;
    public static final int **GUJARATI** ;
    public static final int **GURMUKHI** ;
    public static final int **KANNADA** ;
    public static final int **KHMER** ;
    public static final int **LAO** ;
    public static final int **MALAYALAM** ;
    public static final int **MONGOLIAN** ;
    public static final int **MYANMAR** ;
    public static final int **ORIYA** ;
    public static final int **TAMIL** ;
    public static final int **TELUGU** ;
    public static final int **THAI** ;
    public static final int **TIBETAN** ;
    // Constructors
    private **NumericShaper**(int mask, int key) ;
    // Static methods
    public static NumericShaper **getContextualShaper**(int ranges) ;
    public static NumericShaper **getContextualShaper**(int defaultContext, int ranges) ;

```
    public static NumericShaper getShaper(int singleRange) ;
    // Instance methods
    public boolean equals(Object o) ;
    public int getRanges() ;
    public int hashCode() ;
    public boolean isContextual() ;
    public void shape(int context, int count, int start, char[] text) ;
    public void shape(int count, int start, char[] text) ;
    public String toString() ;
}
```

---

javax.swing.text.html.**ObjectView**

```
public class ObjectView extends ComponentView
{
    // Constructors
    public ObjectView(Element elem) ;
    // Instance methods
    protected Component createComponent() ;
}
```

---

javax.swing.plaf.metal.**OceanTheme** [since 1.5]

```
public class OceanTheme extends DefaultMetalTheme
{
    // Constructors
    public OceanTheme() ;
    // Instance methods
    public void addCustomEntriesToTable(UIDefaults table) ;
    protected ColorUIResource getBlack() ;
    public ColorUIResource getControlTextColor() ;
    public ColorUIResource getDesktopColor() ;
    public ColorUIResource getInactiveControlTextColor() ;
    public ColorUIResource getMenuDisabledForeground() ;
    public String getName() ;
    protected ColorUIResource getPrimary1() ;
    protected ColorUIResource getPrimary2() ;
    protected ColorUIResource getPrimary3() ;
    protected ColorUIResource getSecondary1() ;
    protected ColorUIResource getSecondary2() ;
    protected ColorUIResource getSecondary3() ;
```

}

---

java.awt.font.**OpenType**

---

public interface **OpenType**
{
    public static final int **TAG_ACNT** ;
    public static final int **TAG_AVAR** ;
    public static final int **TAG_BASE** ;
    public static final int **TAG_BDAT** ;
    public static final int **TAG_BLOC** ;
    public static final int **TAG_BSLN** ;
    public static final int **TAG_CFF** ;
    public static final int **TAG_CMAP** ;
    public static final int **TAG_CVAR** ;
    public static final int **TAG_CVT** ;
    public static final int **TAG_DSIG** ;
    public static final int **TAG_EBDT** ;
    public static final int **TAG_EBLC** ;
    public static final int **TAG_EBSC** ;
    public static final int **TAG_FDSC** ;
    public static final int **TAG_FEAT** ;
    public static final int **TAG_FMTX** ;
    public static final int **TAG_FPGM** ;
    public static final int **TAG_FVAR** ;
    public static final int **TAG_GASP** ;
    public static final int **TAG_GDEF** ;
    public static final int **TAG_GLYF** ;
    public static final int **TAG_GPOS** ;
    public static final int **TAG_GSUB** ;
    public static final int **TAG_GVAR** ;
    public static final int **TAG_HDMX** ;
    public static final int **TAG_HEAD** ;
    public static final int **TAG_HHEA** ;
    public static final int **TAG_HMTX** ;
    public static final int **TAG_JSTF** ;
    public static final int **TAG_JUST** ;
    public static final int **TAG_KERN** ;
    public static final int **TAG_LCAR** ;
    public static final int **TAG_LOCA** ;
    public static final int **TAG_LTSH** ;
    public static final int **TAG_MAXP** ;
    public static final int **TAG_MMFX** ;
    public static final int **TAG_MMSD** ;

```
        public static final int TAG_MORT ;
        public static final int TAG_NAME ;
        public static final int TAG_OPBD ;
        public static final int TAG_OS2 ;
        public static final int TAG_PCLT ;
        public static final int TAG_POST ;
        public static final int TAG_PREP ;
        public static final int TAG_PROP ;
        public static final int TAG_TRAK ;
        public static final int TAG_TYP1 ;
        public static final int TAG_VDMX ;
        public static final int TAG_VHEA ;
        public static final int TAG_VMTX ;
        // Instance methods
        public byte getFontTable(int count, int offset, String strSfntTag) ;
        public byte getFontTable(int count, int offset, int sfntTag) ;
        public byte getFontTable(String strSfntTag) ;
        public byte getFontTable(int sfntTag) ;
        public int getFontTableSize(String strSfntTag) ;
        public int getFontTableSize(int sfntTag) ;
        public int getVersion() ;
}
```

---

javax.swing.text.html.**Option**

```
public class Option  implements Serializable
{
        // Constructors
        public Option(AttributeSet attr) ;
        // Instance methods
        public AttributeSet getAttributes() ;
        public String getLabel() ;
        public String getValue() ;
        public boolean isSelected() ;
        public void setLabel(String label) ;
        protected void setSelection(boolean state) ;
        public String toString() ;
}
```

javax.swing.plaf.**OptionPaneUI**

public abstract class **OptionPaneUI** extends ComponentUI
{
    // Constructors
    public **OptionPaneUI**() ;
    // Instance methods
    public abstract boolean **containsCustomComponents**(JOptionPane op) ;
    public abstract void **selectInitialValue**(JOptionPane op) ;
}

javax.swing.**OverlayLayout**

public class **OverlayLayout** implements Serializable, LayoutManager2
{
    // Constructors
    public **OverlayLayout**(Container target) ;
    // Instance methods
    public void **addLayoutComponent**(Component comp, String name) ;
    public void **addLayoutComponent**(Object constraints, Component comp) ;
    public float **getLayoutAlignmentX**(Container target) ;
    public float **getLayoutAlignmentY**(Container target) ;
    public final Container **getTarget**() ; // Since 1.6
    public void **invalidateLayout**(Container target) ;
    public void **layoutContainer**(Container target) ;
    public Dimension **maximumLayoutSize**(Container target) ;
    public Dimension **minimumLayoutSize**(Container target) ;
    public Dimension **preferredLayoutSize**(Container target) ;
    public void **removeLayoutComponent**(Component comp) ;
}

java.awt.image.**PackedColorModel**

public abstract class **PackedColorModel** extends ColorModel
{
    // Constructors

```
    public PackedColorModel(int transferType, int trans, boolean isAlphaPremultiplied, int amask, int
        bmask, int gmask, int rmask, int bits, ColorSpace space) ;
    public PackedColorModel(int transferType, int trans, boolean isAlphaPremultiplied, int alphaMask,
        int[] colorMaskArray, int bits, ColorSpace space) ;
    // Static methods
    // Instance methods
    public SampleModel createCompatibleSampleModel(int h, int w) ;
    public boolean equals(Object obj) ;
    public WritableRaster getAlphaRaster(WritableRaster raster) ;
    public final int getMask(int index) ;
    public final int getMasks() ;
    public boolean isCompatibleSampleModel(SampleModel sm) ;
}
```

---

java.awt.print.**Pageable**

```
public interface Pageable
{
    public static final int UNKNOWN_NUMBER_OF_PAGES ;
    // Instance methods
    public int getNumberOfPages() ;
    public PageFormat getPageFormat(int pageIndex) throws IndexOutOfBoundsException ;
    public Printable getPrintable(int pageIndex) throws IndexOutOfBoundsException ;
}
```

---

java.awt.**PageAttributes** [since 1.3]

```
public final class PageAttributes  implements Cloneable
{
    // Constructors
    public PageAttributes(int[] printerResolution, PageAttributes.PrintQualityType printQuality,
        PageAttributes.OriginType origin, PageAttributes.OrientationRequestedType
        orientationRequested, PageAttributes.MediaType media, PageAttributes.ColorType color) ;
    public PageAttributes(PageAttributes obj) ;
    public PageAttributes() ;
    // Instance methods
    public Object clone() ;
    public boolean equals(Object obj) ;
    public PageAttributes.ColorType getColor() ;
    public PageAttributes.MediaType getMedia() ;
    public PageAttributes.OrientationRequestedType getOrientationRequested() ;
```

```
    public PageAttributes.OriginType getOrigin() ;
    public int getPrinterResolution() ;
    public PageAttributes.PrintQualityType getPrintQuality() ;
    public int hashCode() ;
    public void set(PageAttributes obj) ;
    public void setColor(PageAttributes.ColorType color) ;
    public void setMedia(PageAttributes.MediaType media) ;
    public void setMediaToDefault() ;
    public void setOrientationRequested(PageAttributes.OrientationRequestedType
        orientationRequested) ;
    public void setOrientationRequested(int orientationRequested) ;
    public void setOrientationRequestedToDefault() ;
    public void setOrigin(PageAttributes.OriginType origin) ;
    public void setPrinterResolution(int printerResolution) ;
    public void setPrinterResolution(int[] printerResolution) ;
    public void setPrinterResolutionToDefault() ;
    public void setPrintQuality(PageAttributes.PrintQualityType printQuality) ;
    public void setPrintQuality(int printQuality) ;
    public void setPrintQualityToDefault() ;
    public String toString() ;
}
```

---

java.awt.**PageAttributes.ColorType** [since 1.3]

```
public static final class PageAttributes.ColorType extends AttributeValue
{
    public static final PageAttributes.ColorType COLOR ;
    public static final PageAttributes.ColorType MONOCHROME ;
    // Constructors
    private PageAttributes.ColorType(int type) ;
}
```

---

java.awt.**PageAttributes.MediaType** [since 1.3]

```
public static final class PageAttributes.MediaType extends AttributeValue
{
    public static final PageAttributes.MediaType A ;
    public static final PageAttributes.MediaType A0 ;
    public static final PageAttributes.MediaType A1 ;
    public static final PageAttributes.MediaType A10 ;
    public static final PageAttributes.MediaType A2 ;
```

public static final PageAttributes.MediaType **A3** ;
public static final PageAttributes.MediaType **A4** ;
public static final PageAttributes.MediaType **A5** ;
public static final PageAttributes.MediaType **A6** ;
public static final PageAttributes.MediaType **A7** ;
public static final PageAttributes.MediaType **A8** ;
public static final PageAttributes.MediaType **A9** ;
public static final PageAttributes.MediaType **B** ;
public static final PageAttributes.MediaType **B0** ;
public static final PageAttributes.MediaType **B1** ;
public static final PageAttributes.MediaType **B10** ;
public static final PageAttributes.MediaType **B2** ;
public static final PageAttributes.MediaType **B3** ;
public static final PageAttributes.MediaType **B4** ;
public static final PageAttributes.MediaType **B5** ;
public static final PageAttributes.MediaType **B6** ;
public static final PageAttributes.MediaType **B7** ;
public static final PageAttributes.MediaType **B8** ;
public static final PageAttributes.MediaType **B9** ;
public static final PageAttributes.MediaType **C** ;
public static final PageAttributes.MediaType **C0** ;
public static final PageAttributes.MediaType **C1** ;
public static final PageAttributes.MediaType **C10** ;
public static final PageAttributes.MediaType **C2** ;
public static final PageAttributes.MediaType **C3** ;
public static final PageAttributes.MediaType **C4** ;
public static final PageAttributes.MediaType **C5** ;
public static final PageAttributes.MediaType **C6** ;
public static final PageAttributes.MediaType **C7** ;
public static final PageAttributes.MediaType **C8** ;
public static final PageAttributes.MediaType **C9** ;
public static final PageAttributes.MediaType **D** ;
public static final PageAttributes.MediaType **E** ;
public static final PageAttributes.MediaType **ENV_10** ;
public static final PageAttributes.MediaType **ENV_10X13** ;
public static final PageAttributes.MediaType **ENV_10X14** ;
public static final PageAttributes.MediaType **ENV_10X15** ;
public static final PageAttributes.MediaType **ENV_11** ;
public static final PageAttributes.MediaType **ENV_12** ;
public static final PageAttributes.MediaType **ENV_14** ;
public static final PageAttributes.MediaType **ENV_6X9** ;
public static final PageAttributes.MediaType **ENV_7X9** ;
public static final PageAttributes.MediaType **ENV_9** ;
public static final PageAttributes.MediaType **ENV_9X11** ;
public static final PageAttributes.MediaType **ENV_9X12** ;
public static final PageAttributes.MediaType **ENV_INVITE** ;

```
public static final PageAttributes.MediaType ENV_ITALY ;
public static final PageAttributes.MediaType ENV_MONARCH ;
public static final PageAttributes.MediaType ENV_PERSONAL ;
public static final PageAttributes.MediaType EXECUTIVE ;
public static final PageAttributes.MediaType FOLIO ;
public static final PageAttributes.MediaType INVITE ;
public static final PageAttributes.MediaType INVITE_ENVELOPE ;
public static final PageAttributes.MediaType INVOICE ;
public static final PageAttributes.MediaType ISO_2A0 ;
public static final PageAttributes.MediaType ISO_4A0 ;
public static final PageAttributes.MediaType ISO_A0 ;
public static final PageAttributes.MediaType ISO_A1 ;
public static final PageAttributes.MediaType ISO_A10 ;
public static final PageAttributes.MediaType ISO_A2 ;
public static final PageAttributes.MediaType ISO_A3 ;
public static final PageAttributes.MediaType ISO_A4 ;
public static final PageAttributes.MediaType ISO_A5 ;
public static final PageAttributes.MediaType ISO_A6 ;
public static final PageAttributes.MediaType ISO_A7 ;
public static final PageAttributes.MediaType ISO_A8 ;
public static final PageAttributes.MediaType ISO_A9 ;
public static final PageAttributes.MediaType ISO_B0 ;
public static final PageAttributes.MediaType ISO_B1 ;
public static final PageAttributes.MediaType ISO_B10 ;
public static final PageAttributes.MediaType ISO_B2 ;
public static final PageAttributes.MediaType ISO_B3 ;
public static final PageAttributes.MediaType ISO_B4 ;
public static final PageAttributes.MediaType ISO_B4_ENVELOPE ;
public static final PageAttributes.MediaType ISO_B5 ;
public static final PageAttributes.MediaType ISO_B5_ENVELOPE ;
public static final PageAttributes.MediaType ISO_B6 ;
public static final PageAttributes.MediaType ISO_B7 ;
public static final PageAttributes.MediaType ISO_B8 ;
public static final PageAttributes.MediaType ISO_B9 ;
public static final PageAttributes.MediaType ISO_C0 ;
public static final PageAttributes.MediaType ISO_C0_ENVELOPE ;
public static final PageAttributes.MediaType ISO_C1 ;
public static final PageAttributes.MediaType ISO_C10 ;
public static final PageAttributes.MediaType ISO_C10_ENVELOPE ;
public static final PageAttributes.MediaType ISO_C1_ENVELOPE ;
public static final PageAttributes.MediaType ISO_C2 ;
public static final PageAttributes.MediaType ISO_C2_ENVELOPE ;
public static final PageAttributes.MediaType ISO_C3 ;
public static final PageAttributes.MediaType ISO_C3_ENVELOPE ;
public static final PageAttributes.MediaType ISO_C4 ;
public static final PageAttributes.MediaType ISO_C4_ENVELOPE ;
```

public static final PageAttributes.MediaType **ISO_C5** ;
public static final PageAttributes.MediaType **ISO_C5_ENVELOPE** ;
public static final PageAttributes.MediaType **ISO_C6** ;
public static final PageAttributes.MediaType **ISO_C6_ENVELOPE** ;
public static final PageAttributes.MediaType **ISO_C7** ;
public static final PageAttributes.MediaType **ISO_C7_ENVELOPE** ;
public static final PageAttributes.MediaType **ISO_C8** ;
public static final PageAttributes.MediaType **ISO_C8_ENVELOPE** ;
public static final PageAttributes.MediaType **ISO_C9** ;
public static final PageAttributes.MediaType **ISO_C9_ENVELOPE** ;
public static final PageAttributes.MediaType **ISO_DESIGNATED_LONG** ;
public static final PageAttributes.MediaType **ISO_DESIGNATED_LONG_ENVELOPE** ;
public static final PageAttributes.MediaType **ITALY** ;
public static final PageAttributes.MediaType **ITALY_ENVELOPE** ;
public static final PageAttributes.MediaType **JIS_B0** ;
public static final PageAttributes.MediaType **JIS_B1** ;
public static final PageAttributes.MediaType **JIS_B10** ;
public static final PageAttributes.MediaType **JIS_B2** ;
public static final PageAttributes.MediaType **JIS_B3** ;
public static final PageAttributes.MediaType **JIS_B4** ;
public static final PageAttributes.MediaType **JIS_B5** ;
public static final PageAttributes.MediaType **JIS_B6** ;
public static final PageAttributes.MediaType **JIS_B7** ;
public static final PageAttributes.MediaType **JIS_B8** ;
public static final PageAttributes.MediaType **JIS_B9** ;
public static final PageAttributes.MediaType **LEDGER** ;
public static final PageAttributes.MediaType **LEGAL** ;
public static final PageAttributes.MediaType **LETTER** ;
public static final PageAttributes.MediaType **MONARCH** ;
public static final PageAttributes.MediaType **MONARCH_ENVELOPE** ;
public static final PageAttributes.MediaType **NA_10X13_ENVELOPE** ;
public static final PageAttributes.MediaType **NA_10X14_ENVELOPE** ;
public static final PageAttributes.MediaType **NA_10X15_ENVELOPE** ;
public static final PageAttributes.MediaType **NA_6X9_ENVELOPE** ;
public static final PageAttributes.MediaType **NA_7X9_ENVELOPE** ;
public static final PageAttributes.MediaType **NA_9X11_ENVELOPE** ;
public static final PageAttributes.MediaType **NA_9X12_ENVELOPE** ;
public static final PageAttributes.MediaType **NA_LEGAL** ;
public static final PageAttributes.MediaType **NA_LETTER** ;
public static final PageAttributes.MediaType **NA_NUMBER_10_ENVELOPE** ;
public static final PageAttributes.MediaType **NA_NUMBER_11_ENVELOPE** ;
public static final PageAttributes.MediaType **NA_NUMBER_12_ENVELOPE** ;
public static final PageAttributes.MediaType **NA_NUMBER_14_ENVELOPE** ;
public static final PageAttributes.MediaType **NA_NUMBER_9_ENVELOPE** ;
public static final PageAttributes.MediaType **NOTE** ;
public static final PageAttributes.MediaType **PERSONAL** ;

```
        public static final PageAttributes.MediaType PERSONAL_ENVELOPE ;
        public static final PageAttributes.MediaType QUARTO ;
        public static final PageAttributes.MediaType STATEMENT ;
        public static final PageAttributes.MediaType TABLOID ;
        // Constructors
        private PageAttributes.MediaType(int type) ;
}
```

java.awt.**PageAttributes.OrientationRequestedType** [since 1.3]

```
public static final class PageAttributes.OrientationRequestedType extends AttributeValue
{
        public static final PageAttributes.OrientationRequestedType LANDSCAPE ;
        public static final PageAttributes.OrientationRequestedType PORTRAIT ;
        // Constructors
        private PageAttributes.OrientationRequestedType(int type) ;
}
```

java.awt.**PageAttributes.OriginType** [since 1.3]

```
public static final class PageAttributes.OriginType extends AttributeValue
{
        public static final PageAttributes.OriginType PHYSICAL ;
        public static final PageAttributes.OriginType PRINTABLE ;
        // Constructors
        private PageAttributes.OriginType(int type) ;
}
```

java.awt.**PageAttributes.PrintQualityType** [since 1.3]

```
public static final class PageAttributes.PrintQualityType extends AttributeValue
{
        public static final PageAttributes.PrintQualityType DRAFT ;
        public static final PageAttributes.PrintQualityType HIGH ;
        public static final PageAttributes.PrintQualityType NORMAL ;
        // Constructors
        private PageAttributes.PrintQualityType(int type) ;
}
```

java.awt.print.**PageFormat**

public class **PageFormat** implements Cloneable
{
    public static final int **LANDSCAPE** ;
    public static final int **PORTRAIT** ;
    public static final int **REVERSE_LANDSCAPE** ;
    // Constructors
    public **PageFormat**() ;
    // Instance methods
    public Object **clone**() ;
    public double **getHeight**() ;
    public double **getImageableHeight**() ;
    public double **getImageableWidth**() ;
    public double **getImageableX**() ;
    public double **getImageableY**() ;
    public double **getMatrix**() ;
    public int **getOrientation**() ;
    public Paper **getPaper**() ;
    public double **getWidth**() ;
    public void **setOrientation**(int orientation) throws IllegalArgumentException ;
    public void **setPaper**(Paper paper) ;
}

java.awt.**Paint**

public interface **Paint** implements Transparency
{
    // Instance methods
    public PaintContext **createContext**(RenderingHints hints, AffineTransform xform, Rectangle2D
      userBounds, Rectangle deviceBounds, ColorModel cm) ;
}

java.awt.**PaintContext**

public interface **PaintContext**
{

```
    // Instance methods
    public void dispose() ;
    public ColorModel getColorModel() ;
    public Raster getRaster(int h, int w, int y, int x) ;
}
```

---

java.awt.event.**PaintEvent** [since 1.1]

```
public class PaintEvent extends ComponentEvent
{
    public static final int PAINT ;
    public static final int PAINT_FIRST ;
    public static final int PAINT_LAST ;
    public static final int UPDATE ;
    // Constructors
    public PaintEvent(Rectangle updateRect, int id, Component source) ;
    // Instance methods
    public Rectangle getUpdateRect() ;
    public String paramString() ;
    public void setUpdateRect(Rectangle updateRect) ;
}
```

---

java.awt.**Panel** [since 1.0]

```
public class Panel extends Container implements Accessible
{
    // Constructors
    public Panel(LayoutManager layout) ;
    public Panel() ;
    // Instance methods
    public void addNotify() ;
    public AccessibleContext getAccessibleContext() ; // Since 1.3
}
```

---

javax.swing.plaf.**PanelUI**

```
public abstract class PanelUI extends ComponentUI
{
```

```
    // Constructors
    public PanelUI() ;
}
```

---

java.awt.print.**Paper**

---

public class **Paper** implements Cloneable
```
{
    // Constructors
    public Paper() ;
    // Instance methods
    public Object clone() ;
    public double getHeight() ;
    public double getImageableHeight() ;
    public double getImageableWidth() ;
    public double getImageableX() ;
    public double getImageableY() ;
    public double getWidth() ;
    public void setImageableArea(double height, double width, double y, double x) ;
    public void setSize(double height, double width) ;
}
```

---

javax.swing.text.**ParagraphView**

---

public class **ParagraphView** extends FlowView implements TabExpander
```
{
    protected int firstLineIndent ;
    // Constructors
    public ParagraphView(Element elem) ;
    // Instance methods
    protected void adjustRow(int x, int desiredSpan, ParagraphView.Row r) ;
    public View breakView(Shape a, float len, int axis) ;
    protected SizeRequirements calculateMinorAxisRequirements(SizeRequirements r, int axis) ;
    public void changedUpdate(ViewFactory f, Shape a, DocumentEvent changes) ;
    protected View createRow() ; // Since 1.3
    protected int findOffsetToCharactersInString(int start, char[] string) ;
    protected boolean flipEastAndWestAtEnds(Position.Bias bias, int position) ;
    public float getAlignment(int axis) ;
    public int getBreakWeight(float len, int axis) ;
    protected int getClosestPositionTo(int x, int rowIndex, javax.swing.text.Position.Bias[] biasRet, int
        direction, Shape a, Position.Bias b, int pos) throws BadLocationException ;
```

---

public int **getFlowSpan**(int index) ; // Since 1.3
public int **getFlowStart**(int index) ; // Since 1.3
protected View **getLayoutView**(int index) ;
protected int **getLayoutViewCount**() ;
protected int **getNextNorthSouthVisualPositionFrom**(javax.swing.text.Position.Bias[] biasRet, int
    direction, Shape a, Position.Bias b, int pos) throws BadLocationException ;
protected float **getPartialSize**(int endOffset, int startOffset) ;
protected float **getTabBase**() ;
protected TabSet **getTabSet**() ;
public float **nextTabStop**(int tabOffset, float x) ;
public void **paint**(Shape a, Graphics g) ;
protected void **setFirstLineIndent**(float fi) ;
protected void **setJustification**(int j) ;
protected void **setLineSpacing**(float ls) ;
protected void **setPropertiesFromAttributes**() ;
}

---

javax.swing.text.html.**ParagraphView**

---

public class **ParagraphView** extends ParagraphView
{
    // Constructors
    public **ParagraphView**(Element elem) ;
    // Instance methods
    protected SizeRequirements **calculateMinorAxisRequirements**(SizeRequirements r, int axis) ;
    public AttributeSet **getAttributes**() ;
    public float **getMaximumSpan**(int axis) ;
    public float **getMinimumSpan**(int axis) ;
    public float **getPreferredSpan**(int axis) ;
    protected StyleSheet **getStyleSheet**() ;
    public boolean **isVisible**() ;
    public void **paint**(Shape a, Graphics g) ;
    public void **setParent**(View parent) ;
    protected void **setPropertiesFromAttributes**() ;
}

---

java.awt.image.renderable.**ParameterBlock**

---

public class **ParameterBlock** implements Serializable, Cloneable
{
    protected Vector<Object> **parameters** ;

---

protected Vector<Object> **sources** ;
// Constructors
public **ParameterBlock**(Vector<Object> parameters, Vector<Object> sources) ;
public **ParameterBlock**(Vector<Object> sources) ;
public **ParameterBlock**() ;
// Instance methods
public ParameterBlock **add**(int i) ;
public ParameterBlock **add**(float f) ;
public ParameterBlock **add**(double d) ;
public ParameterBlock **add**(short s) ;
public ParameterBlock **add**(char c) ;
public ParameterBlock **add**(byte b) ;
public ParameterBlock **add**(Object obj) ;
public ParameterBlock **add**(long l) ;
public ParameterBlock **addSource**(Object source) ;
public Object **clone**() ;
public byte **getByteParameter**(int index) ;
public char **getCharParameter**(int index) ;
public double **getDoubleParameter**(int index) ;
public float **getFloatParameter**(int index) ;
public int **getIntParameter**(int index) ;
public long **getLongParameter**(int index) ;
public int **getNumParameters**() ;
public int **getNumSources**() ;
public Object **getObjectParameter**(int index) ;
public Class **getParamClasses**() ;
public Vector<Object> **getParameters**() ;
public RenderableImage **getRenderableSource**(int index) ;
public RenderedImage **getRenderedSource**(int index) ;
public short **getShortParameter**(int index) ;
public Object **getSource**(int index) ;
public Vector<Object> **getSources**() ;
public void **removeParameters**() ;
public void **removeSources**() ;
public ParameterBlock **set**(int index, float f) ;
public ParameterBlock **set**(int index, Object obj) ;
public ParameterBlock **set**(int index, long l) ;
public ParameterBlock **set**(int index, int i) ;
public ParameterBlock **set**(int index, short s) ;
public ParameterBlock **set**(int index, char c) ;
public ParameterBlock **set**(int index, byte b) ;
public ParameterBlock **set**(int index, double d) ;
public void **setParameters**(Vector<Object> parameters) ;
public ParameterBlock **setSource**(int index, Object source) ;
public void **setSources**(Vector<Object> sources) ;
public Object **shallowClone**() ;

}

---

javax.swing.text.html.parser.**Parser**

---

public class **Parser** implements DTDConstants
{
    protected DTD **dtd** ;
    protected boolean **strict** ;
    // Constructors
    public **Parser**(DTD dtd) ;
    // Instance methods
    protected void **endTag**(boolean omitted) ;
    protected void **error**(String err) ;
    protected void **error**(String arg3, String arg2, String arg1, String err) ;
    protected void **error**(String arg2, String arg1, String err) ;
    protected void **error**(String arg1, String err) ;
    protected void **flushAttributes**() ;
    protected SimpleAttributeSet **getAttributes**() ;
    protected int **getCurrentLine**() ;
    protected int **getCurrentPos**() ;
    protected void **handleComment**(char[] text) ;
    protected void **handleEmptyTag**(TagElement tag) throws ChangedCharSetException ;
    protected void **handleEndTag**(TagElement tag) ;
    protected void **handleEOFInComment**() ;
    protected void **handleError**(String msg, int ln) ;
    protected void **handleStartTag**(TagElement tag) ;
    protected void **handleText**(char[] text) ;
    protected void **handleTitle**(char[] text) ;
    protected TagElement **makeTag**(boolean fictional, Element elem) ;
    protected TagElement **makeTag**(Element elem) ;
    protected void **markFirstTime**(Element elem) ;
    public synchronized void **parse**(Reader in) throws IOException ;
    public String **parseDTDMarkup**() throws IOException ;
    protected boolean **parseMarkupDeclarations**(StringBuffer strBuff) throws IOException ;
    protected void **startTag**(TagElement tag) throws ChangedCharSetException ;
}

---

javax.swing.text.html.parser.**ParserDelegator**

---

public class **ParserDelegator** extends HTMLEditorKit.Parser implements Serializable
{

```
    // Constructors
    public ParserDelegator() ;
    // Static methods
    protected static DTD createDTD(String name, DTD dtd) ;
    protected static synchronized void setDefaultDTD() ;
    // Instance methods
    public void parse(boolean ignoreCharSet, HTMLEditorKit.ParserCallback cb, Reader r) throws
        IOException ;
}
```

javax.swing.text.**PasswordView**

public class **PasswordView** extends FieldView
```
{
    // Constructors
    public PasswordView(Element elem) ;
    // Instance methods
    protected int drawEchoCharacter(char c, int y, int x, Graphics g) ;
    protected int drawSelectedText(int p1, int p0, int y, int x, Graphics g) throws BadLocationException
        ;
    protected int drawUnselectedText(int p1, int p0, int y, int x, Graphics g) throws
        BadLocationException ;
    public float getPreferredSpan(int axis) ;
    public Shape modelToView(Position.Bias b, Shape a, int pos) throws BadLocationException ;
    public int viewToModel(javax.swing.text.Position.Bias[] bias, Shape a, float fy, float fx) ;
}
```

java.awt.geom.**Path2D** [since 1.6]

public abstract class **Path2D** implements Cloneable, Shape
```
{
    public static final int WIND_EVEN_ODD ;
    public static final int WIND_NON_ZERO ;
    // Constructors
    private Path2D(int initialTypes, int rule) ;
    private Path2D() ;
    // Static methods
    public static boolean contains(double y, double x, PathIterator pi) ; // Since 1.6
    public static boolean contains(Point2D p, PathIterator pi) ; // Since 1.6
    public static boolean contains(double h, double w, double y, double x, PathIterator pi) ; // Since 1.6
    public static boolean contains(Rectangle2D r, PathIterator pi) ; // Since 1.6
```

```
public static boolean intersects(Rectangle2D r, PathIterator pi) ; // Since 1.6
public static boolean intersects(double h, double w, double y, double x, PathIterator pi) ; // Since 1.6
// Instance methods
public abstract void append(boolean connect, PathIterator pi) ; // Since 1.6
public final void append(boolean connect, Shape s) ; // Since 1.6
public abstract Object clone() ; // Since 1.6
public final synchronized void closePath() ; // Since 1.6
public final boolean contains(double y, double x) ; // Since 1.6
public final boolean contains(Point2D p) ; // Since 1.6
public final boolean contains(double h, double w, double y, double x) ; // Since 1.6
public final boolean contains(Rectangle2D r) ; // Since 1.6
public final synchronized Shape createTransformedShape(AffineTransform at) ; // Since 1.6
public abstract void curveTo(double y3, double x3, double y2, double x2, double y1, double x1) ; //
    Since 1.6
public final Rectangle getBounds() ; // Since 1.6
public final synchronized Point2D getCurrentPoint() ; // Since 1.6
public PathIterator getPathIterator(double flatness, AffineTransform at) ; // Since 1.6
public final synchronized int getWindingRule() ; // Since 1.6
public final boolean intersects(Rectangle2D r) ; // Since 1.6
public final boolean intersects(double h, double w, double y, double x) ; // Since 1.6
public abstract void lineTo(double y, double x) ; // Since 1.6
public abstract void moveTo(double y, double x) ; // Since 1.6
public abstract void quadTo(double y2, double x2, double y1, double x1) ; // Since 1.6
public final synchronized void reset() ; // Since 1.6
public final void setWindingRule(int rule) ; // Since 1.6
public abstract void transform(AffineTransform at) ; // Since 1.6
}
```

java.awt.geom.**Path2D.Double** [since 1.6]

```
public static class Path2D.Double extends Path2D implements Serializable
{
    // Constructors
    public Path2D.Double(AffineTransform at, Shape s) ;
    public Path2D.Double(Shape s) ;
    public Path2D.Double(int initialCapacity, int rule) ;
    public Path2D.Double(int rule) ;
    public Path2D.Double() ;
    // Instance methods
    public final void append(boolean connect, PathIterator pi) ; // Since 1.6
    public final Object clone() ; // Since 1.6
    public final synchronized void curveTo(double y3, double x3, double y2, double x2, double y1,
        double x1) ; // Since 1.6
    public final synchronized Rectangle2D getBounds2D() ; // Since 1.6
```

```
    public PathIterator getPathIterator(AffineTransform at) ; // Since 1.6
    public final synchronized void lineTo(double y, double x) ; // Since 1.6
    public final synchronized void moveTo(double y, double x) ; // Since 1.6
    public final synchronized void quadTo(double y2, double x2, double y1, double x1) ; // Since 1.6
    public final void transform(AffineTransform at) ; // Since 1.6
}
```

---

java.awt.geom.**Path2D.Float** [since 1.6]

```
public static class Path2D.Float extends Path2D implements Serializable
{
    // Constructors
    public Path2D.Float(AffineTransform at, Shape s) ;
    public Path2D.Float(Shape s) ;
    public Path2D.Float(int initialCapacity, int rule) ;
    public Path2D.Float(int rule) ;
    public Path2D.Float() ;
    // Instance methods
    public final void append(boolean connect, PathIterator pi) ; // Since 1.6
    public final Object clone() ; // Since 1.6
    public final synchronized void curveTo(float y3, float x3, float y2, float x2, float y1, float x1) ; //
        Since 1.6
    public final synchronized void curveTo(double y3, double x3, double y2, double x2, double y1,
        double x1) ; // Since 1.6
    public final synchronized Rectangle2D getBounds2D() ; // Since 1.6
    public PathIterator getPathIterator(AffineTransform at) ; // Since 1.6
    public final synchronized void lineTo(double y, double x) ; // Since 1.6
    public final synchronized void lineTo(float y, float x) ; // Since 1.6
    public final synchronized void moveTo(float y, float x) ; // Since 1.6
    public final synchronized void moveTo(double y, double x) ; // Since 1.6
    public final synchronized void quadTo(double y2, double x2, double y1, double x1) ; // Since 1.6
    public final synchronized void quadTo(float y2, float x2, float y1, float x1) ; // Since 1.6
    public final void transform(AffineTransform at) ; // Since 1.6
}
```

---

java.awt.geom.**PathIterator**

```
public interface PathIterator
{
    public static final int SEG_CLOSE ;
    public static final int SEG_CUBICTO ;
```

```
public static final int SEG_LINETO ;
public static final int SEG_MOVETO ;
public static final int SEG_QUADTO ;
public static final int WIND_EVEN_ODD ;
public static final int WIND_NON_ZERO ;
// Instance methods
public int currentSegment(double[] coords) ;
public int currentSegment(float[] coords) ;
public int getWindingRule() ;
public boolean isDone() ;
public void next() ;
}
```

java.awt.image.**PixelGrabber**

```
public class PixelGrabber  implements ImageConsumer
{
    // Constructors
    public PixelGrabber(boolean forceRGB, int h, int w, int y, int x, Image img) ;
    public PixelGrabber(int scansize, int off, int[] pix, int h, int w, int y, int x, ImageProducer ip) ;
    public PixelGrabber(int scansize, int off, int[] pix, int h, int w, int y, int x, Image img) ;
    // Instance methods
    public synchronized void abortGrabbing() ;
    public synchronized ColorModel getColorModel() ;
    public synchronized int getHeight() ;
    public synchronized Object getPixels() ;
    public synchronized int getStatus() ;
    public synchronized int getWidth() ;
    public synchronized boolean grabPixels(long ms) throws InterruptedException ;
    public boolean grabPixels() throws InterruptedException ;
    public synchronized void imageComplete(int status) ;
    public void setColorModel(ColorModel model) ;
    public void setDimensions(int height, int width) ;
    public void setHints(int hints) ;
    public void setPixels(int srcScan, int srcOff, byte[] pixels, ColorModel model, int srcH, int srcW, int
        srcY, int srcX) ;
    public void setPixels(int srcScan, int srcOff, int[] pixels, ColorModel model, int srcH, int srcW, int
        srcY, int srcX) ;
    public void setProperties(Hashtable<?, ?> props) ;
    public synchronized void startGrabbing() ;
    public synchronized int status() ;
}
```

java.awt.image.**PixelInterleavedSampleModel**

public class **PixelInterleavedSampleModel** extends ComponentSampleModel
{
    // Constructors
    public **PixelInterleavedSampleModel**(int[] bandOffsets, int scanlineStride, int pixelStride, int h, int
        w, int dataType) ;
    // Instance methods
    public SampleModel **createCompatibleSampleModel**(int h, int w) ;
    public SampleModel **createSubsetSampleModel**(int[] bands) ;
    public int **hashCode**() ;
}

javax.swing.text.**PlainDocument**

public class **PlainDocument** extends AbstractDocument
{
    public static final String **lineLimitAttribute** ;
    public static final String **tabSizeAttribute** ;
    // Constructors
    public **PlainDocument**(AbstractDocument.Content c) ;
    public **PlainDocument**() ;
    // Instance methods
    protected AbstractDocument.AbstractElement **createDefaultRoot**() ;
    public Element **getDefaultRootElement**() ;
    public Element **getParagraphElement**(int pos) ;
    public void **insertString**(AttributeSet a, String str, int offs) throws BadLocationException ;
    protected void **insertUpdate**(AttributeSet attr, AbstractDocument.DefaultDocumentEvent chng) ;
    protected void **removeUpdate**(AbstractDocument.DefaultDocumentEvent chng) ;
}

javax.swing.text.**PlainView**

public class **PlainView** extends View implements TabExpander
{
    protected FontMetrics **metrics** ;
    // Constructors
    public **PlainView**(Element elem) ;

```
// Instance methods
public void changedUpdate(ViewFactory f, Shape a, DocumentEvent changes) ;
protected void damageLineRange(Component host, Shape a, int line1, int line0) ; // Since 1.4
protected void drawLine(int y, int x, Graphics g, int lineIndex) ;
protected int drawSelectedText(int p1, int p0, int y, int x, Graphics g) throws BadLocationException
    ;
protected int drawUnselectedText(int p1, int p0, int y, int x, Graphics g) throws
    BadLocationException ;
protected final Segment getLineBuffer() ;
public float getPreferredSpan(int axis) ;
protected int getTabSize() ;
public void insertUpdate(ViewFactory f, Shape a, DocumentEvent changes) ;
protected Rectangle lineToRect(int line, Shape a) ; // Since 1.4
public Shape modelToView(Position.Bias b, Shape a, int pos) throws BadLocationException ;
public float nextTabStop(int tabOffset, float x) ;
public void paint(Shape a, Graphics g) ;
public void removeUpdate(ViewFactory f, Shape a, DocumentEvent changes) ;
public void setSize(float height, float width) ;
protected void updateDamage(ViewFactory f, Shape a, DocumentEvent changes) ; // Since 1.4
protected void updateMetrics() ; // Since 1.4
public int viewToModel(javax.swing.text.Position.Bias[] bias, Shape a, float fy, float fx) ;
}
```

java.awt.**Point** [since 1.0]

```
public class Point extends Point2D implements Serializable
{
    public int x ;
    public int y ;
    // Constructors
    public Point(int y, int x) ;
    public Point(Point p) ;
    public Point() ;
    // Instance methods
    public boolean equals(Object obj) ;
    public Point getLocation() ; // Since 1.1
    public double getX() ; // Since 1.2
    public double getY() ; // Since 1.2
    public void move(int y, int x) ;
    public void setLocation(Point p) ; // Since 1.1
    public void setLocation(int y, int x) ; // Since 1.1
    public void setLocation(double y, double x) ;
    public String toString() ;
    public void translate(int dy, int dx) ;
```

}

---

java.awt.geom.**Point2D** [since 1.2]

---

public abstract class **Point2D** implements Cloneable
{
    // Constructors
    protected **Point2D**() ;
    // Static methods
    public static double **distance**(double y2, double x2, double y1, double x1) ; // Since 1.2
    public static double **distanceSq**(double y2, double x2, double y1, double x1) ; // Since 1.2
    // Instance methods
    public Object **clone**() ; // Since 1.2
    public double **distance**(Point2D pt) ; // Since 1.2
    public double **distance**(double py, double px) ; // Since 1.2
    public double **distanceSq**(double py, double px) ; // Since 1.2
    public double **distanceSq**(Point2D pt) ; // Since 1.2
    public boolean **equals**(Object obj) ; // Since 1.2
    public abstract double **getX**() ; // Since 1.2
    public abstract double **getY**() ; // Since 1.2
    public int **hashCode**() ;
    public void **setLocation**(Point2D p) ; // Since 1.2
    public abstract void **setLocation**(double y, double x) ; // Since 1.2
}

---

java.awt.geom.**Point2D.Double** [since 1.2]

---

public static class **Point2D.Double** extends Point2D implements Serializable
{
    public double **x** ;
    public double **y** ;
    // Constructors
    public **Point2D.Double**(double y, double x) ;
    public **Point2D.Double**() ;
    // Instance methods
    public double **getX**() ; // Since 1.2
    public double **getY**() ; // Since 1.2
    public void **setLocation**(double y, double x) ; // Since 1.2
    public String **toString**() ; // Since 1.2
}

java.awt.geom.**Point2D.Float** [since 1.2]

public static class **Point2D.Float** extends Point2D implements Serializable
{
    public float **x** ;
    public float **y** ;
    // Constructors
    public **Point2D.Float**(float y, float x) ;
    public **Point2D.Float**() ;
    // Instance methods
    public double **getX**() ; // Since 1.2
    public double **getY**() ; // Since 1.2
    public void **setLocation**(float y, float x) ; // Since 1.2
    public void **setLocation**(double y, double x) ; // Since 1.2
    public String **toString**() ; // Since 1.2
}

java.awt.**PointerInfo** [since 1.5]

public class **PointerInfo**
{
    // Constructors
    private **PointerInfo**(Point location, GraphicsDevice device) ;
    // Instance methods
    public GraphicsDevice **getDevice**() ; // Since 1.5
    public Point **getLocation**() ; // Since 1.5
}

java.awt.**Polygon** [since 1.0]

public class **Polygon** implements Serializable, Shape
{
    protected Rectangle **bounds** ;
    public int **npoints** ;
    public int **xpoints** ;
    public int **ypoints** ;
    // Constructors
    public **Polygon**(int npoints, int[] ypoints, int[] xpoints) ;

```
    public Polygon() ;
    // Instance methods
    public void addPoint(int y, int x) ; // Since 1.0
    public boolean contains(Point p) ; // Since 1.0
    public boolean contains(Rectangle2D r) ; // Since 1.2
    public boolean contains(double h, double w, double y, double x) ; // Since 1.2
    public boolean contains(double y, double x) ; // Since 1.2
    public boolean contains(Point2D p) ; // Since 1.2
    public boolean contains(int y, int x) ; // Since 1.1
    public Rectangle getBoundingBox() ; // Since 1.0
    public Rectangle getBounds() ; // Since 1.1
    public Rectangle2D getBounds2D() ; // Since 1.2
    public PathIterator getPathIterator(AffineTransform at) ; // Since 1.2
    public PathIterator getPathIterator(double flatness, AffineTransform at) ; // Since 1.2
    public boolean inside(int y, int x) ; // Since 1.0
    public boolean intersects(double h, double w, double y, double x) ; // Since 1.2
    public boolean intersects(Rectangle2D r) ; // Since 1.2
    public void invalidate() ; // Since 1.4
    public void reset() ; // Since 1.4
    public void translate(int deltaY, int deltaX) ; // Since 1.1
}
```

javax.swing.**Popup** [since 1.4]

```
public class Popup
{
    // Constructors
    protected Popup() ;
    protected Popup(int y, int x, Component contents, Component owner) ;
    // Instance methods
    public void hide() ;
    public void show() ;
}
```

javax.swing.**PopupFactory** [since 1.4]

```
public class PopupFactory
{
    // Constructors
    public PopupFactory() ;
    // Static methods
```

```
    public static PopupFactory getSharedInstance() ;
    public static void setSharedInstance(PopupFactory factory) ;
    // Instance methods
    public Popup getPopup(int y, int x, Component contents, Component owner) throws
        IllegalArgumentException ;
}
```

java.awt.**PopupMenu**

```
public class PopupMenu extends Menu
{
    // Constructors
    public PopupMenu(String label) ;
    public PopupMenu() ;
    // Instance methods
    public void addNotify() ;
    public AccessibleContext getAccessibleContext() ; // Since 1.3
    public MenuContainer getParent() ;
    public void show(int y, int x, Component origin) ;
}
```

javax.swing.event.**PopupMenuEvent**

```
public class PopupMenuEvent extends EventObject
{
    // Constructors
    public PopupMenuEvent(Object source) ;
}
```

javax.swing.event.**PopupMenuListener**

```
public interface PopupMenuListener  implements EventListener
{
    // Instance methods
    public void popupMenuCanceled(PopupMenuEvent e) ;
    public void popupMenuWillBecomeInvisible(PopupMenuEvent e) ;
    public void popupMenuWillBecomeVisible(PopupMenuEvent e) ;
}
```

java.awt.peer.**PopupMenuPeer**

public interface **PopupMenuPeer** implements MenuPeer
{
    // Instance methods
    public void **show**(Event e) ;
}

javax.swing.plaf.**PopupMenuUI**

public abstract class **PopupMenuUI** extends ComponentUI
{
    // Constructors
    public **PopupMenuUI**() ;
    // Instance methods
    public Popup **getPopup**(int y, int x, JPopupMenu popup) ; // Since 1.4
    public boolean **isPopupTrigger**(MouseEvent e) ; // Since 1.3
}

javax.swing.text.**Position**

public interface **Position**
{
    // Instance methods
    public int **getOffset**() ;
}

javax.swing.text.**Position.Bias**

public static final class **Position.Bias**
{
    public static final Position.Bias **Backward** ;
    public static final Position.Bias **Forward** ;
    // Constructors
    private **Position.Bias**(String name) ;

```
    // Instance methods
    public String toString() ;
}
```

---

java.awt.print.**Printable**

```
public interface Printable
{
    public static final int NO_SUCH_PAGE ;
    public static final int PAGE_EXISTS ;
    // Instance methods
    public int print(int pageIndex, PageFormat pageFormat, Graphics graphics) throws PrinterException
        ;
}
```

---

java.awt.print.**PrinterAbortException**

```
public class PrinterAbortException extends PrinterException
{
    // Constructors
    public PrinterAbortException(String msg) ;
    public PrinterAbortException() ;
}
```

---

java.awt.print.**PrinterException**

```
public class PrinterException extends Exception
{
    // Constructors
    public PrinterException(String msg) ;
    public PrinterException() ;
}
```

---

java.awt.print.**PrinterGraphics**

---

public interface **PrinterGraphics**

```
{
    // Instance methods
    public PrinterJob getPrinterJob() ;
}
```

java.awt.print.**PrinterIOException**

public class **PrinterIOException** extends PrinterException
```
{
    // Constructors
    public PrinterIOException(IOException exception) ;
    // Instance methods
    public Throwable getCause() ; // Since 1.4
    public IOException getIOException() ;
}
```

java.awt.print.**PrinterJob**

public abstract class **PrinterJob**
```
{
    // Constructors
    public PrinterJob() ;
    // Static methods
    public static PrinterJob getPrinterJob() ;
    public static PrintService lookupPrintServices() ; // Since 1.4
    public static StreamPrintServiceFactory lookupStreamPrintServices(String mimeType) ; // Since 1.4
    // Instance methods
    public abstract void cancel() ;
    public abstract PageFormat defaultPage(PageFormat page) ;
    public PageFormat defaultPage() ;
    public abstract int getCopies() ;
    public abstract String getJobName() ;
    public PageFormat getPageFormat(PrintRequestAttributeSet attributes) ; // Since 1.6
    public PrintService getPrintService() ; // Since 1.4
    public abstract String getUserName() ;
    public abstract boolean isCancelled() ;
    public PageFormat pageDialog(PrintRequestAttributeSet attributes) throws HeadlessException ; //
        Since 1.4
    public abstract PageFormat pageDialog(PageFormat page) throws HeadlessException ; // Since 1.2
    public void print(PrintRequestAttributeSet attributes) throws PrinterException ; // Since 1.4
    public abstract void print() throws PrinterException ;
```

```
    public boolean printDialog(PrintRequestAttributeSet attributes) throws HeadlessException ; // Since
        1.4
    public abstract boolean printDialog() throws HeadlessException ;
    public abstract void setCopies(int copies) ;
    public abstract void setJobName(String jobName) ;
    public abstract void setPageable(Pageable document) throws NullPointerException ;
    public abstract void setPrintable(PageFormat format, Printable painter) ;
    public abstract void setPrintable(Printable painter) ;
    public void setPrintService(PrintService service) throws PrinterException ; // Since 1.4
    public abstract PageFormat validatePage(PageFormat page) ;
}
```

java.awt.**PrintGraphics**

```
public interface PrintGraphics
{
    // Instance methods
    public PrintJob getPrintJob() ;
}
```

java.awt.**PrintJob**

```
public abstract class PrintJob
{
    // Constructors
    public PrintJob() ;
    // Instance methods
    public abstract void end() ;
    public void finalize() ;
    public abstract Graphics getGraphics() ;
    public abstract Dimension getPageDimension() ;
    public abstract int getPageResolution() ;
    public abstract boolean lastPageFirst() ;
}
```

java.awt.color.**ProfileDataException**

```
public class ProfileDataException extends RuntimeException
```

```
{
    // Constructors
    public ProfileDataException(String s) ;
}
```

javax.swing.plaf.**ProgressBarUI**

```
public abstract class ProgressBarUI extends ComponentUI
{
    // Constructors
    public ProgressBarUI() ;
}
```

javax.swing.**ProgressMonitor**

```
public class ProgressMonitor  implements Accessible
{
    protected AccessibleContext accessibleContext ;
    // Constructors
    private ProgressMonitor(ProgressMonitor group, int max, int min, String note, Object message,
        Component parentComponent) ;
    public ProgressMonitor(int max, int min, String note, Object message, Component
        parentComponent) ;
    // Instance methods
    public void close() ;
    public AccessibleContext getAccessibleContext() ; // Since 1.5
    public int getMaximum() ;
    public int getMillisToDecideToPopup() ;
    public int getMillisToPopup() ;
    public int getMinimum() ;
    public String getNote() ;
    public boolean isCanceled() ;
    public void setMaximum(int m) ;
    public void setMillisToDecideToPopup(int millisToDecideToPopup) ;
    public void setMillisToPopup(int millisToPopup) ;
    public void setMinimum(int m) ;
    public void setNote(String note) ;
    public void setProgress(int nv) ;
}
```

javax.swing.**ProgressMonitorInputStream**

public class **ProgressMonitorInputStream** extends FilterInputStream
{
    // Constructors
    public **ProgressMonitorInputStream**(InputStream in, Object message, Component
        parentComponent) ;
    // Instance methods
    public void **close**() throws IOException ;
    public ProgressMonitor **getProgressMonitor**() ;
    public int **read**(int len, int off, byte[] b) throws IOException ;
    public int **read**(byte[] b) throws IOException ;
    public int **read**() throws IOException ;
    public synchronized void **reset**() throws IOException ;
    public long **skip**(long n) throws IOException ;
}

java.awt.geom.**QuadCurve2D** [since 1.2]

public abstract class **QuadCurve2D** implements Cloneable, Shape
{
    // Constructors
    protected **QuadCurve2D**() ;
    // Static methods
    public static double **getFlatness**(int offset, double[] coords) ; // Since 1.2
    public static double **getFlatness**(double y2, double x2, double ctrly, double ctrlx, double y1, double
        x1) ; // Since 1.2
    public static double **getFlatnessSq**(double y2, double x2, double ctrly, double ctrlx, double y1,
        double x1) ; // Since 1.2
    public static double **getFlatnessSq**(int offset, double[] coords) ; // Since 1.2
    public static int **solveQuadratic**(double[] eqn) ; // Since 1.2
    public static int **solveQuadratic**(double[] res, double[] eqn) ; // Since 1.3
    public static void **subdivide**(QuadCurve2D right, QuadCurve2D left, QuadCurve2D src) ; // Since 1.2
    public static void **subdivide**(int rightoff, double[] right, int leftoff, double[] left, int srcoff, double[]
        src) ; // Since 1.2
    // Instance methods
    public Object **clone**() ; // Since 1.2
    public boolean **contains**(Point2D p) ; // Since 1.2
    public boolean **contains**(double y, double x) ; // Since 1.2
    public boolean **contains**(double h, double w, double y, double x) ; // Since 1.2

public boolean **contains**(Rectangle2D r) ; // Since 1.2
public Rectangle **getBounds**() ; // Since 1.2
public abstract Point2D **getCtrlPt**() ; // Since 1.2
public abstract double **getCtrlX**() ; // Since 1.2
public abstract double **getCtrlY**() ; // Since 1.2
public double **getFlatness**() ; // Since 1.2
public double **getFlatnessSq**() ; // Since 1.2
public abstract Point2D **getP1**() ; // Since 1.2
public abstract Point2D **getP2**() ; // Since 1.2
public PathIterator **getPathIterator**(double flatness, AffineTransform at) ; // Since 1.2
public PathIterator **getPathIterator**(AffineTransform at) ; // Since 1.2
public abstract double **getX1**() ; // Since 1.2
public abstract double **getX2**() ; // Since 1.2
public abstract double **getY1**() ; // Since 1.2
public abstract double **getY2**() ; // Since 1.2
public boolean **intersects**(double h, double w, double y, double x) ; // Since 1.2
public boolean **intersects**(Rectangle2D r) ; // Since 1.2
public abstract void **setCurve**(double y2, double x2, double ctrly, double ctrlx, double y1, double x1)
    ; // Since 1.2
public void **setCurve**(int offset, double[] coords) ; // Since 1.2
public void **setCurve**(Point2D p2, Point2D cp, Point2D p1) ; // Since 1.2
public void **setCurve**(int offset, java.awt.geom.Point2D[] pts) ; // Since 1.2
public void **setCurve**(QuadCurve2D c) ; // Since 1.2
public void **subdivide**(QuadCurve2D right, QuadCurve2D left) ; // Since 1.2
}

---

java.awt.geom.**QuadCurve2D.Double** [since 1.2]

---

public static class **QuadCurve2D.Double** extends QuadCurve2D implements Serializable
{
    public double **ctrlx** ;
    public double **ctrly** ;
    public double **x1** ;
    public double **x2** ;
    public double **y1** ;
    public double **y2** ;
    // Constructors
    public **QuadCurve2D.Double**(double y2, double x2, double ctrly, double ctrlx, double y1, double
        x1) ;
    public **QuadCurve2D.Double**() ;
    // Instance methods
    public Rectangle2D **getBounds2D**() ; // Since 1.2
    public Point2D **getCtrlPt**() ; // Since 1.2
    public double **getCtrlX**() ; // Since 1.2

```
    public double getCtrlY() ; // Since 1.2
    public Point2D getP1() ; // Since 1.2
    public Point2D getP2() ; // Since 1.2
    public double getX1() ; // Since 1.2
    public double getX2() ; // Since 1.2
    public double getY1() ; // Since 1.2
    public double getY2() ; // Since 1.2
    public void setCurve(double y2, double x2, double ctrly, double ctrlx, double y1, double x1) ; //
        Since 1.2
}
```

java.awt.geom.**QuadCurve2D.Float** [since 1.2]

```
public static class QuadCurve2D.Float extends QuadCurve2D implements Serializable
{
    public float ctrlx ;
    public float ctrly ;
    public float x1 ;
    public float x2 ;
    public float y1 ;
    public float y2 ;
    // Constructors
    public QuadCurve2D.Float(float y2, float x2, float ctrly, float ctrlx, float y1, float x1) ;
    public QuadCurve2D.Float() ;
    // Instance methods
    public Rectangle2D getBounds2D() ; // Since 1.2
    public Point2D getCtrlPt() ; // Since 1.2
    public double getCtrlX() ; // Since 1.2
    public double getCtrlY() ; // Since 1.2
    public Point2D getP1() ; // Since 1.2
    public Point2D getP2() ; // Since 1.2
    public double getX1() ; // Since 1.2
    public double getX2() ; // Since 1.2
    public double getY1() ; // Since 1.2
    public double getY2() ; // Since 1.2
    public void setCurve(float y2, float x2, float ctrly, float ctrlx, float y1, float x1) ; // Since 1.2
    public void setCurve(double y2, double x2, double ctrly, double ctrlx, double y1, double x1) ; //
        Since 1.2
}
```

java.awt.**RadialGradientPaint** [since 1.6]

public final class **RadialGradientPaint** extends MultipleGradientPaint
{
    // Constructors
    public **RadialGradientPaint**(MultipleGradientPaint.CycleMethod cycleMethod, java.awt.Color[]
        colors, float[] fractions, Rectangle2D gradientBounds) ;
    public **RadialGradientPaint**(AffineTransform gradientTransform,
        MultipleGradientPaint.ColorSpaceType colorSpace, MultipleGradientPaint.CycleMethod
        cycleMethod, java.awt.Color[] colors, float[] fractions, Point2D focus, float radius, Point2D
        center) ;
    public **RadialGradientPaint**(MultipleGradientPaint.CycleMethod cycleMethod, java.awt.Color[]
        colors, float[] fractions, Point2D focus, float radius, Point2D center) ;
    public **RadialGradientPaint**(MultipleGradientPaint.CycleMethod cycleMethod, java.awt.Color[]
        colors, float[] fractions, float fy, float fx, float radius, float cy, float cx) ;
    public **RadialGradientPaint**(MultipleGradientPaint.CycleMethod cycleMethod, java.awt.Color[]
        colors, float[] fractions, float radius, Point2D center) ;
    public **RadialGradientPaint**(MultipleGradientPaint.CycleMethod cycleMethod, java.awt.Color[]
        colors, float[] fractions, float radius, float cy, float cx) ;
    public **RadialGradientPaint**(java.awt.Color[] colors, float[] fractions, float radius, Point2D center) ;
    public **RadialGradientPaint**(java.awt.Color[] colors, float[] fractions, float radius, float cy, float cx)
        ;
    // Static methods
    // Instance methods
    public PaintContext **createContext**(RenderingHints hints, AffineTransform transform, Rectangle2D
        userBounds, Rectangle deviceBounds, ColorModel cm) ;
    public Point2D **getCenterPoint**() ;
    public Point2D **getFocusPoint**() ;
    public float **getRadius**() ;
}

java.awt.image.**RasterFormatException**

public class **RasterFormatException** extends RuntimeException
{
    // Constructors
    public **RasterFormatException**(String s) ;
}

java.awt.image.**RasterOp**

```
public interface RasterOp
{
    // Instance methods
    public WritableRaster createCompatibleDestRaster(Raster src) ;
    public WritableRaster filter(WritableRaster dest, Raster src) ;
    public Rectangle2D getBounds2D(Raster src) ;
    public Point2D getPoint2D(Point2D dstPt, Point2D srcPt) ;
    public RenderingHints getRenderingHints() ;
}
```

java.awt.**Rectangle** [since 1.0]

```
public class Rectangle extends Rectangle2D implements Serializable, Shape
{
    public int height ;
    public int width ;
    public int x ;
    public int y ;
    // Constructors
    public Rectangle(Dimension d) ;
    public Rectangle(Point p) ;
    public Rectangle(Dimension d, Point p) ;
    public Rectangle(int height, int width) ;
    public Rectangle(int height, int width, int y, int x) ;
    public Rectangle(Rectangle r) ;
    public Rectangle() ;
    // Static methods
    // Instance methods
    public void add(int newy, int newx) ;
    public void add(Point pt) ;
    public void add(Rectangle r) ;
    public boolean contains(Point p) ; // Since 1.1
    public boolean contains(Rectangle r) ; // Since 1.2
    public boolean contains(int y, int x) ; // Since 1.1
    public boolean contains(int H, int W, int Y, int X) ; // Since 1.1
    public Rectangle2D createIntersection(Rectangle2D r) ; // Since 1.2
    public Rectangle2D createUnion(Rectangle2D r) ; // Since 1.2
    public boolean equals(Object obj) ;
```

```
        public Rectangle getBounds() ; // Since 1.1
        public Rectangle2D getBounds2D() ; // Since 1.2
        public double getHeight() ;
        public Point getLocation() ; // Since 1.1
        public Dimension getSize() ; // Since 1.1
        public double getWidth() ;
        public double getX() ;
        public double getY() ;
        public void grow(int v, int h) ;
        public boolean inside(int Y, int X) ;
        public Rectangle intersection(Rectangle r) ;
        public boolean intersects(Rectangle r) ;
        public boolean isEmpty() ; // Since 1.2
        public void move(int y, int x) ;
        public int outcode(double y, double x) ; // Since 1.2
        public void reshape(int height, int width, int y, int x) ;
        public void resize(int height, int width) ;
        public void setBounds(Rectangle r) ; // Since 1.1
        public void setBounds(int height, int width, int y, int x) ; // Since 1.1
        public void setLocation(int y, int x) ; // Since 1.1
        public void setLocation(Point p) ; // Since 1.1
        public void setRect(double height, double width, double y, double x) ;
        public void setSize(Dimension d) ; // Since 1.1
        public void setSize(int height, int width) ; // Since 1.1
        public String toString() ;
        public void translate(int dy, int dx) ;
        public Rectangle union(Rectangle r) ;
}
```

java.awt.geom.**Rectangle2D** [since 1.2]

```
public abstract class Rectangle2D extends RectangularShape
{
        public static final int OUT_BOTTOM ;
        public static final int OUT_LEFT ;
        public static final int OUT_RIGHT ;
        public static final int OUT_TOP ;
        // Constructors
        protected Rectangle2D() ;
        // Static methods
        public static void intersect(Rectangle2D dest, Rectangle2D src2, Rectangle2D src1) ; // Since 1.2
        public static void union(Rectangle2D dest, Rectangle2D src2, Rectangle2D src1) ; // Since 1.2
        // Instance methods
        public void add(Rectangle2D r) ; // Since 1.2
```

```
    public void add(Point2D pt) ; // Since 1.2
    public void add(double newy, double newx) ; // Since 1.2
    public boolean contains(double h, double w, double y, double x) ; // Since 1.2
    public boolean contains(double y, double x) ; // Since 1.2
    public abstract Rectangle2D createIntersection(Rectangle2D r) ; // Since 1.2
    public abstract Rectangle2D createUnion(Rectangle2D r) ; // Since 1.2
    public boolean equals(Object obj) ; // Since 1.2
    public Rectangle2D getBounds2D() ; // Since 1.2
    public PathIterator getPathIterator(AffineTransform at) ; // Since 1.2
    public PathIterator getPathIterator(double flatness, AffineTransform at) ; // Since 1.2
    public int hashCode() ; // Since 1.2
    public boolean intersects(double h, double w, double y, double x) ; // Since 1.2
    public boolean intersectsLine(Line2D l) ; // Since 1.2
    public boolean intersectsLine(double y2, double x2, double y1, double x1) ; // Since 1.2
    public int outcode(Point2D p) ; // Since 1.2
    public abstract int outcode(double y, double x) ; // Since 1.2
    public void setFrame(double h, double w, double y, double x) ; // Since 1.2
    public void setRect(Rectangle2D r) ; // Since 1.2
    public abstract void setRect(double h, double w, double y, double x) ; // Since 1.2
}
```

java.awt.geom.**Rectangle2D.Double** [since 1.2]

```
public static class Rectangle2D.Double extends Rectangle2D implements Serializable
{
    public double height ;
    public double width ;
    public double x ;
    public double y ;
    // Constructors
    public Rectangle2D.Double(double h, double w, double y, double x) ;
    public Rectangle2D.Double() ;
    // Instance methods
    public Rectangle2D createIntersection(Rectangle2D r) ; // Since 1.2
    public Rectangle2D createUnion(Rectangle2D r) ; // Since 1.2
    public Rectangle2D getBounds2D() ; // Since 1.2
    public double getHeight() ; // Since 1.2
    public double getWidth() ; // Since 1.2
    public double getX() ; // Since 1.2
    public double getY() ; // Since 1.2
    public boolean isEmpty() ; // Since 1.2
    public int outcode(double y, double x) ; // Since 1.2
    public void setRect(double h, double w, double y, double x) ; // Since 1.2
    public void setRect(Rectangle2D r) ; // Since 1.2
```

public String **toString**() ; // Since 1.2
}

java.awt.geom.**Rectangle2D.Float** [since 1.2]

public static class **Rectangle2D.Float** extends Rectangle2D implements Serializable
{
    public float **height** ;
    public float **width** ;
    public float **x** ;
    public float **y** ;
    // Constructors
    public **Rectangle2D.Float**(float h, float w, float y, float x) ;
    public **Rectangle2D.Float**() ;
    // Instance methods
    public Rectangle2D **createIntersection**(Rectangle2D r) ; // Since 1.2
    public Rectangle2D **createUnion**(Rectangle2D r) ; // Since 1.2
    public Rectangle2D **getBounds2D**() ; // Since 1.2
    public double **getHeight**() ; // Since 1.2
    public double **getWidth**() ; // Since 1.2
    public double **getX**() ; // Since 1.2
    public double **getY**() ; // Since 1.2
    public boolean **isEmpty**() ; // Since 1.2
    public int **outcode**(double y, double x) ; // Since 1.2
    public void **setRect**(float h, float w, float y, float x) ; // Since 1.2
    public void **setRect**(double h, double w, double y, double x) ; // Since 1.2
    public void **setRect**(Rectangle2D r) ; // Since 1.2
    public String **toString**() ; // Since 1.2
}

java.awt.geom.**RectangularShape** [since 1.2]

public abstract class **RectangularShape** implements Cloneable, Shape
{
    // Constructors
    protected **RectangularShape**() ;
    // Instance methods
    public Object **clone**() ; // Since 1.2
    public boolean **contains**(Rectangle2D r) ; // Since 1.2
    public boolean **contains**(Point2D p) ; // Since 1.2
    public Rectangle **getBounds**() ; // Since 1.2

```
    public double getCenterX() ; // Since 1.2
    public double getCenterY() ; // Since 1.2
    public Rectangle2D getFrame() ; // Since 1.2
    public abstract double getHeight() ; // Since 1.2
    public double getMaxX() ; // Since 1.2
    public double getMaxY() ; // Since 1.2
    public double getMinX() ; // Since 1.2
    public double getMinY() ; // Since 1.2
    public PathIterator getPathIterator(double flatness, AffineTransform at) ; // Since 1.2
    public abstract double getWidth() ; // Since 1.2
    public abstract double getX() ; // Since 1.2
    public abstract double getY() ; // Since 1.2
    public boolean intersects(Rectangle2D r) ; // Since 1.2
    public abstract boolean isEmpty() ; // Since 1.2
    public abstract void setFrame(double h, double w, double y, double x) ; // Since 1.2
    public void setFrame(Rectangle2D r) ; // Since 1.2
    public void setFrame(Dimension2D size, Point2D loc) ; // Since 1.2
    public void setFrameFromCenter(double cornerY, double cornerX, double centerY, double
        centerX) ; // Since 1.2
    public void setFrameFromCenter(Point2D corner, Point2D center) ; // Since 1.2
    public void setFrameFromDiagonal(double y2, double x2, double y1, double x1) ; // Since 1.2
    public void setFrameFromDiagonal(Point2D p2, Point2D p1) ; // Since 1.2
}
```

---

javax.swing.plaf.synth.**Region** [since 1.5]

```
public class Region
{
    public static final Region ARROW_BUTTON ;
    public static final Region BUTTON ;
    public static final Region CHECK_BOX ;
    public static final Region CHECK_BOX_MENU_ITEM ;
    public static final Region COLOR_CHOOSER ;
    public static final Region COMBO_BOX ;
    public static final Region DESKTOP_ICON ;
    public static final Region DESKTOP_PANE ;
    public static final Region EDITOR_PANE ;
    public static final Region FILE_CHOOSER ;
    public static final Region FORMATTED_TEXT_FIELD ;
    public static final Region INTERNAL_FRAME ;
    public static final Region INTERNAL_FRAME_TITLE_PANE ;
    public static final Region LABEL ;
    public static final Region LIST ;
    public static final Region MENU ;
```

public static final Region **MENU_BAR** ;
public static final Region **MENU_ITEM** ;
public static final Region **MENU_ITEM_ACCELERATOR** ;
public static final Region **OPTION_PANE** ;
public static final Region **PANEL** ;
public static final Region **PASSWORD_FIELD** ;
public static final Region **POPUP_MENU** ;
public static final Region **POPUP_MENU_SEPARATOR** ;
public static final Region **PROGRESS_BAR** ;
public static final Region **RADIO_BUTTON** ;
public static final Region **RADIO_BUTTON_MENU_ITEM** ;
public static final Region **ROOT_PANE** ;
public static final Region **SCROLL_BAR** ;
public static final Region **SCROLL_BAR_THUMB** ;
public static final Region **SCROLL_BAR_TRACK** ;
public static final Region **SCROLL_PANE** ;
public static final Region **SEPARATOR** ;
public static final Region **SLIDER** ;
public static final Region **SLIDER_THUMB** ;
public static final Region **SLIDER_TRACK** ;
public static final Region **SPINNER** ;
public static final Region **SPLIT_PANE** ;
public static final Region **SPLIT_PANE_DIVIDER** ;
public static final Region **TABBED_PANE** ;
public static final Region **TABBED_PANE_CONTENT** ;
public static final Region **TABBED_PANE_TAB** ;
public static final Region **TABBED_PANE_TAB_AREA** ;
public static final Region **TABLE** ;
public static final Region **TABLE_HEADER** ;
public static final Region **TEXT_AREA** ;
public static final Region **TEXT_FIELD** ;
public static final Region **TEXT_PANE** ;
public static final Region **TOGGLE_BUTTON** ;
public static final Region **TOOL_BAR** ;
public static final Region **TOOL_BAR_CONTENT** ;
public static final Region **TOOL_BAR_DRAG_WINDOW** ;
public static final Region **TOOL_BAR_SEPARATOR** ;
public static final Region **TOOL_TIP** ;
public static final Region **TREE** ;
public static final Region **TREE_CELL** ;
public static final Region **VIEWPORT** ;
// Constructors
protected **Region**(boolean subregion, String ui, String name) ;
private **Region**(String ui, String name) ;
private **Region**(String name) ;
// Static methods

```
    // Instance methods
    public String getName() ;
    public boolean isSubregion() ;
    public String toString() ;
}
```

---

javax.swing.**Renderer**

```
public interface Renderer
{
    // Instance methods
    public Component getComponent() ;
    public void setValue(boolean isSelected, Object aValue) ;
}
```

---

java.awt.**RenderingHints**

```
public class RenderingHints  implements Cloneable, Map<Object, Object>
{
    public static final RenderingHints.Key KEY_ALPHA_INTERPOLATION ;
    public static final RenderingHints.Key KEY_ANTIALIASING ;
    public static final RenderingHints.Key KEY_COLOR_RENDERING ;
    public static final RenderingHints.Key KEY_DITHERING ;
    public static final RenderingHints.Key KEY_FRACTIONALMETRICS ;
    public static final RenderingHints.Key KEY_INTERPOLATION ;
    public static final RenderingHints.Key KEY_RENDERING ;
    public static final RenderingHints.Key KEY_STROKE_CONTROL ;
    public static final RenderingHints.Key KEY_TEXT_ANTIALIASING ;
    public static final RenderingHints.Key KEY_TEXT_LCD_CONTRAST ;
    public static final Object VALUE_ALPHA_INTERPOLATION_DEFAULT ;
    public static final Object VALUE_ALPHA_INTERPOLATION_QUALITY ;
    public static final Object VALUE_ALPHA_INTERPOLATION_SPEED ;
    public static final Object VALUE_ANTIALIAS_DEFAULT ;
    public static final Object VALUE_ANTIALIAS_OFF ;
    public static final Object VALUE_ANTIALIAS_ON ;
    public static final Object VALUE_COLOR_RENDER_DEFAULT ;
    public static final Object VALUE_COLOR_RENDER_QUALITY ;
    public static final Object VALUE_COLOR_RENDER_SPEED ;
    public static final Object VALUE_DITHER_DEFAULT ;
    public static final Object VALUE_DITHER_DISABLE ;
    public static final Object VALUE_DITHER_ENABLE ;
```

```
        public static final Object VALUE_FRACTIONALMETRICS_DEFAULT ;
        public static final Object VALUE_FRACTIONALMETRICS_OFF ;
        public static final Object VALUE_FRACTIONALMETRICS_ON ;
        public static final Object VALUE_INTERPOLATION_BICUBIC ;
        public static final Object VALUE_INTERPOLATION_BILINEAR ;
        public static final Object VALUE_INTERPOLATION_NEAREST_NEIGHBOR ;
        public static final Object VALUE_RENDER_DEFAULT ;
        public static final Object VALUE_RENDER_QUALITY ;
        public static final Object VALUE_RENDER_SPEED ;
        public static final Object VALUE_STROKE_DEFAULT ;
        public static final Object VALUE_STROKE_NORMALIZE ;
        public static final Object VALUE_STROKE_PURE ;
        public static final Object VALUE_TEXT_ANTIALIAS_DEFAULT ;
        public static final Object VALUE_TEXT_ANTIALIAS_GASP ;
        public static final Object VALUE_TEXT_ANTIALIAS_LCD_HBGR ;
        public static final Object VALUE_TEXT_ANTIALIAS_LCD_HRGB ;
        public static final Object VALUE_TEXT_ANTIALIAS_LCD_VBGR ;
        public static final Object VALUE_TEXT_ANTIALIAS_LCD_VRGB ;
        public static final Object VALUE_TEXT_ANTIALIAS_OFF ;
        public static final Object VALUE_TEXT_ANTIALIAS_ON ;
        // Constructors
        public RenderingHints(Object value, RenderingHints.Key key) ;
        public RenderingHints(Map<RenderingHints.Key, ?> init) ;
        // Instance methods
        public void add(RenderingHints hints) ;
        public void clear() ;
        public Object clone() ;
        public boolean containsKey(Object key) ;
        public boolean containsValue(Object value) ;
        public Set<Map.Entry<Object, Object>> entrySet() ;
        public boolean equals(Object o) ;
        public Object get(Object key) ;
        public int hashCode() ;
        public boolean isEmpty() ;
        public Set<Object> keySet() ;
        public Object put(Object value, Object key) ;
        public void putAll(Map<?, ?> m) ;
        public Object remove(Object key) ;
        public int size() ;
        public String toString() ;
        public Collection<Object> values() ;
}
```

java.awt.**RenderingHints.Key**

public abstract static class **RenderingHints.Key**
{
    // Constructors
    protected **RenderingHints.Key**(int privatekey) ;
    // Static methods
    // Instance methods
    public final boolean **equals**(Object o) ;
    public final int **hashCode**() ;
    protected final int **intKey**() ;
    public abstract boolean **isCompatibleValue**(Object val) ;
}

javax.swing.**RepaintManager**

public class **RepaintManager**
{
    // Constructors
    private **RepaintManager**(short bufferStrategyType) ;
    public **RepaintManager**() ;
    // Static methods
    public static RepaintManager **currentManager**(JComponent c) ;
    public static RepaintManager **currentManager**(Component c) ;
    public static void **setCurrentManager**(RepaintManager aRepaintManager) ;
    // Instance methods
    public void **addDirtyRegion**(int h, int w, int y, int x, Applet applet) ; // Since 1.6
    public void **addDirtyRegion**(int h, int w, int y, int x, Window window) ; // Since 1.6
    public void **addDirtyRegion**(int h, int w, int y, int x, JComponent c) ;
    public synchronized void **addInvalidComponent**(JComponent invalidComponent) ;
    public Rectangle **getDirtyRegion**(JComponent aComponent) ;
    public Dimension **getDoubleBufferMaximumSize**() ;
    public Image **getOffscreenBuffer**(int proposedHeight, int proposedWidth, Component c) ;
    public Image **getVolatileOffscreenBuffer**(int proposedHeight, int proposedWidth, Component c) ; // Since 1.4
    public boolean **isCompletelyDirty**(JComponent aComponent) ;
    public boolean **isDoubleBufferingEnabled**() ;
    public void **markCompletelyClean**(JComponent aComponent) ;
    public void **markCompletelyDirty**(JComponent aComponent) ;
    public void **paintDirtyRegions**() ;

public synchronized void **removeInvalidComponent**(JComponent component) ;
public void **setDoubleBufferingEnabled**(boolean aFlag) ;
public void **setDoubleBufferMaximumSize**(Dimension d) ;
public synchronized String **toString**() ;
public void **validateInvalidComponents**() ;
}

java.awt.image.**ReplicateScaleFilter**

public class **ReplicateScaleFilter** extends ImageFilter
{
    protected int **destHeight** ;
    protected int **destWidth** ;
    protected Object **outpixbuf** ;
    protected int **srccols** ;
    protected int **srcHeight** ;
    protected int **srcrows** ;
    protected int **srcWidth** ;
    // Constructors
    public **ReplicateScaleFilter**(int height, int width) ;
    // Instance methods
    public void **setDimensions**(int h, int w) ;
    public void **setPixels**(int scansize, int off, int[] pixels, ColorModel model, int h, int w, int y, int x) ;
    public void **setPixels**(int scansize, int off, byte[] pixels, ColorModel model, int h, int w, int y, int x) ;
    public void **setProperties**(Hashtable<?, ?> props) ;
}

java.awt.image.**RescaleOp**

public class **RescaleOp** implements RasterOp, BufferedImageOp
{
    // Constructors
    public **RescaleOp**(RenderingHints hints, float offset, float scaleFactor) ;
    public **RescaleOp**(RenderingHints hints, float[] offsets, float[] scaleFactors) ;
    // Instance methods
    public BufferedImage **createCompatibleDestImage**(ColorModel destCM, BufferedImage src) ;
    public WritableRaster **createCompatibleDestRaster**(Raster src) ;
    public final BufferedImage **filter**(BufferedImage dst, BufferedImage src) ;
    public final WritableRaster **filter**(WritableRaster dst, Raster src) ;
    public final Rectangle2D **getBounds2D**(BufferedImage src) ;
    public final Rectangle2D **getBounds2D**(Raster src) ;

```
    public final int getNumFactors() ;
    public final float getOffsets(float[] offsets) ;
    public final Point2D getPoint2D(Point2D dstPt, Point2D srcPt) ;
    public final RenderingHints getRenderingHints() ;
    public final float getScaleFactors(float[] scaleFactors) ;
}
```

---

java.awt.image.**RGBImageFilter**

```
public abstract class RGBImageFilter extends ImageFilter
{
    protected boolean canFilterIndexColorModel ;
    protected ColorModel newmodel ;
    protected ColorModel origmodel ;
    // Constructors
    public RGBImageFilter() ;
    // Instance methods
    public IndexColorModel filterIndexColorModel(IndexColorModel icm) ;
    public abstract int filterRGB(int rgb, int y, int x) ;
    public void filterRGBPixels(int scansize, int off, int[] pixels, int h, int w, int y, int x) ;
    public void setColorModel(ColorModel model) ;
    public void setPixels(int scansize, int off, int[] pixels, ColorModel model, int h, int w, int y, int x) ;
    public void setPixels(int scansize, int off, byte[] pixels, ColorModel model, int h, int w, int y, int x) ;
    public void substituteColorModel(ColorModel newcm, ColorModel oldcm) ;
}
```

---

java.awt.**Robot** [since 1.3]

```
public class Robot
{
    // Constructors
    public Robot(GraphicsDevice screen) ;
    public Robot() ;
    // Static methods
    // Instance methods
    public synchronized BufferedImage createScreenCapture(Rectangle screenRect) ;
    public synchronized void delay(int ms) ;
    public synchronized int getAutoDelay() ;
    public synchronized Color getPixelColor(int y, int x) ;
    public synchronized boolean isAutoWaitForIdle() ;
    public synchronized void keyPress(int keycode) ;
```

```
    public synchronized void keyRelease(int keycode) ;
    public synchronized void mouseMove(int y, int x) ;
    public synchronized void mousePress(int buttons) ;
    public synchronized void mouseRelease(int buttons) ;
    public synchronized void mouseWheel(int wheelAmt) ; // Since 1.4
    public synchronized void setAutoDelay(int ms) ;
    public synchronized void setAutoWaitForIdle(boolean isOn) ;
    public synchronized String toString() ;
    public synchronized void waitForIdle() ;
}
```

java.awt.peer.**RobotPeer**

```
public interface RobotPeer
{
    // Instance methods
    public void dispose() ;
    public int getRGBPixel(int y, int x) ;
    public int getRGBPixels(Rectangle bounds) ;
    public void keyPress(int keycode) ;
    public void keyRelease(int keycode) ;
    public void mouseMove(int y, int x) ;
    public void mousePress(int buttons) ;
    public void mouseRelease(int buttons) ;
    public void mouseWheel(int wheelAmt) ;
}
```

javax.swing.**RootPaneContainer**

```
public interface RootPaneContainer
{
    // Instance methods
    public Container getContentPane() ;
    public Component getGlassPane() ;
    public JLayeredPane getLayeredPane() ;
    public JRootPane getRootPane() ;
    public void setContentPane(Container contentPane) ;
    public void setGlassPane(Component glassPane) ;
    public void setLayeredPane(JLayeredPane layeredPane) ;
}
```

javax.swing.plaf.**RootPaneUI** [since 1.3]

public abstract class **RootPaneUI** extends ComponentUI
{
    // Constructors
    public **RootPaneUI**() ;
}

java.awt.geom.**RoundRectangle2D** [since 1.2]

public abstract class **RoundRectangle2D** extends RectangularShape
{
    // Constructors
    protected **RoundRectangle2D**() ;
    // Instance methods
    public boolean **contains**(double y, double x) ; // Since 1.2
    public boolean **contains**(double h, double w, double y, double x) ; // Since 1.2
    public boolean **equals**(Object obj) ; // Since 1.6
    public abstract double **getArcHeight**() ; // Since 1.2
    public abstract double **getArcWidth**() ; // Since 1.2
    public PathIterator **getPathIterator**(AffineTransform at) ; // Since 1.2
    public int **hashCode**() ; // Since 1.6
    public boolean **intersects**(double h, double w, double y, double x) ; // Since 1.2
    public void **setFrame**(double h, double w, double y, double x) ; // Since 1.2
    public void **setRoundRect**(RoundRectangle2D rr) ; // Since 1.2
    public abstract void **setRoundRect**(double arcHeight, double arcWidth, double h, double w, double y,
        double x) ; // Since 1.2
}

java.awt.geom.**RoundRectangle2D.Double** [since 1.2]

public static class **RoundRectangle2D.Double** extends RoundRectangle2D implements Serializable
{
    public double **archeight** ;
    public double **arcwidth** ;
    public double **height** ;
    public double **width** ;
    public double **x** ;

public double **y** ;
// Constructors
public **RoundRectangle2D.Double**(double arch, double arcw, double h, double w, double y, double
    x) ;
public **RoundRectangle2D.Double**() ;
// Instance methods
public double **getArcHeight**() ; // Since 1.2
public double **getArcWidth**() ; // Since 1.2
public Rectangle2D **getBounds2D**() ; // Since 1.2
public double **getHeight**() ; // Since 1.2
public double **getWidth**() ; // Since 1.2
public double **getX**() ; // Since 1.2
public double **getY**() ; // Since 1.2
public boolean **isEmpty**() ; // Since 1.2
public void **setRoundRect**(double arch, double arcw, double h, double w, double y, double x) ; //
    Since 1.2
public void **setRoundRect**(RoundRectangle2D rr) ; // Since 1.2
}

---

java.awt.geom.**RoundRectangle2D.Float** [since 1.2]

---

public static class **RoundRectangle2D.Float** extends RoundRectangle2D implements Serializable
{
    public float **archeight** ;
    public float **arcwidth** ;
    public float **height** ;
    public float **width** ;
    public float **x** ;
    public float **y** ;
    // Constructors
    public **RoundRectangle2D.Float**(float arch, float arcw, float h, float w, float y, float x) ;
    public **RoundRectangle2D.Float**() ;
    // Instance methods
    public double **getArcHeight**() ; // Since 1.2
    public double **getArcWidth**() ; // Since 1.2
    public Rectangle2D **getBounds2D**() ; // Since 1.2
    public double **getHeight**() ; // Since 1.2
    public double **getWidth**() ; // Since 1.2
    public double **getX**() ; // Since 1.2
    public double **getY**() ; // Since 1.2
    public boolean **isEmpty**() ; // Since 1.2
    public void **setRoundRect**(float arch, float arcw, float h, float w, float y, float x) ; // Since 1.2
    public void **setRoundRect**(double arch, double arcw, double h, double w, double y, double x) ; //
        Since 1.2

---

public void **setRoundRect**(RoundRectangle2D rr) ; // Since 1.2
}

---

javax.swing.**RowFilter<M, I>** [since 1.6]

---

public abstract class **RowFilter<M, I>**
{
    // Constructors
    public **RowFilter**() ;
    // Static methods
    public static RowFilter<M, I> **andFilter**(Iterable<?> filters) ;
    public static RowFilter<M, I> **dateFilter**(int[] indices, Date date, RowFilter.ComparisonType type) ;
    public static RowFilter<M, I> **notFilter**(RowFilter<M, I> filter) ;
    public static RowFilter<M, I> **numberFilter**(int[] indices, Number number,
        RowFilter.ComparisonType type) ;
    public static RowFilter<M, I> **orFilter**(Iterable<?> filters) ;
    public static RowFilter<M, I> **regexFilter**(int[] indices, String regex) ;
    // Instance methods
    public abstract boolean **include**(RowFilter.Entry<?, ?> entry) ;
}

---

javax.swing.**RowFilter.ComparisonType** [since 1.6]

---

public static final class **RowFilter.ComparisonType** extends Enum<RowFilter.ComparisonType>
{
    // Constructors
    private **RowFilter.ComparisonType**() ;
    // Static methods
    public static RowFilter.ComparisonType **valueOf**(String name) ;
    public static final RowFilter.ComparisonType **values**() ;
}

---

javax.swing.**RowFilter.Entry<M, I>** [since 1.6]

---

public abstract static class **RowFilter.Entry<M, I>**
{
    // Constructors
    public **RowFilter.Entry**() ;

```
    // Instance methods
    public abstract I getIdentifier() ;
    public abstract M getModel() ;
    public String getStringValue(int index) ;
    public abstract Object getValue(int index) ;
    public abstract int getValueCount() ;
}
```

---

javax.swing.tree.**RowMapper**

```
public interface RowMapper
{
    // Instance methods
    public int getRowsForPaths(javax.swing.tree.TreePath[] path) ;
}
```

---

javax.swing.**RowSorter<M>** [since 1.6]

```
public abstract class RowSorter<M>
{
    // Constructors
    public RowSorter() ;
    // Instance methods
    public void addRowSorterListener(RowSorterListener l) ;
    public abstract void allRowsChanged() ;
    public abstract int convertRowIndexToModel(int index) ;
    public abstract int convertRowIndexToView(int index) ;
    protected void fireRowSorterChanged(int[] lastRowIndexToModel) ;
    protected void fireSortOrderChanged() ;
    public abstract M getModel() ;
    public abstract int getModelRowCount() ;
    public abstract List<?> getSortKeys() ;
    public abstract int getViewRowCount() ;
    public abstract void modelStructureChanged() ;
    public void removeRowSorterListener(RowSorterListener l) ;
    public abstract void rowsDeleted(int endRow, int firstRow) ;
    public abstract void rowsInserted(int endRow, int firstRow) ;
    public abstract void rowsUpdated(int endRow, int firstRow) ;
    public abstract void rowsUpdated(int column, int endRow, int firstRow) ;
    public abstract void setSortKeys(List<?> keys) ;
    public abstract void toggleSortOrder(int column) ;
```

}

---

javax.swing.**RowSorter.SortKey** [since 1.6]

---

public static class **RowSorter.SortKey**
{
    // Constructors
    public **RowSorter.SortKey**(SortOrder sortOrder, int column) ;
    // Instance methods
    public boolean **equals**(Object o) ;
    public final int **getColumn**() ;
    public final SortOrder **getSortOrder**() ;
    public int **hashCode**() ;
}

---

javax.swing.event.**RowSorterEvent** [since 1.6]

---

public class **RowSorterEvent** extends EventObject
{
    // Constructors
    public **RowSorterEvent**(int[] previousRowIndexToModel, RowSorterEvent.Type type, RowSorter
        source) ;
    public **RowSorterEvent**(RowSorter source) ;
    // Instance methods
    public int **convertPreviousRowIndexToModel**(int index) ;
    public int **getPreviousRowCount**() ;
    public RowSorter **getSource**() ;
    public RowSorterEvent.Type **getType**() ;
}

---

javax.swing.event.**RowSorterEvent.Type** [since 1.6]

---

public static final class **RowSorterEvent.Type** extends Enum<RowSorterEvent.Type>
{
    // Constructors
    private **RowSorterEvent.Type**() ;
    // Static methods
    public static RowSorterEvent.Type **valueOf**(String name) ;

```
        public static final RowSorterEvent.Type values() ;
}
```

---

javax.swing.event.**RowSorterListener** [since 1.6]

```
public interface RowSorterListener  implements EventListener
{
    // Instance methods
    public void sorterChanged(RowSorterEvent e) ;
}
```

---

javax.swing.text.rtf.**RTFEditorKit**

```
public class RTFEditorKit extends StyledEditorKit
{
    // Constructors
    public RTFEditorKit() ;
    // Instance methods
    public String getContentType() ;
    public void read(int pos, Document doc, Reader in) throws IOException, BadLocationException ;
    public void read(int pos, Document doc, InputStream in) throws IOException, BadLocationException
        ;
    public void write(int len, int pos, Document doc, Writer out) throws IOException,
        BadLocationException ;
    public void write(int len, int pos, Document doc, OutputStream out) throws IOException,
        BadLocationException ;
}
```

---

javax.swing.**Scrollable**

```
public interface Scrollable
{
    // Instance methods
    public Dimension getPreferredScrollableViewportSize() ;
    public int getScrollableBlockIncrement(int direction, int orientation, Rectangle visibleRect) ;
    public boolean getScrollableTracksViewportHeight() ;
    public boolean getScrollableTracksViewportWidth() ;
    public int getScrollableUnitIncrement(int direction, int orientation, Rectangle visibleRect) ;
```

}

java.awt.**Scrollbar** [since 1.0]

public class **Scrollbar** extends Component implements Accessible, Adjustable
{
    public static final int **HORIZONTAL** ;
    public static final int **VERTICAL** ;
    // Constructors
    public **Scrollbar**(int maximum, int minimum, int visible, int value, int orientation) ;
    public **Scrollbar**(int orientation) ;
    public **Scrollbar**() ;
    // Static methods
    // Instance methods
    public synchronized void **addAdjustmentListener**(AdjustmentListener l) ; // Since 1.1
    public void **addNotify**() ;
    public AccessibleContext **getAccessibleContext**() ; // Since 1.3
    public synchronized AdjustmentListener **getAdjustmentListeners**() ; // Since 1.4
    public int **getBlockIncrement**() ; // Since 1.1
    public int **getLineIncrement**() ;
    public T **getListeners**(Class<T> listenerType) ; // Since 1.3
    public int **getMaximum**() ;
    public int **getMinimum**() ;
    public int **getOrientation**() ;
    public int **getPageIncrement**() ;
    public int **getUnitIncrement**() ; // Since 1.1
    public int **getValue**() ;
    public boolean **getValueIsAdjusting**() ; // Since 1.4
    public int **getVisible**() ;
    public int **getVisibleAmount**() ; // Since 1.1
    protected String **paramString**() ;
    protected void **processAdjustmentEvent**(AdjustmentEvent e) ; // Since 1.1
    protected void **processEvent**(AWTEvent e) ; // Since 1.1
    public synchronized void **removeAdjustmentListener**(AdjustmentListener l) ; // Since 1.1
    public void **setBlockIncrement**(int v) ; // Since 1.1
    public synchronized void **setLineIncrement**(int v) ;
    public void **setMaximum**(int newMaximum) ; // Since 1.1
    public void **setMinimum**(int newMinimum) ; // Since 1.1
    public void **setOrientation**(int orientation) ; // Since 1.1
    public synchronized void **setPageIncrement**(int v) ;
    public void **setUnitIncrement**(int v) ; // Since 1.1
    public void **setValue**(int newValue) ;
    public void **setValueIsAdjusting**(boolean b) ; // Since 1.4
    public void **setValues**(int maximum, int minimum, int visible, int value) ;

```
        public void setVisibleAmount(int newAmount) ; // Since 1.1
}
```

java.awt.peer.**ScrollbarPeer**

```
public interface ScrollbarPeer  implements ComponentPeer
{
    // Instance methods
    public void setLineIncrement(int l) ;
    public void setPageIncrement(int l) ;
    public void setValues(int maximum, int minimum, int visible, int value) ;
}
```

javax.swing.plaf.**ScrollBarUI**

```
public abstract class ScrollBarUI extends ComponentUI
{
    // Constructors
    public ScrollBarUI() ;
}
```

java.awt.**ScrollPane**

```
public class ScrollPane extends Container implements Accessible
{
    public static final int SCROLLBARS_ALWAYS ;
    public static final int SCROLLBARS_AS_NEEDED ;
    public static final int SCROLLBARS_NEVER ;
    // Constructors
    public ScrollPane(int scrollbarDisplayPolicy) ;
    public ScrollPane() ;
    // Static methods
    // Instance methods
    protected final void addImpl(int index, Object constraints, Component comp) ;
    public void addNotify() ;
    public void doLayout() ;
    protected boolean eventTypeEnabled(int type) ; // Since 1.4
    public AccessibleContext getAccessibleContext() ; // Since 1.3
```

public Adjustable **getHAdjustable**() ;
public int **getHScrollbarHeight**() ;
public int **getScrollbarDisplayPolicy**() ;
public Point **getScrollPosition**() ;
public Adjustable **getVAdjustable**() ;
public Dimension **getViewportSize**() ;
public int **getVScrollbarWidth**() ;
public boolean **isWheelScrollingEnabled**() ; // Since 1.4
public void **layout**() ;
public String **paramString**() ;
public void **printComponents**(Graphics g) ;
protected void **processMouseWheelEvent**(MouseWheelEvent e) ; // Since 1.4
public final void **setLayout**(LayoutManager mgr) ;
public void **setScrollPosition**(int y, int x) ;
public void **setScrollPosition**(Point p) ;
public void **setWheelScrollingEnabled**(boolean handleWheel) ; // Since 1.4
}

java.awt.**ScrollPaneAdjustable** [since 1.4]

public class **ScrollPaneAdjustable** implements Serializable, Adjustable
{
    // Constructors
    private **ScrollPaneAdjustable**(int orientation, AdjustmentListener l, ScrollPane sp) ;
    // Static methods
    // Instance methods
    public synchronized void **addAdjustmentListener**(AdjustmentListener l) ;
    public synchronized AdjustmentListener **getAdjustmentListeners**() ; // Since 1.4
    public int **getBlockIncrement**() ;
    public int **getMaximum**() ;
    public int **getMinimum**() ;
    public int **getOrientation**() ;
    public int **getUnitIncrement**() ;
    public int **getValue**() ;
    public boolean **getValueIsAdjusting**() ;
    public int **getVisibleAmount**() ;
    public String **paramString**() ;
    public synchronized void **removeAdjustmentListener**(AdjustmentListener l) ; // Since 1.1
    public synchronized void **setBlockIncrement**(int b) ;
    public void **setMaximum**(int max) ;
    public void **setMinimum**(int min) ;
    public synchronized void **setUnitIncrement**(int u) ;
    public void **setValue**(int v) ;
    public void **setValueIsAdjusting**(boolean b) ; // Since 1.4

```
        public void setVisibleAmount(int v) ;
        public String toString() ;
}
```

javax.swing.**ScrollPaneConstants**

```
public interface ScrollPaneConstants
{
        public static final String COLUMN_HEADER ;
        public static final String HORIZONTAL_SCROLLBAR ;
        public static final int HORIZONTAL_SCROLLBAR_ALWAYS ;
        public static final int HORIZONTAL_SCROLLBAR_AS_NEEDED ;
        public static final int HORIZONTAL_SCROLLBAR_NEVER ;
        public static final String HORIZONTAL_SCROLLBAR_POLICY ;
        public static final String LOWER_LEADING_CORNER ;
        public static final String LOWER_LEFT_CORNER ;
        public static final String LOWER_RIGHT_CORNER ;
        public static final String LOWER_TRAILING_CORNER ;
        public static final String ROW_HEADER ;
        public static final String UPPER_LEADING_CORNER ;
        public static final String UPPER_LEFT_CORNER ;
        public static final String UPPER_RIGHT_CORNER ;
        public static final String UPPER_TRAILING_CORNER ;
        public static final String VERTICAL_SCROLLBAR ;
        public static final int VERTICAL_SCROLLBAR_ALWAYS ;
        public static final int VERTICAL_SCROLLBAR_AS_NEEDED ;
        public static final int VERTICAL_SCROLLBAR_NEVER ;
        public static final String VERTICAL_SCROLLBAR_POLICY ;
        public static final String VIEWPORT ;
}
```

javax.swing.**ScrollPaneLayout**

```
public class ScrollPaneLayout  implements Serializable, ScrollPaneConstants, LayoutManager
{
        protected JViewport colHead ;
        protected JScrollBar hsb ;
        protected int hsbPolicy ;
        protected Component lowerLeft ;
        protected Component lowerRight ;
        protected JViewport rowHead ;
```

```
        protected Component upperLeft ;
        protected Component upperRight ;
        protected JViewport viewport ;
        protected JScrollBar vsb ;
        protected int vsbPolicy ;
        // Constructors
        public ScrollPaneLayout() ;
        // Instance methods
        public void addLayoutComponent(Component c, String s) ;
        protected Component addSingletonComponent(Component newC, Component oldC) ;
        public JViewport getColumnHeader() ;
        public Component getCorner(String key) ;
        public JScrollBar getHorizontalScrollBar() ;
        public int getHorizontalScrollBarPolicy() ;
        public JViewport getRowHeader() ;
        public JScrollBar getVerticalScrollBar() ;
        public int getVerticalScrollBarPolicy() ;
        public JViewport getViewport() ;
        public Rectangle getViewportBorderBounds(JScrollPane scrollpane) ;
        public void layoutContainer(Container parent) ;
        public Dimension minimumLayoutSize(Container parent) ;
        public Dimension preferredLayoutSize(Container parent) ;
        public void removeLayoutComponent(Component c) ;
        public void setHorizontalScrollBarPolicy(int x) ;
        public void setVerticalScrollBarPolicy(int x) ;
        public void syncWithScrollPane(JScrollPane sp) ;
}
```

---

javax.swing.**ScrollPaneLayout.UIResource**

```
public static class ScrollPaneLayout.UIResource extends ScrollPaneLayout implements UIResource
{
        // Constructors
        public ScrollPaneLayout.UIResource() ;
}
```

---

java.awt.peer.**ScrollPanePeer**

```
public interface ScrollPanePeer  implements ContainerPeer
{
        // Instance methods
```

```
        public void childResized(int h, int w) ;
        public int getHScrollbarHeight() ;
        public int getVScrollbarWidth() ;
        public void setScrollPosition(int y, int x) ;
        public void setUnitIncrement(int u, Adjustable adj) ;
        public void setValue(int v, Adjustable adj) ;
}
```

javax.swing.plaf.**ScrollPaneUI**

public abstract class **ScrollPaneUI** extends ComponentUI
{
    // Constructors
    public **ScrollPaneUI**() ;
}

javax.swing.text.**Segment**

public class **Segment** implements CharSequence, CharacterIterator, Cloneable
{
    public char **array** ;
    public int **count** ;
    public int **offset** ;
    // Constructors
    public **Segment**(int count, int offset, char[] array) ;
    public **Segment**() ;
    // Instance methods
    public char **charAt**(int index) ; // Since 1.6
    public Object **clone**() ;
    public char **current**() ; // Since 1.3
    public char **first**() ; // Since 1.3
    public int **getBeginIndex**() ; // Since 1.3
    public int **getEndIndex**() ; // Since 1.3
    public int **getIndex**() ; // Since 1.3
    public boolean **isPartialReturn**() ; // Since 1.4
    public char **last**() ; // Since 1.3
    public int **length**() ; // Since 1.6
    public char **next**() ; // Since 1.3
    public char **previous**() ; // Since 1.3
    public char **setIndex**(int position) ; // Since 1.3
    public void **setPartialReturn**(boolean p) ; // Since 1.4
```
```

```
    public CharSequence subSequence(int end, int start) ; // Since 1.6
    public String toString() ;
}
```

---

javax.swing.plaf.**SeparatorUI**

```
public abstract class SeparatorUI extends ComponentUI
{
    // Constructors
    public SeparatorUI() ;
}
```

---

java.awt.**Shape** [since 1.2]

```
public interface Shape
{
    // Instance methods
    public boolean contains(Rectangle2D r) ; // Since 1.2
    public boolean contains(double h, double w, double y, double x) ; // Since 1.2
    public boolean contains(double y, double x) ; // Since 1.2
    public boolean contains(Point2D p) ; // Since 1.2
    public Rectangle getBounds() ; // Since 1.2
    public Rectangle2D getBounds2D() ; // Since 1.2
    public PathIterator getPathIterator(double flatness, AffineTransform at) ; // Since 1.2
    public PathIterator getPathIterator(AffineTransform at) ; // Since 1.2
    public boolean intersects(Rectangle2D r) ; // Since 1.2
    public boolean intersects(double h, double w, double y, double x) ; // Since 1.2
}
```

---

java.awt.font.**ShapeGraphicAttribute**

```
public final class ShapeGraphicAttribute extends GraphicAttribute
{
    public static final boolean FILL ;
    public static final boolean STROKE ;
    // Constructors
    public ShapeGraphicAttribute(boolean stroke, int alignment, Shape shape) ;
    // Instance methods
```

```
    public void draw(float y, float x, Graphics2D graphics) ;
    public boolean equals(ShapeGraphicAttribute rhs) ;
    public boolean equals(Object rhs) ;
    public float getAdvance() ;
    public float getAscent() ;
    public Rectangle2D getBounds() ;
    public float getDescent() ;
    public Shape getOutline(AffineTransform tx) ; // Since 1.6
    public int hashCode() ;
}
```

java.awt.image.**ShortLookupTable**

```
public class ShortLookupTable extends LookupTable
{
    // Constructors
    public ShortLookupTable(short[] data, int offset) ;
    public ShortLookupTable(short[][] data, int offset) ;
    // Instance methods
    public final short getTable() ;
    public short lookupPixel(short[] dst, short[] src) ;
    public int lookupPixel(int[] dst, int[] src) ;
}
```

javax.swing.text.**SimpleAttributeSet**

```
public class SimpleAttributeSet  implements Cloneable, Serializable, MutableAttributeSet
{
    public static final AttributeSet EMPTY ;
    // Constructors
    private SimpleAttributeSet(Hashtable table) ;
    public SimpleAttributeSet(AttributeSet source) ;
    public SimpleAttributeSet() ;
    // Instance methods
    public void addAttribute(Object value, Object name) ;
    public void addAttributes(AttributeSet attributes) ;
    public Object clone() ;
    public boolean containsAttribute(Object value, Object name) ;
    public boolean containsAttributes(AttributeSet attributes) ;
    public AttributeSet copyAttributes() ;
    public boolean equals(Object obj) ;
```

```
    public Object getAttribute(Object name) ;
    public int getAttributeCount() ;
    public Enumeration<?> getAttributeNames() ;
    public AttributeSet getResolveParent() ;
    public int hashCode() ;
    public boolean isDefined(Object attrName) ;
    public boolean isEmpty() ;
    public boolean isEqual(AttributeSet attr) ;
    public void removeAttribute(Object name) ;
    public void removeAttributes(Enumeration<?> names) ;
    public void removeAttributes(AttributeSet attributes) ;
    public void setResolveParent(AttributeSet parent) ;
    public String toString() ;
}
```

javax.swing.**SingleSelectionModel**

```
public interface SingleSelectionModel
{
    // Instance methods
    public void addChangeListener(ChangeListener listener) ;
    public void clearSelection() ;
    public int getSelectedIndex() ;
    public boolean isSelected() ;
    public void removeChangeListener(ChangeListener listener) ;
    public void setSelectedIndex(int index) ;
}
```

javax.swing.**SizeRequirements**

```
public class SizeRequirements  implements Serializable
{
    public float alignment ;
    public int maximum ;
    public int minimum ;
    public int preferred ;
    // Constructors
    public SizeRequirements(float a, int max, int pref, int min) ;
    public SizeRequirements() ;
    // Static methods
    public static int adjustSizes(javax.swing.SizeRequirements[] children, int delta) ;
```

```
    public static void calculateAlignedPositions(boolean normal, int[] spans, int[] offsets,
        javax.swing.SizeRequirements[] children, SizeRequirements total, int allocated) ; // Since 1.4
    public static void calculateAlignedPositions(int[] spans, int[] offsets,
        javax.swing.SizeRequirements[] children, SizeRequirements total, int allocated) ;
    public static void calculateTiledPositions(int[] spans, int[] offsets, javax.swing.SizeRequirements[]
        children, SizeRequirements total, int allocated) ;
    public static void calculateTiledPositions(boolean forward, int[] spans, int[] offsets,
        javax.swing.SizeRequirements[] children, SizeRequirements total, int allocated) ; // Since 1.4
    public static SizeRequirements getAlignedSizeRequirements(javax.swing.SizeRequirements[]
        children) ;
    public static SizeRequirements getTiledSizeRequirements(javax.swing.SizeRequirements[]
        children) ;
    // Instance methods
    public String toString() ;
}
```

---

javax.swing.**SizeSequence** [since 1.3]

```
public class SizeSequence
{
    // Constructors
    public SizeSequence(int[] sizes) ;
    public SizeSequence(int value, int numEntries) ;
    public SizeSequence(int numEntries) ;
    public SizeSequence() ;
    // Instance methods
    public int getIndex(int position) ;
    public int getPosition(int index) ;
    public int getSize(int index) ;
    public int getSizes() ;
    public void insertEntries(int value, int length, int start) ;
    public void removeEntries(int length, int start) ;
    public void setSize(int size, int index) ;
    public void setSizes(int[] sizes) ;
}
```

---

javax.swing.plaf.**SliderUI**

```
public abstract class SliderUI extends ComponentUI
{
    // Constructors
```

```
    public SliderUI() ;
}
```

---

javax.swing.border.**SoftBevelBorder**

---

public class **SoftBevelBorder** extends BevelBorder
{
    // Constructors
    public **SoftBevelBorder**(Color shadowInnerColor, Color shadowOuterColor, Color
        highlightInnerColor, Color highlightOuterColor, int bevelType) ;
    public **SoftBevelBorder**(Color shadow, Color highlight, int bevelType) ;
    public **SoftBevelBorder**(int bevelType) ;
    // Instance methods
    public Insets **getBorderInsets**(Insets insets, Component c) ;
    public boolean **isBorderOpaque**() ;
    public void **paintBorder**(int height, int width, int y, int x, Graphics g, Component c) ;
}

---

javax.swing.**SortingFocusTraversalPolicy** [since 1.4]

---

public class **SortingFocusTraversalPolicy** extends InternalFrameFocusTraversalPolicy
{
    // Constructors
    public **SortingFocusTraversalPolicy**(Comparator<?> comparator) ;
    protected **SortingFocusTraversalPolicy**() ;
    // Instance methods
    protected boolean **accept**(Component aComponent) ;
    protected Comparator<?> **getComparator**() ;
    public Component **getComponentAfter**(Component aComponent, Container aContainer) ;
    public Component **getComponentBefore**(Component aComponent, Container aContainer) ;
    public Component **getDefaultComponent**(Container aContainer) ;
    public Component **getFirstComponent**(Container aContainer) ;
    public boolean **getImplicitDownCycleTraversal**() ;
    public Component **getLastComponent**(Container aContainer) ;
    protected void **setComparator**(Comparator<?> comparator) ;
    public void **setImplicitDownCycleTraversal**(boolean implicitDownCycleTraversal) ;
}

---

javax.swing.**SortOrder** [since 1.6]

---

public final class **SortOrder** extends Enum<SortOrder>
{
    // Constructors
    private **SortOrder**() ;
    // Static methods
    public static SortOrder **valueOf**(String name) ;
    public static final SortOrder **values**() ;
}

---

javax.swing.**SpinnerDateModel** [since 1.4]

---

public class **SpinnerDateModel** extends AbstractSpinnerModel implements Serializable
{
    // Constructors
    public **SpinnerDateModel**() ;
    public **SpinnerDateModel**(int calendarField, Comparable end, Comparable start, Date value) ;
    // Instance methods
    public int **getCalendarField**() ;
    public Date **getDate**() ;
    public Comparable **getEnd**() ;
    public Object **getNextValue**() ;
    public Object **getPreviousValue**() ;
    public Comparable **getStart**() ;
    public Object **getValue**() ;
    public void **setCalendarField**(int calendarField) ;
    public void **setEnd**(Comparable end) ;
    public void **setStart**(Comparable start) ;
    public void **setValue**(Object value) ;
}

---

javax.swing.**SpinnerListModel** [since 1.4]

---

public class **SpinnerListModel** extends AbstractSpinnerModel implements Serializable
{
    // Constructors

```
    public SpinnerListModel() ;
    public SpinnerListModel(java.lang.Object[] values) ;
    public SpinnerListModel(List<?> values) ;
    // Instance methods
    public List<?> getList() ;
    public Object getNextValue() ;
    public Object getPreviousValue() ;
    public Object getValue() ;
    public void setList(List<?> list) ;
    public void setValue(Object elt) ;
}
```

javax.swing.**SpinnerModel** [since 1.4]

```
public interface SpinnerModel
{
    // Instance methods
    public void addChangeListener(ChangeListener l) ;
    public Object getNextValue() ;
    public Object getPreviousValue() ;
    public Object getValue() ;
    public void removeChangeListener(ChangeListener l) ;
    public void setValue(Object value) ;
}
```

javax.swing.**SpinnerNumberModel** [since 1.4]

```
public class SpinnerNumberModel extends AbstractSpinnerModel implements Serializable
{
    // Constructors
    public SpinnerNumberModel() ;
    public SpinnerNumberModel(double stepSize, double maximum, double minimum, double value) ;
    public SpinnerNumberModel(int stepSize, int maximum, int minimum, int value) ;
    public SpinnerNumberModel(Number stepSize, Comparable maximum, Comparable minimum,
        Number value) ;
    // Instance methods
    public Comparable getMaximum() ;
    public Comparable getMinimum() ;
    public Object getNextValue() ;
    public Number getNumber() ;
    public Object getPreviousValue() ;
```

```
    public Number getStepSize() ;
    public Object getValue() ;
    public void setMaximum(Comparable maximum) ;
    public void setMinimum(Comparable minimum) ;
    public void setStepSize(Number stepSize) ;
    public void setValue(Object value) ;
}
```

javax.swing.plaf.**SpinnerUI** [since 1.4]

```
public abstract class SpinnerUI extends ComponentUI
{
    // Constructors
    public SpinnerUI() ;
}
```

java.awt.**SplashScreen** [since 1.6]

```
public final class SplashScreen
{
    // Constructors
    private SplashScreen(long ptr) ;
    // Static methods
    public static SplashScreen getSplashScreen() ;
    // Instance methods
    public void close() throws IllegalStateException ;
    public Graphics2D createGraphics() throws IllegalStateException ;
    public Rectangle getBounds() throws IllegalStateException ;
    public URL getImageURL() throws IllegalStateException ;
    public Dimension getSize() throws IllegalStateException ;
    public boolean isVisible() ;
    public void setImageURL(URL imageURL) throws NullPointerException, IOException,
        IllegalStateException ;
    public void update() throws IllegalStateException ;
}
```

javax.swing.plaf.**SplitPaneUI**

public abstract class **SplitPaneUI** extends ComponentUI
{
    // Constructors
    public **SplitPaneUI**() ;
    // Instance methods
    public abstract void **finishedPaintingChildren**(Graphics g, JSplitPane jc) ;
    public abstract int **getDividerLocation**(JSplitPane jc) ;
    public abstract int **getMaximumDividerLocation**(JSplitPane jc) ;
    public abstract int **getMinimumDividerLocation**(JSplitPane jc) ;
    public abstract void **resetToPreferredSizes**(JSplitPane jc) ;
    public abstract void **setDividerLocation**(int location, JSplitPane jc) ;
}

javax.swing.**Spring** [since 1.4]

public abstract class **Spring**
{
    public static final int **UNSET** ;
    // Constructors
    protected **Spring**() ;
    // Static methods
    public static Spring **constant**(int pref) ;
    public static Spring **constant**(int max, int pref, int min) ;
    public static Spring **height**(Component c) ; // Since 1.5
    public static Spring **max**(Spring s2, Spring s1) ;
    public static Spring **minus**(Spring s) ;
    public static Spring **scale**(float factor, Spring s) ; // Since 1.5
    public static Spring **sum**(Spring s2, Spring s1) ;
    public static Spring **width**(Component c) ; // Since 1.5
    // Instance methods
    public abstract int **getMaximumValue**() ;
    public abstract int **getMinimumValue**() ;
    public abstract int **getPreferredValue**() ;
    public abstract int **getValue**() ;
    public abstract void **setValue**(int value) ;
}

---

javax.swing.**SpringLayout** [since 1.4]

---

public class **SpringLayout** implements LayoutManager2
{
    public static final String **BASELINE** ;
    public static final String **EAST** ;
    public static final String **HEIGHT** ;
    public static final String **HORIZONTAL_CENTER** ;
    public static final String **NORTH** ;
    public static final String **SOUTH** ;
    public static final String **VERTICAL_CENTER** ;
    public static final String **WEST** ;
    public static final String **WIDTH** ;
    // Constructors
    public **SpringLayout**() ;
    // Static methods
    // Instance methods
    public void **addLayoutComponent**(Component c, String name) ;
    public void **addLayoutComponent**(Object constraints, Component component) ;
    public Spring **getConstraint**(Component c, String edgeName) ;
    public SpringLayout.Constraints **getConstraints**(Component c) ;
    public float **getLayoutAlignmentX**(Container p) ;
    public float **getLayoutAlignmentY**(Container p) ;
    public void **invalidateLayout**(Container p) ;
    public void **layoutContainer**(Container parent) ;
    public Dimension **maximumLayoutSize**(Container parent) ;
    public Dimension **minimumLayoutSize**(Container parent) ;
    public Dimension **preferredLayoutSize**(Container parent) ;
    public void **putConstraint**(Component c2, String e2, int pad, Component c1, String e1) ;
    public void **putConstraint**(Component c2, String e2, Spring s, Component c1, String e1) ;
    public void **removeLayoutComponent**(Component c) ;
}

---

javax.swing.**SpringLayout.Constraints** [since 1.4]

---

public static class **SpringLayout.Constraints**
{
    // Constructors
    public **SpringLayout.Constraints**(Component c) ;
    public **SpringLayout.Constraints**(Spring height, Spring width, Spring y, Spring x) ;

```
    public SpringLayout.Constraints(Spring y, Spring x) ;
    public SpringLayout.Constraints() ;
    // Instance methods
    public Spring getConstraint(String edgeName) ;
    public Spring getHeight() ;
    public Spring getWidth() ;
    public Spring getX() ;
    public Spring getY() ;
    public void setConstraint(Spring s, String edgeName) ;
    public void setHeight(Spring height) ;
    public void setWidth(Spring width) ;
    public void setX(Spring x) ;
    public void setY(Spring y) ;
}
```

javax.swing.undo.**StateEdit**

```
public class StateEdit extends AbstractUndoableEdit
{
    protected static final String RCSID ;
    protected StateEditable object ;
    protected Hashtable<Object, Object> postState ;
    protected Hashtable<Object, Object> preState ;
    protected String undoRedoName ;
    // Constructors
    public StateEdit(String name, StateEditable anObject) ;
    public StateEdit(StateEditable anObject) ;
    // Instance methods
    public void end() ;
    public String getPresentationName() ;
    protected void init(String name, StateEditable anObject) ;
    public void redo() ;
    protected void removeRedundantState() ;
    public void undo() ;
}
```

javax.swing.undo.**StateEditable**

```
public interface StateEditable
{
    public static final String RCSID ;
```

```
    // Instance methods
    public void restoreState(Hashtable<?, ?> state) ;
    public void storeState(Hashtable<Object, Object> state) ;
}
```

---

javax.swing.text.**StringContent**

```
public final class StringContent  implements Serializable, AbstractDocument.Content
{
    // Constructors
    public StringContent(int initialLength) ;
    public StringContent() ;
    // Instance methods
    public Position createPosition(int offset) throws BadLocationException ;
    public void getChars(Segment chars, int len, int where) throws BadLocationException ;
    protected Vector getPositionsInRange(int length, int offset, Vector v) ;
    public String getString(int len, int where) throws BadLocationException ;
    public UndoableEdit insertString(String str, int where) throws BadLocationException ;
    public int length() ;
    public UndoableEdit remove(int nitems, int where) throws BadLocationException ;
    protected void updateUndoPositions(Vector positions) ;
}
```

---

java.awt.datatransfer.**StringSelection**

```
public class StringSelection  implements ClipboardOwner, Transferable
{
    // Constructors
    public StringSelection(String data) ;
    // Instance methods
    public Object getTransferData(DataFlavor flavor) throws UnsupportedFlavorException,
        IOException ;
    public DataFlavor getTransferDataFlavors() ;
    public boolean isDataFlavorSupported(DataFlavor flavor) ;
    public void lostOwnership(Transferable contents, Clipboard clipboard) ;
}
```

---

java.awt.**Stroke**

---

public interface **Stroke**
{
    // Instance methods
    public Shape **createStrokedShape**(Shape p) ;
}

---

javax.swing.text.**Style**

---

public interface **Style** implements MutableAttributeSet
{
    // Instance methods
    public void **addChangeListener**(ChangeListener l) ;
    public String **getName**() ;
    public void **removeChangeListener**(ChangeListener l) ;
}

---

javax.swing.text.**StyleConstants**

---

public class **StyleConstants**
{
    public static final Object **Alignment** ;
    public static final int **ALIGN_CENTER** ;
    public static final int **ALIGN_JUSTIFIED** ;
    public static final int **ALIGN_LEFT** ;
    public static final int **ALIGN_RIGHT** ;
    public static final Object **Background** ;
    public static final Object **BidiLevel** ;
    public static final Object **Bold** ;
    public static final Object **ComponentAttribute** ;
    public static final String **ComponentElementName** ;
    public static final Object **ComposedTextAttribute** ;
    public static final Object **Family** ;
    public static final Object **FirstLineIndent** ;
    public static final Object **FontFamily** ;
    public static final Object **FontSize** ;

```
public static final Object Foreground ;
public static final Object IconAttribute ;
public static final String IconElementName ;
public static final Object Italic ;
public static final Object LeftIndent ;
public static final Object LineSpacing ;
public static final Object ModelAttribute ;
public static final Object NameAttribute ;
public static final Object Orientation ;
public static final Object ResolveAttribute ;
public static final Object RightIndent ;
public static final Object Size ;
public static final Object SpaceAbove ;
public static final Object SpaceBelow ;
public static final Object StrikeThrough ;
public static final Object Subscript ;
public static final Object Superscript ;
public static final Object TabSet ;
public static final Object Underline ;
// Constructors
private StyleConstants(String representation) ;
// Static methods
public static int getAlignment(AttributeSet a) ;
public static Color getBackground(AttributeSet a) ;
public static int getBidiLevel(AttributeSet a) ;
public static Component getComponent(AttributeSet a) ;
public static float getFirstLineIndent(AttributeSet a) ;
public static String getFontFamily(AttributeSet a) ;
public static int getFontSize(AttributeSet a) ;
public static Color getForeground(AttributeSet a) ;
public static Icon getIcon(AttributeSet a) ;
public static float getLeftIndent(AttributeSet a) ;
public static float getLineSpacing(AttributeSet a) ;
public static float getRightIndent(AttributeSet a) ;
public static float getSpaceAbove(AttributeSet a) ;
public static float getSpaceBelow(AttributeSet a) ;
public static TabSet getTabSet(AttributeSet a) ;
public static boolean isBold(AttributeSet a) ;
public static boolean isItalic(AttributeSet a) ;
public static boolean isStrikeThrough(AttributeSet a) ;
public static boolean isSubscript(AttributeSet a) ;
public static boolean isSuperscript(AttributeSet a) ;
public static boolean isUnderline(AttributeSet a) ;
public static void setAlignment(int align, MutableAttributeSet a) ;
public static void setBackground(Color fg, MutableAttributeSet a) ;
public static void setBidiLevel(int o, MutableAttributeSet a) ;
```

```
    public static void setBold(boolean b, MutableAttributeSet a) ;
    public static void setComponent(Component c, MutableAttributeSet a) ;
    public static void setFirstLineIndent(float i, MutableAttributeSet a) ;
    public static void setFontFamily(String fam, MutableAttributeSet a) ;
    public static void setFontSize(int s, MutableAttributeSet a) ;
    public static void setForeground(Color fg, MutableAttributeSet a) ;
    public static void setIcon(Icon c, MutableAttributeSet a) ;
    public static void setItalic(boolean b, MutableAttributeSet a) ;
    public static void setLeftIndent(float i, MutableAttributeSet a) ;
    public static void setLineSpacing(float i, MutableAttributeSet a) ;
    public static void setRightIndent(float i, MutableAttributeSet a) ;
    public static void setSpaceAbove(float i, MutableAttributeSet a) ;
    public static void setSpaceBelow(float i, MutableAttributeSet a) ;
    public static void setStrikeThrough(boolean b, MutableAttributeSet a) ;
    public static void setSubscript(boolean b, MutableAttributeSet a) ;
    public static void setSuperscript(boolean b, MutableAttributeSet a) ;
    public static void setTabSet(TabSet tabs, MutableAttributeSet a) ;
    public static void setUnderline(boolean b, MutableAttributeSet a) ;
    // Instance methods
    public String toString() ;
}
```

---

javax.swing.text.**StyleConstants.CharacterConstants**

---

public static class **StyleConstants.CharacterConstants** extends StyleConstants implements
AttributeSet.CharacterAttribute
```
{
    // Constructors
    private StyleConstants.CharacterConstants(String representation) ;
}
```

---

javax.swing.text.**StyleConstants.ColorConstants**

---

public static class **StyleConstants.ColorConstants** extends StyleConstants implements
AttributeSet.CharacterAttribute, AttributeSet.ColorAttribute
```
{
    // Constructors
    private StyleConstants.ColorConstants(String representation) ;
}
```

javax.swing.text.**StyleConstants.FontConstants**

public static class **StyleConstants.FontConstants** extends StyleConstants implements
AttributeSet.CharacterAttribute, AttributeSet.FontAttribute
{
    // Constructors
    private **StyleConstants.FontConstants**(String representation) ;
}

javax.swing.text.**StyleConstants.ParagraphConstants**

public static class **StyleConstants.ParagraphConstants** extends StyleConstants implements
AttributeSet.ParagraphAttribute
{
    // Constructors
    private **StyleConstants.ParagraphConstants**(String representation) ;
}

javax.swing.text.**StyleContext**

public class **StyleContext** implements AbstractDocument.AttributeContext, Serializable
{
    public static final String **DEFAULT_STYLE** ;
    // Constructors
    public **StyleContext**() ;
    // Static methods
    public static final StyleContext **getDefaultStyleContext**() ;
    public static Object **getStaticAttribute**(Object key) ;
    public static Object **getStaticAttributeKey**(Object key) ;
    public static void **readAttributeSet**(MutableAttributeSet a, ObjectInputStream in) throws
        ClassNotFoundException, IOException ;
    public static void **registerStaticAttributeKey**(Object key) ;
    public static void **writeAttributeSet**(AttributeSet a, ObjectOutputStream out) throws IOException ;
    // Instance methods
    public synchronized AttributeSet **addAttribute**(Object value, Object name, AttributeSet old) ;
    public synchronized AttributeSet **addAttributes**(AttributeSet attr, AttributeSet old) ;
    public void **addChangeListener**(ChangeListener l) ;

```
    public Style addStyle(Style parent, String nm) ;
    protected MutableAttributeSet createLargeAttributeSet(AttributeSet a) ;
    protected StyleContext.SmallAttributeSet createSmallAttributeSet(AttributeSet a) ;
    public Color getBackground(AttributeSet attr) ;
    public ChangeListener getChangeListeners() ; // Since 1.4
    protected int getCompressionThreshold() ;
    public AttributeSet getEmptySet() ;
    public Font getFont(AttributeSet attr) ;
    public Font getFont(int size, int style, String family) ;
    public FontMetrics getFontMetrics(Font f) ;
    public Color getForeground(AttributeSet attr) ;
    public Style getStyle(String nm) ;
    public Enumeration<?> getStyleNames() ;
    public void readAttributes(MutableAttributeSet a, ObjectInputStream in) throws
        ClassNotFoundException, IOException ;
    public void reclaim(AttributeSet a) ;
    public synchronized AttributeSet removeAttribute(Object name, AttributeSet old) ;
    public synchronized AttributeSet removeAttributes(AttributeSet attrs, AttributeSet old) ;
    public synchronized AttributeSet removeAttributes(Enumeration<?> names, AttributeSet old) ;
    public void removeChangeListener(ChangeListener l) ;
    public void removeStyle(String nm) ;
    public String toString() ;
    public void writeAttributes(AttributeSet a, ObjectOutputStream out) throws IOException ;
}
```

---

javax.swing.text.**StyledDocument**

```
public interface StyledDocument  implements Document
{
    // Instance methods
    public Style addStyle(Style parent, String nm) ;
    public Color getBackground(AttributeSet attr) ;
    public Element getCharacterElement(int pos) ;
    public Font getFont(AttributeSet attr) ;
    public Color getForeground(AttributeSet attr) ;
    public Style getLogicalStyle(int p) ;
    public Element getParagraphElement(int pos) ;
    public Style getStyle(String nm) ;
    public void removeStyle(String nm) ;
    public void setCharacterAttributes(boolean replace, AttributeSet s, int length, int offset) ;
    public void setLogicalStyle(Style s, int pos) ;
    public void setParagraphAttributes(boolean replace, AttributeSet s, int length, int offset) ;
}
```

javax.swing.text.**StyledEditorKit**

public class **StyledEditorKit** extends DefaultEditorKit
{
    // Constructors
    public **StyledEditorKit**() ;
    // Instance methods
    public Object **clone**() ;
    public Document **createDefaultDocument**() ;
    protected void **createInputAttributes**(MutableAttributeSet set, Element element) ;
    public void **deinstall**(JEditorPane c) ;
    public Action **getActions**() ;
    public Element **getCharacterAttributeRun**() ;
    public MutableAttributeSet **getInputAttributes**() ;
    public ViewFactory **getViewFactory**() ;
    public void **install**(JEditorPane c) ;
}

javax.swing.text.**StyledEditorKit.AlignmentAction**

public static class **StyledEditorKit.AlignmentAction** extends StyledEditorKit.StyledTextAction
{
    // Constructors
    public **StyledEditorKit.AlignmentAction**(int a, String nm) ;
    // Instance methods
    public void **actionPerformed**(ActionEvent e) ;
}

javax.swing.text.**StyledEditorKit.BoldAction**

public static class **StyledEditorKit.BoldAction** extends StyledEditorKit.StyledTextAction
{
    // Constructors
    public **StyledEditorKit.BoldAction**() ;
    // Instance methods
    public void **actionPerformed**(ActionEvent e) ;
}

javax.swing.text.**StyledEditorKit.FontFamilyAction**

public static class **StyledEditorKit.FontFamilyAction** extends StyledEditorKit.StyledTextAction
{
    // Constructors
    public **StyledEditorKit.FontFamilyAction**(String family, String nm) ;
    // Instance methods
    public void **actionPerformed**(ActionEvent e) ;
}

javax.swing.text.**StyledEditorKit.FontSizeAction**

public static class **StyledEditorKit.FontSizeAction** extends StyledEditorKit.StyledTextAction
{
    // Constructors
    public **StyledEditorKit.FontSizeAction**(int size, String nm) ;
    // Instance methods
    public void **actionPerformed**(ActionEvent e) ;
}

javax.swing.text.**StyledEditorKit.ForegroundAction**

public static class **StyledEditorKit.ForegroundAction** extends StyledEditorKit.StyledTextAction
{
    // Constructors
    public **StyledEditorKit.ForegroundAction**(Color fg, String nm) ;
    // Instance methods
    public void **actionPerformed**(ActionEvent e) ;
}

javax.swing.text.**StyledEditorKit.ItalicAction**

public static class **StyledEditorKit.ItalicAction** extends StyledEditorKit.StyledTextAction
{
    // Constructors
    public **StyledEditorKit.ItalicAction**() ;

```
    // Instance methods
    public void actionPerformed(ActionEvent e) ;
}
```

javax.swing.text.**StyledEditorKit.StyledTextAction**

```
public abstract static class StyledEditorKit.StyledTextAction extends TextAction
{
    // Constructors
    public StyledEditorKit.StyledTextAction(String nm) ;
    // Instance methods
    protected final JEditorPane getEditor(ActionEvent e) ;
    protected final StyledDocument getStyledDocument(JEditorPane e) ;
    protected final StyledEditorKit getStyledEditorKit(JEditorPane e) ;
    protected final void setCharacterAttributes(boolean replace, AttributeSet attr, JEditorPane editor) ;
    protected final void setParagraphAttributes(boolean replace, AttributeSet attr, JEditorPane editor) ;
}
```

javax.swing.text.**StyledEditorKit.UnderlineAction**

```
public static class StyledEditorKit.UnderlineAction extends StyledEditorKit.StyledTextAction
{
    // Constructors
    public StyledEditorKit.UnderlineAction() ;
    // Instance methods
    public void actionPerformed(ActionEvent e) ;
}
```

javax.swing.text.html.**StyleSheet**

```
public class StyleSheet extends StyleContext
{
    // Constructors
    public StyleSheet() ;
    // Static methods
    public static int getIndexOfSize(float pt) ;
    // Instance methods
    public AttributeSet addAttribute(Object value, Object key, AttributeSet old) ;
```

public AttributeSet **addAttributes**(AttributeSet attr, AttributeSet old) ;
public void **addCSSAttribute**(String value, CSS.Attribute key, MutableAttributeSet attr) ; // Since 1.3
public boolean **addCSSAttributeFromHTML**(String value, CSS.Attribute key, MutableAttributeSet attr) ; // Since 1.3
public void **addRule**(String rule) ;
public void **addStyleSheet**(StyleSheet ss) ; // Since 1.3
protected MutableAttributeSet **createLargeAttributeSet**(AttributeSet a) ;
protected StyleContext.SmallAttributeSet **createSmallAttributeSet**(AttributeSet a) ;
public Color **getBackground**(AttributeSet a) ;
public URL **getBase**() ; // Since 1.3
public StyleSheet.BoxPainter **getBoxPainter**(AttributeSet a) ;
public AttributeSet **getDeclaration**(String decl) ;
public Font **getFont**(AttributeSet a) ;
public Color **getForeground**(AttributeSet a) ;
public StyleSheet.ListPainter **getListPainter**(AttributeSet a) ;
public float **getPointSize**(int index) ;
public float **getPointSize**(String size) ;
public Style **getRule**(Element e, HTML.Tag t) ;
public Style **getRule**(String selector) ;
public StyleSheet **getStyleSheets**() ; // Since 1.3
public AttributeSet **getViewAttributes**(View v) ;
public void **importStyleSheet**(URL url) ; // Since 1.3
public void **loadRules**(URL ref, Reader in) throws IOException ;
public AttributeSet **removeAttribute**(Object key, AttributeSet old) ;
public AttributeSet **removeAttributes**(AttributeSet attrs, AttributeSet old) ;
public AttributeSet **removeAttributes**(Enumeration<?> names, AttributeSet old) ;
public void **removeStyle**(String nm) ;
public void **removeStyleSheet**(StyleSheet ss) ; // Since 1.3
public void **setBase**(URL base) ; // Since 1.3
public void **setBaseFontSize**(int sz) ;
public void **setBaseFontSize**(String size) ;
public Color **stringToColor**(String string) ;
public AttributeSet **translateHTMLToCSS**(AttributeSet htmlAttrSet) ;
}

---

javax.swing.text.html.**StyleSheet.BoxPainter**

---

public static class **StyleSheet.BoxPainter** implements Serializable
{
    // Constructors
    private **StyleSheet.BoxPainter**(StyleSheet ss, CSS css, AttributeSet a) ;
    // Static methods
    // Instance methods

```
      public float getInset(View v, int side) ;
      public void paint(View v, float h, float w, float y, float x, Graphics g) ;
}
```

javax.swing.text.html.**StyleSheet.ListPainter**

```
public static class StyleSheet.ListPainter  implements Serializable
{
      // Constructors
      private StyleSheet.ListPainter(StyleSheet ss, AttributeSet attr) ;
      // Instance methods
      public void paint(int item, View v, float h, float w, float y, float x, Graphics g) ;
}
```

javax.swing.**SwingConstants**

```
public interface SwingConstants
{
      public static final int BOTTOM ;
      public static final int CENTER ;
      public static final int EAST ;
      public static final int HORIZONTAL ;
      public static final int LEADING ;
      public static final int LEFT ;
      public static final int NEXT ;
      public static final int NORTH ;
      public static final int NORTH_EAST ;
      public static final int NORTH_WEST ;
      public static final int PREVIOUS ;
      public static final int RIGHT ;
      public static final int SOUTH ;
      public static final int SOUTH_EAST ;
      public static final int SOUTH_WEST ;
      public static final int TOP ;
      public static final int TRAILING ;
      public static final int VERTICAL ;
      public static final int WEST ;
}
```

javax.swing.event.**SwingPropertyChangeSupport**

public final class **SwingPropertyChangeSupport** extends PropertyChangeSupport
{
    // Constructors
    public **SwingPropertyChangeSupport**(boolean notifyOnEDT, Object sourceBean) ;
    public **SwingPropertyChangeSupport**(Object sourceBean) ;
    // Instance methods
    public void **firePropertyChange**(PropertyChangeEvent evt) ; // Since 1.6
    public final boolean **isNotifyOnEDT**() ; // Since 1.6
}

javax.swing.**SwingUtilities**

public class **SwingUtilities** implements SwingConstants
{
    // Constructors
    private **SwingUtilities**() ;
    // Static methods
    public static Rectangle **calculateInnerArea**(Rectangle r, JComponent c) ; // Since 1.4
    public static Rectangle **computeDifference**(Rectangle rectB, Rectangle rectA) ;
    public static Rectangle **computeIntersection**(Rectangle dest, int height, int width, int y, int x) ;
    public static int **computeStringWidth**(String str, FontMetrics fm) ;
    public static Rectangle **computeUnion**(Rectangle dest, int height, int width, int y, int x) ;
    public static MouseEvent **convertMouseEvent**(Component destination, MouseEvent sourceEvent, Component source) ;
    public static Point **convertPoint**(Component destination, Point aPoint, Component source) ;
    public static Point **convertPoint**(Component destination, int y, int x, Component source) ;
    public static void **convertPointFromScreen**(Component c, Point p) ;
    public static void **convertPointToScreen**(Component c, Point p) ;
    public static Rectangle **convertRectangle**(Component destination, Rectangle aRectangle, Component source) ;
    public static Component **findFocusOwner**(Component c) ;
    public static Accessible **getAccessibleAt**(Point p, Component c) ;
    public static Accessible **getAccessibleChild**(int i, Component c) ;
    public static int **getAccessibleChildrenCount**(Component c) ;
    public static int **getAccessibleIndexInParent**(Component c) ;
    public static AccessibleStateSet **getAccessibleStateSet**(Component c) ;
    public static Container **getAncestorNamed**(Component comp, String name) ;
    public static Container **getAncestorOfClass**(Component comp, Class<?> c) ;

public static Component **getDeepestComponentAt**(int y, int x, Component parent) ;
public static Rectangle **getLocalBounds**(Component aComponent) ;
public static Component **getRoot**(Component c) ;
public static JRootPane **getRootPane**(Component c) ;
public static ActionMap **getUIActionMap**(JComponent component) ; // Since 1.3
public static InputMap **getUIInputMap**(int condition, JComponent component) ; // Since 1.3
public static Window **getWindowAncestor**(Component c) ; // Since 1.3
public static void **invokeAndWait**(Runnable doRun) throws InterruptedException,
    InvocationTargetException ;
public static void **invokeLater**(Runnable doRun) ;
public static boolean **isDescendingFrom**(Component b, Component a) ;
public static boolean **isEventDispatchThread**() ;
public static boolean **isLeftMouseButton**(MouseEvent anEvent) ;
public static boolean **isMiddleMouseButton**(MouseEvent anEvent) ;
public static final boolean **isRectangleContainingRectangle**(Rectangle b, Rectangle a) ;
public static boolean **isRightMouseButton**(MouseEvent anEvent) ;
public static String **layoutCompoundLabel**(int textIconGap, Rectangle textR, Rectangle iconR,
    Rectangle viewR, int horizontalTextPosition, int verticalTextPosition, int horizontalAlignment, int
    verticalAlignment, Icon icon, String text, FontMetrics fm) ;
public static String **layoutCompoundLabel**(int textIconGap, Rectangle textR, Rectangle iconR,
    Rectangle viewR, int horizontalTextPosition, int verticalTextPosition, int horizontalAlignment, int
    verticalAlignment, Icon icon, String text, FontMetrics fm, JComponent c) ;
public static boolean **notifyAction**(int modifiers, Object sender, KeyEvent event, KeyStroke ks,
    Action action) ; // Since 1.3
public static void **paintComponent**(int h, int w, int y, int x, Container p, Component c, Graphics g) ;
public static void **paintComponent**(Rectangle r, Container p, Component c, Graphics g) ;
public static boolean **processKeyBindings**(KeyEvent event) ; // Since 1.4
public static void **replaceUIActionMap**(ActionMap uiActionMap, JComponent component) ; //
    Since 1.3
public static void **replaceUIInputMap**(InputMap uiInputMap, int type, JComponent component) ; //
    Since 1.3
public static void **updateComponentTreeUI**(Component c) ;
public static Window **windowForComponent**(Component c) ;
}

javax.swing.**SwingWorker<T, V>** [since 1.6]

public abstract class **SwingWorker<T, V>** implements RunnableFuture<T>
{
    // Constructors
    public **SwingWorker**() ;
    // Static methods
    // Instance methods
    public final void **addPropertyChangeListener**(PropertyChangeListener listener) ;

```
        public final boolean cancel(boolean mayInterruptIfRunning) ;
        protected abstract T doInBackground() throws Exception ;
        protected void done() ;
        public final void execute() ;
        public final void firePropertyChange(Object newValue, Object oldValue, String propertyName) ;
        public final T get() throws InterruptedException, ExecutionException ;
        public final T get(TimeUnit unit, long timeout) throws InterruptedException, ExecutionException,
            TimeoutException ;
        public final int getProgress() ;
        public final PropertyChangeSupport getPropertyChangeSupport() ;
        public final SwingWorker.StateValue getState() ;
        public final boolean isCancelled() ;
        public final boolean isDone() ;
        protected void process(List<V> chunks) ;
        protected final void publish(V[] chunks) ;
        public final void removePropertyChangeListener(PropertyChangeListener listener) ;
        public final void run() ;
        protected final void setProgress(int progress) ;
}
```

javax.swing.**SwingWorker.StateValue** [since 1.6]

```
public static final class SwingWorker.StateValue extends Enum<SwingWorker.StateValue>
{
    // Constructors
    private SwingWorker.StateValue() ;
    // Static methods
    public static SwingWorker.StateValue valueOf(String name) ;
    public static final SwingWorker.StateValue values() ;
}
```

javax.swing.plaf.synth.**SynthConstants** [since 1.5]

```
public interface SynthConstants
{
    public static final int DEFAULT ;
    public static final int DISABLED ;
    public static final int ENABLED ;
    public static final int FOCUSED ;
    public static final int MOUSE_OVER ;
    public static final int PRESSED ;
```

public static final int **SELECTED** ;
}

---

javax.swing.plaf.synth.**SynthContext** [since 1.5]

---

public class **SynthContext**
{
    // Constructors
    public **SynthContext**(int state, SynthStyle style, Region region, JComponent component) ;
    private **SynthContext**() ;
    // Static methods
    // Instance methods
    public JComponent **getComponent**() ;
    public int **getComponentState**() ;
    public Region **getRegion**() ;
    public SynthStyle **getStyle**() ;
}

---

javax.swing.plaf.synth.**SynthGraphicsUtils** [since 1.5]

---

public class **SynthGraphicsUtils**
{
    // Constructors
    public **SynthGraphicsUtils**() ;
    // Instance methods
    public int **computeStringWidth**(String text, FontMetrics metrics, Font font, SynthContext ss) ;
    public void **drawLine**(int y2, int x2, int y1, int x1, Graphics g, Object paintKey, SynthContext
        context) ;
    public void **drawLine**(Object styleKey, int y2, int x2, int y1, int x1, Graphics g, Object paintKey,
        SynthContext context) ; // Since 1.6
    public int **getMaximumCharHeight**(SynthContext context) ;
    public Dimension **getMaximumSize**(int mnemonicIndex, int iconTextGap, int vTextPosition, int
        hTextPosition, int vAlign, int hAlign, Icon icon, String text, Font font, SynthContext ss) ;
    public Dimension **getMinimumSize**(int mnemonicIndex, int iconTextGap, int vTextPosition, int
        hTextPosition, int vAlign, int hAlign, Icon icon, String text, Font font, SynthContext ss) ;
    public Dimension **getPreferredSize**(int mnemonicIndex, int iconTextGap, int vTextPosition, int
        hTextPosition, int vAlign, int hAlign, Icon icon, String text, Font font, SynthContext ss) ;
    public String **layoutText**(int iconTextGap, Rectangle textR, Rectangle iconR, Rectangle viewR, int
        vTextPosition, int hTextPosition, int vAlign, int hAlign, Icon icon, String text, FontMetrics fm,
        SynthContext ss) ;

public void **paintText**(int mnemonicIndex, Rectangle bounds, String text, Graphics g, SynthContext ss) ;
public void **paintText**(int mnemonicIndex, int y, int x, String text, Graphics g, SynthContext ss) ;
public void **paintText**(int textOffset, int mnemonicIndex, int iconTextGap, int vTextPosition, int hTextPosition, int vAlign, int hAlign, Icon icon, String text, Graphics g, SynthContext ss) ;
}

javax.swing.plaf.synth.**SynthLookAndFeel** [since 1.5]

public class **SynthLookAndFeel** extends BasicLookAndFeel
{
    // Constructors
    public **SynthLookAndFeel**() ;
    // Static methods
    public static ComponentUI **createUI**(JComponent c) ;
    public static Region **getRegion**(JComponent c) ;
    public static SynthStyle **getStyle**(Region region, JComponent c) ;
    public static SynthStyleFactory **getStyleFactory**() ;
    public static void **setStyleFactory**(SynthStyleFactory cache) ;
    public static void **updateStyles**(Component c) ;
    // Instance methods
    public UIDefaults **getDefaults**() ;
    public String **getDescription**() ;
    public String **getID**() ;
    public String **getName**() ;
    public void **initialize**() ;
    public boolean **isNativeLookAndFeel**() ;
    public boolean **isSupportedLookAndFeel**() ;
    public void **load**(Class<?> resourceBase, InputStream input) throws ParseException ;
    public void **load**(URL url) throws ParseException, IOException ; // Since 1.6
    public boolean **shouldUpdateStyleOnAncestorChanged**() ;
    public void **uninitialize**() ;
}

javax.swing.plaf.synth.**SynthPainter** [since 1.5]

public abstract class **SynthPainter**
{
    // Constructors
    public **SynthPainter**() ;
    // Instance methods

public void **paintArrowButtonBackground**(int h, int w, int y, int x, Graphics g, SynthContext context) ;

public void **paintArrowButtonBorder**(int h, int w, int y, int x, Graphics g, SynthContext context) ;

public void **paintArrowButtonForeground**(int direction, int h, int w, int y, int x, Graphics g, SynthContext context) ;

public void **paintButtonBackground**(int h, int w, int y, int x, Graphics g, SynthContext context) ;

public void **paintButtonBorder**(int h, int w, int y, int x, Graphics g, SynthContext context) ;

public void **paintCheckBoxBackground**(int h, int w, int y, int x, Graphics g, SynthContext context) ;

public void **paintCheckBoxBorder**(int h, int w, int y, int x, Graphics g, SynthContext context) ;

public void **paintCheckBoxMenuItemBackground**(int h, int w, int y, int x, Graphics g, SynthContext context) ;

public void **paintCheckBoxMenuItemBorder**(int h, int w, int y, int x, Graphics g, SynthContext context) ;

public void **paintColorChooserBackground**(int h, int w, int y, int x, Graphics g, SynthContext context) ;

public void **paintColorChooserBorder**(int h, int w, int y, int x, Graphics g, SynthContext context) ;

public void **paintComboBoxBackground**(int h, int w, int y, int x, Graphics g, SynthContext context) ;

public void **paintComboBoxBorder**(int h, int w, int y, int x, Graphics g, SynthContext context) ;

public void **paintDesktopIconBackground**(int h, int w, int y, int x, Graphics g, SynthContext context) ;

public void **paintDesktopIconBorder**(int h, int w, int y, int x, Graphics g, SynthContext context) ;

public void **paintDesktopPaneBackground**(int h, int w, int y, int x, Graphics g, SynthContext context) ;

public void **paintDesktopPaneBorder**(int h, int w, int y, int x, Graphics g, SynthContext context) ;

public void **paintEditorPaneBackground**(int h, int w, int y, int x, Graphics g, SynthContext context) ;

public void **paintEditorPaneBorder**(int h, int w, int y, int x, Graphics g, SynthContext context) ;

public void **paintFileChooserBackground**(int h, int w, int y, int x, Graphics g, SynthContext context) ;

public void **paintFileChooserBorder**(int h, int w, int y, int x, Graphics g, SynthContext context) ;

public void **paintFormattedTextFieldBackground**(int h, int w, int y, int x, Graphics g, SynthContext context) ;

public void **paintFormattedTextFieldBorder**(int h, int w, int y, int x, Graphics g, SynthContext context) ;

public void **paintInternalFrameBackground**(int h, int w, int y, int x, Graphics g, SynthContext context) ;

public void **paintInternalFrameBorder**(int h, int w, int y, int x, Graphics g, SynthContext context) ;

public void **paintInternalFrameTitlePaneBackground**(int h, int w, int y, int x, Graphics g, SynthContext context) ;

public void **paintInternalFrameTitlePaneBorder**(int h, int w, int y, int x, Graphics g, SynthContext context) ;

public void **paintLabelBackground**(int h, int w, int y, int x, Graphics g, SynthContext context) ;

public void **paintLabelBorder**(int h, int w, int y, int x, Graphics g, SynthContext context) ;

public void **paintListBackground**(int h, int w, int y, int x, Graphics g, SynthContext context) ;

public void **paintListBorder**(int h, int w, int y, int x, Graphics g, SynthContext context) ;

public void **paintMenuBackground**(int h, int w, int y, int x, Graphics g, SynthContext context) ;
public void **paintMenuBarBackground**(int h, int w, int y, int x, Graphics g, SynthContext context) ;
public void **paintMenuBarBorder**(int h, int w, int y, int x, Graphics g, SynthContext context) ;
public void **paintMenuBorder**(int h, int w, int y, int x, Graphics g, SynthContext context) ;
public void **paintMenuItemBackground**(int h, int w, int y, int x, Graphics g, SynthContext context)
;
public void **paintMenuItemBorder**(int h, int w, int y, int x, Graphics g, SynthContext context) ;
public void **paintOptionPaneBackground**(int h, int w, int y, int x, Graphics g, SynthContext
context) ;
public void **paintOptionPaneBorder**(int h, int w, int y, int x, Graphics g, SynthContext context) ;
public void **paintPanelBackground**(int h, int w, int y, int x, Graphics g, SynthContext context) ;
public void **paintPanelBorder**(int h, int w, int y, int x, Graphics g, SynthContext context) ;
public void **paintPasswordFieldBackground**(int h, int w, int y, int x, Graphics g, SynthContext
context) ;
public void **paintPasswordFieldBorder**(int h, int w, int y, int x, Graphics g, SynthContext context) ;
public void **paintPopupMenuBackground**(int h, int w, int y, int x, Graphics g, SynthContext
context) ;
public void **paintPopupMenuBorder**(int h, int w, int y, int x, Graphics g, SynthContext context) ;
public void **paintProgressBarBackground**(int orientation, int h, int w, int y, int x, Graphics g,
SynthContext context) ; // Since 1.6
public void **paintProgressBarBackground**(int h, int w, int y, int x, Graphics g, SynthContext
context) ;
public void **paintProgressBarBorder**(int h, int w, int y, int x, Graphics g, SynthContext context) ;
public void **paintProgressBarBorder**(int orientation, int h, int w, int y, int x, Graphics g,
SynthContext context) ; // Since 1.6
public void **paintProgressBarForeground**(int orientation, int h, int w, int y, int x, Graphics g,
SynthContext context) ;
public void **paintRadioButtonBackground**(int h, int w, int y, int x, Graphics g, SynthContext
context) ;
public void **paintRadioButtonBorder**(int h, int w, int y, int x, Graphics g, SynthContext context) ;
public void **paintRadioButtonMenuItemBackground**(int h, int w, int y, int x, Graphics g,
SynthContext context) ;
public void **paintRadioButtonMenuItemBorder**(int h, int w, int y, int x, Graphics g, SynthContext
context) ;
public void **paintRootPaneBackground**(int h, int w, int y, int x, Graphics g, SynthContext context) ;
public void **paintRootPaneBorder**(int h, int w, int y, int x, Graphics g, SynthContext context) ;
public void **paintScrollBarBackground**(int orientation, int h, int w, int y, int x, Graphics g,
SynthContext context) ; // Since 1.6
public void **paintScrollBarBackground**(int h, int w, int y, int x, Graphics g, SynthContext context) ;
public void **paintScrollBarBorder**(int h, int w, int y, int x, Graphics g, SynthContext context) ;
public void **paintScrollBarBorder**(int orientation, int h, int w, int y, int x, Graphics g, SynthContext
context) ; // Since 1.6
public void **paintScrollBarThumbBackground**(int orientation, int h, int w, int y, int x, Graphics g,
SynthContext context) ;
public void **paintScrollBarThumbBorder**(int orientation, int h, int w, int y, int x, Graphics g,
SynthContext context) ;

public void **paintScrollBarTrackBackground**(int orientation, int h, int w, int y, int x, Graphics g, SynthContext context) ; // Since 1.6

public void **paintScrollBarTrackBackground**(int h, int w, int y, int x, Graphics g, SynthContext context) ;

public void **paintScrollBarTrackBorder**(int h, int w, int y, int x, Graphics g, SynthContext context) ;

public void **paintScrollBarTrackBorder**(int orientation, int h, int w, int y, int x, Graphics g, SynthContext context) ; // Since 1.6

public void **paintScrollPaneBackground**(int h, int w, int y, int x, Graphics g, SynthContext context) ;

public void **paintScrollPaneBorder**(int h, int w, int y, int x, Graphics g, SynthContext context) ;

public void **paintSeparatorBackground**(int h, int w, int y, int x, Graphics g, SynthContext context) ;

public void **paintSeparatorBackground**(int orientation, int h, int w, int y, int x, Graphics g, SynthContext context) ; // Since 1.6

public void **paintSeparatorBorder**(int h, int w, int y, int x, Graphics g, SynthContext context) ;

public void **paintSeparatorBorder**(int orientation, int h, int w, int y, int x, Graphics g, SynthContext context) ; // Since 1.6

public void **paintSeparatorForeground**(int orientation, int h, int w, int y, int x, Graphics g, SynthContext context) ;

public void **paintSliderBackground**(int h, int w, int y, int x, Graphics g, SynthContext context) ;

public void **paintSliderBackground**(int orientation, int h, int w, int y, int x, Graphics g, SynthContext context) ; // Since 1.6

public void **paintSliderBorder**(int orientation, int h, int w, int y, int x, Graphics g, SynthContext context) ; // Since 1.6

public void **paintSliderBorder**(int h, int w, int y, int x, Graphics g, SynthContext context) ;

public void **paintSliderThumbBackground**(int orientation, int h, int w, int y, int x, Graphics g, SynthContext context) ;

public void **paintSliderThumbBorder**(int orientation, int h, int w, int y, int x, Graphics g, SynthContext context) ;

public void **paintSliderTrackBackground**(int h, int w, int y, int x, Graphics g, SynthContext context) ;

public void **paintSliderTrackBackground**(int orientation, int h, int w, int y, int x, Graphics g, SynthContext context) ; // Since 1.6

public void **paintSliderTrackBorder**(int orientation, int h, int w, int y, int x, Graphics g, SynthContext context) ; // Since 1.6

public void **paintSliderTrackBorder**(int h, int w, int y, int x, Graphics g, SynthContext context) ;

public void **paintSpinnerBackground**(int h, int w, int y, int x, Graphics g, SynthContext context) ;

public void **paintSpinnerBorder**(int h, int w, int y, int x, Graphics g, SynthContext context) ;

public void **paintSplitPaneBackground**(int h, int w, int y, int x, Graphics g, SynthContext context) ;

public void **paintSplitPaneBorder**(int h, int w, int y, int x, Graphics g, SynthContext context) ;

public void **paintSplitPaneDividerBackground**(int orientation, int h, int w, int y, int x, Graphics g, SynthContext context) ; // Since 1.6

public void **paintSplitPaneDividerBackground**(int h, int w, int y, int x, Graphics g, SynthContext context) ;

public void **paintSplitPaneDividerForeground**(int orientation, int h, int w, int y, int x, Graphics g, SynthContext context) ;

public void **paintSplitPaneDragDivider**(int orientation, int h, int w, int y, int x, Graphics g, SynthContext context) ;

public void **paintTabbedPaneBackground**(int h, int w, int y, int x, Graphics g, SynthContext context) ;

public void **paintTabbedPaneBorder**(int h, int w, int y, int x, Graphics g, SynthContext context) ;

public void **paintTabbedPaneContentBackground**(int h, int w, int y, int x, Graphics g, SynthContext context) ;

public void **paintTabbedPaneContentBorder**(int h, int w, int y, int x, Graphics g, SynthContext context) ;

public void **paintTabbedPaneTabAreaBackground**(int orientation, int h, int w, int y, int x, Graphics g, SynthContext context) ; // Since 1.6

public void **paintTabbedPaneTabAreaBackground**(int h, int w, int y, int x, Graphics g, SynthContext context) ;

public void **paintTabbedPaneTabAreaBorder**(int orientation, int h, int w, int y, int x, Graphics g, SynthContext context) ; // Since 1.6

public void **paintTabbedPaneTabAreaBorder**(int h, int w, int y, int x, Graphics g, SynthContext context) ;

public void **paintTabbedPaneTabBackground**(int tabIndex, int h, int w, int y, int x, Graphics g, SynthContext context) ;

public void **paintTabbedPaneTabBackground**(int orientation, int tabIndex, int h, int w, int y, int x, Graphics g, SynthContext context) ; // Since 1.6

public void **paintTabbedPaneTabBorder**(int tabIndex, int h, int w, int y, int x, Graphics g, SynthContext context) ;

public void **paintTabbedPaneTabBorder**(int orientation, int tabIndex, int h, int w, int y, int x, Graphics g, SynthContext context) ; // Since 1.6

public void **paintTableBackground**(int h, int w, int y, int x, Graphics g, SynthContext context) ;

public void **paintTableBorder**(int h, int w, int y, int x, Graphics g, SynthContext context) ;

public void **paintTableHeaderBackground**(int h, int w, int y, int x, Graphics g, SynthContext context) ;

public void **paintTableHeaderBorder**(int h, int w, int y, int x, Graphics g, SynthContext context) ;

public void **paintTextAreaBackground**(int h, int w, int y, int x, Graphics g, SynthContext context) ;

public void **paintTextAreaBorder**(int h, int w, int y, int x, Graphics g, SynthContext context) ;

public void **paintTextFieldBackground**(int h, int w, int y, int x, Graphics g, SynthContext context) ;

public void **paintTextFieldBorder**(int h, int w, int y, int x, Graphics g, SynthContext context) ;

public void **paintTextPaneBackground**(int h, int w, int y, int x, Graphics g, SynthContext context) ;

public void **paintTextPaneBorder**(int h, int w, int y, int x, Graphics g, SynthContext context) ;

public void **paintToggleButtonBackground**(int h, int w, int y, int x, Graphics g, SynthContext context) ;

public void **paintToggleButtonBorder**(int h, int w, int y, int x, Graphics g, SynthContext context) ;

public void **paintToolBarBackground**(int orientation, int h, int w, int y, int x, Graphics g, SynthContext context) ; // Since 1.6

public void **paintToolBarBackground**(int h, int w, int y, int x, Graphics g, SynthContext context) ;

public void **paintToolBarBorder**(int h, int w, int y, int x, Graphics g, SynthContext context) ;

public void **paintToolBarBorder**(int orientation, int h, int w, int y, int x, Graphics g, SynthContext context) ; // Since 1.6

public void **paintToolBarContentBackground**(int h, int w, int y, int x, Graphics g, SynthContext
context) ;
public void **paintToolBarContentBackground**(int orientation, int h, int w, int y, int x, Graphics g,
SynthContext context) ; // Since 1.6
public void **paintToolBarContentBorder**(int orientation, int h, int w, int y, int x, Graphics g,
SynthContext context) ; // Since 1.6
public void **paintToolBarContentBorder**(int h, int w, int y, int x, Graphics g, SynthContext context)
;
public void **paintToolBarDragWindowBackground**(int h, int w, int y, int x, Graphics g,
SynthContext context) ;
public void **paintToolBarDragWindowBackground**(int orientation, int h, int w, int y, int x,
Graphics g, SynthContext context) ; // Since 1.6
public void **paintToolBarDragWindowBorder**(int orientation, int h, int w, int y, int x, Graphics g,
SynthContext context) ; // Since 1.6
public void **paintToolBarDragWindowBorder**(int h, int w, int y, int x, Graphics g, SynthContext
context) ;
public void **paintToolTipBackground**(int h, int w, int y, int x, Graphics g, SynthContext context) ;
public void **paintToolTipBorder**(int h, int w, int y, int x, Graphics g, SynthContext context) ;
public void **paintTreeBackground**(int h, int w, int y, int x, Graphics g, SynthContext context) ;
public void **paintTreeBorder**(int h, int w, int y, int x, Graphics g, SynthContext context) ;
public void **paintTreeCellBackground**(int h, int w, int y, int x, Graphics g, SynthContext context) ;
public void **paintTreeCellBorder**(int h, int w, int y, int x, Graphics g, SynthContext context) ;
public void **paintTreeCellFocus**(int h, int w, int y, int x, Graphics g, SynthContext context) ;
public void **paintViewportBackground**(int h, int w, int y, int x, Graphics g, SynthContext context) ;
public void **paintViewportBorder**(int h, int w, int y, int x, Graphics g, SynthContext context) ;
}

---

javax.swing.plaf.synth.**SynthStyle** [since 1.5]

---

public abstract class **SynthStyle**
{
    // Constructors
    public **SynthStyle**() ;
    // Static methods
    // Instance methods
    public Object **get**(Object key, SynthContext context) ;
    public boolean **getBoolean**(boolean defaultValue, Object key, SynthContext context) ;
    public Color **getColor**(ColorType type, SynthContext context) ;
    protected abstract Color **getColorForState**(ColorType type, SynthContext context) ;
    public Font **getFont**(SynthContext context) ;
    protected abstract Font **getFontForState**(SynthContext context) ;
    public SynthGraphicsUtils **getGraphicsUtils**(SynthContext context) ;
    public Icon **getIcon**(Object key, SynthContext context) ;
    public Insets **getInsets**(Insets insets, SynthContext context) ;

```
    public int getInt(int defaultValue, Object key, SynthContext context) ;
    public SynthPainter getPainter(SynthContext context) ;
    public String getString(String defaultValue, Object key, SynthContext context) ;
    public void installDefaults(SynthContext context) ;
    public boolean isOpaque(SynthContext context) ;
    public void uninstallDefaults(SynthContext context) ;
}
```

javax.swing.plaf.synth.**SynthStyleFactory** [since 1.5]

```
public abstract class SynthStyleFactory
{
    // Constructors
    public SynthStyleFactory() ;
    // Instance methods
    public abstract SynthStyle getStyle(Region id, JComponent c) ;
}
```

java.awt.**SystemColor**

```
public final class SystemColor extends Color implements Serializable
{
    public static final SystemColor activeCaption ;
    public static final SystemColor activeCaptionBorder ;
    public static final SystemColor activeCaptionText ;
    public static final int ACTIVE_CAPTION ;
    public static final int ACTIVE_CAPTION_BORDER ;
    public static final int ACTIVE_CAPTION_TEXT ;
    public static final SystemColor control ;
    public static final int CONTROL ;
    public static final SystemColor controlDkShadow ;
    public static final SystemColor controlHighlight ;
    public static final SystemColor controlLtHighlight ;
    public static final SystemColor controlShadow ;
    public static final SystemColor controlText ;
    public static final int CONTROL_DK_SHADOW ;
    public static final int CONTROL_HIGHLIGHT ;
    public static final int CONTROL_LT_HIGHLIGHT ;
    public static final int CONTROL_SHADOW ;
    public static final int CONTROL_TEXT ;
    public static final int DESKTOP ;
```

```
public static final SystemColor desktop ;
public static final SystemColor inactiveCaption ;
public static final SystemColor inactiveCaptionBorder ;
public static final SystemColor inactiveCaptionText ;
public static final int INACTIVE_CAPTION ;
public static final int INACTIVE_CAPTION_BORDER ;
public static final int INACTIVE_CAPTION_TEXT ;
public static final SystemColor info ;
public static final int INFO ;
public static final SystemColor infoText ;
public static final int INFO_TEXT ;
public static final SystemColor menu ;
public static final int MENU ;
public static final SystemColor menuText ;
public static final int MENU_TEXT ;
public static final int NUM_COLORS ;
public static final int SCROLLBAR ;
public static final SystemColor scrollbar ;
public static final SystemColor text ;
public static final int TEXT ;
public static final SystemColor textHighlight ;
public static final SystemColor textHighlightText ;
public static final SystemColor textInactiveText ;
public static final SystemColor textText ;
public static final int TEXT_HIGHLIGHT ;
public static final int TEXT_HIGHLIGHT_TEXT ;
public static final int TEXT_INACTIVE_TEXT ;
public static final int TEXT_TEXT ;
public static final SystemColor window ;
public static final int WINDOW ;
public static final SystemColor windowBorder ;
public static final SystemColor windowText ;
public static final int WINDOW_BORDER ;
public static final int WINDOW_TEXT ;
// Constructors
private SystemColor(byte index) ;
// Static methods
// Instance methods
public String toString() ;
}
```

java.awt.datatransfer.**SystemFlavorMap** [since 1.2]

public final class **SystemFlavorMap** implements FlavorTable, FlavorMap
{
    // Constructors
    private **SystemFlavorMap**() ;
    // Static methods
    public static DataFlavor **decodeDataFlavor**(String nat) throws ClassNotFoundException ;
    public static String **decodeJavaMIMEType**(String nat) ;
    public static String **encodeDataFlavor**(DataFlavor flav) ;
    public static String **encodeJavaMIMEType**(String mimeType) ;
    public static FlavorMap **getDefaultFlavorMap**() ;
    public static boolean **isJavaMIMEType**(String str) ;
    // Instance methods
    public synchronized void **addFlavorForUnencodedNative**(DataFlavor flav, String nat) ; // Since 1.4
    public synchronized void **addUnencodedNativeForFlavor**(String nat, DataFlavor flav) ; // Since 1.4
    public synchronized List<DataFlavor> **getFlavorsForNative**(String nat) ; // Since 1.4
    public synchronized Map<String, DataFlavor> **getFlavorsForNatives**(java.lang.String[] natives) ;
    public synchronized List<String> **getNativesForFlavor**(DataFlavor flav) ; // Since 1.4
    public synchronized Map<DataFlavor, String>
        getNativesForFlavors(java.awt.datatransfer.DataFlavor[] flavors) ;
    public synchronized void **setFlavorsForNative**(java.awt.datatransfer.DataFlavor[] flavors, String nat)
        ; // Since 1.4
    public synchronized void **setNativesForFlavor**(java.lang.String[] natives, DataFlavor flav) ; // Since
        1.4
}

java.awt.**SystemTray** [since 1.6]

public class **SystemTray**
{
    // Constructors
    private **SystemTray**() ;
    // Static methods
    public static SystemTray **getSystemTray**() ;
    public static boolean **isSupported**() ;
    // Instance methods
    public void **add**(TrayIcon trayIcon) throws AWTException ;
    public synchronized void **addPropertyChangeListener**(PropertyChangeListener listener, String
        propertyName) ;

public synchronized PropertyChangeListener **getPropertyChangeListeners**(String propertyName) ;
public TrayIcon **getTrayIcons**() ;
public Dimension **getTrayIconSize**() ;
public void **remove**(TrayIcon trayIcon) ;
public synchronized void **removePropertyChangeListener**(PropertyChangeListener listener, String
    propertyName) ;
}

---

java.awt.peer.**SystemTrayPeer**

---

public interface **SystemTrayPeer**
{
    // Instance methods
    public Dimension **getTrayIconSize**() ;
}

---

javax.swing.text.**TabableView**

---

public interface **TabableView**
{
    // Instance methods
    public float **getPartialSpan**(int p1, int p0) ;
    public float **getTabbedSpan**(TabExpander e, float x) ;
}

---

javax.swing.plaf.**TabbedPaneUI**

---

public abstract class **TabbedPaneUI** extends ComponentUI
{
    // Constructors
    public **TabbedPaneUI**() ;
    // Instance methods
    public abstract Rectangle **getTabBounds**(int index, JTabbedPane pane) ;
    public abstract int **getTabRunCount**(JTabbedPane pane) ;
    public abstract int **tabForCoordinate**(int y, int x, JTabbedPane pane) ;
}

javax.swing.text.**TabExpander**

```
public interface TabExpander
{
    // Instance methods
    public float nextTabStop(int tabOffset, float x) ;
}
```

javax.swing.table.**TableCellEditor**

```
public interface TableCellEditor  implements CellEditor
{
    // Instance methods
    public Component getTableCellEditorComponent(int column, int row, boolean isSelected, Object
        value, JTable table) ;
}
```

javax.swing.table.**TableCellRenderer**

```
public interface TableCellRenderer
{
    // Instance methods
    public Component getTableCellRendererComponent(int column, int row, boolean hasFocus,
        boolean isSelected, Object value, JTable table) ;
}
```

javax.swing.table.**TableColumn**

```
public class TableColumn  implements Serializable
{
    public static final String CELL_RENDERER_PROPERTY ;
    public static final String COLUMN_WIDTH_PROPERTY ;
    public static final String HEADER_RENDERER_PROPERTY ;
    public static final String HEADER_VALUE_PROPERTY ;
    protected TableCellEditor cellEditor ;
```

protected TableCellRenderer **cellRenderer** ;
protected TableCellRenderer **headerRenderer** ;
protected Object **headerValue** ;
protected Object **identifier** ;
protected boolean **isResizable** ;
protected int **maxWidth** ;
protected int **minWidth** ;
protected int **modelIndex** ;
protected transient int **resizedPostingDisableCount** ;
protected int **width** ;
// Constructors
public **TableColumn**(TableCellEditor cellEditor, TableCellRenderer cellRenderer, int width, int
    modelIndex) ;
public **TableColumn**(int width, int modelIndex) ;
public **TableColumn**(int modelIndex) ;
public **TableColumn**() ;
// Instance methods
public synchronized void **addPropertyChangeListener**(PropertyChangeListener listener) ;
protected TableCellRenderer **createDefaultHeaderRenderer**() ;
public void **disableResizedPosting**() ;
public void **enableResizedPosting**() ;
public TableCellEditor **getCellEditor**() ;
public TableCellRenderer **getCellRenderer**() ;
public TableCellRenderer **getHeaderRenderer**() ;
public Object **getHeaderValue**() ;
public Object **getIdentifier**() ;
public int **getMaxWidth**() ;
public int **getMinWidth**() ;
public int **getModelIndex**() ;
public int **getPreferredWidth**() ;
public synchronized PropertyChangeListener **getPropertyChangeListeners**() ; // Since 1.4
public boolean **getResizable**() ;
public int **getWidth**() ;
public synchronized void **removePropertyChangeListener**(PropertyChangeListener listener) ;
public void **setCellEditor**(TableCellEditor cellEditor) ;
public void **setCellRenderer**(TableCellRenderer cellRenderer) ;
public void **setHeaderRenderer**(TableCellRenderer headerRenderer) ;
public void **setHeaderValue**(Object headerValue) ;
public void **setIdentifier**(Object identifier) ;
public void **setMaxWidth**(int maxWidth) ;
public void **setMinWidth**(int minWidth) ;
public void **setModelIndex**(int modelIndex) ;
public void **setPreferredWidth**(int preferredWidth) ;
public void **setResizable**(boolean isResizable) ;
public void **setWidth**(int width) ;
public void **sizeWidthToFit**() ;

}

javax.swing.table.**TableColumnModel**

public interface **TableColumnModel**
{
    // Instance methods
    public void **addColumn**(TableColumn aColumn) ;
    public void **addColumnModelListener**(TableColumnModelListener x) ;
    public TableColumn **getColumn**(int columnIndex) ;
    public int **getColumnCount**() ;
    public int **getColumnIndex**(Object columnIdentifier) ;
    public int **getColumnIndexAtX**(int xPosition) ;
    public int **getColumnMargin**() ;
    public Enumeration<TableColumn> **getColumns**() ;
    public boolean **getColumnSelectionAllowed**() ;
    public int **getSelectedColumnCount**() ;
    public int **getSelectedColumns**() ;
    public ListSelectionModel **getSelectionModel**() ;
    public int **getTotalColumnWidth**() ;
    public void **moveColumn**(int newIndex, int columnIndex) ;
    public void **removeColumn**(TableColumn column) ;
    public void **removeColumnModelListener**(TableColumnModelListener x) ;
    public void **setColumnMargin**(int newMargin) ;
    public void **setColumnSelectionAllowed**(boolean flag) ;
    public void **setSelectionModel**(ListSelectionModel newModel) ;
}

javax.swing.event.**TableColumnModelEvent**

public class **TableColumnModelEvent** extends EventObject
{
    protected int **fromIndex** ;
    protected int **toIndex** ;
    // Constructors
    public **TableColumnModelEvent**(int to, int from, TableColumnModel source) ;
    // Instance methods
    public int **getFromIndex**() ;
    public int **getToIndex**() ;
}

javax.swing.event.**TableColumnModelListener**

public interface **TableColumnModelListener** implements EventListener
{
    // Instance methods
    public void **columnAdded**(TableColumnModelEvent e) ;
    public void **columnMarginChanged**(ChangeEvent e) ;
    public void **columnMoved**(TableColumnModelEvent e) ;
    public void **columnRemoved**(TableColumnModelEvent e) ;
    public void **columnSelectionChanged**(ListSelectionEvent e) ;
}

javax.swing.plaf.**TableHeaderUI**

public abstract class **TableHeaderUI** extends ComponentUI
{
    // Constructors
    public **TableHeaderUI**() ;
}

javax.swing.table.**TableModel**

public interface **TableModel**
{
    // Instance methods
    public void **addTableModelListener**(TableModelListener l) ;
    public Class<?> **getColumnClass**(int columnIndex) ;
    public int **getColumnCount**() ;
    public String **getColumnName**(int columnIndex) ;
    public int **getRowCount**() ;
    public Object **getValueAt**(int columnIndex, int rowIndex) ;
    public boolean **isCellEditable**(int columnIndex, int rowIndex) ;
    public void **removeTableModelListener**(TableModelListener l) ;
    public void **setValueAt**(int columnIndex, int rowIndex, Object aValue) ;
}

javax.swing.event.**TableModelEvent**

```
public class TableModelEvent extends EventObject
{
    public static final int ALL_COLUMNS ;
    public static final int DELETE ;
    public static final int HEADER_ROW ;
    public static final int INSERT ;
    public static final int UPDATE ;
    protected int column ;
    protected int firstRow ;
    protected int lastRow ;
    protected int type ;
    // Constructors
    public TableModelEvent(int type, int column, int lastRow, int firstRow, TableModel source) ;
    public TableModelEvent(int column, int lastRow, int firstRow, TableModel source) ;
    public TableModelEvent(int lastRow, int firstRow, TableModel source) ;
    public TableModelEvent(int row, TableModel source) ;
    public TableModelEvent(TableModel source) ;
    // Instance methods
    public int getColumn() ;
    public int getFirstRow() ;
    public int getLastRow() ;
    public int getType() ;
}
```

javax.swing.event.**TableModelListener**

```
public interface TableModelListener  implements EventListener
{
    // Instance methods
    public void tableChanged(TableModelEvent e) ;
}
```

javax.swing.table.**TableRowSorter\<M>** [since 1.6]

public class **TableRowSorter\<M>** extends DefaultRowSorter\<M, Integer>

```
{
    // Constructors
    public TableRowSorter(M model) ;
    public TableRowSorter() ;
    // Instance methods
    public Comparator<?> getComparator(int column) ;
    public TableStringConverter getStringConverter() ;
    public void setModel(M model) ;
    public void setStringConverter(TableStringConverter stringConverter) ;
    protected boolean useToString(int column) ;
}
```

javax.swing.table.**TableStringConverter** [since 1.6]

```
public abstract class TableStringConverter
{
    // Constructors
    public TableStringConverter() ;
    // Instance methods
    public abstract String toString(int column, int row, TableModel model) ;
}
```

javax.swing.plaf.**TableUI**

```
public abstract class TableUI extends ComponentUI
{
    // Constructors
    public TableUI() ;
}
```

javax.swing.text.**TableView**

```
public abstract class TableView extends BoxView
{
    // Constructors
    public TableView(Element elem) ;
    // Instance methods
    protected SizeRequirements calculateMinorAxisRequirements(SizeRequirements r, int axis) ;
```

```
    protected TableView.TableCell createTableCell(Element elem) ;
    protected TableView.TableRow createTableRow(Element elem) ;
    protected void forwardUpdate(ViewFactory f, Shape a, DocumentEvent e,
        DocumentEvent.ElementChange ec) ;
    protected View getViewAtPosition(Rectangle a, int pos) ;
    protected void layoutColumns(javax.swing.SizeRequirements[] reqs, int[] spans, int[] offsets, int
        targetSpan) ;
    protected void layoutMinorAxis(int[] spans, int[] offsets, int axis, int targetSpan) ;
    public void replace(javax.swing.text.View[] views, int length, int offset) ;
}
```

javax.swing.text.**TabSet**

```
public class TabSet  implements Serializable
{
    // Constructors
    public TabSet(javax.swing.text.TabStop[] tabs) ;
    // Instance methods
    public boolean equals(Object o) ; // Since 1.5
    public TabStop getTab(int index) ;
    public TabStop getTabAfter(float location) ;
    public int getTabCount() ;
    public int getTabIndex(TabStop tab) ;
    public int getTabIndexAfter(float location) ;
    public int hashCode() ; // Since 1.5
    public String toString() ;
}
```

javax.swing.text.**TabStop**

```
public class TabStop  implements Serializable
{
    public static final int ALIGN_BAR ;
    public static final int ALIGN_CENTER ;
    public static final int ALIGN_DECIMAL ;
    public static final int ALIGN_LEFT ;
    public static final int ALIGN_RIGHT ;
    public static final int LEAD_DOTS ;
    public static final int LEAD_EQUALS ;
    public static final int LEAD_HYPHENS ;
    public static final int LEAD_NONE ;
```

```
        public static final int LEAD_THICKLINE ;
        public static final int LEAD_UNDERLINE ;
        // Constructors
        public TabStop(int leader, int align, float pos) ;
        public TabStop(float pos) ;
        // Instance methods
        public boolean equals(Object other) ;
        public int getAlignment() ;
        public int getLeader() ;
        public float getPosition() ;
        public int hashCode() ;
        public String toString() ;
}
```

javax.swing.text.html.parser.**TagElement**

```
public class TagElement
{
        // Constructors
        public TagElement(boolean fictional, Element elem) ;
        public TagElement(Element elem) ;
        // Instance methods
        public boolean breaksFlow() ;
        public boolean fictional() ;
        public Element getElement() ;
        public HTML.Tag getHTMLTag() ;
        public boolean isPreformatted() ;
}
```

javax.swing.text.**TextAction**

```
public abstract class TextAction extends AbstractAction
{
        // Constructors
        public TextAction(String name) ;
        // Static methods
        public static final Action augmentList(javax.swing.Action[] list2, javax.swing.Action[] list1) ;
        // Instance methods
        protected final JTextComponent getFocusedComponent() ;
        protected final JTextComponent getTextComponent(ActionEvent e) ;
}
```

java.awt.**TextArea** [since 1.0]

public class **TextArea** extends TextComponent
{
    public static final int **SCROLLBARS_BOTH** ;
    public static final int **SCROLLBARS_HORIZONTAL_ONLY** ;
    public static final int **SCROLLBARS_NONE** ;
    public static final int **SCROLLBARS_VERTICAL_ONLY** ;
    // Constructors
    public **TextArea**(int scrollbars, int columns, int rows, String text) ;
    public **TextArea**(int columns, int rows, String text) ;
    public **TextArea**(int columns, int rows) ;
    public **TextArea**(String text) ;
    public **TextArea**() ;
    // Static methods
    // Instance methods
    public void **addNotify**() ;
    public void **append**(String str) ; // Since 1.1
    public synchronized void **appendText**(String str) ;
    public AccessibleContext **getAccessibleContext**() ; // Since 1.3
    public int **getColumns**() ;
    public Dimension **getMinimumSize**(int columns, int rows) ; // Since 1.1
    public Dimension **getMinimumSize**() ; // Since 1.1
    public Dimension **getPreferredSize**() ; // Since 1.1
    public Dimension **getPreferredSize**(int columns, int rows) ; // Since 1.1
    public int **getRows**() ; // Since 1
    public int **getScrollbarVisibility**() ; // Since 1.1
    public void **insert**(int pos, String str) ; // Since 1.1
    public synchronized void **insertText**(int pos, String str) ;
    public Dimension **minimumSize**() ;
    public Dimension **minimumSize**(int columns, int rows) ;
    protected String **paramString**() ;
    public Dimension **preferredSize**(int columns, int rows) ;
    public Dimension **preferredSize**() ;
    public void **replaceRange**(int end, int start, String str) ; // Since 1.1
    public synchronized void **replaceText**(int end, int start, String str) ;
    public void **setColumns**(int columns) ; // Since 1.1
    public void **setRows**(int rows) ; // Since 1.1
}

java.awt.peer.**TextAreaPeer**

public interface **TextAreaPeer** implements TextComponentPeer
{
    // Instance methods
    public Dimension **getMinimumSize**(int columns, int rows) ;
    public Dimension **getPreferredSize**(int columns, int rows) ;
    public void **insert**(int pos, String text) ;
    public void **insertText**(int pos, String txt) ;
    public Dimension **minimumSize**(int cols, int rows) ;
    public Dimension **preferredSize**(int cols, int rows) ;
    public void **replaceRange**(int end, int start, String text) ;
    public void **replaceText**(int end, int start, String txt) ;
}

java.awt.font.**TextAttribute**

public final class **TextAttribute** extends AttributedCharacterIterator.Attribute
{
    public static final TextAttribute **BACKGROUND** ;
    public static final TextAttribute **BIDI_EMBEDDING** ;
    public static final TextAttribute **CHAR_REPLACEMENT** ;
    public static final TextAttribute **FAMILY** ;
    public static final TextAttribute **FONT** ;
    public static final TextAttribute **FOREGROUND** ;
    public static final TextAttribute **INPUT_METHOD_HIGHLIGHT** ;
    public static final TextAttribute **INPUT_METHOD_UNDERLINE** ;
    public static final TextAttribute **JUSTIFICATION** ;
    public static final Float **JUSTIFICATION_FULL** ;
    public static final Float **JUSTIFICATION_NONE** ;
    public static final TextAttribute **KERNING** ;
    public static final Integer **KERNING_ON** ;
    public static final TextAttribute **LIGATURES** ;
    public static final Integer **LIGATURES_ON** ;
    public static final TextAttribute **NUMERIC_SHAPING** ;
    public static final TextAttribute **POSTURE** ;
    public static final Float **POSTURE_OBLIQUE** ;
    public static final Float **POSTURE_REGULAR** ;
    public static final TextAttribute **RUN_DIRECTION** ;
    public static final Boolean **RUN_DIRECTION_LTR** ;

public static final Boolean **RUN_DIRECTION_RTL** ;
public static final TextAttribute **SIZE** ;
public static final TextAttribute **STRIKETHROUGH** ;
public static final Boolean **STRIKETHROUGH_ON** ;
public static final TextAttribute **SUPERSCRIPT** ;
public static final Integer **SUPERSCRIPT_SUB** ;
public static final Integer **SUPERSCRIPT_SUPER** ;
public static final TextAttribute **SWAP_COLORS** ;
public static final Boolean **SWAP_COLORS_ON** ;
public static final TextAttribute **TRACKING** ;
public static final Float **TRACKING_LOOSE** ;
public static final Float **TRACKING_TIGHT** ;
public static final TextAttribute **TRANSFORM** ;
public static final TextAttribute **UNDERLINE** ;
public static final Integer **UNDERLINE_LOW_DASHED** ;
public static final Integer **UNDERLINE_LOW_DOTTED** ;
public static final Integer **UNDERLINE_LOW_GRAY** ;
public static final Integer **UNDERLINE_LOW_ONE_PIXEL** ;
public static final Integer **UNDERLINE_LOW_TWO_PIXEL** ;
public static final Integer **UNDERLINE_ON** ;
public static final TextAttribute **WEIGHT** ;
public static final Float **WEIGHT_BOLD** ;
public static final Float **WEIGHT_DEMIBOLD** ;
public static final Float **WEIGHT_DEMILIGHT** ;
public static final Float **WEIGHT_EXTRABOLD** ;
public static final Float **WEIGHT_EXTRA_LIGHT** ;
public static final Float **WEIGHT_HEAVY** ;
public static final Float **WEIGHT_LIGHT** ;
public static final Float **WEIGHT_MEDIUM** ;
public static final Float **WEIGHT_REGULAR** ;
public static final Float **WEIGHT_SEMIBOLD** ;
public static final Float **WEIGHT_ULTRABOLD** ;
public static final TextAttribute **WIDTH** ;
public static final Float **WIDTH_CONDENSED** ;
public static final Float **WIDTH_EXTENDED** ;
public static final Float **WIDTH_REGULAR** ;
public static final Float **WIDTH_SEMI_CONDENSED** ;
public static final Float **WIDTH_SEMI_EXTENDED** ;
// Constructors
protected **TextAttribute**(String name) ;
// Instance methods
protected Object **readResolve**() throws InvalidObjectException ;
}

java.awt.**TextComponent** [since 1.0]

public class **TextComponent** extends Component implements Accessible
{
    protected transient TextListener **textListener** ;
    // Constructors
    private **TextComponent**(String text) ;
    // Instance methods
    public void **addNotify**() ;
    public synchronized void **addTextListener**(TextListener l) ;
    public void **enableInputMethods**(boolean enable) ; // Since 1.2
    public AccessibleContext **getAccessibleContext**() ; // Since 1.3
    public Color **getBackground**() ; // Since 1.0
    public synchronized int **getCaretPosition**() ; // Since 1.1
    public InputMethodRequests **getInputMethodRequests**() ;
    public T **getListeners**(Class<T> listenerType) ; // Since 1.3
    public synchronized String **getSelectedText**() ;
    public synchronized int **getSelectionEnd**() ;
    public synchronized int **getSelectionStart**() ;
    public synchronized String **getText**() ;
    public synchronized TextListener **getTextListeners**() ; // Since 1.4
    public boolean **isEditable**() ; // Since 1.0
    protected String **paramString**() ;
    protected void **processEvent**(AWTEvent e) ;
    protected void **processTextEvent**(TextEvent e) ;
    public void **removeNotify**() ;
    public synchronized void **removeTextListener**(TextListener l) ; // Since 1.1
    public synchronized void **select**(int selectionEnd, int selectionStart) ;
    public synchronized void **selectAll**() ;
    public void **setBackground**(Color c) ; // Since 1.0
    public synchronized void **setCaretPosition**(int position) ; // Since 1.1
    public synchronized void **setEditable**(boolean b) ; // Since 1.0
    public synchronized void **setSelectionEnd**(int selectionEnd) ; // Since 1.1
    public synchronized void **setSelectionStart**(int selectionStart) ; // Since 1.1
    public synchronized void **setText**(String t) ;
}

java.awt.peer.**TextComponentPeer**

public interface **TextComponentPeer** implements ComponentPeer
{
    // Instance methods
    public long **filterEvents**(long mask) ;
    public int **getCaretPosition**() ;
    public Rectangle **getCharacterBounds**(int i) ;
    public int **getIndexAtPoint**(int y, int x) ;
    public InputMethodRequests **getInputMethodRequests**() ;
    public int **getSelectionEnd**() ;
    public int **getSelectionStart**() ;
    public String **getText**() ;
    public void **select**(int selEnd, int selStart) ;
    public void **setCaretPosition**(int pos) ;
    public void **setEditable**(boolean editable) ;
    public void **setText**(String l) ;
}

java.awt.event.**TextEvent** [since 1.1]

public class **TextEvent** extends AWTEvent
{
    public static final int **TEXT_FIRST** ;
    public static final int **TEXT_LAST** ;
    public static final int **TEXT_VALUE_CHANGED** ;
    // Constructors
    public **TextEvent**(int id, Object source) ;
    // Instance methods
    public String **paramString**() ;
}

java.awt.**TextField** [since 1.0]

public class **TextField** extends TextComponent
{
    // Constructors

```
        public TextField(int columns, String text) ;
        public TextField(int columns) ;
        public TextField(String text) ;
        public TextField() ;
        // Static methods
        // Instance methods
        public synchronized void addActionListener(ActionListener l) ; // Since 1.1
        public void addNotify() ;
        public boolean echoCharIsSet() ;
        public AccessibleContext getAccessibleContext() ; // Since 1.3
        public synchronized ActionListener getActionListeners() ; // Since 1.4
        public int getColumns() ; // Since 1.1
        public char getEchoChar() ;
        public T getListeners(Class<T> listenerType) ; // Since 1.3
        public Dimension getMinimumSize(int columns) ; // Since 1.1
        public Dimension getMinimumSize() ; // Since 1.1
        public Dimension getPreferredSize(int columns) ; // Since 1.1
        public Dimension getPreferredSize() ; // Since 1.1
        public Dimension minimumSize() ;
        public Dimension minimumSize(int columns) ;
        protected String paramString() ;
        public Dimension preferredSize() ;
        public Dimension preferredSize(int columns) ;
        protected void processActionEvent(ActionEvent e) ; // Since 1.1
        protected void processEvent(AWTEvent e) ; // Since 1.1
        public synchronized void removeActionListener(ActionListener l) ; // Since 1.1
        public void setColumns(int columns) ; // Since 1.1
        public void setEchoChar(char c) ; // Since 1.1
        public synchronized void setEchoCharacter(char c) ;
        public void setText(String t) ;
}
```

java.awt.peer.**TextFieldPeer**

```
public interface TextFieldPeer  implements TextComponentPeer
{
    // Instance methods
    public Dimension getMinimumSize(int columns) ;
    public Dimension getPreferredSize(int columns) ;
    public Dimension minimumSize(int cols) ;
    public Dimension preferredSize(int cols) ;
    public void setEchoChar(char echoChar) ;
    public void setEchoCharacter(char c) ;
}
```

---

java.awt.font.**TextHitInfo**

public final class **TextHitInfo**
{
    // Constructors
    private **TextHitInfo**(boolean isLeadingEdge, int charIndex) ;
    // Static methods
    public static TextHitInfo **afterOffset**(int offset) ;
    public static TextHitInfo **beforeOffset**(int offset) ;
    public static TextHitInfo **leading**(int charIndex) ;
    public static TextHitInfo **trailing**(int charIndex) ;
    // Instance methods
    public boolean **equals**(Object obj) ;
    public boolean **equals**(TextHitInfo hitInfo) ;
    public int **getCharIndex**() ;
    public int **getInsertionIndex**() ;
    public TextHitInfo **getOffsetHit**(int delta) ;
    public TextHitInfo **getOtherHit**() ;
    public int **hashCode**() ;
    public boolean **isLeadingEdge**() ;
    public String **toString**() ;
}

---

java.awt.font.**TextLayout**

public final class **TextLayout** implements Cloneable
{
    public static final TextLayout.CaretPolicy **DEFAULT_CARET_POLICY** ;
    // Constructors
    private **TextLayout**(float justifyRatio, float[] baselineOffsets, byte baseline, TextLine textLine) ;
    public **TextLayout**(FontRenderContext frc, AttributedCharacterIterator text) ;
    public **TextLayout**(FontRenderContext frc, Map<?, ?> attributes, String string) ;
    public **TextLayout**(FontRenderContext frc, Font font, String string) ;
    // Static methods
    // Instance methods
    protected Object **clone**() ;
    public void **draw**(float y, float x, Graphics2D g2) ;
    public boolean **equals**(TextLayout rhs) ;
    public boolean **equals**(Object obj) ;
    public float **getAdvance**() ;

```
    public float getAscent() ;
    public byte getBaseline() ;
    public float getBaselineOffsets() ;
    public Shape getBlackBoxBounds(int secondEndpoint, int firstEndpoint) ;
    public Rectangle2D getBounds() ;
    public float getCaretInfo(TextHitInfo hit) ;
    public float getCaretInfo(Rectangle2D bounds, TextHitInfo hit) ;
    public Shape getCaretShape(Rectangle2D bounds, TextHitInfo hit) ;
    public Shape getCaretShape(TextHitInfo hit) ;
    public Shape getCaretShapes(TextLayout.CaretPolicy policy, Rectangle2D bounds, int offset) ;
    public Shape getCaretShapes(Rectangle2D bounds, int offset) ;
    public Shape getCaretShapes(int offset) ;
    public int getCharacterCount() ;
    public byte getCharacterLevel(int index) ;
    public float getDescent() ;
    public TextLayout getJustifiedLayout(float justificationWidth) ;
    public LayoutPath getLayoutPath() ; // Since 1.6
    public float getLeading() ;
    public Shape getLogicalHighlightShape(int secondEndpoint, int firstEndpoint) ;
    public Shape getLogicalHighlightShape(Rectangle2D bounds, int secondEndpoint, int firstEndpoint)
        ;
    public int getLogicalRangesForVisualSelection(TextHitInfo secondEndpoint, TextHitInfo
        firstEndpoint) ;
    public TextHitInfo getNextLeftHit(TextLayout.CaretPolicy policy, int offset) ;
    public TextHitInfo getNextLeftHit(int offset) ;
    public TextHitInfo getNextLeftHit(TextHitInfo hit) ;
    public TextHitInfo getNextRightHit(int offset) ;
    public TextHitInfo getNextRightHit(TextHitInfo hit) ;
    public TextHitInfo getNextRightHit(TextLayout.CaretPolicy policy, int offset) ;
    public Shape getOutline(AffineTransform tx) ;
    public Rectangle getPixelBounds(float y, float x, FontRenderContext frc) ; // Since 1.6
    public float getVisibleAdvance() ;
    public Shape getVisualHighlightShape(TextHitInfo secondEndpoint, TextHitInfo firstEndpoint) ;
    public Shape getVisualHighlightShape(Rectangle2D bounds, TextHitInfo secondEndpoint,
        TextHitInfo firstEndpoint) ;
    public TextHitInfo getVisualOtherHit(TextHitInfo hit) ;
    protected void handleJustify(float justificationWidth) ;
    public int hashCode() ;
    public TextHitInfo hitTestChar(Rectangle2D bounds, float y, float x) ;
    public TextHitInfo hitTestChar(float y, float x) ;
    public void hitToPoint(Point2D point, TextHitInfo hit) ; // Since 1.6
    public boolean isLeftToRight() ;
    public boolean isVertical() ;
    public String toString() ;
}
```

java.awt.font.**TextLayout.CaretPolicy**

public static class **TextLayout.CaretPolicy**
{
    // Constructors
    public **TextLayout.CaretPolicy**() ;
    // Instance methods
    public TextHitInfo **getStrongCaret**(TextLayout layout, TextHitInfo hit2, TextHitInfo hit1) ;
}

java.awt.event.**TextListener** [since 1.1]

public interface **TextListener** implements EventListener
{
    // Instance methods
    public void **textValueChanged**(TextEvent e) ;
}

java.awt.font.**TextMeasurer** [since 1.3]

public final class **TextMeasurer** implements Cloneable
{
    // Constructors
    public **TextMeasurer**(FontRenderContext frc, AttributedCharacterIterator text) ;
    // Instance methods
    protected Object **clone**() ;
    public void **deleteChar**(int deletePos, AttributedCharacterIterator newParagraph) ;
    public float **getAdvanceBetween**(int limit, int start) ;
    public TextLayout **getLayout**(int limit, int start) ;
    public int **getLineBreakIndex**(float maxAdvance, int start) ;
    public void **insertChar**(int insertPos, AttributedCharacterIterator newParagraph) ;
}

javax.swing.plaf.**TextUI**

public abstract class **TextUI** extends ComponentUI

```
{
    // Constructors
    public TextUI() ;
    // Instance methods
    public abstract void damageRange(Position.Bias secondBias, Position.Bias firstBias, int p1, int p0,
        JTextComponent t) ;
    public abstract void damageRange(int p1, int p0, JTextComponent t) ;
    public abstract EditorKit getEditorKit(JTextComponent t) ;
    public abstract int getNextVisualPositionFrom(javax.swing.text.Position.Bias[] biasRet, int
        direction, Position.Bias b, int pos, JTextComponent t) throws BadLocationException ;
    public abstract View getRootView(JTextComponent t) ;
    public String getToolTipText(Point pt, JTextComponent t) ; // Since 1.4
    public abstract Rectangle modelToView(Position.Bias bias, int pos, JTextComponent t) throws
        BadLocationException ;
    public abstract Rectangle modelToView(int pos, JTextComponent t) throws BadLocationException ;
    public abstract int viewToModel(javax.swing.text.Position.Bias[] biasReturn, Point pt,
        JTextComponent t) ;
    public abstract int viewToModel(Point pt, JTextComponent t) ;
}
```

java.awt.**TexturePaint**

```
public class TexturePaint implements Paint
{
    // Constructors
    public TexturePaint(Rectangle2D anchor, BufferedImage txtr) ;
    // Instance methods
    public PaintContext createContext(RenderingHints hints, AffineTransform xform, Rectangle2D
        userBounds, Rectangle deviceBounds, ColorModel cm) ;
    public Rectangle2D getAnchorRect() ;
    public BufferedImage getImage() ;
    public int getTransparency() ;
}
```

java.awt.image.**TileObserver**

```
public interface TileObserver
{
    // Instance methods
    public void tileUpdate(boolean willBeWritable, int tileY, int tileX, WritableRenderedImage source) ;
}
```

javax.swing.**Timer**

public class **Timer** implements Serializable
{
    protected EventListenerList **listenerList** ;
    // Constructors
    public **Timer**(ActionListener listener, int delay) ;
    // Static methods
    public static boolean **getLogTimers**() ;
    public static void **setLogTimers**(boolean flag) ;
    // Instance methods
    public void **addActionListener**(ActionListener listener) ;
    protected void **fireActionPerformed**(ActionEvent e) ;
    public String **getActionCommand**() ; // Since 1.6
    public ActionListener **getActionListeners**() ; // Since 1.4
    public int **getDelay**() ;
    public int **getInitialDelay**() ;
    public T **getListeners**(Class<T> listenerType) ; // Since 1.3
    public boolean **isCoalesce**() ;
    public boolean **isRepeats**() ;
    public boolean **isRunning**() ;
    public void **removeActionListener**(ActionListener listener) ;
    public void **restart**() ;
    public void **setActionCommand**(String command) ; // Since 1.6
    public void **setCoalesce**(boolean flag) ;
    public void **setDelay**(int delay) ;
    public void **setInitialDelay**(int initialDelay) ;
    public void **setRepeats**(boolean flag) ;
    public void **start**() ;
    public void **stop**() ;
}

javax.swing.border.**TitledBorder**

public class **TitledBorder** extends AbstractBorder
{
    public static final int **ABOVE_BOTTOM** ;
    public static final int **ABOVE_TOP** ;
    public static final int **BELOW_BOTTOM** ;
    public static final int **BELOW_TOP** ;

public static final int **BOTTOM** ;
public static final int **CENTER** ;
public static final int **DEFAULT_JUSTIFICATION** ;
public static final int **DEFAULT_POSITION** ;
protected static final int **EDGE_SPACING** ;
public static final int **LEADING** ;
public static final int **LEFT** ;
public static final int **RIGHT** ;
protected static final int **TEXT_INSET_H** ;
protected static final int **TEXT_SPACING** ;
public static final int **TOP** ;
public static final int **TRAILING** ;
protected Border **border** ;
protected String **title** ;
protected Color **titleColor** ;
protected Font **titleFont** ;
protected int **titleJustification** ;
protected int **titlePosition** ;
// Constructors
public **TitledBorder**(Color titleColor, Font titleFont, int titlePosition, int titleJustification, String title, Border border) ;
public **TitledBorder**(Font titleFont, int titlePosition, int titleJustification, String title, Border border) ;
public **TitledBorder**(int titlePosition, int titleJustification, String title, Border border) ;
public **TitledBorder**(String title, Border border) ;
public **TitledBorder**(Border border) ;
public **TitledBorder**(String title) ;
// Static methods
// Instance methods
public int **getBaseline**(int height, int width, Component c) ; // Since 1.6
public Component.BaselineResizeBehavior **getBaselineResizeBehavior**(Component c) ; // Since 1.6
public Border **getBorder**() ;
public Insets **getBorderInsets**(Insets insets, Component c) ;
protected Font **getFont**(Component c) ;
public Dimension **getMinimumSize**(Component c) ;
public String **getTitle**() ;
public Color **getTitleColor**() ;
public Font **getTitleFont**() ;
public int **getTitleJustification**() ;
public int **getTitlePosition**() ;
public boolean **isBorderOpaque**() ;
public void **paintBorder**(int height, int width, int y, int x, Graphics g, Component c) ;
public void **setBorder**(Border border) ;
public void **setTitle**(String title) ;
public void **setTitleColor**(Color titleColor) ;
public void **setTitleFont**(Font titleFont) ;
public void **setTitleJustification**(int titleJustification) ;

public void **setTitlePosition**(int titlePosition) ;
}

---

javax.swing.plaf.**ToolBarUI**

---

public abstract class **ToolBarUI** extends ComponentUI
{
    // Constructors
    public **ToolBarUI**() ;
}

---

java.awt.**Toolkit** [since 1.0]

---

public abstract class **Toolkit**
{
    protected final Map<String, Object> **desktopProperties** ;
    protected final PropertyChangeSupport **desktopPropsSupport** ;
    // Constructors
    public **Toolkit**() ;
    // Static methods
    public static synchronized Toolkit **getDefaultToolkit**() ;
    protected static Container **getNativeContainer**(Component c) ;
    public static String **getProperty**(String defaultValue, String key) ;
    // Instance methods
    public void **addAWTEventListener**(long eventMask, AWTEventListener listener) ; // Since 1.2
    public void **addPropertyChangeListener**(PropertyChangeListener pcl, String name) ; // Since 1.2
    public abstract void **beep**() ; // Since 1.1
    public abstract int **checkImage**(ImageObserver observer, int height, int width, Image image) ;
    protected abstract ButtonPeer **createButton**(Button target) throws HeadlessException ;
    protected abstract CanvasPeer **createCanvas**(Canvas target) ;
    protected abstract CheckboxPeer **createCheckbox**(Checkbox target) throws HeadlessException ;
    protected abstract CheckboxMenuItemPeer **createCheckboxMenuItem**(CheckboxMenuItem target)
        throws HeadlessException ;
    protected abstract ChoicePeer **createChoice**(Choice target) throws HeadlessException ;
    protected LightweightPeer **createComponent**(Component target) ;
    public Cursor **createCustomCursor**(String name, Point hotSpot, Image cursor) throws
        IndexOutOfBoundsException, HeadlessException ; // Since 1.2
    protected abstract DesktopPeer **createDesktopPeer**(Desktop target) throws HeadlessException ; //
        Since 1.6
    protected abstract DialogPeer **createDialog**(Dialog target) throws HeadlessException ;

public T **createDragGestureRecognizer**(DragGestureListener dgl, int srcActions, Component c, DragSource ds, Class<T> abstractRecognizerClass) ;

public abstract DragSourceContextPeer **createDragSourceContextPeer**(DragGestureEvent dge) throws InvalidDnDOperationException ;

protected abstract FileDialogPeer **createFileDialog**(FileDialog target) throws HeadlessException ;

protected abstract FramePeer **createFrame**(Frame target) throws HeadlessException ;

public abstract Image **createImage**(URL url) ;

public abstract Image **createImage**(ImageProducer producer) ;

public abstract Image **createImage**(int imagelength, int imageoffset, byte[] imagedata) ; // Since 1.1

public abstract Image **createImage**(String filename) ;

public Image **createImage**(byte[] imagedata) ; // Since 1.1

protected abstract LabelPeer **createLabel**(Label target) throws HeadlessException ;

protected abstract ListPeer **createList**(List target) throws HeadlessException ;

protected abstract MenuPeer **createMenu**(Menu target) throws HeadlessException ;

protected abstract MenuBarPeer **createMenuBar**(MenuBar target) throws HeadlessException ;

protected abstract MenuItemPeer **createMenuItem**(MenuItem target) throws HeadlessException ;

protected abstract PanelPeer **createPanel**(Panel target) ;

protected abstract PopupMenuPeer **createPopupMenu**(PopupMenu target) throws HeadlessException ; // Since 1.1

protected abstract ScrollbarPeer **createScrollbar**(Scrollbar target) throws HeadlessException ;

protected abstract ScrollPanePeer **createScrollPane**(ScrollPane target) throws HeadlessException ; // Since 1.1

protected abstract TextAreaPeer **createTextArea**(TextArea target) throws HeadlessException ;

protected abstract TextFieldPeer **createTextField**(TextField target) throws HeadlessException ;

protected abstract WindowPeer **createWindow**(Window target) throws HeadlessException ;

public AWTEventListener **getAWTEventListeners**(long eventMask) ; // Since 1.4

public AWTEventListener **getAWTEventListeners**() ; // Since 1.4

public Dimension **getBestCursorSize**(int preferredHeight, int preferredWidth) throws HeadlessException ; // Since 1.2

public abstract ColorModel **getColorModel**() throws HeadlessException ;

public final synchronized Object **getDesktopProperty**(String propertyName) ;

public abstract String **getFontList**() ;

public abstract FontMetrics **getFontMetrics**(Font font) ;

protected abstract FontPeer **getFontPeer**(int style, String name) ;

public abstract Image **getImage**(URL url) ;

public abstract Image **getImage**(String filename) ;

public boolean **getLockingKeyState**(int keyCode) throws UnsupportedOperationException ; // Since 1.3

public int **getMaximumCursorColors**() throws HeadlessException ; // Since 1.2

public int **getMenuShortcutKeyMask**() throws HeadlessException ; // Since 1.1

protected MouseInfoPeer **getMouseInfoPeer**() ; // Since 1.5

public PrintJob **getPrintJob**(PageAttributes pageAttributes, JobAttributes jobAttributes, String jobtitle, Frame frame) ; // Since 1.3

public abstract PrintJob **getPrintJob**(Properties props, String jobtitle, Frame frame) ; // Since 1.1

public PropertyChangeListener **getPropertyChangeListeners**() ; // Since 1.4

public PropertyChangeListener **getPropertyChangeListeners**(String propertyName) ; // Since 1.4

public Insets **getScreenInsets**(GraphicsConfiguration gc) throws HeadlessException ; // Since 1.4
public abstract int **getScreenResolution**() throws HeadlessException ;
public abstract Dimension **getScreenSize**() throws HeadlessException ;
public abstract Clipboard **getSystemClipboard**() throws HeadlessException ; // Since 1.1
public final EventQueue **getSystemEventQueue**() ;
protected abstract EventQueue **getSystemEventQueueImpl**() ;
public Clipboard **getSystemSelection**() throws HeadlessException ; // Since 1.4
protected void **initializeDesktopProperties**() ;
public boolean **isAlwaysOnTopSupported**() ; // Since 1.6
public boolean **isDynamicLayoutActive**() throws HeadlessException ; // Since 1.4
protected boolean **isDynamicLayoutSet**() throws HeadlessException ; // Since 1.4
public boolean **isFrameStateSupported**(int state) throws HeadlessException ; // Since 1.4
public abstract boolean **isModalExclusionTypeSupported**(Dialog.ModalExclusionType
    modalExclusionType) ; // Since 1.6
public abstract boolean **isModalityTypeSupported**(Dialog.ModalityType modalityType) ; // Since
    1.6
protected Object **lazilyLoadDesktopProperty**(String name) ;
protected void **loadSystemColors**(int[] systemColors) throws HeadlessException ; // Since 1.1
public abstract Map<TextAttribute, ?> **mapInputMethodHighlight**(InputMethodHighlight highlight)
    throws HeadlessException ; // Since 1.3
public abstract boolean **prepareImage**(ImageObserver observer, int height, int width, Image image) ;
public void **removeAWTEventListener**(AWTEventListener listener) ; // Since 1.2
public void **removePropertyChangeListener**(PropertyChangeListener pcl, String name) ; // Since
    1.2
protected final void **setDesktopProperty**(Object newValue, String name) ;
public void **setDynamicLayout**(boolean dynamic) throws HeadlessException ; // Since 1.4
public void **setLockingKeyState**(boolean on, int keyCode) throws UnsupportedOperationException ;
    // Since 1.3
public abstract void **sync**() ;
}

---

javax.swing.**ToolTipManager**

---

public class **ToolTipManager** extends MouseAdapter implements MouseMotionListener
{
    protected boolean **heavyWeightPopupEnabled** ;
    protected boolean **lightWeightPopupEnabled** ;
    // Constructors
    private **ToolTipManager**() ;
    // Static methods
    public static ToolTipManager **sharedInstance**() ;
    // Instance methods
    public int **getDismissDelay**() ;
    public int **getInitialDelay**() ;

```
    public int getReshowDelay() ;
    public boolean isEnabled() ;
    public boolean isLightWeightPopupEnabled() ;
    public void mouseDragged(MouseEvent event) ;
    public void mouseEntered(MouseEvent event) ;
    public void mouseExited(MouseEvent event) ;
    public void mouseMoved(MouseEvent event) ;
    public void mousePressed(MouseEvent event) ;
    public void registerComponent(JComponent component) ;
    public void setDismissDelay(int milliseconds) ;
    public void setEnabled(boolean flag) ;
    public void setInitialDelay(int milliseconds) ;
    public void setLightWeightPopupEnabled(boolean aFlag) ;
    public void setReshowDelay(int milliseconds) ;
    public void unregisterComponent(JComponent component) ;
}
```

---

javax.swing.plaf.**ToolTipUI**

```
public abstract class ToolTipUI extends ComponentUI
{
    // Constructors
    public ToolTipUI() ;
}
```

---

java.awt.datatransfer.**Transferable**

```
public interface Transferable
{
    // Instance methods
    public Object getTransferData(DataFlavor flavor) throws UnsupportedFlavorException,
        IOException ;
    public DataFlavor getTransferDataFlavors() ;
    public boolean isDataFlavorSupported(DataFlavor flavor) ;
}
```

javax.swing.**TransferHandler** [since 1.4]

public class **TransferHandler** implements Serializable
{
    public static final int **COPY** ;
    public static final int **COPY_OR_MOVE** ;
    public static final int **LINK** ;
    public static final int **MOVE** ;
    public static final int **NONE** ;
    // Constructors
    protected **TransferHandler**() ;
    public **TransferHandler**(String property) ;
    // Static methods
    public static Action **getCopyAction**() ;
    public static Action **getCutAction**() ;
    public static Action **getPasteAction**() ;
    // Instance methods
    public boolean **canImport**(TransferHandler.TransferSupport support) ; // Since 1.6
    public boolean **canImport**(java.awt.datatransfer.DataFlavor[] transferFlavors, JComponent comp) ;
    protected Transferable **createTransferable**(JComponent c) ;
    public void **exportAsDrag**(int action, InputEvent e, JComponent comp) ;
    protected void **exportDone**(int action, Transferable data, JComponent source) ;
    public void **exportToClipboard**(int action, Clipboard clip, JComponent comp) throws
        IllegalStateException ;
    public int **getSourceActions**(JComponent c) ;
    public Icon **getVisualRepresentation**(Transferable t) ;
    public boolean **importData**(Transferable t, JComponent comp) ;
    public boolean **importData**(TransferHandler.TransferSupport support) ; // Since 1.6
}

javax.swing.**TransferHandler.DropLocation** [since 1.6]

public static class **TransferHandler.DropLocation**
{
    // Constructors
    protected **TransferHandler.DropLocation**(Point dropPoint) ;
    // Instance methods
    public final Point **getDropPoint**() ;
    public String **toString**() ;
}

javax.swing.**TransferHandler.TransferSupport** [since 1.6]

public static final class **TransferHandler.TransferSupport**
{
    // Constructors
    public **TransferHandler.TransferSupport**(Transferable transferable, Component component) ;
    private **TransferHandler.TransferSupport**(DropTargetEvent event, Component component) ;
    // Instance methods
    public Component **getComponent**() ;
    public DataFlavor **getDataFlavors**() ;
    public int **getDropAction**() ;
    public TransferHandler.DropLocation **getDropLocation**() ;
    public int **getSourceDropActions**() ;
    public Transferable **getTransferable**() ;
    public int **getUserDropAction**() ;
    public boolean **isDataFlavorSupported**(DataFlavor df) ;
    public boolean **isDrop**() ;
    public void **setDropAction**(int dropAction) ;
    public void **setShowDropLocation**(boolean showDropLocation) ;
}

java.awt.font.**TransformAttribute**

public final class **TransformAttribute** implements Serializable
{
    public static final TransformAttribute **IDENTITY** ;
    // Constructors
    public **TransformAttribute**(AffineTransform transform) ;
    // Instance methods
    public boolean **equals**(Object rhs) ; // Since 1.6
    public AffineTransform **getTransform**() ;
    public int **hashCode**() ; // Since 1.6
    public boolean **isIdentity**() ; // Since 1.4
}

java.awt.**Transparency**

public interface **Transparency**
{
    public static final int **BITMASK** ;
    public static final int **OPAQUE** ;
    public static final int **TRANSLUCENT** ;
    // Instance methods
    public int **getTransparency**() ;
}

java.awt.**TrayIcon** [since 1.6]

public class **TrayIcon**
{
    // Constructors
    public **TrayIcon**(PopupMenu popup, String tooltip, Image image) ;
    public **TrayIcon**(String tooltip, Image image) ;
    public **TrayIcon**(Image image) ;
    private **TrayIcon**() ;
    // Static methods
    // Instance methods
    public synchronized void **addActionListener**(ActionListener listener) ;
    public synchronized void **addMouseListener**(MouseListener listener) ;
    public synchronized void **addMouseMotionListener**(MouseMotionListener listener) ;
    public void **displayMessage**(TrayIcon.MessageType messageType, String text, String caption) ;
    public String **getActionCommand**() ;
    public synchronized ActionListener **getActionListeners**() ;
    public Image **getImage**() ;
    public synchronized MouseListener **getMouseListeners**() ;
    public synchronized MouseMotionListener **getMouseMotionListeners**() ;
    public PopupMenu **getPopupMenu**() ;
    public Dimension **getSize**() ;
    public String **getToolTip**() ;
    public boolean **isImageAutoSize**() ;
    public synchronized void **removeActionListener**(ActionListener listener) ;
    public synchronized void **removeMouseListener**(MouseListener listener) ;
    public synchronized void **removeMouseMotionListener**(MouseMotionListener listener) ;
    public void **setActionCommand**(String command) ;
    public void **setImage**(Image image) ;

```
    public void setImageAutoSize(boolean autosize) ;
    public void setPopupMenu(PopupMenu popup) ;
    public void setToolTip(String tooltip) ;
}
```

java.awt.**TrayIcon.MessageType** [since 1.6]

```
public static final class TrayIcon.MessageType extends Enum<TrayIcon.MessageType>
{
    // Constructors
    private TrayIcon.MessageType() ;
    // Static methods
    public static TrayIcon.MessageType valueOf(String name) ;
    public static final TrayIcon.MessageType values() ;
}
```

java.awt.peer.**TrayIconPeer**

```
public interface TrayIconPeer
{
    // Instance methods
    public void displayMessage(String messageType, String text, String caption) ;
    public void dispose() ;
    public void setToolTip(String tooltip) ;
    public void showPopupMenu(int y, int x) ;
    public void updateImage() ;
}
```

javax.swing.tree.**TreeCellEditor**

```
public interface TreeCellEditor  implements CellEditor
{
    // Instance methods
    public Component getTreeCellEditorComponent(int row, boolean leaf, boolean expanded, boolean
        isSelected, Object value, JTree tree) ;
}
```

javax.swing.tree.**TreeCellRenderer**

public interface **TreeCellRenderer**
{
    // Instance methods
    public Component **getTreeCellRendererComponent**(boolean hasFocus, int row, boolean leaf,
        boolean expanded, boolean selected, Object value, JTree tree) ;
}

javax.swing.event.**TreeExpansionEvent**

public class **TreeExpansionEvent** extends EventObject
{
    protected TreePath **path** ;
    // Constructors
    public **TreeExpansionEvent**(TreePath path, Object source) ;
    // Instance methods
    public TreePath **getPath**() ;
}

javax.swing.event.**TreeExpansionListener**

public interface **TreeExpansionListener** implements EventListener
{
    // Instance methods
    public void **treeCollapsed**(TreeExpansionEvent event) ;
    public void **treeExpanded**(TreeExpansionEvent event) ;
}

javax.swing.tree.**TreeModel**

public interface **TreeModel**
{
    // Instance methods
    public void **addTreeModelListener**(TreeModelListener l) ;

```
    public Object getChild(int index, Object parent) ;
    public int getChildCount(Object parent) ;
    public int getIndexOfChild(Object child, Object parent) ;
    public Object getRoot() ;
    public boolean isLeaf(Object node) ;
    public void removeTreeModelListener(TreeModelListener l) ;
    public void valueForPathChanged(Object newValue, TreePath path) ;
}
```

javax.swing.event.**TreeModelEvent**

```
public class TreeModelEvent extends EventObject
{
    protected int childIndices ;
    protected Object children ;
    protected TreePath path ;
    // Constructors
    public TreeModelEvent(TreePath path, Object source) ;
    public TreeModelEvent(java.lang.Object[] path, Object source) ;
    public TreeModelEvent(java.lang.Object[] children, int[] childIndices, TreePath path, Object source)
        ;
    public TreeModelEvent(java.lang.Object[] children, int[] childIndices, java.lang.Object[] path,
        Object source) ;
    // Instance methods
    public int getChildIndices() ;
    public Object getChildren() ;
    public Object getPath() ;
    public TreePath getTreePath() ;
    public String toString() ;
}
```

javax.swing.event.**TreeModelListener**

```
public interface TreeModelListener implements EventListener
{
    // Instance methods
    public void treeNodesChanged(TreeModelEvent e) ;
    public void treeNodesInserted(TreeModelEvent e) ;
    public void treeNodesRemoved(TreeModelEvent e) ;
    public void treeStructureChanged(TreeModelEvent e) ;
}
```

javax.swing.tree.**TreeNode**

public interface **TreeNode**
{
    // Instance methods
    public Enumeration **children**() ;
    public boolean **getAllowsChildren**() ;
    public TreeNode **getChildAt**(int childIndex) ;
    public int **getChildCount**() ;
    public int **getIndex**(TreeNode node) ;
    public TreeNode **getParent**() ;
    public boolean **isLeaf**() ;
}

javax.swing.tree.**TreePath**

public class **TreePath** implements Serializable
{
    // Constructors
    protected **TreePath**() ;
    protected **TreePath**(int length, java.lang.Object[] path) ;
    protected **TreePath**(Object lastPathComponent, TreePath parent) ;
    public **TreePath**(Object lastPathComponent) ;
    public **TreePath**(java.lang.Object[] path) ;
    // Instance methods
    public boolean **equals**(Object o) ;
    public Object **getLastPathComponent**() ;
    public TreePath **getParentPath**() ;
    public Object **getPath**() ;
    public Object **getPathComponent**(int index) ;
    public int **getPathCount**() ;
    public int **hashCode**() ;
    public boolean **isDescendant**(TreePath aTreePath) ;
    public TreePath **pathByAddingChild**(Object child) ;
    public String **toString**() ;
}

javax.swing.event.**TreeSelectionEvent**

public class **TreeSelectionEvent** extends EventObject
{
    protected boolean **areNew** ;
    protected TreePath **newLeadSelectionPath** ;
    protected TreePath **oldLeadSelectionPath** ;
    protected TreePath **paths** ;
    // Constructors
    public **TreeSelectionEvent**(TreePath newLeadSelectionPath, TreePath oldLeadSelectionPath,
        boolean isNew, TreePath path, Object source) ;
    public **TreeSelectionEvent**(TreePath newLeadSelectionPath, TreePath oldLeadSelectionPath,
        boolean[] areNew, javax.swing.tree.TreePath[] paths, Object source) ;
    // Instance methods
    public Object **cloneWithSource**(Object newSource) ;
    public TreePath **getNewLeadSelectionPath**() ;
    public TreePath **getOldLeadSelectionPath**() ;
    public TreePath **getPath**() ;
    public TreePath **getPaths**() ;
    public boolean **isAddedPath**(int index) ; // Since 1.3
    public boolean **isAddedPath**(TreePath path) ;
    public boolean **isAddedPath**() ;
}

javax.swing.event.**TreeSelectionListener**

public interface **TreeSelectionListener** implements EventListener
{
    // Instance methods
    public void **valueChanged**(TreeSelectionEvent e) ;
}

javax.swing.tree.**TreeSelectionModel**

public interface **TreeSelectionModel**
{
    public static final int **CONTIGUOUS_TREE_SELECTION** ;

```
    public static final int DISCONTIGUOUS_TREE_SELECTION ;
    public static final int SINGLE_TREE_SELECTION ;
    // Instance methods
    public void addPropertyChangeListener(PropertyChangeListener listener) ;
    public void addSelectionPath(TreePath path) ;
    public void addSelectionPaths(javax.swing.tree.TreePath[] paths) ;
    public void addTreeSelectionListener(TreeSelectionListener x) ;
    public void clearSelection() ;
    public TreePath getLeadSelectionPath() ;
    public int getLeadSelectionRow() ;
    public int getMaxSelectionRow() ;
    public int getMinSelectionRow() ;
    public RowMapper getRowMapper() ;
    public int getSelectionCount() ;
    public int getSelectionMode() ;
    public TreePath getSelectionPath() ;
    public TreePath getSelectionPaths() ;
    public int getSelectionRows() ;
    public boolean isPathSelected(TreePath path) ;
    public boolean isRowSelected(int row) ;
    public boolean isSelectionEmpty() ;
    public void removePropertyChangeListener(PropertyChangeListener listener) ;
    public void removeSelectionPath(TreePath path) ;
    public void removeSelectionPaths(javax.swing.tree.TreePath[] paths) ;
    public void removeTreeSelectionListener(TreeSelectionListener x) ;
    public void resetRowSelection() ;
    public void setRowMapper(RowMapper newMapper) ;
    public void setSelectionMode(int mode) ;
    public void setSelectionPath(TreePath path) ;
    public void setSelectionPaths(javax.swing.tree.TreePath[] paths) ;
}
```

---

javax.swing.plaf.**TreeUI**

```
public abstract class TreeUI extends ComponentUI
{
    // Constructors
    public TreeUI() ;
    // Instance methods
    public abstract void cancelEditing(JTree tree) ;
    public abstract TreePath getClosestPathForLocation(int y, int x, JTree tree) ;
    public abstract TreePath getEditingPath(JTree tree) ;
    public abstract Rectangle getPathBounds(TreePath path, JTree tree) ;
    public abstract TreePath getPathForRow(int row, JTree tree) ;
```

```
    public abstract int getRowCount(JTree tree) ;
    public abstract int getRowForPath(TreePath path, JTree tree) ;
    public abstract boolean isEditing(JTree tree) ;
    public abstract void startEditingAtPath(TreePath path, JTree tree) ;
    public abstract boolean stopEditing(JTree tree) ;
}
```

javax.swing.event.**TreeWillExpandListener**

```
public interface TreeWillExpandListener  implements EventListener
{
    // Instance methods
    public void treeWillCollapse(TreeExpansionEvent event) throws ExpandVetoException ;
    public void treeWillExpand(TreeExpansionEvent event) throws ExpandVetoException ;
}
```

javax.swing.**UIDefaults**

```
public class UIDefaults extends Hashtable<Object, Object>
{
    // Constructors
    public UIDefaults(java.lang.Object[] keyValueList) ;
    public UIDefaults(float loadFactor, int initialCapacity) ;
    public UIDefaults() ;
    // Instance methods
    public synchronized void addPropertyChangeListener(PropertyChangeListener listener) ;
    public synchronized void addResourceBundle(String bundleName) ; // Since 1.4
    protected void firePropertyChange(Object newValue, Object oldValue, String propertyName) ;
    public Object get(Object key) ; // Since 1.4
    public Object get(Locale l, Object key) ; // Since 1.4
    public boolean getBoolean(Object key) ; // Since 1.4
    public boolean getBoolean(Locale l, Object key) ; // Since 1.4
    public Border getBorder(Locale l, Object key) ; // Since 1.4
    public Border getBorder(Object key) ;
    public Color getColor(Locale l, Object key) ; // Since 1.4
    public Color getColor(Object key) ;
    public Locale getDefaultLocale() ; // Since 1.4
    public Dimension getDimension(Locale l, Object key) ; // Since 1.4
    public Dimension getDimension(Object key) ;
    public Font getFont(Object key) ;
    public Font getFont(Locale l, Object key) ; // Since 1.4
```

```
    public Icon getIcon(Object key) ;
    public Icon getIcon(Locale l, Object key) ; // Since 1.4
    public Insets getInsets(Locale l, Object key) ; // Since 1.4
    public Insets getInsets(Object key) ;
    public int getInt(Locale l, Object key) ; // Since 1.4
    public int getInt(Object key) ;
    public synchronized PropertyChangeListener getPropertyChangeListeners() ; // Since 1.4
    public String getString(Locale l, Object key) ; // Since 1.4
    public String getString(Object key) ;
    public ComponentUI getUI(JComponent target) ;
    public Class<?> getUIClass(String uiClassID) ;
    public Class<?> getUIClass(ClassLoader uiClassLoader, String uiClassID) ;
    protected void getUIError(String msg) ;
    public Object put(Object value, Object key) ;
    public void putDefaults(java.lang.Object[] keyValueList) ;
    public synchronized void removePropertyChangeListener(PropertyChangeListener listener) ;
    public synchronized void removeResourceBundle(String bundleName) ; // Since 1.4
    public void setDefaultLocale(Locale l) ; // Since 1.4
}
```

---

javax.swing.**UIDefaults.ActiveValue**

```
public static interface UIDefaults.ActiveValue
{
    // Instance methods
    public Object createValue(UIDefaults table) ;
}
```

---

javax.swing.**UIDefaults.LazyInputMap** [since 1.3]

```
public static class UIDefaults.LazyInputMap  implements UIDefaults.LazyValue
{
    // Constructors
    public UIDefaults.LazyInputMap(java.lang.Object[] bindings) ;
    // Instance methods
    public Object createValue(UIDefaults table) ;
}
```

javax.swing.**UIDefaults.LazyValue**

```
public static interface UIDefaults.LazyValue
{
    // Instance methods
    public Object createValue(UIDefaults table) ;
}
```

javax.swing.**UIDefaults.ProxyLazyValue** [since 1.3]

```
public static class UIDefaults.ProxyLazyValue  implements UIDefaults.LazyValue
{
    // Constructors
    public UIDefaults.ProxyLazyValue(java.lang.Object[] o, String m, String c) ;
    public UIDefaults.ProxyLazyValue(java.lang.Object[] o, String c) ;
    public UIDefaults.ProxyLazyValue(String m, String c) ;
    public UIDefaults.ProxyLazyValue(String c) ;
    // Instance methods
    public Object createValue(UIDefaults table) ;
}
```

javax.swing.**UIManager**

```
public class UIManager  implements Serializable
{
    // Constructors
    public UIManager() ;
    // Static methods
    public static void addAuxiliaryLookAndFeel(LookAndFeel laf) ;
    public static void addPropertyChangeListener(PropertyChangeListener listener) ;
    public static Object get(Object key) ;
    public static Object get(Locale l, Object key) ; // Since 1.4
    public static LookAndFeel getAuxiliaryLookAndFeels() ;
    public static boolean getBoolean(Object key) ; // Since 1.4
    public static boolean getBoolean(Locale l, Object key) ; // Since 1.4
    public static Border getBorder(Object key) ;
    public static Border getBorder(Locale l, Object key) ; // Since 1.4
```

public static Color **getColor**(Locale l, Object key) ; // Since 1.4
public static Color **getColor**(Object key) ;
public static String **getCrossPlatformLookAndFeelClassName**() ;
public static UIDefaults **getDefaults**() ;
public static Dimension **getDimension**(Locale l, Object key) ; // Since 1.4
public static Dimension **getDimension**(Object key) ;
public static Font **getFont**(Locale l, Object key) ; // Since 1.4
public static Font **getFont**(Object key) ;
public static Icon **getIcon**(Locale l, Object key) ; // Since 1.4
public static Icon **getIcon**(Object key) ;
public static Insets **getInsets**(Object key) ;
public static Insets **getInsets**(Locale l, Object key) ; // Since 1.4
public static UIManager.LookAndFeelInfo **getInstalledLookAndFeels**() ;
public static int **getInt**(Object key) ;
public static int **getInt**(Locale l, Object key) ; // Since 1.4
public static LookAndFeel **getLookAndFeel**() ;
public static UIDefaults **getLookAndFeelDefaults**() ;
public static PropertyChangeListener **getPropertyChangeListeners**() ; // Since 1.4
public static String **getString**(Locale l, Object key) ; // Since 1.4
public static String **getString**(Object key) ;
public static String **getSystemLookAndFeelClassName**() ;
public static ComponentUI **getUI**(JComponent target) ;
public static void **installLookAndFeel**(UIManager.LookAndFeelInfo info) ;
public static void **installLookAndFeel**(String className, String name) ;
public static Object **put**(Object value, Object key) ;
public static boolean **removeAuxiliaryLookAndFeel**(LookAndFeel laf) ;
public static void **removePropertyChangeListener**(PropertyChangeListener listener) ;
public static void **setInstalledLookAndFeels**(javax.swing.UIManager.LookAndFeelInfo[] infos)
    throws SecurityException ;
public static void **setLookAndFeel**(LookAndFeel newLookAndFeel) throws
    UnsupportedLookAndFeelException ;
public static void **setLookAndFeel**(String className) throws ClassNotFoundException,
    InstantiationException, IllegalAccessException, UnsupportedLookAndFeelException ;
}

---

javax.swing.**UIManager.LookAndFeelInfo**

---

public static class **UIManager.LookAndFeelInfo**
{
    // Constructors
    public **UIManager.LookAndFeelInfo**(String className, String name) ;
    // Instance methods
    public String **getClassName**() ;
    public String **getName**() ;

```
    public String toString() ;
}
```

javax.swing.undo.**UndoableEdit**

```
public interface UndoableEdit
{
    // Instance methods
    public boolean addEdit(UndoableEdit anEdit) ;
    public boolean canRedo() ;
    public boolean canUndo() ;
    public void die() ;
    public String getPresentationName() ;
    public String getRedoPresentationName() ;
    public String getUndoPresentationName() ;
    public boolean isSignificant() ;
    public void redo() throws CannotRedoException ;
    public boolean replaceEdit(UndoableEdit anEdit) ;
    public void undo() throws CannotUndoException ;
}
```

javax.swing.event.**UndoableEditEvent**

```
public class UndoableEditEvent extends EventObject
{
    // Constructors
    public UndoableEditEvent(UndoableEdit edit, Object source) ;
    // Instance methods
    public UndoableEdit getEdit() ;
}
```

javax.swing.event.**UndoableEditListener**

```
public interface UndoableEditListener  implements EventListener
{
    // Instance methods
    public void undoableEditHappened(UndoableEditEvent e) ;
}
```

javax.swing.undo.**UndoableEditSupport**

public class **UndoableEditSupport**
{
    protected CompoundEdit **compoundEdit** ;
    protected Vector<UndoableEditListener> **listeners** ;
    protected Object **realSource** ;
    protected int **updateLevel** ;
    // Constructors
    public **UndoableEditSupport**(Object r) ;
    public **UndoableEditSupport**() ;
    // Instance methods
    public synchronized void **addUndoableEditListener**(UndoableEditListener l) ;
    public synchronized void **beginUpdate**() ;
    protected CompoundEdit **createCompoundEdit**() ;
    public synchronized void **endUpdate**() ;
    public synchronized UndoableEditListener **getUndoableEditListeners**() ; // Since 1.4
    public int **getUpdateLevel**() ;
    public synchronized void **postEdit**(UndoableEdit e) ;
    public synchronized void **removeUndoableEditListener**(UndoableEditListener l) ;
    public String **toString**() ;
    protected void **_postEdit**(UndoableEdit e) ;
}

javax.swing.undo.**UndoManager**

public class **UndoManager** extends CompoundEdit implements UndoableEditListener
{
    // Constructors
    public **UndoManager**() ;
    // Instance methods
    public synchronized boolean **addEdit**(UndoableEdit anEdit) ;
    public synchronized boolean **canRedo**() ;
    public synchronized boolean **canUndo**() ;
    public synchronized boolean **canUndoOrRedo**() ;
    public synchronized void **discardAllEdits**() ;
    protected UndoableEdit **editToBeRedone**() ;
    protected UndoableEdit **editToBeUndone**() ;
    public synchronized void **end**() ;
    public synchronized int **getLimit**() ;

```
    public synchronized String getRedoPresentationName() ;
    public synchronized String getUndoOrRedoPresentationName() ;
    public synchronized String getUndoPresentationName() ;
    public synchronized void redo() throws CannotRedoException ;
    protected void redoTo(UndoableEdit edit) throws CannotRedoException ;
    public synchronized void setLimit(int l) ;
    public String toString() ;
    protected void trimEdits(int to, int from) ;
    protected void trimForLimit() ;
    public synchronized void undo() throws CannotUndoException ;
    public void undoableEditHappened(UndoableEditEvent e) ;
    public synchronized void undoOrRedo() throws CannotRedoException, CannotUndoException ;
    protected void undoTo(UndoableEdit edit) throws CannotUndoException ;
}
```

java.awt.datatransfer.**UnsupportedFlavorException**

```
public class UnsupportedFlavorException extends Exception
{
    // Constructors
    public UnsupportedFlavorException(DataFlavor flavor) ;
}
```

javax.swing.**UnsupportedLookAndFeelException**

```
public class UnsupportedLookAndFeelException extends Exception
{
    // Constructors
    public UnsupportedLookAndFeelException(String s) ;
}
```

javax.swing.text.**Utilities**

```
public class Utilities
{
    // Constructors
    public Utilities() ;
    // Static methods
```

public static final int **drawTabbedText**(int startOffset, TabExpander e, Graphics g, int y, int x, Segment s) ;
public static final int **getBreakLocation**(int startOffset, TabExpander e, int x, int x0, FontMetrics metrics, Segment s) ;
public static final int **getNextWord**(int offs, JTextComponent c) throws BadLocationException ;
public static final Element **getParagraphElement**(int offs, JTextComponent c) ;
public static final int **getPositionAbove**(int x, int offs, JTextComponent c) throws BadLocationException ;
public static final int **getPositionBelow**(int x, int offs, JTextComponent c) throws BadLocationException ;
public static final int **getPreviousWord**(int offs, JTextComponent c) throws BadLocationException ;
public static final int **getRowEnd**(int offs, JTextComponent c) throws BadLocationException ;
public static final int **getRowStart**(int offs, JTextComponent c) throws BadLocationException ;
public static final int **getTabbedTextOffset**(int startOffset, TabExpander e, int x, int x0, FontMetrics metrics, Segment s) ;
public static final int **getTabbedTextOffset**(boolean round, int startOffset, TabExpander e, int x, int x0, FontMetrics metrics, Segment s) ;
public static final int **getTabbedTextWidth**(int startOffset, TabExpander e, int x, FontMetrics metrics, Segment s) ;
public static final int **getWordEnd**(int offs, JTextComponent c) throws BadLocationException ;
public static final int **getWordStart**(int offs, JTextComponent c) throws BadLocationException ;
}

javax.swing.tree.**VariableHeightLayoutCache**

public class **VariableHeightLayoutCache** extends AbstractLayoutCache
{
    // Constructors
    public **VariableHeightLayoutCache**() ;
    // Instance methods
    public Rectangle **getBounds**(Rectangle placeIn, TreePath path) ;
    public boolean **getExpandedState**(TreePath path) ;
    public TreePath **getPathClosestTo**(int y, int x) ;
    public TreePath **getPathForRow**(int row) ;
    public int **getPreferredHeight**() ;
    public int **getPreferredWidth**(Rectangle bounds) ;
    public int **getRowCount**() ;
    public int **getRowForPath**(TreePath path) ;
    public int **getVisibleChildCount**(TreePath path) ;
    public Enumeration<TreePath> **getVisiblePathsFrom**(TreePath path) ;
    public void **invalidatePathBounds**(TreePath path) ;
    public void **invalidateSizes**() ;
    public boolean **isExpanded**(TreePath path) ;
    public void **setExpandedState**(boolean isExpanded, TreePath path) ;

```
    public void setModel(TreeModel newModel) ;
    public void setNodeDimensions(AbstractLayoutCache.NodeDimensions nd) ;
    public void setRootVisible(boolean rootVisible) ;
    public void setRowHeight(int rowHeight) ;
    public void treeNodesChanged(TreeModelEvent e) ;
    public void treeNodesInserted(TreeModelEvent e) ;
    public void treeNodesRemoved(TreeModelEvent e) ;
    public void treeStructureChanged(TreeModelEvent e) ;
}
```

javax.swing.text.**View**

```
public abstract class View  implements SwingConstants
{
    public static final int BadBreakWeight ;
    public static final int ExcellentBreakWeight ;
    public static final int ForcedBreakWeight ;
    public static final int GoodBreakWeight ;
    public static final int X_AXIS ;
    public static final int Y_AXIS ;
    // Constructors
    public View(Element elem) ;
    // Instance methods
    public void append(View v) ; // Since 1.3
    public View breakView(float len, float pos, int offset, int axis) ;
    public void changedUpdate(ViewFactory f, Shape a, DocumentEvent e) ;
    public View createFragment(int p1, int p0) ;
    protected void forwardUpdate(ViewFactory f, Shape a, DocumentEvent e,
        DocumentEvent.ElementChange ec) ; // Since 1.3
    protected void forwardUpdateToView(ViewFactory f, Shape a, DocumentEvent e, View v) ; // Since
        1.3
    public float getAlignment(int axis) ;
    public AttributeSet getAttributes() ;
    public int getBreakWeight(float len, float pos, int axis) ;
    public Shape getChildAllocation(Shape a, int index) ;
    public Container getContainer() ;
    public Document getDocument() ;
    public Element getElement() ;
    public int getEndOffset() ;
    public Graphics getGraphics() ; // Since 1.3
    public float getMaximumSpan(int axis) ;
    public float getMinimumSpan(int axis) ;
    public int getNextVisualPositionFrom(javax.swing.text.Position.Bias[] biasRet, int direction, Shape
        a, Position.Bias b, int pos) throws BadLocationException ;
```

```
    public View getParent() ;
    public abstract float getPreferredSpan(int axis) ;
    public int getResizeWeight(int axis) ;
    public int getStartOffset() ;
    public String getToolTipText(Shape allocation, float y, float x) ; // Since 1.4
    public View getView(int n) ;
    public int getViewCount() ;
    public ViewFactory getViewFactory() ;
    public int getViewIndex(Shape allocation, float y, float x) ; // Since 1.4
    public int getViewIndex(Position.Bias b, int pos) ; // Since 1.3
    public void insert(View v, int offs) ; // Since 1.3
    public void insertUpdate(ViewFactory f, Shape a, DocumentEvent e) ;
    public boolean isVisible() ;
    public abstract Shape modelToView(Position.Bias b, Shape a, int pos) throws BadLocationException
        ;
    public Shape modelToView(Shape a, Position.Bias b1, int p1, Position.Bias b0, int p0) throws
        BadLocationException ;
    public Shape modelToView(Shape a, int pos) throws BadLocationException ;
    public abstract void paint(Shape allocation, Graphics g) ;
    public void preferenceChanged(boolean height, boolean width, View child) ;
    public void remove(int i) ; // Since 1.3
    public void removeAll() ; // Since 1.3
    public void removeUpdate(ViewFactory f, Shape a, DocumentEvent e) ;
    public void replace(javax.swing.text.View[] views, int length, int offset) ; // Since 1.3
    public void setParent(View parent) ;
    public void setSize(float height, float width) ;
    protected boolean updateChildren(ViewFactory f, DocumentEvent e,
        DocumentEvent.ElementChange ec) ; // Since 1.3
    protected void updateLayout(Shape a, DocumentEvent e, DocumentEvent.ElementChange ec) ; //
        Since 1.3
    public int viewToModel(Shape a, float y, float x) ;
    public abstract int viewToModel(javax.swing.text.Position.Bias[] biasReturn, Shape a, float y, float
        x) ;
}
```

javax.swing.text.**ViewFactory**

```
public interface ViewFactory
{
    // Instance methods
    public View create(Element elem) ;
}
```

javax.swing.**ViewportLayout**

public class **ViewportLayout** implements Serializable, LayoutManager
{
    // Constructors
    public **ViewportLayout**() ;
    // Instance methods
    public void **addLayoutComponent**(Component c, String name) ;
    public void **layoutContainer**(Container parent) ;
    public Dimension **minimumLayoutSize**(Container parent) ;
    public Dimension **preferredLayoutSize**(Container parent) ;
    public void **removeLayoutComponent**(Component c) ;
}

javax.swing.plaf.**ViewportUI**

public abstract class **ViewportUI** extends ComponentUI
{
    // Constructors
    public **ViewportUI**() ;
}

java.awt.image.**VolatileImage** [since 1.4]

public abstract class **VolatileImage** extends Image implements Transparency
{
    public static final int **IMAGE_INCOMPATIBLE** ;
    public static final int **IMAGE_OK** ;
    public static final int **IMAGE_RESTORED** ;
    protected int **transparency** ;
    // Constructors
    public **VolatileImage**() ;
    // Instance methods
    public abstract boolean **contentsLost**() ;
    public abstract Graphics2D **createGraphics**() ;
    public abstract ImageCapabilities **getCapabilities**() ; // Since 1.4
    public Graphics **getGraphics**() ;
    public abstract int **getHeight**() ;

```
    public abstract BufferedImage getSnapshot() ;
    public ImageProducer getSource() ;
    public int getTransparency() ; // Since 1.5
    public abstract int getWidth() ;
    public abstract int validate(GraphicsConfiguration gc) ;
}
```

java.awt.**Window** [since 1.0]

```
public class Window extends Container implements Accessible
{
    // Constructors
    public Window(GraphicsConfiguration gc, Window owner) ;
    public Window(Window owner) ;
    public Window(Frame owner) ;
    private Window() ;
    private Window(GraphicsConfiguration gc) ;
    // Static methods
    public static Window getOwnerlessWindows() ; // Since 1.6
    public static Window getWindows() ; // Since 1.6
    // Instance methods
    public void addNotify() ; // Since 1.0
    public void addPropertyChangeListener(PropertyChangeListener listener, String propertyName) ;
    public void addPropertyChangeListener(PropertyChangeListener listener) ;
    public synchronized void addWindowFocusListener(WindowFocusListener l) ; // Since 1.4
    public synchronized void addWindowListener(WindowListener l) ;
    public synchronized void addWindowStateListener(WindowStateListener l) ; // Since 1.4
    public void applyResourceBundle(String rbName) ;
    public void applyResourceBundle(ResourceBundle rb) ;
    public void createBufferStrategy(BufferCapabilities caps, int numBuffers) throws AWTException ;
        // Since 1.4
    public void createBufferStrategy(int numBuffers) ; // Since 1.4
    public void dispose() ;
    public AccessibleContext getAccessibleContext() ; // Since 1.3
    public BufferStrategy getBufferStrategy() ; // Since 1.4
    public boolean getFocusableWindowState() ; // Since 1.4
    public final Container getFocusCycleRootAncestor() ; // Since 1.4
    public Component getFocusOwner() ;
    public Set<AWTKeyStroke> getFocusTraversalKeys(int id) ; // Since 1.4
    public GraphicsConfiguration getGraphicsConfiguration() ; // Since 1.3
    public List<Image> getIconImages() ; // Since 1.6
    public InputContext getInputContext() ; // Since 1.2
    public T getListeners(Class<T> listenerType) ; // Since 1.3
    public Locale getLocale() ; // Since 1.1
```

public Dialog.ModalExclusionType **getModalExclusionType**() ; // Since 1.6
public Component **getMostRecentFocusOwner**() ; // Since 1.4
public Window **getOwnedWindows**() ; // Since 1.2
public Window **getOwner**() ; // Since 1.2
public Toolkit **getToolkit**() ;
public final String **getWarningString**() ;
public synchronized WindowFocusListener **getWindowFocusListeners**() ; // Since 1.4
public synchronized WindowListener **getWindowListeners**() ; // Since 1.4
public synchronized WindowStateListener **getWindowStateListeners**() ; // Since 1.4
public void **hide**() ;
public boolean **isActive**() ; // Since 1.4
public final boolean **isAlwaysOnTop**() ; // Since 1.5
public boolean **isAlwaysOnTopSupported**() ; // Since 1.6
public boolean **isAutoRequestFocus**() ; // Since 1.7
public final boolean **isFocusableWindow**() ; // Since 1.4
public final boolean **isFocusCycleRoot**() ; // Since 1.4
public boolean **isFocused**() ; // Since 1.4
public boolean **isLocationByPlatform**() ; // Since 1.5
public boolean **isShowing**() ;
public void **pack**() ;
public boolean **postEvent**(Event e) ;
protected void **processEvent**(AWTEvent e) ;
protected void **processWindowEvent**(WindowEvent e) ;
protected void **processWindowFocusEvent**(WindowEvent e) ; // Since 1.4
protected void **processWindowStateEvent**(WindowEvent e) ; // Since 1.4
public void **removeNotify**() ;
public synchronized void **removeWindowFocusListener**(WindowFocusListener l) ; // Since 1.4
public synchronized void **removeWindowListener**(WindowListener l) ;
public synchronized void **removeWindowStateListener**(WindowStateListener l) ; // Since 1.4
public void **reshape**(int height, int width, int y, int x) ;
public final void **setAlwaysOnTop**(boolean alwaysOnTop) throws SecurityException ; // Since 1.5
public void **setAutoRequestFocus**(boolean autoRequestFocus) ; // Since 1.7
public void **setBounds**(Rectangle r) ; // Since 1.6
public void **setBounds**(int height, int width, int y, int x) ; // Since 1.6
public void **setCursor**(Cursor cursor) ; // Since 1.1
public void **setFocusableWindowState**(boolean focusableWindowState) ; // Since 1.4
public final void **setFocusCycleRoot**(boolean focusCycleRoot) ; // Since 1.4
public void **setIconImage**(Image image) ; // Since 1.6
public synchronized void **setIconImages**(List<?> icons) ; // Since 1.6
public void **setLocationByPlatform**(boolean locationByPlatform) ; // Since 1.5
public void **setLocationRelativeTo**(Component c) ; // Since 1.4
public void **setMinimumSize**(Dimension minimumSize) ; // Since 1.6
public void **setModalExclusionType**(Dialog.ModalExclusionType exclusionType) ; // Since 1.6
public void **setSize**(int height, int width) ; // Since 1.6
public void **setSize**(Dimension d) ; // Since 1.6
public void **setVisible**(boolean b) ;

```
    public void show() ;
    public void toBack() ;
    public void toFront() ;
}
```

java.awt.event.**WindowAdapter** [since 1.1]

```
public abstract class WindowAdapter  implements WindowFocusListener, WindowStateListener,
WindowListener
{
    // Constructors
    public WindowAdapter() ;
    // Instance methods
    public void windowActivated(WindowEvent e) ;
    public void windowClosed(WindowEvent e) ;
    public void windowClosing(WindowEvent e) ;
    public void windowDeactivated(WindowEvent e) ;
    public void windowDeiconified(WindowEvent e) ;
    public void windowGainedFocus(WindowEvent e) ; // Since 1.4
    public void windowIconified(WindowEvent e) ;
    public void windowLostFocus(WindowEvent e) ; // Since 1.4
    public void windowOpened(WindowEvent e) ;
    public void windowStateChanged(WindowEvent e) ; // Since 1.4
}
```

javax.swing.**WindowConstants**

```
public interface WindowConstants
{
    public static final int DISPOSE_ON_CLOSE ;
    public static final int DO_NOTHING_ON_CLOSE ;
    public static final int EXIT_ON_CLOSE ;
    public static final int HIDE_ON_CLOSE ;
}
```

java.awt.event.**WindowEvent** [since 1.1]

public class **WindowEvent** extends ComponentEvent

```
{
    public static final int WINDOW_ACTIVATED ;
    public static final int WINDOW_CLOSED ;
    public static final int WINDOW_CLOSING ;
    public static final int WINDOW_DEACTIVATED ;
    public static final int WINDOW_DEICONIFIED ;
    public static final int WINDOW_FIRST ;
    public static final int WINDOW_GAINED_FOCUS ;
    public static final int WINDOW_ICONIFIED ;
    public static final int WINDOW_LAST ;
    public static final int WINDOW_LOST_FOCUS ;
    public static final int WINDOW_OPENED ;
    public static final int WINDOW_STATE_CHANGED ;
    // Constructors
    public WindowEvent(int id, Window source) ;
    public WindowEvent(int newState, int oldState, int id, Window source) ;
    public WindowEvent(Window opposite, int id, Window source) ;
    public WindowEvent(int newState, int oldState, Window opposite, int id, Window source) ;
    // Instance methods
    public int getNewState() ; // Since 1.4
    public int getOldState() ; // Since 1.4
    public Window getOppositeWindow() ; // Since 1.4
    public Window getWindow() ;
    public String paramString() ;
}
```

---

java.awt.event.**WindowFocusListener** [since 1.4]

```
public interface WindowFocusListener  implements EventListener
{
    // Instance methods
    public void windowGainedFocus(WindowEvent e) ;
    public void windowLostFocus(WindowEvent e) ;
}
```

---

java.awt.event.**WindowListener** [since 1.1]

```
public interface WindowListener  implements EventListener
{
    // Instance methods
    public void windowActivated(WindowEvent e) ;
```

```
    public void windowClosed(WindowEvent e) ;
    public void windowClosing(WindowEvent e) ;
    public void windowDeactivated(WindowEvent e) ;
    public void windowDeiconified(WindowEvent e) ;
    public void windowIconified(WindowEvent e) ;
    public void windowOpened(WindowEvent e) ;
}
```

---

java.awt.peer.**WindowPeer**

```
public interface WindowPeer  implements ContainerPeer
{
    // Instance methods
    public boolean requestWindowFocus() ;
    public void setAlwaysOnTop(boolean alwaysOnTop) ;
    public void setModalBlocked(boolean blocked, Dialog blocker) ;
    public void toBack() ;
    public void toFront() ;
    public void updateFocusableWindowState() ;
    public void updateIconImages() ;
    public void updateMinimumSize() ;
}
```

---

java.awt.event.**WindowStateListener** [since 1.4]

```
public interface WindowStateListener  implements EventListener
{
    // Instance methods
    public void windowStateChanged(WindowEvent e) ;
}
```

---

javax.swing.text.**WrappedPlainView**

```
public class WrappedPlainView extends BoxView implements TabExpander
{
    // Constructors
    public WrappedPlainView(boolean wordWrap, Element elem) ;
    public WrappedPlainView(Element elem) ;
```

```
    // Instance methods
    protected int calculateBreakPosition(int p1, int p0) ;
    public void changedUpdate(ViewFactory f, Shape a, DocumentEvent e) ;
    protected void drawLine(int y, int x, Graphics g, int p1, int p0) ;
    protected int drawSelectedText(int p1, int p0, int y, int x, Graphics g) throws BadLocationException
        ;
    protected int drawUnselectedText(int p1, int p0, int y, int x, Graphics g) throws
        BadLocationException ;
    protected final Segment getLineBuffer() ;
    public float getMaximumSpan(int axis) ;
    public float getMinimumSpan(int axis) ;
    public float getPreferredSpan(int axis) ;
    protected int getTabSize() ;
    public void insertUpdate(ViewFactory f, Shape a, DocumentEvent e) ;
    protected void loadChildren(ViewFactory f) ;
    public float nextTabStop(int tabOffset, float x) ;
    public void paint(Shape a, Graphics g) ;
    public void removeUpdate(ViewFactory f, Shape a, DocumentEvent e) ;
    public void setSize(float height, float width) ;
}
```

---

javax.swing.text.**ZoneView** [since 1.3]

```
public class ZoneView extends BoxView
{
    // Constructors
    public ZoneView(int axis, Element elem) ;
    // Instance methods
    protected View createZone(int p1, int p0) ;
    public int getMaximumZoneSize() ;
    public int getMaxZonesLoaded() ;
    protected int getViewIndexAtPosition(int pos) ;
    public void insertUpdate(ViewFactory f, Shape a, DocumentEvent changes) ;
    protected boolean isZoneLoaded(View zone) ;
    protected void loadChildren(ViewFactory f) ;
    public void removeUpdate(ViewFactory f, Shape a, DocumentEvent changes) ;
    public void setMaximumZoneSize(int size) ;
    public void setMaxZonesLoaded(int mzl) ;
    protected void unloadZone(View zone) ;
    protected boolean updateChildren(ViewFactory f, DocumentEvent e,
        DocumentEvent.ElementChange ec) ;
    protected void zoneWasLoaded(View zone) ;
}
```

Index